Saul Bass

SAUL BASS

ANATOMY OF FILM DESIGN

JAN-CHRISTOPHER HORAK

UNIVERSITY PRESS OF KENTUCKY

Scholarly publisher for the Commonwealth,
serving Bellarmine University, Berea College, Centre College of Kentucky,
Eastern Kentucky University, The Filson Historical Society, Georgetown
College, Kentucky Historical Society, Kentucky State University,
Morehead State University, Murray State University, Northern Kentucky
University, Transylvania University, University of Kentucky, University of
Louisville, and Western Kentucky University.
All rights reserved.

Editorial and Sales Offices: The University Press of Kentucky
663 South Limestone Street, Lexington, Kentucky 40508-4008
www.kentuckypress.com

Library of Congress Cataloging-in-Publication Data

Horak, Jan-Christopher.
  Saul Bass : anatomy of film design / Jan-Christopher Horak.
    pages cm. — (Screen classics)
  Includes bibliographical references and index.
  Includes filmography.
  ISBN 978-0-8131-4718-5 (hardcover : alk. paper)—
  ISBN 978-0-8131-4720-8 (pdf)—ISBN 978-0-8131-4719-2 (epub)
  1. Bass, Saul—Criticism and interpretation. I. Title.
  PN1998.3.B377H68 2014
  741.6092—dc23   2014020826

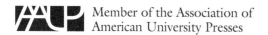

Contents

Introduction: *Qui êtes-vous*, Saul Bass?   1

1. Designer and Filmmaker   33

2. Film Titles: Theory and Practice   71

3. Creating a Mood: *Pars pro toto*   129

4. Modernism's Multiplicity of Views   191

5. The Urban Landscape   227

6. Journeys of Discovery: Seeing Is Knowledge   265

7. Civilization: Organizing Knowledge through Communication   305

Acknowledgments   357

Filmography   361

Notes   369

Selected Bibliography   421

Index   441

Illustrations follow page 225

Introduction

Qui êtes-vous, Saul Bass?

The Forty-First Academy Awards ceremony took place on 14 April 1969 at the Dorothy Chandler Pavilion, on what used to be Bunker Hill in downtown Los Angeles. It was the first Oscar ceremony to be broadcast worldwide and the first held at that location. As usual, it was a star-studded affair. Katharine Hepburn was nominated as best actress for the second year in a row, this time for *The Lion in Winter*, an award she would have to share with Barbra Streisand for *Funny Girl*—the only time there has been a tie in this category. Saul and Elaine Bass, too, were present at the awards ceremony, since the designer was nominated in the best documentary short category for *Why Man Creates* (1968). The couple rode to the Chandler in a rented limousine together with USC graduate student and Bass advisee George Lucas, who had been an assistant on the production. Bass's competitors were *The House that Amanda Built* (Fali Bilimoria), *The Revolving Door* (Lee R. Bobker), *A Space to Grow* (Thomas P. Kelly Jr.), and *A Way out of the Wilderness* (Dan E. Weisburd). Given his longtime work in the film industry, Bass was heavily favored to win. At the ceremony, Bass sat in an aisle seat at stage left, ten rows from the podium; Elaine was next to him in a light-colored chiffon dress. Actors Diahann Carroll and Tony Curtis read out the names of the nominees for best documentary and best short documentary, respectively. When Tony Curtis called out Bass's name as the winner, he bounced up to the stage, despite the wooden cane that preceded his every step. Curtis handed the Oscar to Bass, who was wearing a traditional tuxedo, in contrast to Curtis's mod outfit. Bass took the Oscar in his right hand while balancing his weight with his left hand on the cane. He bent over the microphone and, in an uncharacteristic moment of brevity, said, "Thank you, thank you very much." Then he quickly walked offstage.[1] No thanks to his staff, no thanks to his wife, no thanks to the Academy. More important, Bass failed

1

to mention Kaiser Aluminum and Chemical Corporation, the film's sponsor and original producer, causing mini-scandal to erupt at corporate headquarters. Did Bass just forget, due to nerves or under pressure to keep his acceptance speech short? We will probably never know. The oversight may not have been accidental, however, given the huge fights with Kaiser over the film's final structure, laboratory costs, and even the title. Bass hated the title because he thought it promised more than he could deliver.[2]

In hindsight, we can see that Bass deserved to win for what would be his greatest cinematic achievement, although his largely avant-garde work certainly challenged the Academy's notions of genre. Indeed, the category "Best Documentary, Short Subjects" hardly describes Bass's free-form essay, a hodgepodge of film notes that asks many more questions than it answers. And what makes it a documentary? The film includes several forms of animation and mostly staged sequences. In fact, it is a modernist romp, at moments seemingly incoherent and yet also brilliant in its open-endedness; its fragmentation forces the viewer to engage in the construction of meaning, thus fulfilling the promise of every modernist work to make the audience an active participant. In addition to the Academy Award, *Why Man Creates* won numerous film festival and other awards, as well as being placed on the National Film Registry of the Library of Congress in 2002, designating it a national treasure.[3]

But the somewhat tortured production history of the film also points out the pitfalls of having a corporate sponsor for such a personal and highly idiosyncratic project. In Bass's most cynical evaluation of the film, he admitted to a group of AT&T executives: "I think now—that the most creative thing about the film was that I found a rationalization that enabled me to convince the client, to allow me to make the film."[4] Even if the film was not a direct advertisement for Kaiser, the company covered all the production costs, and the corporate executives and Bass often had vastly different ideas about what kind of film they were financing. The designer usually argued that because sponsored films didn't have to sell anything, they were preferable to commercials or industrial film productions, where the filmmaker was at the mercy of the client. But Bass wanted to have it both ways: complete freedom to produce artistic work, and complete financing by a corporate sponsor that would pay all the bills, including a substantial honorarium to support Bass's office. Unlike most other avant-garde filmmakers, Bass was not willing to self-finance or to take on contract work to pay for his own personal films. After all, Bass had grown up in the Hollywood film industry, where no one invested their own money. Paradoxically, despite the insider status that an Academy Award seemingly represented, Bass remained an outsider in the movie industry, for several reasons. First, he was a graphic designer who had essentially created his own job description in a highly regulated system of film production. Second, his own aesthetic ambitions to bring high art to an often resistant Hollywood industry set him apart. Third, he sought the company of like-minded professionals, mostly producer-directors who had declared their independence from the classic Hollywood studio system.

Seen from our perspective in the twenty-first century, Saul Bass seems to define an era. As a designer of studio publicity, movie posters, title sequences and montages, commercials, and corporate logos from the 1940s to the 1990s, Bass heavily influenced the look of both film advertising and Hollywood films. Bass's poster designs and his credit sequences for Hollywood feature films were extremely innovative in terms of their formal design, use of iconography, and narrative content. His graphic work resembled no one else's in Hollywood, and his film credits changed forever how audiences looked at the opening minutes of a film. Simultaneously, all his film-related work incorporated aesthetic concepts borrowed from modernist art, translating them into new commercial modes of address and thereby transforming film industry conventions that had remained relatively stagnant for decades. Bass's designs influenced not only other studio publicity designers and filmmakers but also a whole generation of young designers that he personally trained in his studio. Among those who started their careers with Saul Bass were Thurston Blodgett, Paul Bruhwiler, Vincent Carra, John Casados, Morton Dimondstein, Vahe Fattal, Augustine Garza, Joel Katz, Karen Lee, Henry Markowitz, Michael Mills, Dave Nagata, Ted Piegdon, Gay Reinecke, Clarence Sato, Arnold Schwartzman, Mamoru Shimokochi, G. Dean Smith, Jay Toffoli, Todd Walker, Don Weller, and Howard York.

At a time when Hollywood's Taylorized system of film production called for extreme specialization within the work flow, Saul Bass was, uniquely, a generalist. He burst onto the creative floors of the film production factory and argued for the importance of the designer in the production process. Because of his aesthetic influences and the particular moment of his arrival in a changing Hollywood, Bass was able to cross over into other fields of film production, from designing advertising and publicity posters to creating title sequences and montages and eventually directing a Hollywood feature film. Bass's career trajectory thus exemplified a trend in 1950s Hollywood and beyond that allowed designers to raise their status in the caste system that pervaded the Los Angeles film studios. Bass's intervention into the Hollywood film production process through creative titling complicates our notions of who is responsible for the filmic text in the still rather structured Hollywood system: the director or a collective? But it also complicates our ability to read that text, given that its muddled authorship opens it up to multiple narrative interpretations. Bass's high art sensibility in all his work for the American studios demands attention, particularly because his strategy of elevating a production's aesthetic value furthered product differentiation in the marketplace, which became a necessity once the Paramount Consent Decree ended studio control of the movie theaters. In fact, Bass's career can only be understood within the context of the breakdown of the old Hollywood studio system, which was eventually replaced by a system of freelance artists under contract. Bass, as an outsider, was at the forefront of this development.

Saul Bass presents a particular challenge for film studies because his work in Hollywood has fallen through the cracks to some extent. Academic studies focus mainly on directors, screenwriters, and occasionally cinematographers—those considered central to the creative process of filmmaking. Technical specialists, whether costume and set designers or designers of film titles and montage sequences, such as Saul Bass and Slavko Vorkapich before him, only occasionally come under scrutiny. Reading film texts as semantic constructions independent of any authorial intentions, genre, semiotic, and structuralist studies have been unable to account for such specialists. This study takes the position that Bass, as a designer and filmmaker who intervened in film texts signed by others, demands a more nuanced approach involving both cinema studies and art history methodologies. This book is therefore neither a biography nor an analysis of individual films; rather, it proposes to read Bass's work in its totality as a metatext, defining the public screen persona of Saul Bass the designer, regardless of whether his chosen medium was advertising, titles, or independent films. Just as actors develop screen identities that are an amalgamation of screen images and the public discourse around them, Bass developed a designer persona. I refer to this persona as the Bass brand, regardless of whether he or his office staff actually held the pencil or pen on any particular design. Such an approach demands a high degree of cross-disciplinary analysis, which is why the present project is structured neither chronologically nor by medium; instead, it attributes formal and intellectual commonalities to the Bass brand across media.

The morning after the Oscars, Bass arrived late at the Saul Bass & Associates office on La Brea. The staff had gathered to congratulate the boss and themselves on their success, which, it was hoped, would move Bass's filmmaking career to a new level. Bass noticed that Art Goodman, his right-hand man for more than ten years, was signing reproductions of sketches for staff members, since he had drawn the "Edifice" animation sequence for *Why Man Creates*. Saul took his trusted designer aside and told him that he couldn't sign his own name to the sketches: he worked for Bass, and only Bass was allowed to sign artwork.[5] A day later, an anonymous cartoon of Bass with his Oscar and Moses' tablets appeared in the office, probably drawn by Goodman. Bass is shown saying, "Voice of whom?" implying that even God had to make an appointment. Goodman, who was as mild-mannered as they come, worked for almost forty years in the Bass office. Bass was the front man for some of Goodman's best work, but Art never complained about the slight.

Indeed, even though Bass was known to be a screamer, there were few fights between Bass and Goodman, because Art always deferred to Saul as the head of the design studio. That's the way it was. This was not Hollywood per se, where one's last credit was often the only way to get one's next job. This was an American commercial design studio, where it was common practice for only the head designer to sign the work. A British designer-filmmaker who worked briefly for Bass noted that he was shocked by the practice until he realized that's the way it was in America.[6] Bass had his reasons for insisting on a Los Angeles street address for the office, which was nominally in "Hollywood." He always thought of himself as a designer with interests far beyond the film community. And Bass was nothing if not a master at creating and controlling his own brand. It was the key to his success.

In terms of his movie titles, Bass has been acknowledged to the point of cliché as the master innovator. Even in the twenty-first century, filmmakers and title designers pay homage to Bass's achievements. For example, producer Matthew Weiner's opening credits for the cable television series *Mad Men*, about a Madison Avenue advertising firm in the 1960s, is a specific tribute to Bass and *North by Northwest* (with a little *Casino* thrown in). As noted by Steve Fuller, creative director for Imaginary Force, the firm that designed the title sequence: "I'm a huge Saul Bass fan . . . I like to think that it's kind of an update of Saul Bass."[7] New York title designer Peter Himmelstein suggests that title designers study "every title sequence Saul Bass ever did" to educate themselves about the medium's history: "Bass had this integrity of design from project to project, regardless of theme or content."[8] Likewise, Ty Mattson's titles for season 8 of the television series *Dexter* are another homage to Bass: "The poster series that I created for *Dexter* was inspired by mid-century modern design and particularly the work of Saul Bass."[9] Mattson actually "borrows" an almost exact replica of the disembodied hand from the titles to Bass's *The Facts of Life* (1960). Other modern film titles influenced by Bass include *Ed Wood* (1994, Tim Burton), *Se7en* (1995, David Fincher), *Bad Education* (2004, Pedro Almovodar), *Kiss Kiss Bang Bang* (2005, Shane Black), *The Kingdom* (2007, PIC Agency [Pamela Green, Jarik Van Sluijs]), *Zombies, Zombies, Zombies . . .* (2008, Jason Murphy), and *Argo* (2012, Ben Affleck), to name only a few. Kyle Cooper, who has been called the new Saul Bass of movie titles, created titles for *Se7en*, *The Island of Dr. Moreau* (1996, John Frankenheimer), and *Donnie Brasco* (1997, Mike Newell), among more than seventy others.[10] Like Bass, Cooper insists that title sequences are an integral part of the movie.[11] For *Catch Me If You Can* (2002, Steven Spielberg), the French design firm Kuntzel & Deygas created another specific homage to Bass; the film, like *Mad Men*, takes place in the early 1960s, when Bass was at the top of his game. Modern title designers have a huge technical advantage over Bass, however; they can use digital tools to create many of the effects Bass had to create painstakingly in the analog era.

Posters also reflect Bass's influence. For instance, Sidney Lumet's *Before the Devil Knows You're Dead* (2007) was designed by the Los Angeles–based advertising agency Coldopen after producer Mark Urman told Lumet he wanted "something Saul Bass-y . . . something simple and strong with lots of room for review quotes."[12] Another recent poster that riffed on Bass is *A Huey P. Newton Story* (2001, Spike Lee), designed by Art Sims; earlier, Sims had "plagiarized" the *Anatomy of a Murder* poster for Spike Lee's *Clockers* (1995). Other posters that play with the Bass style include *Burn after Reading* (2008, Ethan and Joel Cohen), designed by P+A/Mojo; *In the Loop* (2009, Armando Iannucci), designed by Crew Creative Advertising; *Precious* (2009, Lee Daniels) and *Buried* (2010,

Rodrigo Cortés), both designed by Ignition Print; and, most recently, the pre-release poster for *Django Unchained* (2012, Quentin Tarantino), designed by BLT Communications. These random selections attest not only to the longevity and distinctiveness of the Bass brand but also to the fact that twenty-first-century Hollywood design firms have embraced that style when it suits their purposes.

Given his multidimensional talents and unique ability to bring together high art and commercialism, Bass represents a long-standing reality in the Hollywood industry—namely, that artists fight for aesthetic issues and sometimes actually succeed, thereby establishing their independence, or, when they lose, they compromise and salvage what they can. In the case of Bass, this meant either signing his name to the work or taking his name off the design, but getting paid and working steadily nevertheless. Bass often accompanied his signature with a stamp of the Bass logo: a fish (a bass) with the designer's physiognomy. It is both a playful and a literal image (designed by Don Weller). Bass became Hollywood's most prominent designer precisely because he jealously guarded his brand—a brand so tied up with his own personality that Bass/Yager & Associates was not sustainable after the designer's demise.

Creating Saul Bass

In interviews, Saul Bass liked to say, "I always knew I was going to be Saul Bass, commercial artist."[13] But what did that mean, and how did it work? In an article on creativity, Bass related a funny anecdote about his Jewish mother, who asked him what he did for a living. She, like most laypersons, had little concept of what commercial design work entailed. Bass showed his mother an advertisement he had designed and explained that he had done neither the photography nor the typography, which confused her. Finally, he said, "Well, you see, I conceive the whole thing, and then I get all these people together and get them to carry out the process." His mother responded, "Oh—you devil!"[14] In other words, a designer didn't necessarily create an actual advertisement or brochure or billboard or logo; he or she created the concepts and then assigned others to physically carry out the tasks. A design office might have many designers and technicians working in it, but at its head was the designer whose name was on the door. It was that individual who conceptualized ideas, talked to clients, approved designs, and established the firm's identity. Designer Lorraine Wild has connected this strategy to the post–World War II movement of young American modernist designers, trained mostly by German Jewish émigré designers-artists from the Bauhaus, to legitimize their work in the commercial arena of American capital: "They found that a most efficient way to connect to their clients as consultants was to tie their own identity as artists and individual creators (or 'stars') to the work that they produced. Like movie stars or famous artists (figures more easily understood by commercial/popular culture), their work was increasingly championed on the basis of personal authorship (even if the work was actually the product of a 30-person office), rather than for its merits."[15]

In other words, no matter how many designers worked for Bass, he was the controlling intelligence who defined the look and the brand, because clients insisted on star quality. A consistent brand not only guaranteed quality, as far as clients were concerned, but also allowed them to know exactly what they were paying for. Individual designers could make significant contributions, but they worked for the firm. Bass himself explained his design team as follows: "So it's not 'Saul Bass & Associates' like a company, but Saul Bass and his associates . . . I have a whole group of guys who are all up to our ass in all kinds of interesting things."[16] Or, as an unpublished official biography put it: "Rather than trying to be a never-diminishing font of symbols, a kind of superhuman Trademark Man, Bass shares the creative doodling with a bullpen of designers, acting as a combination competitor, editor, nudge, shaman, gadfly, guru and fearless leader. His success as an inspiration and constructive arbiter of the ideas of others is almost as important to the trail of trademarks he has laid down over the years as is his own originality."[17]

Bass utilized a ruthless process of elimination, whittling down possibilities and always keeping his eyes on the prize, which was to produce a consistent product that met the client's needs. Art Goodman characterized the collaborative process similarly: "A lot of what ifs, out of which Bass will eventually coax a solution. No matter how nutty an idea may sound, Saul encourages people to say it. To me Saul has always been a true editor. He can find something that others don't see."[18] Arnold Schwartzman described the process as designers throwing out ideas until Bass decided, "Let's work on that."[19] Another employee who worked for Bass in the 1960s, Mike Lonzo, noted that Bass could be completely oblivious to others when he worked, even if they were contributing ideas. He was obsessive about work, and although he could be extremely generous on a personal level, he rarely thanked anyone for their design work. As far as he was concerned, it was their job.[20] Bass usually worked until late at night, and staff members were expected to do the same. Although he considered Bass a mentor and a friend, Schwartzman left the office after only six months because he couldn't work through the night, as Saul required.[21] Designing at Saul Bass & Associates did not occur only during normal business hours. As Bass himself noted, creativity "cannot operate from nine to five every day and not at any other time."[22]

Bass's own office was meticulously neat, filled with armies of ancient stone figures and animal fetishes, organized like a mini–museum exhibit; his awards, including the Oscar; and examples of his work and family photographs hanging on the wall. The rooms were usually kept at near-frigid temperatures, whether winter or summer, because Bass thought if it was too warm, the staff might be lulled to sleep. If anyone complained about the temperature, Bass would throw him or her a sweater from a pile in the corner.[23] Many of Bass's employees remember him fondly as a friendly and brilliant raconteur, but also as a nervous nail-biter and an occasional screamer. Not surprisingly, most designers eventually left to set up their own design firms if they had any ambition, the exception being Art Goodman.

Goodman, despite being an unbelievably talented designer, stayed because he felt comfortable. Both he and Bass were former New Yorkers who shared a Jewish upbringing and sense of humor, and they often played practical jokes on each other. Both loved pre-Columbian and other forms of "primitive" art, and they undoubtedly shared a common design aesthetic. Goodman treated Bass like a father figure, while Bass treated Goodman like a brother. Goodman worked on numerous corporate identity and packaging campaigns and developed many of the logos that Bass became famous for; he also drew movie and event posters. Because Bass's hand was apparently unsteady, Goodman prepared many of the final storyboards for Bass's animated titles and films. According to designer Mamoru Shimokochi, "Art's drawings were unique and extraordinary, always characterized by humor and a strong simple message."[24]

When he first moved to Los Angeles after World War II, Goodman worked for Hal Friedman and then opened his own office. Goodman joined Bass's firm initially as a freelancer and then as a full-time designer— at less pay than he had been making. The advantage for Goodman was that he didn't have to run his own office; he was uncomfortable with the business, hustling side of design work. Naturally shy and reticent, and self-conscious about a war wound that had crippled his writing hand, Good-man would get stage fright with clients.[25] Bass, in contrast, was a master at communicating ideas to clients and could sell them almost anything. Lou Dorfsman, a longtime friend and colleague, was in awe of Bass's ability to make the pitch. This is how he described Bass's conversation with Kodak executives during the planning stages of the 1964 New York World's Fair:

> Saul and Will Burtin—a superb thinker and designer—were both working for Eastman Kodak projects. Burtin gave a presentation of what he was planning, and there was a big yawn from the board of directors. . . . He talked in highly abstracted aesthetical and philosophical terms. Then Saul came on with the kind of know-how that moves people—Americans. He was talking about the cash register. He was talking about aesthetics and beauty—and the cash register! The cash register they all understood, and they lit up. I watched Saul at work, and I learned more from watching him: I know how to talk to CEOs and presidents of companies because of my observations of Saul at work. He was fabulous, so convincing. Those people could hear the cash register ringing from the sales of film—and Saul got through.[26]

After Herb Yager joined the firm, he became a major force in the company, not only finding new clients but also paying attention to the bottom line; he managed the corporate design work, ensuring that certain standards of quality were maintained, even on smaller projects that did not necessarily warrant Bass's valuable time. Yager had previously worked for Carson Roberts, but when that firm was bought by Ogilvy Public Relations, Yager was forced to look for new opportunities. A friend of his had interviewed for the job of business manager with Bass, but when he learned what the salary was, he declined and recommended Yager. During their interview, he and Bass discovered that they had attended the same elementary, middle, and high schools in the Bronx, only fifteen years apart. It was as if Yager were already family. Yager agreed to take the salary but proposed that after a year's probation, he would become a co-owner of the firm. Bass reacted with a comment about chutzpah, but Yager said that in a year's time, Bass could decide—yes or no, in or out.[27] Yager must have significantly increased revenue, because the firm's name was soon changed to Bass/Yager & Associates. Thereafter, Yager kept the firm profitable, even if it meant subsidizing Bass's filmmaking with corporate design work.

Another important personality in the Bass office, especially in the 1980s and at the end of Bass's career, was his second wife, Elaine Maka-tura. When she was hired as a secretary, Bass was still married, but she soon won his heart. In the late 1970s she became a steady collaborator on films and film title work and actually received codirector credit with Bass, although she was never involved in any of the graphic design and identity campaign work that constituted the center of the business.[28] Their fights in the 1980s were legendary, although they perceived the bickering as part of the creative process.[29] Indeed, by the 1990s, when Bass was becoming fragile, Elaine Bass moved into a position of greater authority and may have taken the lead on later titles such as *Age of Innocence, Mr. Saturday Night*, and *Cape Fear*. She brought a level of feminine sensuousness and tactility to the Bass brand that had previously been absent. Saul was all geometry, whereas Elaine introduced curves and undulations, like the glistening water's surface in *Cape Fear*, as well as long takes that contrasted with Bass's montage technique.

Some argue that Elaine's contributions to Saul's work from the 1960s onward cannot be underestimated and that in some cases she was responsible for the product.[30] The creative relationship between husband and wife has been characterized as equal to that of Ray and Charles Eames, a comparison that former employees in the Bass office have described as overstated. It seems doubtful that, in her position as an assistant, Elaine would have had much influence on design decisions in the early years, and later she was present at the office only intermittently, having taken on the responsibility of raising their two children.[31] Not that there aren't traces of Elaine, even early on. In the credits of *West Side Story*, Bass inserted the initials "SB-EM," barely visible on a wall of graffiti, but took sole credit for the title work. A Bass office press release from 1979 notes that Elaine assisted on the titles for *West Side Story* and *Walk on the Wild Side* and on the films *From Here to There* and *The Searching Eye*.[32] Once the children were older and required less attention, "she felt there was more time available to devote to filmmaking and returned to more active involvement."[33]

According to a staff member who worked in the office in the late 1970s, Elaine continually pressed Saul for full credit on film work, which may explain why the 35mm theatrical release of *The Solar Film* credits only Bass as director, whereas the Pyramid nontheatrical version released later credits both of them.

However, until the late 1970s, Bass never mentioned his wife as an equal collaborator in any published interviews. Elaine's name did not come up in Bass's 1978 interview film, *Bass on Titles*, nor in an American Film Institute (AFI) seminar in May 1979, despite the fact that the subject of the seminar was filmmaking.[34] According to Owen Edwards, who interviewed Bass extensively for a book in the late 1980s, he never sensed that Elaine was important to the office's design work; nor was she present at the interviews, other than to serve tea.[35] Furthermore, in the estate collection, there are no surviving staff photographs of Elaine. In a 1980 interview, however, Bass acknowledged: "That is why my collaboration with my wife Elaine in the film work is so important to me. She is the only person that I completely trust in terms of her judgment, and her sense of appropriateness—and this has been tested over a long period of time."[36] Indeed, after 1979, Bass more consistently mentioned Elaine in connection with their film work, but the corporate identity and design work remained Saul's exclusive purview. This is substantiated in an unpublished official biography from 1993, which quotes Saul: "Elaine is not an aggressive, confrontational person, while that sort of thing is very easy for me on a movie set. So we have an understanding when we're shooting. I tend to be the mouthpiece, I've got the loud voice, and if there's any yelling to do I'm the one who does it."[37]

It seems clear that, given his relationship with his other designers (even Art Goodman), Saul Bass never relinquished artistic control because he was protecting his brand. As Yager conceded, Bass had great difficulty sharing credit with any of his designers, including his wife. Until the late 1970s, Elaine Bass's contributions in the film arena must therefore be considered in the same light as those of all the other designers who worked in the Bass office and never received credit, even if her actual influence as a sounding board was not insubstantial. After 1979 the Bass brand, at least in the filmmaking arena, evolved into "Saul & Elaine Bass." This book therefore attributes credit to "Saul Bass" not as the biological and biographical individual but as a design entity, a consistent brand, a label. The number of employees in Bass's design office fluctuated, depending on the work, but he may have employed as many as forty individuals at any one time, none of whom received credit.

Branding Saul Bass

After Bass moved to the West Coast in 1946, he quickly learned that relentless self-promotion was not only the rule in Hollywood; it was also a necessary survival skill. If Bass wanted to create a design brand that appealed to Hollywood's self-styled artistic elite, he needed to constantly market himself and his office. Such promotion included a show reel that had to be kept up-to-date for potential clients, press releases, attendance at design conferences and lectures, continuous submissions for Art Directors Club awards, occasional articles authored by the designer, and, most important, articles about Bass by "objective" third parties. One staff member in the Bass office was responsible for promptly sending out photo materials requested by journalists, magazine editors, and clients. Sample reels also kept changing, depending on Bass's latest work and on the evolving master narrative of his career.[38] Even in his own films, Bass promoted his own work. For example, in a 1969 AT&T corporate film, he used his own Continental, Westinghouse, and other Bass-designed corporate logos to illustrate points he was making about good logo design, in an attempt to sell his new corporate identity campaign to the rank and file. Indeed, much of the published work on Saul Bass was orchestrated to some degree by Bass himself through interviews, visual materials, his own essays, and company public relations materials. In this way, Bass maintained the integrity of the brand while creating an official Saul Bass biography and mythology.

Bass's success in keeping his name in the public eye is illustrated by the sheer number of articles about him in the highbrow design and art press. Profiles of Bass began to appear in the early 1950s and provided a level of legitimacy, class, and visibility that he required to attract corporate and Hollywood clients. Between 1954 and his passing in 1996, more than sixty-five articles or profiles on Bass, almost always including quotes from the designer, were published in European, Japanese, and American design and art journals such as *Communication Arts, Design Week, Graphis, IDEA, Industrial Design, Gebrauchsgraphik,* and *Print.* Since the 1920s, foreign art journals such as the Berlin-based *Gebrauchsgraphik* had not only propagated Bauhaus art and design principles to the American design community (it included English translations) but also enhanced the respectability of commercial art, a fact not lost on Bass.[39] Even an informal survey of these art journals indicates that few, if any, other American designers received as much attention as Bass did.

As early as November 1948, Bass published a cover design for the prestigious journal *Arts & Architecture*. In a blurb accompanying and explaining his contribution, Bass wrote: "Man's conflicts are expressed by the confusion and indirection of the background against which is projected the highly integrated nature-machine, the egg; a symbol not only of order but also of purposeful growth."[40] It might as well have been a manifesto for the evolving Bass brand: keep the design simple, utilize geometric forms, and don't overload the background with information that becomes only "noise." In 1953 Bass published a short, heavily illustrated article on movie advertising in the Swiss design journal *Graphis*,[41] which would become one of his biggest supporters. Founded in 1944, the trilingual (English, German, and French) journal was a Bass stronghold for decades; it published more than fifteen Bass-themed articles, including what were essentially promotion pieces on Bass written by Yager and Bass's friend Henry Wolf.[42] In 1954, two years after going independent, Bass was profiled in the storied journal *American Artist*. The author emphasized the designer's high aesthetic aspirations, even when working for hire: "For him there is no conflict of 'commercial' vs. 'fine art.' He has simply chosen an area of activity which enables him to communicate with many, rather than with a few."[43] Three years later, in a lengthy article on West Coast designers, *Industrial Design* highlighted Bass, writing: "Equally at home in the abstract world of ideas and the tangible world of the eye, Saul Bass has become an undisputed leader in the western graphics world with work that is fresh, lithe, charming."[44] What is most striking in these articles is the degree to which Bass is positioned as something more than a commercialist. Like the field of design as a whole, which in post–World War II America was demanding academic respectability, Bass was consistently stylized as an intellectual, a thinker, and an artist.

Bass was getting this kind of attention not only because of the quality and originality of his work but also because he had been busy establishing contacts in the field. In particular, his involvement in the Art Directors Clubs of New York and Los Angeles made the field take notice. Bass won his first New York Art Directors Club award in 1945 for an advertisement for Tylon Cold Wave, which he may have produced as a class assignment in Gyorgy Kepes's design seminar at Brooklyn College. Through the New York club, Bass later made contact with modernist designers Herbert Bayer, Alexey Brodovitch, Will Burtin, Herbert Matter, and Paul Rand.[45] From 1948 until 1962, examples of Bass designs—whether produced for commercial or movie clients—appeared year after year in the New York club's *Annual of Advertising and Editorial Art and Design*. In 1949 Bass was involved in a serious car accident on the way to the Los Angeles Art Directors Club awards ceremony, where he was to receive a gold medal and two certificates of merit.[46] Over the next ten years, Bass would win dozens of awards from Art Directors Clubs in New York, Cleveland, Chicago, and Los Angeles. In 1981 he won the prestigious AIGA Medal "in recognition of his exceptional achievements in the field of design."[47]

Meanwhile, Bass also became involved in the International Design Conference in Aspen (IDCA), joining its program committee in 1953. The conference had been founded in 1951 by Walter Paepcke of Container Corporation of America, the most high-profile supporter of modernist design among America's corporate CEOs; Paepcke had underwritten Moholy-Nagy's New Bauhaus School in Chicago in 1938. The conference's stated goal was to bring designers and business leaders together to discuss the value of good design, but also to make contacts. Bass was a featured speaker at the 1954 conference, when the topic was "Planning: The Basis of Design"; other speakers included Richard Neutra, Russell Lynes, Burns W. Roper, Edgardo Contini, and Robert Saudek.[48] Bass attended the conference virtually every year until his death, becoming one of the éminences grises of Aspen, whether as a speaker or as a filmmaker presenting his work at the Wheeler Opera House at evening screenings. By the 1970s, he was a longtime member of the IDCA's Board of Directors, and he sometimes conducted workshops at the conference. For example, at his 1991 workshop titled "Bare Bones Filmmaking," his students produced a spoof of the ape sequence in Stanley Kubrick's *2001: A Space Odyssey*.[49] In 1996, two months after his death, the IDCA (which was focusing on the history of German design that year) organized a tribute for Bass.[50]

In reference to his film work in Hollywood, Bass took pains to remain visible in industry trade journals, sending notes to *Variety* about his activities. After 1956 and the success of *The Man with the Golden Arm*, Bass became a vocal proponent of what *Variety* termed "the avant-garde approach to film ad and title design."[51] Never shy, Bass had no qualms about attacking conservative distributors, exhibitors, or heads of studio publicity departments for their reluctance to try anything new. By the 1960s, Bass's name and illustrations of his work were also appearing in film journals. The designer's business strategy in Hollywood was to create something new that would make waves in the trades but could be marketed again and again, establishing an iconic Bass brand. In other words, there was a constant push and pull with the film industry—attacking when strong, then compromising. In this regard, it is interesting to examine which images Bass chose when sending out samples of his work to journalists.

His most published work by far, whether in art journals or film magazines, came from *The Man with the Golden Arm*; examples of the poster or titles appeared in at least sixty publications.[52] This makes sense, given that Bass dated the beginning of his Hollywood career with this film by Otto Preminger, despite the fact that he had already designed a number of titles and had already worked in movie industry advertising for eighteen years. Title stills or posters from *Anatomy of a Murder*, *Bonjour Tristesse*, and *Exodus*—all of them Preminger films—were also popular, appearing in more than thirty publications. The inclusion of *Bonjour Tristesse* is a bit surprising, given the film's failure at the box office, but of course, Bass's association with the famous producer-director and with a well-known French novel added to his own prominence. Preminger was considered serious and highbrow by the industry and the press. Indeed, illustrations from all the Preminger titles Bass worked on, including *Saint Joan*, *The Cardinal*, *Bunny Lake Is Missing*, and *Advise and Consent*, were published at least ten times. Surprisingly, Alfred Hitchcock's *North by Northwest* merited fewer than five published illustrations, while *Psycho* was seen in at least twenty publications and *Vertigo* in twenty-five or more. Only four other films (not including Bass's own films *Why Man Creates* and *Phase IV*) achieved double digits in terms of frequency of publication: *Storm Center*, *West Side Story*, *Spartacus*, and *Walk on the Wild Side*. The number of illustrations for his other film work falls off dramatically, seemingly based on Bass's submission of whatever he happened to have finished at the moment, rather than on an attempt to build the Bass brand. Once he was established as a title designer, Bass stopped sending samples of his movie advertisements from before 1956, including his first poster for *Carmen Jones*, possibly because he felt the Bass brand was not pure enough in this early work.

Thus, Bass supplied the same images to countless publications in an effort to establish his brand, while simultaneously attaching his name to films and directors who were considered legitimate auteurs, with Preminger trumping Hitchcock in this regard.[53]

The centrality of *The Man with the Golden Arm* to the Bass brand is connected to the construction of what might be termed the official biographical narrative of Saul Bass. In countless interviews, Bass claimed that before his work on that film, he had previously worked only as a graphic designer. After becoming the self-styled father of modern film titles, Bass decided to make his own films in the mid-1960s, while also designing corporate logos. Later, he and his wife Elaine returned to filmmaking and film titles in the late 1970s and mid-1980s, respectively. The narrative of Bass's professional journey from graphics to live-action film to corporate design is seen in its purest form in the self-produced film *Bass on Titles*. At an AFI seminar, Bass stated: "My entry into the film world grew out of my graphic work. When I came to California, I began to design symbols for motion pictures, for Otto Preminger on *The Man with the Golden Arm*. . . . So, I was well established in my career as a graphic designer before I began working in film. . . . I began my film experience by pushing graphic design stuff around and then got more immersed in the idea of live action and became, in a sense, a filmmaker via that route."[54] He later admitted in some oral histories that he actually began working in film advertising in 1938, more than fifteen years before his "official" start in the business. However, Bass's own chronology from posters to film credits to films to corporate identity breaks down: he was directing commercials and industrial films long before his first official film, *The Searching Eye*, and his corporate identity work dates from the early 1950s, immediately after he opened his own design studio.

Interestingly, given Bass's obvious desire to manipulate and control his own life story, two authorized biographies were commissioned in the last years of his life, neither of which was published. Bass had approached a representative of Harry Abrams & Company about a book as early as 1980.[55] Bass initially wanted Herb Yager to write his biography; Yager had authored the *Graphis* article (1978), had been heavily involved in the special Bass issue of the Japanese design magazine *Idea* (1979), and had acted as interlocutor in *Bass on Titles* (1978). But Yager thought he would be seen as too biased, given that he was Bass's business partner.[56] In the late 1980s Owen Edwards, the founding editor of *American Photogra-*

pher, was commissioned to write a long essay for a heavily illustrated book about Saul Bass as part of a new projected series on photographers and designers.[57] After he completed the piece, Edwards got a call from Bass stating that he would not approve the essay because it "didn't go deep enough."[58] The manuscript, which amounted to less than a hundred pages, quotes Bass extensively, as well as Art Goodman, but Bass's editing of his own quotes indicates he was not particularly happy with what he had said to Edwards during their interviews.[59] The project was quickly abandoned by the publisher, who refused to pay the author more than 25 percent of his advance.

Bass and Yager must have decided that the time was ripe for a Bass book, however, because a short time later they hired NPR film critic Joe Morgenstern to write a biography. Morgenstern's first draft was completed in April 1994.[60] The 150-page manuscript is broken down into twenty-five chapters with titles such as "A Subway Scholar Finds Betty Grable," "Saul & Elaine," "Seeing Things Fresh," and "Personal Handwriting." The brevity of both Morgenstern's and Edwards's manuscripts indicates that they were meant to be accompanied by numerous illustrations in a coffee table–style book. Although Morgenstern focuses on Bass's film work, including the two phases of his title-making career, the author also dedicates chapters to corporate campaigns such as those for Celanese, Lawry's, United Airlines, Getty, Avery, and the Girl Scouts.

Publishers, however, were not buying it, even after the second draft, with changes by Yager and Bass, was completed. Don Congdon Associates, a literary agent, noted in October 1994 that the manuscript needed work, and a rejection letter from Simon and Schuster soon followed.[61] Yager continued to shop the manuscript around, but Abrams, Viking Studio Books, John Macrae Books, W. W. Norton, and Universe Publishing all sent their regrets. In all likelihood, the problem was that Morgenstern had basically ghostwritten an autobiography in the guise of a biography; in other words, Morgenstern's manuscript was based solely on his interviews with Bass and papers and other materials provided by Bass's office. Meanwhile, Yager and Morgenstern got into a major tussle. In April, Morgenstern had been promised payment for his work.[62] But in July, Yager told Morgenstern he was withholding the writer's $5,000 fee because the manuscript was only a draft, additional changes needed to be made, and it was six months late. In the same letter, apparently sent in reaction to Morgenstern's complaints about not being paid, Yager noted acrimoniously: "Your letter amazed me. I am embarrassed. In one bizarre and completely unnecessary overreaction, you obliterated our friendship. As for Saul, he deserved better."[63] By then, Bard College professor Pat Kirkham had started her own Saul Bass research project with a published interview with Saul and Elaine Bass in April 1994. Thus, the decision was made (probably sometime in 1995) to hire her to write the biography. Bass continued to work on the layout and selection of images for this book until his death.

Bass's official biographical narrative was finally published posthumously in 2011. *Saul Bass: A Life in Film and Design* is a richly illustrated tome that covers all facets of Bass's career—his film title designs, corporate identity campaigns, and independently produced films. The most original portion of the book is Pat Kirkham's well-researched essay on Bass's childhood and early career. Apart from the survey of Bass's career, this large-format volume includes hundreds of illustrations, a listing of the design studio's projects for hire, and a bibliography. The book does not highlight the work of any other designers in the Bass office (except for Elaine Bass), yet for any Bass scholar, it is a rich source of documentation, even if it perpetuates much of the Bass mythology.

No other full-length book study has been published, although Andreas A. Timmer's 1999 dissertation, "Making the Ordinary Extraordinary: The Film-Related Work of Saul Bass," deserves mention. After discussing modernist graphic design and Bass's application of those principles to film titles, Timmer focuses on Bass's collaborations with Preminger, Hitchcock, and Martin Scorsese, presenting close readings of some Bass title sequence images but largely ignoring Bass's use of typography. He then discusses Bass's work as a visual consultant on *Psycho*, *Spartacus*, and *Grand Prix*, followed by analyses of Bass's *Why Man Creates*, *Notes on the Popular Arts*, and *Phase IV*. However, Timmer is a bit too telegraphic in his discussion of Bass's work, which may be why the dissertation has not been published. Timmer concludes:

Following his model Kepes while simultaneously establishing his own approach, Bass describes himself as a "visual communicator" and not an artist with a capital A. What does this mean for a designer working in the context of the entertainment industry? In terms of high concept advertising it means art with a practical and informational purpose. Bass succeeded in keeping titles functional while at the same time elevating them into an art form. Many of his credit sequences have a poetic quality that both serves and transcends their functionality. What makes Bass a master in his field is his ability to combine highly original designs with popular appeal.[64]

Popular articles on Saul Bass have been limited to brief biographical narratives, with only one short, formal analysis of a few Bass-created title sequences in the mix.[65] Other articles and interviews available on the Internet do not go beyond the kind of hagiography Bass consistently encouraged. One exception is Emily King's master's thesis, "Taking Credit: Film Title Sequences, 1955–1965," which includes chapters on *The Man with the Golden Arm*, *Vertigo*, and *Spartacus*, as well as Maurice Binder's *From Russia with Love* and Richard Williams's *What's New Pussycat*. Although King recognizes and celebrates the revolutionary aspect of the title designs created by Saul Bass and others, she remains ambiguous about their long-term influence:

> While title sequences which translated static graphic idioms onto the screen were commonplace in the 1960s, they never became the dominant mode of movie titling, nor were they ever completely displaced. From the late 1960s until now there has been huge variety in styles of movie titling, from Woody Allen's theatre-style "cards" to the innovative computer animation in films such as *Superman* (1978). Rather than either reflecting a shift in the conventional relationship between Hollywood and modern design, or amounting to a new element in the vocabulary of the mainstream film-maker, the titles sequences addressed in this thesis were part of the widespread changes in film-making which were eventually to render any single Hollywood formula redundant.[66]

There has been little academic research on the history of film studio publicity campaigns, the marketing of film products, or Hollywood titling practices, all of which could provide context for Bass's work. Most publications have, in fact, centered on issues of censorship and exploitation.[67] Although Emily King's *A Century of Movie Posters: From Silent to Art House* devotes several pages to Saul Bass, it is concerned mainly with film directors rather than poster artists.[68] Finally, a number of collectors and fans have published books of movie posters for the nostalgia market. These may be good visual resources, but they hardly constitute serious academic analysis.

A Designer in Hollywood

Bass's film career challenges our theoretical assumptions about authorship on a number of levels. Whether one designates the director, the producer, or some other authority figure as the auteur of a film, Bass's titles or other interpolated sequences represent the only minutes of a film for which an entity other than the "author" can claim sole credit for the text. But even if we have given up on the notion of an author or the existence of a single film text, as structuralist and post-structuralist theory articulates, the question remains, how do we evaluate Bass's contribution as a designer? As Ross Melnick recently posited, not only is the issue of a unified film text in question; film historians must also consider those elements that can no longer be recuperated, such as the actual live performance.[69] Meanwhile, film historians and theorists often conflate the physical film and all other texts surrounding it (publicity, posters, trailers, advertising), reading them as a master text guided by the producer, the director, or both. But I argue that Bass's intervention into that master text—whether titles, advertising, television commercials, posters, or trailers—represents a unified vision, outside that of the implied author's master text. Nowhere is this more apparent than in the controversy surrounding *Psycho*, which continues to this day.

Uncontested is the fact that Bass is credited in the film for the titles and as "visual consultant," having acted in that capacity not only for the opening credits but also for the storyboards for the infamous shower sequence. When François Truffaut asked Hitchcock about Bass's participation in the production of *Psycho*, Hitchcock replied that Bass had delivered sketches for the murder of the detective and had actually shot the montage of him going up the stairs, but Hitchcock subsequently discarded it all. He said not one word about the shower sequence, which by the mid-1960s had made *Psycho* famous.[70] Possibly in reaction to Hitchcock's niggardly apportionment of credit, or possibly because he was now a feature film director himself (*Phase IV*) looking for credibility, Bass dropped a bombshell in an interview with the *London Sunday Times*: "When the film came out everyone went wild about the shower-bath murder which I'd done, almost literally shot by shot, from my storyboard. And then Hitchcock had second thoughts."[71] Since then, endless printer's ink has been devoted to the issue, and even Bass's own statements are somewhat of a moving target. At an AFI seminar in 1979, he all but took credit for directing, without saying it outright: "I storyboarded it, and literally supervised the shooting of it. Hitchcock was on the set, and I thought Hitch was going to direct it. But when I came to the set, he was very generous and insisted I direct the shots. I got a short course with Hitch on that picture."[72] Bass later insisted that Hitchcock had directed the sequence: "But the truth of the matter is, it *was* and *is* Hitch's film. It's all his, no matter what I did."[73]

Unfortunately, all the eyewitness accounts, many of which have denied any Bass involvement in the direction of the shower sequence, are unreliable, since all were articulated long after the fact.[74] Here, I briefly summarize the major positions and offer my own take on the subject. Stephen Rebello has criticized both Hitchcock and Bass for overstating their positions, but he ultimately comes down on the side of the film's director.[75] Interestingly, in the recent Hitchcock biopic based on Rebello's book, Bass has been all but written out of the story.[76] Pat Kirkham, in contrast, makes a forceful case for Bass's authorship of the shower sequence; although it seems very convincing, it is based more on speculation and formal design than on any hard evidence.[77] The late Raymond Durgnat skirts the question altogether, commenting on Bass's titles but analyzing the shower sequence from an auteurist-formalist and psychoanalytic perspective, without even mentioning the authorship controversy.[78]

Based on evidence from various sources, I believe that Bass may have set up a few shots under Hitchcock's supervision, and Bass did design the storyboards, almost all of which ended up as images in the final edit. Hitchcock also allowed Bass to shoot 16mm tests, which Bass describes with some precision, as well as suggest an edit. As far as directing, Bass later conceded that Hitchcock invited him to set up the first and second shots, but probably no more than that.[79] Thus, it is likely that Hitchcock hired Bass to create an Eisensteinian montage for the first murder because he envisioned a shockingly sudden demise for his leading lady and needed a montage specialist, which he decidedly was not. But in the end, Alfred and Alma Hitchcock worked out the final edit after the first previews, so *Psycho* was ultimately not only Hitchcock's financial risk but also very much his own work.

So why did Bass start this controversy? One must wonder whether it was a public relations ploy, since Bass made no claims about directing the shower sequence until he had become a feature film director himself with *Phase IV*. Maybe the publicity was just too good to turn down, given that Bass could, with some credibility, challenge the authorship of one of the few film directors who was truly a household name in America, and given that his business was starting to go south. Or was it merely a casual remark that got out of hand? We will never know, but I'm assuming that for Bass it was a branding issue, in the sense that he wanted to reestablish his expertise as a director and a montage specialist, having previously designed or produced sequences for Stanley Kubrick, Vincente Minnelli, Carl Foreman, and John Frankenheimer, among others.

Like these directors, most of Bass's Hollywood clients were or wanted to be seen as auteurs. As I argue here, Saul Bass (and the role of the designer) came into prominence as the studio system was crumbling and independent producer-director hyphenates were on the rise. These independents, whether Otto Preminger, Stanley Kramer, Billy Wilder, or Stanley Kubrick, had high artistic aspirations for their films and employed Bass to give their work cachet. That was possible because of the gradual breakdown of the studio system and the ebbing of power held by studio production and publicity departments. Nevertheless, Bass's style and techniques were still considered avant-garde by many in the industry, and his efforts to realize his design ideas were always subject to pressure from the more traditional elements in the Hollywood system.

Rather than seeing any artistic production within the commercial film industry as "selling out," and thus substantiating the romantically inflected dichotomy between art and commerce, newer film and media histories have advanced the notion that it was possible to work in Hollywood but still participate in avant-garde practices. David James notes that avant-garde filmmakers and Hollywood have always had a symbiotic relationship: "Even when the concerns of minority cinemas are quite specific, often their expression creates cultural forms whose difference, more or less reworked, can be productively assimilated by other groups or by the industry. But this function of the avant-garde as the research and development branch of the cultural industry is reciprocated in the latter's utility for the avant-garde. Minority practices are inevitably framed by the dominant industry and determined by its overall structure."[80]

With regard to Bass's commercial design work, whether in movie publicity, filmmaking, or advertising, I would characterize it as a modernist avant-garde practice constituted within Hollywood rather than in opposition to it. This seems not only advisable, given the formal innovation and consistent branding apparent in all of Bass's work, but also necessary, given the designer's education. Directly indebted to teachers who had studied and worked at the Bauhaus in Weimar Germany, Bass translated the Bauhaus ethic and aesthetic into an American idiom, just as Walter Gropius, Laszlo Moholy-Nagy, and Gyorgy Kepes transplanted Bauhaus ideals to Chicago and New York in post–World War II America. Indeed, the central Bauhaus notion of art and design having both aesthetic and functional applications was put into practice in 1920s Germany and 1950s America.

To illuminate not only how that process of aesthetic translation worked but also its historical and cultural coordinates (specifically in terms of Saul Bass, and generally in terms of high modernism's infiltration of American cultural practice), it might be productive to invoke a concept such as vernacular modernism. As Miriam Hansen notes, "modernism encompasses a whole range of cultural and artistic practices that register, respond to, and reflect upon processes of modernization and the experience of modernity, including a paradigmatic transformation of the conditions under which art is produced, transmitted, and consumed. In other words, just as modernist aesthetics are not reducible to the category of style, they tend to blur the boundaries of the institution of art in its traditional, eighteenth- and nineteenth-century incarnation that turns on the ideal of aesthetic autonomy and the distinction of 'high' vs. 'low,' of autonomous art vs. popular and mass culture." Hansen argues that the high modernist canon—with its specific "single-logic" genealogy from "Cubism to Abstract Expressionism," from Brecht to the theater of the absurd, from Eisenstein to Godard or Walter Ruttmann to Stan Brakhage—essentialized the role of the artist while denying modernism's infiltration of many commercial genres and "vernacular" forms of cultural practice entailing "connotations of discourse, idiom, and dialect, with circulation, promiscuity, and translatability." What Hansen is getting at here is that many forms of mass culture, whether Hollywood film narratives or their advertising, communicate in a dialogue with diverse and divergent consumers. And while I'm hesitant to accept Hansen's notion that all Hollywood narrative cinema in its classical phase imbricates with the modernist project, I agree that the very act of constituting what is almost always a partial or overdetermined discourse in Hollywood resulted in varying degrees of self-reflexivity; further, this awareness of engaging in a discourse is the raison d'être of modernist art. As Hansen writes: "The reflexive dimension of Hollywood films in relation to modernity may take cognitive, discursive, and narrativized forms, but it is crucially anchored in sensory experience and sensational affect, in processes of mimetic identification that are more often than not partial and excessive in relation to narrative comprehension."[81]

Saul Bass's film work, whether titles created for independent producer-directors or his own films, must therefore be seen as a continual effort to bring avant-garde practices to Hollywood. His design elements exude modernism not only because of the Bauhaus influence but also because Bass himself preferred a more fragmented approach that left interpretive spaces open, allowing the audience to read film texts subjectively.

The Bass Brand

According to Pat Kirkham, Bass saw and loved Maya Deren's *Meshes in the Afternoon* (1945), as well as other avant-garde films. Over the course of his career, Bass consistently worked with American avant-garde filmmakers such as. the Whitney brothers and Pat O'Neill. Bass's personal films contributed to the essay film genre pioneered by Chris Marker and Jean-Luc Godard, but with precedents in Dziga Vertov.[82] Indeed, Bass films such as *The Searching Eye* and *Why Man Creates* question audiences directly and provide possible but not definitive answers; they consciously communicate knowledge through vision. Jean-Pierre Gorin's dictum regarding the essay film certainly pertains to these Bass titles: it is "the meandering of an intelligence that tries to multiply the entries and the exits into the material it has elected (or by which it has been elected)."[83] And just as montage is central to the aesthetic of the essay film, with the hand of the editor crafting a way of seeing and hearing, the visual tropes of the eye (vision) and the hand (creating form) are central to the Bass brand.

As early as 1957, we see Bass utilizing pure abstraction in his credit sequence for Billy Wilder's *The Seven Year Itch*. This sequence is all the more striking because its relationship to the narrative is as abstract as abstract art. Was Bass thinking of the New York City brownstones that are the locale for the film's action? What interests me here is the way Bass limits his color palette to black, white, and various hues from red to brown, making the sequence nothing if not a study of a limited corner of the color wheel. The sequence recalls both the American abstract expressionists (who were being recognized in the 1950s as the most avant-garde artists in the world) and the German painters of and around the Bauhaus school, such as Paul Klee.

Paul Klee's *Flora in the Sand* is one of a series of paintings by the artist that reduce topographies to various squares and rectangles of color. It is this concept of using flat planes of color to visualize geographic space that connects this 1927 painting to Bass's titles for *The Seven Year Itch*. And while it may be foolhardy to make a direct link between these two works, as I have here, the possibilities are rich in terms of comparing the works of many Bauhaus artists with Bass's work. Certainly, Bauhaus art courses and aesthetics theorized that geometry and abstraction were central elements of composition within the two-dimensional frame, even if the objects depicted were less abstracted or even photographic. Photography was, of course, taught in the basic Bauhaus art course, and Bauhaus photography workshops were extremely active. Almost all Bauhaus artists took up photography at one point or another, and Moholy-Nagy was possibly the most active of the group.

Abstraction thus became a major design element in the photographic work of the Bauhaus artists. Lotte Beese's 1927 photograph of a loom (Anni Albers ran the textile workshop at the Bauhaus and would become one of the most famous textile designers in America) reduces the machine to an abstract play of light, line, and form. Indeed, its original function as a loom is completely lost in the photographic image. However, what we do see is an image that, despite its abstraction, manages to create a sense of depth and the impression of a machine, even if we don't know what that machine does. Compare this image with Saul and Elaine Bass's title sequence for *Casino* (1995; see chapter 5), which frames Las Vegas neon in such a way as to create nothing more than abstract patterns of light, making it virtually impossible to identify. The sequence becomes a cacophony of light and color, revealing neither the content (specific casino signs) nor the locale but nevertheless conveying the sense of endless activity that is Las Vegas. For Bass, the formal design elements, the use of circles, squares, and lines of movement, were the heart of any design.

Saul Bass's design work in cinema and film publicity must be seen first and foremost as a graphic art, evolving from his training as a graphic artist. As the following chapters show, Bass conceptualized film as a two-dimensional space, composing his images for a frame rather than for the window into the world theorized by André Bazin and other realists. His title sequences, as well as his films, communicate meaning through composition, creating graphics in motion that are astounding today because they were produced with analogue technology rather than digital, computer-generated programs. Indeed, Bass's designs in film presage cinema's return in the twenty-first century to animation and painting, as theorized by Lev Manovich: "The manual construction of images in digital cinema represents a return to nineteenth century pre-cinematic practices, when images were hand-painted and hand-animated. At the turn of the twentieth century, cinema was to delegate these manual techniques to animation and define itself as a recording medium. As cinema enters the digital age, these techniques are again becoming the commonplace in the filmmaking process. Consequently, cinema can no longer be clearly distinguished from animation. It is no longer an indexical media technology but, rather, a sub-genre of painting."[84]

Bass's interest in Bauhaus design elements also led him to become a film montage specialist. One can argue that Bass's designs incorporated montage before he ever touched a foot of film. By the 1950s, he was working closely with editors to learn about editing. Bass loved the endless possibilities of montage, of putting together a syntactic unit of film images; he loved thinking in terms of montage. As a result, camera movements in Bass's film titles and films are few and far between, even in his later films such as *The Solar Film* and *Quest*. It was not until the 1980s, possibly due to the influence of Elaine Bass, that camera movement became more prominent in his titles; for instance, the titles for *War of the Roses* and *Mr. Saturday Night* both feature long, horizontal camera tracks, exploring landscapes. In contrast, Art Goodman's animation sequences in *Why Man Creates* and *The Solar Film* are explorations through time, but they are constructed as camera movements through space, based, of course, on the illusion of movement through animated images.

Camera movement implies a journey, and journeys through time and space were central to the Bass universe. His end title sequence for *Around the World in 80 Days* was the first of many quest narratives Bass would design and execute. The quest, whether intellectual or physical, became the structuring presence in many of his own films: *From Here to There, The*

Searching Eye, Why Man Creates, Phase IV, and *Quest*. Like the quests of classical mythology, visual metaphor transforms these journeys into a search for knowledge. Indeed, vision and sight become synonymous with knowledge, especially when the communication of knowledge is visual rather than verbal.

Bass created more than modernist designs; he consciously created a brand that was recognizable to both industry professionals and laypersons. The work of Saul Bass & Associates must be understood as a brand created by a design office with numerous contributing individuals, even if Saul (and later Elaine) was the controlling intelligence behind that brand. The Bass brand was rigorously maintained by limiting the design palette to a certain number of techniques and design elements. Regardless of whether he was working on movie advertising campaigns, film titles, short films, corporate logos, or corporate identity campaigns, the integrity of the Bass identity had to be maintained. Incorporating modernist and avant-garde designs into the Bass brand, however, did not imply improvisation. In fact, quite the opposite was true: nothing was left to chance. Once a concept had been agreed on, often after endless discussion, the Bass office or often Bass himself storyboarded everything, down to the blocking of actors.[85] Even if the titles and films were supposed to look like they had been spontaneously constructed, the product of experimentation or fiddling around, as Bass called it, they were always consciously developed and executed.

Saul Bass's designs have been held in high esteem for decades by his peers, as well as by specialists in other fields, yet the time is ripe for a critical reevaluation of all of Bass's work. Certainly, his designs were valued in the commercial marketplace, where he commanded fees that might have priced him out of the Hollywood market, at least until he made a comeback in the late 1980s. Now, more than fifteen years after the designer's death, it is time to measure Bass's contribution to the field, beyond some of the mythologies associated with him. My historical analysis of the Saul Bass legacy seeks to contextualize his work within the historical coordinates of Hollywood film production and movie publicity—specifically, the evolution of film posters from the earliest days to the present, his advertising work, his film titles, and his films. Finally, Bass must be seen in the context of the larger social developments in post–World War II America—namely, the increase in intellectual respectability among the design profession, its recognition by society as a legitimate profession, and the upward mobility of designers in the financial hierarchy of rewards and withholdings. As previously demonstrated by others, it was the influx of European-born or -trained designers (many of them German-Jewish exiles) into 1950s America that vastly expanded the palate for and the palette of acceptable design in this country. Furthermore, I contend that Bass was keenly aware of the pioneering role he played in his chosen field, sometimes even relishing his part as agent provocateur in Hollywood's conservative guild system, yet producing seminal aesthetic work that largely conformed to the system's needs. The designer can truly claim a place next to the greats of mid-twentieth-century American design: Ivan Chermayeff, Milton Glaser, Paul Rand, Ikko Tanaka, and Henryk Tomaszewski.[86]

Analyzing Saul Bass Designs in Film

In the chapters that follow, I analyze the design work of Saul Bass & Associates as it pertained to the film industry. Although I quote Saul Bass, when relevant, to indicate some form of intentionality, my ultimate goal is to define the designer through his work. Therefore, my analyses often begin with a formalist approach, presenting what is actually on the page or on the screen, then bringing in larger social, political, or contextual issues. As a result, the portrait that evolves may have little to do with the flesh-and-blood human being who was Saul Bass. Rather, I'm interested in the way his work created design standards in the film industry that are still valid today, more than fifteen years after his death. The Bass brand, as I argue, has a tangible existence in the work that survives, as well as in the work of designers who followed him.

Chapter 1, "Designer and Filmmaker," begins with a brief biography of Saul Bass and then pursues the intellectual and aesthetic roots of the Saul Bass brand. It is not enough to simply invoke the Bauhaus, as other writers have done. Instead, I demonstrate how Bass appropriated and internalized Bauhaus concepts as articulated by Moholy-Nagy and Kepes, primarily through the visual examples published in the seminal work of both these designers. Given that Bass spent at least fifteen years involved in movie advertising, I then present a short history of the field to tease out what was different about Bass's designs once he began to find his own voice and create what would become the Bass brand. I conclude first with definitions of the Bass design style and brand, focusing finally on the many recurring visual motifs in his design work.

Chapter 2, "Film Titles: Theory and Practice," focuses on the history and practice of producing film titles or credit sequences. Arguably, this is where Bass's influence was most strongly felt. After briefly analyzing Bass's titles for *That's Entertainment II*, his own informal history of titles, I lay out the technical and aesthetic development of titles in Hollywood and then turn to the theories underlying all titling. Unlike virtually every other commentator on Bass's title work, I initially privilege typography and the role of the modernist design grid as an aesthetic precept in his titles. I next turn to the many production strategies employed in his title work. Although some titles were purely graphic in design, others utilized various forms of animation or photographic montages, yet almost all referenced modern art. Indeed, Bass was consciously incorporating not only European modernist design standards but also contemporary American art (e.g., Abstract Expressionism) into his work in an effort to raise the bar in Hollywood.

Chapter 3, "Creating a Mood: *Pars pro toto*," digs deeper into the Bass methodology, particularly his penchant for creating pithy symbols for his posters and film publicity—logo-like forms that functioned symbolically like his corporate identity designs. I also present a brief history of movie posters to illustrate what was revolutionary about Bass's designs. Then I demonstrate how his posters, especially those created for Otto Preminger, consciously quoted modernist art and artists in order to imbue his movie publicity campaigns with a seriousness of purpose. Next I tease out not only the formalist aspects of his movie design work but also recurring thematic elements, as expressed in selected film title designs. Interestingly, for all his modernist aspirations, Bass was equally drawn to an almost mystical conception of signs, the elements of fire and water, and the concrete world of objects and landscapes morphing into abstract notions of the mind.

Chapter 4, "Modernism's Multiplicity of Views," moves from the single image to Bass's construction of meaning through montage. The designer's penchant for dissecting and then reanimating body parts comes into play almost everywhere in his work—the disembodied hand being an almost obsessive visual trope—but particularly in his titles for *Anatomy of a Murder*. Bass's methodology for constructing meaning in film was based on Eisensteinian concepts of montage, whereby the body of a film consists of a stitching together of countless moving images. In this connection, I first analyze Bass's previously neglected work in television commercials, where he cut his film production teeth. Then I discuss title sequences based on montage and the way they contribute to the initial impression of the film. The chapter concludes with a close reading of his independently produced environmental film *The Solar Film,* which largely functions non-verbally through a montage of images.

Chapter 5, "The Urban Landscape," explores what I believe to be one of the ur-sites of modernist art and avant-garde films: the modern cityscape. Bass's titles here move from modernist abstraction and graphics to documentary montages, as developed in the avant-garde city films of the 1920s and 1930s. I then analyze another ubiquitous visual trope in Bass's work involving the urban environment—namely, city lights, as articulated in film titles and his first short animated film. I conclude with the image of the city in Bass's commercials for National Bohemian Beer.

Chapter 6, "Journeys of Discovery: Seeing Is Knowledge," further explores the notion of travel and the quest as forms of knowledge, based on visual perception. A number of Bass's film titles are structured as journeys, yet for the most part, it is the audience that experiences intellectual growth, not the characters engaged in the journey. That position changes radically with Bass's independent short films, which are all structured as journeys during which the audience learns to see and perceive what lies beneath the surface. What is also apparent in his short films, especially *The Searching Eye* and *Quest,* is the way Bass has transformed himself from an urban Jewish modernist into a California nature enthusiast with seemingly mystical and spiritual leanings.

Finally, Chapter 7, "Civilization: Organizing Knowledge through Communication," highlights Bass's work as a communicator of ideas and history, whether in his opening credits, montage sequences, or films. Beginning with his previously unknown promotional film *Apples and Oranges,* which visualizes the findings of an important study comparing television and magazine advertising, I then discuss his animated short, *100 Years of the Telephone.* Next, I analyze what I perceive to be his magnum opus, *Why Man Creates,* which encapsulates many of Bass's ideas about art and civilization and is presented in a form that gives the viewer freedom to contribute to the film's meaning. In other words, it is a truly modernist work of art. I conclude with his lone feature film, *Phase IV,* which, despite its unhappy production and release history, has been celebrated as a complex science fiction film that in many ways explodes notions of genre while asking the question, what makes us human?

1

Designer and Filmmaker

One of the most striking aspects of Saul Bass's epically successful career as a designer was that he was essentially an autodidact without formal academic training. While his official biographies note that he studied with Howard Trafton and Gyorgy Kepes (the latter a superstar designer in his own right), the fact was that Bass's "studies" were limited to a handful of night-school courses. Bass was always very modest on this point, reminding interviewers that there were few opportunities to study graphic design in America at that time because "commercial art" was considered a lowly profession.[1] Though it is true that some colleges were offering degrees in graphic design, the economic pressures of the Depression played a role in Bass's decision to enter the workforce rather than attend college. Not surprisingly, Bass was skeptical about the value of an academic education: "I don't see artists as engaging in esoteric activity, but as a worker, engaged in a particular kind of skill."[2] Bass certainly never played the role of an intellectual; rather, he epitomized the engaged craftsman of quality, which may have been why he fit into the classical Hollywood paradigm so well: there, almost everyone learned by doing rather than by attending school. As Bass noted in 1990: "I guess what makes me uncomfortable is the word 'philosophy.' For me design is a 'craft.' And I try very hard to be a good craftsman."[3]

Like many Hollywood practitioners (and many commercial designers), Bass later affected an aversion to any kind of theorization or analysis of his work. In interviews he threw out a few theoretical bones, such as his notion of revitalizing clichés or a theoretical explication of reductionist modes of creativity, but they were part of his official narrative. Any analytic discussion of the formal characteristics of a particular work got sidetracked into whether the design caught anyone's attention. Douglas Bell, in a regrettably unfinished oral history, tried valiantly to engage Bass in a dialogue about the formal elements of his campaign for *The Champion*

(1949), an early example of what would become the Bass brand. Bell kept suggesting meanings, which Bass lobbed right back without comment, focusing instead on the incredible impact his advertising campaign had had in Hollywood. When Bell mentioned Kepes's concept of "dynamic iconography" as a theoretical tool for understanding Bass's unconventional use of graphic space in *The Champion* campaign, Bass retorted that such terms are "so general as to be meaningless." Unperturbed, Bell tried another tactic and got this response: "Well, you could read a lot into it." Finally, Bass got curt: "You have to be careful about theories and about so-called principles. I don't know what the principles are, Doug." He then explained that when he was younger he had been insecure, but now he believed only in intuition. Bass closed the discussion with a coup de grace: "Fruitless to speculate about it, except that it's amusing to talk about it. But you can't deal with it seriously, other than as sort of an intellectual arabesque."[4] Sounding a bit like John Ford in his famous interview with Peter Bogdanovich,[5] Bass was not about to reveal his trade secrets or intellectualize his own work. When another interviewer questioned his philosophy of design, Bass shot back: "Theories are very dangerous, and philosophy is theory. God help you if you do your next piece based on a theory, you are lost."[6]

Ironically, early in his career, the Hollywood community perceived Bass as somewhat of a New York egghead. And he was not averse to intellectual discussions about design. According to Al Kallis, Bass loved to discuss theory and process, engaging in endless philosophical and aesthetic debates about why it was better to lay out an ad one way or another.[7] Bass was not lying about his intuitive grasp of good design. But then, Bass learned by intuition. A year before his death, a profile on Bass noted: "The self-knowledge he has from all the years of practice is that his art and craft, so often praised and followed, is not a science, but something more intuitive."[8] Bass's burning ambition in life was to become "Saul Bass," so he consumed art and design with a vociferous appetite. Asked about his influences, he mentioned one of his mentors: "I watched Paul Rand, five years my senior, like a hawk."[9] Rand, for his part, was worried that Bass was copying him.[10]

Saul Bass: A Brief Biography

Bass was born in the Bronx, New York, on 8 May 1920 to Jewish, Yiddish-speaking parents who had emigrated from the Romanian-Ukrainian shtetl. He graduated from James Monroe High School at age fifteen, already winning awards for his art and draftsmanship.[11] A precocious child, Bass was fascinated by the Egyptian exhibits at the Metropolitan Museum of Art. Indeed, archaeology and ancient cultures would become a lifelong fascination; the designer, who believed in reincarnation, thought he either had been an archaeologist in a former life or would become one in the next life.[12] Bass began working for a freelance designer in an entry-level position—getting coffee, picking up supplies, and the like. He also received a scholarship from the Art Students League, and in September 1936 he enrolled in an evening class, Layout and Design for Industry, taught by Howard Trafton; Bass continued to take art classes at night until at least late 1940.[13] Trafton focused heavily on fine art, but he also gave his students training they could use in commercial art, being a practitioner himself. As Bass stated to biographer Joe Morgenstern: "Intuitively, I understood that if I wanted to come to grips with design, i.e. with so-called commercial art, I really had to understand the principles that made fine art work."[14]

Meanwhile, in 1938 Bass moved to a small New York firm that produced trade advertisements for United Artists and then for Warner Brothers (for twice the money). He married Ruth Cooper and had two children: Robert in 1942 and Andrea in 1946. In 1941 Bass was promoted to 20th Century–Fox as a layout man; he earned excellent wages but had little freedom to design advertisements that deviated from the depressing norm.[15] According to Pat Kirkham, Bass was so unhappy with the movie publicity business that he quit in 1943 and took a job at half pay at an advertising agency, Blaine Thompson Company, "with the proviso that he not work on movie studio ads."[16] However, when the agency ran into trouble with its Warner Brothers account, Bass was brought in to help.[17] Thus, Bass received an extensive apprenticeship in film advertising that lasted more than ten years. He learned not only the standard practices of the day but also what he, as a designer, did not want to do. By this time, Bass had already joined the Screen Publicists Guild, participating in June 1942 in a Civilian Defense Information Bureau demonstration at Macy's as a quick-sketch artist.[18]

Sometime in late 1944 Bass discovered Gyorgy Kepes's *The Language of Vision*.[19] According to another early interview,[20] Bass first read Laszlo Moholy-Nagy's *The New Vision: From Material to Architecture*.[21] In any case, Bass learned that Kepes was teaching around the corner at Brooklyn

College and apparently enrolled in his class. Kepes, a former collaborator of Moholy-Nagy's, had studied at the Bauhaus in Weimar Germany before being forced by the Nazis to immigrate to the United States via London. Kepes and, by extension, Moholy-Nagy would exert an enormous influence on Bass, turning the budding adman's vague artistic aspirations into a concrete set of goals and principles that would become hallmarks of the Bass brand. When asked in an interview how Kepes had influenced him, Bass noted that his work had become more dynamic and abstract: "I began to deal with non-illustrative formal elements in addition to the formal elements . . . it was a very dramatic step for me."[22] Bass was particularly struck by an exercise Kepes had his students do after a discussion of Mondrian and the tension between color fields moving forward or backward. Bass stated: "His classes changed everything for me. In a way, I was trying to open the door, pulling and pushing the knob. Kepes said, 'Turn it,' and I stepped through."[23]

In 1946 Bass was lured away by Buchanan & Company, the fifth largest advertising agency in the United States. He was hired to be an art director in its newly established West Coast offices, where Paul Radin was creative director. (As a producer, Radin would later hire Bass to direct *Phase IV*.) Buchanan handled the substantial Paramount Pictures account, as well as the advertising for other major American firms, so the twenty-six-year-old Bass moved to Hollywood. As he noted in a 1981 interview: "I decided that New York was not only very cold but very dull and that I needed to warm up."[24] His first West Coast workplace was the fabled "Garden of Allah," at the southwest corner of Sunset and Crescent Heights. In a May 1947 advertisement in *Variety*, Buchanan & Company announced its new address on Canon Drive in Beverly Hills and its staff, which included John Krimsky as manager of the motion picture division, with Radin and Bass reporting to him.[25] Bass later claimed there were two reasons for his preference for California: one was the movie business, and the other was that the corporate business culture in California was "primitive," meaning "there has been little time for the stifling institutionalization and stratification which strangles creativity in many, very old or established business."[26] Bass understood that his chances of breaking into the commercial design business were far greater in California than in New York, where long-established WASP design firms dominated Madison Avenue.

In February 1949 Bass was involved in a terrible automobile accident in Pasadena on his way to Art Directors Club awards ceremony, where he was supposed to pick up one gold medal and two certificates of merit. Instead, he ended up at Temple Hospital with a shattered hip.[27] A subsequent infection caused his hip to become necrotic, and he suffered from the aftereffects for the rest of his life.[28] Given that such injuries tend to be adversely affected by cold and dampness, the warm California weather was an added incentive to stay in the West.

By July 1950 Bass was Buchanan's executive art director, handling, among other things, the United Artists account.[29] Although much of the film advertising he did was still ho-hum, Bass began to push the boundaries, especially when working with the independent producer-directors who would soon help upend the studio system. They allowed him to incorporate new ideas about advertising design into his work. But Bass knew the studio system too well, and he understood that studio politics rarely changed: "Once you work for a studio you get caught up in the 'group decision' mentality. Nobody wants to take the responsibility for anything, so everybody plays it safe and criticizes."[30] Most of his United Artists clients were independents, including Stanley Kramer Productions, for which Bass designed advertisements and premiere invitations for *Champion* (1949), *Death of a Salesman* (1951), and *The Sniper* (1952), among others.[31] He worked simultaneously with directors Mark Robson and Edward Dmytryk, who would both later hire him for movie title work, as would Kramer. He also created advertising designs for Joseph Mankiewicz's *No Way Out* (1950) and *All About Eve* (1950), Fred Zinnemann's *The Men* (1950) and *High Noon* (1952), and Anatole Litvak's *Decision before Dawn* (1951), all of which displayed elements of the evolving Bass style.[32] As an employee, Bass was not yet signing his name to his work, unlike Paul Rand, whose poster for *No Way Out* demonstrated the lockstep in design concepts between the two men.

Meanwhile, Bass continued to design advertisements and selected print material for other Buchanan clients, including Rexall Drugstores, Reynolds Aluminum, and Western Airlines. By August 1951 Bass was ready to move on again and took a position at Foote, Cone & Belding; the advertising agency was going through a major reorganization after the departure of one of its founders, Emerson Foote.[33] Bass was brought in to handle the account for RKO, a movie studio owned at the time by eccentric billionaire Howard Hughes. Bass enjoyed relating anecdotes about midnight meetings with the reclusive Hughes in limousines. Once he got

Hughes's approval on RKO's advertising campaigns, Bass would be unceremoniously dumped on a street corner and left to find his own way home.[34]

Bass worked for Hughes until late 1952, when he quit after allegedly being denied a salary raise. Bass then founded his own firm, and over the next several years he designed mostly from home as he attempted to establish his brand, sometimes bringing in other freelancers. He earned a steady income from his freelance movie ads and tried to break free of the conventions that demanded every square inch of ad space be filled with content. With Bass, it was all about designing clean, legible, unique material. Although Bass had done his own lettering and calligraphy during his years of apprenticeship, he used other artists once he became an art director. According to Al Kallis, who worked with Bass for several years in the mid-1950s, Bass conceptualized the layout and design, while Kallis drew the art and Maury Nemoy handled the typography and calligraphy.[35] Another steady collaborator on film titles was Harold Adler, who created the lettering for *Carmen Jones, Man with the Golden Arm, The Seven Year Itch*, and the Hitchcock titles.

Bass continued to maintain an office at Foote, Cone, & Belding for a while. Then he shared digs in Hollywood (at Highland and Franklin) with Maury Nemoy and another freelance designer, Phyllis Tanner, with whom he also collaborated, before finally setting up his own design office at 1778 Highland Avenue.[36] However, Bass worked largely from home in the mid-1950s, and a contemporary article on West Coast designers mentions Bass splitting his time between Hollywood and an Altadena studio, the latter in his home.[37] Meanwhile, his wife Ruth raised the two children and worked on a PhD in physiology at the University of Southern California. In 1959 Bass's firm moved to 7758 Sunset Boulevard, which was a small house that had been converted to office spaces. The two-car garage doubled as a film studio, with a 16mm Steenbeck, projectors, and a white wall for screenings. In 1965 Saul Bass Associates moved to 7039 Sunset Boulevard in West Hollywood, which included a larger warehouse space in the back. By then, about ten to twelve people worked in the office. The front office was always "neat as a pin," and the walls were painted, at Bass's insistence, ocher and olive green.[38] Bass was particularly meticulous about his little menagerie of pre-Columbian fetish statues, which could not be moved under any circumstances.[39]

In 1957, shortly after moving to Highland Avenue, Bass hired Elaine

A. Makatura as his secretary.[40] After divorcing his first wife, Ruth, Saul and Elaine were married on 30 September 1961 and eventually had two children, Jennifer and Jeffrey. Other longtime employees who joined the Bass team in 1960 included artist-animator Art Goodman, who had started working as a freelancer for Bass in 1956 and became his "right hand man."[41] Photographer George Arakaki and production manager Nancy von Lauderbach also worked for Bass. Morrie Marsh, a former printing company salesman who had known Bass professionally since the early 1950s, became Bass's business manager, a position he maintained until he was—in his opinion—ruthlessly pushed aside by Herb Yager.[42] Numerous other filmmakers and photographers worked on individual projects on a freelance basis, including the Whitney brothers, Bill Melendez, Pat O'Neill, Herb Klynn, Jules Engel, Bob Willoughby, and Jerry Fruchtman.

Lightcraft of California was the first company that hired Bass to conceive a corporate identity campaign. From there, Bass broadened his market base to include numerous commercial clients for which he designed "space advertisements, package design, merchandise and point-of-sales displays, exhibitions, direct mail pieces, and company stationery."[43] His commercial clients included Brett Lithographing Company, Glide windows, General Pharmaceutical Corporation, Frank Holmes Laboratories, Flo-Ball pens, Madre Selva cosmetics, Pabco paint, Carson-Roberts Company, and John W. Westley Associates.[44] It is no accident that Bass went independent at this time, expanding his base and design services beyond the movie advertising business. According to designer and Bass intimate Lou Dorfsman, "In 1949, the advertising/communications business, which had been very white, Anglo-Saxon, Protestant, broke wide open. You suddenly had Jews, Greeks, all kinds of people in the business, who gave it an incredible shot in the arm."[45] Indeed, Bass's corporate identity campaign for ALCOA (along with Rand's campaign for IBM) pioneered these efforts in American marketing and made Bass a household name in design. His rebranding of AT&T in the late 1960s was the largest such effort in U.S. corporate history.[46] Unlike the very modest fees earned for film design work (less than $30,000), corporate logos and corporate identity campaigns could bring in millions of dollars.[47]

With the rise of independent film production, the trend in Hollywood was to move away from big advertising agencies, with their anonymous workforces, and toward boutique operations led by designers who would cater to individual client's needs and be more flexible and faster, given the tighter production schedules.[48] An incredible showman, Bass utilized his verbal acuity to make the pitch to potential clients in Hollywood and dove into the booming postwar Southern California economy. Less than a decade after his move to Los Angeles, Bass would be hailed by a Swiss design journal as a leader of California modernism.[49]

It was in 1954 that Bass first tried his hand at designing title sequences for films. He had been hired by Otto Preminger to create the publicity art for *Carmen Jones*, including the poster, and was then given the opportunity to do the titles as well. For decades, Hollywood studios had treated credit sequences as an afterthought, usually employing standardized graphics with the company logo. However, some independent Hollywood producers had begun to experiment with new graphic elements and animated sequences to create a particular mood or feeling before the film's actual narrative commenced. Saul Bass was in the forefront of this development, and his credit sequences utilized graphic elements from his advertising campaign designs. For the first time in Hollywood's modern era, a graphic designer (Bass) received onscreen credit for title work. As the press book for *Carmen Jones* notes: "There's been a lot of talk among those who have seen *Carmen Jones* . . . about the unusual credits which precede the film. Unusual in itself, the designer of the titles is credited—one Saul Bass. They are distinctive in terms of modern design, for their neat, clean, open look."[50]

In fact, Bass received almost instant recognition for his innovative title work, as evidenced by an article in the *New York Times* in December 1957, barely two years after he entered the movie title field.[51] Using the same designer to create both the film titles and the publicity meant that a film could be "branded." According to Bass: "My initial thoughts about what a title can do was to set mood and the prime underlying core of the film's story, to express the story in some metaphorical way. I saw the title as a way of conditioning the audience, so that when the film actually began, viewers would already have an emotional resonance with it."[52] More important, Bass's titles allowed product differentiation for individual films. This was a must after the Paramount Consent Decree in 1948, which required films to be sold to theaters individually and based on their own merit, rather than as part of a studio package. In the latter case, theater owners had to take only the films offered by a studio's distribution arm, making it more important to brand the studio than the individual film. It was the independent producers, rather than studio publicity departments, who first understood the ramifications of this change.

While Bass's simple flickering flame and clean graphics for *Carmen Jones* impressed critics, it was his title sequence for Preminger's follow-up film, *The Man with the Golden Arm* (1955), that really garnered attention. Bass would go on to design every credit sequence for every Preminger film between *Saint Joan* (1957) and *Bunny Lake Is Missing* (1965), including *Porgy and Bess* (1959), although his designs were not used. Bass's titles and ad campaigns for *Bonjour Tristesse* (1958), *Anatomy of a Murder* (1959), *Exodus* (1960), and *Advise and Consent* (1962) were legendary, and he contributed designs for posters, lobby cards, and other publicity material as well. Bass also designed the cover for Preminger's autobiography, although the idea to put the back of Preminger's bald head on the cover came from Herb Yager. The former president of the Academy of Motion Picture Arts and Sciences, Sid Ganis, started his career in the publicity department at 20th Century–Fox and, by the 1980s, was head of worldwide publicity for Paramount. Ganis recalled that when Bass and Preminger worked together, the director would give Bass numerous suggestions, which the designer would listen to quite seriously and even jot down notes, promising to get to work on Preminger's ideas right away. Weeks later, when Bass presented his designs for the title sequence or the publicity campaign, Preminger would remark with astonishment that his ideas were nowhere to be seen, whereupon Bass would apologize and say that he had tried, but they just hadn't worked out. Bass had a slightly different take on working with the autocratic director. With regard to their infamous verbal fisticuffs over the titles for *The Man with the Golden Arm*, Bass noted: "I discovered that what we wound up with together was better than what I started with on my own. Otto was [a] very tough and bullheaded kind of person. . . . In a funny way it worked for me."[53]

Another high-profile client was Alfred Hitchcock. Bass worked as a visual consultant for Hitchcock while the director was producing his films independently at Paramount. Bass designed the credit sequences for *Vertigo* (1958), *North by Northwest* (1959), and *Psycho* (1960), cementing his reputation as a gifted auteur of titles, even if the megalomaniacal Hitchcock was unwilling to give the designer credit for his role in conceptualizing the shocking shower sequence. Bass created the storyboards and designed the editing of the shower sequence, and he may have directed some setups, but Hitchcock infamously downplayed Bass's contribution, characterizing Bass as a mere assistant he happened to humor.[54] Meanwhile, in the 1960s Bass continued to design material for Preminger, Billy Wilder, Robert Aldrich, Stanley Kramer, John Frankenheimer, Stanley Kubrick, and other directors.

By the time Bass moved to his new offices, he had established himself not only in the film world but also as one of the most important designers in the United States, a representative of what was called the modern American style. He was designing houses in association with Buff, Straub and Hensman Architects, hi-fi systems for Stephans Tru-Sonic, playgrounds for the Longwood Redevelopment Corporation, and floor and wall tiles for Pomona Tile Company. He also expanded his corporate identity and logo work, designing a new look for Speedway Petroleum Company, which owned a chain of gasoline stations.[55] A critic writing in the prestigious *Industrial Design*, discussing how West Coast modernism was suffusing American design, noted: "Equally at home in the abstract world of ideas and the tangible world of the eye, Saul Bass has become an undisputed leader in the western graphics world with work that is fresh, lithe, charming, and free of the bonds of a single 'style.'"[56] Other highbrow design journals, many of them published in Europe, concurred.[57] Another sign of Bass's public recognition was the number of prizes he began to amass for his work: in 1957–1958 he won the National Society of Art Directors' Art Director of the Year Award, the New York Art Directors Club Gold Medal, a San Francisco Art Directors Club medal, and a Los Angeles Art Directors Club medal and several other awards.[58]

In 1955 the corporate rebranding work for Speedway Petroleum got Bass involved in making television commercials for the company, an experience that would serve him well in terms of both editing film for titles and directing short industrial films. Two years later, Bass made commercials for Blitz beer and National Bohemian beer, followed in the 1960s by Rainier beer. Some of these beer commercials consisted of only a couple of shots, but the "Andy Parker regular Joe" series for National Bohemian beer followed a white-collar worker from the office to his local bar, where he enjoyed a cold brew as he relaxed after work.[59] Bass produced the titles for Frank Sinatra's first television program, *The Frank Sinatra Show* (1957), which also involved creating a television promo; a year later he directed promos for ABC Television's fall lineup. Commercials for Chevrolet, Dixie Cup, Mattel, Rayovac, RCA, Olin Mathieson, Bridgestone tires, and others would follow, but his masterpiece is undoubtedly his Mennen Baby Magic commercial (1962), for which he won the grand prize at the Cannes Advertising Film Festival.[60]

From there, it was only a short step to corporate and industrial films. In fact, Bass was highly successful in finding corporate financing for his work, even when the films were more educational than commercial and did not advertise a company's products. In 1961 he produced a short animated film for a Stan Freberg television special, *The Sale of Manhattan*, which showcased Bass's typically urbane, Jewish humor. In 1962 Bass designed *Apples and Oranges* for CBS Television, a promotional film that was intended to convince clients that television commercials were more effective than print advertising.[61] In addition, Bass may have collaborated with Ray Bradbury, Jules Engel, and Herb Klynn on the Oscar-nominated animated film *Icarus Mongolfier Wright* (1962).[62] The same year, he produced a series of infomercials for IBM, including one on using computers for cancer research and another humorous animated piece on "Why Computers Are Good"—a mini-version of the history of invention he produced for *Why Man Creates*. Two Bass-directed short films were released in 1964: *From Here to There* for United Airlines and *The Searching Eye* for the Eastman Kodak Company, which were screened at the New York World's Fair in the Transportation and Travel and the Kodak Pavilion, respectively.[63] His next short, *Why Man Creates* (1968), was sponsored by Kaiser Aluminum; it won an Academy Award and, like the previous films, concerned both the act of seeing and the production of art. Other corporate projects followed: an untitled AT&T corporate identity film (1969); *One Hundred Years of the Telephone* (1977), an animated film for AT&T; and *Windows* (1977) for Warner Communications (later retitled *Notes on the Popular Arts*). Meanwhile, Bass also became a montage expert, much as Slavko Vorkapich had been a generation earlier. He created either storyboards or actual film sequences for *Psycho, Spartacus, West Side Story, The Four Horsemen of the Apocalypse*, and *Grand Prix* and consulted on *Apocalypse Now* (1974).[64] Two films for the educational market followed: *Bass on Titles* (1978), in which Bass discusses his by-then legendary film title sequences, and *The Solar Film* (1980), financed by Robert Redford's Wildwood Productions to advocate the development of solar energy sources.

Bass's interest in social issues had led him to develop a forty-minute film in the late 1960s about modernity's impact on human society, to be called *Notes on Change*. He was hoping to find the kind of enlightened corporate sponsorship that had made *Why Man Creates* possible; in other words, even in the absence of direct advertising for the company, the film "could reflect corporate responsibility and sensitivity just by the fact of sponsorship." Unfortunately, the project was preempted when Alvin Toffler's best seller *Future Shock* was published eight months into Bass's preproduction work, apparently leading to the project's demise.[65] The script was written by Mayo Simon, the cowriter of *Why Man Creates*; he would go on to script Bass's science fiction feature film *Phase IV* (1974), which takes its cues from *The Hellstrom Chronicles* (1971) and other ecological disaster movies, although it is much more thoughtful than some other epigones. *Phase IV* tells the story of mutated ants that have evolved into highly intelligent beings with the ability to coordinate mass attacks on civilization. The film was mishandled by Paramount, its distributor, and the advertising was targeted toward the horror-film audience. Most critics agree, however, that it was an intelligent experiment more akin to a European art film than a grind-house exploitation horror film, and it suffered from weak dialogue and acting. Even before Bass's original ending—a free-form phantasmagoria of images—was rediscovered, the film had achieved cult status, yet it was a financial loser in 1974, failing to recoup its expenses (but only barely). The film ended Bass's career as a Hollywood feature filmmaker, although that was not immediately apparent. In an interview published in September 1975, Bass still expressed optimism about future film projects: "Frankly, I'm looking to the future with great excitement. There are so many stories that need telling."[66] Three years later, he was still looking for a feature film project, noting in the trades, "It is hard to find properties."[67]

Elaine and Saul Bass codirected another short science fiction film, *Quest* (1983). It was based on "Frost and Fire," an original story by Ray Bradbury, who also supplied the script. With a production budget of approximately $1 million, the film was financed by M. Okada International Association. Despite winning numerous prizes at American film festivals, the film was not commercially released in the United States, probably due to resistance from the Japanese financiers, although it was distributed nontheatrically.[68]

Meanwhile, in 1974 Bass hired marketing expert Herb Yager, a one-time partner in Alan Landsburg Productions. Yager eventually became a full partner, and the firm's name was changed in September 1978 to Saul

Bass/Herb Yager & Associates.[69] Over the years, Bass had considered bringing in other partners, including Lou Dorfsman, who stated: "I went into business with Saul Bass three times, seriously, with lawyers and everything, but as you can see, [I] never actually picked up and left [CBS]."[70] The firm's reorganization was precipitated by the fact that the business was just limping along. Bass had been undercharging for his services, and finances were apparently a mess, especially after Bass spent at least two years almost exclusively on *Phase IV*. Yager shifted the focus to the more lucrative corporate identity campaigns, and he apparently succeeded in putting the business in order, as reflected by his promotion to partner. The same sense of aesthetic minimalism that had influenced Bass's posters and graphic designs now came into play in the design of corporate logos for United Airlines, AT&T, United Way, Alcoa, Dixie Paper, Rockwell International, Quaker Oats, Lawry's Seasoning, the Girl Scouts, the YWCA, and Warner Communications. Many of these logos are still instantly recognizable by most ordinary Americans. Bass earned large sums for these corporate logos and for the corporate identity campaigns, which involved designing everything from gas station fuel pumps to uniforms. However, Bass's studio also worked pro bono, designing many posters for the Academy Awards as well as artwork for film festivals, art exhibitions, social action causes, and the like, thus giving expression to his sense of social responsibility.

In the late 1980s Bass made his Hollywood comeback. A younger generation of filmmakers, including Martin Scorsese, Steven Spielberg, and James L. Brooks, appreciated his title designs of thirty years earlier and now wanted a similar look for their own films.[71] Scorsese, in particular, admired Bass's work with Hitchcock and Preminger and would encourage Bass and company to achieve new heights in title design with *Goodfellas* (1990), *Cape Fear* (1991), *Age of Innocence* (1993), and *Casino* (1995). Elaine Bass received equal credit on these titles, and her influence is clearly visible. *Casino* was Bass's last credited work. He died of non-Hodgkin's lymphoma at Cedars-Sinai Medical Center in Los Angeles on 25 April 1976, shortly before his seventy-sixth birthday. By then, he and Elaine had sold the company to Citigate (a UK public relations firm with global connections—now Citigate Dewe Rogerson), but Bass Yager Citigate, as it was called, was not sustainable without Saul. Unlike advertising firms, which establish brands that long outlive their founders (e.g., J. Walter Thompson), design firms are too focused on the talents and personality of the designer-owner to survive the founder's demise.[72]

The Bauhaus and 1950s American Design

In the mid-1940s Bass came under the spell of Bauhaus design philosophies, as communicated in two seminal books: Moholy-Nagy's *The New Vision: From Material to Architecture* and Gyorgy Kepes's *The Language of Vision*. Bass imbibed the lessons of the Bauhaus aesthetic and applied them to American commercial art design in his subsequent work. Moholy-Nagy and Kepes were Hungarians, the latter a student and close collaborator of the former in Berlin from 1930 to 1932, when they both worked at the Bauhaus. Along with other Bauhaus alumni, their influence on post–World War II American design is incalculable.

The Bauhaus was established in Weimar in 1919 as a state-operated institution of higher learning for architecture and other related arts. Architect Walter Gropius was its first director and gave the arts and crafts school its name. In April 1919 Gropius published the Bauhaus manifesto, which featured a woodcut by Lyonel Feininger on its title page. Gropius called for an end to distinctions between high and low art: "Let us therefore create a new guild of craftsmen without the class-distinctions that raise an arrogant barrier between craftsmen and artists! Let us desire, conceive, and create the new building of the future together."[73] Architecture, typography, carpentry, metalwork, weaving, sculpture, wall painting, and theater design all had workshops at the Bauhaus, since art was not just an object for ruling-class patronage; it was meant to embrace all aspects of human interaction. Furthermore, through the workshop method, Bauhaus professors taught that each real-world design problem had its own solution based on specific social and economic conditions, and that strict adherence to a design ideology was counterproductive. Such pragmatism fit seamlessly into the emerging ideology of the postwar visual communications industry in America, which understood itself to be in the service of consumer capitalism. Jettisoned in a process of transatlantic acculturation were the more radical ideological underpinnings of the Bauhaus design aesthetic, leaving formalist design principles: "The European modernists and their American counterparts found clients who were willing to put the theories into practice for commercial use; there was neither time nor necessity for the manifestos or ideology that had characterized the movement in Europe. Even clients such as the Container Corporation of America, which patronized modern design in part because of the progressive social values it held, were doing so primarily because of the forward looking image they could achieve by associating themselves with contemporary art."[74] One can imagine that such an aesthetic would also appeal to a young designer slaving away in the movie advertising business but with higher aspirations.

Historians agree that many of the most influential designers of the twentieth century taught or studied at the Bauhaus. In architecture, there was Gropius himself, as well as Mies van der Rohe; in interior and furniture design, Marcel Breuer became a household name; and Herbert Bayer became a master of graphic design and photography. Moholy-Nagy did it all—painting, photography, sculpture, architecture, typographic design, bookmaking, and film. Oskar Schlemmer was synonymous with revolutionary theater design, Anni Albers and Gunta Stölzl developed the new field of textile design, and Marianne Brandt and Wilhelm Wagenfeld forever changed product design. Famous photographers included Lux and Lyonel Feininger, Heinz Loew, Lucia Moholy, Walter Peterhans, Joost Schmidt, and Otto Umbehr (Umbo). Working alongside them were some of the greatest artists of the century, including Paul Klee, Josef Albers, and Wassily Kandinsky. The Bauhaus continued to operate until 1933, when the Nazis shut it down as a bastion of degenerate art. However, it underwent numerous changes over the years of its existence—geographic (moving from Weimar to Dessau in 1925 and then to Berlin in 1932), institutional (Hannes Meyer became director in 1928, Ludwig Mies van der Rohe in 1930, and Laszlo Moholy-Nagy in 1932), and philosophical (evolving from a focus on painting to the incorporation of all the other arts, and from limited aesthetic concerns to greater community engagement). Some of these changes were brought about by the continual controversies and scandals generated by the institution; some were the result of mounting political pressures from the conservative and Nazi factions of the ideological spectrum; and others were caused by internal strife, such as the complaints of women students that they were being herded into weaving and ceramics workshops.

Born in Bacsborosod, Hungary, in 1895, Laszlo Moholy-Nagy was trained as a lawyer but became a self-taught artist. After a brief foray into writing and poetry, he took up painting shortly before the end of World War I. Once he was demobilized from the army in 1918, Moholy-Nagy finished his law degree in Budapest but soon became interested in art production, joining the constructivist-influenced left-wing group MA, for which he wrote articles and manifestos. Although he was probably not directly involved in the Hungarian Soviet Republic of Bela Kuhn in 1919, Moholy-Nagy followed most of MA's members into exile when that short-lived government gave way to a fascist dictatorship. From Vienna, where MA regrouped, Moholy-Nagy moved in 1920 to Berlin, which was evolving into one of the most cosmopolitan cities in Europe. That same year, he attended the first Dadaist congress in Berlin and became friends with such leading Dadaists as Hannah Höch and Hans Richter. As the German representative of MA, Moholy-Nagy nurtured contacts with Van Doesburg and De Stijl in Holland, Karl Teige and the Czech Devestil group in Prague, and Alexander Rodchenko and the Soviet productivists in Moscow. Although, as movements, Constructivism (in its Soviet and Hungarian manifestations), Dadaism, Suprematism, Productivism, and Neoplasticism displayed somewhat different national and ideological characteristics, they had much in common, especially in their modernist fragmentation.

In spring 1923, Moholy-Nagy was awarded a professorship at the Bauhaus, initially replacing Johannes Itten in the metallurgy workshop. However, he soon became a significant force in all aspects of the school, teaching the basic introductory course that all first-year students had to complete, where he insisted that art and design must meet the needs of a modern industrial society. His published books in the Bauhaus series— *The Theatre of the Bauhaus* (No. 4, 1925), *Painting, Photography, Film* (No. 8, 1925), and *The New Vision: From Material to Architecture* (No. 14, 1929)—became hugely influential. All of them were republished numerous times, and *The New Vision* eventually morphed into *Vision in Motion* (1947), which was republished posthumously by his wife, Lucia Moholy.[75]

Born in Selyp, Hungary, in 1906, Gyorgy Kepes graduated from the Budapest Royal Academy of Arts in 1928. He decided to give up painting for film after falling under the influence of the Hungarian left-wing poet and painter Lajos Kassak. Kepes gravitated to Berlin, where he designed the cover for Rudolf Arnheim's seminal work on film theory, *Film as Art*. Knowing that Moholy-Nagy had written for Kassak's publications, Kepes wrote to the master and was invited to join his workshop in 1929, where he remained until 1932. At the time, Moholy-Nagy had just completed his first avant-garde film and was working on others, including *Berlin Still-Life* (1931) and *Gypsies* (1932), both of which not only experimented with new cinematic devices but also actively critiqued existing political and social conditions.[76] The artistic collaborators later reconnected in London, where both had emigrated to flee the Nazis.

In 1937 Moholy-Nagy invited Kepes to run the Color and Light Department at the New Bauhaus in Chicago, sponsored by industrialist and philanthropist Walter Paepcke. After its failure in 1938, the school morphed into the Institute of Design, where Kepes stayed until 1943. He was recruited that year by Serge Chermayeff, who had begun to transform the Art Department of Brooklyn College after his appointment as chair in 1942. Chermayeff had previously been associated with Kepes and Moholy-Nagy when he lectured at the Institute of Design in 1941. At Brooklyn College, the renowned Russian-born, London-educated architect invested the curriculum with ideas central to the Bauhaus movement, noting that "a liberal arts education could play an important part in restoring art to its proper relationship with contemporary life by developing a sense of reality and responsibility with a free creative and critical capacity."[77] Environmental design was part of the curriculum for all art students, who were encouraged to apply their aesthetic talents to the urban environment of Brooklyn. In 1946, at the recommendation of Walter Gropius, Chermayeff became Moholy-Nagy's successor at the Institute of Design in Chicago, while Kepes moved to the Massachusetts Institute of Technology. He remained there until 1974 and established the Center for Advanced Studies in 1967.

Although the Bauhaus influence was cut short in Germany due to the rise of National Socialism and the school's closing in 1933, Bauhaus faculty and alumni had a seismic impact on American art, architecture, and especially design. Moholy-Nagy's huge sphere of influence in Chicago included Marli Ehrman, who headed the Weaving Workshop at the Institute of Design, and Hin Bredendieck, who later became director for industrial design at George Tech. Other notables included architect Mies van der Rohe, after his immigration to Chicago; Walter Gropius and Marcel Breuer at the Harvard Graduate School of Design, where they trained Philip Johnson, I. M. Pei, Lawrence Halprin, and Paul Randolph; Naum Gabo at Harvard's School of Architecture; Werner Drewes in the Art Department at Columbia University; Josef and Anni Albers, as well as Trude Guermonprez, at Black Mountain College; Herbert Beyer at the

Aspen Institute; and Will Burtin at *Fortune Magazine*. In addition, a number of former Bauhaus artists became American artists, including Lux and Lyonel Feininger, Wassily Kandinsky, Piet Mondrian, and Paul Klee.

The influence of the Bauhaus on American design went far beyond the personal connections between these artists and their American students. Three central Bauhaus ideas were easily translated into the American idiom because they seamlessly conformed to American conceptions of pragmatic problem solving, an ideological free-trade zone in the arts, and Taylorist notions of industrial efficiency and time management. First, the Bauhaus emphasized utilitarian art production in order to reverse the perception of manufacturing and its products as soulless and ugly; design had to be elegant and close to everyday life. Second, the Bauhaus sought to reunite intellectual pursuits and aesthetic theory with practical skills; the Bauhaus artists saw themselves as craftspersons solving the problems of a modern industrial society. The old hierarchy of the arts, which placed painting and fine art above all, was considered obsolete and inadequate for the twentieth century. Finally, the Bauhaus workshop system, which privileged experimentation not for its own sake but to solve real-world problems, became a model for art education at American universities in the post–World War II era. Is there any better way to describe Bass's own view of himself than as a craftsperson solving the problems of society?

It is not an exaggeration to state that the very concept of a graphic designer embracing the mechanization of image production came from the Bauhaus. At that ground zero, the new profession's identity began to evolve, culminating in the field's establishment through such organizations as the Art Directors Club of America. Many Bauhaus designers, but especially Moholy-Nagy, privileged the process of "selecting, editing, creating in the mind, rather than producing with the hand."[78] Saul Bass would embrace all these ideas, even if he was not necessarily conscious of or willing to acknowledge their origins. In the Bass studio, the hand could be that of Saul, as in *Why Man Creates*, or it could be that of Art Goodman or a number of other designers, but the intellectual process of selecting, editing, and creating the Bass look was Saul's alone.

Moholy-Nagy and Kepes: Point, Line, Circle

Bass's incredible success as a designer was due in no small part to his ability to take the Bauhaus philosophy and its design conceptions and translate them into a working method that yielded a consistent brand and look while communicating simple, direct messages for his clients. For Bass, reading the Bauhaus texts gave his design work a new, deeper level of meaning, beyond the immediate objective of creating an advertisement to sell a product. As Catherine Sullivan notes in an early piece on Bass, the Bauhaus emphasis on art as experience, its melding of art theory and practice, and its insistence that art, science, and technology are not mutually exclusive but intermingled spoke volumes to the young designer.[79] Bass suddenly understood that even the most crass commercial ventures, like film advertising, could benefit from good design solutions. He was probably also impressed by the Bauhaus attitude toward technology, which viewed technological progress as a positive expansion of human sensory perception rather than a dehumanizing element in society. Trained from the ground up as an apprentice designer with little academic background, Bass must have felt validated by Moholy-Nagy's and Kepes's belief that the boundaries between high art and popular or commercial art should be negligible, at least in terms of their aesthetic value.

Furthermore, Bass embraced the idea that we human beings are the sum of our learned experiences and that human communication through art, design, and literature is what makes us human. As Moholy-Nagy notes in *The New Vision*: "Everyone is equipped by nature to receive and assimilate sensory experiences. Everyone is sensitive to tones and colors, has sure touch and space relations, etc. This means that by nature everyone is able to participate in all the pleasures of sensory experiences." Later in that same text, he formulates the link between art and communication even more precisely: "It (art) is the most intimate language of the senses, a direct linking of man to man."[80] Moholy-Nagy repeatedly implies that the most efficient forms of human communication are rooted in biology, in forms that tap directly into the human psyche and are experienced physiologically rather than through the intellect. Moholy-Nagy speaks of biology (nature) interacting with technology (mechanical manipulation) to create functional solutions to design problems (because these are closest to the possibilities inherent in the natural form). Such notions must have been very appealing to Bass, who also cultivated a strong humanistic impulse and later seemingly gravitated from material concerns to more mystical ones.

American advertisers had already accepted Harold Laswell's theory of stimulus-response, which postulated that the consuming public was receptive to certain stimuli that could elicit a specific response, ultimately leading to the purchase of goods. But exactly how that worked remained unclear. *The New Vision* provided practical answers for Bass, just as it had profoundly influenced Paul Rand by theorizing that design was subject to order and a system.[81] In particular, Bass embraced Moholy-Nagy's dictum that each new work demanded a specific set of design solutions in order to achieve maximum functionality as an object whose purpose was to communicate meaning. Design was therefore based on practical solutions inherent in the material, rather than on abstract, theoretical principles. Like many American designers, Bass adopted the formal principles of clean, uncluttered design based on sans serif type and basic geometric shapes (intended to communicate modernity and a contemporary feel to postwar consumers) and jettisoned the theory. In interviews, Bass was always loath to articulate the theories underlying his work. He would concede that his method of work was reductionist rather than expansive, paring down elements to their most essential function rather than adding superfluous ornamentation, which is a central concept in Moholy-Nagy's book.[82]

Of particular help to Bass in terms of analyzing specific design problems and solutions was Moholy-Nagy's breakdown of the materials used in the design process into four elements: structure, texture, surface aspect, and massing (mass arrangement). Structure pertains to the physical characteristics of the material—for instance, fibers for paper and cloth, and grain for wood. Texture helps the designer understand the look and feel of design materials on the surface. Surface aspect differs from texture in that it is subject to manipulation by the artist—for example, a metal's texture may be hard and smooth, but an artist's hammer can create patterns on the surface that change the texture. Massing, according to Moholy-Nagy, has to do with the arrangement of surface treatments in groups.[83]

Overall, *The New Vision*'s illustrations probably exerted the most influence on Bass. All of Moholy-Nagy's books feature a montage of brief, almost telegraphed texts in juxtaposition to images, with many pages consisting exclusively of images. The photographic images in *The New Vision* must have been a never-ending source of inspiration for Bass, because his later designs abound with similarities. As an intuitive and visual learner, Bass assimilated the photographic illustrations in both *The New Vision* and Kepes's *The Language of Vision*, understanding them not merely as illustrations of theoretical concepts but, more importantly, as powerful visual designs to be filed away in his own personal catalog for future use. One particularly striking example is a view from an airplane that shows the structure of a mountain range, which Moholy-Nagy calls a "macrophotograph" because it reveals the large-scale relationships of geographic formations.[84] Though two-dimensional, the photograph reveals through light, density, color, and form a geology that is otherwise hidden to the human eye situated, as it were, on the earth's surface. That image could have been the template for the infinite variety of geologic structures seen from the sky in Bass's film *From Here to There* (1964). It also figures prominently in *The Searching Eye* (1964), where the filmmaker positively revels in the landscape's changing colors, tones, and textures, and again in Bass's introductory sequence for *NBC: The First 50 Years* (1976). Another example of such inspiration can be found in the manipulated photographic image of an elevator shaft by O. Firle (1928), which uses multiple exposures to create a spiral effect that sucks the eye into the black vortex of the image. Did Bass have that photograph in mind when he created the graphic Lissajous form design for *Vertigo*, whose hero has a paranoid fantasy of falling down the stairs of a church tower?

Despite Moholy-Nagy's influence, the core concepts of Bass's work as a designer originated more directly from his declared mentor Gyorgy Kepes and his seminal book on the theory of art, *The Language of Vision*. Kepes articulated Bauhaus principles that had previously been wedded to theories of Gestalt psychology. Both Kandinsky and Klee had incorporated Gestalt theories in their basic Bauhaus courses, including the notion of the whole being greater than the sum of its parts. Utilizing the senses to decode a purely visual language was also central to Kepes's aesthetics, as articulated in *Language of Vision*. The language of line, shape, and color is perceived as a system of visual communication that is analogous to written language, based on the human ability of perception. Art is seen not as a matter of "artistic" inspiration but as a discipline governed by scientific principles that can be articulated, the production of art as a matter of experience, and the perception of formal order. According to Gestalt psychology, the *whole*, whether in art or in nature, is composed of an interrelationship of its constituent parts, whereby the whole is always more than the sum of its parts. As a result, according to Kepes, "The experience of an image is a creative act of integration. Its essential characteristic is that by plastic power an experience is formed into an organic whole."[85] Kepes, in fact, expressly acknowledges his indebtedness to

Gestalt psychologist Max Wertheimer and his assistants Kurt Koffka and Wolfgang Kohler at the beginning of *Language of Vision*.

As early as 1938, Kepes outlined his goals for his design students: "As the eye is the agent of conveying all impressions to the mind, the achieving of visual communication requires a fundamental knowledge of the means of visual expression. Development of this knowledge will generate a genuine 'language of the eye,' whose 'sentences' are created images and whose elements are the basic signs, line, plane, halftone gradation, color, etc."[86] What Kepes offered Bass was heady stuff. *Language of Vision* posits not only an international language based solely on the visual, on a system of signs and significations in images, but also a scientific worldview of art. Ironically, Gestaltists today no longer propagate a physiological theory undergirding the biological origins of Gestalt thinking, but it is unclear to what degree Bass believed or even perceived these pseudoscientific elements of Gestalt theory. As he later admitted, he didn't really understand Kepes's book: "Now, I didn't understand the book, but I knew it was the answer. I knew it was the word. It was very vague, for me, and very ambiguous and very mysterious."[87] In fact, Bass internalized Kepes's philosophy and declared it intuition—which it was, up to a point, given its naturalization within Bass's worldview.

As a strategy for facilitating communication, Kepes's Gestalt provided both simple and direct instructions for communicating, as well as a methodology for distilling complexity into hieroglyphics. Bass's lifelong fascination with Egyptology added the emotional kick. This was undoubtedly a powerful tool in the hands of an American designer whose clients sought intuitive methods of persuasion to harness the inchoate nature of audience desire. Bass admitted that his design work after his exposure to Kepes became "more dynamic and more abstract."[88]

There seems to be a clear contradiction, then, between the influence of Bauhaus theories and proscriptions, as clearly evidenced by the dramatic turn in Bass's work after his involvement with Kepes, and his later assertions that his work was intuitive and there were no rules. In point of fact, it is likely that Bass assimilated images and concepts from Kepes and Moholy-Nagy to the point that they became second nature and therefore seemed "intuitive" to the designer. Bass probably also sympathized with Kepes and other Bauhaus practitioners because of his humanistic-Jewish background. All the practitioners of Gestalt were optimistic, liberal, and largely the product of a German-Jewish symbiosis. They were literally transplanted from Weimar to the New World, and those left behind perished in the Shoah. The Bauhaus ideology incorporated a strong sense of social responsibility, making it all the more appealing to a kid from the Bronx who had seen and experienced the poverty of the Depression. Most important in terms of Kepes's influence on Bass, *Language of Vision*'s final chapters explicate the way the idioms of modern painting can be translated into the medium of advertising. Not being hamstrung by traditional forms, advertising can employ the most heterogeneous elements—whether through language, graphics, photography, or abstract shapes—to communicate meaning: "Posters on the streets, picture magazines, picture books, container labels, window displays . . . could disseminate socially useful messages, and they could train the eye, and thus the mind, with the necessary discipline of seeing beyond the surface of visible things."[89]

Kepes changed everything for Bass because *The Language of Vision* offered practical design solutions that Bass applied to his commercial work. Kepes taught Bass that the visual field of any design consists of objects placed in space, where color, brightness, texture, size, and the relationship of points, lines, and areas create spatial forces that interact with the background. The eye assimilates these various spatial forces and organizes their visual differences into a whole. But again, what may have impressed Bass more than the concepts were the illustrations, which demonstrate how impactful isolated visual elements such as squares, circles, and lines can be on a blank, white page.[90] These geometric shapes not only manifest dynamic movement by creating actual force fields, depending on their placement, but also become powerful tools in guiding the eye toward the design's most important message.

According to Gestalt psychology, as explained by Kepes, several laws are at work in this process of perceiving the "plastic image": the law of proximity or nearness, which groups elements together when they are placed close by; the law of continuance, which groups elements along a line or progression; the law of closure, whereby the eye may add invisible elements to complete a regular figure; the law of symmetry, which privileges figure-ground relationships; and the law of common fate, by which elements moving in the same direction are perceived collectively.[91] All other aspects of Kepes's design theory flow from these principles, which are based on the active perception and assimilation of visual data by the viewer: "The final task of plastic organization is, then, the creation of an optical structure of movement that will dictate the direction and progression of plastic relationships until the experience reaches full integration."[92]

Just how well Bass absorbed these lessons can be demonstrated by comparing Kepes's illustration of the varying placement of squares within rectangles in *The Language of Vision* with Bass's trade journal invitation to the premiere of *All About Eve* (1950) at Grauman's Chinese Theatre in Hollywood. The latter diagonally stacks white rectangles for the invitation, envelope, and tickets, respectively, on a black background, while a less obtrusive red sans serif type above announces "the motion picture event of the year."[93] Or, as Bass admitted to Douglas Bell, the trade advertisement for *Return to Paradise* (1953) was "a Bauhaus ad, absolutely inappropriate for the subject, but it tells you how obsessive I was about the whole thing."[94] In another example, "Equation," images of a script + studio/location + director = movie; it transitions from Bauhaus ideograms to large rectangular blocks of text that form the horizontal base for the vertical tower of images and math.

While the first section of Kepes's book concerns the plastic organization of the image, the next section falls under the heading of visual representation, which "operates by means of a sign system based upon a correspondence between sensory stimulations and the visible structure of the real world."[95] Kepes theorizes that it becomes the designer's task to find correspondences between spatial relationships in reality and those on the two-dimensional page to signify meaning. Thus, in medieval paintings, there was a direct relationship between the size of objects and their importance and power; this relationship was destroyed with the institutionalization of a Renaissance perspective, only to be reestablished in modernist art. Kepes advocates a movement away from the single, closed perspective of the vanishing point on the horizon to either a linear perspective that opens space for the beholder in all directions or multiple, even overlapping perspectives that reflect the many subjectivities of viewers assimilating the image: "The image became once more a dynamic space experience instead of a dead inventory of optical facts."[96]

One of the most important concepts Bass took away from his reading of *The Language of Vision* was the notion of reduction and simplicity. It was a key concept in what would become the Bass brand and one that Bass repeatedly referenced in interviews. Kepes develops his argument for simplicity and intensity by noting that the modern urban environment represents an overabundance of visual stimulation and a "turmoil of events." Because the human attention span is too short, it becomes necessary to pare down details to their essential shape and meaning. Like a traffic signal on a busy city street, the designed message must be direct, simple, and intense.[97] Bass often spoke of his own reductive point of view, his preference for simplification of design rather than layered complexity. His increasing use of logo-like, reductive metaphorical images, especially after the success of the first Otto Preminger campaigns, was the direct result of his intuitive understanding of what was necessary for effective modern product advertising, given the plethora of conflicting messages bombarding the consumer.

This reduction of sensory perception engages the subjectivity of the consumer—an absolute must for successful advertising. According to Kepes's final section on "dynamic iconography," visual experience is much more than a bundle of sensory stimulants working on the eye and ear; rather, these visual sensations are imbricated with human memory and subjectivity.[98] The more generalized an iconic image becomes, the better it engages with the subject's memory of other similar objects. Just as multiple perspectives invalidated the one-dimensional perspective of post-Renaissance art, the new freedom achieved through plastic organization allows for multiple meanings, releasing "associative energies inherent in every visible fragment of reality."[99]

Finally, Kepes sees advertising as a perfect playing field for "testing representational images in combination with pure plastic units and verbal elements."[100] Kepes peppers his book with illustrations of modern paintings, photographs, architecture, and design, as well as examples of dynamic advertising. Modern American designers represented in *The Language of Vision* include Lester Beall, Joseph Binder, Will Burtin, Joseph Feher, Morton Goldsholl, and Ladislav Sutnar. I suspect that Bass studied these illustrations from the advertising world with particular intensity. For example, Kepes demonstrates how the fixed Renaissance perspective of traditional art can be transformed into multiple perspectives by cutting up an image and reassembling it on an open field, allowing the eye to fill in the missing information to create a dynamic whole. Kepes illustrates this principle with two photomontages by M. Halberstadt and Clifford Eittel, which undoubtedly inspired Bass's photomontage in an innovative trade advertisement for *Attack!* (1956), which announces the completion of principal photography with three words placed in a zigzag pattern in the spaces between image fragments.[101] Bass would use the technique repeatedly, including in some of his designs for *Anatomy of a Murder* and possibly in a trade advertisement for Red Skelton on CBS Radio as early as 1951.[102]

A Paul Rand advertisement from 1941 illustrates Kepes's discussion of the relative size of objects in any design. Several more Rand designs appear later in the book, one of which is visually juxtaposed with a Picasso drawing. As we know, Bass watched Rand like a hawk, and the connection between modernist art and advertising must have shocked Bass, who was used to moving in the vulgar circles of movie trade advertising. Likewise, an A. M. Cassandre advertisement from 1937 for Container Corporation of America (Walter Paepcke's company) is visually juxtaposed with a Braque still life. Kepes also includes his own advertisement for Container Corporation of America—a 1938 image of a disembodied hand in motion that would become a key image in Bass's own catalog of iconography. A photomontage for Herbert Bayer's 1939 design class (of another disembodied hand) became the inspiration for one version of Bass's trade advertisement for *Decision before Dawn* (1951), and E. McKnight Kauffer's painting *The Early Bird* (1919) became the template for the birds in flight depicted on Bass's Keio Department Store wrapping paper.[103] Indeed, Saul Bass became a brand not only because he used a limited canon of stylistic devices but also because he created a catalog of iconographic images and forms that appeared repeatedly across media and were recognized as elements of the Saul Bass brand.

A Short History of Movie Advertising

Saul Bass's ideal was to publicize something without actually selling a product. According to Al Kallis, advertising work in the traditional movie business didn't appeal to Bass because he didn't want to apply the hard sell; his goal was to devise more creative campaigns that were themselves works of art. "Bass wanted his label to be as important as the advertising itself," said Kallis.[104] Bass therefore attempted to obtain funding for his documentary projects from enlightened capitalist corporations that were eager to have their names associated with a unique visual experience that did almost anything except sell a tangible product. Bass would argue that such films brought prestige to the company, enhancing its public identity. Ironically, Bass cut his teeth on movie advertising, and it was during the time he spent slaving away as a lettering man on thousands of standard, anonymously designed movie ads that Bass read Kepes and Moholy-Nagy and began to dream of a different kind of work. Over a period of a decade, Bass would experiment with new designs that ran the gamut from the largely traditional, figurative ads common to the genre to very clean, wholly modernist ads and other movie collateral, the latter produced mostly for movie companies, directors, or actors rather than to advertise individual films. Bass's innovations must be contextualized within the history of Hollywood movie advertising. He made an impact because studio advertising had stagnated for at least two decades.

Even though the invention of the movies and the "age of advertising" occurred simultaneously, film industry advertising was initially limited to film company names and movie genres. Programs of short films changed multiple times a week, and cinema owners never knew in advance what they would receive from the film exchange. Posters and handbills were the earliest form of film publicity. Advertising in newspapers commenced in the early 1910s, when film companies began to distribute prepared stories, photos, and ads to exhibitors for publication in local newspapers.[105] After the narrative feature film became the dominant form of cinema around 1915, advertisements in newspapers followed the lead of poster designs, often replicating a single signature scene or image from the film: John Wilkes Booth jumping from the balcony of the Ford Theatre in *Birth of a Nation* (1915) or the ape and the girl on top of a skyscraper in *King Kong* (1933). Although some advertisements actually included film stills, most used specially created artwork featuring portraits of the stars.[106] In fact, traditional movie advertising was made up almost entirely of pen-and-ink artwork and hand-lettered typography, as the use of halftone reproductions had not yet been perfected.[107]

By the 1930s, however, pen-and-ink drawings had been almost wholly supplanted by halftone photographs. Hollywood advertising was now a riot of text, artwork, and photographs from the film or portraits of the stars. Every square inch of the advertisement had to be filled with content: at the bottom, small text replicating news stories; in the middle, visual images, titles, and stars; at the top, the film's tagline. Warner Brothers' advertisement for *So Big* (1932), directed by William Wellman and starring Barbara Stanwyck, is typical. The ad's most obvious design feature is a sun pattern consisting of a circular portrait of Stanwyck, various artwork depicting scenes from the film projecting outward like rays, and Stanwyck and *So Big* on opposite sides of the orb. The film's tagline, "For five years . . ." appears above that, while the white space below is filled with a box containing the names of ten actors in a column, the Warner Brothers logo, Edna Ferber's name in large, bold type, and a quasi–newspaper story with movie factoids filling all the voids in between.[108]

As the 1930s and 1940s progressed, little changed in advertising design, except that the typography and art for the film title was often more innovative, conforming to the title design in the film credits.[109] Furthermore, newspaper-style text was replaced with more images, and there was less text overall. By the 1950s, text was limited to taglines, the title, and the major stars and technical credits, but advertising designs were still overloaded with content.

While Bass continued to design advertisements that resembled those of his colleagues, he also experimented with open designs that left white spaces on the page, limiting his visuals to one or two themes. His 1951 trade advertisement for Anatole Litvak's World War II drama about a sympathetic German deserter, *Decision before Dawn*, documents the designer's self-assuredness in implementing this principle. Employing what Kallis called Bass's mastery of scale, the photomontage emphasizes giant hands as emblems of physical danger, while time is represented by running bodies, thereby replicating a Kepes design principle involving mass weight and spatial organization. Sullivan comments on the way the *Decision before Dawn* ad conveys so simply the narrative of a chase in a single two-dimensional space: isolating the tragic hero and overlaying bureaucratic-looking stamps with the film title, thus visually communicating the character's subjugation by the *Schreibtischtäter* (desk-bound perpetrators) of Nazi Germany.[110] Interestingly, the ad published in *American Artist* in 1954 is slightly less abstract than the version reproduced in Bass and Kirkham's 2011 biography: losing the grasping hands, the hero is seen much closer in the foreground as well as in the extreme background, connoting a temporal relationship between the two images; there is also a village on the horizon, creating a visual cross with the hero's temporal image, while another space is visually filled with the official-looking stamps. By the most economical visual means, Bass communicates the essence of the film's story.

Bass also experimented with Bauhaus design concepts in some of the unsigned movie advertising he created for Howard Hughes and RKO. For example, his trade advertisement for *Hard, Fast, and Beauti-*

ful (1951), a film directed by Ida Lupino at RKO, is immediately recognizable as a Bauhaus-influenced design.[111] Like *The Champion* ad Bass designed for Stanley Kramer, the design concept here is open, featuring a mostly red canvas. Extending below is a visual arch made up of three different monochromatic black images from the film, while the words "HARD / FAST and / BEAUTIFUL" in white typewriter lettering cut over the lower end of the arch. All the other type is black or gray and extremely small, so it almost bleeds into the background area. The overall graphic impression resembles a large semicolon dominating the picture surface, creating a downward movement that unites the individual images of the film; the white text identifying the film floats above these images but also stabilizes the visual field as a whole. Given that all three images display female bodies, the film's tagline—placed in tiny black cursive handwriting below the white type "BEAUTIFUL"—seemingly originates from the hand of the artist: "a story about women . . . *for men!*" Bass specifically addresses the male audience because this was a "woman's melodrama" by a female director, so the female audience was already in the bag; the goal here was to expand the audience to include their male dates. The meticulous attention to weight and balance in the ad, with open spaces reserved for red fields of color, would become hallmark features of the Bass brand, and a specific red hue was ubiquitous.

But this move toward a cleaner style of advertising was not automatic; nor was it consistent. A number of movie advertisements from the early 1950s seemingly conform to the Bass brand and give the impression that Bass had completely abandoned the conventions of the industry. However, these ads are not for individual films; they are generalized advertisements for production companies (Blaustein/Taradash), directors (Robert Aldrich), and actors (Jack Palance). In his movie advertising work with Al Kallis between 1953 and 1957, one can see that Bass is still struggling to break away from the industry's figurative and realistic representations of a film's visual elements in advertising. Kallis himself subscribed to that traditional aesthetic, although he also worked on overtly modernist advertising campaigns for Bass, such as his print ads for Quantas (1956) and Blitz beer (1957). Kallis also drew both the fire and rose logo for *Carmen* and the hot pink rendition of Dorothy Dandridge as Carmen featured on the poster and in much of the advertising—a poster design Bass stopped taking credit for at some point. Even in the advertising campaigns that are still heavily figurative (e.g., for *The Racers*, *On the Threshold of Space*, *Mister Roberts*, and *Magnificent Obsession*), Bass restricts the number of images or scenes depicted and integrates them into a larger, abstract design. One Bass ad for *Magnificent Obsession* features a cut-up image (per Kepes), as did his early *No Way Out* advertisement, but it also creates a montage of successive film frames. An ad for *The Virgin Queen* is dominated by a vertical axis, consisting of a single illustration, and a horizontal axis of typography, with the film's title anchoring the vertical axis. For *A Star Is Born*, Bass plays with a logo of a star: it is at the center of one ad, with an illustration of Judy Garland inside; it appears in a much smaller version, with only text inside, over a dominating scene of Garland in front of a theater curtain; and it is used merely as a tiny silhouette logo, anchoring a pencil drawing of Garland and James Mason. In another version, Bass jettisons the logo altogether in favor of a star constructed of text in Broadway lights. What all these advertisements have in common is a severe reduction in images and text compared with more conventional, ballyhoo advertising; in addition, Bass is beginning to work out strategies for implementing logos.

A 1955 trade advertisement for producer Benedict Bogeaus's *Pearl of the South Pacific* (which Bass was proud enough to publish in an early article about himself, despite the film's Saturday matinee ambitions) illustrates Bass's ability not only to layer space in multiple planes on the page, each carrying its own semantic weight, but also to create a narrative through five separate panels.[112] Later, I address the ad's use of cinematic montage in the Eisensteinian sense, but here I consider Bass's equally remarkable construction of spatial planes for a South Seas island relic and objet d'art that must connote geography and generic narrative tropes yet is isolated on a white background, emphasizing its museum quality, even as the words "Technicolor" and "Superscope" take us back to the genre's guarantees. The photographed body parts seen in the five panels, along with the narrative text, are likewise laid against a white background, isolating their physicality while emphasizing their function as visual signs. Through text insertions on two other recurring planes, Bass develops narratives while simultaneously addressing the reader through graphic design in multiple spaces: the museum, the cinema, the street (walking with a date along Broadway).

Thus, Bass's movie advertising work in the late 1940s and early 1950s became a testing ground for many of the design concepts culled from his spiritual mentors Gyorgy Kepes and Laszlo Moholy-Nagy. Bass attempted not only to unclutter the standard design practices of the day but also to move away from figurative and photographic images, favoring instead abstract, logo-like designs.

The Bass Brand: Simplicity, Rhythm, Balance, Repetition

Examining the work of Saul Bass & Associates (later Bass/Yager & Associates) over a fifty-year period, the consistency of the look is striking. This is not to say that the design studio didn't evolve over the decades to keep up with modern design trends and technologies, but Bass understood that brand identity was the key to his success. Like the companies for which Bass created identifiable logos and corporate identities, like the films for which Bass's studio designed pithy images and introductions, Bass's own brand needed to be recognizable to potential clients. Such branding not only differentiated his work from that of his competitors but also garnered attention to the extent his designs deviated from the norms and clichés of the day. Certainly, that was the lesson learned from early unsigned movie advertisements such as those for *The Champion*, which caused a sensation, according to Bass, because they looked so different from conventional movie advertising.

Bass's work displayed the characteristics that would become associated with his brand: strong graphic elements, modern typography, geometric ordering of the two-dimensional space on multiple spatial planes, a limited color palette (either mostly primary colors or coordinated pastels), and a simple iconographic element at its center. Bass used a catalog of "house" images and pared down the cluttered, circus-sideshow look of most movie ads. Other designers working at the major Hollywood studios sought to catch the consumer's eye with sensational images cribbed from the film and reproduced photographically as major visual elements in an overcrowded, typographic design scheme. In contrast, Bass incorporated his absorption of modern art techniques—specifically, the concepts of Bauhaus design—into his advertising work.

The first tenet of the evolving Bass brand, then, was simplicity of expression. The visual field had to be open and uncluttered, allowing text and images enough space to create a dynamic impression on the consumer that would communicate a clear message. The consumer's mind and eye would no longer be distracted by the noise of multiple messages directed to diverse audiences; instead, there would be one direct and unambiguous message intended to appeal to all audiences. Bass noted in an interview after the release of *Bonjour Tristesse*: "The basic problem in all kinds of design has been that everybody tries to say too much. You have to say something simple, but something that moves people."[113] A simple design with emotional appeal was the foundation of the Bass brand. Graphic elements and text needed space within the frame's visual field to develop their own dynamic force, without conflicting with other graphic elements and thus complicating the message. Another hallmark of the Bass brand was the use of large fields of color (or lack of color) to create an open space for the design elements within. Bass noted: "I tend to simplification, looking for the one powerful, provocative image that takes the notion of whatever you are trying to communicate and does something to it, and forces you to exam it. And is sufficiently seductive to pull you into it."[114]

The notion of getting pulled into an image depended on the second characteristic of the Bass brand—namely, the creation of dynamic rhythms within the field of vision. Each design element, whether image, object, or text, created a directional sense of movement through the act of reading. While the open field of color created the prerequisite for the design element to develop its dynamic force, that force had to be seen in relation to other forces within the field, creating the image's overall rhythm. It was here that the message gained its emotional effectiveness. Such emotive and dynamic rhythms would become extremely important in Bass's film title work, as well as a guiding principle in the way he edited films; however, they were also important considerations in his graphic designs. For example, a trade advertisement for Robert Aldrich's *Vera Cruz* (1954) features the legs, hips, and elongated shadow of a gunslinger facing a rival in a shoot-out; the legs and shadow slice the oblong background diagonally, creating a strong sense of instability and movement. Denying the reader the identity of the human depicted also instills a sense of anticipation about the event's outcome. Yet the text—placed, for the most part, in the upper right and lower left quadrants of the field of vision—overlays the image with a counterdiagonal that stabilizes the image, turning it into a self-enclosed hieroglyphic that is both figurative and abstract.

Another characteristic of the Bass brand originating in Bauhaus thinking, then, was the establishment of balance and symmetry within the image or from image to image, as in films. Each graphic element brought its own dynamic force that had to be harnessed within the visual field to guide the eye to the essential information. Although Bass never talked about it, it seems clear from an analysis of his design work that he, like the European Bauhaus designers before him, relied heavily on a grid structure to work out the various design elements on a two-dimensional plane. The trade advertisement for *Hard, Fast, and Beautiful* is a perfect example of the underlying grid at work in Bass's design. A central horizontal axis allows Bass to balance the text-heavy film title and tagline across the bottom half of the frame, while the invisible central vertical axis guides the black arch of images and stabilizes, through symmetry, the white text of the title within the red field. The result is an image of movement and stasis that draws the eye to its center and then guides it to the images and text.

The final characteristic of the Bass brand was his ability to create a cogent design element, image, or logo that could be utilized repeatedly across different media and had the ability to cement the identity of a product within that iconography. This mode of operation was obviously a necessary step in designing corporate logos and identity campaigns, as Bass conceived them. However, the Bass-designed iconic images for film advertising, whether the crooked arm for *The Man with the Golden Arm* or the *Vertigo* spiral, were something completely new, functioning in exactly the same way as corporate logos but also tapping into deeper levels of collective psychology. Bass's employment of repetitive design elements to enhance product identification went far beyond establishing logos. Indeed, some critics have complained that "the frequent recourse to California rainbows, also lay him open to charges of repetition."[115]

For example, Bass's campaign for Pabco paints utilized its corporate identity of rainbow colors (established in the 1920s) to design a series of simple line drawings on a black background, whereby the rainbow-colored line was seemingly drawn by a single paintbrush.[116] Rainbows or rainbow-color motifs also appeared, logically, in a campaign for Fuller paints; as design elements in Bass's own Bass/Yager & Associates logo, the entrance to the Bass design studio, and posters for the Chicago International Film Festival; in the identity campaigns for Japan Energy Corporation (1994) and United Airlines (1974); in the invitation to the premiere of *The Pride and the Passion* (1957); in the logos for Frank Holms Laboratories (1954), United Way (1972), Paul Harris (1973), Pomona College (1987), and Special Olympics (1989); in the electronic, moving logos for Hanna-Barbera (1979), Kibun (1984), and the National Film Registry (1989); and as a cover image for *IDEA* magazine (1990). Bass even designed a monochromatic rainbow typography.[117] Rainbows are both pure color and deeply embedded in our collective imagination of fairy tales and magic and the glory of nature after a sudden rainstorm on a hot summer's day. One can assume that because Bass used a rainbow for his own corporate logo, he associated the rainbow with creativity, endless possibilities, and the freedom to go anywhere. Likewise, such associations would have been seen as positive elements in the messages his clients wanted to communicate.

Simultaneously, the repetition of design elements such as rainbows allowed Bass to employ archetypal iconographies and motifs to address audience desire, while defining the Bass brand for clients. Indeed, Bass returned to certain images and forms almost obsessively throughout his career, indicating that they held some deeper meaning for him that went beyond the requirements of a particular design problem or campaign. In fact, the Bass iconography tapped into archetypal images of the elements of fire, water, wind, and earth, as well as visual jokes about modernity.

Recurring Visual Motifs

One of the most striking aspects of Saul Bass's work as a designer is the consistency of his look, his style, and his brand across media, whether graphic art in his print ads and posters, two- and three-dimensional identity campaigns, commercials, film titles, or films. Certainly, over his nearly fifty-year career, Bass strove to be at the forefront of modern design and experimented with new techniques and new technologies, such as video and digital imaging. But at the same time, there were consistencies in his work that made Saul Bass Bass. He was a relentless promoter and understood the first rule of mass communications: to create a brand, you need to repeat the message. And once that brand is created, it has to be rigorously maintained by limiting the design palette to a certain number of techniques and design elements. Whether consciously or unconsciously— the designer himself consistently resisted any attempt to define or analyze his design elements—Bass drew from a well of images and iconographies that appeared repeatedly in his work. Such brand consistency served several purposes. First, like all branding, it associated a particular product with certain qualities that would sell an item. Like Hollywood and its endless remakes and sequels, Bass reutilized and repurposed successful design elements. One concept that became an integral part of the Bass brand was the creation of logo-like images that, in their stripped-down simplicity, defined and encapsulated an entire film. As Bass noted, the core of modern advertising is simplicity, requiring concentration on a single point to drive the message home and have the product positively identified.[118] Second, logos for corporate clients, similar to the logo-like images created for films, identified the company or the product in a specific way that made it recognizable and desirable to potential clients. Having said that, Bass would also reuse images and motifs in a variety of contexts that furthered the goal of the Bass brand more than the goal of any one product. This gave clients a notion of what they could expect when they hired the design firm for a specific project. The reuse of images would not have been immediately apparent to clients because of the variety of contexts in which they were utilized. For example, Bass employed an identical globe with arms extended from inside the globe (and an almost identical color scheme) in advertisements for the *Detroit News* (1961) and the titles for *It's a Mad, Mad, Mad, Mad World* (1963).[119] Given that the first usage was strictly local, whereas the later film titles reached a national audience, and given that two different media were involved, Bass's reuse can be seen as part of the effort to create his own brand.

The globe image points to one of the most common design elements in all of Bass's work: circles. They were often a prominent, formal design element, whether images of setting or rising suns, representations of the earth, abstracted globes, or pupils as a metaphor for vision. According to Jeff Okun, Bass was interested in simple shapes more than anything, which is why he chose circles as the center of so many designs. Indeed, he was more focused on graphic design and compositional elements than on any semantic meaning.[120] Gestalt psychologist Rudolf Arnheim identifies the circle as one of the simplest visual patterns. Its perfection attracts attention because humans are genetically predisposed to a perceptual preference for round shapes. Interestingly, Arnheim, like Bass, connects the circular form to vision and the eye, noting that "the animal eye is one of the most striking visual phenomena in nature."[121] For Gestalt psychology, then, the graphic element of the circle elicits a physiological response that is deeply ingrained in biology and the survival of the species, since the perception of a predator's eye can mean life or death for the prey. At the more mundane level of graphic design, if Bauhaus theory stipulates that a line represents the motion of a pencil guided by the hand of an artist across a page, the circle represents continuous or infinite movement around a central axis. The circle is a self-enclosed form, conveying a strong sense of autarky, and is considered by Bauhaus artists to be one of the basic formal elements of design, along with squares and lines. Moholy-Nagy encapsulates all three design elements in his painting *Yellow Circle* (1921), which places a yellow sun in the bottom left quadrant of the image, overlaid with x- and y-axes (lines), and a square; this composition shifts the balance to just below the painting's center. In Moholy-Nagy's nonrepresentational painting, the yellow circle is an abstraction, a plane of yellow color, yet even here, cultural meaning reverberates through the image.

There is something primeval about the circle, given that it was probably one of the first shapes perceived by primitive humans looking up at the moon and the sun, which are typically associated with deities. Those first humans would have been able to take a stick and draw a circle in the sand to communicate the notion of a cosmic force or unity greater than mortal man. For millennia, the Native American hoop or medicine wheel has signified the universe and nature—the *Wakan Tanka*, in the language of the Sioux. Images of the sun, in particular, carry implications of the orb's life-giving force, its ability to produce warmth, to grow food, and so forth. The spiritual dimensions of the sun (the ancient Greeks and many other cultures considered the sun a deity) imbue the circle with rich symbolic meaning as something universal, sacred, divine, and infinite. It follows that the divine energy of the circle also connects the form to fertility, whether for growing food or for procreation of the species. In addition, because circles enclose and separate an inside space from an outside space, they imply safety and protection—whether in Celtic mythology, where Stonehenge's giant protective circle demarcates a privileged space, or more mundanely in western movie mythology, where the wagons form a circle to defend against an attack by Indians. All these cultural and emotionally charged associations reverberate in Bass's utilization of images of the sun.

Bass employed the image of a yellow sun in an orange-red sea for his poster of the William Wyler western *The Big Country* and, more surrealistically, in his poster for the "Sixth Israel Film Festival in the USA" (1989).

A setting sun turns up almost obsessively as an image in nature, whether in *That's Entertainment II* or in his films *Why Man Creates* and *Quest*. We can trace this image through numerous works in multiple media. Abstracted, the image of the sun first appears in Bass's corporate identity campaign for Lightcraft of California (1952), in a television commercial for Sun detergent (1956), and on the cover of the sound-track album for *Hurry Sundown* (1967). While all three renderings are different in style, they have in common a playful execution. Likewise, the opening sequence for *NBC: The First 50 Years* (1976) begins playfully with a young boy drawing a simple, abstracted sun with chalk on a blackboard, which represents the universe; this dissolves to an actual image of the sun flaring out from behind the earth, then cuts to aerial images of a fertile earth. The sequence can be interpreted as a visual metaphor for the history of NBC from the childlike innocence of early television to the mature and bountiful programs of the 1970s. But it can also be seen as an expression of Bass's own mystical relationship to nature, which seemed to grow stronger over time.

In his Bohemian beer commercials (1950s), the sun is a force that must be blocked for proper brewing, while in the credit sequence for *Something Wild* (1961), the sun seems to be an almost alien force, surviving in a concrete jungle of skyscrapers. In *The Searching Eye* (1964), the camera zooms in on the eye of the boy protagonist as he makes a telescope with a sheet of paper, then cuts to a reverse shot in a perfectly matched image of a glowing yellow-orange sun as it sets in the ocean. As in the NBC special, Bass is allowing us to view nature and the beauty of the world through the eyes of a child, hoping to capture some of the innocence, exuberance, and emotional wonder of such a vision. That particular constellation of signifiers is also at the center of Bass's poster for *Why Man Creates* (1968), which again features a huge yellow sun, surrounded by a field of red, with a single human in silhouette in the foreground. But that figure, which has a very small head and hugely elongated arms and legs, looks like it was drawn by a child or by a modernist artist like Giacometti. Virtually the same image appears in the film proper, introducing a sequence that concerns primitive and ancient humans' attempt to depict nature in art. Bass essentially remakes the image in his poster for *The Solar Film* (1980), which visualizes a rising yellow sun in a blue sky; a toddler in diapers in the foreground walks toward the sun, framed in exactly the same way the stick figure was framed in the earlier poster for *Why Man Creates*. While the visual imagery is the same, the semantics of the image have changed; here, the child walking toward the sun represents the future world powered by solar energy.

In a Bridgestone commercial from the 1960s, a girl skips rope in front of a red-yellow sun; it also turns up in a Security Pacific Bank commercial from 1979. In some work, such as Bass's credit sequence for *That's Entertainment II* (1976) or his film *Notes on the Popular Arts* (1977), a setting sun seems to denote nothing more than a happy ending, while elsewhere, the setting and rising sun is imbued with the mystical force of nature, such as in *Phase IV* (1974), *Quest* (1983), a Matsushita commercial (late 1970s), and the credit sequence for *The Silk Road* (1988). Finally, for advertisements for the documentary *The Naked Eye* (1957), Bass puts an eye inside a sun image, thus uniting two of his favorite icons.

This repeated use of photographic representations of the sun in multiple media indicates that the image held more than a passing interest for Bass; it tapped into some deep-seated emotions that went well beyond the imperatives of branding. This aspect of Bass's design work is explored in later chapters, where the focus is on reading individual films and other works involving moving images. The next chapter returns to the origins of the designer's film work: credit sequences for Hollywood films. It is in this arena that Bass may have had his greatest impact as a designer, since he has been rightfully acknowledged as the father of modern title sequences not only by historians but also by the present generation of title producers.

2

Film Titles

Theory and Practice

Having previously branded himself as the most innovative designer of modern Hollywood film titles, Saul Bass took a twenty-year hiatus. Between *Seconds* (1966) and *Broadcast News* (1987), he designed only a couple of titles for Otto Preminger, as well as *That's Entertainment II* (1976).[1] He took his name off the credits for *Looking for Mr. Goodbar* (1977) after a monumental fight with director Richard Brooks, but by then, title work was no longer a factor in the Bass studio business. Apparently, title work on several films in the late 1960s fell through, including a planned prologue and title for *Hawaii* (1966) and *The Party* (1968).[2] According to Jeff Okun, Bass had stopped creating credit sequences because his partner Herb Yager argued that titles were labor intensive and never made any money. Given that the office was in financial trouble, Bass was supposedly allowed to take credits work only if the more lucrative corporate identity work didn't suffer.[3] Since Yager didn't join the firm until 1974, Bass's ambition to become a director of shorts and feature films probably explains the lack of involvement in title credits in the preceding decade. However, even in the 1960s, Bass, who was not a talented businessman, was constantly overspending and getting into conflicts with his business manager Morrie Marsh. Mike Lonzo, who worked with Bass in the mid-1960s, got the feeling that Bass enjoyed creating titles more as a hobby because they were so labor intensive and such money losers.[4]

As Bass stated in an interview, after setting off "a Renaissance in titles," he simply "got bored with the activity and had to get out of it, mainly because I did want to go on to other things."[5] In another interview, he stated that Hollywood film directors began to exert total control over their films (much like their European counterparts) and were thus no longer willing to turn titles over to someone else.[6] In his American Film Institute seminar in 1979, he claimed he got out of the title business because titles "were beginning to get irresponsible and irrelevant."[7] However, this argument seems unlikely, given that Bass's clients were auteurs, both before (Preminger) and after (Scorsese) the hiatus. Finally, in his film *Bass on Titles*, Yager asks Bass straight out whether he has abandoned his work on titles. Bass's answer indicates that he has closed that chapter of his career and moved on to filmmaking: "My work on titles was a marvelous opportunity to learn about filmmaking. I touched on every aspect of the process, both creatively and technically. I worked with many wonderful people. But there are always new challenges."

Two other factors may have played a part in Bass's break from titles. It is possible that some filmmakers began to shy away from Bass because his titles were too successful, leading numerous critics to state that the title sequences were better than the films that followed.[8] According to James Pollack, head of titling services for the National Screen Service (NSS), which produced the Bass-designed titles for Billy Wilder's *The Seven Year Itch*, Wilder never again worked with NSS (or Bass, for that matter) on a title sequence after a film critic wrote, "If the film had lived up to the titles, it would have been a good picture."[9] *Time* magazine noted that more than half the New York film critics observed that Bass's titles for *A Walk on the Wild Side* were better than the film: "Suggesting the story's themes of harlotry, perversion and vengeance, it set the mood that the ensuing picture tried but failed to match."[10] Bass remembered having a very uncomfortable lunch with director Edward Dmytryk after the reviews appeared.[11] When *The Searching Eye* was shown at the Chicago Film Festival in 1964, one critic quipped: "But Saul Bass, whose credits alone have made some of the worst movies worth the price, was almost enough to redeem the evening."[12] Bass was quickly becoming a stereotype of himself. *Variety* went so far as to say that Bass might no longer find work in the title field: "There has been a somewhat too frequent use of the line 'The best thing about the film is the Saul Bass credits'—and Bass is apt to wonder that anyone will ever hire him again."[13] In fact, he did worry about that.[14]

It may also be true that Bass had priced himself out of the market.[15] However, this is a matter of conjecture, given that all financial records from before the 1970s were apparently lost, and Bass kept mum about his fees.[16] Fortunately, a letter survives (in the Gregory Peck Papers) in which Bass summarizes for an anxious producer the production costs for his previous title work, excluding his $15,000 design fee and the advertising campaign:

"Carmen Jones" (color & Cinemascope)	$4,500
"Man with the Golden Arm" (black & white)	3,500
"Saint Joan" (black & white)	6,000
"Seven Year Itch" (color & Cinemascope)	8,000
"Attack" (black & white)	1,700
"Storm Center" (black & white)	3,300
"The Pride and the Passion" (color)	7,000

As you will note there is a wide divergence and range reflecting different problems of production. As I indicated in our conversation I could not estimate the production cost of a title for "The Big Country" until a clear picture existed of what was to be done. But, as you know, almost anything interesting that you would do (especially in color) tends to run to considerable amounts. . . . To restate the situation: In projecting costs for the title, the only additional amount to calculate is my design fee. The rest of the costs remain generally the same as they would be were I not involved in the matter.[17]

American Cinematographer noted in 1960 that the cost of Bass's elaborate title design for *Around the World in 80 Days* was so high in order "to discourage all but the most ambitious producers."[18] That title is conspicuously absent from Bass's list.

According to internal memos in the Stanley Kramer Collection, Bass charged a $10,000 fee for *The Pride and the Passion*, which equaled his standard fee for his work with Preminger.[19] That jibes with the fees reported by Stephen Rebello; he notes that Bass was paid $10,000 to design the credits for the low-budget *Psycho*, which cost $21,000 to produce, or approximately 3 percent of the total $800,000 budget.[20] According to a 1964 *Variety* article, the average price for movie titles was $7,500 to $8,000 for a quality film, with animated titles (such as Freleng's *Pink Panther* titles) running closer to $25,000. With his design fees, Bass titles were on the expensive side, but not overly so. An exception was the whopping $45,000 Universal paid for Bass's *Spartacus* titles.[21] Bass also refused to put out bids, which was becoming the industry norm in the 1960s, as many producers trawled for the lowest bidder. Presentations for bids could cost a designer anywhere from $300 to $3,000, with no way to recoup any of that investment if the job went elsewhere.

There was also a backlash against inventiveness in credit design, first from the industry and then from at least one well-known critic. As early as 1957, *Variety* expressed a prevalent view in the industry: "There are those who feel that credit originality can be overdone. . . . However, there's some suspicion that an offbeat credit runoff, while pleasing to the patrons, does an injustice to the talent since the audience's attention is diverted from the names."[22] Bass's independence could be taken two ways: positively, as an attempt to be a trailblazer, or negatively, as an effort to assert too much control over the production process. As Fred Foster wrote in *American Cinematographer*, Bass keeps "a close vigil on every title project until it is fully cut, in order to maintain the original concept."[23] In a piece about a hypothetical film *Poncho* (aka *The Sundowners*), critic Vincent Canby described the vagaries of the ad campaign in which Bass's "classy layouts" and "simple striking designs in the modern manner" are upended by "the company topper" who loves them at first and then desperately needs images of the love scene.[24]

Beyond industry voices, there were film critics. In a piece on the newly developing art-house audience for high-quality European cinema, Pauline Kael, ever the faux populist, attacked Bass by name:

> And so American movies now often come, packaged as it were, with several minutes of ingenious, abstract, eye-catching titles. This send-off—the Swiss-graphics look provided by Saul Bass and other designers—has virtually nothing to do with style or mood of the picture, but makes the movie look more *modern*. (How can the picture be dismissed as trash when it looks like your own expensive living room?) This type of design, using basic colors and almost no soft lines, was, of course, devised so that advertising would be clear and effective with a minimum of cost. In movies, a photographic medium, complexity and variety of shadings of beauty are no more expensive than simplification. But modern graphic design, which has built an aesthetic on advertising economics, has triumphed.[25]

74

The backlash continued a few years later in the *New York Times*, no less, when a critic noticed that movie titles had increased in length from one minute in the 1930s to six minutes in the 1960s, concluding that the credits "were getting out of hand."[26] But the writer conveniently forgot to mention that industry standards had radically changed since the studio era, and many more individuals were receiving screen credit.

Ken Coupland commented laconically on Bass's evolving reputation in movie land: "His fall from favor in the film industry was apparently due to a combination of factors, part aesthetics, part economics—and part hubris."[27] Be that as it may, today Saul Bass is recognized as "the father of modern film title design."[28]

That's Entertainment II

According to Saul Bass, he took on the titles for *That's Entertainment II* (1976) as a personal favor to Gene Kelly, who asked him to do it.[29] It was a sequel to *That's Entertainment* (1974) and a compilation of great screen moments from Metro-Goldwyn-Mayer's storied history. Bass solved the problem of having to list almost every famous actor in MGM's golden-age roster by creating titles that parodied conventional credit sequences as they had been produced since the 1930s. Bass described his task as follows:

> The opening consisted of the recreation and montaging of all the great old title devices that we used "way back when." The wave washes upon the shore obliterating the names lettered in the sand. The scroll unrolls revealing the names and is consumed in flames. The names are formed by flower petals floating on water as the breeze scatters them. The names recede into the glorious sunset . . . are branded on wood . . . are cast in gold letters on red velvet . . . are rung up on an old cash register, etc., concluding with a pull back from snow covered mountains revealing the title of the film in monumental snow covered granite against the heavens.[30]

As the credits unspool, the viewer is exposed to a series of clichés associated with films, genres, or even studios, in a mash-up that itself becomes a meditation on the semantics of titles.

As Bass notes, clichés function as visual shorthand: "Clichés are terribly important, because they communicate in an extraordinary way, that's what turns them into clichés, because they get used again and again until you tire of them."[31] Elsewhere, Bass states that he "used ideas, which had not been appropriate for other films."[32] This was Bass at his most playful, yet he also managed to insert at least one of his signature images to identify the sequence as a Bass product. In fact, Bass was most interested in Hollywood's mythic reality, so he inserted titles that might never have been done but were "the kind of thing that should have been done."[33] As one critic wrote of the titles: "He'd retain the very qualities which dated them and gave them their own special charm and naïveté—flat lighting, slight clumsiness, funny colour."[34]

The film begins with a quasi-biographical montage of Fred Astaire and Gene Kelly, the two cohost-narrators of the film.[35] It opens with a color image of an embossed, brown, leather-bound scrapbook whose first page reproduces the MGM "Ars Gratia Artis" logo; the image bleeds to black and white and then cuts to a series of gold-framed photographic portraits of Astaire and Kelly from babyhood to adulthood. These are interlaced with stock shots of trains, closing suitcases, disembodied chorus-girl legs, theater marquees, and clapping audiences, sutured with rapid dissolves that typically indicate a rise to stardom in classical Hollywood films—the kind of montage Slavko Vorkapich excelled in producing.[36] Bass would reuse the device of tracking along family portraits in his contribution to the credits for *A River Runs through It* (1992), directed by Robert Redford, for which Wayne Fitzgerald ultimately got credit.[37]

The last two photos include the signatures of Astaire and Kelly, and the next image returns to color: the USC marching band forming (in fast motion) the word "AND" on a football field, replicating a similar shot in Moholy-Nagy's *The New Vision*.[38] The Vorkapich-style "rise-to-stardom" montage not only pays homage to his fellow Angelino but also recalls Bass's mastery of the form in both commercials (Mennen Baby Magic) and titles (*The Victors*). Apart from introducing the film's narrators, the montage sequence also references the transition from silent films to musicals, the most popular film genre at the beginning of the 1930s. The marching band scene is clearly a joke, given its out-of-proportion ratio between production effort and semantic content.

The sequence cuts to three names scrawled in the sand, which are then washed away by the surf. Each group of names that follows is presented in a different style with an appropriate typography: a medieval parchment is opened by disembodied hands, revealing Gothic script, and then burns away; names appear as pebbles in a tropical pool before they float away; a setting yellow sun in a red sky (Bass's signature image) appears behind scrawl credits in white block letters that disappear into a vanishing point just above the orb; the red sky dissolves to red velvet, and the camera tracks over gold-plated three-dimensional letters that sparkle in the light; turning pages of a book reveal Book Antiqua typography; handwritten names are part of a message in a bottle in the surf; names pop up on an old-time manual cash register; credits are typed on a manual typewriter by invisible hands; an open file drawer reveals names on the files; names are branded into wood with western music; "Lassie" is marked on dominoes that fall; names appear and dissolve on a Chinese gong (familiar as J. Arthur Rank's logo). The sequence ends with the camera panning up a painted cartoon image of a mountain with the film's title seemingly chiseled in the rock.

First, it should be noted that while the opening title sequence lists all the actors who appear in archive footage, it does not include any behind-camera credits, unlike Bass's other title sequences. Those names appear in the end credits, which are conventional and were apparently designed without Bass's input. Rather than having a unified look, as credits normally would, the title sequence's heterogeneity mirrors the hodgepodge of film clips that follow. Yet there seems to be little correlation between the actors listed and the style of the individual title; for example, Judy Garland and Mickey Rooney starred together in numerous musicals but never with Bing Crosby, yet all three are listed in a sand-and-surf shot.[39] Another onscreen couple, Spencer Tracy and Katharine Hepburn, are listed on a giant gong but are seen only in behind-the-scenes footage in *That's Entertainment II*.[40] Furthermore, whereas the styles of the titles seem to refer to every genre—from comedy to epic drama, from musicals to film noirish crime dramas and westerns—*That's Entertainment II*'s clips focus almost exclusively on musicals and comedies. More logically, listing Robert Taylor on medieval parchment recalls his participation in such epics as *Ivanhoe* (1952) and *The Knights of the Round Table* (1953), while the old-fashioned cash register names comedians Abbott and Costello, Jack Benny, Robert Benchley, Laurel and Hardy, and the Marx Brothers, alluding to a jack-in-the-box. In at least two cases, the Bass re-creation correlates to particular actors' credits: Nelson Eddy and Jeanette MacDonald appeared in the musical *Maytime*, which had similar credits that floated away, while the western-style title lists Betty Hutton and Howard Keel, who starred together in *Annie Get Your Gun* (1952), the only example in which the generic reference correlates to an actual clip in the film.

It is also worth noting what Bass omitted from his over-the-top survey of title styles. Given his own pioneering work in Hollywood, the absence of any form of animation is particularly striking, as is the lack of any experimental modes, whether in typography or graphic design.[41] Animation is only hinted at in camera movement in the final title image. Postproduction special effects are limited to a roll title and an occasional dissolve. Indeed, the titles are much more aesthetically conservative than Bass's other work and even more conservative than much of Hollywood's commercial production in the 1960s. Contemporary critics certainly picked up on the parody in Bass's opening sequence. Charles Michener of *Newsweek* commented: "The title sequence, designed by old master Saul Bass, lists the stars in a send up of just about every title sequence ever contrived to fit a genre."[42] An English film critic went even further: "Saul Bass has designed the blissfully parodic main titles, as if to imply that what we are about to watch is all part of a grandiose vulgarity no longer to be taken very seriously by people as sophisticated as we are assumed to have become."[43]

Limiting his palette to clichéd forms increased the likelihood of a self-reflexive reading by audiences, but the question remains: Was Bass consciously excluding innovative title design not only to emphasize the cliché but also to tap into the conservative nostalgia that had apparently appealed to the blockbuster audiences of the original *That's Entertainment?* Or was it a manifestation of the nonthreatening style required by the moribund studio brass? In any case, Bass was consciously commenting on a particular style of titles in the late classical era, before the appearance of the narrative, atmospheric titles he would promulgate. At the same time, the self-conscious regurgitation of visual clichés in title design allowed Bass to theorize that film titles are an important device in the construction of film meaning, even in their most simplistic form.

Indeed, Saul Bass emphasized again and again in interviews that film titles should be integral to the film's overall aesthetic construction: "My initial thoughts about what a title can do was to set the mood and the prime underlying core of the film's story, to express the story in some metaphorical way. I saw the title as a way of conditioning the audience, so that when the film actually began, viewers would already have an emotional resonance with it."[44] In other words, rather than seeing a film's credit sequence as extraneous to the film proper or, at best, as a transitory stage before the actual film narrative commences, Bass insisted on titles' primacy as a means of engaging the viewer. This was a revolutionary concept in the film industry. In the late 1940s a title practitioner still had to imagine a future where "the ideal title will indicate the mood of that picture in the most simple and direct means."[45]

According to a *New York Times* piece in 1957, Bass had tried to convince several movie producers in the early 1950s that credit sequences could be more than just a list of names: "No one seemed to understand what I had in mind, because it had never been done before. I hardly knew myself, except that I had this constant, vague, irritating feeling there must be some way to make the titles an exciting accessory to the picture."[46]

Ironically, by the early 1960s, the term "Bass-ish" was understood in the industry to mean "any esoteric title comprising a sequence of frenetically gyrating forms."[47] But Bass, possibly unconsciously, also made a theoretical point when he said: "My idea is the first frame of the film is the first frame of the film and the film begins then."[48] Indeed, David Bordwell has argued similarly that no matter how primitive the titles, the reading of the film begins with the first frame.[49] As a critic in *American Cinematographer* put it more mundanely in 1960: "A number of directors and artists have taken a new approach to titling their productions—1) let titles serve as a positive introduction to the story by setting an appropriate mood, or tempo; 2) make them interesting; and 3) make them easily readable."[50] This idea probably came from Bass (especially the legibility issue, which would be a concern only to designers), since much of the rest of the article discusses Bass's pioneering title sequences. It seems clear that Bass expressed the notion of titles "setting a mood" very early in his career, causing the industry itself to adopt that terminology.[51]

Although the designer might seemingly envision the audience as malleable and passive, Bass's title sequences were in fact constructed to engage the viewer in active readership of the film. In other words, the sea change in title design brought about by Bass and some of his cohorts involved a shift in the semantic and syntactical weight of the credit sequence in relation to the narrative proper. Geoff McFetridge, a third-generation title designer very much indebted to Bass, has succinctly summarized the Bass legacy: "Titles are looked at on a few different levels. . . . Like how the piece is going to fit into the film, how it works to change the film, and how it works independently of the film as an abstract impression of the film."[52] Thus, in keeping with the gradual breakdown of classical narrative tropes and styles, Bass's work demanded an active reader rather than an audience that could lose itself in narrative. To explicate Bass's aesthetic, as well as his place in the history of Hollywood title design, it will be useful to unpack theoretically how title design informs the film viewing experience.

Theoretical Models

Anyone who grew up in the 1950s or earlier, before multiplexes dominated cinema culture, remembers that the projectionist invariably began a film with the theater curtain down, projecting the studio's logo, the film's title, and sometimes other credits on the curtain as it rose. Raising the curtain after the projector had been engaged emphasized the theatrical experience and gave the opening an anticipatory and ritualistic staging for audiences. In larger theaters, the house organist would finish his or her preshow performance with a flurry as the lights dimmed, the projector was thrown into gear, and the curtain began its slow rise. This was a clear indication of the status of film titles in the classical era: they represented a transitional moment between the cartoon, the newsreels, the trek to the concession stand, and the actual movie. Undivided attention was not required because, in the eyes of the audience (and the projectionist, as a representative of the industry), the film's narrative had not yet begun. When *The Man with the Golden Arm* was sent to theaters, it included a note to the projectionist "to pull curtain before titles" so the audience could actually see the titles.[53] That started a revolution.

Producers failed to discourage the earlier practice because the titles addressed the audience directly, communicating information about the making of the film, whereas in classical Hollywood, modes of address of necessity took an indirect approach through mechanisms of viewer identification. Titles therefore seemed more closely aligned with newsreels and other more self-conscious prefilm offerings than with the film's diegetic construction. In fact, as film theorist André Gardies has noted, film titles always serve a double function that is, to a certain degree, at cross-purposes, especially in classical cinema.[54] In one sense, titles inform the viewer about the behind-the-scenes history of a film's production: who is appearing in the film, from the stars down to the supporting roles;

who directed the actors; who manipulated the camera; who wrote the story; who designed the costumes; and so forth. The credits also communicate copyright and other legal information, gauge the relative importance of the individual participants through their graphic and syntactic placement, and even hint at a film's budget, depending on how elaborate the title sequence is. All this information was considered extraneous to the subsequent narrative and indeed delayed the moment when the viewer could be coaxed into the narrative via identification with a character. However, this nondiegetic content can also contribute to the production of narrative meaning. For instance, if the film stars an actor with a well-defined screen persona (e.g., it's a John Wayne film) or if it was directed by an auteur with a consistent set of obsessions and a particular style, the audience will be reminded of the artist's previous work. In this sense, film credits also function as a transition between the film being projected and all other films previously made by the production team. Furthermore, in the classical period, the studio's opening logo, as well as the style of the credits that followed, branded the studio and its total output rather than an individual film.

At the same time, film credits lead the viewer into the diegesis through visual and auditory cues that foreshadow the narrative. Rather than visualizing a specific narrative iteration, they speak to the viewer by harnessing generic expectations—for example, by putting a set of laughing masks in the corner of the title frame to indicate a comedy. Indeed, typeface and decorative embellishments have been correlated with genre since the first decade of cinema's existence. Typographic features became highly conventionalized; after *The Mask of Fu Manchu* (1932), the use of pseudo-Chinese Latin characters became de rigueur for all subsequent Asian-themed Hollywood films.[55] Credits rolling over a live-action or still image might also connote genre, foreshadowing an important location or creating a particular atmospheric mood, such as the image of a night train screaming through a deserted, highly lit suburban train station seen over the opening credits of *Brief Encounter* (1946). Thierry Kuntzel begins his close textual and Freudian analysis of Ernest B. Schoedsack and Irving Pichel's *The Most Dangerous Game* (1931) with the film credits, where images of a door and a door knocker—both prominent in the film to come—provide a background to the title graphics.[56] Especially in the silent period, actors' credits were often printed over moving images of the principal players in costume, bowing to the audience—another self-conscious device that simultaneously delayed and presaged the narrative to come.

In other words, title sequences have always served both diegetic and nondiegetic functions. What has changed is the ratio between the two. In the classical period, the credits' emphasis was on branding the studio and its players within an ongoing production schedule, not on individual film narratives, which were often interchangeable. It was only with the rise of independent producer-directors after World War II that the need to differentiate each individual film began to take precedence, moving the focus away from studio recognition and toward the crafting of an engaging narrative hook, beginning with the titles. This shift in the ratio between diegetic and nondiegetic content made sense, given that independent producers usually had all their financial eggs in one basket—namely, the film at hand—and only its success would guarantee further productions. Each film therefore had to be marked by and marketed through its own unique identity.

As the above theses indicate, film titles are also distinguished from the main narrative by the fact that they communicate knowledge through multiple media rather than simply through graphics and sound. Credit sequences might employ numerous techniques such as animation, live-action shots, still images, distorted lenses, postproduction special effects, rapid montages, or slow tracking shots. In this sense, film titles can be much more experimental than the body of a film, and they even influenced classical film style.[57] Film titles are always of necessity logocentric, whereas the film proper may communicate over broad stretches with little dialogue or no words at all. Typography, composition and layout, movement, color, design, and underlying images (or the lack thereof) all contribute to the overall design of film titles. Bass, in particular, explored the potentialities of moving graphics to keep the audience's attention, incorporating little "narrative" surprises or graphic anomalies in his typography. However, a fundamental tension between word and image remained. As Tom Conley notes: "Writing is never the film itself, but both the image and script are together, within each other, in various degrees of tension that cannot be resolved."[58] And although typography was largely standardized in the interest of a branded house style during much of the classical period, it would become an important element in the differentiation of individual films once the studio system began to break down in the late 1940s.

Given the heterogeneous nature of film credits and their need to communicate through multiple media, reading film titles is and was a much more conscious activity than film viewing. Even in the classical studio period, when any artifice was seen as an impediment to viewer identification with the narrative, film titles delayed the moment of view identification (1) because the narrative proper usually began with the first scene and (2) because reading credits demanded that the viewer become conscious of his or her own position as subject-viewer outside the film. This positioning of the subject outside the narrative would continue even after title designers began to incorporate more elements of the narrative proper into the opening credits and even when the film's narrative began before the credit sequence and then continued as the credits rolled. Such an intermingling of narrative and film titles became possible only after the tenets of classical Hollywood style had given way to more self-conscious narratives, often at the edge of parody. This latter phenomenon would reach its apotheosis with Maurice Binder's titles for the James Bond films and the opening credit sequence for Sergio Leone's *Once upon a Time in the West* (1968), which runs for more than six minutes and has only four lines of dialogue. Within a few years, these aesthetic changes would accelerate with the introduction of digital technology, leading to an anything-goes attitude.

Returning to film titles' dual function as communicators of both diegetic and nondiegetic information, pushing and pulling the viewer in and out of the narrative, we might theorize that film titles ultimately naturalize any diegetic space by contrasting their artifice to the film's story.[59] Thus, although film titles may suppress their own artifice by employing narrative devices—the turning of pages or the burning of a parchment—the remaining structural artificiality always highlights the continuous flow of images and synchronous dialogue that follows (the film) as a more natural form of perception—that is, as more real than the credits. Whereas the narrative proper is subject to continuity editing (more or less, depending on the film's style), credit sequences are often segmented into individual, self-contained frames in which the semantic content or even style often changes drastically from frame to frame, as seen in many of Bass's film titles.

Modern film titles themselves are now subject to a variety of placements within a film's total length, whether at the beginning, middle, or end. Indeed, film credits were almost always divided between the beginning and end of a film, even in the classical period, when the end credits usually listed the players and their roles. In the late classical period and certainly in the modern era, film titles appear at both the beginning and end of a film. The demise of the studio system necessitated that every participant in a film's production be listed in the credits as evidence of employment. Previously, many studio workers who were under contract remained anonymous, and the credits named only the principals or the department heads. The post–studio system industry, consisting largely of freelance labor, demanded credit for all. As the earlier discussion of *That's Entertainment II* illustrates, it was up to the individual producer whether the title designer was responsible for the end credits. In the case of *The Seven Year Itch* (1955) and *Advise and Consent* (1962), Bass designed humorous end titles; for *That's Entertainment II* and other films, he did not.

Finally, a film's titles must be understood in relation to all the print and broadcast publicity that precedes their unspooling, as well as the trailers that announce a film's arrival.[60] Such collateral material creates audience expectations that can be either fulfilled or denied in a film's opening moments, depending on its construction and design. In the classical period, the studio's marketing department was responsible for posters, lobby cards, press books, and magazine, trade, and newspaper advertisements, as well as film credits. At Metro-Goldwyn-Mayer, this meant that film title designers worked under Howard Dietz, the head of publicity, and Hal Burrows, the studio's art director in New York, before the final designs were sent to Culver City for production and insertion into the film.[61] It is no accident that Bass began in publicity, moved to titles, and, as a designer, often handled both aspects of a film. His ambition to identify a film for its potential audience through the simplest, most identifiable forms took branding to a new level, especially in title design.

A Short History of Titles

The first film titles appeared in the silent era more than 100 years ago. Surprisingly, a comprehensive history of title design has yet to be written, although the subject has been covered in several works and a few isolated essays on the Internet.[62] As a result, Bass's claim that title design remained unchanged for decades until he entered the field has seldom been challenged. Authorized Bass biographer Pat Kirkham notes: "In U.S. films of the early-to-mid 1950s, the majority of what then were often called title backgrounds consisted of a fairly short list of credits, often in unimaginative lettering, rolling over a static image that suggested the genre of the film."[63] Similarly categorical is Peter Hall's statement: "The film title came of age in 1955."[64] Ken Coupland argues: "It's no exaggeration to say that Bass . . . invented the modern movie title as we know it."[65] Gemma Solana and Antonio Boneu call Bass "the putative father of all of today's credit designers."[66] In point of fact, the history of title design is much more complex than such a one-dimensional model indicates. Deborah Allison, in a more nuanced reading of the history of film titles, argues that gradual changes in style occurred long before Bass and other 1950s designers initiated a sea change in title design. For example, she points to the elaborate titles in George Cukor's *The Women* (1939), which introduced the exclusively female cast with little vignettes, including images of animals that physically or emotionally resembled the characters they played: Joan Crawford was represented by a leopard; Joan Fontaine, a lamb; and Marjorie Main, a horse. Furthermore, Allison notes that such a visual introduction of the actors was not uncommon in the 1930s.[67] In fact, introducing actors by having them appear from behind a theatrical curtain or in the midst of some emblematic activity was a common convention in the silent era. For example, Cecil B. DeMille's title sequence for *The Cheat* (1915) featured actors Sessue Hayakawa, Fannie Ward, and Jack Dean looking at the camera while performing a bit of business key to their characters. Establishing such precedents for innovative title design does not lessen the achievement of Saul Bass; it merely acknowledges that title design was considered an important activity long before Bass's arrival on the scene.

Indeed, although the earliest films by the Edison and Biograph companies from 1892 to 1900 featured neither head titles nor explanatory or dialogue titles, title cards listing the film's title and the production company became a standard practice after 1900, when films were no longer than a single shot or two. Since films in this period were sold by producers directly to exhibitors by the foot or the meter, the production company, title, and copyright date were considered sufficient to identify the work. During the silent era, titles usually featured white or light-colored typography on a black background, typically framed by company-specific designs and the company logo. Including company logos and copyright information became an absolute necessity because the illegal duping of films for resale was endemic in the early years of the industry.[68] However, because head titles could be separated from the film, film companies were often forced to incorporate logos into their sets, so they couldn't be easily removed.

Early film companies often adopted specific fonts for titles and intertitle cards, such as Pastel (BB&S, 1892), National Old Style (ATF, 1916), and Photoplay (Samuel Welo's Studio, 1927).[69] The head title for Edwin S. Porter's *The Great Train Robbery* (1903) employed elaborate lettering for the title but also included both the company logo and the copyright notice in two different corners of the frame. By the early 1910s, film companies were adding the name of the director-producer to the head title, as well as that of the screenwriter. They also started to standardize the look of the titles to brand the film production company, as the Biograph Company did for all films made by D. W. Griffith between 1908 and 1914.

By the 1920s, the basic information included on the head title had expanded to include the names of writers, producers, and sometimes cameramen; the names of the stars had been added to head titles as early as 1913. Film companies created increasingly complex head titles, overcrowding the graphic look with the names of producers, writers, directors, and actors, as well as company logos and source material; in addition, drawn or photographic images were often included in the head title's background. Once narratives became more complex, films featured both credit titles at the beginning and intertitles that reproduced dialogue or other narrative information and often featured elaborate illustrations, both as decoration and as commentary on the film.

The titles themselves were often hand-drawn on glass, then rephotographed against an artfully constructed background. With the invention of optical printers in the early 1920s, and their improvement by Linwood G. Dunn in the early 1930s, filmmakers could rephotograph other pieces of film or multiple film images, allowing even more complex montages. An optical printer would have been necessary to insert live-action background images behind titles, which, according to Bordwell, was introduced in 1923 with Universal's *The Merry-Go-Round* (Rupert Julian and Erich von Stroheim); animated titles were featured in *The Speed Spook* (Charles Hines) the following year.[70] Jack Jarmuth's titles for *The Jazz Singer* (1927) relied on optical printing and were produced by Pacific Title and Art Studio, which had a virtual lock on title work in Hollywood.[71] Subsequent title cards would include additional technical credits, as well as a complete list of credited actors and their roles.

As Allison notes, the practice of bunching up numerous credits on a single title card continued in the 1930s, after the introduction of sound. Some credits also featured live-action or still background images, and others utilized animation and other moving graphic forms. Many also employed a studio house style; for example, the MGM lion in stone relief appeared in the background of many of the studio's film credits.[72] Deviations from the studio style were achieved most often through typography and layout, which were tailored stylistically to match the film's generic and narrative characteristics. Indeed, studio lettering artists were extremely inventive in employing novel typefaces and hand-lettering styles in conjunction with painted or photographed backgrounds to give each title sequence its own identity. Looking over the numerous head titles collected by Steven Hill,[73] it is clear that both fonts and layout remained very traditional throughout the classical period, with few artists looking to modernism or modernist graphic design for inspiration. As late as 1947, a practitioner in the field of title design complained that the mandate to fill the entire screen with text, no matter what the background, "puts the designer somewhat in the position of the singer who must continuously sing at full voice."[74] Not surprisingly, given its vulgarization of modernist architecture, *The Fountainhead* (1949, King Vidor) has titles that mimic modernist design. Typical of all title sequences from the 1930s and 1940s is their relative brevity, with most running under one minute.[75]

Allison cites several examples of innovative and even self-reflexive film credits. *What Price Hollywood?* (1932, Raoul Walsh), *The Cat and the Fiddle* (1933, William K. Howard), and *You'll Never Get Rich* (1941, Sidney Lanfield) place their credits on roadside billboards, seen from the point of view of a moving vehicle. Similarly, Otto Preminger's *Where the Sidewalk Ends* (1950) has a camera track a man walking along a sidewalk, where the head titles are written in white paint on the pavement; subsequent credits appear over a nighttime street scene as plainclothes detectives drive down the road. The head title for *Sunset Boulevard* (1950, Billy Wilder) appears stenciled on a street curb. *The Great Ziegfeld* (1936, Robert Z. Leonard) created titles out of Broadway marquee lights, a style Saul Bass would imitate in several films, including *Ocean's Eleven* (1960, Lewis Milestone).[76] Title designer Everett Aison discusses *Of Mice and Men*'s (1939) titles, which appear several minutes into the film and are scrawled in chalk on the side of a freight train the protagonists have just hopped.[77] The graphic layout and typography of *Criss Cross* (1949, Robert Siodmak) are conventional, but they literally melt off the screen, like the protagonist's dream. The head title of Samuel Fuller's *Scandal Sheet* (1952, Phil Karlson) appears under the masthead as a newspaper headline, and credits are inserted into various columns. Finally, the act of making a credit sequence is visualized in *Carefree* (1938, Mark Sandrich), where disembodied hands draw the titles in finger-paint style on a glass surface painted black. In *I Love Melvin* (1953, Don Weis), Debbie Reynolds writes the film's title in lipstick on a mirror, presaging Bass films that depict the act of writing or lettering, such as *Why Man Creates* (1968).

Despite these and other early examples of innovative film titles, most film historians agree that Saul Bass precipitated a major paradigm shift in the way the industry viewed credit sequences. As one critic put it: "It is mainly due to Bass that people have come to believe we are in the midst of a Renaissance in title design."[78] Beginning in the mid-1950s, film titles would become a new, specialized field for designers, allowing them greater freedom to experiment and create specific identities for every film. As Bass noted in 1960 in a short piece in *Graphis*: "I have approached the titles with the objective of making them sufficiently provocative and entertaining to induce the theater inhabitants to sit down and watch, because something is really happening on the screen. It then may become possible to project a symbolic foretaste of what is to come, and to create a receptive atmosphere that will enable the film to begin on a higher level of audience rapport."[79]

As noted, economic factors, especially the breakdown of the studio system, led to conditions that could accommodate an independent artist like Saul Bass. Whereas in the classic studio era it was Jack Warner at Warner Brothers or Darryl Zanuck at 20th Century–Fox or Howard Dietz at MGM who decided on the look and lettering of film titles,[80] independent producers gravitated to independent designers who could brand their clients. Furthermore, the Hollywood strike of 1946 had precipitated the founding of the Scenic and Title Artists Local 816, a union for graphic artists and designers, which acknowledged that these individuals made significant contributions to the look and feel of a film.[81] Finally, the font size for individual credits was contractually enforced by studio agreements via so-called billing sheets, thus limiting the title artist's choices. Independent producers like Otto Preminger had the leeway to give their designers more space, if they chose to do so.

By the 1960s, most of the studios had given up their titling operations, and a new subindustry emerged that focused on title design and production; this situation continues today, with a new computer-trained generation of film title designers. Bass first worked with National Screen Service, which produced not only film titles but also a large percentage of the "paper"—that is, the posters, stills, lobby cards, and other collateral advertising for a film. But NSS was nowhere near the largest firm in the business. That distinction was held by Pacific Title and Art Studio, which was responsible for nearly 50 percent of all titles and worked almost exclusively for Warner Brothers, MGM, Fox, and Universal. Other companies competing for the remaining titling business included Consolidated, Howard Anderson, Ray Mercer, and DePatie-Freleng.

Over the next forty years, title design would continue to evolve from the simple reproduction of film credits to elaborate prefilms that were intended to be perceived as separate from the film proper. Technological innovations also occurred, with glass-plate lettering and matte titling (optical printing) eventually giving way to video and then digital effects, all of which opened up multifarious possibilities for creative design.

The next generation of prominent designers would include Wayne Fitzgerald, Pablo Ferro, Maurice Binder, Robert Brownjohn, and many others. Just how quickly the industry changed is evidenced by the title sequence for *Silk Stockings* (1957, Rouben Mamoulian), a musical remake of Greta Garbo's *Ninotchka* (1939, Ernst Lubitsch). The title could be mistaken for a Bass design, particularly the way the screen is divided into an ever-changing array of colored rectangles. But *Silk Stockings* was designed by Wayne Fitzgerald, who began working at Pacific Title in 1951 and stayed through 1967, before going freelance. Indeed, Fitzgerald credits Bass with "changing everything" when it comes to titles.[82] The *Silk Stockings* title sequence takes its cue from the "Satin and Silk" musical number in the film. Fabric bolts in various pastel colors roll either horizontally or vertically over the previously listed credits, never completely covering the preceding bolts as a new set of credits appears. Thus, at one point, powder blue satin rolls up from the bottom, covering the right half of the frame, while white, pink, and blue fabrics remain visible in horizontal and vertical strips. The strict geometric construction of the screen space, the use of a limited pastel color palette, the use of all capital letters for names and credits, and the dynamic layout of justified text are all characteristic of Bass's style. Pacific Title's layout, based on studio billing sheets, remained rigidly centered and in the vertical safety zone of one-third above and one-third below the horizontal axis. Bass, probably because he was working in wide-screen formats, chose to use left and right justification at the extreme edges of the screen frame to demarcate his typographic space. Fitzgerald began to play with the same idea in *Silk Stockings*.

Once the first generation of title designers, including Bass, had opened up the process aesthetically, new technologies began to evolve. In the 1970s video techniques and computer programming made inroads among designers of title sequences, such as Dan Perri's titles for *Star Wars* (1977) or Richard and Robert Greenberg's titles for *Superman* (1978). With the introduction of desktop computer graphics programs like Adobe After Effects, designers could design, animate, and composite credit sequences on their own workstations, giving them a whole new level of control.[83] Kyle Cooper's titles for *Se7en* (1995) have repeatedly been cited as representative of the new possibilities of digital title design. Other designers working in the field in the 1990s included Michael Riley, Karin Fong, Robert Dawson, Garson Yu, Randy Balsmeyer and Mimi Everett, Bob Freeman, Carla Swanson, and Melissa Elliot.[84] A wholly digitally trained generation of title designers has emerged since the turn of the twenty-first century, including Nic Bends (Momoco), Jeremy Cox (Imaginary Forces), Pamela B. Green (PIC Agency), Erin Sarofsky, Smith & Lee Design, and Steve Viola.

Design and Typographic Theory

Film credit sequences utilize both words and images, so there is a relationship between typography and visual design. What is the nature of that relationship, and why do designers choose one particular typographic style or font over another? Visual design creates meaning through the aesthetics of composition, layout, and images in connection with the semantic meanings of the text. Whereas design is more concerned with aesthetics, typography is usually more concerned with legibility. In addition to font, type size, and kern, typography is about the placement and graphic design of the text: the spacing of words, sentences, and columns within the frame.[85]

Design and typographic theory should answer questions about why some designs work and others don't, but few answers have been forthcoming. Indeed, although a set of prescriptive rules seemingly exists as a result of decades of practice and the need to formalize conventions, little has been published in the realm of design theory. Designers are loath to theorize about their work, seeing each design problem as unique—form following function, to use a cliché. When asked whether he had a philosophy of design, Bass responded: "Theories are very dangerous, and philosophy is theory."[86] Bass's colleague Paul Rand put it differently: "There is no formula for good design; each problem is unique, as is each solution."[87] Also typical is the statement of typography designer Peter Bil'ak: "Type design, however, seems to resist attempts to establish an encompassing theory by its very nature. Type design is not an intellectual activity, but relies on a gesture of the person and his ability to express it formally. Even if a theory existed, it would not be very useful, since type design is governed by practice. There might be detailed 'how to' instructions, but those do not qualify as general or abstract principles for creating type."[88]

The argument that design is intuitive and therefore not subject to the kind of abstraction demanded by theory seems logical at first, until one applies the same notion to art, which is also largely intuitive but for which there is a large body of theory. Developing directly from the modernist art movements of the early twentieth century, art theory focuses on perception, utilizing Gestalt psychology to undergird prescriptive rules for production that are supposedly justified by human biology. Rudolf Arnheim and Gyorgy Kepes, among others, explicate design as an abstract formal activity originating in visual perception and divorced from the linguistic interpretation of texts.[89] Indeed, Kepes's *The Language of Vision* is, shockingly, completely devoid of any discussion of typography and texts in visual design, as if cultural meaning were of no importance, as if historical-social context contributed nothing to perception. Yet even theorists of typography tend to slip into naturalistic metaphors when trying to explicate good design: "In a badly designed book, the letters mill and stand like starving horses in a field. . . . In a well-made book, where designer, compositor and printer have all done their jobs, no matter how many thousands of lines and pages, they must dance in the margins and aisles."[90] Such statements notwithstanding, this same theorist goes on to establish some principles of typographic design. The first is that the inner logic of the text must be reflected in the inner logic of the typography. In other words, what does the text say, and how can that meaning be best expressed in type? This principle can also be applied to typography in film credits, where the goal is to create an inner logic between the content and meaning of the film and the typography of the credits. Second, typography should make visible the relationship between the text and the other elements (e.g., photography, diagrams, notes). In title design, therefore, relationships exist between typography and background images, animation, optical effects, and the like, all of which make up the total visual design of the frame.[91]

One unwritten rule of the Hollywood film title business was that the material used in film tiles had to be different from anything actually seen in the film.[92] It might therefore be productive to look at Saul Bass's typography and compositional design strategies over a broad range of film credit sequences before analyzing individual titles. If we can identify consistencies in the Bass style, design motifs, and brand, then we can begin to read the designer's work in its specific historical context—its moment in history—as well as understand how it speaks to the contemporary generation, spawning countless homages and imitations.

Bass on Titles

Saul Bass's most comprehensive comments on his movie title work were captured in a thirty-two-minute film he created for Pyramid Films, a distributor of educational short films for the 16mm nontheatrical market. Bass had approached Pyramid about financing such a film, arguing that, given the number of invitations he received to lecture on titles, there was an educational market for a film on that subject. Discussions about a title reel started in the Bass office as early as October 1968, but research began in earnest in March 1973, when Morrie Marsh, Bass's office manager, approached Bob Bouchet at Pyramid. At first, both film and television credits were going to be included. As Marsh noted in an internal memo to Bass, such a film would "accommodate an interest . . . by every school that has a film, theatrical or design department," and it would "therefore [be made] not so much for the purposes of entertainment as it is an important piece of research material."[93]

Two major issues slowed the preproduction work significantly. First, there was the matter of obtaining clearances from the rights holders for the long clips that would be necessary if the titles were to be shown in their entirety (it had been decided that only "unabridged" titles would serve an educational purpose). As late as May 1977, just months before the film's release, six of the ten titles had not yet been cleared. Interestingly, several titles were initially rejected because of "insufficient visual interest," including *The Seven Year Itch*, *North by Northwest*, and *Spartacus*.[94] Surprisingly, the rights were eventually obtained at no cost to the producers, and the approximately $30,000 it cost to make the film was split between production expenses and Bass's design fee. An even bigger issue was the fact that many of the studios had discarded the original production materials for the titles chosen. According to Jeff Okun, he joined the Bass office in 1976 to remake elements for *It's a Mad, Mad, Mad, Mad World*, *Spartacus*, *Walk on the Wild Side*, and *Seconds*, utilizing surviving outtakes and cribbing the music from sound-track albums.[95] The film was released on 15 September 1977 and was shown at various film festivals over the next several years, including in Rotterdam (1981) and Venice (1982); in the latter city, "producers and directors flocked" to attend a packed midnight show.[96]

Bass on Titles follows the official Bass narrative. The designer makes brief statements about ten credit sequences, ordered not chronologically but according to their supposed technical complexity. The off-camera interviewer, Herb Yager, begins by referencing *Man with the Golden Arm* as the first animated logo in a credit sequence. *In Harm's Way* and *Seconds* are then presented as "the next logical step" in terms of moving to live-action images. *West Side Story* and *It's a Mad, Mad, Mad, Mad World* are discussed as very long titles, while *The Big Country*, *The Victors*, and *Grand Prix* represent titles that function as temporal prologues, "further integrating the title into the film." In fact, the sequence shown for *The Victors* is not the end credits (which is interesting in its own right) but a prologue occurring before the head title. Finally, the titles for *Nine Hours to Rama* and *A Walk on the Wild Side* illustrate the "most challenging aspect of any creative endeavor, and that is dealing with ordinary things," or making the ordinary stand out anew. The film ends with Bass's closing statement about being a filmmaker. As this brief synopsis shows, the narrative structure of *Bass on Titles* is more anecdotal than theoretical. A review in the Educational Film Library Association's journal was mixed: "A worthy tribute to Saul Bass, and a nice chance to see his work collected for examination. A unique presentation of an aspect of filmmaking which is rarely explored. Live sequences with

Bass could have been staged more imaginatively than just a 'talking head.'"[97]

While the viewer learns something about the original impetus for a specific title sequence, Bass's brief comments do little to explain his methodology or theoretical thinking. Bass reiterates his often-articulated statement that he uses titles in a new way "to actually create a climate for the story that is about to unfold." In other words, Bass reinforces the notion that the credits should be considered a portion of the narrative proper, a notion he then develops with his examples of sequences as prologues. Furthermore, Bass places his symbols—whether the golden arm, a watch, or a cat—at the center of his content discussion but says nary a word about his techniques. For instance, he mentions the globe at the center of *It's a . . . Mad World* but fails to discuss its animation; nor does he explain the slow-dissolve technique of *Nine Hours to Rama* or how specific techniques are appropriate for specific projects.

Indeed, the film is a perfect example of Hollywood's strategy of dazzling with technique without revealing the actual labor taking place behind the curtain. Unfortunately, given 16mm film's normal aspect ratio, the wide-screen credits for *West Side Story, In Harm's Way, Nine Hours to Rama, It's a . . . Mad World,* and *Grand Prix* have been severely cropped to fit the frame, making it all but impossible to study Bass's design. Because Yager is both interlocutor and producer of *Bass on Titles,* it is not far-fetched to see the film as part and parcel of his efforts to revitalize the Bass brand and drum up new business opportunities. That might explain Bass's closing statement, which highlights his experience in short films, features, commercials, and work for hire, not just film titles. Though the film's original intention may have been educational, its pitch is more in keeping with an industry demonstration reel. The film's limited value as an educational tool thus resides in its documentation of heretofore disparate title sequences and Bass's statements about them, allowing students to discuss the Bass style.

The Saul Bass Style

Not surprisingly, given his modernist mentors, Bass gravitated toward modernist and geometric typefaces rather than Renaissance, Baroque, or Romantic font styles, which he used only occasionally and for specific reasons. Unlike some Hollywood title designers, Bass eschewed all forms of iconographic typography as well as most abstracted typography, probably for reasons of legibility. Such ornamentation was thought to be very old school by modernist designers. Nor did Bass employ any three-dimensional typeface styles. Geometric modernist typefaces communicated a more contemporary feel; a precise product of the machine age, they were cleaner and more legible. Typography had to stand out boldly, given the many other visual elements competing for the viewer's attention. Such font styles also correlated more closely with Bass's overall design aesthetic, which sought to establish balance, harmony, and contrast through the simplest geometric forms and a geometrically precise construction of screen space. For example, the strong diagonal design elements in *The Man with the Gold Arm*, correlating with the film's narrative of drug addiction, are stabilized for reader legibility through the use of a modern font that stresses horizontal and vertical axes. The typography for *Seconds* functions similarly, although in this case, the contrast is between optically distorted and irregular photographic images and a clean, modern typeface. In *Bunny Lake Is Missing*, the ripped black paper creates very irregular forms, while the typography underneath is clearly supported by a grid.

In a sampling of fifty-three credit sequences, Bass preferred sans serif type, which he used in thirty-seven sequences. Geometric typefaces eliminated serifs and were thought to look cleaner and project modernity. Indeed, sans serif type styles were preferred by modernist designers at the Bauhaus and became a hallmark of the international style that influenced Bass and other American designers after World War II. Thanks to their simple, legible form, sans serif typefaces were considered more contemporary than the ornamental type styles associated with Art Nouveau and other nineteenth-century art movements.[98] In addition, the choice of type may have been influenced by the film medium itself, since elaborate serifs might hinder legibility on a screen with moving images.

In those cases in which Bass chose a serif type, the film subjects were often historical in nature: *Around the World in 80 Days, Cowboy, The Pride and the Passion, A Walk on the Wild Side*, and *The Age of Innocence*. In addition, *Spartacus* features a Roman serif type—appropriate because the slaves' uprising against Rome occurred just as serif type was becoming established in Latin inscription.[99] Similarly, utilizing an italicized serif type for *Age of Innocence* allowed the Basses not only to re-create the elaborate late-nineteenth-century serifs of Art Nouveau, thus immersing the viewer in the period from the very start, but also to mimic the calligraphy of Edith Wharton's original hand-written manuscript of her novel of the same name. However, there were exceptions to Bass's use of serifs to signify history, as *Saint Joan*'s sans serif type demonstrates.

Interestingly, except for the handwritten typography credits for *Advise and Consent*, *In Harm's Way*, *Why Man Creates*, and *100 Years of the Telephone*, Bass usually eschewed handcrafted lettering to mimic calligraphy. He preferred to create block-print typefaces that were slightly imperfect (*Saint Joan* and *Exodus*); looked scrawled, like writing on a blackboard or graffiti on a brick wall (*Not with My Wife, You Don't* and *West Side Story*, respectively); or were written by his own hand (*Why Man Creates* and *A Personal Journey with Martin Scorsese*). Such hand-produced typography, which had fallen out of fashion earlier in the century, had been revived by fine artists working in design in the 1950s.[100] The title *Bunny Lake Is Missing* is also handmade in slightly irregular block print that changes color on the last word, reflecting the film's ambiguous narrative, while the credits use a modernist geometric font. The credit sequence for *Around the World in 80 Days* ends with a highly stylized cursive title card, giving it a romantic, nineteenth-century air of adventure (in keeping with Jules Verne), although all the previous credits used a print typography. Finally, the title sequence for *The Seven Year Itch* utilizes a handcrafted print with extreme serifs and very fanciful lettering; this lack of modernist simplicity contrasts with the high-art modernism of Bass's color boxes, which pay homage to Paul Klee. In the case of these hand-produced types, Bass deviated from the Bauhaus model, which sought to eliminate the hand of the individual artist in favor of a more mechanical, objective style.[101] Indeed, Bass emphasized the creative hand of the artist in all his work, most prominently in *Why Man Creates*.

Bass also strove to create a typographical look that created large geometric fields balanced across the screen space. To give the text a block look, Bass demonstrated a preference for large and small capital letters in his title sequences. Because capital letters have a uniform height, the letters and lines of text look almost box-like, thereby emphasizing the rectangular shape of the screen space occupied by text; lowercase letters, in contrast, create lines with irregular contours at the top.[102] Modernist typography designers from the 1920s, such as Herbert Bayer and Jan Tschichold, advocated abolishing upper- and lowercase altogether for the sake of simplicity and legibility.[103] In his title sequences, Bass employed capital letters either exclusively (*Anatomy of a Murder*, *Storm Center*, *Saint Joan*, *A Bronx Tale*, and *Casino*) or in conjunction with a more conventional capitalization scheme, choosing to designate either names or credits in all caps (*Carmen Jones*, *Attack! The Racers*, *Something Wild*, *Around the World in 80 Days*, *Walk on the Wild Side*, *Exodus*, *Nine Hours to Rama*, *Bunny Lake Is Missing*, *In Harm's Way*, *The War of the Roses*, and *Mr. Saturday Night*). For *The Pride and the Passion*, Bass used all caps only for the names in the technical credits.

Bass preferred white lettering on dark, multicolored, or moving surfaces, although he employed black type when confronted with a white surface, as in *Bunny Lake Is Missing* and *The War of the Roses*. The former necessitated a switch from black to white for the director's credit, whereas in *The Big Knife*, the director's credit switched from white to black type. Bass sometimes alternated between black and white lettering, as in *Cowboy*. He rarely employed a variety of colors (an exception was *Not with My Wife, You Don't*), possibly in reaction to the garish and oversaturated reds used for numerous film titles in the 1950s. Indeed, Hollywood films shot in color in the 1950s and 1960s overwhelmingly utilized reds and strong yellows for their title credits. Bass employed those colors in his images, not in his texts. Not until the 1990s would Elaine and Saul Bass use red typography for films, such as *Goodfellas* and *Higher Learning*. The preference for white type makes sense in terms of legibility, not only for black-and-white films but also for the busyness of color cinematography, particularly if the backgrounds consist of live-action images. Colored type lacks contrast or, conversely, creates an unwanted illusion of dimension.[104] Black lettering threatens to get lost in the background, whereas white lettering tends to pop forward, as if it is above the background image (this occurs because black absorbs light, while white reflects it). Also, because color can have a whole set of symbolic associations, as well as communicate emotions such as intensity, excitement, or calmness, Bass may have been reluctant to give the text such emotional weight.[105] Finally, Bass's layout of the typography within the screen frame privileged a geometric ordering of the text, balancing right and left, and with text fields rigorously structured along central vertical and horizontal axes.

The size of the screen frame changed radically during the 1950s with the new wide-screen aspect ratios of Hollywood films. When the decade began, the "Academy aperture" was still the absolute norm; wide-screen formats with different aspect ratios—from Cinerama (2.6:1) to Cinemascope (2.55:1)—were introduced after 1953, before Bass created his first titles for *Carmen Jones*. For decades, the Academy aspect ratio (1.37:1) had been considered ideal because it was thought to conform more or less to the golden mean, as defined by some introductory film texts.[106] The "golden section" or "divine proportion" (a/b = b/[a + b], where *a* is the short side and *b* is the long side of a rectangle) was used by mathematicians and architects, going back to the ancient Egyptians, to establish harmony and order, and it was a design principle of classical painting, architecture, and graphic design.[107] In fact, the ratio of the golden mean (1.66:1) is identical to the flat, wide-screen format of many modern European films and closer to the format of flat, wide-screen American films (1:85:1) than to Academy aperture; yet for decades, cinematographers argued that the Academy ratio was the most aesthetically pleasing for dramatic content. Although some of Bass's credit sequences were for films that still used the Academy ratio (*The Big Knife*, *Storm Center*, *Edge of the City*), most had transitioned to wide-screen formats, which may have encouraged Bass to play with unconventional text placements.

Whether filmed in Academy aspect ratio or wide-screen formats, Bass's titles achieved a unified look by organizing the design elements asymmetrically on a mathematically precise grid, employing sans serif type, and utilizing right or left justification (mirroring the screen's frame), just as Bauhaus artists and post–World War II International Typographic Style designers had done.[108] The basis for a mathematical screen grid was the establishment of a horizontal axis and a vertical axis, cutting the frame into four equal rectangles, which allowed Bass to create architectural structures within the two-dimensional screen space. The underlying grid was largely invisible, but in *North by Northwest*, the grid is taken from a building façade and then abstracted to allow the text to move along its lines. Given that film credits have to be clearly legible and create a hierarchy of names and positions, Bass employed text fields within the larger space of the frame. Allowing text sizes to be dictated by overall design, opening up the screen to permit "empty" areas without text, creating text blocks and patterns, and paying strict attention to typography were all revolutionary concepts in an industry where attention to the details of title design was an anomaly.

But using a graphic designer's grid also meant that Bass's title designs were overwhelmingly two-dimensional; he only rarely utilized the third dimension of cinematic space, as some contemporary designers have done. Indeed, while some graphic designers (e.g., typographer Jan Tschichold) attempted to create the illusion of a third dimension on the page in their print work, Bass's title work remained resolutely two-dimensional, even when he employed live-action images behind his titles. Even those that depicted three-dimensional spaces (e.g., *The Big Country, The Cardinal*) flattened the image, treating the frame conceptually as a two-dimensional space. Bass almost always preferred lateral, horizontal movement or background images that flattened out space through their design. This attitude, which film theorists have characterized as seeing the cinematic screen as a two-dimensional frame rather than as a window onto a three-dimensional space, also characterized Bass's work as a film director and was in keeping with his preference for montage over long takes and extended camera movement.

Bass's titles almost always gave preference to lines and blocks of text above the frame's horizontal axis or directly below it, which conformed to the conventions established by studio and Pacific Title designers. But there were exceptions. For *The Big Country*, most of the credits are located in the bottom quarter of the screen, probably because Bass and Wyler wanted to communicate the vastness of the western landscapes in the background images. For *Advise and Consent*, the main actors' credits also appear centered at the bottom of the screen, while the top half is covered with the continual, uneven movement of the stripes of an American flag, as if it were waving in the wind. This creates a dynamic contrast between the symbolic weight of the flag, as an icon of American democracy, and the actors who play participants in the drama of that democracy. For technical credits, Bass more often created blocks of text in the lower half of the frame with a smaller typeface, giving the text a foundational weight. In a number of sequences, Bass utilized the horizontal axis as a railroad along which to move text from offscreen space, as in *Psycho* or, more prominently, *Goodfellas*. With *The Cardinal*, Bass centered the head title, then used dissolves to move the main actors' credits along the horizontal axis, a device he repeated in *Cape Fear.*

In title sequences from early in his career, Bass rarely centered the credits (which was the conventional practice), except when only one credit appeared on the screen. Rather, Bass rigorously utilized a vertical axis to balance text on the left and right sides of the frame, often alternating text from one side to the other. For example, in the titles for *Anatomy of a*

Murder, the credits are placed inside or around various cutout shapes of body parts that cross the vertical axis with every new title. Even the head title, with its abstracted corpse cut in half by the vertical axis, seems less than centered because the title is read on two lines screen left and one line screen right. *Age of Innocence*, like so many other Bass credits, also alternates text left and right from title to title. Such a back-and-forth movement forces the viewer to move his or her gaze left and right, actively searching for the text. It also connects one frame to the next in a much more dynamic fashion than just leaving the viewer to stare at evolving texts centered squarely in the frame. This principle is already evident in Bass's first title sequence for *Carmen Jones*, where he alternates between single lines of text on the horizontal axis and lists of credits to the right of the vertical axis, then places left- and right-justified text along both edges of the frame for the technical credits.

Bass was extremely consistent in his use of right- or left-justified text for multiple credits. With *Carmen Jones*, this left and right justification caused the center justification to be ragged, leaving space in the center frame for the sequence's image of a burning flame and also mimicking the movement of the flame. Numerous other sequences feature technical credits that alternate between left and right justification from title to title. In some cases, such as when Bass is dealing with two columns of text, he employs a center justification for the two columns, giving the impression of order at the center and a ragged feeling at the edges. According to one design theorist, such a flush-left, ragged-right composition evokes "the continued flirtation with order and chaos."[109] Indeed, the push and pull between stability and motion must have been central to Bass's design concept for film titles: there is not one example of justified text (where the spacing between letters and words is irregular) blocks (rather than single lines of text) in Bass's work. Completely unjustified text is only slightly less rare, appearing in *The Seven Year Itch* and *The Man with the Golden Arm*. In the former case, the credits appear in rectangular boxes, mitigating the impression of the unjustified text; in the latter case, the horizontal typography contrasts with the strong diagonal lines, mirroring a narrative of drug addiction.

Thus, we can conclude that Bass rejected the conventional, centered film titles that Hollywood had been producing for decades. He sought to create dynamic movement that fluctuated between stability and disorder by utilizing the entire frame as his canvas, creating weight and counterweight with blocks of text and left or right justification. Bass's designs, like those of the Constructivists in the Soviet Union, the German Bauhaus artists, and De Stijl designers in Holland, were based on mathematical grids.[110] The use of grids is standard procedure for book and magazine designers, allowing them to organize content on a page and ensure that margins and other features are considered in relation to text. Such grids can be visible or invisible, directing the eye to various points on the page. According to Martin Solomon, creating a grid "to break down your space mathematically, you become aware of the energy forces within each segment and how the size and shape of each element relates to the whole."[111] At the same time, Bass often turned the seriousness of the undertaking on its head, ending his title sequences with a humorous coda or a visual pun that acted as a final exclamation point to the sequence. A perfect example of this stylistic device, which Bass implemented repeatedly, is the visual and aural spring that pops Billy Wilder's directorial credit out of the sequence's abstract color grid like a jack-in-the-box, cuing the audience to the fact that *Some Like It Hot* is a comedy.

Moving Graphics: *Psycho, Higher Learning, Goodfellas*

After hiring Bass to create the titles for *Vertigo* and *North by Northwest*, Hitchcock again turned to him not only to design the titles but also to act as a visual consultant for particular scenes in *Psycho* (1960), sending him the first twenty pages of the script on 10 November 1959. Valuing the innovative eye of the designer, Hitchcock was particularly interested in having Bass storyboard several problem areas rather than asking his staff illustrator, Joseph Hurley, to do so.[112] These included the shower scene, the Arbogast murder, the revelation of Mother, and the view of the haunted house. Bass was supposed to be paid $10,000 for thirteen half days of work over thirteen consecutive weeks, as well as $2,000 extra for the storyboards, but he ultimately took home $17,000 for all his work on the film.[113] The titles were done at National Screen Service at a cost of $21,000.

Although Bass designed most if not all of his titles with an invisible grid (as simple as x- and y-axes), the grid construction itself is a manifest and self-reflective theme in the credit sequence for *Psycho*. Here (and not for the last time) Bass creates credits that are virtually pure graphics in motion. The text functions on a semantic level as well as visually, moving, constantly forming and re-forming in different patterns. Bass described the project as follows: "The entire title is designed on a module of black bars of equal weight, which slide onto the screen horizontally or vertically in various patterns. Parts of each credit are carried on different bars. When they are in proper conjunction, the typographic elements line up to create a legible credit designation. The entire effect is harsh, strident, and some-what unpredictable, as a reflection of those qualities that give the film its particular character."[114]

The thick gray and black lines that form vertically and horizontally at varying rates, as well as the fractured white typography that flows from illegibility to legibility and back again, move along evenly spaced, verti-cally and horizontally structured axes. Likewise, Bass contrasts the invisi-ble central axis, from which lines emanate or into which they are absorbed, to the ragged edges formed by the lines moving offscreen. This theme of order and chaos manifests itself as soon as the film's head title rolls into view: Bass slices the white typography of "ALFRED HITCHCOCK'S" into three horizontal chains of typographical fragments that enter the screen space on parallel tracks from opposite directions, so that only when the middle chain is in place in the center of the screen does the type become legible. The typography is thus first understood by the viewer as pure form, decipherable only at the point of perception and reception, surrounded, as it were, by abstracted moving forms. Bass constructs a visual symphony in dissonant tones that Raymond Durgnat correctly identifies as "extending the tradition of Eggeling, Ruttmann, Lye, MacLaren."[115]

After the typography breaks up again and moves offscreen as frag-ments, "PSYCHO" becomes legible in the center of the screen in the same manner, moving from data to message. Bass adds a tickler by having the tripartite typography shudder or stutter before disappearing into black; it then reappears, now sliced horizontally in two, with half moving up offscreen and the other half moving down offscreen. This type of little surprise is not uncommon in Bass's title work, presaging here the surprises revealed in the film. James Counts quotes Harold Adler, who describes how this complicated work was done before the digital age:

The production team for the *Psycho* credit sequence settled on a configuration of over thirty parallel bars for each field. Adler, who handled the horizontal bar movements, explained, "We got six foot-long aluminum bars and sprayed them black. We worked on a large white painted plywood board with push-pins to guide the bars. The bars had to follow a straight line and couldn't wiggle. Paul (Stoleroff) and I manually pushed in each bar at predetermined distances and speeds. Each bar was precisely timed by numbers of frames per second, called 'counts.' Each bar had to be pushed in and shot separately. Once a bar had gone across the screen, it was tied down. There were lots of retakes because they'd come in crooked."[116]

The letters that split into two halves and move offscreen in different directions also function as a trope for the deeply schizophrenic state of the central protagonist, whose personality has split to make room for his dead mother. Such animated typography can be read by the audience as "creepy," in keeping with the horror film to follow, just as the severed parts of meaningful words can be seen as a trope for the bodies of the victims in the narrative to come. Bernard Herrmann's strikingly dissonant opening music punctuates the credits with shrill sections corresponding to the breakup of the letters. That auditory and visual cue signals the mental breakdown of the central character. Bass thus submits to the strict confines of the grid in his movement of lines and type, but he is also aware of the unpredictability of time within his constructed space, giving birth to moments of chaos.

Throughout the following credits, Bass continues the push and pull between order and instability. While most of the main actors' credits are centered and solitary on the screen, the stability of block lettering for legibility is brief; the hustle and bustle of movement soon continues. Bass sticks to white typography, which he divides into capital letters of two different sizes and weights—larger for names, and smaller for job titles or special remarks. Along with the sans serif, modernist block typeface, capital letters give the impression of fitting easily into the grooves that carry text to and away from their destination on the screen. In contrast, Bass creates weak vertical axes by having some of the technical credits center-justified with two columns of text, creating unstable ragged edges of text that are always threatening to fall over if the base is too narrow. These invisible vertical axes constructed of center-justified text are themselves sometimes placed off center, adding to the compositional instability. And yet these same vertical axes sometimes explode outward, with text flying, or are forged from the collision of text. Bass increases the unpredictability quotient by having text move either vertically or horizontally off the grid; the switch occurs without apparent logic, like the murders themselves. For example, the name John Gavin appears on a vertical axis but moves offscreen on a horizontal one.

Bass engages in formal play with the grid by actually constructing its visible form through color typography (i.e., a letter's density, measured on a gray scale). Here, Bass articulates levels of visibility and contrast in typography by alternating gray and black lines; the gray appears to be white until actual white typography glides along the gray and black grid. Bass also has the screen go totally black, establishing a new zero point for any colored lettering to come. The horizontal construction of space into light and dark lines of equal size creates a venetian blind effect in the credits that can be interpreted as a trope for the film's theme of observation and punishment.[117] Indeed, the film's first few live-action shots explicitly suggest this theme, as the camera zooms in on a darkened hotel window with venetian blinds that are mostly closed, then raised in the next scene as Marion's illicit lover opens the blinds after they've had sex. Here, the viewer is explicitly placed in the uncomfortable position of being a voyeur, a Peeping Tom viewing a primal scene. As elsewhere in the narrative, the blinds create a barrier to vision but also allow those inside to gaze out without being seen. In the first scene, the blinds form a pattern of gray and white lines on the faces of the lovers, a typical film noir visual trope that signifies the characters' moral ambiguity but also mirror the titles. Finally, the blinds remind us of Bass's graphic design work, where he would often slice a photographic image into strips, forcing the viewer to reconstruct the whole image mentally (e.g., his trade advertisement for *Attack!* or his window cards for *Anatomy of a Murder*).

Horizontal lines thus govern a symphony of movement along a strict grid, but the highlighted typography is always more unstable than stable, always attempting to achieve stability of form and then falling into chaos. Just as the film's narrative leads the viewer to identify with a character (played by Janet Leigh) and then eliminates her, throwing the viewer into turmoil, the titles oscillate between legibility and illegibility, order and chaos. And to make that point, the horizontal grid itself deconstructs after Hitchcock's severed directorial credit simultaneously moves up and down the grid into offscreen space, while bars slowly disappear into a central horizontal axis. Only then does a live-action shot of a sun-baked city dissolve out of the wreckage. Thus, through purely graphic means, Bass's *Psycho* titles create an objective correlative to Hitchcock's fractured narrative.

Thirty-five years later, Bass (and his wife Elaine) would construct a similar grid-based title sequence, again employing moving type in shades of black, white, and gray, but without the metaphoric elements featured in *Psycho*. For John Singleton's third feature, *Higher Learning* (1995), Bass would reuse some of *Psycho*'s formal design elements to the tune of a hip-hop sound track, while turning the grid forty-five degrees to create strong diagonal movement within the film's frame. One might argue that the diagonal movement of text on- and offscreen mirrors the learning curve experienced by the racially and culturally diverse students in the film as they try to accept one another as human beings and live together harmoniously on campus. However, the titles here have seemingly little symbolic meaning in relation to the film's narrative. This was not always the case.

As Bass's initial design proposals demonstrate, he originally wanted to begin with a word cloud that visualized racial prejudice by articulating various racial slurs: First the word "nigger" appears in the top left quadrant in white text on an all-black screen, followed by "White Boy" in the opposite quadrant, slightly lower. Then "fag," "kike," and "lesbo" appear above the first two words, while "bitch" and "skinhead" appear below. More and more pejorative terms appear until the screen is literally filled with them, except for a black space in the center of the screen. (Bass used the same idea in *Why Man Creates*, where numbers gradually blacken a white screen.) As the white typography begins to fade, the word "unlearn" appears in red at the center. Bass and Singleton thus offer a solution to racial prejudice and other forms of discrimination to both the audience and the characters. When all the other words have faded to black, the "un" disappears and is replaced by the film's title in red: *Higher Learning*.[118] This "teaser" before the head title was apparently still planned as late as two months after initial discussions between Bass and the producers, but was not included in the final production in November.[119] The use of such crude language was apparently too inflammatory for the producers at Columbia, because all that remains of the concept is the film's final image: an American flag over which the word "unlearn" is typed in black Times New Roman letters. That word then dissolves into the same bright red of the head title before fading out for the non-Bass end titles.

The film's approved title sequence also ends with the American flag. After Singleton's directorial credit zooms offscreen, the chimes of a campus clock are heard while the screen remains black for a couple of seconds before cutting to an American flag that fills the screen; then the camera pans 180 degrees to reveal a student demonstration. The full-screen flag, with its strong horizontal red and white stripes, functions first as a visual shock after the powerful diagonals and monochromatic design of the previous titles, jolting the viewer kinesthetically, as the original opening design would have done intellectually. More important, bracketing *Higher Learning*'s narrative with the American flag signals that the multiethnic campus of Columbus University is a microcosm for the nation as a whole.

Formally, the tiles remain consistent with the Bass brand in terms of both the grid construction and the layout of text on the screen. Utilizing a modern block font, Bass contrasts the black screen with white type for names and gray type for designations. The letters are all capitals and sans serif, probably the Compacta font discussed with the producers.[120] The film opens with hip-hop music and a black screen; then each word shoots diagonally into the frame from the bottom left corner, covering that whole quadrant of the screen: "COLUMBIA PICTURES PRESENTS." The words then shoot up the same diagonal line and exit the frame at the top, screen right. "A FILM BY JOHN SINGLETON" enters from the bottom at the same angle but shifted to the right, so it is slightly off center, and exits as before. The red head title, dissected horizontally, enters from the top and bottom of the screen diagonally, coming to rest and forming legible words just off center, in the same place as the previous credit. The head title is the only one in which Bass utilizes the same kind of horizontally split lettering used in *Psycho*; it also changes color, while all the other titles are monochromatic. Here, the split seems to have no metaphoric function. Its legibility is delayed until the title comes to rest, while the change to red may be intended only to make the title pop or to connect formally with the American flag that follows.

The following actors' credits all move similarly onto and off this diagonal grid, coming to rest at various points on the screen either individually or in groups, alluding to the similarities and differences of the students who are the subject of the film. The next set of technical credits switches to a strictly horizontal and vertical grid, appearing right-justified on either the left or right side of the screen, just above the horizontal axis. These include the single screen credit for Saul and Elaine Bass, indicating the importance of their work in the context of the whole production. After the music credit for jazz musician Stanley Clarke, the titles return to a diagonal grid for the production designer and subsequent major credits, including Singleton's credit for writing and directing. As in the case of *Psycho*, the credits are constantly moving (except for a brief moment to allow the viewer to read them), with Bass giving explicit instructions to "start each title card immediately after the previous one exits. No black between cards."[121] Indeed, the text's movement is driven by the steady beat of the hip-hop music.

Finally, Bass and Singleton's decision to create titles that eschew images and use only words suggests, like the rejected teaser, that the film itself is very much about language. Words are used both to hurt, by prejudiced students, and to educate and enlighten, by the likes of Laurence Fishburne, who plays an African American college professor and campus wiseman. With *Higher Learning*, then, Bass not only makes the movement of text within a grid the most important design element in his titles; he also emphasizes the logocentric nature of the college learning experience.

The Martin Scorsese film *Goodfellas* (1990) is another example of Bass's love of mathematically precise grids and purely graphic titling, here, framing Scorsese's visual and narrative sensibility. Opening his film with a deceptively simple visual concept that has Bass's signature all over it, the director pays tribute to one of his personal idols while simultaneously interpolating a raw and brutal live-action scene of a mob killing, a Scorsese trademark. Reducing his grid to a single horizontal axis, Bass again moves his typography to play the game of illegibility-legibility.

Scorsese was always a huge Bass fan. The director states the following in his foreword to the Bass and Kirkham book: "Saul Bass. Before I ever met him, before we worked together, he was a legend in my eyes."[122] Elsewhere, Scorsese relates that, as a teenager, he would storyboard Bass's titles, not even knowing who the artist was.[123] Scorsese appreciated Bass's vision and his ability to find unique solutions to the problem of film titles: "His title sequences are films in and of themselves. . . . They have the ability to capture the tone of a work in actual images. Like candy, a constant originality." Scorsese probably would have worked with Bass sooner, but he didn't know whether Bass was still in the business or even alive. According to one source, Scorsese had hired Kyle Cooper to do the titles for *Goodfellas*, but Cooper was having trouble coming up with a metaphor.

When the director expressed regret that Bass was no longer working, Cooper informed him that Bass was still around and promptly talked himself out of a job.[124] Scorsese relates his rediscovery of Bass differently: "I saw *War of the Roses* (1989) and saw that Bass was still working. On *Goodfellas*, I knew where the credits were going to go, but couldn't make them work with the typography we had. I told Barbara de Fina, we need to get Bass here and within one or two tries, he got it."[125] In another interview, Scorsese confided that when he saw *Big* (1988), he realized Bass was still alive and working.[126]

In fact, preliminary designs in the Saul Bass Collection demonstrate that he made a number of proposals that were apparently rejected. Several designs re-created the look of *Bunny Lake Is Missing*, whereby each new title was ripped away by hand and then replaced with the following title. Another design utilized block type and a thick white line under each major credit, similar to Bass's titles for *Big*. A third design was significantly more complicated and involved putting each credit onscreen twice. The first time, the credit appeared as gray block capital letters, tightly bunched up and completely filling every square inch of the screen, almost like a background image. The second, more legible version of the credit appeared in white sans serif lettering in normal-sized type with only the first letter in caps.[127] Here, Bass was riffing on an idea he had worked out in the poster for *The Cardinal*. It is unclear whether Bass shared these designs with Scorsese and they were rejected, or whether they were just preliminary sketches.

The film opens with the words "WARNER BROTHERS PRESENTS" in light gray Helvetica modern type zooming along a horizontal track just above the center frame from screen right, coming to rest at center frame, then zooming off, screen left, like a car passing in the night; in fact, a car is heard driving on the sound track.[128] All the letters are uppercase, creating a train-in-the-night effect, or a rectangular design, when the typography comes to rest. The next above-the-title credit—"AN IRWIN WINKLER PRODUCTION"—enters from screen right along the same horizontal track and exits screen left, as does "A MARTIN SCORSESE PICTURE." The following major actors' credits appear from screen left and exit screen right. While the credits are moving, the typography is blurred and illegible until it rests at center screen. Once again, Bass is playing with the legibility-illegibility dichotomy, utilizing the vertical axis as his train station. One critic compared the brief moment when the typography comes to rest with the later freeze frames that introduce flashbacks: "At various moments, Scorsese freezes Henry's life in mid-action, usually so that Henry can narrate how significant the moment was to his life at the time."[129]

Once the title for Paul Sorvino exits screen right, a white title fades in (rather than moving in), announcing that the following is a true story. The film then cuts to a live-action shot of a late 1960s American car (presumably the one heard on the sound track) pulling away into the darkness, followed by another white title on a black background indicating that the story takes place in New York, 1970. In the following live-action sequence, a group of gangsters driving in a car stops to get out and shoot a noisy, struggling body wrapped in white sheets in the car's trunk. Cutting from a shot of the blood-splattered bedsheets in the trunk, the camera comes to rest in close-up on actor Ray Liotta—playing the "hero," Henry Hill—his face bathed in a red glow emanating from the car's tail lights, before fading out to black. The credits then resume with the film's title, in capital letters and bright red type, zooming from screen left to center frame and then exiting screen right. The remaining major credits follow, moving in and out of frame (sometimes changing direction) in the same fashion, but in white type and with the names in capital letters and the designations in regular script.[130] In some cases, the designation appears on a second line above the credit, but it moves through the frame in sync with the name.

The decision by Bass and Scorsese to move the typography along a single track in and out of the frame, interrupted by an incredibly violent action scene, can be interpreted in several different ways. First, the stark simplicity and mathematical precision of the typography contrast with the messy, ugly, and banal illogic of the murder that occurs in the film's opening moments, just as the black and white of the titles contrasts with the color action scene. The sound track of the moving car and the black background mirroring the nighttime scene create continuity and a semantic connection. Second, the linearity and one-dimensionality of the typographical movement express a degree of inevitability in the narrative. Once on a train, there is no changing course after it has left the station; likewise once one has chosen the life of a gangster, there is no way out. In this context, one might interpret the movement of titles from left to right, and then from right to left, as reflecting the two first-person narratives that structure the diegesis: that of Henry and his Jewish wife, Karen.

Another critic has noted that the horizontal movement of the titles reflects Hill's inability to move up through the ranks of the Mafia because he is only half Italian and can't be "made."[131] Ironically, gangster Henry Hill eventually turns state's evidence, thus beating the odds of getting out of the "life." Indeed, the viewer later realizes that it is this first messy killing that leads Hill to rethink his life in the Mafia.

The visual connection between the blood on the sheet covering the corpse in the trunk, Hill's red-tinted face (reflecting the car's brake lights), and the red typeface of the film's title reinforces the notion that the life of a gangster is exceedingly violent and possibly fatal. Given Scorsese's Catholic background, one might also argue that the viewer is witnessing a scene from hell or a warning that committing a mortal sin (murder) will lead to hell. At the same time, the intimacy of the scene—in particular, Scorsese's close-up of Hill—not only reflects the hero's realization (revealed much later) that he is metaphorically in hell but also implicates the viewer as a witness to the murder and thereby complicit in it. Finally, the metaphoric quality of the title design as a moving train contrasts with the two static, diegetic titles that identify the narrative's time and place. Employing normal typography rather than stylized capital letters for these two titles increases their credibility, as does the fact that Scorsese captures the murder scene with what appears to be available light and a handheld camera. In the film that follows, Scorsese observes with documentary precision a group of "wise guys" over a thirty-year career. Bass's achievement was to encapsulate that experience into a single formal metaphor for the titles, as he had done so often before.

Animation: *Bonjour Tristesse, The Pride and the Passion*

As in the case of the titles for *Saint Joan,* which Bass had produced for Preminger a year earlier, his titles for *Bonjour Tristesse* (1958) expanded his repertoire of techniques beyond the grid, creating a visually stimulating background rather than animating the credits themselves. Both credit sequences are structured the same way: typography appears over a background of animated objects, with the final title reproducing the signature image-logo used in the poster and the advertising campaign.[132] In the case of *Saint Joan,* ringing church bells morph into the sword and truncated body armor of the heroine. In the popular imagination, bells have always signified the arrival of good or bad news or warnings of danger; here, they proclaim the arrival of France's tragic liberator.[133] In *Bonjour Tristesse*, flowers turn into a single teardrop on an abstracted, gender-neutral face, with hearts in its eyes and a tabula rasa mouth, signifying the melancholy of the human condition. Placement of the typography in both cases was still subject to an underlying grid, with text appearing in relation to both a horizontal and a vertical axis. Thus, in *Bonjour Tristesse*, Bass constructs a dichotomy between the formalized structure of the text and the seemingly serendipitous, playful flow of colored objects, the latter associated with the subjective musings of the teenage girl at the center of François Sagan's novel and Otto Preminger's film. Bass himself noted in an early *New York Times* interview: "I tried to evolve an image which would have the full meaning of the words 'good morning sadness' and would immediately convey the feeling of a young girl robbed of the normal joys of youth, who has lived a lifetime during her adolescence."[134] Preminger thus films the past in color and the present in black and white, since Cecile (Jean Seberg) cannot overcome the melancholy resulting from her role in the death of Anne (Deborah Kerr), the woman her father (David Niven) had hoped to marry.

Saul Bass's career as a title designer had begun only three years earlier, and he was already carving out a reputation in Hollywood. As one critic wrote of the teardrop-adorned face of a young girl that would function as the poster and the final image in Bass's titles for *Bonjour Tristesse*: "It is the special translation of a tall, crew-cut, 37-year-old industrial designer, Saul Bass, whose drawings among artistic and captivating movie titles and credits on the screen have attracted unprecedented attention in recent seasons."[135] *Variety* critic Gene Moskowitz also commented favorably on Bass's "colorful and clever" titles, while giving the film itself a decidedly mixed review for its "script deficiencies and awkward reading."[136]

Bonjour Tristesse opens with the words "OTTO PREMINGER PRESENTS" placed just below the central horizontal axis (Bass's favorite location for titles) in a wide-screen (Cinemascope) space. Placing the typography below the horizontal axis gives it weight within the compositional space of the screen. The white, sans serif, block capital letters begin just to the left of the central vertical axis; the text is right-justified, anchoring the title and leading the eye to an offscreen space. To mitigate the imbalance created between the left and right screen halves, Bass creates an upside-down arc of four cutout circles that appear sequentially in shades of dirty yellow, brown, and off-white, just above the horizontal axis but starting at the frame's right edge and continuing to the vertical axis. The resulting composition contrasts objects and text—the arc versus the straight line, color versus black and white (as in the film)— yet it also creates compositional balance. This composition does not remain stable for long, however. Rather, we see multicolored circles as well as hand-drawn crosses and stars that flash on and off irregularly above the title, in the top half of the wide-screen space. Bass described what he was doing:

> The title signals the diverse mode of gaiety and sadness in the film itself. It opens with random forms popping which are gay in color and playful in tempo. At first, one form predominates and then another. Slowly the mood changes and the color deepens and becomes more somber. As it begins to assume more forbidding tones, the forms, which were vaguely flower-like, become more specifically so, developing petal-like shapes. The petals form an overall pattern of dropping petals, which cover the screen at one point. Finally only one petal is left. The face (the symbol for the entire campaign) forms around it and we see that the petal is really a tear.[137]

This after-the-fact description does not necessarily jibe with the emotional experience of viewing. In fact, the yellow-brown colors are associated with the girl, in particular, her bathroom. And rather than expressing "gaity," they appear during moments of anger and jealousy. Furthermore, the continual appearance-disappearance of the shapes functions as a metaphor for the violently variable moods of the teenager. Yet, like the film itself, which begins in the present before transitioning to flashbacks, the overall tenor is that of melancholy.

As the opening credit fades out, it is replaced by a credit for Deborah Kerr, placed on the same horizontal axis but justified at screen right. Objects continue to be seen above it, mostly in the top right quadrant, again balancing the composition. Next, David Niven's credit appears at center screen but well below the central horizontal axis, framed screen right by seven irregularly placed circles and crosses. As the major actors' credits continue to fade in and out, singly or in groups, they always appear in relation to the central axes, with the cutout icons placed strategically around the typography and sometimes overlapping each other. With the final set of actors' credits, the button-like shapes change color to blue and purple and create a transition to the film's head title: "IN BONJOUR TRISTESSE." The title is placed in the same position as the opening credit, but screen right, with several burnt red and blue stars to the right, above the title, and one star below the title at screen left, again balancing the overall composition.

The following major credits continue this pattern, appearing as black-and-white text in various quadrants of the frame, counterbalanced and framed by blue flower shapes. These blue flowers begin to open up into four distinct petals; then individual petals start dropping down off the screen as the white typography of the technical credits appears over them, left-justified. As in the case of the major credits (other than actors), the designations appear in capital letters but in a smaller type size than the names. Once again, the use of small and large capital letters creates two-dimensional spaces of color out of typography, allowing Bass to contrast rectangular and irregular shapes within the frame. The petals turn into blue raindrops—some lighter, some darker; some seemingly closer and others farther away—as the technical credits roll. One critic has described the "narrative arc" of the sequence: "The themes of passion, metamor-phosis, sexual awakening, and melancholy that mark the progress of the film all find resonance in these titles."[138] Bass thus aligns virtually abstract, slightly anthropomorphic shapes with the conflicting emotions of Cecile. Indeed, some of the shapes resemble the roses that ornament the hero-ine's mirror, which she uses to abuse herself in a moment of self-loathing.

The final image of the face with a single teardrop perched on its cheek—the face light blue and the tear a darker blue—forms a cross with Preminger's credit as producer and director, which appears on the hori-zontal axis. The drawing, unlike the previous abstract shapes, was accom-plished with no more than a few bold strokes of oil paint or chalk, recalling Picasso in its utter simplicity, with echoes of so-called primitive art as fil-tered through the early-twentieth-century French modernists. The same image is repeated over the end credit, this time with the tear in purple-red. Bass's *Bonjour Tristesse* poster of the iconic physiognomy features an olive green background and a muted blue face with a black teardrop, colors that only increase the melancholy of the image. Thus, the colors for *Bon-jour Tristesse* mirror the psychological state of the pubescent heroine. But the titles, like the poster design, also reference high modernist art. An abstract painting in the fiancée's bedroom features two misshaped circles of color on a black background, echoing the abstract shapes in Bass's title design. Since Anne is an accomplished designer herself, the modernist art titles also presage what father and daughter will lose with her death—namely, a seriousness of purpose.

Produced and directed by Stanley Kramer, *The Pride and the Passion* was released between *Saint Joan* and *Bonjour Tristesse*, but Bass probably produced the titles around the same time as the former. As noted earlier, Bass had designed numerous advertising campaigns for Kramer beginning in the late 1940s. Unlike the titles for the Preminger films, which use animation to move objects in the background, Bass's titles for *The Pride and the Passion* create an animated effect by moving the camera over static artwork to imbue a sense of dynamic movement. Bass also inserts animated objects over and around the text as dramatic emphasis, while his typography seems less slavishly beholden to the underlying grid structure. Quite surprisingly, given Bass's antipathy for colored typography, he employs yellow text and yellow interpolated objects in an overall red scheme of background images—the two colors, of course, representing the Spanish flag. Most unusually, Bass uses the drawings of another famous artist for his background images—in this case, Francisco Goya—rather than having his own creative team draw the art. It is unclear whether this was a requirement of Kramer or Bass. As a result, the titles have an uncharacteristic busyness, given the visual density of Goya's prints.

The Pride and the Passion is a costume film, taking place during the Napoleonic occupation of Spain. It tells the story of a Spanish citizen army that is loyal to the Bourbon monarchy and captures and transports a giant cannon to attack the French stronghold of Avila in 1810. This is the backdrop for a love triangle involving Sophia Loren and Frank Sinatra, who incongruously play Spanish peasants, and Cary Grant, playing a stranded English naval officer. Shot on location in Spain in VistaVision and Technicolor with a $4 million budget, Kramer's film was heavily supported by the fascist government of Generalissimo Franco, which undoubtedly appreciated the many unmotivated scenes of Catholic pomp and circumstance, as well as the film's overt nationalist ideology. In fact, the Spaniards are vaguely stylized as nascent democrats, while the evil French are depicted as the authoritarian enemy, even though the historical reality was the exact opposite—that is, the Spaniards supported a reactionary monarchy against the liberal democratic ideals of the French Revolution.

As in the case of the Preminger films preceding and following it, Bass was initially hired to design not only the titles but also all the other elements of the campaign, including the trailer and advertising. Indeed, the template for the contract with Bass was based on a Preminger contract, according to preproduction documents. However, there was resistance to Bass's hiring within the United Artists organization, particularly from Max E. Youngstein, one of UA's owners. In a memo to Kramer, Myer P. Beck noted: "As I believe Max has advised you, he objects to Saul Bass on *The Pride and the Passion* for $10,000. Max does not feel that Saul is right for this picture."[139] Bass's fee was supposed to cover "all advertising and promotion material, plus the Fredenthal theatrical subject."[140] Ultimately, Bass designed only the premiere invitation, the titles, and the trailer.

Ironically (to the knowing viewer), Bass reproduces etchings from Goya's *The Disasters of War* as background images. This cycle of eighty-two prints, which the artist completed between 1810 and 1820 but was not published in his lifetime, expressed his own ambivalence about the French invasion. Goya was a Spanish patriot, but as a political liberal, he was enthusiastic about Napoleonic human rights reforms. Goya's work has thus been interpreted as an antiwar statement in which there are only victims and losers—no winners. But Kramer's film can hardly be called pacifist. In particular, Bass utilizes five prints: No. 5 ("And They Are Like Wild Beasts"), No. 7 ("What Courage"), No. 26 ("One Can't Look"), No. 35 ("Nobody Knows Why"), and No. 52 ("No Hagen a Tiempo"; used in the end credits). As Bass notes in his description of the titles: "The film concerns itself with the Napoleonic invasion of Spain. The title consists of a series of etchings from Goya's 'The Disasters of War,' overlaid with flat transparent colors in the sepia, red, orange, brown range. As we shift from one drawing to another, there is a corresponding color change."[141] Bass is apparently confusing the title sequence with the trailer, since the title background images are in fact tinted end-to-end in red, except for the end credit, which bleeds to orange. But Bass also uses at least one severely cropped image ("Look What a Tailor Can Do!") from another cycle of etchings, *Los Caprichos* (1799), as background for his head title. And Bass's final image in the title sequence comes from an 1820 series of etchings, *Prisoner in Chains*, showing a peasant shackled and bound, his body contorted as the chains pull him in two directions. All of Goya's images utilized in the titles emphasize subjugation and violence against the common people, setting the stage for Kramer's peasant liberation narrative.

The credit sequence opens with an all-red screen on which yellow serif type (possibly Times New Roman) fades in just above the horizontal axis, filling the left of the screen to just beyond the central vertical axis: "STANLEY KRAMER PICTURES PRESENTS." That text dissolves to "Cary Grant" on the same line, but double in size and right-justified, and to Goya's print No. 26 of peasants being executed by French troops. The camera pans right from the Spaniards to the bayonets pointing at them from the extreme right of the frame. As the camera comes to rest on a close-up of the rifles, Grant's name fades out and Frank Sinatra's name fades in on the same line, but left-justified. Interestingly, the bayonets are not reproduced from Goya's print; as a close comparison reveals, they have been redrawn, possibly to produce a more balanced composition between image and text. That title dissolves to "Sophia Loren in" on the same horizontal line, from the center to screen right. This is accompanied by the cropped image from *Los Caprichos*, whereby the etching of a woman praying dominates the center of the frame, while screen left features outlines of other praying peasants and screen right remains in darkness. The connection between the image and the text is obvious, given Loren's role as a Spanish peasant, but the cropping from a vertical to a horizontal Cinemascope frame has eliminated the top half of Goya's image, which depicts a giant scarecrow. In fact, Bass takes Goya's supremely anticlerical print—the tailor of the title represents Spain's reactionary ruling class, which keeps the people down through superstition and ignorance—and turns it into a view of religious martyrdom, which is more in keeping with the film's overall ideology.[142]

While this image stays onscreen, the text fades out, followed by the sequential appearance of at least fourteen irregular bullet holes in yellow above and below the horizontal axis, followed by the sequential appearance of the title words, with "The Pride" and "Passion" above the central axis, and the intervening "and the" below it, all accompanied by rousing Spanish-inflected orchestral music. The re-created muskets and die-cut bullet holes are also featured on the cover of the program booklet that Bass designed for the world premiere at the Screen Directors Guild Theatre on 26 June 1957; the inside pages reproduce the Goya prints in various colors.[143] (Bass had already used small die-cut circles as bullet holes over red images of war to great effect in his trade advertisements for

Attack! [1956], and he would use them again for an unpublished trade ad for John Sturges's western *The Magnificent Seven* [1960].)[144] Two of the bullet holes cover the woman's face, possibly foreshadowing the death of the female lead, but also abstractly visualizing the narrative outcome of the first Goya image of peasants being executed. This image dissolves to a close-up of a cannon, a cropped and flipped image from Goya's print No. 7, with a column of supporting actors' credits unjustified, screen right, and in much smaller type. The camera slowly pans left along the cannon's barrel, which forms the horizontal axis of the frame, coming to rest on the woman firing the cannon; once she fills the right side of the screen, various major credits fade in and out above and below the axis. The title ends with animated lightning bolts (in yellow) emanating from the cannon's vent.

The credits then dissolve to a cropped image of a woman thrusting a lance into the right side of the frame (Goya's No. 5), the weapon again forming the central horizontal axis, while the credit for composer George Antheil becomes visible. Then the camera begins a slow pan to the right as columns of technical credits, half the size of the previous credits, dissolve in and out, justified either left or right (including Bass's credit: "titles designed by"). As more technical credits appear, uncharacteristically unjustified in the bottom half of the screen, the camera zooms in on the female cannoneer's head. As the last credit fades out, the woman's head fills the screen and is then obscured by numerous yellow lances entering at very slight diagonals from screen right and apart from the central horizontal axis, where "produced and directed by Stanley Kramer" appears in white text over the right two-thirds of the frame in the same size as the previous major credits but still much smaller than the starring credits. These remain onscreen as the background image dissolves to an extreme close-up of the Goya print *Prisoner in Chains*, depicting the legs and arms of a shackled peasant. Then, as the credit fades out and the camera pans vertically up the peasant's legs, the narrative begins: "It is 1810. . . . The French legions of Napoleon smash across Spain." Bass completes the sequence by wiping the image from the top and bottom until it disappears at the horizontal axis, the red bleeding out to reveal a Technicolor image of an army on the march. At the film's end, the image bleeds to red and a final Goya print (No. 52) of a hooded peasant woman cradling a dead girl; the end credits fade in, with two justified columns listing the actors and their roles, and red dissolves to orange. A final credit for the "SPANISH

PEOPLE IN THE TENS OF THOUSANDS WHO MADE POSSIBLE THIS MOTION PICTURE" is punctuated by another strafing of bullet holes, placed as earlier.

Clearly, Bass chose his background images and cropped them to focus on women as both victims and aggressors, as well as to highlight the film's thesis that the Spanish peasant armies were composed of soldiers of both genders. But one must also note that the filmmaker eschews the most violent and surrealist images in the *Disasters of War* cycle, and Goya's antiwar sentiment is downplayed in the interest of a nationalist epic. Both the camera's movement and Bass's animated bullet holes and lances are interpolated to abstractly signify the military action at the narrative's center. Finally, although Bass employs his trademark central horizontal axis and balanced left and right screen halves to structure the typography, the use of unjustified serif type and the overall busyness of the frame—filled with text, image, and action animated through camera movement—seem uncharacteristic of Bass's other work. That is, unless one looks at the trailer.

The original trailer for *The Pride and the Passion* is credited onscreen as follows: "THE TRAILER: DRAWINGS BY DAVID FREDENTHAL DESIGN BY SAUL BASS."[145] This is apparently the only trailer Bass ever signed, although visual material from his titles was reused in numerous trailers, especially for films by Preminger. Bass also claimed responsibility for the trailer for *The Man with the Golden Arm*, which intercuts the titles with shots from the film, but it is unsigned.[146] Most strikingly, the trailer for Stanley Kramer's film employs neither material from the Bass titles nor live-action scenes from the film; instead, it presents a synopsis of the film, wholly illustrated with pencil drawings by David Fredenthal in the style of Goya. The three-minute trailer opens with a slow zoom onto a drawing of a Spanish village nestled in a wide-open countryside, while Bizet's *Carmen* overture plays and a narrator begins the story of peasants in revolt. As the film dissolves to a guitar player (the tint transitioning from yellow to red), yellow bullet holes flash across the screen to the sound of castanets, a dead giveaway that Bass is the author. The bullet holes and red tint continue to appear as the camera pans along a line of solders and the narrator intones, "The shadow of Napoleon sweeps across a once happy land." The trailer then zooms in on the disembodied, gnarled hand of a corpse (another trademark Bass image), before cutting to drawn portraits of Cary Grant and the principal actors in costume, the tints dissolving from red to blue and purple to red. In the next section, the camera pans along a column of peasants dragging the monster cannon, with yellow diagonal bars punctuating the image, much as they do in the title sequence. Yellow bars are also used in conjunction with music to signify explosions, as the French open fire. Finally, as the title appears at the end over a red-tinted drawing of the cannon's giant wheel, yellow lightning streaks from the gun—another visual punctuation seen in the titles. Utilizing standard cinematic techniques, such as crosscutting between long shots and close-ups, moving the camera, and tinting, Bass animates the two-dimensional drawings to visualize the story and characters of *The Pride and the Passion* and create a three-dimensional narrative space. The sound track, certainly not written by Bass, establishes the film as a standard Hollywood epic of oppressed people yearning for liberty. Nevertheless, this is possibly the most nonconformist trailer produced in Hollywood at the time, and it is a strong indication of Bass's growing ability not only to design two-dimensional flat spaces but also to construct narratives though editing.

Cartoons: *Around the World in 80 Days*; *It's a Mad, Mad, Mad, Mad World*

Although some of the titles discussed above required relatively simple forms of cell animation, Bass collaborated with animators on more complex projects, such as the mini-cartoon he created for Michael Todd's *Around the World in 80 Days*. Bass humorously reframes the whole three-hour epic narrative as an animated epilogue in which the principal characters appear allegorized as cartoon figures. Once his steady collaboration with Art Goodman began in the mid-1950s, Bass's films and titles would regularly feature animated sequences, but for this film he worked with Disney animator Shamus Culhane and with Bob Curtis, Barry Geller, and Ron Maidenberg (all of whom were uncredited). The extreme length of the credits (given the large number of cameos) forced the filmmakers to put them at the end of the film as an epilogue, which was highly unusual at the time and a real gamble. As Bass wrote in 1960 about the genesis of the sequence: "The epilogue represented unusual problems of integration between the story line and character designation. There was a great need for a lively and relatively brief statement to counteract the surfeit of desire to look at additional film after completing several hours of viewing."[147] Bass noted his nervousness when the film opened: "My credits came at the *end* of the movie. When the story was over, people began getting up to leave. I wanted to shout: 'Hey, wait! Back, everybody! Sit down!' Then, slowly, they did stop and sure enough, sat down again to watch. It was the crucial test for me."[148] Ironically, it would not be Bass's central character (and symbol) in the titles, a running timepiece with legs, but rather his balloon from the Paris-to-Spain sequence (an invention not found in Verne's novel) that would become the central motif for Todd's conventional advertising campaign.

Michael Todd was an extremely successful Broadway producer who never did anything that wasn't gargantuan, and so it was with *Around the World in 80 Days*, his first film production. Supposedly involving 68,894 individuals in thirteen different countries, the film consumed 680,000 feet of color film and was shot on 140 sets and 112 natural settings at a then staggering cost of $6 million.[149] Among its cast of tens of thousands were four leading roles, ninety-eight uncredited feature players, and forty-two stars in what were termed "cameos," a word that has since entered the entertainment industry lexicon.[150] Given that all the genuine stars had to be named in the title sequence, Todd decided to put it at the end of the film as an epilogue—he already had a prologue with Edward R. Murrow—and to have it animated. Unfortunately, by the time the film was in postproduction, Todd was so far in debt that his creditors demanded that the film's negative be kept in escrow. Bass's weekly payments abruptly ceased and did not resume for several months.[151] Finances may or may not have played a role in Bass's decision in July 1956, roughly four months before the film's opening, to obtain a release from his contract to design the advertising and promotional materials along with the titles; it is possible that he was simply overwhelmed by the production of the epilogue.[152]

The credit sequence reportedly cost $60,000, not including Bass's fee—an enormous sum at the time and the price of an entire low-budget feature film.[153] The gamble paid off, however, not only in terms of the film's numerous Academy Awards and $33 million in box-office receipts but also in terms of the favorable reviews Bass received for his work. As Jack Harrison wrote in the *Hollywood Reporter*: "And Saul Bass rates a special credit for his epilogue design, which carries all the film's credits in an interesting manner that will also entertain audiences through the use of color, cartoons, fireworks and caricatures."[154] Then again, there were critics who thought the film was already too long and boring and that

Bass's "amusing animated titles add[ed] an extra five or six minutes."[155] However, as Hollis Alpert noted a few years later, Bass received plenty of applause for his work: "For the first time in movie history, the audience gladly sat through titles."[156] Although negative reviews seemed to hold sway for several decades after its initial release, renewed interest in early cinema travelogues, Hale's Tours films, and nineteenth-century panoramas has led some recent Internet commentators to rehabilitate the film because its 70mm, wide-screen traveling shots mimic early cinematic forms.[157]

Shortly after the film opened, Animation Inc. filed a lawsuit against Michael Todd and Saul Bass, claiming that Bass had been "falsely credited" with authorship of the epilogue. Earl Klein, the president of Animation, maintained that the company had created 100 storyboards that had been given to and plagiarized by Todd without due credit or payment.[158] Bass countersued for libel and for $600,000, and the case was settled out of court shortly before going to trial.[159] According to reports, "Undisclosed cash settlement was made, with Animation's acknowledgement that Bass was the proper one to get screen credit."[160] In Hollywood, screen credit is often bestowed on the last talent to work on a project, not necessarily on everyone who did so. Given the cash settlement, it is likely that Bass inherited some of the visual material for the project.

The title sequence features a limited animation style with cutout static figures moving in stop-motion through space—a style popularized by United Productions of America (UPA). The cell animated figures involved in the chase move horizontally in endless repetition through broad swaths of color overlaid with cutout images. What strikes the eye are the constantly changing spatial geographies created out of walls of color, humorously demarcating various segments of the narrative. Each sequence, representing another leg of the journey, has its own color scheme but also mimics certain film genres, such as the jungle adventure, the western, or the Dickensian melodrama. There is a surrealistic quality to much of the imagery, a lot of it seemingly copied from newspaper illustrations. Some images are employed to illustrate narrative relationships, while others are strongly reminiscent of the photo art montages of Moholy-Nagy, such as *Leda* (1926). This surrealist view is particularly pronounced in the ocean sequence, where underwater objects are signified as illustrations because their size relations are not of the real world. Indeed, like the walls of color, these animations emphasize two-dimensional space, thereby calling attention to their own artifice.

The title sequence begins abstractly with a meandering red line, made by a yellow penny-farthing bicycle, moving across, up, and down the left side of the screen. When the bicycle's giant front wheel reaches the exact middle of the screen, just below the horizontal axis, a play on words in white typography fades in under the line's arch—"WHO WAS SEEN IN WHAT SCENE . . . ," followed by " . . . AND WHO DID WHAT"—as the bicycle continues its circuitous path out of the frame at screen right. The division of the wide screen into two halves and the use of the circle as a design element reappear at the film's end, where two circles depict an open pocket watch at the bottom center of the frame, dividing the Todd–AO 70mm wide screen into exactly two halves. While the left circle encloses the elaborately cursive title of Jules Verne's novel, as if it were an engraved inscription on a gold watch, the right circle reveals the timepiece's moving gears. Metaphorically, we can interpret the two joined circles as the fulfillment of the film's heterosexual union, a notion confirmed by Bass's figures representing the would-be lovers colliding, inaugurating the scene just described. The coda symbolically reaffirms the union: the exposed watch works explode, revealing a beating heart in the remaining circle.

Like the film narrative itself, the six-minute animation behind the titles is conceived of as a race in which a top-hatted timepiece with legs, representing Phileas Fogg (David Niven), and a penny-farthing bicycle, representing Fogg's manservant Passepartout (Cantinflas), are seen relentlessly moving from left to right across the screen, conforming to the journey from London to Asia to America and back to London (i.e., from west to east). Having already viewed a nearly three-hour epic, audiences immediately recognized these symbols, since Fogg is depicted as an unbelievably pedantic time-control freak, and Passepartout is introduced riding a penny-farthing, which in the nineteenth century was the exclusive domain of brash young men. The yellow bicycle passes through a bright red screen and then continues through an abstract landscape of swaths of vertical color. These become wider in the abstract gentlemen's club sequence, where a row of open-faced cards are constantly morphing into other cards. Each of the following sequences, visualizing a different geographic locale, is introduced with musical cues from that region's folk culture. Bass utilizes re-creations of nineteenth-century newspaper illustrations but adds humorous bits throughout, such as Peter Lorre's Japanese servant chasing a butterfly or the angel of Jules Verne dropping the novel on a bobby's head.

Cantinflas is the first credit to appear onscreen (left), after the bicycle rides out of the frame screen right. Niven's credit and symbol are seen only after a playing card sequence, representing the members of the gentlemen's club (Finlay Currie, Robert Morley, Ronald Squire). In the following sequences, the names of actors are only loosely associated with the animation, and their order is not necessarily tied to their importance. For example, in the balloon sequence, Martine Carol, Fernandel, Charles Boyer, and Evelyn Keyes are listed, but only Boyer is actually a balloonist; the others merely appear in the Paris locations. Likewise, José Greco, Luis Dominguin, Gilbert Roland, and Cesar Romero have cameos in the Spanish locations but not necessarily in the bullfighting sequence depicted. Alan Mowbry and Robert Newton, the latter playing the detective who pursues Fogg across the globe, are introduced with an Egyptian pyramid, and Cedric Hardwicke, Reginald Denny, Ronald Colman, and Robert Cabal are shown with Indian elephants in the next leg of the journey. However, Melville Cooper's credit also appears in the elephant sequence, even though his cameo as a ship's steward on the RMS *Mongolia* occurs before Fogg and Passepartout reach Cairo. The film's last major character, Shirley MacLaine as Indian princess Aouda, rescued from a funeral pyre, gets her own screen and is represented abstractly by a riot of floating veils in various shades of blue, with green eyes and a vermilion Tilaka mark on the implied forehead. Her symbol then joins the bicycle and the timepiece in the subsequent chase around the world, as does the mustache belonging to the detective who is on the hero's tail.

That the typography is actually integrated into the animated action, rather than over it, is another innovation. Credits appear on balloons, out of fireworks in the election day sequence, or when a saloon door is opened and closed, as in the San Francisco Barbary Coast sequence.[161] Other cameos are credited in a similar fashion as the animated narrative moves from India to Japan to the United States and then to London. Bass breaks with Hollywood convention by interspersing the behind-the-scenes credits with the stars' cameo credits, rather than grouping the former after the latter. Thus, the first set of technical credits fades in sequentially on a dark background while a wooden Siamese longboat in flaming red and yellow floats through the bottom of the frame. The next set of credits for music, screenplay, and other technical personnel is superimposed over the San Francisco political campaign rally and subsequent train journey across the American plains, while the final set of technical credits (including "Titles by Saul Bass") and those for producer, director, and novelist are inserted in the London Salvation Army and jail sequences. The jail sequence benefits from a similar bars and turnkey design created by Bass for the promotional material for Stanley Kramer's *My Six Convicts* (1952).[162] The film's head title also appears, against convention, at the very end.

Despite the relentless movement of the cartoon action from left to right, signifying the chase against time (with time depicted as a fluttering butterfly), Bass's credits conform to a grid with horizontal and vertical central axes. Interestingly, Bass uses the 70mm screen to his advantage, emphasizing the extreme width through continuous lateral movement. He eschews left and right justification (his usual practice) because that would have created a visual "wall" blocking movement. As a result, nearly all the credits are placed in reference to the horizontal axis, thereby visually complementing the eastward flow of the action. The exceptions are several credits where the designations and the names form two- and three-pronged forks, the typography mimicking the fireworks in the sky while the ballyhoo of the political campaign is depicted (and heard) at the bottom of the frame. More in keeping with the Bass brand, the final credits for Michael Todd, Michael Anderson, and Jules Verne appear as a split screen in pastel colors, with the vertical axis functioning as a door that is opened by a nineteenth-century London bobby who inserts a key into a lock, mirroring Phileas Fogg's own "gaol" release. Verne's credit is accompanied by a faded outline of an angel hovering above the central horizontal axis on the vertical axis, paying visual tribute to the novel's author. Bass remains faithful to his emerging brand by utilizing a white serif type to undergird the historical subject matter and by presenting all credited names in capital letters and all designations in lowercase type.

Bass's animated visualizations are both narrative and nonnarrative, referencing art and art illustrations, flattening space to emphasize the conscious construction of images. In keeping with the notion of self-conscious imagery, Passepartout can be translated from German or French to mean "mat," as in a border surrounding a work of art, so here, Bass frames each vignette as a cliché of the nineteenth-century European vision of the world—the Sphinx in Egypt, the elephant caravan in India—while simultaneously engaging in a play of symbols in an imaginary space.[163] Finally, Bass inserts the red heart into the pocket watch as a coda or visual exclamation at the end of the sequence, proclaiming the Hollywood "happy ending." Here, then, Bass delves into narrative more concretely than in almost all his other work, since the titles' intelligibility depends on a constant reference to the previous narrative.

Like *Around the World in 80 Days*, the credit sequence for Stanley Kramer's *It's a Mad, Mad, Mad, Mad World* (1963) had to accommodate a huge list of supporting actors and cameos attached to an extremely long film (190 minutes) presented in Cinerama.[164] In both cases, Bass chose to create an animated cartoon, but for the latter film, he shortened the titles to just over four minutes and placed them at the beginning of the film. Given that *It's a . . . Mad World* is an essentially plotless slapstick comedy about a random group of motorists searching for a buried cache of stolen money, Bass decided to go with a single joke idea rather than retell the narrative, as he had done in the earlier film. His idea was to take a drawing of a globe (the mad world of the title) and transform it into various objects. As Bass described it: "The title is a series of visual puns on a symbol of the world. The symbol becomes, in turn, a ping pong ball, a balloon, a top, a yo-yo, an egg. . . . It is bounced, kicked, inflated, tossed, hatched . . . and it is zipped open, cracked, sawed, flapped, unhinged."[165] Each visual joke is accompanied by another set of credits. As noted earlier, Bass had used the same idea in a series of billboards for the *Detroit News*.[166] In one, an arm reaches out from inside the globe; in another, a male figure looks down into a globe that has been sliced in half. Both ideas are reutilized in the film's titles.

For *It's a Mad, Mad, Mad, Mad World*, ten actors appear "above the title," beginning with Spencer Tracy; thirty-eight more appear below the title, ending with Jimmy Durante "& a few more surprises." Once source actually lists a total of seventy-one actors, including fifty-two cameos.[167] The film presented special problems because it was shot on Ultra Panavision 65mm negative, and no one had ever created an animated film in that wide-screen format. Given that the film was set to premiere at the newly opened Pacific Cinerama Dome Theatre on Sunset Boulevard in Los Angeles, the animators faced a number of challenges, including creating more than 5,000 animated cells that had to be redrawn to fit an extremely wide screen with an aspect ratio of 2.76:1 (70mm projection prints).[168] Bass worked with veteran animator Bill Melendez of Playhouse Pictures (who would later become famous for the *Peanuts* and Charlie Brown films).

The drawings were simple black ink on clear acetate, which Bass placed against various colored backgrounds—mostly red, but also orange, purple, and pink.[169] Bass gets his own credit for title design, but Melendez and his team of animators seemingly remain uncredited, unless the credit sequence is frozen at the moment the globe (which is being inflated with a bicycle pump) explodes to reveal names like so much confetti: Bill Melendez, Ed Levitt, Bernard Gruver, Bob Carlson, Carl Pederson, and Ade Woolery. Surprisingly, Bass was not credited in the film's press book,[170] so he received few mentions in reviews. An exception was Philip K. Scheuer, who wrote in the *Los Angeles Times* that "Saul Bass' opening titles are inspired, but then they are cartoons," making the point that the human characters lack depth.[171] *Daily Variety* ended its review with the following statement: "Titles by Saul Bass are clever and dizzying, aptly igniting the fuse for an explosive motion picture experience."[172] By August 1965, *It's a Mad, Mad, Mad, Mad World* had grossed more than $30 million in road shows and regular theatrical runs, yet United Artists' estimated net profit was only $610,200.[173]

The title sequence begins with the opening credit—"STANLEY KRAMER PRESENTS A UNITED ARTISTS RELEASE"—centered and center-justified in white sans serif capital letters. This title had to remain on the screen for twenty-two seconds while the oversized Cinerama curtain rose.[174] Next, a male figure wearing a black hat and carrying a huge globe with extreme difficulty enters from frame left, moves to the center of the image, then disappears underneath the weight of the orb. The figure is almost identical to the character of the canvasser measuring responses to advertising in Bass's *Apples and Oranges* (1962) or in a series of trade advertisements for *Some Like It Hot* (1960). A hand then saws a square hole from inside the globe and waves a flag with Spencer Tracy's name on it. Two disembodied hands appear from the top of the screen and nail the hole shut, setting up the basic cartoon situation: the "hands of God" are manipulating the globe, and the humans inside the globe are trying to get out. Subsequent credits for starring roles appear when the hands from on high produce a key for opening a can of Spam and proceed to open the globe similarly, while smaller hands inside the globe throw out names that appear in a column at screen left. When the inside hands start manically rearranging the names' order, the hands of God close up the globe and bounce the credits offscreen. The globe then splits in two horizontally and fireworks explode outward, revealing the film's title in yellow dots resembling Broadway lights, another recurring Bass visual trope. The hand from above manages to cap the gusher and screw the top of the globe back into place, leading to the next joke: As the globe withers in size to form an egg, a giant hen sits on it. The egg cracks open to reveal more actors' credits; then the two halves morph into a shell game to expose additional credits. The globe then changes into a tire for a unicycle, with two legs from above peddling through the frame, leaving a row of white lettering in its wake, and then back again. Just as it is about to leave the frame, the tire springs a leak and deflates. The hands from above pump it up until it completely fills the frame and explodes, showering names over the whole frame until only a handful of actors' credits remain, which are picked up by a hand from inside the globe.

For the subsequent technical credits, the globe is wound up with another key and begins spinning like a top. While a male figure holds on to the top for dear life, a crowd of figures is catapulted in all directions like the spinning disk ride at Coney Island, which Bass might have remembered from childhood. Once the globe stops spinning, a number of black bodies lift off the top of the globe and walk off screen left, revealing more technical credits, including "Titles by Saul Bass." For the music credits, a small figure appears from inside the globe and begins to sing the title song but is immediately silenced when the hand of God slaps the door shut. Those same hands then cut up the globe to create a row of paper dolls, with one doll consisting of typography. The hand next turns the globe into a yo-yo to reveal major credits. Then a small figure uses a ladder to open another door in the globe, from which a mob merges and tramples the figure underfoot as Stanley Kramer's final credit for producing and directing rolls.

Like the film itself, which starred virtually every comedian working in Hollywood at the time, Bass's title sequence is pure slapstick—a series of sight gags that have no direct connection to the film's plot but prepare the audience for the madcap car chase to follow. Similarly, the film implies that it is every man (and woman) for himself (and herself) in the race for the money, and the invisible hand of fate will intervene to help or hinder the participants in a chase to end all chases. The disembodied hands that keep entering from various sides of the frame to manipulate the globe may be read as Bass's version of the "fickle finger of fate," influencing the ever-changing amalgamations of antagonists pursuing the money. Here, then, Bass reveals his genuine sense of humor, which first made an appearance in the *Sale of Manhattan* sequence Bass created with Stan Freberg, as well as in *Some Like It Hot*, it is featured more prominently in the credit sequence for *Not with My Wife, You Don't* (1966), the civilization sequence in *Why Man Creates* (1968), and *Notes on the Popular Arts* (1977).

To delve deeper into the Bass style and brand as they pertain to his title sequences, it might be productive to return to Bass's poster and advertising work for the major Hollywood studios, in particular, his insistence on utilizing modern forms of product advertising to promote new films to the public and to the entertainment industry. In traditional film advertising as Bass had practiced it from the late 1930s through the mid-1940s, the goal was to reach as much of the film-going public as possible by filling an ad with multiple messages. Bass subsequently gravitated toward creating a single visual or graphic identity for a film that, if successful, could "sell" the film much more efficiently than the previous scatter-shot approach.

3

Creating a Mood

Pars pro toto

Bauhaus and Gestalt aesthetics influenced Saul Bass's art, nowhere more visibly than in his film posters, which often reduced a film's narrative content to a single iconic image. The designer's later reputation as a creator of pithy corporate logos provides a clue to his method: Bass had an extreme talent for capturing the essence of a film's narrative in a single abstract, highly iconographic image; this image, through its metonymic quality, would then become the central visual idea or logo for an advertising campaign. Most historians credit Bass as being the inventor of the film logo, which "is the figurative representation of a film's meaning, its title, its plot."[1] Bass was always looking for metonymies—the parts standing in metaphorically for the whole, *pars pro toto*—as prescribed by Gestalt theory. Furthermore, by the mid-1950s, Bass had designed a number of logos for corporate clients, including Lightcraft, Frank Holmes Laboratories, and KLH Research, so he was well acquainted with the trademark principle. Bass was in fact at the forefront of a new trend toward corporate identity campaigns.[2] For his film advertising campaigns, Bass designed what he called "visual slogans" that identified a film for the potential audience with a single image.[3]

Interestingly, we find Bass's most extensive theoretical statements on what constitutes a good logo design not in an interview or an essay but in his AT&T corporate identity campaign film (1969). There, Saul Bass notes that many clean, new products feature modernist designs. The goal of any logo is to "break through and help unclutter the visual environment." A trademark is central to any advertising campaign, and Bass identifies three types of trademarks: abbreviations; words; and word and image, called logo type. In the last case, an image identifies the company, while the words underneath may indicate subsidiaries. According to Bass, a logo must be contemporary, and simple forms can remain contemporary over a long time—for instance, the Mercedes-Benz star was designed eighty-five years ago. Finally, logo, typeface, and a specific and constant color scheme can combine to create multiplying signifiers, as in the case of the AT&T stripes with the bell logo—the stripes signifying competition and speed in contemporary usage.[4] How to stand out in a crowd was the question. Bass's answer was to leave space around his logos, invariably placing them in monochromatic fields of color that framed them and allowed them to breathe, away from the visual clutter of other advertising.

Such identity-based advertising campaigns in the film industry became possible once the Hollywood studio system began to break down in the early 1950s. This allowed independent producer-directors such as Otto Preminger to take control of their films' publicity, rather than turning the marketing over to anonymous studio advertising departments or, worse, local theater chain owners. One critic pinned the advent of the movie logo on "an era of cost-cutting on the part of the studios and other moviemakers," since logos could be utilized in smaller, cheaper advertisements, and stated that Bass was the "acknowledged master of the art form."[5] After experiencing major difficulties with the Motion Picture Producers and Distributors Association (MPPDA) and United Artists over the campaign for *The Moon Is Blue* (1953), Preminger decided he needed to stay involved with his film's advertising. Joseph Breen, head of the Motion Picture Production Code Office, had denied the film its seal of approval for allegedly being pornographic, and United Artists' advertising campaign treated the film as if it actually *were* pornographic, featuring a naked woman looking at the moon.[6] Livid that his gentle sex comedy would be sold as an exploitation film, Preminger claimed he hired Bass to create a more subtle approach (although there is some question about this). Bass supposedly drew two doves on a windowsill with the shade drawn, an idea he would also use in his poster for Billy Wilder's *Love in the Afternoon* (1957) and the titles for *Ocean's Eleven* (1960), but the design was not widely implemented for *The Moon Is Blue*.[7] In the advertising campaign for *Carmen Jones*, Bass created a logo that was used in the title sequence, but it was not carried through consistently in the advertising. For *The Man with the Golden Arm*, Preminger insisted that the campaign maintain a consistent look and message, creating a revolution in the industry that was not welcomed on all fronts.

For his first logo-only campaign, Bass envisioned a contorted arm for *The Man with the Golden Arm*. The publicity effort began in December 1955 with a 540-foot billboard mounted above the Fox Beverly in Los Angeles.[8] Next, the city was plastered with 164 billboards (twenty-four sheets) and 6,000 six-sheet posters.[9] The crooked arm symbol also appeared on movie theater marquees without any additional title information, including at the Victoria Theatre on Broadway, where the film premiered—a first in the industry. Since the symbol had been so widely disseminated by the time of the film's opening, the gimmick worked.[10] However, some advertisers had grave doubts because neither of the film's stars, Frank Sinatra and Kim Novak, was named or seen anywhere in the images. Indeed, when some theater owners threatened to add photographs of Sinatra, Preminger told them he would pull the film.[11] The one-sheet poster eventually included small images of the principal actors. In the end, the campaign for *The Man with the Golden Arm* was a huge success, despite intense pressure from United Artists to make it more conventional. In fact, the distributor relented only because the filming of the controversial novel had caused a firestorm in the press, and the movie was still in production just weeks before its 16 December 1955 opening.[12] On 27 December the *Hollywood Reporter* published a seven-page advertisement for the film, opening with the poster and followed by full-page photos of Frank Sinatra, Eleanor Parker, Richard Conte, and Kim Novak, while Lewis Meltzer and Elmer Bernstein got tribute pages. Strangely, there was no page for Preminger.[13]

The Bass-Preminger logo campaign was repeated for other films, including *Anatomy of a Murder* (1959). *Variety* columnist Robert Landry noted that Bass's logo for the campaign had been designed even before Preminger shot the film on location in Michigan. The logo, a highly abstracted image of what was assumed to be a corpse— "known in the trade already as 'the horizontal man'"—was "stuck all over the American scenery." The campaign premiered in Los Angeles with billboards of just the logo; these were then posted over with the stars and the logo, and finally with the logo and full billing. The logo was also printed on more than 100,000 postcards to advertise the paperback reissue of Robert Traver's novel, on which the film is based.[14] Much of the original trailer either intercuts the titles or superimposes the credits over live-action scenes from the film; it may have been produced by Bass, although he receives no credit.[15]

Indeed, the visual logos created by Bass for particular movie advertising campaigns are unforgettable. The rose in flames for *Carmen Jones* (1954) illustrates the central character's temperament and beauty. The fractured arm for *The Man with the Golden Arm* (1955) symbolizes the principal character's use of intravenous drugs. The chain-mail leggings and broken sword of a medieval knight for *Saint Joan* (1957) represent Joan's status as a French warrior arrested by the English invaders. The face and teardrops in *Bonjour Tristesse* (1957) metaphorically illustrate the emotional state of the film's teenage heroine. The swirling vortex design for *Vertigo* (1958) visualizes the central character's fear of heights. The Van Gogh–esque desert sun in *The Big Country* (1958) dwarfs a tiny posse on the horizon, emphasizing the film's vast geographic space. The disembodied corpse (post autopsy) for *Anatomy of a Murder* (1959) becomes a metonymy for the defense attorney's legal analysis at a murder trial. The arm holding up a sword in *Spartacus* (1960) and a rifle in *Exodus* (1960) represents two well-known uprisings, Roman slaves and the Haganah. The disembodied woman carrying three balloons in *One, Two, Three* (1961) symbolizes the many surprises experienced by an American Coca-Cola executive in Cold War Berlin. The logo-image of *West Side Story* visualizes an urban tenement with attached fire escape and exuberant dancers. The exposed dome of the U.S. Capitol implies that *Advise and Consent* (1962) is an inside look into the workings of Congress.[16] The stopwatch in *Nine Hours to Rama* (1963) collapses the narrative's frantic search for a would-be assassin into a race against the clock. The cash-carrying balloon in *It's a Mad, Mad, Mad, Mad World* (1963) embodies the film's madcap race to find the hidden prize money. For *The Cardinal* (1963), Bass employed only typography: the letters "Cardinal" overshadowed by "The," signifying the overwhelming power of the Vatican.[17] The extended arm of an admiral for *In Harm's Way* (1965) encapsulates the military's power to send men to their deaths in war. The cutout doll for *Bunny Lake Is Missing* (1965) represents the mother's search for her lost child. The folded legs of a reclining female nude in *Such Good Friends* (1971) refer to the many lovers of a dying man (as discovered by his wife). With *Rosebud* (1975), Bass reprises the armed extremity from *Exodus*, this time carrying a knife, a grenade, a gun, and a corkscrew—the weapons belonging to the Palestinian terrorists who kidnap five wealthy young women. For *Brothers* (1977), a film about an Angela Davis–type character who is in love with an imprisoned Black Panther, Bass imagines two holding hands, one in shackles. For Preminger's last film, *The Human Factor* (1979), Bass employs a telephone receiver with a long cord hanging down off the hook to represent a secret agent's mysterious disappearance in the first scene, setting the convoluted spy plot in motion. And finally, in the poster (drawn by Art Goodman) for *The Double McGuffin* (1979), a group carries away a bound corpse on their shoulders, referencing the disappearance of a body found by a group of boys in the woods.

These logos achieved instant recognition by simplifying their semantic content to basic geometric forms, eliminating all details to become two-dimensional silhouettes that could be printed in any monochromatic color. The logos functioned as a central design element in the posters, but they were also utilized in all other publicity materials, creating a moment of instant visual perception before the brain had a chance to decipher the verbal text. Taking his cues from Gestalt notions of reductiveness, Bass's ambition was to distill everything "down to one image that was both provocative and metaphorical, and yet somewhat ambiguous and seductive, and still true to the film."[18] No other contemporary designer made such heavy use of these logo-like images that spoke to "the language of the eye." Furthermore, while most movie publicity designers still relied on photographic images to denote the film's content, Bass's logos were much more abstract and thus more effective in creating a recognition effect in the consumer. With the campaigns for Warner Brothers' *Batman* (1989) and Steven Spielberg's *Jurassic Park* (1993), modern movie publicity caught up with this concept.

We can even find Bass logos on posters he did not take credit for. For example, at first glance, the window cards and other advertising for the American release of *Spartacus* demonstrate what Bass would *not* have done: there are far too many characters in the design, although the notion of putting a character's likeness on Roman coins may have come from Bass. But the coins themselves are too realistic, as are the photographically reproduced faces. Also, there is no balance or dynamic in the composition: the coins are ordered taxonomically, rather than in a visually arresting fashion. However, the typography of the title *Spartacus* and the figure that marks its visual end point in the lower right-hand corner are clues to Bass's input: the Roman torso in silhouette with the outstretched arm and sword mirrors the outstretched arm with a rifle in *Exodus*'s design and is inverted on *The Man with the Golden Arm*'s publicity. In fact, Universal Studios handled all the designs for *Spartacus* without Bass's participation, except for that logo.[19] Ironically, the logo does not appear in the Bass-designed credit sequence for *Spartacus*, although he had previously included logos in his title sequences for *The Man with the Golden Arm*, *Bonjour Tristesse*, and other films. It should also be noted that Bass did not design logos for many of the films he worked on as a title designer; nor did he employ such logos in his own films.

The utilization of logos implied an extremely focused advertising campaign, which contradicted standard studio and entertainment industry practice. Traditional studio ballyhooers employed a scattershot approach, attempting to reach as many potential audiences as possible with mixed messages (and images), including the names and head shots of the stars and some emblematic scenes from the film. Bass, in contrast, employed the trademark principle, hammering home a single point to the broadest possible audience, forcing them to actively engage and not just consume; as readers, they were expected to decode the abstract, seemingly ubiquitous image. This approach had its pitfalls. Such an advertising campaign could never rescue a box-office failure (such as *Saint Joan*), but, Bass observed, it might "help push a mediocre film over the line."[20] It was a gamble, however: "If it catches on, you're a hero. If it doesn't, all's lost and you take the entire blame."[21] In fact, Bass did get the blame for the failed *Vertigo* advertising campaign, which initially used the spiral logo he designed. That logo apparently didn't catch on with the public, so Paramount switched to a conventional sell, utilizing the logo only for the modified one-sheet posters. Changing an advertising campaign midstream was not uncommon, although the redesigned ads could also be hits or misses.[22] In this case, the new campaign substantially improved attendance, leading Paramount to reaffirm the right of studio executives to turn "a deaf ear" to independents with their own campaign angles.[23] Nevertheless, Bass continued to make posters with logo-like designs for Preminger and other clients.

A Short History of Movie Posters

Ervine Metzl states in *The Poster: Its History and Its Art* that a great poster exemplifies both good art and good advertising.[24] Saul Bass's movie posters fulfilled the first rule of good poster design by grabbing the attention of passersby with their bright colors and logo-like images that were both recognizable and mysterious, encouraging viewers to look more closely. Posters had been used to attract audiences since the turn of the twentieth century, when the film industry was in its infancy. Modern poster printing technology—namely, the use of stone lithography—had been invented in 1798 by Alois Senefelder in Germany, but it was not until 1866, when Jules Chéret began creating multicolor stone lithos in Paris, that posters became a popular medium for legitimate theater advertising.[25] In Europe, artists such as Henri de Toulouse-Lautrec, Alphonse Mucha, Pierre Bonnard, and Aubrey Beardsley soon dominated street scenes with their Art Nouveau posters. By the beginning of the twentieth century, posters were an established medium of public communication with its own infrastructure consisting of poster clubs, poster galleries, poster critics, and even journals such as *Das Plakat* (Berlin) and *The Poster* (New York).[26]

Before 1910, movie posters were generic, advertising a film company's total output or a particular genre rather than any one film, and individual nickelodeons often produced their own hand-painted posters. With the establishment of the Motion Picture Patents Trust in 1908 under the guise of the General Film Company, movie poster production was centralized and subject to strict internal censorship. The General Film Company hired A. B. See Lithograph Company of Cleveland to print posters and advertising materials for all its member companies, including Biograph, Edison, Essanay, Kalem, Kleine, Selig, and Vitagraph;[27] however, other companies, such as the Metro Litho Company of New York, also served the film industry. The General Film Company's Poster Department also standardized poster sizes, some of which already existed for other kinds of entertainment, especially the one-sheet (27 by 41 inches), three-sheet (41 by 81 inches), six-sheet (81 by 81 inches), and twenty-four-sheet (246 by 108 inches) formats. New formats designed specifically to dress up theater lobbies included lobby cards (11 by 14 inches), half sheets (22 by 28 inches), and insert cards (14 by 36 inches); in the 1910s, these were printed in a brown and white rotogravure process, but by the 1920s, a photo-gelatin or heliotype printing process became the norm.[28] Larger stone lithographic posters remained a rarity until the advent of feature films around 1915. For example, Universal advertised its Lois Weber production of *The Merchant of Venice* (1914) with a special six-sheet poster, illustrating a scene from the film.[29] One-sheets were sold by A. B. See to cinema owners for fifteen cents apiece.[30] Early trade articles about "paper"—as poster advertising was known in the industry—focused on the often lurid visual content of posters, which seldom did justice to the films.[31] Some people complained that the actors' faces on the posters were too generic (remedied by sending photos of the actors to the lithographer's artists) or that the scenes were too generic, leading patrons to think they had already seen the film, even if it had just been released.[32]

Once the star system established itself in America in the early 1910s, posters began to name actors more frequently. As early as 1912, film companies began to offer posters of their stars; for example, Crystal Films sold "the first ever five color poster on an individual performer," featuring Pearl White.[33] By 1916–1918, posters of individual films and their stars were commonplace, even in billboard size. One trade journal suggested that exhibitors use a generic twenty-four-sheet billboard advertising Pauline Frederick at Paramount, then papering over it with a six-sheet poster in the corner to advertise her latest release.[34] Posters featuring the star of the movie in costume remained standard throughout the 1920s, but a new offset color printing process introduced at the end of the decade by the Morgan Litho Company eventually supplanted most stone lithography film poster production.[35] The offset process allowed poster designers to reproduce photographs on posters, significantly changing their look, although artists' renditions remained popular until at least the 1970s.

In the 1930s film posters became more varied stylistically in terms of their content, with each studio developing its own house style. Posters created in studio shops were usually not the work of a single artist; rather, they were produced by several illustrators, each of whom had his own specialty (e.g., faces or women or western scenes). Artists at 20th Century–Fox, working with Tooker Litho, continued to produce stone lithographs until the 1950s, with busy mixtures of colors, stars, film scenes, and credits. Columbia produced illustrated posters under art director Jack Meyers until the 1940s; then, to cut costs, it switched to a process of using colorized black-and-white still images for posters. MGM's advertising department under Hal Burrows preferred a clean and simple look consisting of portraits of stars, plain white or one-color backgrounds, and red-black or red-blue typography; it relied heavily on freelance illustrators such as Al Hirschfeld, Clayton Knight, William Galbraith Crawford, Louis Fancher, and Alvan Cordell "Hap" Hadley. Paramount posters featured bigger faces and more color variety, but they were generally less sophisticated than MGM's, displaying the artwork of Herman Heyer, Constantin Alajalov, Peter Arno, Buford Tune, and Frederick Siebel. Under art director David Strumf, RKO emphasized subtle designs and often employed soft watercolor washes, but it also produced some colorful and brash posters, especially those created by Abe Burnbaum, Frank Bensing, Russell Paterson, and William Rose. Universal's art department was headed by Phillip Cochrane until 1937 (and by Maurice Kallis after 1942); it turned out posters with very bold colors and very little white space and employed artists such as Karl Godwin, A. M. Froelich, Frank Snapp, and Harry Fur. Warner Brothers under Charles Einfeld had the cheapest looking paper after it switched from multicolor to two-color printing at the end of the 1930s; it often reproduced a montage of photographs rather than original artwork.[36] However, common to almost all studio posters was a traditional style of realistic illustration that harked back to N. C. Wyeth; the more high art–inflected styles were limited to European film posters. Virtually all movie poster design work remained anonymous, although a few well-known designers occasionally received contracts, including Alberto Vargas for *Moon over Miami* (1941), Thomas Hart Benton for *The Grapes of Wrath* (1939), Norman Rockwell for *The Magnificent Ambersons* (1942) and *The Song of Bernadette* (1943), and Paul Rand for *No Way Out* (1950). Some well-known designers, such as Milton Glaser and Herb Lubalin, left the industry in disgust because their designs were rarely used. The problem was that the advertising campaigns, including posters, were subject to approval by a studio hierarchy that insisted on making design decisions.[37] Only after obtaining such approval was the artwork sent to the printers, which, beginning in 1940, forwarded the final product to the National Screen Service for distribution to exchanges and theaters.

National Screen Service, a producer of movie trailers for the studios, had been in business since 1920, but in 1940 it made a deal to once again centralize the distribution of all movie paper.[38] At first, some of the studios, such as Paramount, turned over all their paper production to NSS; however, they soon regained artistic control of their advertising, utilizing NSS merely to distribute posters to exhibitors.[39] National Screen Service's greatest innovation was to add a date code and release number in the lower right-hand corner of every movie poster it distributed (e.g., 65/136 for *In Harm's Way*, indicating that this was the 136th film distributed by NSS in 1965). Not until 1984 did NSS lose its monopoly, and the studios resumed control over poster distribution.

Meanwhile, styles changed little, with scenes from films and stars' names dominating movie poster content. Studios did experiment, however, with different versions of a poster for a given film, with style A being more prevalent than style B (in rare cases, there was even a style C). Bass usually designed style A, but in some cases his were designated style B; for example, for *The Big Country*, the style A poster is dominated by conventional pencil sketches of the four principal actors. In the 1960s and 1970s illustrations and typography were usually printed on white backgrounds, a style that gave way to full-color photographic images as a background for text in the post-1980 period. As in the case of titles sequences, Saul Bass bucked these trends with his poster designs, which not only eschewed realistic illustrations but also drew their inspiration from modernist art.

Saul Bass Posters

It's unclear when Bass designed his first movie poster. He won a New York Art Directors Club medal for a design for *Carmen Jones* (the artist was Al Kallis, Maurice Kallis's son) that is identical to the film's one-sheet poster, which was probably his first.[40] The *Carmen Jones* poster seems fairly traditional at first glance, with its realistically painted central figure of the African American Carmen. Indeed, photographs or artwork depicting the stars, so prevalent in the movie posters of the era, are almost completely absent from Bass's work, except when they were added after the fact, as in the case of the posters for *The Man with the Golden Arm*. However, typical for Bass is the Bauhaus box design, where the bars of the bedpost create rectangular frames, similar to his *Return to Paradise* trade ads or Panaview Company advertising. The bottom 20 percent of the frame is stark black, with white and some blue typography; in contrast, the upper 80 percent is flaming orange, with the black bars framing Carmen in hot pink on the right half of the poster's frame. Carmen and the bed promise sex, but they also boil down the visual imagery to a bare minimum to focus on the film's theme. The black bedpost allows Bass to abstractly divide his space, giving the illusion of order or a woman in her place, but simultaneously emphasizing the garish and conflicting colors that suggest murder and mayhem. The poster does not include the Bass-designed logo of the rose and the flame, although the title lobby card for *Carmen Jones* is all logo, with a tiny Kallis-painted figure of Dorothy Dandridge in the lower right-hand corner.

Saul Bass posters were without precedent in the American film indus-try. Since at least the 1930s, studio publicity departments had tried to cram as much information as possible into a poster, overcrowding the space with both too much typography (and different styles of type) and too many images. Bass reduced the message to a minimum, presenting even large amounts of text in such a way as to make it part of the abstract design of the whole. As one poster historian put it: "Extracting a basic symbol from his credit sequences, Bass interpreted the nature of film in simple graphic terms, making his posters instantly recognizable and strik-ing."[41] Another critic called his film posters "the most distinguished motion picture graphics in the United States."[42]

However, according to at least once source, Bass's style of poster fell out of fashion in the late 1960s,[43] yet he continued to produce occasional movie posters into the late 1970s. One challenge was that as actors took increasing control of their own careers in the 1960s and beyond, contracts often dictated the exact placement of the stars' images and text on all pub-licity, precluding Bass-style designs that featured only logos and mono-chromatic backgrounds.[44]

Such industry-mandated parameters, or the fact that his original proofs were changed, may have been why Bass has "disowned" an inde-terminate number of his poster designs. For example, the A-style poster for *Carmen Jones* was designed by Bass and painted by Al Kallis. Another example: the A-style poster for Stanley Kramer's *Judgment at Nuremberg* (1961) features a black background with extremely high-contrast, ink-drawn profile portraits of the principals (as if part of a jury) in a thick col-umn along the vertical axis; it is framed at the top by a tagline in yellow type and at the bottom by the names of the actors, running perpendicular to the images, with Kramer's name and the film's title in yellow at the very bottom. It is a striking poster, and the title's placement and size make it even more unconventional.[45] For unknown reasons, Bass never took credit for either poster, or perhaps he just forgot he had designed them. However, Bass's authorship of the latter seems undeniable when com-pared with a trade advertisement (possibly unpublished) for *The Shrike* drawn by Al Kallis. It employs the exact same design concept: an extreme high-contrast profile portrait in white at the center of a black background. The portrait group on the *Nuremberg* one-sheet poster reappears in vari-ous other media, including the six-sheet (but not the three-sheet) foreign poster designs (Denmark, Germany) and the sound-track album cover, where the image is utilized as if it were a logo, another indication that Bass was the designer. Furthermore, the black-and-white color scheme with a touch of yellow, possibly referring to the yellow armbands Jews were forced to wear in Nazi Germany, gives the poster a kind of gravitas, in keeping with the grim subject matter, and again points to Bass. Finally, the layout of the text, with the actors' names justified left and right to create a solid block, anchoring the visual image with the title modestly placed below, is typical of Bass, as evidenced by his subsequent poster for *In Harm's Way*. Conversely, the poster for *West Side Story* has been credited to Bass by numerous historians, and a case can be made that it conforms to the Bass style; however, either Bass disowned it or it was created without his participation as a faux Bass poster.[46] How many other Bass posters remain unidentified?

Bass actually signed numerous film festival and special event posters, which he continued to produce almost until he died, such as the Academy Award posters in the 1990s. The great majority of this work for nonprofits was pro bono and was often carried out by subordinates like Art Goodman. Nevertheless, Bass's classic posters created for Preminger, Hitchcock, and Wilder in the 1950s and 1960s have rightfully entered into the art market as prized objects, commanding significantly higher prices than other poster collectibles.[47]

Bass experimented with minimalist design concepts in his movie trade advertisements, but his posters moved beyond good design to poster art. The goal of a movie poster, according to Bass, is "to evoke a mood, an atmosphere, and a feeling that is appropriate to the character of the film. It must symbolize and summarize in the most succinct and memorable form what the film is essentially about."[48] Thus, Bass's creations had to fulfill all the criteria of modernist conceptions of good poster design: "visibility, simplicity of message, originality of forms, singularity of color scheme and intellectual clarity."[49] Bass's not quite monochromatic color choices guaranteed visibility. The logos and content-appropriate typography spoke to simplicity and originality. Finally, the unified approach was evidence of great intellectual clarity.

Employing logos as trademarks to identify individual films, Bass demonstrated an almost exclusive preference for uniformly red or red-orange backgrounds for his posters. This not only attracted viewer attention but also highlighted the usually black logo designs: *Carmen Jones*, *Edge of the City*, *The Big Country*, *Vertigo*, *West Side Story*, *Advise and Consent*, *One,*

Two, Three; Nine Hours to Rama (never used); *It's a Mad, Mad, Mad, Mad World; The Human Factor; Such Good Friends; Brothers; The Double McGuffin; The Shining;* and the unpublished *Tonkô*. Apart from the film's title, all other typography for stars and credits was placed at the bottom of the poster, usually in very small, almost invisible print so that attention was focused on the logo. The logos themselves varied from abstractions to concrete, iconographic images, but at least eight of them directly referenced high modernist art imagery.

The Big Country's style B poster features a bright yellow sun in an orange desert landscape, painted in the style of Van Gogh's moon in *Starry Night*. The sun backlights a line of tiny black riders on the implied horizon, while the almost translucent typography above (except for the black title) seems to be nothing more than a desert cloud.[50] The poster for Billy Wilder's *One, Two, Three* is cartoonish and roughly drawn by Art Goodman's hand, as if it were a twentieth-century modernist interpretation of "primitive art" (both Bass and Goodman had an affinity for pre-Columbian art). The woman's face and disembodied arm in stark black frame the balloons that dominate the center of the image. For *Such Good Friends*, the logo-image of a woman's legs as she lies horizontally seemingly references the rounded female forms of Hans Arp, Henry Moore, or Henri Matisse's *Blue Nude II* (1952); in the last work, the position of the legs and the angle of view are strikingly similar to Bass's poster. For the *Why Man Creates* poster, Bass places a Giacometti-like human figure in silhouette against an orange sun in a red landscape, an image that today has more of a science-fiction than a modern art feel, given its similarity to later alien images such as ET. The connection to modernist art is even more apparent in Bass's most famous posters.

The posters for *The Man with the Golden Arm, Saint Joan, Bonjour Tristesse*, and *Anatomy of a Murder* stand out in American film poster history. Quite apart from the uniqueness of their design (particularly their trademark semantics), these posters consciously pay homage to modernist, abstract art. Interestingly, although the development of logos has been discussed ad nauseam by both journalists and serious commentators in the Bass literature, no one has mentioned that Bass's posters for these early Preminger films utilize large areas of color abstractly, mirroring the work of Abstract Expressionists in the United States and European modernist painters. Indeed, some of these posters can be cited as examples of color field painting, since the impression of color is at least as important as the logos within them. Color field painters evolved in the 1950s and included Mark Rothko, Ad Reinhardt, Clifford Still, Adolph Gottlieb, Barnett Newman, and Robert Motherwell. These American painters privileged large areas of uniform color on their abstract canvases, downplaying the role of brushstrokes and the action of painting in favor of pure color as a subject on a flat surface.

To take the most obvious example, Saul Bass's poster for *Anatomy of a Murder* is an almost exact reimaging of Mark Rothko's painting *Orange and Yellow* (1956). Both images feature a large rectangular field of yellow-orange color over a rectangle of orange-red. The hues may not be exactly the same, but both painting and poster have slightly irregular rectangles; Rothko's borders are indistinct, while Bass's have a hand-drawn look with broken lines. The original Rothko has a slightly larger field of color as a base, covering approximately 60 percent of the frame, whereas Bass reverses the scheme: his yellow field (with the corpse logo) is a bit top-heavy, giving the composition an imbalance, in keeping with the film's theme. According to Rothko, his abstract paintings and colors "express . . . basic human emotions—tragedy, ecstasy, doom. . . . The people who weep before my pictures are having the same religious experience I had when I painted them."[51] One can imagine that Bass wanted to communicate similar emotions abstractly, especially rage and jealousy, which are important motivations in the murder trial that is the subject of the film. Utilizing large swaths of color, whether all red or other strong colors, certainly attracted visual attention, whether on a billboard or a one-sheet poster. But associating Preminger's film with the modern art of Rothko and Abstract Expressionism gave it added cachet as both a serious and an extremely contemporary work. Duke Ellington used Bass's poster in the background of his 1962 television special in *The Art of Ellington!* Host Raymond Burr compared Ellington's jazz to the modern art of Picasso, Cezanne, and Gauguin.[52] The black logo itself—the "horizontal man," as the industry trades dubbed it—was constructed of disconnected body parts lying in an orange field; this referenced not only the wooden models used by art students to learn how to draw proper proportions but also modern art methods of depicting the body, as evidenced by the above-mentioned *Blue Nude II*.

Likewise, Bass's poster design for *Saint Joan* places the film's logo at the center of an abstract painting consisting of small squares in various shades of red, yellow, blue-gray, and off-white on a red background. Like the central logo of a knight's leggings and broken sword, the squares have an unfinished look, as if they were created by a single imperfect brushstroke or were badly printed. The logo seems to represent Joan herself: a military leader broken by the enemy, like her sword, which lies at the figure's feet. In contrast, Bass's use of arrows on the ends of the *S* and *J* of the title's white typography is less readable, resembling devils' tails more than the directional signs he would later use for *West Side Story* or his Alcoa campaign. Was Bass expressing the irony of a saint being accused of consorting with the devil? The forest of squares can be read literally as a brick wall or as an abstract representation of Joan's ragtag army. Bass himself likened the squares of color in a red field to a "medieval stained-glass effect" as background for the historical film.[53] However, the overall impression of a mosaic of reds and blues on a flat red field seems to reference Ad Reinhardt's painting *Red* (1950) as well as an otherwise uncharacteristic Piet Mondrian painting, *Composition Chequerboard Dark Colours* (1919), consisting of red and blue squares. Again, the logo's placement over an abstract field of color has strong associations with modernist art, especially Abstract Expressionism, which was in vogue at the time; this would have spoken to the kind of educated audience that might be interested in a historical film about a thirteenth-century Catholic martyr. Indeed, the logo's sensibility, reminiscent of carbon rubbings off a medieval tomb, is consciously juxtaposed with the background's modernity, a paradox Preminger's movie promised but seldom delivered.

Bass's poster for *The Man with the Golden Arm* is a product of his first total identity campaign, with the crooked arm used as a trademark logo for all media, including the film titles and advertising. Yet, as in the preceding example, Bass inserts his logo into a white square at the center of an abstract field of rectangular colors of blue, black, and purple.[54] Although there are no direct precedents for Bass's colors and design, the impression created by the irregular and oddly shaped monochromatic rectangles on a white field, dividing the flat space of the poster into an abstract geometric pattern that looks painted, recalls both Mondrian's geometric paintings and Josef Albers's *Homage to a Square* series, which he started in 1950 and was obsessed with for decades. I think Bass chose blues and purples because these colors were thought to be cool, like the jazz on the film's sound track (Bass would use similar colors for an Elmer Bernstein music album), in contrast to the hot reds representing the flaming passions of *Saint Joan* and *Anatomy of a Murder*. Interestingly, Bass substituted brighter colors in some of his collateral materials featuring the same design. The abstracted arm, of course, remains at the center of the design, but in the officially released version of the poster, black-and-white photographic images of the stars are placed strategically within the rectangles, so they do not disturb the overall abstract graphic impression. Bass considered these images a perversion of his original design.

The poster design for *Bonjour Tristesse* references modern art not only in its overall color scheme but also in its logo design. As noted in the previous chapter, a face is seen at the end of the title sequence, drawn with a few simple strokes.[55] This also became the logo for the film's advertising campaign. Interestingly, Bass implemented a number of different color schemes in different media. The one-sheet poster places the blue-green lines of the face—eyes, eyebrows, nose, mouth—in a field of olive green with a black teardrop. The olive green bleeds through the rough brushstrokes of the line and the teardrop, creating a sense of both melancholy, through the dominant color, and dissonance, due to the clash of the green hues. Such color dissonance was a stylistic device used by the German Expressionists to create a clash of emotions. However, there may have been other versions of the one-sheet poster with a more pleasingly contrasting blue line against the olive green.[56] The window card utilizes a pink line drawing on a blue background—colors more readily associated with the sex scene in the photograph at the bottom of the frame.[57] A square formatted advertisement is all hot pink with a blue face, the logo hovering below two photographic images of near-naked sex between the principal characters; the black teardrop is the only remaining signification of *Tristesse*.

The line drawing of a face and a teardrop in the left eye is reminiscent of Picasso's well-known series of simple line drawings *Le Visage de la Paix* (1950), which feature the bare outlines of a woman's face and a dove of peace. The way a single line connects the nose and the eyebrow is the same in both, but inverted: Bass anchors the eyebrow that must carry the weight of the black teardrop with the bridge of the nose, thus balancing the composition. Bass's line painting remains symmetrical and is therefore more conventional than Picasso's brilliantly off-kilter view of the world. The Bass image of the face, in its very sparseness of detail (like a mask), also referenced African art through the filter of European modernism; African masks had become a huge source of inspiration for European modernist painters, whether Picasso, Modigliani, Klee, or the mature Matisse.[58] Indeed, Bass makes this connection visually in *Why Man Creates* when he cuts from the film's signature image of a Giacometti-like human figure against an orange sun to prehistoric human figures cut from sandstone or from a Picasso painting of a face to an ancient stone sculpture (he pays homage to Picasso by zooming in on his signature, preceded by signatures of Degas and Rembrandt). In this context, Bass's use of brown-toned, uppercase type for the principal actors' names, as well white type of the same size for the title, *Bonjour Tristesse*, both irregularly centered, gives the text a kind of primitive corporality under the mask. Further down, in much smaller type, Bass lays out the crew's credits in unobtrusive block text, so that the overwhelming impression of the poster is indeed the face and the teardrop.

There are, in fact, numerous examples of images and sequences in Bass's film work that reference abstract modern art, as discussed later. But Bass's most radical attempt to create abstract art may be his unpublished title sequence for Otto Preminger's *Porgy and Bess* (1959).[59] Although it is unclear at what stage the production of these titles was halted in favor of a more conventional credit sequence (not by Bass), surviving visual tests in the Saul Bass Papers reveal nothing less than a high art, wholly abstract, experimental film. Some shots were seemingly created by overlaying cutouts of color folios, and some are simply photographs of painted abstract patterns. Other abstract shapes seem to have been computer generated, constructed by optically printing individual abstract shapes, or achieved through masking and colored light. The colors are bright—intense greens, pinks, purples, and blues—which is fitting, given the film's exaggerated, cakewalk-style costumes. These abstract and utterly modernist color forms, referencing such experimental animators as Walter Ruttmann (*Opus I–IV*), Oskar Fischinger, and Len Lyle (*Colour Box*), were probably created by John Whitney, since some of the images strongly resemble his 1942 film *Variations on a Circle*. They contrast sharply with the folksy style of the film's narrative, which reflects Broadway's on-again, off-again enchantment with its own view of African American culture. Based on the surviving evidence, Bass was gambling that he could convince Preminger to move beyond the graphic but still representational designs for his *Saint Joan* and *Bonjour Tristesse* titles to completely abstract ones. What can't be established is how Bass was planning to marry the abstract animation in the tests to the concrete titles for *Porgy and Bess*. In the end, though, the carnivalesque quality of the George Gershwin opera and Preminger's decision to stage it as a costume film mitigated against any such modernist art experimentation.

That Bass was consciously quoting modernist art as a branding strategy becomes apparent in another unpublished piece: a preview poster for *Storm Center* (1956).[60] Against a burnt orange background, the bottom of the frame features "BETTE DAVIS IN STORM CENTER" in red and white sans serif type; in the upper two-thirds of the frame, a painted image of a face, in a slightly rougher brushstroke than for *Bonjour Tristesse*, appears half on the remains of a burnt piece of paper and half on the monochrome orange background, with a slice of a Thomas Jefferson quote in very small type, mimicking an art museum label, just below. The poster as a whole was just too sophisticated for any commercial distributor, given its modernist art message communicating both the danger to art when free speech is threatened and art's recuperative properties. Instead, the industry-trained publicists got what they wanted with an A-style poster featuring lots of images and even a hurricane-like swirl thrown into the mix, the kind of cluttered canvas Bass was trying to wean the industry of. The fact that Bass's *Storm Center* poster was never published as publicity, but was released only later as a piece of Saul Bass art, indicates yet again that Bass was way ahead of his time and still an industry outsider.

There is, in fact, a whole category of movie posters within the Bass canon that could be called the gallery versions. Bass published these posters independently, long after the films' actual release. They are his preferred versions, his purest idea of how the films' posters should have looked. Some were rejected by the distributor or producer as publicity; some may have been designed after the fact and self-published by Bass in various journals. Indeed, with the development of an art poster market in the early 1980s, Bass also began to reprint his posters as silk screens for sale. The Bass-designed but distributor-rejected posters for *Storm Center*, *The Magnificent Seven*, *Grand Prix*, *Nine Hours to Rama*, *Seconds*, *The Fixer*, *Tonkō*, and *Schindler's List* fall into this category.

Saul Bass's personal versions of his film posters strove for the greatest level of abstraction while still using iconic signs to communicate the spirit of the film. This process of whittling away visual details to focus on the simplest and most abstract forms is evident in his publicity work for *Nine Hours to Rama*, which also illustrates how complicated the question of authorship can be in commercial design work. Bass's first designs were published just before Paul Bacon's cover design for the original novel by Stanley Wolpert appeared in March 1962. Surprisingly, Bacon's design consists of Bass's trademark red-orange background; the novel's title in black sans serif capitals, centered on the page; and the author's name just below in white caps.[61] This is an example of Bacon's "big book look," for which he became famous. Similar to Bass's *pars pro toto* aesthetic, Bacon sought to find "something that would be a synthesis graphically of what the story was about."[62] Surrounding the typography, Bacon places a multitude of small human figures with their backs to the viewer; they seem to be running toward some unseen point in the background. Other than defining them as possible followers of Mahatma Gandhi, there are few other semantic markers to help deconstruct the image, but it is essentially a figurative and realistic illustration that uses central perspective.

In contrast, Bass's pre-release poster, published in January 1962, utilizes a monochromatic and significantly abstracted image of an Indian guru in the foreground with arms raised; behind him, masses of black human silhouettes are seen running up an endless staircase.[63] The arms and especially the outstretched hands frame the stairs and the teeming masses, while "NINE HOURS TO RAMA" appears in white caps just below the image. The question is, who influenced whom? Did Bass see the book design before its publication, or did Bacon see Bass's publicity work for the film? The idea of the masses running away from the implied observer-guru is common to both designs, but Bass's image is both more semantically concrete (a leader animates the masses) and more abstract through the monochromatic coloring. Bass would try a similar design for the poster of *The Cardinal* but would ultimately reject it.[64] The design concept reappeared, however, on the face of the timepiece that illustrates several other pieces of collateral material, including the later paperback edition of the book.[65] Bass's gallery version of the *Nine Hours to Rama* poster reduces the content even further: it is an image of Gandhi himself, shot and lying on the ground, only his forearms, hands (holding a rose), and head visible within the frame as black silhouettes in a reddish-brown background. Indeed, this logo-like image captures the essence of the film's narrative much better than the previous versions, which are difficult to read semantically. But of course, this version was too modern for the producers to consider.

Bass also began circulating "improved versions" of certain posters (e.g., *The Man with the Golden Arm*, *Exodus*, *In Harm's Way*), which to him meant removing their most obvious advertising features—photos and credits. Bass began this practice quite early, as Metzl's description in a 1963 book demonstrates. The author describes Bass posters as having "succeeded in relegating the inescapable and egocentric credits to a single line of small type at the bottom of the poster," which can only refer to some of Bass's preferred designs.[66] When the British Film Institute staged a Bass poster show in 2001, these authorized Bass reprints were exhibited rather than the original posters for the films' release, a practice that continued with a Kemistry Gallery exhibition in London in 2004.[67] It is understandable that Bass wanted to get his original visions in circulation, publishing the whole series years after the films in question were released; however, as a consumer and a poster collector, one would have hoped he would have been more forthcoming about their provenance.

Although Bass enjoyed a Hollywood comeback as a title designer in the last decade of his life, he did not return to film posters after designing the one for Stanley Kubrick's *The Shining* (1980). Like his poster for *The Cardinal*, *The Shining*'s is conceptualized around typography—in this case, Art Goodman's ghostly image in "THE." Bass did, however, produce a significant number of film festival posters and posters for various social causes, usually volunteering his own and his studio's time. These posters have a much greater stylistic variety than his film posters, incorporating photographic images for the first time. For example, his French Bicentennial poster (1989) reprises in toto his trade ads for *Storm Center*, to highlight human rights. His photomontage for the 1984 U.S. Olympiad shows an extremely foreshortened diver hurtling through space like Superman; the same concept, but with a foreshortened strip of film hurtling toward a bright yellow-orange sun, turned up two years later in the Directors Guild of America Golden Jubilee poster. Equally surrealistic is Bass's 1985 Filmex (Los Angeles) poster, where a film can hovers like a spaceship from *Close Encounters of the Third Kind* above the California palms, with a hazy orange-red sun on the horizon. The 35mm aluminum film can idea also showed up in a number of other film festival posters, such as the United States Film Festival (1988), the Sundance Film Festival's earlier incarnation, and the Israel Film Festival in the USA. There were also some purely graphic art posters, such as those for the Music Center Unified Fund (1979), the Sinfonia Varsovia World Tour (1987), the Twenty-Fifth Chicago Film Festival (1989), and the Special Olympics (1989). Many of these were handled by Art Goodman, while Bass concentrated on the corporate identity campaigns and, later, the second wave of film titles.

Although a number of early Bass posters, like the one for *Edge of the City*, have only recently been identified by poster dealers as the work of Saul Bass, his published movie posters constitute a stylistically unique, modernist art–influenced body of work without equal. Yet for Bass, such posters were only one element of a broader identity campaign that involved "paper," newspaper advertising, and title sequences. Common to all was the notion of *pars pro toto*, parts standing in for the whole. This was first demonstrated in Bass's campaign for *The Man with the Golden Arm*. The great irony is that the twisted arm and hand that would become the film's logo in the advertising campaign made an appearance only at the end of the titles, with Otto Preminger's credit. Preminger, of course, knew that the logo would emphasize, without being censurable, the still taboo subject of drug use in America. The logo thus functions *pars pro toto* for the film's advertising campaign but as only a coda for the titles, which develop a much more layered and ambiguous narrative that more closely mirrors the film's narrative complexity.

The Man with the Golden Arm

Saul Bass liked to end his title sequences with a little surprise, a graphic or visual punctuation mark to end the sequence and, usually, to emphasize the director's credit. In the case of *The Man with the Golden Arm*, this takes the form of the distorted and crooked arm that appears at the end of the sequence, where previously we have seen only straight moving lines. Likewise, the logos for both *Saint Joan* and *Bonjour Tristesse* fade in at the end of the title sequence with Preminger's directing credit. The Billy Wilder credit in a white rectangle jumps out of the two-dimensional space, attached to a spring like a jack-in-the-box, in *The Seven Year Itch*. The titles for *Around the World in 80 Days* end with an exploding pocket watch. In *Advise and Consent*, the dome of the Capitol opens up, like the lid of a pot, to reveal Preminger's credit. In the *Spartacus* title sequence, the Roman statuary visualized in the background cracks and breaks apart, like the Roman Empire itself. Yellow flames engulf the screen with the appearance of Preminger's final credit in *Exodus*, possibly a visual trope for the Holocaust. *Walk on the Wild Side* ends with a catfight between the black "hero" of the title sequence and a white interloper. Bass thus gives the audience visual and often auditory cues (apart from the director's credit) to demarcate the end of his work as title designer and the beginning of the filmmaker's creative effort.

As noted earlier, the poster for *The Man with the Golden Arm* privileges the film's logo at the center of an abstract painting in the style of Mondrian or the Abstract Expressionists. Most commentators (and Bass himself) have focused on the logo as a metaphor for the central character's heroin addiction.[68] The titles themselves have also been discussed in terms of the dominant drug theme: "Bass' titles for the film feature spiny, cut-out projectiles, vaguely redolent of veins and syringes that manage to be disconcerting despite the accompaniment of Elmer Bernstein's rather brassy jazz score."[69] Another critic has suggested that the white bars refer to the character Frankie's drumsticks,[70] and Bernstein's cool jazz score, a Hollywood popularization of bebop, certainly underscores the abstract rhythm of the moving graphics. However, one could also read the white square as a poker table surrounded by players and spectators, and the arm might represent the dealer, who is playing a crooked game. The placement of the photos in the release poster actually supports such a reading. Likewise, the title sequence—with its abstract play of straight white lines on a black background, the logo morphing out of a straight line only at the end of the sequence—can also be read in terms of gambling, rather than as a metonymy for drug addiction. Indeed, when Frankie is called "the man with the golden arm" in the film, it is a gambler referencing the card dealer's professional skills, not his drug addiction.

Preminger understood that the drug theme would scandalize the film and sell theater tickets, but both he and Bass were as interested in Frankie's career as a poker player. The game became a metaphor for success or failure in the modern world. Frankie has a golden arm because of his dealing skills and his ability to control his environment, reflected in the strict geometry of fifty-two cards. However, he is able to function only when he is high on heroin. His skill and his addiction are intertwined, as least in his own mind, despite evidence (which the viewer is privy to) that his skills expand when he is sober. The richness of meaning in Bass's titles for *The Man with the Golden Arm* thus lies in the many contradictions inherent in the character of Frankie Machine, expressed by the symbolic abstraction of animated white bars and static typography, set to Bernstein's jazz score.

The titles open with an off-center (left), not quite perpendicular, thick white line entering the screen from the top and ending just above the horizontal axis, while "OTTO PREMINGER PRESENTS" appears horizontally, just below, mostly in the upper left quadrant. Apart from pointing directly to the important information, the visual design is both stable (x-y axes) and unstable, due to the bar's slight diagonal orientation. Three more bars of varying lengths then appear in a row at the top, again slightly diagonal, but together they create a stable block around the vertical axis, while the names of the three principal actors appear on the horizontal axis below. Here, the bars might be understood as symbolic of individuals, the way one might draw four lines and then cross them with a fifth when keeping count. Next, all but one of the bars fade out, along with the credits; they are replaced sequentially with three more bars that enter clockwise from the three sides of the frame, while the film's title fades in between the four bars, creating an almost square whose right and bottom borders form the x-y axes for the upper left quadrant. This visual design, which is quite stable but has slight irritations, can be read much more productively as a visual trope for a poker table with four players rather than in terms of drugs.

All but the right horizontal bar fade out; the remaining line then extends across the whole screen to form the horizontal axis, followed by a short bar and a long bar above and below that are slightly off axis. Two irregular columns of credits in smaller-type (all caps) slide in from screen left for the secondary actors, above and below the central axis. These horizontal bars might be interpreted as shuffling cards, again emphasizing Frankie's role as a card shark. The following credits are universally stable above and below the horizontal axis, while the accompanying animated bars around them are slightly off, as if someone were peeking at their cards. Finally, one bar shifts forty-five degrees to a perpendicular position, just off the vertical axis, as columns of technical credits slide in from the left and the right to stabilize the image. Visually, Bass is continually playing with stability and instability in his composition, mirroring Frankie's states of being sober and stoned. Thus, while the environment of illegal gambling fuels the poker dealer's addiction (as would the music business, if he were to break in), Bass and Preminger downplay the film title's more lurid association with heroin addiction by performing an abstract ballet of moving bars in the title sequence that metaphorically visualizes a poker game—the game itself being a metaphor for Frankie's struggle with both his addiction and his surroundings. Indeed, the narrative is very much about the Sinatra character's inability to escape from a profession he is very good at.

Only the final four vertical bars separating the technical credits at screen left and right mutate into the jagged hand of a drug addict or a crooked card player, protruding down from the top of the frame and ending at Preminger's horizontal directing credit. Frankie's crooked card dealing is never made completely clear in the film's narrative, but it may explain why his employers insist that he deal the cards in a high-stakes game with out-of-towners. Such a reading of the title animation obviously contradicts almost everything Bass has said about his work, but it can be supported by the overall design as well as other production facts. For example, because the film lacked a seal from the Motion Picture Production Code Office, there was an incentive to devise visual strategies to finesse local censorship boards, which were likely to be sensitive to realistic depictions of sexuality and violence. Bass and Preminger felt that, given the controversy over the filming of Nelson Algren's well-known novel about drug addiction, they would be well advised to avoid any overt visual references to the topic, as well as any exploitive taglines such as "I was a drug addict!"[71] Abstraction in the titles and the ad campaign permitted knowing winks to consumers without upsetting the guardians of social morality.

Interestingly, in his own after-the-fact description of the title sequence, Bass, too, emphasized the topic of drugs: "Intent was to create a spare, gaunt, intensity that would reflect, in spirit, the character of the film, about drug addiction."[72] However, this rereading of the sequence may have occurred after the film's drug theme caused such a scandal.[73] Bass may have forgotten that his original intention was to capture the film's entire narrative about the antihero's profession as a gambler and his attempts to become a musician—a goal frustrated by his drug addiction. Instead, Bass liked to recall an argument he had with Preminger over whether the graphics in *The Man with the Golden Arm* should move. It bears quoting in full because of what it reveals about Bass's ability to focus attention on process without revealing anything about their discussions of content and design:

At one point, having created the symbol, Otto and I looked at each other and said: "Why not put it at the head of the film and make it move." And zaaap!!! I was launched on my parallel career as a filmmaker! I did a title for *The Man with the Golden Arm*.

Now—Otto liked my idea for the title. But he thought it should be a series of non-moving images. I thought it had to move. We disagreed. The exchange became volatile. Finally, I stalked out. Went back to my office. And sulked. I sat there, still steaming. Time went by. I calmed down. I began to think . . . "Gee, I blew it!! I really do want to do that title!" I thought a little. "Hmmmmm . . . non-moving images . . . it could have a certain kind of stylistic character and emotional effect . . . static images . . . sharp cuts . . . kinetic movement . . . hmmm." . . . I began to warm up to the idea. I began to like it.

The phone rang. It was Otto. "Hello, Saul—you know, you are right. It should move!"

"But wait a minute Otto, it's really more interesting if it doesn't. It could [give] us a kind of kinetic. . . ." —Bam! That started another altercation.

Finally, he said: "I insist! And you will see how wrong you are!"

And he was right. And I was right.[74]

Indeed, the titles caused a sensation in the industry and the press and possibly among audiences, although there are no hard data to back up the latter assertion. Both *Variety* and the *Hollywood Reporter* explicitly praised the credits in their reviews of the film, a unique occurrence up to that time, with the latter noting that the titles "give it the distinction of a carefully fashioned book."[75]

Bass's advertising campaign and credit sequence for *The Man with the Golden Arm* are still considered the official start of his Hollywood career, even though it was neither his first film logo campaign nor his first title work (honors for both belong to *Carmen Jones*). In fact, he had been involved in Hollywood film advertising since the late 1930s. However, the controversial nature of the film and the modernist simplicity of Bass's stark black-and-white moving graphics in the title sequence catapulted the designer into the center of the Hollywood scene. From that point on, Bass would, with more or less authority and with varying degrees of success, attempt to develop a new brand for each film project he worked on, often employing recurring images and tropes that would eventually constitute the Saul Bass brand. Ironically, despite Bass's modernist aesthetics, the designer often employed visual themes that have traditionally been associated with the elements of nature and various primitive forms of spirituality: fire, water, earth, and air. Some commentators have argued that Bass changed after he moved to California—a smart, urban Jew transformed into a cowboy hat–wearing westerner with a strong pagan bent. Indeed, the rainbow imagery discussed earlier perfectly encapsulates the epistemological contradiction between the materialist concerns of modernism and the mystical-spiritual thrust of many of Bass's recurring motifs; this contradiction is also inherent in Gestalt theory and design, as understood and practiced by Moholy-Nagy and Kepes. However, one might also theorize that, in its American corporate incarnation, modernist design itself became hybridized with nativist and romantic imagery and that this was especially true of California modernism. Indeed, a similar phenomenon is apparent with regard to early American avant-garde cinema as well as the post–Maya Deren film avant-garde: "If we theorize that many of the city films of the American avant-garde constructed a mixture of modernist formal elements and romantic desires, then the avant-garde's depiction of nature seems to be a more direct expression of American romantic sensibilities. . . . What connected the American avant-garde filmmakers to Romanticism, however, was their interest not only in depicting nature, however abstracted, but more importantly, in utilizing nature as a visual metaphor for the expression of human (mostly male) subjectivity."[76]

Fire Signs: *Carmen Jones, Storm Center, Exodus*

The advertising campaign and titles for *Carmen Jones* marked the first time Saul Bass employed an image of fire. He would return to that elemental sign repeatedly in his design work and as an image in his films, ending with his last, *Casino*. Like the pre-Socratic Greek philosophers who believed that water, air, earth, and fire were the elemental constituents of the universe, Bass was fascinated by the cultural iconographies attached to these elements. One might have thought the mystical features of such a *Weltbild* would seem alien to someone who grew up in a cosmopolitan environment. Yet in Bass's films, images of fire often appear as a life-giving force associated with the heat and light of the sun—for example, in the scientific "creation of the universe" sequences in *The Searching Eye*, *Why Man Creates*, and *The Solar Film*. Here, fire's power is far beyond the control and comprehension of human beings; it is an elemental power of nature required to fuel all life on the planet. When the sun's energy is withdrawn or is no longer available, as in *Quest*, human life collapses. Ironically, whereas the sun has always been depicted in symbolic abstractions as a circle, fire and flames cannot be visually contained by the frame. Unlike circles, squares, and lines, its form is imprecise, constantly shifting and changing; it is an image in motion even when it is static and two-dimensional. Some of Bass's interest in images of fire, then, must be attributed to his formal sense, utilizing fire's undulating form and intense color as a counterweight to the ordered and controlled presentation of his typography or simply reveling in the glory of uncontrollable image making, just as fire symbolizes unbridled passion to the point of self-destructiveness.

Employing a drawing of a flame and a feather in a perpendicular relationship, Bass's first use of a fire sign was in the logo for Phoenix Corporation, an independent production company owned by film producers Daniel Taradash and Julian Blaustein.[77] At the time, Bass was designing titles for the company's film *Storm Center*, which also features fire imagery. Placing his symbols on vertical and horizontal axes, Bass hoped to signify a dichotomy: the anarchic force of nature versus the written, communicating, and civilizing word. With a slight semantic shift, a painted flaming torch symbolizes purity and passion in the Bass-designed poster for UNESCO's Human Rights Week in 1963, the prominent red flames and typography depicting freedom.[78] Here, Bass taps into powerful collective imagery to give symbolic meaning to fire, a meaning associated with a salutary Promethean myth. However, fire's physical properties also allow it to be understood symbolically as a destructive force of nature that can extinguish life. For example, in *Phase IV*, a farming family attempts to defend themselves against invading ants by lighting a perimeter trench filled with oil and creating a wall of fire. Bass's poster for *Exodus* has flames at its center to signify both the Holocaust, in which Jewish bodies were burned en masse in furnaces, and the revolutionary struggle of the young Israeli state. And in *Carmen Jones*, Bass communicates the passion of sexual desire and its destructive power through the iconography of flames.

Bass's first noncorporate logo, specifically designed for a movie campaign, was the black rose in flames for Otto Preminger's *Carmen Jones*. Although the logo was not used on every piece of advertising for the film, it did appear on Preminger's stationery, the title lobby card, and the record album. It also appeared as a graphic element in the B-style poster but was not included in the better-known A-style poster (also designed by Bass), which utilized a striking painting by Albert Kallis of Carmen in a red dress, looking sultry between the bedposts. It is unclear why Bass chose not to include the logo, but he may have understood that Kallis's figure would have suffered, as it did when it was reduced in size with the logo appended on one version of the one-sheet poster. The logo made a solo appearance on the title card of the lobby card set and, along with the Kallis figure, on the window card; it was featured exclusively on the cover of the sound-track album and on Preminger's production stationery. The logo consisted of a hand-drawn outline of a black rose against a background of red flames; however, some posters, such as the French lobby card distributed by 20th Century–Fox, included only the outline of the rose against a white background.

The Bass-designed logo of the rose in flames communicates a rich and layered iconography dating back to the ancient Egyptians. The rose was associated with the goddess Isis, whose beauty and power were venerated. Given this religious pedigree, it is not surprising that Greco-Roman cultures also used a rose to symbolize the beauty of Aphrodite, the goddess of love—an association that plays a central role in *Carmen Jones*'s iconography. In Christian iconography, as manifested in medieval painting, the rose is a sign of Christ's suffering on the cross. Fire, in contrast, is associated with both the destructive and life-giving forces of nature, fueling love and passion and serving as a method of ritual purification.

As played by Dorothy Dandridge, Carmen Jones is an African American sexpot. She appears with a red rose between her teeth and another in her hair, both mirroring her flaming red skirt—the color associated with passion. Carmen Jones is thus marked as a creature who consumes men with abandon, living only for her own pleasure. The flames communicate sexual heat and desire but also the fact that those who give in to unbridled passion will eventually be consumed and destroyed, including Carmen and her hapless lover Joe, played by Harry Belafonte. Fire is also associated with alchemy and magic, turning Carmen into a sorceress who is able to bewitch men with her feminine wiles. Indeed, Dandridge, who was previously associated with rather cool, nonsexual roles (e.g., in *Bright Road*), not only changed her personal iconography with *Carmen Jones* but also began a passionate love affair with director Otto Preminger.[79]

Bass's titles for *Carmen Jones* play with many of these signifiers. The center of the black frame is dominated by a red flame that shoots up from the bottom and cuts the wide-screen image perpendicularly at the vertical axis. The flame is in constant motion but generally keeps its long, narrow shape while it burns in an otherwise black space. The outline drawing of a black rose is visible within the red flame; its flower is placed just below the horizontal axis, and its stem protrudes from the bottom of the frame. The image communicates both movement and stasis, the force of nature in the flames and the mark of beauty in the iconic rose. The white, all-caps, serif typography either cuts the flame horizontally around the center axis (for the major credits) or is placed in columns on the left-hand side of the screen or at both screen left and right, leaving the flame continuously visible. Given that we hear Bizet's overture to *Carmen* on the sound track as the typography fades in and out, it is natural that Bass chose a more archaic-looking serif type. The surprise of the subsequent live-action scene is that the film is staged in modern dress.

As in so many of Bass's posters, only three colors—red, black, and white—are visible in the titles. The red flame (created with red filters) seemingly burns in darkness, thus highlighting the white names in the credits. There is something uncanny about the stringent, formal composition of the visual elements and the flame that emits no light. Here, the flame is both unreal and very much a controlled burn; it is visually identical to an eternal flame, Bass having devised a symbolic rendering of the dead Carmen's cemetery monument. Such a reading of Bass's titles would reframe the ensuing narrative as a flashback and cast a sense of doom over the story of a woman who has paid for her sins—not necessarily a spoiler, given that Bizet's work is well known to opera lovers. Thus, while the color red symbolizes Carmen's passion and desire, the flame here may signify the quiet peacefulness of a grave.

Flames and fire take on a specific historical meaning in Bass's credit sequence for *Storm Center* (1956). The film concerns a small-town librarian who refuses to take a book off the shelf despite pressure by the community, even after she is unjustly branded a Communist. Indeed, the flames that engulf the screen near the end of the titles refer directly to the evening of 10 May 1933, when Nazi organizations staged book burnings in all the major German cities, consigning some of the greatest books of the nineteenth and twentieth centuries to the flames. Among the eighty-seven authors whose works were burned were Walter Benjamin, Bertolt Brecht, John Dos Passos, Theodore Dreiser, Albert Einstein, Sigmund Freud, André Gide, Ernest Hemingway, James Joyce, Franz Kafka, Karl Marx, Marcel Proust, Erich Maria Remarque, Arthur Schnitzler, H. G. Wells, and Stefan Zweig. The books of many of these same authors will burn in the town's library at the end of the film's narrative.

Stanley Kramer began this project in 1951, when the film was titled *The Library* and Mary Pickford was slated to play the lead. The title was changed to *Circle of Fire*, and production began in mid-September 1952. However, production came to a halt after the first day's shoot: Pickford refused to return to the set because the film was in black and white.[80] It is possible that Pickford pulled out because of the controversial subject matter and because the House Un-American Activities Committee was at its most powerful. Barbara Stanwyck was brought in to replace Pickford, but the film was ultimately shelved. It was picked up several years later by Daniel Taradash and Julian Blaustein's production company, which hired Bette Davis for the starring role. Another screenwriter, Eric Moll, was brought in to revise Kramer's script. Shot almost entirely in Santa Rosa, California, the film was budgeted at $750,000.[81] Since Bass had designed stationery for the company, it was not surprising that he was asked to do the titles.

The background of the white typography in the titles consists of three elements. First, there is an open book with two columns of text spilling over into the left and right sides of the frame; the white inside margins create a wide, empty swath, with a line at the "spine" on the vertical axis. The margins of the text are slightly off center, as if they really were pages in a book. The text is slightly out of focus, so the audience cannot actually read it, but the typography clearly denotes a book; it also functions within the title frame as two blocks over which the credits can be seen. The production company and Bette Davis's name above the title appear sequentially at center screen, before Bass dissolves to a double exposure of a young boy's face and the book page, followed by the film's title. Of all the facial features, the boy's eyes (the second element) are privileged within the composition of the frame. The eyes move right and left, then look directly at the camera, seemingly reading the text the audience sees. By visually overlapping the book and its reader, Bass devises a visual trope for the act of reading and the acquisition of knowledge through reading. However, that first impression is wrong: the eyes are looking far beyond the text to an invisible horizon, as if searching for danger. The eyes are the most important organ in Bass's world. Thus, one might also read the eyes as belonging to the librarian, their movement a metaphor for her vigilance over the books, freedom of speech, and personal liberty. Seeing is knowledge. And yet the gender ambiguity of the face is heightened by the fact that the image is cut off below the bridge of the nose, effectively rendering the subject mouthless and therefore speechless. Are these renderings of the dead who cannot speak, those whose writings are being silenced by bans and book burnings?

As the credits continue to fade in and out (all caps, sans serif type, justified to the frame, placed on a grid), the book begins to burn at the bottom right corner. At first, only a small flame is visible; then the page is burned away, revealing an uncharred page below. Here is the third element in Bass's design: fire. The fire coincides with a column of technical credits at screen left, followed by a second left-justified column, including "Titles by Saul Bass." As the next credits appear, the page is slowly engulfed in flames, leaving behind the charred black pages of the book and the face. One eye remains visible through the flames. The superimposition signifies that both the book and the human subject are burning. Here, then, Bass brilliantly visualizes Heinrich Heine's dictum: where they burn books they will sooner or later burn people. By the time the director's credit appears, the screen is a raging inferno, with the eye of the subject only faintly visible in the darkness, an apt if abstract metaphor for the Shoah. The explicit reference to the Shoah in the titles is supported by the fact that the more legible text in the identically designed trade ads is printed in Hebrew. *Storm Center*, then, is a cautionary, liberal-hearted tale of American democracy, the First Amendment, and intellectual freedom—not exactly popular topics at the height of the anti-Communist witch hunts. The Catholic Legion of Decency gave the film a special negative rating in 1956, something it had done only once before in the case of *Blockade* (1938), William Dieterle's thinly veiled Spanish Civil War story. It noted: "Propaganda film offers a warped, oversimplified and strongly emotional solution to the complex problem of civil liberties in America."[82] Bass, through the montage of three distinct images, abstractly visualizes the Holocaust, implying, like Heine, that the elimination of free speech can lead to genocide and mass murder.

However, Bass's advertising campaign for *Storm Center* uses the same visual elements to offer a slightly different message. In full-color trade ads, the monochromatic eyes and face of a woman form the background, while the ad's vertical axis is a line of fire in natural colors that splits the face in half and forms a cross with "BETTE DAVIS [red type] in STORM CENTER [white lettering]" on the horizontal axis. The advertisement's right side also features a column of book text and a brownish-orange tint, further visually dividing the woman's face. The photographic image of the woman, the book text (whose left side is burning), and the typography create layers of signifiers over signifiers. All the previous clusters of meaning surrounding books, knowledge, and the Holocaust are played out here; in addition, the splitting of the physiognomy, which doesn't occur in the titles, allows us to read the image as a split in the human psyche, whereby good and evil can coexist, thus articulating at least one theory of why (wo)man shows such inhumanity to (wo)man. The largely rectangular image becomes the anchor for many of the trade advertisements, which sport a large black space above the image and the statement: "In all the years no picture has said this!" In some of these ads, Davis and the title appear as a typographical border, separating the black space above from the logo-like image below. Other advertisements, which do not look like Bass designs, feature a circular vortex to designate the storm, which is reminiscent of *Vertigo* but much cruder.

If *Storm Center*'s visual trope signifying the Shoah is subtle enough to be missed by the less visually literate members of the audience, then Bass's advertising campaign for *Exodus* was even less explicit, with the equally abstract iconography of fire applicable to a variety of interpretations. By having a photographic image burn off on the *Exodus* poster and other visual collateral, Bass borrows directly from his *Storm Center* titles, charring the bottom edge of the photo (rather than a book page) as the flame consumes it. At the same time, Bass places his *Exodus* logo at the center of the poster and in the opening title, again juxtaposing, as with *Carmen Jones*, an abstract logo and a realistic image of fire.

Exodus began life as a film pitch when the production head of Metro-Goldwyn-Mayer, Dore Schary, hired Leon Uris to write a screenplay about the Jewish struggle to establish a homeland in Israel. Uris's agent, Ingo Preminger (Otto's brother), convinced Schary to fund the writer's research in Israel.[83] By the time the novel was completed, Schary had been fired; Abe Vogel, MGM's new head, was less than enthusiastic about a highly political, anti-British film. Otto Preminger, however, was excited about the project and purchased the screen rights in May 1958, four months before the novel was published; it became an international best seller and was the most popular novel in the United States since *Gone with the Wind*. Uris felt taken advantage of by the Preminger brothers because Otto paid MGM only its original investment of $75,000, rather than the six figures the screen rights would have been worth after publication of the novel. Preminger next went to Arthur Krim at United Artists to secure a $4 million budget for the film.[84] Then he hired blacklisted writer Dalton Trumbo to write the screenplay, giving Trumbo his first official screen credit in more than a decade and helping to break the blacklist.[85] By the first day of production on 29 March 1960, Bass had designed and UA had published advertisements in the trades, featuring the *Exodus* logo, announcing advance ticket sales for the Warner Theater in New York, a Chicago theater, and the Fox Wilshire in Los Angeles on 21 December 1960, the day of the premiere.[86] Bass had also hired John Whitney to do film tests for the *Exodus* titles, which, ironically, were built not around the theme of fire but of water—specifically, footage of the surf.[87] Bass and Preminger may have been thinking about illegal immigrants to Palestine landing on the beach, which is in fact the way the film begins.

Bass's *Exodus* logo plays off his *Spartacus* logo, designed only months earlier for that film's September 1960 release. The *Spartacus* logo, which was used only sparingly on posters and other publicity, features the silhouette of a Roman gladiator's torso and raised arm brandishing a sword. *Exodus*'s logo highlights arms outstretched toward the sky, with one arm holding a rifle perpendicular. Both logos communicate armed struggle and revolution, but the rifle signifies that *Exodus* is not a biblical epic, as the title might imply, but a contemporary story. Visualizing multiple arms rather than a single arm denotes that this struggle is that of a whole people rather than a charismatic individual, as in *Spartacus*. The logo is anchored to the title directly below, appearing in all capitals and a sans serif, military stencil font,[88] which communicates the martial nature of this exodus. In the 1980s Bass started printing and selling an authorized version of the *Exodus* poster with the black logo on an Israeli blue background, but for the film's official release poster, he added the element of fire.

Printed on a white background, the central image consists of the abstract logo in black and the military stenciled title in white, printed on top of what appears to be a sky blue photograph that is burning behind the title but also partially obscuring the logo. The flames consuming the photo are seen only in that image, so if we assume the photograph is depicting some level of reality, the photo both captures the flames and is simultaneously destroyed by them. Unlike the credit sequence, though, where the flame is more like a torch, the fire on the poster art covers the whole bottom of the image. The poster thus functions at various semantic levels and juxtaposes unlike signifiers, such as an iconic image of real fire and the symbolic logo. The yellow flames can therefore be understood as both the flames of revolt for the Jewish nation in Palestine and the raging fire of the Holocaust, out of which arose the Jewish survivors' struggle to find a homeland.

Bass's titles start with a monochromatic royal blue background over which the words "OTTO PREMINGER PRESENTS" appear in white caps and centered. A moment later, a yellow flame licks up from the bottom of the frame, exactly at the center axis; this fire seemingly starts below the visible image. As the first title fades out, it is replaced by the black *Exodus* logo at the vertical axis and just above the horizontal axis; this is followed by the white, apparently hand-drawn title in caps, just below the horizontal axis and the logo, mirroring Bass's preferred poster design, but with the yellow flame flickering over both. Here again, Bass limits his color palette to black and white and two complementary colors, blue and yellow, allowing the typography and the moving image of the flame to stand out. Next, both logo and title disappear, and the names of the principal actors fade in and out on the horizontal axis, alternating between screen left and screen right. As the grid-based credits continue, the yellow flame moves to the right or left across the bottom of the frame, making room for columns of credits on either side. Only after the credit for producer and director Otto Preminger appears on the screen does the flame spread out over the entire bottom of the frame; it then engulfs the whole screen and partially obscures the last credit, which finally fades out, leaving the screen an inferno. Thus, for much of the two-and-a-half-minute title sequence, the image of fire resembles an eternal flame, as seen at war memorials and other commemorative sites, and indeed, this film is a memorial to those who fought and died in the first Israeli war. The closing image, however, cannot help but conjure up the Holocaust, the last remnants of typography symbolizing 6 million dead, just as the lone eye does in *Storm Center*.[89]

Bass would include an inferno in the opening credits one last time for Martin Scorsese's *Casino*, which would also prove to be Bass's last screen credit. In that film, a firebomb opens the proceedings, but for the most part, the titles are about the phantasmagoric lights of Las Vegas rather than corpses rotting in shallow desert graves.

Water Signs: *In Harm's Way, Cape Fear*

Saul Bass's poster for *In Harm's Way* features the outstretched arm of a U.S. Navy admiral pointing off into the distance, implying that the officer is responsible for sending many men to their deaths on the battlefields of Iwo Jima, Guadalcanal, and Okinawa. For visual emphasis, the arm is white, cutting through the otherwise black background at the horizontal axis, while blue typography lists the principal actors. Since the black rectangle covers only the top two-thirds of the one-sheet poster, a second logo—now with a black arm and the film's title slanting upward, as if attached to the arm—is centered in the white space below. This is the only time Bass used a logo twice on the same poster. Adding the title to the logo literalizes the message of the military power structure sending soldiers in harm's way, but that may have been necessary to guarantee the legibility of the "trademark," as *Variety* called it, if it were to function as publicity before audiences were familiar with the film's narrative. In fact, the *In Harm's Way* logo and "one world" ad campaign concept were designed and approved before the film even began shooting.[90] This was a strategy Bass and Preminger used repeatedly, at least as far back as *Anatomy of a Murder.* Interestingly, the smaller Bass logo-title seemingly anchors the black rectangle above, as Bass again applies the Bauhaus lessons of balance and counterbalance, as well as visual repetition.

Given that the design phase was completed before film production began, it's not surprising that there is little connection between the iconic message of the logo and Bass's titles. The poster's logo and typography were both handled by Art Goodman, with Bass functioning as art director.[91] The logo does, however, appear with the film's title—seemingly drawn in white chalk onto a live-action image of the film's opening location—but the remaining titles come at the end of the film. Unlike the logo, which is a concrete and symbolic representation of a generally understood nonverbal gesture, the closing title sequence uses water in its various forms as a metaphor for the film's temporal arc from peace to war and back to peace; concrete images of war appear only at the end of the sequence, with shots of an atom bomb exploding over Hiroshima and

Nagasaki. Bass himself described the titles as follows: "This opening consists of a symbolic live-action montage, which parallels roughly the historical span of the film. Starting just before the Japanese attack on Pearl Harbor, it chronicles the United States entry and participation in the war against Japan, and ends with the explosion of the Hiroshima Bomb."[92] The titles' typography and design conform completely to the Bass style: white sans serif type, capital letters placed on a grid, with left and right justification. Of more interest are the visuals.

Like American avant-garde filmmakers Ralph Steiner (*H_2O*, 1928), Henwar Rodakiewicz (*Portrait of a Young Man*, 1931), and Slavko Vorkapich (*Moods of the Sea*, 1942), Saul Bass traffics in highly romantic metaphors of nature. The credits open with images of a glistening surf on a quiet beach; the surf and the waves increase in size and strength as the credits proceed and reach an initial crescendo as the water forms a monster funnel, sucking everything into its vortex. The montage highlights water in motion, abstractly, as pure movement; water flows horizontally to the right, then the view is from under the waves, an abstract symphony of water movement. The credits fade in and out as if in concert with the light and dark of a turbulent sea, increasing their legibility. Then the storm breaks loose and the viewer is on an invisible ship, riding out a tremendous storm that culminates in huge explosions on the water for the major behind-the-scenes credits. This is followed by an oil fire, shot from above, just as Otto Preminger's usual credit as producer and director appears. If we accept Bass's historical chronology of the title sequence, the explosions and atom bomb come at war's end. The previous images of the storm are purely metaphorical signifiers of war, without any concrete historical references. Such images of nature have the potential effect of naturalizing images of war. However, the ensuing shots of billowing clouds of burning oil directly reference well-known newsreel footage of U.S. Navy ships burning out of control in Pearl Harbor, although we never see any ships in Bass's footage.

Unfortunately, the cut to the atom bomb might make sense as a historical marker, but it appears to be a sudden and undue visual and conceptual escalation from the previous images of explosions. Bass may not have intended it, but it is possible to read the montage of images referencing Pearl Harbor and the atom bomb as punishment of the Japanese people for the crime of aggression. The shots of bombs exploding can also be read as unnatural acts in what is otherwise the natural order of things.

Whether the God-like point of view in the shots of burning oil was meant to be an inside joke on Preminger remains a matter of speculation, but once the credit fades out, Bass cuts in the footage of an atom bomb explosion, followed by a full-moon shot and a return to the glistening and now calm ocean surf. Bass thus constructs a circular narrative by opening and closing on identical images of a calm and peaceful sea. However, the intercutting of an image of a full moon between the bomb and the beach is more perplexing. The moon and water are soul mates in some mythologies, but in any case, the image of a full moon feminizes the progression of signifiers. Then again, the shot may function only as visual punctuation, signifying a moment of rest before nature again takes its course.

Thus, while the titles depict the phrase "the gathering storm," taken from Sir Winston Churchill's multivolume history of World War II, it is unclear whether audiences made the connection as envisioned by Bass. They may have understood the title sequence as replicating the subjective experience of sailors at sea during World War II. Conversely, the use of water and storm imagery implies that war is a natural, possibly unavoidable phenomenon. No matter how the images are interpreted metaphorically, the montage of seawater harks backward and forward to the film avant-garde.

Ironically, Bass employs water to communicate a completely different, ominous sense of dread in *Cape Fear*. Rather than crashing waves, as in *In Harm's Way*, he uses water's reflective qualities on a calm surface. The changing surface creates abstract patterns of movement in muted browns, greens, and golds, which resemble an Abstract Expressionist painting in motion but also reproduce images in Ralph Steiner's H_2O. The slightly agitated movement of the water renders the surface opaque, making it possible for Bass to superimpose black-and-white images that seem to undulate under the water's surface; though they are never completely hidden, they are not distinctly visible either, adding to the sense of dread, especially in conjunction with Bernard Herrmann's ominous music as orchestrated by Elmer Bernstein.

Cape Fear was the first Saul Bass title sequence in decades to receive specific comment in contemporary film reviews. Leonard Maltin noted on his television program *Entertainment Tonight*: "When I started watching *Cape Fear* and the titles came on, I was mesmerized. Watching those titles reminded me of how much a creative title sequence can do to set the tone of the film." The *Hollywood Reporter*'s film critic chimed in: "A shimmeringly eerie title sequence, pulses and punctuates with steady, coursing energy. Depths of praise to title-ists Elaine and Saul Bass for the surging undercurrents." Finally, *New York Magazine* commented on Bass's uncanny ability to set the stage for the violent action to follow, without ever showing any violence: "From its opening shots of scary faces wavering beneath placid water, under the sensational fractionalized title sequence by Elaine and Saul Bass, *Cape Fear* palpitates with dread."[93] Such notices documented that Bass had indeed made a Hollywood comeback.

The film opens on a dark screen with the sound of rain falling and low rumbling thunder, followed by a fade-in to a mostly green body of water, the wind creating horizontal patterns on its surface while the names of the production companies appear in white caps at screen left, punctuated by the blast of horns and strings on the sound track. Other names that appear above the title include Martin Scorsese (screen left) and the principal actors' names, which are placed in succession from left to right on a horizontal axis (a Bass trademark), while the coloration of the water's surface creates a zigzag vertical axis. Before the actors' names appear, however, the image of an eagle is superimposed on the water; it flies closer and closer, its claws threatening, as if it were hovering over the water. The shot is identical to an image Bass used in the original final sequence from *Phase IV*; before that, he used a variation in *Why Man Creates*. The image dissolves to a closer shot of the water, with blues, oranges, and dirty greens shifting to and fro as the film's title appears centered on the screen. As he did with *Psycho* thirty years earlier, Bass slices the typography in two horizontally, shifting one layer ever so slightly to create a stronger sense of discontinuity. Once the title fades out, a close-up black-and-white moving image of a distorted eye appears, as if it is under the water's surface.

The titles for *Cape Fear* thus consist of four distinct elements: (1) the sans serif typography with the visual hiccup; (2) the play of abstract color and light on the water's surface, moving from horizontal to vertical patterns (the switch coming with Saul and Elaine Bass's credit) and then back to horizontal patterns as indistinct shadows darken and then lighten the water's surface; (3) barely visible monochromatic moving images, their shapes distorted as if the light beneath the waves has been broken—an eye, a mouth with teeth, a head, a body; and (4) Elmer Bernstein's score, which uses strings and woodwinds to increase the sense of dread inherent in the visuals.

The double exposures of shimmering color images of water and high-contrast black-and-white images are subject to multiple interpretations. One reading might theorize them as akin to subliminal images, their legibility so limited behind the shimmering water that audiences might miss their actual content altogether, yet they communicate an uncanny sense of danger that comes from under the water. The distorted eye and head recall Bass's *Seconds* as well as *Vertigo*'s titles; all three films feature apparently weak central characters who aren't strong subjects for audience identification. Bass was quite vocal about his intentions with regard to the titles: "Our concept for the film was based on the notion of submerged emotions—the back potentials of the psyche. The spine of the concept was water. The entire title consists of water, and the water changes: it becomes more and more abstract, until what you see are flickering reflections. . . . Then we began to introduce other images that added levels of unease and uncertainty. Using simple optical devices, we put the images under water and distorted them. Eventually the water becomes the emotional whiplash of form and color with disturbing emotional undercurrents."[94]

Using water's physical qualities to reflect, refract, and absorb light, Bass creates a canvas in motion that can be mistaken for a piece of Abstract Expressionist art. It is an inspired idea, given that Abstract Expressionism is all about expressing emotion, and given Bass's interest in visualizing emotional and psychological states. At a purely formal level, the play with light on the water's surface pays homage to the film avant-garde, especially Steiner's H_2O and a number of Steiner films from the 1960s. Water images are both an index of a real geographic place, the houseboat home of the family at the narrative's center, and a metaphor for emotional and psychic states of mind that reside below the surface of consciousness. One film critic misremembered the camera rising up out of the swamp, which doesn't actually happen until much later in the film. However, the characterization of the water as a swamp is relevant because swamps signify danger. Swamps may look calm on the surface, but underneath lurk all kinds of dangerous wildlife. But it is also relevant because swamps are metaphors for moral corruption, which defines both the protagonist and the antagonist. Water's transparency and simultaneous opacity make it a perfect metaphor for the human mind. This point is confirmed by the last titles, when the water's dirty greens give way to blood-red tints filling the screen, as Martin Scorsese's directorial credit appears and a negative image of Juliette Lewis's eyes fades in as she begins her first-person narrative. It is a horrific moment, the red screen referencing blood (as it did in *Goodfellas*) and also foreshadowing the film's climactic finale, the image of the eye indicating that there are witnesses to the horror.

Ironically, unlike Bass's fire imagery, his water imagery lacks any of the usual life-affirming and life-renewing connotations of water. Instead, his water imagery functions on a metaphorical level as a dangerous and unknowable space, whether it serves as a naturalized signification of war or as a visual metaphor for the conscious and unconscious mind. In *Cape Fear*, Bass may also be depicting the phrase "return of the repressed," since it is Max Cade's return, after he has been forgotten by the protagonist, that functions as the narrative's central event. The utilization of water imagery allows Bass to create formalist film montages that are indistinguishable from avant-garde films. Meanwhile, Bass also demonstrates a fascination with ordinary objects, which he wants us to see in a new light, tearing them out of their everyday, almost invisible context. Throughout his career, Bass repeatedly returned to this exercise of turning the commonplace into the extraordinary.

Objets Trouvés: *Advise and Consent, Nine Hours to Rama, The War of the Roses, The Age of Innocence*

Saul Bass was a master of creating visual symbols or logos for the advertising campaigns he devised for Otto Preminger, among others. Part of that talent involved finding an object or sign that could represent the film as a whole. The same *pars pro toto* aesthetic inherent in creating logocentric advertising campaigns and posters was also at work in conceptualizing title sequences that placed everyday objects at the center of their design. Referencing *Nine Hours to Rama*, Bass notes in his own film, *Bass on Titles*, that "one of the most challenging aspects of any creative endeavor is dealing with ordinary things, dealing with things we know so well, we cease to see them." Bass liked to take everyday objects and make them strange, forcing us to look at them anew with a different set of eyes. These found objects are imbued with symbolic and metaphorical weight in various title sequences: an American flag in *Advise and Consent*; a globe–beach ball in *It's a Mad, Mad, Mad, Mad World*; a timepiece in *Nine*

Hours to Rama; a white handkerchief in *The War of the Roses*; roses and lace in *The Age of Innocence*. Beyond his manipulation of the commonplace to extract symbolic meaning, Bass implements methodologies from avant-garde cinema to reimagine such objects in a formalist play of light, color, and movement.

Advise and Consent begins with Bass's logo for the advertising campaign in light gray against a black background: a visual rendition of the U.S. Capitol's dome opening up, like a teapot with an attached lid, to reveal the film's title underneath.[95] For this black-and-white film, Bass uses all capital, white, sans serif lettering to create a block of type that fits within the confines of the open dome, indicating to the viewer that the film will expose the inner workings of Congress—in this case, the Senate. The logo-title then dissolves to the image of a billowing American flag, its stripes filling the screen horizontally. The American flag, of course, is associated with a whole array of symbolic meanings, the most obvious being a signifier for American democracy. Indeed, the film's narrative revolves around a corrupt southern senator who leads a personal vendetta against the president's nominee for the post of secretary of state, invoking anti-Communist rhetoric to cover up his own impure motives. A moment later, the shot dissolves to a similar image of the American flag, now filling the screen above the horizontal axis and leaving room below for the names of the fourteen principal actors, which appear centered and sequentially through dissolves. Interestingly, the names are designed in white cursive typography, almost as if they were signatures, possibly to contrast the government, as represented by the flag, and the individuals who make up that body. The subsequent credits for supporting actors are in sans serif type in columns at screen right, as are all the later technical credits, which switch from screen left to right to top; the major behind-the-scenes credits for music, production design, and cinematography are again in cursive type at center screen. Meanwhile, the stripes of the flag dissolve to screen left, then right, then bottom, always leaving room on the opposite side for the white credits. The penultimate credit dissolves to a black image with the *Advise and Consent* logo at center frame, which opens to reveal Otto Preminger's credit as producer and director (another little Bass visual joke).

Given that the film is in black and white, the question arises why Bass chose to show only the stripes of the flag and not the blue field and stars. One explanation may have to do with the fact that the flag's stripes represent the original thirteen colonies, the blue field represents the president, and the stars the present states in the Union. Bass and Preminger may have wanted to indicate that the film tells a story about the representatives of the states, rather than the national government. The colors in the flag did not carry any symbolic meaning when the flag was first created in 1777. Only with the adoption of the "Great Seal" in 1782 did the colors red, white, and blue become imbued with specific symbolic meaning: "White signifies purity and innocence, Red, hardiness & valor, and Blue, the color of the Chief signifies vigilance, perseverance & justice."[96] In light of these symbolic associations, Bass's use of only "red" and white stripes may be seen as an ironic comment on the Senate, since the subsequent narrative illustrates a total lack of purity, innocence, hardiness, or valor among its elected members.

Alternatively, the image of the American flag billowing in an invisible wind from one credit to the next, the view of the flag changing to make room for new credits but also indicating the passage of time, may in fact signify that the institution of American democracy will persevere through internal and external crises. Similarly, the flag survived the Battle of Baltimore during the War of 1812, still waving over Fort McHenry the morning after and inspiring Francis Scott Key to write "The Star-Spangled Banner." In fact, the image of the flag waving in the wind cannot help but conjure up associations with the national anthem, patriotism, and the longevity of American democracy. Indeed, Preminger's film ends with the senator's retirement after the final vote of confirmation, the implication being that the business of the government and democracy will continue the next day.

Not the American flag but a timepiece is at the center of the credits for Mark Robson's *Nine Hours to Rama*, which visualizes nine hours in the life of the assassin of Mahatma Gandhi. Bass in fact discusses the *Nine Hours to Rama* titles in *Bass on Titles*, expressing the desire that audiences see ordinary, everyday objects in a new light. The film's complex plot revolves around preparations for Gandhi's murder, on the one hand, and a race against time as a police inspector tries to prevent the assassination attempt, on the other hand. Bass's titles focus on the outer and inner workings of a pocket watch, which is actually seen in the film, allowing him to create suspense by zeroing in on the element of time. From the very start, Bass's titles are a moving-image documentation of a finely tuned instrument made by human hands, structured as a visual symphony. Referencing similar visual works in the style of *Neue Sachlichkeit*, the titles can also be read as a formal study of color, movement, and time. In fact, it is camera vision—presenting a view made possible only by camera optics—that allows the audience to see the everyday anew. Photography, which highlights the beauty of modern technology, had its precedents in the work of German New Realists in the 1920s and American photographers such as Paul Strand. But Bass ratchets up the emotions by throwing Expressionist lighting and strong emotional colors into the mix, creating a sense of anticipation as the clock ticks.

As early as October 1961, Robson hired Bass to design a logo for the film's ad campaign and the cover of the paperback version of Stanley Wolpert's novel (published in 1963), as well as the titles. By January 1962, Bass had designed a preproduction poster, which he signed but does not correspond to the Bass gallery version. Meanwhile, filming in India had been completed, and studio production was about to commence at the MGM studios at Elstree, England.[97] Designer Dave Nagata handled most of the work on the *Nine Hours to Rama* titles. The film premiered a year later, on 21 February 1963, in London. Again, reviewers went out of their way to mention and praise Bass's titles, including James Powers at the *Hollywood Reporter*, Harrison Carroll at the *Los Angeles Herald Examiner*, Philip K. Scheuer of the *Los Angeles Times*, and the reviewer for *Variety*. Most effusively, Raymond Levy wrote in *Motion Picture Herald*: "Saul Bass has effected one of his most unique jobs of establishing a mood in his backgrounds to the credit cards—a motif of the time element mounting in intensity and excitement before the story opens."[98] Many reviewers hated the film, even if they liked the titles, including this acidic British critic: "What strengthens Mr. Bass' claims on our attention is, of course, the rueful fact that his little inventions so frequently pulse on in the memory when the works they set out to preface have quite, quite faded. And certainly nothing so becomes dreadful NINE HOURS as its inception, a Bass magnification of the clicking, lunging innards of a clock. After this vibrant stuff, suspense curls up and dies."[99]

Interestingly, the titles open with a Gandhi quote and the standard historical disclaimer (which is usually found near the back of the titles) in white block type, while two purple-red letters in Sanskrit fill the center of the black screen. That text is replaced by a block of red text in Hindi, which then dissolves to one line of large Hindi text filling the bottom half of the screen below the horizontal axis. The above-the-title credits appear in white sans serif caps.

The film's title is centered just above the horizontal axis on a black background, while the top half of a red-tinted stopwatch creates a 180-degree arch directly below the title. The camera then begins a slow zoom into the exact center of the watch's face, until the screen is completely red; white credits for the supporting actors fade in and out in a column at screen left. Bass lights the watch from the right side, so that the hands and the center peg throw deep shadows onto the watch's face, multiplying the moving parts in the image. The camera then cuts to a microscopic close-up of the tip of the minute hand moving slowly toward twelve o'clock and, finally, to an even closer shot as the credits for the principal behind-the-camera talent appear on the horizontal axis. The next twelve shots present microscopic views of the pocket watch's mechanical movement—its springs and gears. The one-minute sequence is photographed in high key lighting, so the yellow-brown parts appear and disappear out of the surrounding darkness, while the major and technical credits continue. The final five shots of the title sequence return to the face of the watch. The last image is of a small round dial within the larger watch face, with the director's credit dissolving in a perfectly matched cut to the wheel of a steam engine as the narrative commences.

If the watch measures and signifies time, it does so through the movement of its constituent parts. Indeed, time can be visualized in film only through movement—that is, action. Technically, the microphotography of the sequence would be simple in the digital era, but given that these images are analog, they are nothing short of extraordinary. Utilizing a design concept similar to Moholy-Nagy's *A Lightplay: Black, White, Grey* (1930), in which the moving parts of a machine reflect abstract light patterns, Bass's central montage of the watch's movement can be mistaken for an abstract avant-garde film. In particular, the play of shadows, as the tiny second hand steadily makes its 360-degree journey and the camera moves ever closer to the watch's face, recalls abstract avant-garde films from the 1920s. And like many New Realist photographers in the 1920s, Bass celebrates the beauty of technology, the precision of the watch works, just as Ralph Steiner did in *Mechanical Principles* (1930) or Paul Strand did in his Akeley camera series. In keeping with the Bass style, the designer also limits his color palette to reds, dark yellows, and blacks, accentuating the dark, foreboding quality of the visuals. Time stops for no one, so the movement also communicates a sense of the inevitability of fate and the assassin's bullet.

Unlike the body of the film, which utilizes music composed by Englishman Malcolm Arnold, Bass chooses authentic Indian music. The element of time is thus first measured by sound, not images; the beat of the tabla and sitar marks time as the first title appears. The heavily rhythmic Indian music only intensifies the acute sense of the passage of time expressed in the images. Simultaneously, the use of Indian music not only foreshadows the film's narrative but also adds another exotic element to the visuals, since such music would have been alien to most Western audiences in 1963 (i.e., before the counterculture and before the Beatles discovered Ravi Shankar).

Bass's ability to manipulate an ordinary object and make it strange reached new heights with his titles for Danny DeVito's *The War of the Roses* (1989). Here, a seemingly white landscape is revealed to be nothing more than a handkerchief. The concept for the titles was Saul's, although both he and Elaine are credited.[100] The titles open on a gray screen with wisps of light moving in undefined patterns over the screen as we see the above-the-title credits, including those of the three principal actors: Michael Douglas, Kathleen Turner, and Danny DeVito. That background continues as a single red rose and a long green stem underline the title shot. As the supporting actor credits fade in and out, the highlights become more defined, forming a landscape that seems to have ridges and valleys, while the camera continuously tracks to the right. As the major behind-the-camera credits appear, the focus becomes even sharper on the background; the light and shadow landscape now appears to have a definite texture, forming half-circle patterns. For once, Bass employs black typography rather than white, but true to his style, all the letters are sans serif capitals; the narrow font is atypical of Bass's earlier title work and may reflect Elaine's influence. The typography with the credits centered on the horizontal axis is extremely elegant, as is the discreet gray-white background. However, contrary to the Bass style, which usually avoids diagonal lines, the light forms diagonals that roll gently around the typography. The sequence ends with a typical visual joke when the camera pulls back to reveal that the white and gray background is actually a handkerchief, into which the film's narrator, played by Danny DeVito, blows his nose. This led the critic for the *Nation* to write of the film: "The high point of *The War of the Roses* is the title sequence, directed by Elaine and Saul Bass. The camera peers and pokes through the folds of a snow-white fabric, at last revealing it to be a handkerchief. Then comes the first scene, in which the director of the rest of the film, Danny DeVito, puts the handkerchief to use, in effect smearing snot all over the audience—which is pretty much what he does for the following two hours as well."[101]

Given that the film is a vicious satire of Hollywood romantic comedies—a couple meet, fall in love, fall out of love, and then wage a relentless war against each other—such a reading is not without merit. Another critic saw the titles as visual echoes of an all-white wedding: "Visually, we could be looking at a variety of things: the train to a wedding dress, clean linen sheets signifying the unpolluted slate of a new life together, or the black titles as place cards over a tablecloth."[102] Such readings emphasize the irony of the difference between romantic notions of marriage in Hollywood films and the reality of most American marriages, which end in divorce at least as often as in "happily ever after." Both critics, however, miss the important element of the moving camera, which seemingly dollies from left to right on its own horizontal axis, as if traveling through a white landscape of snow or sand. In fact, some of the background images could be mistaken for the sand dunes of a desert landscape.

The title sequence was in fact shot by having the camera track along an extremely long, unbroken bolt of white cloth that had been tastefully crumpled to give it the texture of a landscape. Conceptually, the design can be compared to Bass's earlier titles for *Alcoa Premiere*, in that camera movement rather than editing allows a vacillating perception between the concrete and the abstract. Here, the titles become a visual metaphor for the Roses' cold and barren marriage, the diagonals indicating a kind of movement without movement; their marriage is indeed on the rocks, despite the red rose underlining the film's title, which is usually associated with romantic love. Whatever the interpretation, Bass's title sequence for *The War of the Roses* and its closing joke depend on initially misperceiving an ordinary object: a white handkerchief.

Elegant (but without a distasteful joke at the end) also describes Bass's titles for Martin Scorsese's *The Age of Innocence* (1993). Based on Edith Wharton's 1920 Pulitzer Prize–winning novel of fin de siècle upper-class New York society, *The Age of Innocence* depicts an unhappy love affair between two people who cannot marry because of the rigid social conventions of the American Gilded Age. According to Bass, Scorsese gave him and Elaine virtually complete freedom: "We would show him a few scribbles and a few storyboard frames and, based on that, we went ahead and produced it."[103]

The credit sequence features a visual symphony of roses blooming behind a veil of Victorian lace, as the overture to Charles Gounod's mid-nineteenth-century opera *Faust* is heard on the sound track (thus aurally introducing the opening scene at the Metropolitan Opera). As the music slowly builds to a crescendo, the roses open ever more furiously, ending with the image of a dandelion seed head at the moment Scorsese's directorial credit appears onscreen. It is a perfect metaphor for the eruption of sexual passion and its end; simultaneously, it reverberates with the director's Catholicism, connecting the emotional suffering of the protagonists with the Passion. The dominant colors used in the sequences—from deep violet to coral pink, red, and purple and finally vivid yellows—signify intense emotionality. This is underscored by the highly romantic music, which, in its operatic orchestration, also conveys a sense of melancholy and unhappiness, especially since the final image in the sequence is seemingly a metaphor for death and decay.

The title sequence begins with a black screen as the first credits for the production companies appear in a white serif typeface centered on the horizontal axis. The first above-the-title actor credit for Daniel Day Lewis is framed above and below by lines of beautifully handwritten calligraphy, more or less illegible in violet against the black background but possibly meant to be a reproduction of Wharton's original manuscript (though her hand was not quite as elegant) or perhaps a love letter. Following Michelle Pfeiffer's credit, the underlying manuscript turns a dark pink before Winona Ryder's credit fades in and out, indicating that the first two stars will constitute the narrative's central romance. Then a coral rose in almost the same hue as the text fades in and slowly begins to open as the text turns black and the film's title appears in white, surrounded by a white ornamental design of interlocking loops. As that rose gives way to a second rose and then another in red and yellow, the moving images seem to be photographed through lace, while the supporting actors' credits appear in white, screen left, left-justified and then screen right, right-justified. The major behind-the-scenes credits follow, again on the horizontal axis and centered, accompanied by ever-larger dissolving images of roses and lace. Finally, the screen becomes completely red, with small roses visible at the bottom of the screen, as the credits for producer, novelist, and scriptwriters appear. As the screen turns dark yellow, with a dandelion seed head and dark calligraphy replacing the lace, Scorsese's credit as director fades exactly perpendicular to the margins of the handwritten text, forming a cross.

Bass himself called the title design highly metaphoric: "The title was deliberately ambiguous and metaphorical. The kinds of notions we had in mind involved an attempt to project the romantic aura of the period and still signal its submerged sensuality and hidden codes. . . . The continuous series of long dissolves from flower to flower creates a sensuous overlay to the notion of Victorian innocence."[104] And indeed, one can interpret the lace as superficially associated with Victorian society, just as the music identifies the film's time and place. *The Age of Innocence* opens at a Metropolitan Opera performance of *Faust*, where Gounod's work had its American premiere in October 1883, creating an aural continuity with Bass's title sequence. It is also possible to interpret the operatic track heard offscreen, which visualizes Faust's unnatural pact with the devil to achieve social success, as an allegory for the hero's contract with society to gain status and wealth, despite his libidinal urges and his love for a woman he can't have.

Given the film's narrative of conflict between sexual desire and strict moral codes, it might be more productive to see the images of roses as unbridled nature and the intricate lace patterns as a metaphor for the strictures of a rigid class society. Indeed, it is impossible not to interpret the blooming roses sexually, given the centuries-long tradition of such iconography going back to the Kama Sutra, in which the female organ is represented through flowers. The ever-quickening pace of the opening petals thus replicates the rhythms of sexual orgasm. Ironically, Scorsese's film is much more about the repression of erotic desire than about sexual joy.

Bass was fascinated by the time-lapse cinematography that allowed him to make the invisible visible, as in the case of a rose opening its petals. That technology had been discovered shortly after the birth of cinema, but it was the 1920s avant-garde filmmakers and theorists such as Moholy-Nagy and Hans Richter who championed time-lapse as a specifically cinematic vision. Bass had used similar shots of flowers blooming in a Rainier beer commercial in 1966 and, more prominently, in *The Searching Eye* (1964). In both cases, flowers represent nature's beauty and fertility. An eerily otherworldly blue rose opens its petals in Bass's original ending for

Phase IV, expressing the notion that nature has survived but in a different form since the arrival of the ants. A rose closing its petals marks the transition to "Phase III," when human life has changed forever. Interestingly, Bass's shot of the dandelion seed head in *The Age of Innocence* is recycled from *Why Man Creates*, where it has a completely different semantic meaning. Whereas the dandelion in Bass's earlier film designates a fertility of ideas, in *The Age of Innocence* it visualizes the death of the flower and the drying up of desire. Calligraphy replaces lace in this last image, thus framing the credit sequence and pointing to the literary origins of the text, but also to the film and its emotional conflicts as narrative.

States of Mind: *The Big Knife, The Shrike, Vertigo, Bunny Lake Is Missing, Seconds*

Utilizing images of objets trouvés symbolically, Saul Bass invokes a *pars pro toto* strategy to capture a film's essence in a found object. When dealing with films that are about the psychology of their characters, though, such a strategy becomes more problematic. How can one reduce complex emotional or psychological states of mind to a single object? Bass therefore experimented with a variety of conceptual and intellectual solutions to individual design problems, moving from a kind of documentary realism to symbolic representations to pure abstraction. Nevertheless, he continued to focus on letting parts stand in for the whole when depicting psychological states of mind. For *The Big Knife* (1955), Bass presents the anguished face of an actor in extreme close-up to convey his emotional conflict. *The Shrike* (1955) employs blatantly Freudian symbolism for a story about emotional subjugation. With the credits for *Vertigo* (1958), Bass references abstract, experimental film imagery to communicate the central character's fear of heights. Bass's titles for *Bunny Lake Is Missing* (1965) invoke playtime in the nursery but also reveal a darker, violent streak. In *Seconds* (1966) the distorted camera lens mirrors the central character's physical and psychological journey. In each case, concrete images reference psychological states of mind that cannot be directly depicted but only implied through imagery.

Although *The Big Knife* was only Bass's fifth title sequence, it already bore the characteristics that would become associated with the Bass brand. Radio commentator Shirley Thomas said, "I'd like to give special thanks to Saul Bass for the opening titles of the film. . . . They are wonderfully imaginative and immediately establish the mood of the drama."[105] Bass had been hired by Robert Aldrich, who was producing the film independently and with whom Bass had previously worked on the publicity campaigns for *Vera Cruz* (1954) and *Kiss Me Deadly* (1955). The film was based on Clifford Odets's play about a mentally fragile actor who is bullied into submission by a Hollywood studio boss. The play starred John Garfield, was directed by Lee Strasberg, and ran on Broadway at the National Theatre from February to May 1949. Although Aldrich's film adaptation bombed, the *film maudit* has become a cult classic, owing in large measure to its anti-Hollywood stance. According to Aldrich, the character of the studio executive, played by Rod Steiger, was a mixture of Louis B. Mayer, Jack Warner, and Harry Cohn, none of whom ever forgave Aldrich for his indiscretion and all of whom blacklisted him at their respective studios.[106]

The titles for *The Big Knife* are deceptively simple. After the producers are named in white lettering on a black background, a high-angle image of Jack Palance's head and naked shoulders comes into view at the bottom of the frame. The film's title then appears centered, just above the horizontal axis, slicing the very top of the actor's head, which indistinctly melds into the black background. After Palance's starring credit appears on the same line, the music increases in volume to a sharp, annoying whine, while the actor moves his hands up to his forehead in a gesture of anguish and frustration. As more acting and technical credits appear on the right half of the screen, right-justified, Palance continues to look down; only his forehead, eyebrows, and nose remain visible, but the features of his face are distorted. After the credit for Clifford Odets, several white horizontal and vertical lines divide the screen into seven uneven rectangles; the white lines grow thicker until white fills the screen and the final credit for Robert Aldrich as producer and director appears in black lettering.

The image of the naked actor in the title sequence, holding his head in his hands, clearly indicates that the film is about a tormented and possibly depressed human being. The audience knows this because the codes of photographic realism indicate that the camera can capture human emotions on a face. Indeed, the cinematic close-up was perfected by Hollywood cameramen to allow the audience to experience and identify with a character's emotions, as expressed by the physiognomy. Furthermore, the actor's raised arms and hands form a human gesture that is also intelligible as a sign of suffering, while the bare shoulders seemingly increase the character's vulnerability, since he is naked to the world.

Bass had designed a series of trade advertisements extolling Jack Palance's acting talents and featuring a pretty head shot in 1953.[107] Bass had also employed a similar composition and design concept in his trade advertisements for Stanley Kramer's *Death of a Salesman* (1951). There, Fredric March is shown from a high angle, bringing his hand up to his eyebrows. The emotion in both is the same: existential angst brought about by the inability to influence or control their physical existence and psychological well-being. The *Salesman* advertisement also includes an image fractured into five uneven pieces, as does a trade ad for *The Racers*; both images indicate a breakup, as does the final image of the *Spartacus* titles.

But here, Bass also seems to be playing with various attitudes about human psychology—in particular, the ability to discover hidden emotions as expressed in the face. For this purpose, cinematography was much more useful than photography. The late nineteen century had in fact seen a flood of scientific treatises on the study of physiognomy, providing exact descriptions and visual evidence that allowed one to "accurately" trace human character traits, including criminal behavior.[108] Specific facial features, according to such studies, could be read as racial characteristics (a favorite of anti-Semites) or could be used to predict genetic deficiencies or behavioral patterns, including alcoholism and criminality. Ironically, if the eyes are a "window to the soul," then Bass's titles for *The Big Knife* reveal nothing, because the angle of vision hides Palance's eyes underneath his black eyebrows, leaving the audience to ascribe whatever emotions they wish to the actor's mysterious facial expression. But if the audience has any doubts that the character's anguish will lead to a crack-up, Bass obliterates them by graphically visualizing his mental breakdown with broken white lines that split the image into distinct pieces. Indeed, just as the image of Palance disappears before Aldrich's directorial credit, the character he plays disappears off the stage of life when he commits suicide at the end of the film.

The Shrike was the third title Bass designed, and the film was so low-tech that is was considered an indie or avant-garde production. Like the titles for *Carmen Jones* and *The Seven Year Itch*, those for *The Shrike* were totally different from anything else being done at the time. Cost-conscious Universal produced the film, which was directed by high art–minded José Ferrer, who had previous ties to the Pulitzer Prize–winning play by Joseph A. Kramm. When the play premiered on Broadway at the Cort Theatre in 1952, Ferrer served as producer, director, and star,[109] while Kramm's wife, Isabel Bonner, played the female lead.[110] The play broke box-office records, earning a return on its investment in a mere nine weeks.[111] Ferrer was also attached to film rights, which were bartered between RKO and Louis B. Mayer before being acquired by Universal's Aaron Rosenberg. Judith Anderson and Ida Lupino were considered for the female lead, but June Allyson eventually won the role.

The play takes place in a mental hospital, where a supposedly brilliant theatrical director has been institutionalized. As the play's narrative reveals, he has been driven there by his shrewish wife. When others are present, she pretends to be sweet and pliable, but her change in demeanor is an indication of her extreme manipulation of her husband's fragile emotions. Jim Downs has attempted suicide with barbiturates, and he might also be addicted to them, which is why he is locked up. The play alternates between scenes in the mental hospital and flashbacks of Jim when he was healthy and "sane." In the original play, the wife leaves her husband to rot in the mental ward while she enjoys his wealth, but Universal apparently decided that June Allyson's screen persona was incompatible with such heartlessness, so in the film, the wife brings her husband home to care for him. Considered highly misogynist in more contemporary readings,[112] *The Shrike* supports the 1950s American stereotype that behind every successful man is a woman—and that woman could be a castrating super-housewife, once Freud's theories had made their way into the American bedroom. According to A. H. Weiler in the *New York Times*, although *The Shrike* as a film "warped into a somewhat clinical study of a man terrified and almost mortally wounded by his unconsciously designing spouse, it emerges as an uncommonly absorbing and provocative drama."[113]

A pair of long metal scissors placed horizontally on a black background in high-key light appears in the first shot. A disembodied female hand (judging from the fingernails) enters from screen left and grabs the scissors. A side view of hand and scissors fills the length of the screen on the central horizontal axis, slicing the surrounding darkness of the frame in half. The female hand turns the scissors forty-five degrees in order to cut a white paper band, resembling a grocery store cash register receipt, entering from the top of the screen like a phallus with José Ferrer's name typed horizontally on it. Another strip with "THE SHRIKE" in Times New Roman is held at the top of the screen by a different female hand, as the hand manipulating the scissors slips out of frame left while cutting off the extremity. The scissors glisten in the high-key light, menacing the viewer in a lesson learned from Alfred Hitchcock's playbook. At the same time, the horizontal scissors, the vertical paper strip at the far right side of the frame, and the darkness in between them form a Mondrian-like geometric pattern of light and dark lines and rectangles. This composition remains steady while each new paper strip with additional credits enters the frame from the top, at least until the scissors complete their work, dismembering the vertical white column as the paper falls out of the frame.

Bass's title sequence is all about castration. The scissors are a classic icon in the Freudian psychoanalytic paradigm, making their earliest cinematic appearance in G. W. Pabst's *The Secret of the Soul* (1924). There, they function as fetishes of the fear of castration, as they do in Salvatore Dali's dream sequence in Alfred Hitchcock's *Spellbound* (1944). In Catholic countries during Mardi Gras, women are allowed to cut off men's ties with a pair of scissors, a folk tradition that again plays out the castration scenario. The snipping of each credit by female hands mirrors each soul-defeating comment Anne Downs hurls at her husband's damaged psyche, but it is also understood as a manifestation of his fear of castration. Bass thus employs classic Freudian iconography, which he assumes to be common cultural currency in 1950s America. The joke lasts for 1:45 minutes, with the directorial credit being slashed in a more violent flurry of cuts, just as the theater director will be destroyed by his own wife.

But one wonders whether the title sequence is also a metaphor for the studio's censorship of the original play, as evidenced by the altered ending. The title image resembles in striking detail other culturally circulated images of a pair of scissors cutting celluloid filmstrips as a metaphor for the censorship process. For example, the cover of Murray Schumach's study of film censorship, *The Face on the Cutting Room Floor*, features a pair of scissors cutting through a strip of 35mm film.[114] Bass later admitted that he didn't like the sequence, possible because its Freudian metaphor was a bit too obvious.[115]

Vertigo is considered Alfred Hitchcock's masterpiece and the greatest film of all time, according to the British Film Institute's 2012 poll of film critics (*Psycho* is tied at number 34, and *North by Northwest* is number 53).[116]

These BFI polls, taken every ten years since 1952, are indicative of contemporary aesthetic value. *Vertigo* unseated Orson Welles's *Citizen Kane*, which had been number 1 since the original poll. Yet *Vertigo* was not even in the top ten until 1982; it moved up to fourth place in 1992 and second in 2002, largely due to the general critical reevaluation of Hitchcock since his death in 1980. Although Bass made some brilliant titles for some mediocre films, in the case of *Vertigo*, his titles are a symbolic microcosm of Hitchcock's multitextured film as a whole. Color design, imagery, and the computer-generated spiral design translate Hitchcock's obsessions into both avant-garde abstraction (i.e., *cinema pur*) and iconic imagery of vision—both elements of the Bass brand, even though the typography for the above-title credits and the title deviates from this usual style.

At the same time, Bass was designing equally abstract titles for Otto Preminger's *Porgy and Bess*. Those titles were never used and probably never moved beyond the testing stage; however, the surviving footage, sans actual graphic titles, is a riot of abstract color footage. Not surprisingly, Preminger chose a different route, and John Whitney, who probably worked with Bass on the project, got involved in *Vertigo*, creating the electronic spirals for the title sequence.[117] Whitney would also help Bass on the opening titles for the Bob Hope and Dinah Shore television shows.[118]

Vertigo was a much better fit for Bass's own avant-garde ambitions.[119] Indeed, the Lissajous mathematical light form at the center of the credit sequence, doubling as *Vertigo*'s logo, is at the core of the film's visual design. Bass relates how he got the idea to use the spiral design: "I wanted to achieve that very particular state of unsettledness associated with vertigo and also a mood of mystery. I sought to do this by juxtaposing images of eyes with moving images of intense beauty. I used Lissajous figures, devised by a French mathematician in the nineteenth century to express mathematical formulae, which I had fallen in love with several years earlier. You could say I was obsessed with them for a while—so I knew a little of what Hitch was driving at. I wanted to express the mood of this film about love and obsession."[120]

As Donald Spoto notes, the spirals, as abstract visualizations of vertigo, found their objective correlative in "the winding Staircase of the bell tower at the Mission, Carlotta Valdes' single lock of spiraling dark hair . . . the spiraling journey of the two cars on San Francisco's hilly streets . . . the camera spiraling around Judy as she composes a letter to Scottie."[121] The idea to connect spiral shapes to a fear of falling may have come from O.

Firle's photograph "Elevator Shaft" (1928), reprinted in Moholy-Nagy's *The New Vision*.[122] Spoto's observation gains credence in light of Bass's *Vertigo* poster, in which a male figure is depicted falling into the vortex of the spiral. Bass's own after-the-fact description also reads the title rather one-dimensionally: "Vertigo is a sense of dizziness (the tendency towards dizziness), usually associated with heights. The manifestation of this affliction in the life of the main character is a pivotal element in the story of this film. The introductory credits attempt to recreate this feeling in symbolic, abstract terms."[123] In the first important reevaluation of Hitchcock's work, Robin Wood not only identifies *Vertigo* as the director's most perfect masterpiece but also points to the importance of Saul Bass's titles, particularly the close-up of the face and eyes. This introduces an important theme in the film, namely, "the inscrutability of appearances: the impossibility of knowing what goes on behind the mask."[124] Furthermore, Wood discusses Hitchcock's attraction-repulsion complex toward beautiful women, who are unknowable because of the masks they hide behind, just as Bass focuses on the face as a mask. But there is also a confluence of much richer imagery at work here, giving the title sequence its own mysterious, intellectual depth.

The titles begin with a color close-up shot of Kim Novak's mouth, left cheek, and nose. The unconventional framing of the photograph, revealing only half a face, could be a direct reference to the cover photo of Franz Roh and Jan Tschichold's 1929 book *Foto-Auge, Photo-Eye, Oeil et Photo*.[125] Bass then pans and zooms the camera, holding his frame on the woman's mouth, eyes, and left eye, respectively, for the above-the-title credits for Jimmy Stewart, Kim Novak, and Alfred Hitchcock. The reframing of each shot, as the camera momentarily comes to rest before zooming further into the female physiognomy, is consciously artificial and arty, an almost analytic dissection of female anatomy that suddenly goes blood red in the last tinted shot, while the film's title fades in and moves from background to foreground (Bass would later repeat the red tint on a shot of Juliette Lewis's eyes in *Cape Fear*). Once the title fades out, the camera zooms in farther; the Lissajous form becomes visible deep in the woman's pupil and then grows to fill the screen, repeating the same movement as the typography for *Vertigo*. To the audience, however, it also appears as if the camera is zooming into the darkness of the eye, metaphorically entering the mind. While the spiral changes color and shape, mutating into an electronic mandala and then back to numerous Lissajous forms, but always staying dead center in the frame, the remaining actors' and technical credits unspool over the animation. In a reverse motion shot, a spiral shrinks in size, as if receding, and the red-tinted eye returns, now with Alfred Hitchcock's director's credit.

The continuous camera movement in the opening sequence, as well as the abstract animation that creates the illusion of moving into spaces that morph into other spaces, represents to the audience a movement into the psyche of a woman, making manifest the adage that the eye is a window to the soul. This may be a partial explanation for the blood-red tinting, which breaks into the naturalistically colored image like a menstrual cycle of tidal wave proportions. Bass, of course, loved red because of its raw emotional power and its high visibility. But doesn't the red tint also clearly depict Hitchcock's phobia: fear of the same cold, aloof, blonde goddesses he also promotes? The blood-red tint may be an expression of Hitchcock's physical abhorrence of female genitalia, as well as of his own obese form. The unknowable in women is reinforced by the eyes shifting from left to right as the camera passes over them. The abstract spirals that emerge from Judy's inner eye are a visualization of the workings of her mind, not just a symbol of Scottie's fear of heights. In their pseudoscientific distribution, such Lissajous forms entered the semantics of psychology in general, becoming metaphors for mental processes. Indeed, educational films often used simplified graphs to visualize mental processes, and avant-garde cinema, as practiced by Mary Ellen Bute, the Whitney Brothers, and Jordan Belson, used scientific tools such as the oscilloscope to create art. These uses supported an audience's reading of abstract, moving designs as symbols of brain activity, thoughts, and feelings. Bass liked the Lissajous forms, and he would use them again in *Phase IV*, when his desert scientists measure a completely different kind of intelligence, that of ants.

However, just as the film's central male character is unable to decipher the words and actions of the woman he is infatuated with, in Hitchcock's most eloquent confession of his own weaknesses, the audience sees but does not necessarily understand what the spiral patterns mean; they remain abstract, colorful designs that never coalesce into concrete images of thought, even though the animation seems to be a roller-coaster ride through the central nervous system. For the audience, then, there is another kind of anxiety at work here: fear of being unable to decode the images in front of them. That anxiety is heightened by the color red, which tints a realistic image and turns it into an image of horror and violence—an image of violence against women, just as happens in the film.

Bunny Lake Is Missing marks for Bass yet another foray into Freudian psychology, this time orchestrated by Otto Preminger. Ostensibly a suspense thriller about the kidnapping of a little girl, the film spends much of its time questioning the single mother's sanity. Thus, when her brother is revealed to be the kidnapper, it is an extreme case of an overdetermined ending, and the film failed in the United States due to a lack of credibility. Two distinct readings, neither of which is completely cogent, emerge: it is either the story of a neurotic woman whose child is a figment of her imagination, compensating for her failed marriage and sexual inadequacies, or it is about an incestuous brother-sister relationship, causing the jealous sibling to kidnap the child that has come between them. This structural weakness was never resolved over the film's six-year gestation period, despite the fact that no fewer than seven scriptwriters had a hand in the screenplay.[126] Bass designed the paper doll, which became the logo for the film and the poster, even before the film began shooting in April 1965, as indicated by a trade advertisement.[127] Although the film received mixed reviews, critics again praised Bass for his titles.[128] The designer's own description of the title sequence is ambiguous, unless one already knows that the brother is the kidnapper: "The key protagonist in the film is a deeply emotionally disturbed person who is involved in the disappearance of the child, Bunny. The opening reflects this psychotic state of mind."[129]

The first frame of the credit sequence reveals a disembodied hand that reaches in from frame right and tears away black paper in the upper left-hand corner to expose a white field with black capital lettering, "OTTO PREMINGER PRESENTS." The hand is shot from below with very high-key light, adding a noirish effect but also replicating the opening shot of *Sparatcus*.[130] Bass would later attempt to reutilize the same tear-away technique in his titles for the first version of *Goodfellas* (1991), unsuccessfully, and for the British television movie *Under Suspicion* (1994), successfully; it was also a design element in his poster for Preminger's *Tell Me that You Love Me, Junie Moon* (1970) and in a company logo for Magdalena Productions (1994). The unevenly torn paper is shaped almost like a dagger, indicating that violence is lurking. The subsequent credits are accompanied by a loud tearing noise on the sound track that is vaguely threatening; it overpowers the flutes playing a tune that might be associated with childhood. In the next shot, the hand reaches from below and tears off the right side of the frame at roughly the vertical axis, showing the title in hand-drawn capitals, with the last four letters of "MISSING" fading to almost white. In this manner, the hand continues to tear away black paper, entering from either left or right, to reveal subsequent titles. The uneven white, horizontal field created by the tears stands in visual opposition to the clean black typography and right- or left-justified credits. Before the final credit, the disembodied hand tears out a paper doll at the extreme left frame, while Preminger's producer-director credit fades in white, just above the horizontal axis. Bass's trade-mark surprise ending comes when the hand reappears out of the darkness, screen right, and tears away the blackness to reveal the opening live-action scene. This highly self-reflexive moment tells the audience that what follows is only a movie. Bass turns this into a circular device at the end of the film when a black mask in the shape of the torn paper-doll cutout covers the live-action image of the mother, now reunited with her daughter, and the disembodied hand replaces the black paper, creating a black screen and allowing the end credits to roll.

Who does the hand belong to? Although never completely visible, it appears to be a male hand. At one level, the credits merely represent a nursery school activity—making paper dolls. But these are cut, not torn. Bass is reworking a paper-doll concept he first developed for an invitation he designed pro bono for Hollywood for SANE in 1960.[131] In that earlier design, the paper-doll chain signified community solidarity, whereas in Bunny Lake's ad campaign and titles, the doll is torn from black paper (as clearly indicated by the shadowing), giving it both the sophistication of modern art and a "primitive" childlike quality—not the work of a child but iconographically linked to childhood. The grating sound adds a tinge of perversity, in keeping with the slightly creepy characters that populate the film. If the hand belongs to the psychotic brother, the doll may repre-sent his own distorted image of the child as a plaything that can be dis-carded after playtime, allowing the incestuous pair to continue their love affair. In such an Oedipal narrative, the child must be eliminated so as not to disturb the central relationship, however perverted it may be. Such a reading is supported by the fact that a broken doll brought to the doll hospital leads to the kidnapper. Conversely, the doll might symbolize an imaginary child created in the mind of the mother, just as toddlers often make up invisible friends to articulate their own desires. Is the imaginary child the symbolic consummation of the incestuous relationship? Such a reading is made manifest at the end of the film, when only mother and daughter are seen cheek to cheek inside the doll shape. The final shot, then, symbolically takes back the "happy ending," questioning whether anything in the film is real. For some critics, such as Andrew Sarris, the film's ambiguity was what made it enjoyable.[132]

With the titles for *Seconds*, Bass returns to a study of physiognomy, but this time through a distorted lens—perverted like the science in the film that promises new identities for old minds and bodies. The plot revolves around a bored sixty-year-old businessman who hires a corporation to give him a new body and a new identity, so it stages his death and turns him into a Malibu-based artist. Thus, the plot takes literally the middle-aged desire to start life anew. Working again with John Frankenheimer (Bass had done the titles for *The Young Stranger* and *Grand Prix*), Bass employs both experimental and horror film techniques in the credits, mirroring *Seconds'* own mix of genres—part science fiction, part thriller, part 1960s youth cult film. Indeed, this mix of genres and the film's extremely bleak ending led to its box-office failure, although the film has since been recuperated by film historians as one of the director's most interesting works.[133] Based on surviving storyboards, Bass's original designs for the title sequence used the same visual idea he had developed for the poster (which was apparently rejected), in which he played with notions of an old-young Janus face and the making of human copies, as in a printing press.[134] In creating a montage of distorted images of Art Goodman's face,[135] Bass moved closer to Frankenheimer's and cinematographer James Wong Howe's visual design for the overall film, making liberal use of handheld cameras, jump cuts, extreme close-ups, first-person point of view shots, and fish-eye lenses. Working with Howard Anderson Opticals and Art Goodman, Bass shot footage that was then projected via a rear-process projector onto an aluminum plate, which could be bent to create visual distortions.[136]

The titles begin with a completely abstract, extreme close-up of an unidentifiable black-and-white object that is seemingly moving around its own axis. This is revealed to be an eye once the camera comes to rest (actually, it dissolves to a close-up of an eye), with the black circle of the pupil dominating the middle of the frame. After Rock Hudson's sans serif credit appears in white capitals and disappears screen right, the lens again stretches the image, similar to a fun-house mirror.[137] Alienating, atonal electronic music accompanies the image as the eyeball splits into two parts and is rejoined in the convex lens before Frankenheimer's above-the-title credit fades in, followed by a dissolve to a dark, out-of-focus orifice—a mouth—as the title appears in the center of the frame. The camera continues to zoom in on the mouth and teeth, which then dissolve into a series of images in which the lips and facial features are seemingly multiplied in (invisible) split-screen montages as the actors' credits fade in, left-justified at screen left. Subsequent shots focus on the nose and then Goodman's face, but they are shot from an extremely low angle, from under the chin. Either the camera seemingly zooms in on various orifices or the image is stretched or contracted in the mirror, becoming an abstract play of black, gray, and white shadows. The final horrific image before Frankenheimer's directorial credit consists of the face under a surgical mask, cutting to a close-up shot of the hole where the mouth should be as "directed by JOHN FRANKENHEIMER" fades in (an image strangely reminiscent of Bass's 1962 commercial for Mennen Baby Magic).

Given that the film is about plastic surgery and the creation of new identities, Bass's decision to visually explore a man's physiognomy in a way that is both unsettling and mysterious seems appropriate. The camera is like an instrument probing various facial orifices, and the film is about the invasion of the body by medicine; however, the image distortions indicate that there is something unhealthy about this particular brand of medicine. The subject seems to understand this, because in one shot the eye darts back and forth in fear, just as the final shot of the white cotton mask instills in the audience an apprehension about what is to come. The split-screen shots multiply certain lines on the face, indicating that the attached body is rather old. Utilizing black-and-white film stock also emphasizes abstraction, making it more difficult for the audience to decode the indexical content of the images and thus further unsettling them. Finally, the camera distortions undermine the usual montage process, which allows the viewer to construct an image of the human face from separate close-up shots. As a result, any exploration of human psychology through the study of photographic physiognomy (as in *The Big Knife*) is impossible.

The film that follows demonstrates the replacement of an old face with a new face and body and even the transition to a new physical identity, but nothing can change the thoughts of the mind within. The final two images of the mask can thus be read as occurring either after the subject's first operation, when he receives his new face, or before his second operation (i.e., as a death mask), when his body will be given to a new client. Ironically, no contemporary or modern critics have posited that the film may be an allegory for spiritual, religious, and psychological self-help cults such as Esalen, all of which promised youth, peace, and happiness for those who were willing to give up their previous lives and accept new identities. Ironically, Bass himself would be involved with Esalen in the 1970s, lecturing at its Big Sur campus.

As these examples demonstrate, Saul Bass had a particular genius for creating title sequences from images of everyday objects, inviting audiences to look beyond their ordinary meanings and find beauty in their form or in their uncommon symbolic meanings. Whether referencing events, physical facts, or psychological states of mind, Bass almost always found concrete images that could represent more complex issues, just as his logos symbolically captured whole films. The fact that he returned to this strategy of utilizing parts for the whole throughout his career indicates how productive this design aesthetic could be in the creation of advertising campaigns and title sequences. A *pars pro toto* aesthetic would also play a significant role in Bass's almost obsessive use of body parts in all his design work.

4

Modernism's Multiplicity of Views

If one important conceptual strategy for Saul Bass's design work was *pars pro toto* (finding a single image to stand for the whole), then another strategy he developed early on was creating wholes out of many individual parts. Photomontages were important in the Bauhaus, with Moholy-Nagy creating some of the most striking examples, because they taught design students about spatial proportions within the frame and the juxtaposition of intellectual content. Bass's movie advertisements demonstrate that he was a master at both. Montage on a two-dimensional surface takes the form of a multiplicity of images often separated into panels on a single page, as seen in some of his advertising campaigns. Cinematic montage consists of the editing of individual shots to create a synthetic whole, as in Bass's commercials and independent films. Bass also understood the value of Sergei Eisenstein's concept of montage as a juxtaposition of images to create meaning. And in a 1990 interview he discussed Hitchcock's use of a shock cut in *The Lady Vanishes*—open mouth + train whistle = scream—as the origin of what has become a cliché.[1] Eisenstein had similarly differentiated between these two aesthetic strategies, defining one as internal montage, which involves putting together dynamic elements within the composition of a single shot, and the other as metric or rhythmic montage, in which different shots are syntactically ordered to create meaning.[2]

In contrast to his official biographical narrative, Saul Bass's interest in filmmaking surely predated his first official films in the mid-1960s. Even as a teenager in the 1930s, he attended screenings of Russian films at New York's Fifty-Fifth Street Playhouse, including *Potemkin* (1925) and *Mother* (1926); he might have seen early American avant-garde films there as well, such as Ralph Steiner's H_2O.[3] Apart from his growing experience in producing title sequences, Bass's cinematic thinking began to invade his design work as early as the 1950s. His design for a trade advertisement for *Magnificent Obsession* (1954) slices an ostensibly moving image (painted by Al Kallis) of a couple kissing into four slightly different rectangular panels, each panel resembling a frame from a film, allowing the consumer to "see" the action move forward toward the kiss. A 1955 trade advertisement for producer Benedict Bogeaus's *Pearl of the South Pacific* consists of five oblong panels, each featuring a different "close-up" to visualize audience reaction to the film—shaking hands (male and female), holding hands (same), high-heeled female legs upended, a woman's surprised profile, an elegantly gloved feminine hand—while below the text box a South Seas statue refers to the film.[4] In both cases, the text between the images and the design encourage a syntactical reading from top to bottom (i.e., from left to right), as if they were frames of a film. Ironically, the visual information in the latter ad—the upscale clothing and jewelry, a statue that might be found in an art museum—speaks to a sophisticated audience, although Allan Dwan's adventure film was geared more toward the Saturday matinee crowd. But Hollywood's reach has always exceeded its grasp.

Saul Bass quickly developed into a master of montage, cutting together his title sequences and commercials out of numerous individual shots whose meaning could be read only through their syntactical juxtaposition. Early on, Bass started working with veteran editor Albert Nalpas, who spent his days at National Screen Service cutting trailers and then moonlighted for Bass. NSS letterman Harold Adler also worked for Bass after hours. Like Bass, Nalpas was extremely meticulous. Bass would select the shots after reviewing rushes, and Nalpas would do a first cut and fine-tune subsequent edits, based on Bass's instructions.[5] Bass expressed his feelings about editing in an interview: "I love the editing process, because it's a ritualistic kind of thing, a process of which you have complete control. . . . Partly it's the sensation of craft—I like to run a moviola, to set up the film, to run it, to stop, to go back, to look; just as some people like to work wood."[6] Even more revealing is his statement about montage at an American Film Institute seminar in 1979, where craft is supplanted by an intellectual and intuitively visual process: "What I'm saying is that montage editing is in your head, you're really creating the thing. The choices are arbitrary."[7]

While Bass's early live-action titles for *The Racers, The Big Knife,*

Johnny Concho, and *Storm Center* consist of essentially single takes over which the titles are superimposed, beginning with *Attack!* (1956), Bass utilized continuity editing, as he would with the titles for *Edge of the City* (1957) and subsequent films. Bass's commercials for National Bohemian beer (1957) also demonstrate a high degree of sophistication in terms of their editing, as discussed later. As Bass stated in a television interview: "I like putting something together out of many individual parts. Like a mosaic, they eventually all fit together to make a whole."[8]

Bass's understanding of quick-cutting montage was certainly why Hitchcock hired him to design the shower sequence for *Psycho*, and it is the major reason why the sequence has become so famous (even though Bass did not direct it, as he once stated). The forty-eight storyboard frames of Bass's design correspond almost directly to the film as shot and edited, with only minor tweaks. But if there is any doubt about Bass's prowess in cutting together film, one need look no further than his commercial for Mennen Baby Magic (1962), which is a model of Eisensteinian montage, a symphony of baby body parts that avoids showing a whole baby within a single frame.

Bass was apparently fascinated by body parts, and they pervade his design work and films. Conforming to Eisensteinian montage theory, Bass uses images of individual body parts to either create dynamic conflict within a single frame or to give the impression of a synthetic whole. There are numerous examples of disembodied body parts in the work of the Bauhaus. Indeed, Bauhaus photographers attempted to abstract both objects and bodies in their work, and these exercises were often done with an eye toward creating advertising photos. For example, in an advertisement titled "Young People: Come to the Bauhaus," designed by Hannes Meyer in 1929 (when he was director of the Bauhaus), we see the image of a disembodied hand. That image encapsulated the Bauhaus educational model, which focused on hands-on workshops where students could actively experiment in conjunction with their teachers. At the Bauhaus, the hand thus became a metaphor for the production of art. But this hand, like so many of Bass's hands, is also an action figure. The hand "walks" toward the viewer, thus following the advice of the slogan: "Come to the Bauhaus." The hand is a functional tool, as illustrated by Moholy-Nagy in a photograph juxtaposing a pair of pliers and a hand gripping an object.[9] The trope of the hand, in particular, is ubiquitous within the Bauhaus and the German avant-garde.

Emblematic is Lucia Moholy-Nagy's 1926 photo-portrait of her husband, his open hand stretching toward the camera. For the Bauhaus artists, the hand represented the artist and his craft; for example, Moholy-Nagy's "Photogram" (1926) juxtaposes a hand with a paintbrush. Herbert Beyer created a series of surrealistic photomontages utilizing hands and eyes, including "Hands Act" (1932) and "Lonely Metropolitan" (1932), where disembodied hands function independently of bodies. Bauhaus student Munio Weintraub (Amos Gitai's father) made at least two photographs for a Bauhaus workshop in 1930 that show disembodied hands in action.[10] Stella Simon's film *Hände* (1928) employs hands to stage a cinematic ballet, while Albert Viktor Blum's film *Hände* (1928) is a montage of proletarian hands at work.

But in Bass's work, the disembodied hand, seemingly unconnected to a human body, appears most often. For example, his aborted titles for *Looking for Mr. Goodbar* (1977, Richard Brooks) feature disembodied female and male hands doing a pas de deux around a candle and glasses of wine and beer on a bar table.[11] Here, as almost everywhere in Bass's work, the hands are indexical signs of human action and emotion; they lack the individuality of hands attached to faces and are generalized, so to speak, to represent Every(wo)man. Bass had previously done an animated courtship of male and female hands in *The Facts of Life*. Such hands also turn up in the following Bass designs: *Decision before Dawn* (advertisement), Pabco paint (billboard), *The Man with the Golden Arm* (credits), Manufacturers National Bank (advertisement), "Let Him Die" (*Saturday Evening Post* illustrations), *Love in the Afternoon* (poster), RCA "The Kid" (commercial), *Anatomy of a Murder* (credits), Hollywood for SANE (poster), *Spartacus* (credits), *One, Two, Three* (poster), Mennen Baby Magic (commercial), *Exodus* (trade advertisements), *It's a Mad, Mad, Mad, Mad World* (credits), *The Victors* (prologue), *Bunny Lake Is Missing* (credits), *Facts of Life* (credits), *In Harm's Way* (poster), *Hurry Sundown* (sound-track album cover), Bell Telephone campaign (film), *Why Man Creates* (film), *Rosebud* (poster), *Phase IV* (film), *Brothers* (poster), *Talk Radio* (poster), *Tonkô* (poster), and *Mr. Saturday Night* (credits). I'm sure there are more.

What attracted Bass to the image of the human hand? Was it his belief in the creative hand, the hand of the artist, his own sure hand, as in the case of the Bauhaus? Was this obsessive reworking of hand imagery connected to Art Goodman, who was Bass's "right-hand man," drawing with his right hand because his left had been rendered useless by a war wound? Was it the hand of fate or some higher force, as in *It's a Mad, Mad, Mad, Mad World*? Or were these hands simply stand-ins for offscreen characters? Interestingly, what connects almost every Bass image of a disembodied human hand is that they are active—accomplishing a task, reaching into the frame to influence the action, manipulating the graphic design. Hands communicate anguish in the face of war in *The Victors* and send men to war in *In Harm's Way*; hands point accusingly in *Decision before Dawn* and protect in *Love in the Afternoon* (poster); hands rise up in revolt in *Exodus* and are raised, voting in unity, in the Bell Telephone film.

Body Parts

Clearly, Bass's most famous use of body parts was in the logo, poster, and title sequence for *Anatomy of a Murder*. The logo became so well known as part of the Bass brand that the designer successfully stopped Spike Lee from using a similar image for his film *Clockers* (1995). Otto Preminger took immediate action when he first saw Art Sims's design for the *Clockers* poster, and Universal quickly withdrew the image with an apology.[12] Ironically, Bass's first design for the *Anatomy of a Murder* title sequence involved a series of straight lines running vertically and horizontally through the frame, which at first glance looks exactly like the *Psycho* credits. Preminger apparently rejected the design, leading Bass to resell the idea thirteen months later to Alfred Hitchcock for *Psycho*.[13] The *Psycho*-like titles seem odd, given that Bass designed the *Anatomy* poster and logo before film production began. However, the B-style one-sheet, the half-sheet, and other foreign poster designs, including the French poster, show traces of the line design; their strongest visual element is lines slicing through black-and-white images, another example of montage on a single page.[14] For *Anatomy of a Murder*, Bass was responsible for designing the whole collateral package, including trade advertisements, letterhead, invitation to the premiere, album cover, and some of the posters,[15] so one wonders whether he was initially trying to marry the dismembered corpse with the venetian blind images of Stewart and other principals. Bass's own description of the title sequence is of little help here, since it was apparently written after the fact and is purely descriptive: "This film was based on the symbol (the segmented figure) designed by Saul Bass for use in the general advertising and promotion of the film. Working within the framework of a contemporary jazz score by Duke Ellington, a staccato and fragmented style was developed for the title."[16] The word *anatomy* (originating from the Greek for "to cut") has several definitions in the dictionary, including analysis of phenomena (the title's meaning), as well as the physical dissection of a body into parts, which may have given Bass the idea.[17]

Like every other black-and-white Preminger film, the title sequence for *Anatomy of a Murder* begins with a monochromatic gray screen on which "OTTO PREMINGER PRESENTS" appears in white capital letters. The typography is then slowly covered by the legs, arms, head, and torso of a body that seems to be cut out of rough black paper, and the title of the film appears in white letters inside the legs and torso of the corpse. The images are accompanied by Duke Ellington's jazzy score, which, like Elmer Bernstein's music for *Man with the Golden Arm*, immediately gives the film a contemporary feel; moreover, the aural entrance of horns, drums, and saxophones matches the appearance of various body parts, increasing their shock value. All the body parts then disappear, except for the head; in a subsequent shot, the head moves from right to left while enlarging to fill the screen, with James Stewart's credit appearing inside. In the next frame, two legs become visible at screen right, followed by the credits for Lee Remick and Ben Gazzara. For the subsequent actors' credits, various hands, arms, and legs jut into the frame from the left or the right; the subsequent major credits are accompanied by a torso and head combination moving into the frame, followed by more arms. Like the supporting actors' credits, the technical credits are placed outside the body parts; in the latter case, a leg, head, and hand are also sliced into several pieces, entering from the bottom, left, and right. Finally, two outstretched arms move in from the bottom of the image and black out the whole frame for Preminger's final credit as producer-director. The final pair of outstretched arms are almost identical to the arms in the *Exodus* poster. The animation for the head title, the stars, and Otto Preminger were also cut into the film's original trailer.[18]

In *Anatomy of a Murder*, Preminger focuses on a small-town lawyer (Stewart) from the Upper Peninsula of Michigan who likes fishing more than legal work. However, he takes the case of a soldier accused of killing a man, allegedly for raping his wife. Preminger focuses on the mechanics of the trial and the legal system, including the gathering of evidence, jury selection, examination and cross-examination, and the importance of finding legal precedents through research. Indeed, Preminger brilliantly analyzes the American legal system, similar to the way he dissects the workings of Congress in *Advise and Consent*. One can therefore interpret the body parts as bits of testimony. Like the body, which is never seen as a whole, the individual bits of testimony make the search for the truth difficult. The lawyers can either embrace as true or attempt to discredit the various pieces of testimony. But, as in the trial itself, there is a game of truth and illusion going on in the titles. On the one hand, all the various body parts, which have been cut from rough paper, enter from the left or the right, as if coming from either the prosecution or the defense. They are abstractions that can hardly be mistaken for real bodies. Indeed, as with Bass's poster, the corpse is a modern art construction, decidedly graphic and two-dimensional. On the other hand, the legs are dragged out of frame, as if they are attached to real bodies, while the hands and arms actively push credits out of frame, again, as if being manipulated by a real body, emphasizing the real–not real dichotomy that is at the center of the drama.

Likewise, Bass's title sequence for *Spartacus* begins with an image of a disembodied hand, but it is the hand of a statue from antiquity. Indeed, the opening sequence is presented as a series of still lifes of Roman statues. Bass's design consists of a montage of statues and credits, similar to Eisenstein's *October* and Dziga Vertov's *The Man with the Movie Camera*. The film, based on a novel by blacklisted author Howard Fast and a script by blacklisted writer Dalton Trumbo (whom Kirk Douglas hired and gave screen credit to), was originally supposed to be directed by Anthony Mann, but he was fired after two and a half weeks and replaced by Stanley Kubrick.[19] Bass, who had been hired before production began to do the titles and design the climactic battle sequence, was one of the few members of the crew to remain after Mann's departure.[20] Although critics such as Hedda Hopper attacked the film for its alleged Communist inspiration, and although at $12 million it was one of the most costly films ever produced up to that time, *Spartacus* eventually became Universal's biggest moneymaker when it went into general release in 1962. It was also nominated for six Academy Awards and won four, although Kubrick later disowned the film.[21] The reviews were decidedly mixed, due in part to the market's oversaturation with sword-and-sandal epics and in part to the film's expense. Typical was the review in *Monthly Film Bulletin*: "It is disappointing therefore to find that despite enormous expenditure, technical resources and an unusually talented team, so much of *Spartacus* falls into the old ruts of cliché and sentiment."[22] In 1991 *Spartacus* was restored by

Robert A. Harris, including twenty-three minutes cut from the re-release in 1967 and fourteen minutes that had been censored, leading to a growing critical recognition of the film as a flawed masterpiece.

Unlike other projects Bass worked on at the time, he produced only the title sequence for *Spartacus* and was not responsible for any of the publicity material. This is clear from the posters, which have far too many elements. However, Bass was responsible for designing the battle sequences and therefore received special screen credit as a design consultant, as he had on *Psycho*, although it is unclear whether Kubrick actually utilized the Bass storyboards.[23]

The titles open with a hand pointing left, near center screen but moving slightly to the left, and lit directly from above in a brown light. As a result, most of the screen remains in darkness, with only the tops of the thumb and three fingers visible as "BYRNA PRODUCTIONS, INC." appears in white capitals on the horizontal axis. Meanwhile, Alex North's drum-heavy martial music makes its presence felt on the sound track. A second clenched hand with the iron bracelet of a slave becomes visible screen left, while Kirk Douglas's name appears to the right of the vertical axis. Next, a statue of a Roman eagle fades in at center screen, behind Laurence Olivier's credit, which is replaced by a clay jug in a woman's hand for Jean Simmons's credit; the Charles Laughton and Peter Ustinov credits are also accompanied by carved stone hands, the latter with the head of a snake. The last above-the-title credit for John Gavin includes a hand holding a perpendicular sword just off center, now in a gray-green tint, the camera panning down the sword's shaft after the credit fades out. It is replaced by the head title, a second sword pointing up from the bottom along the vertical axis and forming a cross with the typography. Another open hand, its palm facing the camera, as if greeting, and a close-up of lips accompany the remaining actors' credits in columns at screen left, while Tony Curtis's credit is seen over two open hands reaching out to welcome. The major artistic and technical credits are then presented in blue tints over images of large and small Latin text chiseled into stone, including Saul Bass's credit directly under the large roman type "ECXXI" (from 121). Alex North's credit includes the back of a Roman head, followed by Kirk Douglas's executive producer credit, which is accompanied by a young Roman head with its face half in shadow. Bass then creates several Janus heads bathed in purple light, through superimpositions, before cutting to subsequent heads for Edward Lewis's and Stanley

Kubrick's credits, which are also bathed in half light. After Kubrick's credit fades out, the statue develops cracks and falls apart as the camera zooms in on the stone head's remaining eye socket.

Some have agreed that Elaine Bass may have been responsible for much of the *Spartacus* sequence because, at the time, Saul was in Japan at a design conference.[24] However, there is documentation only that she handled the research and shot some of the artwork at the Norton Simon Museum. Roman statues for the sequence were found at the Los Angeles County Museum, the Getty Museum, the Anthropological Museum at Berkeley, and the Norton Simon, while the Roman fist with shackles and the final cracked head were manufactured by a local artist from plaster.[25] Given that most of the Roman imagery depicts heads and hands, it seems likely that Bass left instructions and ultimately made all the decisions, just as he would have if any of his other designers had been assisting him on the project. As noted earlier, the breakup of the statue is a Bass-branded formal device, going back to his *Death of a Salesman* ads. In any case, the imagery, the typography, and the overall design based on a grid indicate that the *Spartacus* title sequence is pure Saul Bass, and possibly one of his most elegant.

Most striking in the title sequence is the extremely high-key lighting, so that only parts of the statues are visible. The disembodied heads and hands seemingly rise up out of darkness, their indistinct contours adding to their mystery. Their origins, Bass seems to be suggesting, are buried in the darkness of the past. In addition, the various color tints, going from flashy browns to gray-green, light baby blue, turquoise blue, purple, and back to blue, add relief to the images and convey the sense that these statues are very old, but these colors also allow the white typography to stand out. The 3:38-minute title sequence is divided into three sections: the first section through the title credit features hands; Latin typography functions as background for the major and technical credits; and Roman heads accompany the credits for music, production, and direction. Each section metaphorically delineates a different aspect of *Spartacus*'s overall narrative. Yet, despite these narrative elements, the title sequence is very much a work of graphic art, a montage of static images rather than cinematic motion—images that are illustrative of actual history and therefore capable of producing knowledge.

The first pair of hands is lit in flesh tones, visualizing the transition from the real humans in history to their aesthetic representations in stone.

Each hand and the object it holds represent a character named onscreen: a hand in shackles for Spartacus, a hand carrying a jug for Varinia, a hand holding a sword for Julius Caesar. Ustinov's Batiatus is obviously a villain, holding a symbolic snake in his hand, while Crassius's eagle represents Rome's patrician past. Typical of Bass, these are hands in action, and here they begin to define characters and conflicts. Between them all is an extreme close-up of large, sensuous male lips (harking back to *The Young Stranger*), possibly referencing the film's homoerotic subplot. The second section consists of lines of Latin text alternating with roman numerals dominating the screen. The Latin, some of it drawn to appear chiseled in stone, has been chosen less for content than for design, the typography and language seemingly strange and remote but also vaguely familiar; we understand that it is a Roman text. As the great religions teach us, the word is law, so here the text represents the law, but ironically, there is a conflict between natural law, represented by Spartacus (and later codified in the French and American revolutions), and the written (Roman) law at the heart of the film. The final section is a study in patrician heads, moving from young to old. Through double exposures, Bass also creates Janus heads that symbolize Roman patrician society as both noble and doomed to extinction. The latter idea is also communicated visually by the dark shadows that split the faces in half. The visual breakup of the final aged visage is Bass's interpretation of Karl Marx's (and Dalton Trumbo's) dialectical materialism, because the ruling class will inevitably be swept away by the proletarian masses that Spartacus represents. But one can also read the three sections as the law mitigating between the hand and the mind, between the intuitive and the animalistic, the rational and the intellectual, with language being the crucial civilizing influence. It is a theme Bass returns to again and again.

The same year Bass completed the *Spartacus* titles for Kubrick, the *Psycho* titles for Hitchcock, and the *Exodus* titles for Preminger, he also designed titles for the Norman Panama and Melvin Frank production *The Facts of Life* (1960), starring Bob Hope and Lucille Ball. This was the third film starring Ball and Hope (the others were *Fancy Pants* and *Sorrowful Jones*), but it was the first after Ball's divorce from Desi Arnaz and the cancellation of their television show. Numerous accidents, including a nasty fall by Ball, marred the production.[26] Frank and Panama had made a name for themselves as producer-writer-director hyphenates for Bob Hope and Danny Kaye comedies, and here they attempted to craft a sex comedy about married neighbors who fall in love—in other words, a film about adultery. The film received very good reviews and was nominated for five Oscars, including best screenplay.

Bass's titles consist of a live-action sequence in which the illicit lovers meet at the airport, leading Lucille Ball to reminisce about how a middle-aged mom came to be involved in an extramarital affair. Bass then cuts to the head title and an extended animated sequence for the remaining credits, integrating the typography into a series of visual jokes about love and courtship. As in the case of *It's a Mad, Mad, Mad, Mad World*, Bass humorously employs disembodied hands that reach into the image from offscreen to manipulate the scene. Again, the critics took notice, with one writing in *Limelight*: "Saul Bass, who never seems to run out of ideas, gets the fun off to an early start."[27] The film was a box-office hit.[28]

The most striking element of the head title is that while the film's title is centered in white sans serif letters on a gray background, just above the horizontal axis, the individual letters are placed slightly askew, each letter on its own axis. The title is then replaced by daisies in a bunch, followed by a male hand with stems, which reaches into the frame from screen left until each stem is attached to a flower. The male hand is withdrawn, and a female hand comes from screen right to take the bouquet out of the frame. Next, the male hand reaches in from screen left with a box of chocolates, and the secondary leads are revealed when the female hand removes the bonbons. The costars are listed between a stack of presents held by the male, which the female again snatches. The male hand next offers a necklace made up of additional names, which the female grabs and stretches into a straight line. The names of the scriptwriters appear next to highball glasses at the bottom, as ice cubes are dropped in; the male and female hands each grab a glass to make a toast. The male hand lights the female's cigarette, creating an associate producer credit in the ash. A black telephone generates notes for the song credits, while a heart-shaped card presents more major credits. The technical credits are shaped as coats and suitcases; the latter idea was reused for the *Advise and Consent* poster and publicity.[29] Bass's credit for the titles appears on the label of an LP record, which the male hand puts on a turntable. Finally, the producer credit is seen on a lamp shade as the male hand turns off the light, followed by the female hand turning on the light for the director's credit and the male turning it off again—a pas de deux before bedtime sex. Bass would rework the idea of male and female hands at a candlelighted table in a "meat factory"—as pickup bars were called in the 1970s—for *Looking for Mr. Good-bar*. But the manipulation of the image from frames left and right also recalls the titles for *Anatomy of a Murder*.

Bass's title sequence for *The Facts of Life* humorously depicts the various steps in a typical American courtship ritual, leading to sex if not marriage. As soon as the animated title sequence begins, Eydie Gormé and Steve Lawrence begin singing the Johnny Mercer title song, which runs the full length of the titles. The opening title and daisies signal that this is a comedy, and Bass seemingly eschews the grid design in favor of diagonals. Bass divides the screen into a male space (screen left) and a female space (screen right), visualizing the objects exchanged between the disembodied hands of the partners. The succession of objects shown onscreen chronicles the stages of an increasingly serious seduction: flowers, candy, pearls, boxes of presents, telephone conversations, cigarettes, drinks, mood music. The coat rack and suitcases, then, mark the transition to the bedroom, which is represented by a table lamp. The fact that the male hand turns off the light and the female turns it back on implies that the woman is still ambivalent about taking the final step and having sex (i.e., committing adultery). Indeed, the film's comedic narrative centers on the couple's frustrated attempts to have sex, and it remains unclear—given that this is 1960, and given Lucille Ball's reluctance to be perceived as an adulteress—whether they ever make it into bed. It is also the first time that Bass was allowed to give himself screen credit on a separate title card, indicating the designer's growing visibility as a Hollywood player.

Commercials

By the early 1960s, Bass had gained significant experience as a filmmaker, not only by editing live-action title sequences for *Attack!*, *The Big Country*, and *North by Northwest* but also through his commercials, such as those for Speedway 79 gasoline (1955) and National Bohemian beer (1957). In comparison to filmmakers attached to Madison Avenue ad agencies such as J. Walter Thompson, Bass made relatively few commercials.[30] He hated the hard sell in movie advertising and probably felt the same about television commercials. According to Al Kallis, who worked with Bass in the mid-1950s, the designer preferred a gentler approach to consumers, one that respected their intellectual capabilities and sold lifestyle rather than a specific product. Bass and Kirkham quote the designer:

"I feel there is more than one way to do a selling job. . . . There is a positive, consistent, coherent way, one that respects the intelligence, good taste and capacity of an audience."[31] The IBM infomercials of the early 1960s were more to Bass's liking. A similar strategy operated in *From Here to There* and subsequent Bass shorts: they were financed by clients that did not require the sale of a specific product. Bass preferred to avoid direct sales pitches in his commercials, but that was hardly possible, given that their sole purpose is to sell goods and services to consumers.

Commercials had gone through a long apprenticeship on the radio and were rapidly becoming more sophisticated on television, with a marriage of aural and visual media. There was a move away from live television commercials, when spots were announced onstage during live television broadcasts, and toward filmed commercials over which the sponsor had more control and that could employ more sophisticated forms of communication, other than directly addressing the viewer. Commercials had to entertain and be memorable if they were going to convince consumers to purchase a particular product. The sales pitch had to be loud and clear. Interestingly, some Bass commercials featured the Bass family, almost like home movies.

Bass's two commercials for Mennen's Baby Magic lotion and Mennen's Genteel Baby Bath soap (1962) are like little cinematic masterpieces, symphonies of baby body parts that owe much to Eisenstein's concepts of associative montage. Indeed, Bass's Baby Magic commercial won the Grand Prize at the Cannes Advertising Film Festival in 1963.[32] The commercial was apparently a family project, and it starred Elaine Bass. Most striking in comparison to similar commercials from the period, which usually featured medium shots of a whole baby, Bass's commercials consist almost exclusively of images of baby body parts that seem almost abstract, at least until they are imagined together with other images.

The commercial opens with the camera looking down on a naked baby, while a heartbeat is heard on the sound track.[33] The camera slowly tracks in closer as very sheer sheets, almost like gauze, are pulled away, one layer after another. "A baby is born," says the soft, comforting voice of the offscreen narrator, followed by the piercing shrill of a baby screaming, cut against an image of the gaping yaw of the baby's mouth—a black hole in the center of the frame, recalling an almost identical shot of Janet Leigh in the *Psycho* shower sequence. That somewhat horrific image is onscreen for less than two seconds, replaced by an image of tiny feet and the narrator's soothing voice: "New born." Other close-ups of the baby's feet and hands follow. Then the mother's face enters the frame to kiss the nape of the baby's neck, followed by a close-up of Mennen Baby Magic lotion. Next we see the mother's hands take the lotion and rub it on various parts of the baby's body, while the narrator calmly assures the consumer that Mennen's baby lotion helps replace nature's own moisture, and the baby gurgles happily. After Elaine Bass kisses the baby on the cheek, the baby yawns and her eyes fall closed, while a disembodied hand closes the bottle of Baby Magic.

This one-minute black-and-white commercial consists of a total of nineteen different shots. This is striking in itself, given that another contemporary commercial for a Mennen baby product makes do with only a handful of shots held for a long time—a baby is seen in a home setting, playing happily in a tub with a crib and other baby accessories in the background.[34] In Bass's commercial, the first shot of the baby lying on a white sheet is held for twelve seconds as the camera slowly zooms in through the translucent fabric, as if penetrating layers of skin, thus preparing the viewer for the narrator's suggestion that Baby Magic will protect that soft baby skin. The remaining eighteen shots have an average screen length of three seconds or less. However, the shots do not seem to be that short because Bass connects every shot with dissolves rather than straight cuts, except for a straight cut from the first to the second shot of the gaping mouth crying. (Ironically, Bass inserts an almost identical image of a gaping mouth in his title sequence for *Seconds*.) The dissolves are held for half a second, giving the impression that the images flow from one to the other without breaks, while the white of the sheets and the mother's white hair band are only barely distinguishable from the gray, amorphous masses of baby flesh that fill the screen. Each shot taken individually remains an abstraction, since the images provide no environmental context, no set design, unlike standard commercials. Dramatically, the baby's cry alerts the viewer to danger and the need to protect the baby from harm—a need fulfilled by the product. After Baby Magic lotion is applied, the baby sleeps peacefully. Thus, Bass's commercial pitches a product, but the sell is as soft as a baby's bottom. It functions on one level as nothing more than an abstract play of human baby forms, which, thanks to the soothing voice of the narrator, communicate security and safety for the child.

Bass's commercial for Mennen Genteel Baby Bath soap from the same period utilizes many of the same images from the Baby Magic commercial and consists of twenty-three images in one minute, thanks to a shorter opening shot.[35] Like the first commercial, a heartbeat and layers of translucent sheets accompany the image, followed by various baby body parts. Here, the sixth shot features a crying baby mouth, before the mother undresses the baby and prepares her bath. A shot of the faucet and water running horizontally through the frame seems to present the baby's point of view, followed by shots of the invisible mother's hand washing various parts of the baby's body. As in the first advertisement, a soothing male voice and dissolves give the whole sequence a smooth flow, and in the final images, the baby yawns and falls asleep. As in the first commercial, Bass zooms in on the baby like a microscope focusing on a specimen (an idea he would use again in *Phase IV*), then deconstructs the body into parts without ever putting them back together. It is an Eisensteinian exercise in montage that passes as a commercial. Thus, although these commercials may have been too arty to serve as effective product advertising, they are brilliant examples of Bass's ability to edit film abstractly, creating a mood from many separate images that are connected through formal composition.

In 1969 Saul Bass was hired by the Mattel Toy Company, and there are a number of Mattel commercials in the Bass Collection; however, it is unclear which were directed by Bass.[36] The exception is a Mattel Baby Tenderlove commercial, which features a five-year-old girl with a doll. In a series of intense close-ups, the girl is shown playing with her baby doll, sending it down a slide, walking with it, counting fingers that actually bend, feeding the doll baby food and then a bottle, washing the baby, combing its hair, and putting it to bed with a good-night kiss. All the while, the girl is talking to the doll, like a mother chatting with her baby, until the narrator pipes in, "Baby feels like a real baby, makes you feel like a real mom." As in the Mennen commercials, Bass frames his shots in a series of intense close-ups; the girl is almost always in the center of the frame, except when the close-ups are of doll parts. A final close-up of a Band-Aid on the doll's arm dissolves to Mattel's red logo. As he did in the Mennen commercials, Bass removes everything extraneous from view, focusing on the mother and the baby—or, in this case, on the girl and her Baby Tenderlove doll. Whereas the Mennen commercials depict a mother's care for a baby whose response is rudimentary (sleep), Bass's montage establishes a relationship between child and doll, as if the latter were human. Indeed, the Mattel commercial can be seen as a virtual remake of the first two Mennen commercials. Finally, until the narrator is heard and the logo is seen in the final seconds of the one-minute ad, one hardly knows what product is being advertised. Ironically, commercials that leave one guessing about the product would become very popular decades later in American television.

Not surprisingly, then, another commercial Bass made at this time was not a product advertisement but an image advertisement. Known as the RCA "The Kid" commercial (1968),[37] the sixty-second spot consists of thirteen separate shots depicting a young boy (played by Jeffrey Bass, Saul's youngest son) tying his shoe. Crosscutting between the intense stares of the toddler in close-up and his efforts to navigate the shoelaces on his sneakers, the commercial relies on extreme close-ups of both fingers and laces. Again, Bass reduces the audience's field of vision to subject and object, seer and seen, as in the Mattel commercial. And like the Mennen commercials, Bass opens with an establishing shot—here, a slow tracking shot from the boy's entire body, sitting in front of giant building blocks, to an extreme close-up of his sneaker. Over the next twelve shots, Bass depicts the boy's slow but steady progress as he learns to tie his shoes, alternating only two shots, reinforcing audience identification through close-ups of a cute kid with blond hair. In contrast to Baby Tenderlove, though, "The Kid" is narrated throughout by an adult male voice that exudes confidence and charisma: "Figuring out all new ways to make things work. . . . Finding ways to meet his changing needs in every field from education to medicine. From space to entertainment. This is RCA today." RCA is presented as a company with a future because it is dealing in cutting-edge, modern technologies. The narrator talks about RCA's research and development in computers and other communication systems "to make a better world." But there is also the implication that RCA will doggedly pursue new avenues of research, will remain open to fresh ideas, like an innocent child. That idea is reinforced through the dominant narrative of the montage: a boy successfully ties his shoe, which is the first step on the road to success, as the audience knows when they see the last close-up of a smile on the child's face. Experiencing the child's success touches the heart of every parent, another core audience for this commercial. And if they are touched, maybe they will trust RCA, whose rainbow logo fades in over that final smile.

The Mennen and RCA shorts were not the only commercials Bass produced with children, nor were they the only ones that overtly played with cinematic form. In 1962 Bass produced a black-and-white commercial for Band-Aid that employed optical, step-and-repeat printing to visualize children at play. Listed in the Bass Collection as the "Band-Aid—Pogo Stick" commercial, the thirty-second spot juxtaposes images of children with images of animated Band-Aids.[38] The commercial begins somewhat perversely, as the camera peers through a chain-link fence onto a school playground where children are seen; the fence is real, but the playground is obviously a studio set. Simultaneous zigzag wipes from the left and right obliterate that image, followed by two shots of a girl on swing and a boy on a pogo stick. The action of the children is captured in a stroboscopic effect through the experimental step-and-repeat opticals, seemingly breaking down motion into its constituent parts. Bass had first seen such images as stills in Kepes's *The Language of Vision*, particularly his discussion of the representation of movement.[39] Six years later, Norman McLaren would release his avant-garde masterpiece *Pas de deux*, which used the same step-and-repeat optical printing process to intensify the movements of a ballet. The visual effect on film had its precedent in Marcel Duchamp's Cubist masterpiece *Nude Descending a Staircase No. 2* (1912). The shot of the boy on his pogo stick is captured in a split screen, the other half showing a colorful Band-Aid strip spinning around its own axis. Next, we see a girl jumping rope through the frame and a boy on roller skates; the initial movement of the children is multiplied in countless individual images printed within the same frame. After the second pair of children, Bass inserts a series of shots of Band-Aids with many different patterns and in various sizes, moving in unison. Here, Bass is employing stop-motion animation, as if in an Oskar Fischinger avant-garde film about children playing. Interspersed are different Band Aid boxes, while children speak on the sound track, commenting about how pretty their Band-Aids are. Despite the avant-garde origins of both the step-and-repeat and the stop-motion animation, the two parts of the commercial don't necessarily fit together. One could, however, read the first shot behind the fence as entering into a childhood world of fantasy, with the animated Band-Aids (injury being a fact of life with kids) and the children's play each functioning on different, unconnected levels of fantasy, papering over the fact that Band-Aids are needed in times of crisis and hurt. In contrast to the other commercials discussed, it is interesting that Bass eschews close-ups of body parts to visualize the myriad uses of Band-Aids; instead, he contrasts long shots of wholesome young children engaging in exercise and play with close-ups of Band-Aids. So, in effect, bodies and Band-Aids are the same size onscreen, visually linking activities that might result in scrapes and bruises and their remedy—an interesting experiment that may never have actually appeared on television.

Live-Action Montage

Like Otto Preminger, producer-director Robert Aldrich prized his independence from the major Hollywood studios, and his collaboration with Saul Bass began almost immediately after Aldrich went independent. Bass was responsible for the advertising campaigns for Aldrich's second and third features, *Vera Cruz* (1954) and *Kiss Me Deadly* (1955), both of which were recognized at the time by French critics François Truffaut and Jean-Luc Godard as masterpieces and are still considered among the most important American films of the 1950s. For Aldrich's next film, *The Big Knife* (1956), Bass took over duties for the titles and some trade ads, while apparently leaving the release campaign to others. For Aldrich's fifth independent production, *Attack!* (1956), he hired Bass again to handle the titles and contribute design elements to the ad campaign, although Bass received no screen credit.[40] The film is based on a 1954 Broadway play titled *Fragile Fox*, and United Artists paid Aldrich $22,000 just to change the name to *Attack!*

Although not the first film in the Bass canon to do so, *Attack!* features an extended live-action sequence before the credits that sets the stage for the film's conflict between a World War II platoon leader and his weak and vacillating company commander, whose failure to support the platoon's action has led to the death of some of his men. As a result of this highly dramatic scene, the team of Bass and Aldrich decided to insert the titles over a live-action sequence that does not move the narrative forward, as later Hollywood title sequences would, but does provide a montage of atmospheric shots of soldiers at rest behind the lines after the heat of battle. This was not the first time Bass placed live-action footage behind his titles, but the previous cases (*The Shrike, The Racers, The Big Knife*) had involved single, more or less compositionally static shots, whereas *Attack!*'s titles consist of a montage of twenty-one separate shots in a two-minute sequence. The editing construction bears some analysis for what it accomplishes in terms of producing meaning and for Bass's grasp of film editing, even at this early date. Bass constructed the sequence out of outtakes rather than shooting any footage himself, yet he achieves a striking sense of narrative and compositional unity.[41]

The title sequence, which is in black and white (as is the film), begins with the camera panning as the helmet of a fallen soldier rolls down a hill and comes to rest next to a lone flower. The production company credits appear in a column at the frame's extreme left, with each word on its own line. This highly metaphoric image of death and life alerts the audience (if the precredit sequence hadn't already done so) that this will be an antiwar narrative. As Aldrich formulated it, the film is about "the terribly corrupting influence that war can have on the most normal, average human beings, and the terrible things it makes them capable of that they wouldn't be capable of otherwise."[42] Bass then cuts to a slow zoom on the face of platoon leader Lieutenant Costa, played by Jack Palance, as his above-the-title credit appears at extreme right; Bass then cuts back to the helmet being strafed by machine-gun fire as Eddie Albert's credit appears screen left, alluding to the fact that his character (Captain Cooney) is responsible for the death represented by the helmet. This shot–reverse shot construction continues with another close-up of Costa as he disappears behind a partially destroyed wall, while the film's title appears screen right. Bass then cuts again to the reverse angle, an extreme close-up of the helmet and flower, as Lee Marvin's costarring credit is seen. The shot dissolves to a matched cut from the helmet to a large, round loudspeaker that fills the frame as swing music blares out. The above-title credits therefore complete the precredit sequence, while transitioning to an after-battle scene in which all the other credits roll.

As the title sequence continues, the filmmakers intercut shots of Lieutenant Woodruff (William Smithers) as he walks from right to left through a village with close-ups of soldiers drinking and eating in an open-air mess. However, just as the pretitle action sequence never reveals the face of Captain Cooney (only parts of his body), the soldiers also remain faceless (except for Woodruff, who is one of the only characters to survive). They are depicted by a hand holding a cup, a mess kit resting in a lap, walking boots, or hands warming themselves at a fire, emphasizing the anonymity of war, the soldiers' status as cannon fodder, and the fact that Cooney's predicament is a result of corruption in the system rather than his own individual weakness. Unlike most Hollywood filmmakers, who tended to deflect political criticism of the system by blaming "one bad apple," Aldrich was not one to pull punches when criticizing social inequalities and political inadequacies. Furthermore, Bass's trademark circle motif—the dead soldier's helmet, the loudspeaker (shown three times), and finally a shot through a giant wagon wheel—ties the sequence together but also undergirds the indivisibility of the system (the army) and its parts (soldiers), as the audience hears a disembodied voice emanating from the speaker. The final frame, with Aldrich's producer and director credit, is seen over a bird's-eye view of a military truck in the town square, possibly a visual joke on the director's god-like status.

Bass again visually differentiates the credit designations, which are white, serif, small capital letters, from the names, which are large caps. The layout of the typography is based on a grid, with the major credits fading in above or below the central horizontal axis, sometimes in a long, straight line across the width of the screen. However, there are some uncharacteristic exceptions. As for the opening production company credit, Bass inserts an unjustified column of text in a darkened archway at screen right for cameraman Joseph Biroc, while similarly placing the music and orchestra credit for Frank Devol inside the loudspeaker from which the diegetic music blares. In the first case, the placement seems to be based on legibility, but in the second case, the placement seems at least partially motivated by the image's content. The other secondary technical credits are left-justified; opposite them, Bass places the standard copyright verbiage, which is right-justified, again conforming to the grid. Thus, the overall design of the titles conforms to the Bass style, but he expands his cinematic vocabulary to include the montage of live-action images for narrative continuity.

Bass's first titles in a Cinerama film were for *It's a Mad, Mad, Mad, Mad World*, which was shot in Ultra Panavision 70mm. In that film, he solved the problem of an extremely wide screen, which encompassed peripheral vision, by using the entire screen as a canvas for his animated characters and events, as he had for *Around the World in 80 Days*, shot in Todd-AO. John Frankenheimer's *Grand Prix* (1966) was produced using the slightly less wide Super Panavision 70mm spherical lens process, which had an aspect ratio of 2.21:1.[43] Bass, who had already created the titles for *Exodus*, the second Super Panavision 70mm film ever produced, accommodated the wide screen in *Grand Prix* by creating multi-image montages that split the screen into as many as sixty-four different frames. Thanks to his World's Fair experience in multimedia presentations, Bass was the ideal candidate to explore the formal capabilities of a wide-screen, split-screen technology to undergird the dramatic aims of Franken-heimer's overall narrative. Interestingly, *Grand Prix*'s publicists argued that Bass's split-screen technique allowed viewers to experience past and present simultaneously: "Saul Bass has created an innovation in motion picture main titles for MGM's Cinerama presentation of the John Fran-kenheimer film, *Grand Prix*, with the novel design of special 'triptych' effects for the titles. Effect combines parallel action sequences of film while also permitting simultaneous flash-backs."[44] In fact, Bass was hired in the summer of 1966 not only to create the titles for *Grand Prix* but also to function as a second unit director, designing montages of the major Formula I races that constitute the film's background.[45]

Frankenheimer and producer Edward Lewis first signed a deal with Cinerama and MGM in November 1964, with Lewis John Carlino tapped to write the original story. When the production team announced the same MGM-Cinerama deal almost a year later, Carlino had been jetti-soned in favor of a script by Robert Allen Arthur based on Robert Daley's novel *The Cruel Sport*.[46] Shooting commenced in May 1966, six weeks before Bass was brought in for the action sequences.[47] According to notes in the Bass Papers, Bass actually restaged some of the races: "The racing sequences were shot under the direction of Saul Bass, who subsequently edited several races, and set the editing style for the remainder of these sequences. Under the direction of Mr. Bass, nine cameras were used in a documentary coverage of the actual races at Monte Carlo, Spa, Clermont-Ferrand, Brands Hatch, Zandvoort, and Monza. He then restaged the races using the production company's own fleet of Formula I cars and the actual drivers from the real races."[48] Bass was involved in other technical innovations as well. For example, a special high-speed camera developed for NASA was used to shoot 600,000 feet of negative from inside the For-mula I racing cars, capturing the driver's point of view.[49] Both the speed-ing car shots and the split-screen technology sparked fads in Hollywood, such as the split-screen scenes in Richard Fleischer's *The Boston Strangler* (1968) and Norman Jewison's *The Thomas Crown Affair* (1968), the lat-ter designed by Pablo Ferro, another well-known title designer.

The film premiered on 22 December 1966 at the Hollywood Pacific Cinerama Dome on Sunset Boulevard and became a hit, earning more than $1 million in forty-three weeks at that theater alone. The film cost $8 million to make,[50] and Cinerama, as cofinancier, reportedly earned $5 million of the total $20.8 million gross. Indeed, *Grand Prix* was one of the ten highest-grossing films of the year and won three Oscars for techni-cal achievements. The film and Bass's montages, in particular, received enthusiastic reviews.[51] However, Pauline Kael, who apparently really dis-liked Bass, wrote the following nasty comment: "After the first few min-utes of *Grand Prix* (MGM), my companion leaned over and said, 'Now you know what it's like to be run over.' Saul Bass had got hold of heavy tires and Cinerama: you don't go to this movie, it comes after you. And you're not rid of Bass after the titles, he keeps coming back with mon-tages—little World's Fair–type documentaries, simple-minded and square, that pad out the three hours."[52]

New York Times critic Bosley Crowther also commented on the World's Fair look of the split-screen montages, but much more positively: "Triple and quadruple panels and even screen-filling checkerboards full of appropriate and expressive racing-world images hit the viewer with stimu-lations that optically generate a sort of intoxication with racing."[53] In fact, Frankenheimer had visited the New York World's Fair and seen Charles and Ray Eames's seventeen-screen slide show titled "Think" in the IBM Pavilion. Ironically, as happened so often, Bass's montage work was praised, while Frankenheimer's direction of the actors in the off-track melodrama was derided, a view that persists today.[54]

Bass's titles for *Grand Prix* chronicle the last few minutes before the beginning of the Grand Prix Formula I race in Monaco. They consist of more than 100 shots (including split screens, which count as a single shot) in 4:25 minutes, producing an average shot length of less than three sec-onds. It is an absolutely breathtaking sequence that captures all the excite-ment, noise, and anticipation of one of the world's great auto races. Bass begins the sequence with a dark screen, listing the above-the-title credits for the distributor, James Garner, Eva Marie Saint, Yves Montand, and Toshiro Mifune in very light blue, capital, sans serif letters exactly cen-tered in the wide-screen frame. He then pulls back to reveal that the dark-ness comes from the inside of a tailpipe, its circular form filling center screen and encompassing the film's title. At the moment the tailpipe becomes visible, the film's orchestral music is overpowered by the sound of the engine as the tailpipe image splits into six images. While the follow-ing actors' credits appear center-justified at the horizontal axis, Bass cuts to extreme close-ups of the Formula I tires rolling into place, shots of the crowd, and close-ups of mechanics tightening various bolts (which are again multiplied to thirty-two and sixty-four images in split screen).

Behind the next set of major credits for music, cinematography, and production design, Bass cuts in more shots of the crowd and more technical preparations (e.g., measuring tire pressure), as the incessant revving of engines blows out the sound track. Next we hear the racetrack announcer identifying the drivers who will become the film's protagonists, as Bass intercuts close-up shots of the drivers putting on their helmets, the loudspeakers, and the crowds as the secondary technical credits and the names of real Formula I racers fade in and out, right-justified on the right half of the screen. As a French announcer begins the countdown, Bass swiftly cuts together extreme close-ups of the drivers fixing their gloves; then the track goes silent, except for a heartbeat, as the drivers put on their goggles in slow motion and Bass's credit as "Visual Consultant, Montages and Titles" appears centered onscreen, followed by credits for screenplay, production, and director.[55] Frankenheimer's credit, also centered, brings back the engine noise, followed by a final montage of hands at the wheel, goggles, spectators, stopwatches, the racing official counting down, and smoking tires.

More than any other title sequence designed by Bass, the credits for *Grand Prix* are a technical tour de force, employing rapid editing, split screens, slow-motion photography, multiple exposures, and montages. Overall, the title sequence narrative is broken down into three large sections. The first section (1:38) involves moving the cars into place, making technical preparations, and the drivers getting to their cars. In the second section, the drivers and their backstories are identified by the diegetic announcer, who appears in the first shot of this section (1:47). The final section (1:10) depicts the countdown and the start of the race. Surprisingly, the whole title sequence includes not a single establishing shot or long shot, except for the last image of the cars crossing the start line. Indeed, the title sequence is constructed almost exclusively of close-ups and even extreme close-ups of parts—whether car parts or human body parts such as heads and hands—the montage rhythmically following the beat of revving engines as the hands of a stopwatch tick away. Even the eight shots of the crowd in the sequence are medium shots of heads, so the audience never gets a sense of the scene as a whole. Many of the images are so close that it takes a moment to actually read them. Split screens, which were ostensibly created to present two or more images simultaneously in time, are utilized here to multiply single close-up shots of objects, whether tailpipes, bolts, tire caps, RPM gauges, loudspeakers, or thumbs in the air. The images are thus defamiliarized, functioning as a abstract play of light, movement, and color. Given the extreme width of the Super Panavision screen, the use of close-ups seems counterintuitive. Filmmakers working in such wide-screen formats tended to prefer vistas and extreme long shots that remained onscreen for a significant amount of time, rather than Russian-style montages. However, given Bass's intention to build suspense and interest in the race from the first frame of the film, his method of juxtaposing tightly composed shots of very short duration makes sense, and it worked, because the audience is kept extremely busy reading the rapid progression of moving images. No wonder the drama off the track seemed lifeless.

Bass and Frankenheimer's montages in four of the subsequent five racing sequences are equally impressionistic, attempting not a realistic documentation of real racing events but rather a cinematic construction of a fast and dangerous sport. In each, Bass highlights different aspects of the race. For the Monaco Grand Prix, Bass engages in numerous split-screen experiments, including utilizing only one-third of the wide-screen space and then opening wide to fill the frame. Bass's split screens also show evidence of many spatial and temporal breaks, indicating that he is worried not about continuity in space or time but only about continuity in visual design. With the French Grand Prix, an hour into the film, Bass focuses on shots of the crowd, especially amateur filmmakers and photographers pointing cameras at Bass's camera. This level of self-reflexivity is increased in the race itself, which is presented as a visual symphony. Bass juxtaposes slow-motion images of cars, multiple exposures, and split-screen shots dissolving into other split screens, accompanied by symphonic music rather than the roar of engines. The Belgian Grand Prix sequence, in contrast, features moving camera shots tracking the cars or subjective shots from inside the cars. When the camera is very low on the ground, the speed of the vehicles is accentuated, making this sequence all about the race from the driver's point of view. Finally, the Dutch Grand Prix sequences utilize the split-screen technique to create frames of varying sizes while depicting different spaces and persons, whether competing drivers or their cars' owners. Thus, Bass's montages of the various races are less about furthering the film's overall narrative or realistically portraying an actual race than about creating highly impressionistic, cinematic vignettes of the sport of Formula I racing.

If *Grand Prix*'s titles are all about breaking down a big event like an international automobile race into its constituent parts, then *Mr. Saturday Night* returns us to a microcosm of the family home. Starring and cowritten and directed by Billy Crystal, *Mr. Saturday Night* is a fictional biopic of an over-the-hill entertainer who is now reduced to performing at Jewish retirement homes in the Catskills. Crystal first developed his Buddy Young Jr. character—a typical borscht-belt comedian in the mold of Alan King or Milton Berle (known as "Mr. Television")—on *Saturday Night Live*. Buddy Young's fatal flaw is that he can tell jokes as fast as anyone, but he doesn't listen to his audience, insulting them with a kind of brash ethnic chutzpah that was common among stand-up comics in the 1990s, when the film was made, but would have alienated 1950s audiences who were used to white-bread television comedy. Buddy is also an ambitious bastard who uses people—most of all, his long-suffering brother. For the titles, Bass again focuses on parts rather than wholes, cutting together close-up shots of a Jewish mother's hands preparing a holiday meal (Elaine Bass played the role, but only her hands are seen) and the empty dishes remaining after the meal, accompanied by Buddy Young's nonstop patter on the soundtrack. His often fecal humor is a subject from the first image, and this is the most word-heavy title sequence Bass ever created.

Earning less than $14 million at the domestic box office, *Mr. Saturday Night* was a flop, despite mildly good reviews.[56] As one trade industry analyst noted, "Audiences simply weren't interested in a film that was mostly about a testy, cantankerous old man—even if he was played by Billy Crystal."[57] David Paymer was nominated for a Best Supporting Actor Oscar in 1992 for his portrayal of Buddy's brother, Stan, but by then, the film had died commercially. Interestingly, several critics began their reviews by praising the titles as a way of pointing out what was wrong with the film. Reaching back to their own childhoods in the 1930s, Elaine and Saul Bass re-create a Jewish High Holiday feast heavy on sentimentality. Marilyn Moss describes it most directly in *Box Office*: "The camera trolls lovingly over a feast of rich Jewish food: chicken filled with stuffing, fatty brisket, potatoes swimming in gravy and stuffed kishke. It all adds up to schmaltz, a perfect metaphor for this film by first time director Crystal."[58] The *Wall Street Journal* is just as blunt: "It's all there—Mom, matzo balls and lots of schmalz, the chicken fat that gives traditional Jewish cuisine its particular pungency—and it's [*sic*] heaviness. The title sequence—brilliantly designed by Saul and Elaine Bass—makes exactly this point. The humor, like the food, is delicious and satisfying, and always, no matter what's being served, loaded with schmalz."[59] The *New Yorker* likewise mentions "platter after platter of fatty food."[60]

Even before the first image, as the production company credits, centered in white letters above the horizontal axis on a dark screen, fade in and out, Billy Crystal as Buddy Young is heard offscreen—"My mother was trying to kill us . . . "—followed by a close-up of a cannonball of matzo dough plopping onto a wooden kitchen table. The line immediately gets one's attention and is followed by the punch line: ". . . with fat," accompanied by Klezmer music and the young interviewer laughing at Buddy's jokes. Over the next two minutes, Bass edits together twenty-two shots of a pair of fleshy, middle-aged female hands preparing matzo soup; cutting onions and tomatoes; stuffing sausages, chickens, and cabbage; cutting and salting brisket; grinding chopped liver; mashing potatoes with fat; frying latkes; and then serving meat, challah, soup, smoked fish, stuffed cabbage, noodles, potatoes, apples, and tea.[61] Billy Crystal's above-the-title credit, the title, and the credits for Paymer and costar Julie Warner appear centered on the horizontal axis in capital letters, with the first letter one size larger, over the first and second images of the mother making matzo. Since the title sequence is essentially a flashback to the 1930s, Bass chooses an old-school serif type. The subsequent acting credits as well as the major behind-the-camera credits fade in and out well below the horizontal axis, alternating between screen left and right. "Title Sequence Saul & Elaine Bass" appears over the image of the meat grinder oozing out chopped liver. The final thirty-five seconds is a continuous close-up tracking shot moving from left to right (with two "invisible" dissolves) past dinner plates with food remnants, ending on an image of a still smoking cigar butt in an ashtray, as the producer, writer, and director credits roll and the comedian discusses his after-dinner performances for his family.

The title sequence is therefore all about a shared Jewish identity. Just as the mother's hands prepare foods that are associated with eastern European Jewish kitchens, Buddy Young gabs and jokes about his family's roots in Russia, where "they had no food." No topic is too bad or too disgusting for the comedian, who turns his father's premature death into a joke and lists the bodily functions of certain relatives. The images, meanwhile, have their own zaftig quality, sometimes gross (stuffing a chicken) and sometimes almost sexual (stuffing sausages). The fact that Bass chooses to show only the mother's hands and the objects she touches again exemplifies the designer's *pars pro toto* aesthetic. Here, close-ups of ethnic noshes function as a metaphor for Jewish family life and culture. However, the mother's lack of individuality also allows her to become a universal image of the Jewish mother and underlines how the comedian's nonstop monologue objectifies his family and keeps the attention on his own giant ego, just as the film demonstrates how Buddy Young destroys his relationships with his brother, wife, and daughter.[62] Furthermore, the long track down the empty table, revealing the perfect skeletal remains of a fish, communicates a sense of emptiness and loss, contrasting with the comedian's narrative of his rise to fame from a Brooklyn dinner table to CBS television in 1956. It is a sequence that contrasts nostalgia and aggressive humor, the warm colors of the family meal onscreen and the abrasive narrative of the comedian offscreen. Finally, we see here Bass's utilization of two kinds of montage: editing close-up details from shot to shot to depict the chronological preparation and serving of the holiday meal, and the internal montage as the camera glides past the culinary ruins on the table. Such lateral tracks appear fairly infrequently in the Bass canon, but they are central to the design of his titles for *West Side Story*, *Alcoa Premiere*, and, much later, *War of the Roses*, as well as this latter portion of *Mr. Saturday Night*. Since Saul preferred montage, it seems likely that Elaine was responsible for the long tracking shot, just as she may have been involved in the *War of the Roses* titles.

The Solar Film

Sergei Eisenstein and Vsevolod Pudovkin both theorized that editing— that is, montage, or the physical joining together of shots—is the very essence of film art, an aesthetic position they developed from the work of their teacher, Lev Kuleshov. Pudovkin put it most succinctly: "The work of the director is characterized by thinking in filmic pictures; by imagining events in that form in which, composed of pieces joined together in a certain sequence, they will appear upon the screen."[63] Saul Bass's own films— that is, those he directed—are all the product of an intense editing process; they are usually constructed out of heterogeneous visual material that Bass and his editors have given shape through editing. To put it more directly, Bass, like Eisenstein and Pudovkin, constructed meaning through the montage of mostly short shots. In fact, Bass almost never included long takes in his nonfiction films, and even *Phase IV* and *Quest* are highly edited works. Indeed, the only film in the Bass Collection that has long scenes with a continuously running video or film camera—other than *Bass on Titles*, which has extensive talking-head footage of Bass himself—is *The Party* (1975), which in all probability was not directed by Bass. This fifteen-minute film was sponsored by Westinghouse and consists of many historical personages from the company's ninety-year existence mingling at a cocktail party. *The Party* was produced by Bass, but the small budget probably caused him to delegate the work.[64]

Beginning with *The Searching Eye*, Bass constructs his narratives, his intellectual threads, by treating images almost like words, developing segments around visual themes and then building up individual segments into larger montages of images and ideas. Bass preferred montage over mise-en-scène, to use André Bazin's theoretical dichotomy between filmic styles, because, as a designer, he was more comfortable composing two-dimensional images than constructing long sequences composed in a three-dimensional space. Utilizing long takes, which are dependent on moving actors or information in and out of a space or moving the camera through a given physical space, requires both a different kind of spatial thinking and a different composition than Bass was accustomed to as a designer of print media and even film titles, which tend to be graphic and flat. The exceptions to this rule are the animated sequences in Bass's films and titles, which create the illusion of moving through space and/or time without cuts. However, even in these cases, it can be argued that, conceptually, a process of montage is at work to communicate complex historical relations.

The Solar Film certainly conforms to the Bass style in terms of its editing structure, overarching narrative, inclusion of the obligatory animation sequence, and relationship to its intellectual content. As noted earlier, Bass preferred film projects funded by sponsors that were more interested in advocacy or image building than in selling a specific product. Neither *From Here to There* nor *The Searching Eye* overtly references products sold by the commercial financiers, United Airlines and Eastman Kodak, respectively; rather, they create consumer interest in activities associated with these companies. As a result, Bass's short documentaries are highly episodic meditations on particular issues, engaging the viewer in an active process of thinking about the subject at hand. Bass's rhetorical methodology concentrates on editing together individual images around a specific theme or concept, then building up larger sequences to construct a narrative.

Saul Bass's involvement in *The Solar Film* project likely began in December 1977, after he was approached directly by Robert Redford. However, Redford did not announce that Bass had been hired until September 1978, probably after Bass's first script had been approved.[65] Redford's participation came about through Consumer Action Now, an environmental advocacy group founded in 1970 by his then-wife Lola Redford and Ilene Goldman to disseminate useful information to consumers on environmental issues.[66] The earliest film script, dated November 1976, carried the working title "Caging the Sun." That script, which Redford himself had a hand in writing, focused exclusively on documenting new solar-powered communities, with a nod to ancient versions such as Montezuma's Castle in Arizona and Stonehenge (the only images to survive in Bass's version).[67] Redford's production company, Wildwood Enterprises, produced the film with fifty-fifty financing from philanthropist Norton Simon and Warner Communications, once they had a workable script from Bass. Simon, who owned Hunt-Wesson Foods, Avis, and Canada Dry, among other companies, also funded the Norton Simon Art Museum in Pasadena. The documentary had an approved budget of $317,699 plus a 10 percent contingency fee; this did not include Bass's $50,000 fee as coproducer and director or $35,000 in preproduction costs, which included his $10,000 script honorarium.[68] Warner Communications, which had just financed Bass's *Windows* (aka *Notes on the Popular Arts*), also distributed the film theatrically when the National Association of Theater Owners agreed to screen the short film with Redford's feature *The Electric Horseman* (1979, Sydney Pollack).[69] The film was in production from 24 May to 3 September; editing took place in October, followed by postproduction sound work. Approximately 20 percent of the film's seventy-one shots or scenes consisted of stock shots.[70]

The Solar Film premiered at the John F. Kennedy Center in Washington on 17 March 1980 and was subsequently screened in 8,000 theaters across the country—quite an accomplishment, given that shorts had all but disappeared from theatrical screens more than a decade before.[71] For Redford, it was important to get the film out to audiences who would not normally have access to it: "Most of the time, movies like this go on PBS and speak to a group that already understands the situation. Or it is seen only by those in the energy trade."[72] The premiere was a star-studded affair and garnered significant press attention, largely because of Redford's personal participation. It was subsequently nominated for an Oscar in the live-action short film category, even before its official premiere, and it won several prizes at film festivals.[73] More surprising, *The Solar Film* was actually reviewed in the press. The *Los Angeles Times* commented: "There are inspired moments, others not so inspired."[74] Charles Champlin, also writing in the *Los Angeles Times*, liked the film: "Never was so much urgent information communicated so painlessly, and the encouraging last note is that progress is being made."[75] Another critic reviewing Academy Award–nominated shorts took issue with the film: "Bass, who has made his reputation filming dazzling opening credit sequences for feature films, has assembled a hodge-podge of solar commercials, animation and dramatic footage into a 12 minute film that confuses more than it elucidates."[76] Stanley Mason in *Graphis* described *The Solar Film* as "full to the brim with stirring and fascinating images."[77]

Bass was supposed to earn 30 percent of the net profits, but unfortunately, the film actually lost money for Bass/Yager.[78] Apparently, Norton Simon was disappointed that Warner Brothers had done so little to promote the film.[79] Days after the premiere, Sheldon Renan from Pyramid Films offered to distribute the film nontheatrically, and Pyramid promoted the film tirelessly in the summer of 1980, even though it was still in theatrical distribution.[80] Strangely, Pyramid eventually agreed to let Warner Brothers distribute to the educational market. In a letter to Pyramid, Michael Britton wrote: "You have authorized him to arrange for distribution of *The Solar Film* to colleges and schools. We agree with you that the idea is now to have the film seen by as many people as possible."[81]

Given his own personal obsession with images of the sun and his growing interest in environmental issues, Bass naturally gravitated to the subject matter offered by Redford. But Bass also had his doubts about a film on solar energy; he was not convinced that the technology was viable. According to a statement by Bass in the film's official press release: "Elaine and I did a crash course to find out for ourselves and as we went along, an interesting thing happened. We began to feel that solar advocacy was not only valid but important. It added a level of determination, because we realized how significant it was to really help people understand more about the subject. It seemed clear to us that a well made film could counteract misinformation. What we learned is that the conventional wisdom—that solar is distant and at best its contribution to our energy needs would be minimal, is simply not true." Once he was convinced, Bass sought to produce a film that would avoid "a dreary finger pointing approach," common to many advocacy and propaganda films, and instead "encourage people to think more and more about the subject."[82]

The original theatrical release was called *The Solar Film*, but the subsequent nontheatrical release in 16mm was advertised in all publicity as *A Short Film about Solar Energy*. There are two apparent differences between the films: First, the original release was eleven minutes long and included a "talk show" scene; this scene was excised from the more tightly edited nine-minute version distributed by Pyramid Films. Second, *The Solar Film* credits Saul Bass as director, while the later version adds Elaine to the credits: "Directed by Elaine & Saul Bass."[83] This was Elaine's first joint directorial credit with her husband on any project. Apparently, there were major differences of opinion between the Basses on the film's edit. According to Jeff Okun, Elaine changed the whole central section of the film while Bass was in Japan working on another project. When Bass returned, Okun showed him the new concept, even though Elaine had given strict instructions not to do so unless she was there to frame it. The next day, Bass looked at the footage as if he had never seen it. He then made some small changes over several weeks to get it back to the way he wanted it.[84]

According to the production notes for *The Solar Film*, it was divided into three parts of approximately equal length. The first part visualizes the formation and creation of the earth, as well as primitive man's relationship to the burning orb in the sky, whether characterized by fear, awe, or insanity. The second part, an animated section produced by Art Goodman and Herb Klynn, chronicles the Industrial Revolution, theorizing that it was the result of finding and exploiting new energy sources such as coal, oil, and natural gas. The third part suggests that the limitless energy of the sun might be a more sustainable source of energy than coal or oil to meet future electric power needs. Thus, while the first and last live-action sections mirror each other, both in their visual style and in their focus on essentially utopian visions of man's relationship to the sun, the middle animated section introduces a highly dystopian view of human civilization's relationship to the earth.[85]

The first shot in *The Solar Film* is a signature Bass image: the earth's curvature cuts through the center of the fame, starting slightly below the horizontal axis at the left and ending slightly above it at the right, as the sun appears as a point of light that grows until the flare fills the frame. Off-screen, a narrator states: "The sun rose on a barren earth, where vast and profound changes occurred." Bass then cuts to rainstorms, shots of microscopic organisms in the sea beginning the evolutionary process, followed by a montage of leaves and plants. Bass thus opens the film with a montage that suggests the earth's creation myth as postulated by Darwin, a sequence he had previously developed in almost identical form in *The Searching Eye*. The next segment cuts together images of Neanderthal man (an actor, shot from an extremely low angle, framed against the sky), followed by shots of Stonehenge, the Egyptian pyramids, and the Navajo cliff dwelling called Montezuma's Castle, as examples of how our ancestors reacted architecturally to the power of the sun. The section ends with a close-up image of a human hand and a compass drawing the solar system on graph paper, which forms a bridge to the subsequent animated sequence. Bass thus achieves a narrative arc from the dawn of time to a Copernican view of the universe.

A close-up of a barefoot human walking through the forest dissolves to a shot underground and then to the three-minute animation sequence, during which the camera moves toward a distant horizon at the top of the frame, where the sun is rising. A farmer picks up a piece of coal he has dug from the ground and notes that the stuff burns very well, followed by hundreds of identical miners throwing the same piece of coal into the air.[86] As the camera tracks forward, the miners are replaced by coal towers that morph into factories surrounded by houses, and cars and trucks drive on the roads between the factories. One road stretching to the horizon dissolves into railroad tracks, as trains fill the horizon. Next, the camera swoops down on another man who is digging and strikes oil; oil derricks sprout over the landscape, turning into endless oil refineries. The camera then tracks an oil pipeline through an agricultural landscape and into a city, where the pipeline is transformed into a congested highway and cars suck gas from the pipeline. "Remember the good old days, when we could just go driving?" the narrator asks, as Bass visualizes the inflation of fuel prices with a shrinking dollar bill as a magic carpet; its passengers parachute into a gridlocked city intersection, where other humans converge and fill the screen.

The Solar Film then cuts to a "live" television talk show titled *Answers to the Energy Problem*, where a panel of experts that includes politicians, environmentalists, and academics is formally introduced. The so-called experts then look around in embarrassed silence, until the moderator cuts to a commercial break. The joke falls a bit flat, which may be why Bass cut the sequence from the nontheatrical version. The final segment begins with shots of humans enjoying and making use of the sun (to dry laundry, to make adobe bricks), accompanied by the sound of Mike Oldfield's "Tubular Bells," a popular rock instrumental at the time. Next, Saul Bass himself speaks on the track: "One thing I really like about solar energy is that it is really clean, and that we are not at the mercy of those foreign oil producers." He then constructs another montage of solar panels on roofs and the lightbulbs they illuminate, followed by industrial-level solar-panel energy farms. The final image of a toddler in diapers walking toward the setting (or rising) red sun was also used for the film's poster, adding to its symbolic weight. A roll text appears over the image of the baby:

> The sun gave us a world.
> It stands ready to give us a future.
> Everyone agrees: Solar energy is good.
> The problem is, it waits last in line
> To receive research and development money.
> If we put some economic muscle behind it now,
> Solar energy could make a major
> Contribution to our energy needs by 1985.
> What are we waiting for?[87]

The three-part segmentation of *The Solar Film* thus develops the following argument: The sun has always been a life-giving force on earth, providing the energy to create life itself. When those same life-forms died, they became the basis for fossil fuels, which created modern civilization but also contributed to the chaos of unchecked urban development. In the future, if civilization is to survive, it will have to find more efficient and cleaner sources of energy, like solar power. However, solar energy research is massively underfunded at present, and increasing research and development of solar energy sources could have a major effect on the world's environment within five years.

Needless to say, thirty-some years later, the film's utopian vision is only slightly more real than it was in 1980. Interestingly, unlike today's solar power advocates, who contrast the finiteness of fossil fuels to the limitlessness of solar energy, Bass's argument in *The Solar Film* is based on economics: the United States is dependent on foreign oil producers, who can charge whatever price they wish. In Goodman's animated sequence, there seems to be a sleight of hand, because urban gridlock is presented as an outcome of unchecked fossil fuel consumption rather than faulty urban planning. Neither the finite supply of fossil fuels nor their carbon waste is addressed. According to Bass, "The understanding with the production company was that it should not be critical of other energy sources but should take a positive, even joyous approach to the use of solar energy."[88]

The argument for the cleanliness of solar energy is made visually, through the final montage, rather than verbally. Just as the first segment's live-action montage is constructed of a limited but carefully composed set of images, the final segment is a deliberately composed montage in which not a single image is superfluous and each one makes an intellectual point. At the same time, the live-action images in the first and third sections are composed abstractly, as if they were images in an art film rather than a documentary. Thus, in the first and third sections, Bass repeatedly returns to compositions that privilege circles, whether the sun itself or solar panels arranged in circular designs. This communicates that whereas the earth's evolution in the first section is a natural progression of life, and the development of solar energy in the third section is in harmony with nature, the intervening second section chronicles developments that destroy nature (no circular forms). For example, the film's opening shot of the sun rising above the earth's curved surface has an almost mirror image in the final sequence: the sun rises above a hilltop, its light (energy) falling on a grove of ripening peaches, indicating the constancy and consistency of the sun's power to give life. The sun is ever present in the lives of humanity, even when civilization is focused elsewhere (on fossil fuels). The animated sequence depicts travel through space and time toward a horizon—forward movement toward the future, the sun, and a more sustainable environment. This is mirrored in the final image of the toddler waddling toward that same horizon, signifying that the solar energy industry is in its infancy and is taking baby steps toward the future. Like a human child, the solar energy industry needs to be nurtured and protected if it is to grow and mature into an entity that will be productive for civilization as a whole.

In conclusion, Saul Bass's repeated use of images of body parts, particularly hands, originated first in his aesthetic strategy of *pars pro toto*. He was always looking for efficient ways to encapsulate ideas and processes in a single metaphoric image. Moving from graphic designs consisting of single images, advertisements, or posters to moving-image sequences and complete film works, Bass intuitively gravitated toward montage as a method of constructing image sequences that could communicate complex human and environmental processes. Like the Russian Constructivists, Bass saw the film frame not as a window into an unlimited space beyond the frame but as a discreet graphic unit that could communicate information through both the composition of a single shot and, more importantly, the juxtaposition of images in montage sequences. As the European modernists of the 1920s, including Bauhaus theorists, realized, fragmenting views into multiple perspectives was particularly conducive to visualizing the urban environment. And Bass, as a child of New York City, had a particular affinity for depicting urban spaces, as examined in the next chapter, even if his move to California resulted in a gradual shift in his emotional attachment toward natural landscapes, as documented in his last nonfiction film, *The Solar Film*.

Art Goodman drawing of Bass with his Oscar. (Courtesy of James Hollander)

Dexter season 8 posters, designed by Ty Mattson. (Courtesy of Ty Mattson)

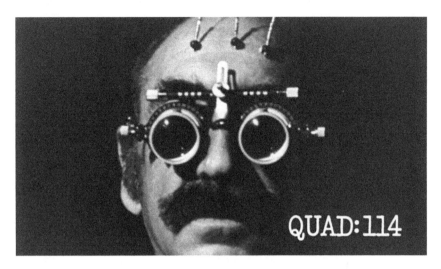

Saul Bass in *Phase IV*, original ending. (Courtesy of Paramount Pictures)

Paul Klee's *Flora in the Sand* (1927). (© 2013 Artists Rights Society [ARS], New York)

Poster for *One, Two, Three* (1961). (Courtesy of MGM Media Licensing)

Cover of Gyorgy Kepes's *The Language of Vision*. (Courtesy of Gyorgy Kepes estate)

Laszlo Moholy-Nagy's *Vision in Motion* (1947).
(© 2013 Artists Rights Society [ARS], New York/
VG Bild-Kunst, Bonn)

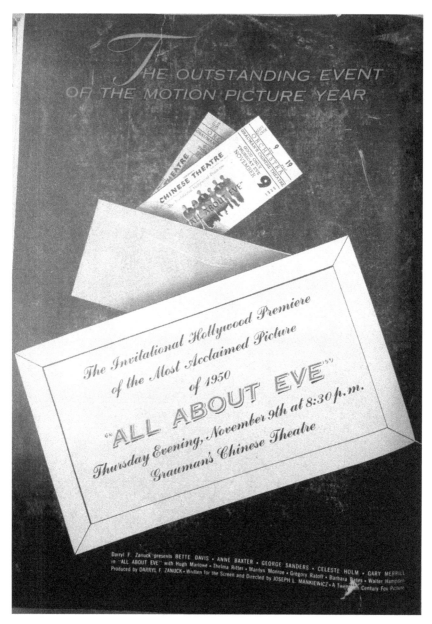

Trade advertisement for *All About Eve* (1950).

Trade advertisement for *Hard, Fast, and Beautiful* (1951).

Trade advertisement for *The Big Country* (1958).

Titles for *Advise and Consent* (1962). (Courtesy of Mrs. Victoria Preminger)

Titles for *Psycho* (1960). (Courtesy of Universal Studios)

Titles for *Higher Learning* (1995). (© 1995 Columbia Pictures Industries, Inc. All Rights Reserved. Courtesy of Sony Pictures Post Production Services, Inc.)

Titles for *The Pride and the Passion* (1957). (Courtesy of MGM Media Licensing)

Titles for *Around the World in 80 Days* (1956). (Licensed by: Warner Bros. Entertainment Inc. All Rights Reserved)

Titles for *It's a Mad, Mad, Mad, Mad World* (1963). (Courtesy of MGM Media Licensing)

Poster for *The Man with the Golden Arm* (1955). (Courtesy of Mrs. Victoria Preminger)

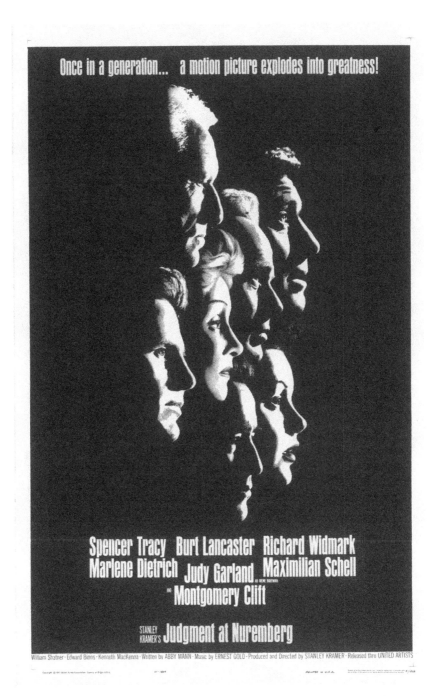

Poster for *Judgment at Nuremberg* (1961). (Courtesy of MGM Media Licensing)

Trade advertisement for *The Shrike* (1955).

Poster for *Anatomy of a Murder* (1959). (*Anatomy of a Murder* © 1959, renewed 1987 Otto Preminger Films, Ltd. All Rights Reserved. Courtesy of Columbia Pictures)

Mark Rothko, *Orange and Yellow* (1956), oil on canvas. (© 1998 Kate Rothko Prizel and Christopher Rothko/ Artists Rights Society [ARS], New York)

Poster for *Saint Joan* (1957). (Courtesy of Mrs. Victoria Preminger)

Title tests for *Porgy and Bess* (1959).

film editors FERRIS WEBSTER · DAVID NEWHOUSE

Titles for *Seconds* (1966). (Courtesy of Paramount Pictures Corporation)

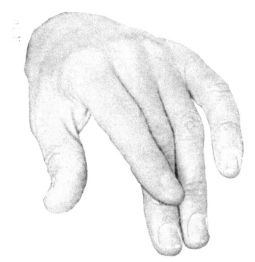

junge menschen
kommt ans bauhaus!

Advertisement for *Junge Menschen kommt ans Bauhaus* (1929). (© 2014 Artists Rights Society [ARS], New York / VG Bild-Kunst, Bonn)

Titles for *Anatomy of a Murder* (1959). (*Anatomy of a Murder* © 1959, renewed 1987 Otto Preminger Films, Ltd. All Rights Reserved. Courtesy of Columbia Pictures)

Titles for *Spartacus* (1960). (Courtesy of Universal Studios)

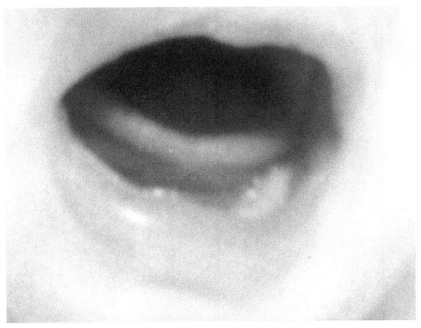

Television commercial for Mennen baby oil (1962).

Band-Aid commercial (1962).

Titles for *North by Northwest* (1959). (Licensed by: Warner Bros. Entertainment Inc. All Rights Reserved)

Titles for *Alcoa Premiere* (1961).

Opening sequence for *West Side Story* (1961). (Courtesy of MGM Media Licensing)

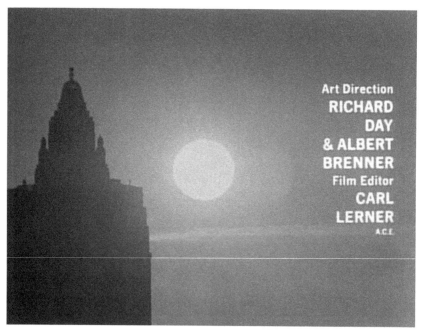

Titles for *Something Wild* (1961). (Courtesy of Jack Garfein)

Titles for *PM East/PM West* (1961–1962).

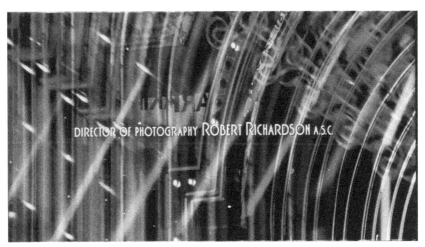

Titles for *Casino* (1995). (Courtesy of Universal Studios)

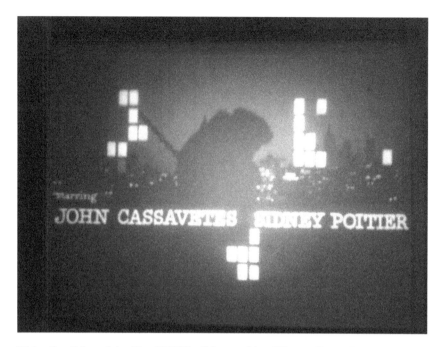

Titles for *Edge of the City* (1957). (Licensed by: Warner Bros. Entertainment Inc. All Rights Reserved)

Poster for *Edge of the City* (1957). (Licensed by: Warner Bros. Entertainment Inc. All Rights Reserved)

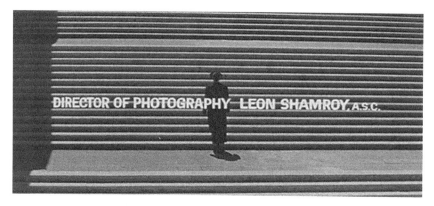

Titles for *The Cardinal* (1963). (Courtesy of Mrs. Victoria Preminger)

Titles for *Walk on the Wild Side* (1962). (*Walk on the Wild Side* © 1962, renewed 1990 Columbia Pictures Industries, Inc. All Rights Reserved. Courtesy of Columbia Pictures)

Photograph from Moholy-Nagy's *Vision in Motion*. (© 2013 Artists Rights Society [ARS], New York/VG Bild-Kunst, Bonn)

The Chronicle.

CHICAGO, FRIDAY MORNING, MARCH 25, 1872.

FOR SALE

DICK YORK   VICTOR MANUEL MENDOZA   RICHARD JAECKEL
KING DONOVAN   VAUGHN TAYLOR   DONALD RANDOLPH
JAMES WESTERFIELD   EUGENE IGLESIAS   FRANK de KOVA

Appleby & Matlack

Five Dollars Reward

An Affortment in his ufual Way,

Almonds.

FIGS.

Titles for *Cowboy* (1958). (*Cowboy* © 1958, renewed 1986 Columbia Pictures Industries, Inc. All Rights Reserved. Courtesy of Columbia Pictures)

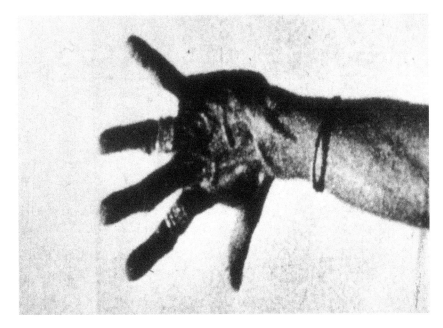

Unpublished montage for *The Four Horsemen of the Apocalypse* (1962).

Titles for *The Victors* (1963). (*The Victors* © 1963, renewed 1991 Columbia Pictures Industries, Inc. All Rights Reserved. Courtesy of Columbia Pictures)

Apples and Oranges (1962), animated CBS public relations film.

Still photograph from *Phase IV* (1974). (Courtesy of Paramount Pictures Corporation)

5

The Urban Landscape

Saul Bass lived in New York City until 1946, when he was twenty-six years old. At the time, it was still the most modern urban environment in the world. Indeed, going back to the turn of the twentieth century, European and American modernists considered New York the modern city par excellence. Walt Whitman sang its praises in his poem "Mannahatta," first published in the 1860 edition of *The Leaves of Grass*: "High growths of iron, slender, strong, splendidly uprising toward clear skies." Paul Strand, Alfred Stieglitz, and Alvin Langdon Coburn captured not only the explosion of skyscrapers before World War I but also how the new urban topography changed perceptions of the world in their photographs "Wall Street" (1910), "Two Towers" (1913), and "The Octopus" (1912), respectively. Visiting New York for the first time in September 1915, Marcel Duchamp exclaimed, "New York is a work of art, a complete work of art."[1] Between the world wars, Bernice Abbott's series of New York photographs, such as "Untitled (New York City)" (1929), and Charles C. Ebetts's iconic "Lunch atop a Skyscraper" (1932) continued to document the new vision of the urban landscape. Paul Strand and Charles Sheeler's *Manhatta* (1921), an avant-garde film portrait of the city, defined the city film genre forever after, privileging the extreme high and low angles of vision that the vertical thrust of modern architecture forces on the urban flaneur.[2] Russian Constructivist painter Kazimir Malevich's 1924 photomontage, *Architekton in Front of a Skyscraper (Suprematist Transformation of New York)*, mixed painting and a photographic image of Lower Manhattan's skyscrapers to privilege the extreme vertical and horizontal grids that are part and parcel of the urban landscape.

New York, especially at night, offered European modernists a phantasmagoric vision of the urban landscape. When Sergei Eisenstein first visited New York in 1931, he exclaimed: "All sense of perspective and of realistic depth is washed away by a nocturnal sea of electric advertising. Far and near, small (in the *foreground*) and large (in the *background*), soaring aloft and dying away, racing and circling, bursting and vanishing—these lights tend to abolish all sense of real space, finally melting into a single plane of colored light points and neon lines moving over a surface of black velvet sky."[3] Gyorgy Kepes, too, discovered the unique visual experience that artificial light affords an urban environment: "Buildings that were modeled under the sun into a clear sculptural form, under the simultaneously acting artificial light-sources lose their three-dimensional quality. Contours are obscured. The light spots, coming from inside and outside simultaneously, and the fusion of luminosity and chiaroscuro, break up the solid form as a unit of space."[4] Modernist artists thus picked up on two ways in which the perception of space changes in an urban environment: skyscrapers obliterate the horizon, making extreme angle views up, down, or through buildings necessary; and electric illumination at night flattens space to create purely abstract forms.

Not surprisingly, cityscapes became a major inspiration for the work of Saul Bass, yet his depictions of urbanity seem reductionist. In particular, Bass repeatedly favors two visual tropes to signify urban landscapes. On the one hand, the grid structure in his design work mirrors the perpendicular lines of urban architecture in the twentieth century, just as his visualization of cities privileges vertical-horizontal movement. On the other hand, Bass seems to be fascinated by urban nightscapes, with their perpendicular arrangement of spots of light reducing a city's architecture to light spectacles, as seen on Broadway theater marquees. This reduction of the urban landscape to visual clichés seems inexplicable, given Bass's upbringing in the New York megalopolis. One explanation may be that Bass was never very fond of New York, given his personal associations with the city: his parents' unassimilated, Yiddish-speaking home; the family's poverty after the death of his father; the years of toiling in the movie advertising business at the bottom of the totem pole. Unlike most New Yorkers who go to Hollywood seeking fame and fortune and then flee back to the city as soon as they can—Woody Allen's pro–New York/anti-Hollywood attitude being typical—Bass seemingly loved the open, natural environment of Los Angeles and eventually morphed into a cowboy hat–wearing westerner.[5] As early as 1954, a journalist wrote: "The Basses . . . show no signs of homesickness for the East."[6] As a result, there are few documented statements about the designer's New York experience, other than that he loved to visit art museums and lived "on the other side of the tracks."[7]

Cityscapes

Saul Bass employed a variety of strategies to depict the urban landscape in his title sequences, moving from the pure modernist art abstraction of *Seven Year Itch* (1955) and the indexical abstraction of *Four Just Men* (1959) to the live-action geometric designs of *North by Northwest* (1959), *Something Wild* (1961), and *Alcoa Premiere* (1961), the visual chaos of big-city graffiti in *West Side Story* (1961), and the flashing lights of his two Las Vegas movies, *Ocean's Eleven* (1960) and *Casino* (1995). Interestingly, although the degree of abstraction shifts from one title sequence to the next, all demonstrate some level of formalist design, especially in terms of their visual composition and editing.

Bass's titles for *The Seven Year Itch* are the most nonrepresentational of his career. They reference modernist painting directly, as does his poster for *Anatomy of a Murder*, but they also spoof abstract painting as it had developed since the turn of the twentieth century. Given that this was only Bass's third title sequence, the credits for *The Seven Year Itch* are both astonishingly original and self-assured. The play of the same name, written by George Axelrod, was the biggest comedy hit of the 1952–1953 season. Metro-Goldwyn-Mayer wanted to purchase the screen rights as a vehicle for June Allyson and Van Johnson,[8] but instead they were purchased for $225,000 by Charles K. Feldman, a former agent turned independent film producer. A year later, Feldman announced that he had signed a joint production deal with 20th Century–Fox and that Billy Wilder would coproduce and direct the film version.[9] The titles were contracted out to National Screen Service, Hollywood's biggest producer of posters and a major contractor for screen titles; NSS apparently hired Bass to create the titles for the film, perhaps at Wilder's behest. NSS, however, was more than willing to take credit for the titles after numerous reviewers commented favorably on them; the company even purchased advertisements in the trades to crow its achievement.[10] Until that time, reviewers commenting specifically about film titles was unheard of, but it would happen again and again when Bass was behind the product.

As would happen repeatedly, Bass's titles were praised, but the film itself received mixed reviews, mostly because critics were disappointed that Axelrod's biting sex comedy had been watered down owing to the Motion Picture Production Code and the Catholic Legion of Decency.[11] Indeed, as a play, *The Seven Year Itch* was a frank, funny, adult meditation on marital infidelity, whereas the film was about only the *desire* to commit adultery; following through would have required punishing the adulterer, at least as far as Joseph Breen and the MPPC Office were concerned, which would hardly be compatible with a comedy. Nevertheless, the film became the fourth highest grossing of 1955, earning $7.8 million. Although Bass received screen credit for the titles, neither the studio press materials nor reviewers mentioned his name. The one exception was *Variety*, which wrote: "Saul Bass' main title, a series of hinged and perambulatory patches on a multi-colored field attracted audience comment at the Broadway preview Wednesday at Loew's State. Remarked one lady: 'Credits arranged this way are very interesting—and you don't have to read them.' Which is the sort of crack which gives New Yorkers a bad name in Hollywood where screen credits come first before the wife and the trust fund."[12]

Jack Moffitt in the *Hollywood Reporter* also commented on Wilder's many production innovations, including the "novel and amusing" title cards, while *Showman's Trade Review* concluded: "The picture deserves at least a variant of an Academy Award for its extremely effective head title." Finally, in keeping with Bass's often-stated intentions, *Motion Picture Daily* commented that the boxed credits set the tone for the picture.[13] Bass himself witnessed audience reaction to the titles at Loew's State in New York: "As the main title appeared there was a sudden buzz of excitement, murmurs of approval while everyone sat up in their seats awaiting the opening shots. It was a very special experience."[14]

Bass's titles begin with a black Cinemascope screen in which an orange vertical rectangle appears, which is then attached to a yellow horizontal rectangle. On the sound track, the audience hears orchestral music with plenty of horns, which is immediately recognizable as connoting the hustle and bustle of the big city. As the music continues, the film frame is filled with twenty-one adjoining boxes in various sizes and shades from almost white to pink to dark reddish brown. As the last rectangle moves around the frame, it falls into place in the last remaining black space, only to open again to reveal elaborate white, handcrafted serif type on a black background, spelling out Charles K. Feldman's above-the-title producer credit. After the "door" closes again, three boxes on the left and one on the right open to reveal the film's title. All subsequent credits, beginning with those of the stars, Marilyn Monroe and Tom Ewell, appear in these boxes as they open to black. In keeping with Bass's trademark surprise ending, Billy Wilder's directorial credit pops out of the flat space on a spring and bounces around like a jack-in-the-box.

As early as 1955, then, we see Bass utilizing pure abstraction in his credit sequence for *The Seven Year Itch*. The rectangle pattern mimics the grid of urban streets and parks, as if looking straight down at a map (or Google Earth), a more abstract version of *West Side Story*'s prologue (described later). In fact, the concept of using flat planes of color to visualize topographies links Bass's titles for *The Seven Year Itch* to modernist painting. The sequence recalls both American Abstract Expressionists and German painters of the Bauhaus, particularly Paul Klee. Klee's *Flora on Sand* (1927), for example, is one of a series of topographic paintings that reduce the picture frame to variously sized squares and rectangles of muted color, similar to Bass's titles. Yet one can also argue that Bass's color palette is at some level representational, since the browns, ochers, yellows, and lavenders are reminiscent of the New York City brownstones that are the setting of the film. Similarly, the music is abstract yet also representational of traffic, a theme picked up in the film's first image of male commuters racing around the now womanless city streets in August. At the same time, the way Bass limits his color palette to black, white, and hues ranging from red to brown makes the sequence nothing if not a study of a limited segment of the color wheel, just as Klee's 1930 painting *Farbtafel* (Color Chart), which uses more regularized squares, is also a meditation on pure abstract color. Certainly, as Bass would have learned from Kepes, Bauhaus art aesthetics emphasize geometry and abstraction as central elements of composition within the two-dimensional frame. Clinching the reference to modernist abstract art, Bass places his own credit in the lower right-hand corner of the frame, as if he were signing a painting.

In apparent contradistinction to such references to modern art, the typography of the credits, with its extreme serifs and curlicues, eschews the modern look of Swiss sans serif fonts and instead emphasizes serendipity and comedy, more in keeping with Wilder's humorous narrative. When the film's title comes on, the *t* in *Itch* gives a little shake—an almost literal visualization of the word. The spring attached to the final directorial credit propels it forward off the two-dimensional frame of the color field; in addition to representing Bass's trademark surprise ending, this may be a literary reference to Georges Feydeau, a hugely popular French belle époque playwright of sex farces.[15] Billy Wilder certainly would have seen Feydeau's *The Girl from Maxim's* (1899) and *A Flea in Her Ear* (1907), both of which were repeatedly staged in Germany and France in the interwar period. Very much like Ernst Lubitsch, whom Wilder adored, Feydeau loved sudden narrative reversals and coincidences, leading one contemporary critic to comment on the jack-in-the-box construction of his plays—an observation Bass literalizes in his final image. However, the joke may also be on modernist abstract art, which lay critics often poohpoohed as empty and contentless, something a child could paint. Bass visually illustrates the notion that there is nothing behind the art, just an empty black space. Ironically, Wilder was a collector of modernist art, including paintings by Picasso, Giacometti, Calder, Renoir, and Dufy.[16]

Somewhat less abstract renditions of a cityscape are seen in Bass's titles for the British television series *Four Just Men* (1959–1961). Based on characters created by author Edgar Wallace, the crime series follows the exploits of four friends who met in the Italian campaign during World War II. A professor of law (Richard Conte), a member of Parliament (Jack Hawkins), a foreign correspondent (Dan Daily), and a hotelier (Vittorio De Sica), they now live in New York, London, Paris, and Rome, respectively, and work essentially as vigilantes fighting international crime. All four appeared in the pilot episode, establishing their relationship. Thereafter, they starred individually in episodes filmed on location in their respective home cities. Given its international cast of major stars, none of whom had previously worked in television, *Four Just Men* was one of the most expensive and ambitious shows broadcast in the United Kingdom. However, since the thirty-nine half-hour episodes broadcast on ITV failed to find an American sponsor and were therefore not shown on network television, the series did not deliver a return on investment and was quickly canceled.[17]

The credit sequence begins with a black "1" inside a small white circle on a gray field, with lines moving out in every direction from the center.[18] The same sequence repeats itself three more times with the numbers 2, 3, and 4 at the center. The graphic then adds two more white circles in the right top quadrant of crisscrossing lines to enclose the words "Just Men," while Bass's credit appears on a horizontal line at frame left, below the horizontal axis. The graphic for each number then reappears, but with the name of a city in the circle and a black-and-white close-up photograph of the star behind it. The graphic then fades out and is replaced by the star's name, centered in white, sans serif capital letters above the horizontal axis.

The graphic clearly represents an abstract version of a street map for each of the major metropolitan areas featured in the series. However, while the city names are identified and the constellation of lines appears to be different for each city, it is not possible to graph the title design on an actual map of those cities. The representation of the city through the circle and lines is thus indexical in the sense of representing a real place, but it is also a graphic abstraction. Bass used a similar abstract design for a billboard advertisement for British Airways in 1957.[19] The intersecting lines, as in the title graphic, also represent the personal interconnections between the principal characters. Bass thus creates an effective and extremely simple graphic design that is instantly readable to a large number of viewers as representing an urban landscape.

The most striking aspect of Bass's titles for Alfred Hitchcock's *North by Northwest* (1959) is that they begin with a graphic design and then dissolve to live-action shots that make concrete what had previously been rendered abstractly. This mixture of media was probably the result of budgetary constraints, which similarly impacted Bass's titles for John Frankenheimer's *The Young Stranger* (1957) and later Otto Preminger's *The Human Factor* (1979), both of which utilize graphic designs in the opening titles before transitioning to credits over live-action shots.[20] Indeed, Hitchcock's production was apparently close to $1 million over budget before the titles were even produced, so Bass was paid "a ridiculously low amount" and crafted the live-action portion of the titles from second-unit outtakes of Manhattan streets.[21] Despite the striking look of his graphic opening, it was nevertheless a rehash of ideas he had tried to sell to Preminger for *Anatomy of a Murder* and would reutilize in a different form for *Psycho*. Another anomaly is the fact that the titles use the standard grid in conjunction with strong diagonals, a design element Bass would not return to until *Higher Learning* (1995) at the end of his career.

The *North by Northwest* titles open with a black-and-white version of Metro-Goldwyn-Mayer's lion logo that is matted, uncharacteristically, on a green background that remains on the screen after the logo dissolves away. It is replaced by thin dark-blue lines that stream in first diagonally and irregularly from the left side of the frame and then vertically from the bottom, creating a diagonal grid at a forty-five-degree angle to the vertical axis, as Bernard Herrmann's frenetic orchestral score is heard on the sound track. The vertical axis then serves as a track on which white capital letters ride up and down, beginning with "METRO-GOLDWYN-MAYER" entering from the top and "PRESENTS" from the bottom; the lettering is centered but resting diagonally. Bass then more than doubles the size of the sans serif type for the above-the-title credits for Cary Grant, Eva Marie Saint, and Alfred Hitchcock, as well as for the film's title. Each title rides up or down into the frame, the movement of the typography offset by the countermovement of a short white bar to the left or right. Next, the costarring credits enter from the top and bottom as the green background dissolves to an image of a skyscraper; the grid is revealed to be the pattern on the building's all-glass facade, while New York City street traffic is reflected in the windows. The major artistic and technical credits continue to rise from the bottom and the top, always accompanied by a white bar moving in the opposite direction. The names are all in one font size, and the all-capital designations are half that size but also centered within the frame, appearing almost three-dimensional due to their placement on the diagonal grid. Bass then cuts to closer shots of crowds walking out of the building's entrance and down a staircase,[22] as the standard disclaimer about events and characters being fictitious slides in from the left, just below the screen's horizontal axis. More street shots follow, including two women fighting over a taxi, as Hebert Coleman's associate producer credit and Alfred Hitchcock's director credit slide into the frame and then out the other side. The final credit is accompanied by a shot of a city bus halting at a bus stop and then pulling away, just as the master himself makes his trademark cameo and misses the bus, followed by another shot of the building's entrance—in fact, the same shot seen earlier with a woman in a blue dress leaving the premises—beginning the narrative proper.

In *North by Northwest*, then, Bass works with three separate design elements: the diagonal grid structure that morphs into an urban skyscraper, the images of big-city human and vehicular traffic, and the movement of the typography. The last actually mimics the vertical movement of an elevator inside the building, as indicated by the ever-present bar moving in the opposite direction and signifying the elevator's counterweight.[23] Alternatively, Donald Spoto interprets the vertical movement as "prefiguring the final clinging and falling from the sheer rocks" at the end of the film, creating a circular narrative structure.[24] The diagonal grid structure on a "violent green" background serves not only as a device for the movement of text but also as a simile for all urban architecture.[25] The diagonal view, in keeping with natural vision in a crowded urban environment, and the grid structure reflect abstracted cityscapes as imagined by Bass. However, the symbolism of green, which is a shade darker than green's baseline, is less clear. Indeed, the use of blue and green may at first seem counterintuitive because they are natural colors that soothe and calm the spirit. However, the color makes sense as a starting point for a narrative arc from order and stability to chaos and disorder, indicated by the dissolve to the face of the actual building, which is at first visually difficult to read, given the distortions resulting from the images reflected in the uneven pieces of glass. The dominant color in the glass, other than gray (reflecting the cliffs at the end?), is the yellow of the taxi cabs, a color signifying danger. Once he moves to images of the teeming, anonymous masses, Bass starts to play with visual tropes of the city, which he will repeatedly use in other title sequences and his own films. In his titles, then, Bass is creating a visual shorthand for the narrative of a New York City advertising executive (Cary Grant) whose ordinary life is thrown into chaos when he is mistaken for an assassin. Hitchcock's cameo as a frustrated commuter, just after the directorial credit, is yet another example of Bass's trademark surprise ending, and it was not the first time Hitch played a traveler on public transportation.[26]

If *North by Northwest* delivers a graphic representation of urban architecture before dissolving to an actual building in New York, then Bass's titles for the television show *Alcoa Premiere* (1961–1962) vacillate between abstract graphic designs and an almost utopian vision of a modern city created solely with miniatures in what is structured as a 180-degree view of a concrete and steel landscape. The mostly dramatic, omnibus-type series was hosted by Fred Astaire, who faded in from Bass's titles to introduce each week's episode. Alcoa had previously sponsored three television programs since 1955, all of which had slightly different omnibus formats; this one featured revolving casts and stories. The program was not tied to New York or any other urban landscape, since some episodes were modern westerns and others were historical, but it tackled some serious and controversial subjects. In reviewing the opening show, *Variety* called it "one of the best dramas on ABC-TV this season" because it tackled a "difficult, unpleasant theme." But it then went on to say that the show was no better than "some of the middlin' successful stanzas done in

the old days" on *Playhouse 90*.[27] Numerous better-known directors par-
ticipated, including John Ford, John Brahm, Alan Crosland Jr., George
Schaeffer, and Norman Lloyd, as well as writers Lionel Trilling and Peter
Tewksbury. Actors making guest appearances included Lee Marvin,
Jimmy Stewart, Keir Dullea, Dana Andrews, George Kennedy, Shelley
Winters, and Kurt Kasznar.[28]

The deal for *Alcoa Premiere* was probably set up by MCA's Lew Wasserman, who had made clients Ronald Reagan (*General Electric Theater*)
and Alfred Hitchcock (*Alfred Hitchcock Presents*) rich as two-minute hosts
and partial "owners" of their respective shows, guaranteeing them a percentage of the profits.[29] Wasserman was also Astaire's agent, and production costs were kept low by shooting at Revue Studios, owned by MCA.
But the program folded after only two seasons and fifty-eight episodes,
unlike Reagan's and Hitch's seven- and ten-season jackpots. The Alcoa
company magazine *Al-Zalean* reported in spring 1963 that *Alcoa Premiere*'s last show would be on 12 September. Alcoa then began sponsoring the Huntley-Brinkley news show. The back cover of the September–
October 1964 issue of *Al-Zalean* announced that the company would
sponsor a new show, *Alcoa Preview*, hosted by Douglas Fairbanks Jr.[30]

Bass got involved in *Alcoa Premiere* because he had been hired in
March 1961 to redesign Alcoa's corporate identity, having previously
designed a brochure for the company in 1959.[31] The new identity, called
the "Mark of Alcoa," was introduced with a full-page advertisement in the
Wall Street Journal in February 1963.[32] *Alcoa Premiere*'s first show aired
on 10 October 1961, so Bass must have completed the titles that summer,
before the new logo had been designed or approved. According to a company report, in 1961 Alcoa formed a "graphics committee" headed by
T. M. Hunt, general manager of advertising and promotion, to oversee
the design of a new corporate logo by Saul Bass.[33] Bass also suggested
changing the company's primary name to ALCOA (all caps), whereas
previously it had always used "Alcoa" on the logo in conjunction with the
complete name, Aluminum Company of America.[34] In December 1962 a
newly designed company logo was presented to employees in *Al-Zalean*.
The new logo and name was rolled out to the general public in January
1963, when Bass created a series of thirty-second television spots,
"ALCOA New Mark," which were broadcast during episodes of *Alcoa
Premiere*. The spots feature moving camera shots (as if taken from a car)
of various directional road signs, both freestanding and in the pavement;

they end with the new ALCOA logo—a geometric design that could very well be a road sign—while a narrator states that ALCOA is moving in a new direction with a new mark.[35] Bass had already tested some of these design ideas in *Something Wild* (tracking the camera along the pavement) and *West Side Story* (utilizing street signs). He reused the design of the "New Mark" commercials in his opening titles for the prestigious British ITV weekly newsmagazine *This Week* (1965), as well as for lead-ins and promos.[36]

The *Alcoa Premiere* titles begin with free-floating white dashes that grow in size as they move from the background to the foreground, followed by oval-shaped discs repeating the motion. "ALCOA" then appears center screen in capital letters, turning around its own horizontal axis; the name zooms forward as the oval discs disappear, filling the screen. Behind "ALCOA," "PREMIERE" appears upside down in the background, repeating the movement of the first word until the typography covers the horizontal axis of the screen. While "PREMIERE" continues to stretch and then fade out, white ovals and dashes repeat their original movement forward, until changes in the lighting reveal the dashes to be the high-contrast roofs of skyscrapers. The camera zooms in and moves horizontally past the facades of numerous skyscrapers. Panning right to reveal giant gray cylinders behind the model skyscrapers, the camera suddenly changes direction, quickly panning up and over the cylinders to a vertical shot straight down, where five rooftops form the letters A L C O A, columns surrounded by circles, squares, and rectangles. The announcer is heard off camera: "*Alcoa Premiere*. Brought to you by the Aluminum Company of America." Next, the camera zooms in to a close-up on the *O*, whose center dissolves to an image of palm trees and the ocean; the zoom continues until the ocean view fills the screen. The end title sequence essentially reverses the motion, zooming out from the *O* to ALCOA and then to the model cityscape. As the episode credits appear onscreen, the camera begins a ninety-degree track around the model; then, through dissolves, the sequence cuts between similar tracking shots left and zooms in on the model. Bass's own credit appears on the very last title, just above the guild logos.

As in the case of *North by Northwest*, Bass's titles for *Alcoa Premiere* transition from purely graphic two-dimensional representations to three-dimensional architectural renderings. Here, the transition occurs from a two-dimensional space created by television special effects to a three-dimensional space created by models of a metropolitan cityscape. Similarly, the abstract and pliable designs of the former morph into a seemingly real space because the facades are constructed of photographs glued to columns of varying heights, simulating a dense urban landscape. Happily, set photographs of the three-dimensional cityscape model were published, allowing us to see exactly how Bass shot the sequence.[37] By employing very high-key lighting, continuously changing the pools of light illuminating the model structures, and keeping the background dark, even when shooting straight down on the model, Bass creates the illusion that the tops of the "buildings" are white. He thus ingeniously sutures the two segments by perfectly matching cuts from free-floating forms to the concrete rooftops of his artificial cityscape. Bass painted the cardboard and plaster models with a highly reflective paint to give them a metallic quality, in keeping with the sponsor's product. Interestingly, because some of the buildings have photographed facades, while others appear to be architectural models, Bass consciously creates a vision of an urban environment that is both modern and modern art, concrete in an indexical sense and purely abstract. Furthermore, by bundling his signifiers of modernity—vertically thrusting buildings with clean lines; tall, round columns morphing into purely abstract forms, changing with the light—Bass communicates not only something about the television show to come but also something about its sponsor. Whether the columns are actually made of aluminum is less important than the fact that they could be. ALCOA is therefore identified with modern abstract art, with modern urban architecture, and with aluminum products. It is the kind of sequence that can only work in black and white, because the transformation of the image relies heavily on changing light patterns of black, gray, and white. Just as Moholy-Nagy used his light modulator to similar effect, Bass employs a camera to create a study in light and form that visualizes the modern city. Bass in fact designed a "city" on a set, and it moves from a concrete reality to an abstraction in steel and aluminum that is pure Bauhaus.

The breathtaking opening sequence and closing credits for *Alcoa Premiere*, with its horizontal camera movement past skyscrapers, can be seen as a continuation of the cosmic lateral track in *West Side Story* (1961), where the camera is looking straight down on New York buildings and transforming the city into a geometric topography.[38] Furthermore, like *Alcoa Premiere* and *North by Northwest*, Bass begins his opening title for *West Side Story* as a pure abstraction, which then dissolves into a real image.[39] Bass is credited in *West Side Story* for the titles and as a visual consultant; he was directly responsible for the opening sequence over the overture, the helicopter shots of New York, and the closing titles. Inspired by William Shakespeare's *Romeo and Juliet*, the Broadway musical was written by Arthur Laurents, with lyrics by Steven Sondheim and music by Leonard Bernstein. It premiered at the Winter Garden Theatre on 26 September 1957 and ran for 732 performances. The film rights were purchased by Walter Mirish for $375,000, after Seven Arts bowed out of the project; Mirish then approached Robert Wise to produce and direct alongside Jerome Robbins, the original director on Broadway.[40] However, after only a third of the film had been completed, including the opening musical number, Mirish fired Robbins because the novice film director had supposedly gone overbudget by demanding endless takes.[41] The film was completed in early summer 1961 and premiered on 18 October 1961. Costing more than $6 million, the 155-minute film was the most successful movie of the year, earning $12 million from a $43 million gross and garnering eleven Academy Awards—more than any other musical in history.

The reviews were very positive, with plenty of credit going to Wise and the technical crew. In particular, reviewers commented on the Bass overture and the opening sequence, high over New York. Arthur Knight wrote in the *Saturday Review*: "One can only say that Saul Bass, the visual consultant, and/or Boris Leven, the production designer, have made this film as exciting pictorially as it is musically and dramatically—aided of course, by the magnificent color photography of Daniel Fapp."[42] James Powers congratulated Bass on his "moody introductory frames," while *Variety*'s critic thought the titles and credits were novel.[43] However, it was the opening montage of helicopter shots that most impressed the critics, even in retrospect. As Todd McCarthy indicates: "Even now, after all the years, the film's opening minutes—the abstracted representation of Manhattan against changing colors and eventual pullback to reveal the title, backed by a magnificent orchestration of the most thrilling overture in movie musical history, followed by the quiet aerial shots looking directly down on the city—by themselves provide emotional frissons beyond anything emanating from the stage show."[44]

Bass and Kirkham claim that Saul was not responsible for the signature poster for *West Side Story*, although in terms of color, spatial construction, and the logo of two dancing juvenile delinquents that appeared in virtually all the film's collateral, it certainly conforms to the Bass style.[45] The sheet music for the musical's hit song "Tonight"; the lobby cards; the one-, three-, and six-sheet posters; and the promotion brochure all utilized Bass designs and colors, while many foreign posters and United Artists' re-release in 1968 used the same basic design but changed the colors, inserting multicolored images in the typography.[46] From the existing documentation, it is unclear whether Bass merely disowned the poster after it might have been altered by the studio publicity department or whether it was a copycat design. With Bass's minimalist color scheme of black-and-white typography on a red background, the space below the horizontal axis is taken up with the title, "WEST SIDE STORY," each word stacked above the other and spelled out in a military stencil, sans serif type that creates an edifice, much like a New York tenement neighborhood. The designer here uses typography architecturally, something Bass would repeat in his poster for *The Cardinal.* The visual impression of a slum is strengthened by attaching abstracted, metal fire-escape ladders to the right side of the typography and having two white-silhouetted dancers on the fire escape. The white dancers find their opposite in a pair of black silhouettes dancing at the top right-hand corner of the poster, signifying the Jets and the Sharks. Perfectly balancing the black dancers against the red background and the black title below is a triangle of white credits in a simple, modern type, the base of the triangle matching the "roof" of the building. The poster and advertising thus have all the characteristics of the Bass brand: a clean, simple design; strong colors; modern typography; and an image that is both abstract and iconographic.

The storyboards designed by Bass for the opening musical number have been published, but since there is no one-to-one correlation between the storyboards and what Robbins shot, the authorship remains hazy.[47] The sequence has indications of Bass's influence, especially the montage of bodies in motion, constantly changing direction, and the use of fences and other objects in the foreground, exaggerating the movement of the camera and of the actors in the background; Bass would use a similar technique in his titles for *A Walk on the Wild Side.* Wise asked Bass to conceive and produce the opening title sequence because he did not want Bernstein's beautiful overture to be muffled behind the curtain—the practice at the time was to play the overture with the curtain down. Therefore, he needed something visual onscreen if the curtain was to be raised.[48] Wise, however, claimed that the helicopter shots of New

York were his idea: "One of the solutions was the opening of the film, the flight over New York. That was my idea, I wanted to show New York as a real city, because that's where our story is taking place. At the same time, by shooting straight down in the patterns and forms the city gave us, we delivered this 'real' New York in an abstract way."[49] The idea may have been Wise's, but the execution, especially the composition of the cityscape, bears all the hallmarks of the Bass style, and Bass took credit for shooting the helicopter footage.[50] Meanwhile, the credits were put at the end of the film because there were so many of them, given the need to credit both the theater and film productions. Furthermore, as Bass states in *Bass on Titles*, because a major character dies at the end, the producers thought the audience might need a moment to collect themselves after such an emotional finale, and the end credits would allow them to do that. Bass also opined that the graffiti-style credits grew out of the visual violence in the film.

In place of the opening credits, a yellow-tinted graphic appears consisting of a pattern of very thin vertical lines of extremely variable lengths; it covers the top half of the frame, forming an irregular semicircle whose circumference begins and ends at the top of the frame. The lines have a strong similarity to computer graphics, but they remain static; meanwhile, the background tint changes over the course of the overture from yellow to red, orange, purple, and blue. Four and a half minutes into the overture, the camera slowly zooms out, and the graphic diminishes in size but also takes on mass. The lines form rectangles in a darker blue, while the film's title appears in caps at the bottom of the frame in a font created from the same vertical lines, which then turn white as the blue intensifies. Through a perfectly matched dissolve, the graphic pattern at the top morphs into a live-action view of Lower Manhattan, as the title fades out and the overture ends.

The aerial view of Manhattan cuts to an overhead shot of a bridge surrounded by water, its road dissecting the frame just below the horizontal axis as the camera moves left. Through movement and form, Bass matches that cut to another bridge, its left side forming a circular ramp that fills the left side of the screen. A docked ocean liner is seen next, its hull matched to the bridge. The camera continues to move left in the next five bird's-eye-view shots of Manhattan. More shots follow: the United Nations building (reprising *North by Northwest*), the Empire State Building, parking lots, Yankee Stadium, Columbia University, and housing projects.

The last image of Hell's Kitchen plunges in a swift camera zoom to the ground, then cuts to a large basketball court where the first confrontation–dance number between the Jets and the Sharks occurs.

While the opening sequence tracks continuously to the left, the closing credits reverse the movement and basically track right, along an old brick wall covered with "WEST SIDE STORY" in block letters. The camera zooms in to the "directed by" credit for Wise and Robbins, which is written in chalk; then it tracks left to the screenplay and other credits, all tagged as graffiti. Bass dissolves to an abandoned storefront whose windows have been whited out with glass wax, and the production credits appear to be written with a finger. Next, the camera zooms in on a wooden fence, where more credits are scrawled, and then dissolves to a stucco wall with the principal actors' credits, the camera panning up from one to the next. The supporting roles appear as white, justified text onscreen, with another wall as background; the camera then pans right and down to reveal more production credits as graffiti. Indeed, all the remaining production credits alternate between graffiti on walls, doors, and street signs and white, justified text onscreen, while themes from the overture are replayed on the track. The idea of titles as urban graffiti and the camera tracking along a brick wall had previously been used in an Ealing comedy, *Hue and Cry* (1947, Charles Crichton), which Bass may have seen, since the film was released in the United States in 1951.[51]

Thus, *West Side Story*'s narrative is sandwiched between the opening, soaring high over the city, and the closing credits, which take the audience to the depths—that is, between heaven and hell. Bass's opening swoops down from the bird's-eye view to the urban basketball court that is the setting for the opening number and a central character's death, a movement into the urban hell. The film's trailer follows an identical arc, abridging Bass's opening montage.[52] While the view from on high reveals a geometric and almost godly order, each image carefully composed to express balance and symmetry, lines and squares, the end credits are hidden in the visual chaos and disorder of street graffiti. The camera must search for the credits among huge amounts of extraneous visual noise, leaving the impression of a city run amok—an impression that not even the white, justified credits onscreen (conforming to all the Bass principles of design) can alleviate. The color tints during the overture are synchronized to the moods and themes of the musical's songs; for example, for "Tonight," the screen turns Bass's favorite fire-engine red, then transitions through orange and pink to blue for "Maria" and then to orange for Bernstein's "Mamba." Expressing color as pure emotion in relation to song, Bass designs a palette of mostly primary colors that evolves to the more muted colors of an urban New York topography: grays, browns, blues, greens, and spots of other primary colors. The end titles, which also mark class distinctions, are reduced to the drab grays, browns, blacks, and chalk whites of urban street graffiti. This steady draining of color implies a narrative of decay, just as the paint is peeling on the first tenement wall, where "WEST SIDE STORY" once glowed. The film's narrative is thus encapsulated in the movement from high, colorful aspirations of both love and democracy to an underworld of gang violence and anarchy, a tragedy not of noble birth but of violence.

Even the alteration between screen and scene text, between hand-scrawled letters and modernist typography, seems as random as the killing that concludes the film. The view from on high is a tourist's view of a great metropolitan city; the quick zoom down to the playground is an indication that the audience will see the dark underside of the urban environment. The camera movement in the end titles is highly controlled to appear erratic, always searching its next target rather than knowing where to find it, like Orpheus in the dark. I may be reading too much of a literary countermyth into Bass's symbolic use of color here, but Shakespeare's *Romeo and Juliet* is not about ethnic and class warfare; it is about rivalries within the ruling class. Finally, unlike the street signs and pavement markings that confidently and optimistically point the way in Bass's commercials for ALCOA or even in his titles for *Something Wild*, the street signs in the end credits of *West Side Story* are useless discards, randomly tossed in a dark corner and leading to nowhere. Just as the urban dilemmas of poverty, housing, and labor had become increasingly contentious topics in 1961, given the burgeoning civil rights movement, Bass's signage no longer points the way.

While Alfred Hitchcock's *North by Northwest* opens inside the United Nations building in New York City, Jack Garfein's *Something Wild* (1961) begins with an image outside the UN. Similarly, while the titles for *North by Northwest* focus on one busy Midtown Manhattan skyscraper, Bass's titles for *Something Wild* present a portrait of New York that focuses on urban architecture, traffic, and teeming masses of pedestrians in the first three-quarters and city lights in the last quarter, thus employing Bass's two favorite urban tropes. Based on the novel *Mary Ann* (1958), by Alex Karmel, the production was independently financed by Garfein and his then-wife, actress Carroll Baker, who starred; the film was distributed by United Artists. Hollywood still relied almost exclusively on studio production, but *Something Wild* was shot wholly on location in New York City in the summer of 1960, and it was shot chronologically, another anomaly for Hollywood but a growing trend among independent features. Although the *New York Times* listed the budget as $900,000, Garfein later pegged it at $350,000, more like an independent film.[53] Saul Bass was hired a year later, in June 1961, indicating that there may have been production or financial problems; in addition, Aaron Copland was hired in September 1961 to write the film's score after the previous composer, Morton Feldman, was fired.[54] Garfein had survived a Nazi concentration camp as a child, immigrating to the United States after the war and then joining the Actors' Studio, where he became a disciple of method acting (hence the chronological shoot). He had directed one previous film, *The Strange One* (1957), the story of a mobbing at a southern military academy for boys. Garfein ran into trouble with the studio censors at Columbia, however, because he insisted on shooting a scene with African American actors.[55] In a 1963 profile, Albert Johnson called Garfein "America's angriest young director."[56]

Garfein seemed to court controversy. The film begins with an on-camera rape scene, shows brief nudity, and features a happy ending that includes marriage, even though the male lead kidnaps the heroine and keeps her locked up for months against her will in his apartment. Not surprisingly, the black-and-white film was roundly panned and flopped miserably, not even playing in major markets after its New York premiere on 23 December 1961. Disappointed reviewers apparently expected an arty, European-flavored independent feature but got an overdetermined Hollywood ending instead.[57] However, there were exceptions. Jonas Mekas called *Something Wild* "the most interesting American film of the quarter; it may become the most underestimated film of the year."[58] Recently, the film has been rehabilitated as a weird but fascinating piece, possibly because the so-called Stockholm syndrome has made the film's narrative credible.[59] At the time, though, it was just another case of praise for Bass titles attached to a bad film, with one reviewer noting that the titles "were the most original item about the whole production."[60] Albert Johnson called the title designs of New York City "stunning."[61] However, another critic disliked the credits, calling them "some of the most absurd credit titles Saul Bass has so far perpetrated."[62]

Bass's opening shot of the United Nations is followed by various abstracted images of urban architecture; it ends with the camera panning down a building, the movement accelerating by switching to longer focal lengths, as the above-the-title credits for the production company and Carroll Baker appear onscreen in white sans serif type. The movement comes to an abrupt halt on a bird's-eye view of a city street; trolley tracks slice the image at the horizontal axis, and the film's title appears centered just above as Aaron Copland's blaring horns signify city traffic. Bass cuts in more shots of pedestrians from the same angle, then goes to street level as Ralph Meeker's name appears. Subsequent shots of automobile traffic from both bird's-eye and ground views, much of it in fast motion, accompany the remaining actors' credits in left-justified black type at screen left. The horizontal motion of the cars is picked up by the camera swish-panning right over white lines in the pavement, coming to a quick halt as shadows of pedestrians pass and the screenplay credits appear on the horizontal axis. Close-up images of flying pigeons transition to shots of the sky, with the sun at the exact center of the frame, as the credits for Eugene Schüfftan's cinematography and Copland's music are centered one-third above and below the sun, respectively. The sun remains in the center, growing incrementally from shot to shot but now framed to the left and right by urban architecture and the major technical credits, either left- or right-justified. The sun then match-dissolves to a headlight and an urban nightscape, followed by images of Times Square news tickers that are increasingly enlarged and abstracted, morphing into out-of-focus headlights as the minor technical credits and producer's credit are seen across the bottom of the screen. That image dissolves again to a shot taken from a subway train entering an underground station for Garfein's director's credit, followed by a shot of blurred subway windows as the train leaves the station.

The titles for *Something Wild* are among the most mathematically precise of Bass's career. The 2:45-minute title sequence is exactly divided into three sections of 65 seconds, 65 seconds, and 35 seconds (or 37.5 percent, 37.5 percent, and 25 percent). The opening section, during which the above- and below-the-title actors' credits are seen, focuses on the facades of New York buildings and pedestrian and vehicular traffic. The second section inserts images of the sun, sky, and nature (pigeons) into the urban environment, over which the major behind-the-scenes credits appear. The shorter third section, consisting of city and subway lights, accompanies the final credits, including those for the producer and director. The proportions correspond almost exactly to Gustav Freitag's triangle of dramatic structure for a five-act play, which in turn is derived from Plato's concept of the Golden Proportion: exposition, rising action, climax, falling action, dénouement. In this scheme, then, the cacophony of city sounds and fast-moving traffic mark the exposition and rising action, the static images of nature and the sun mark the climax and falling action, and the nightscapes mark the dénouement.

Bass's editing structure within each sequence is equally precise. He cuts consistently on form and movement, transitions compositionally from stable to unstable, from stasis to movement, while utilizing a whole catalog of avant-garde film techniques, including extreme camera angles, multiple exposures, fast motion, changing focal lengths, and blurred focus. Interestingly, unlike many visions of the city that emphasize the verticality of form (skyscrapers) and movement, Bass sticks almost exclusively to horizontal movement—either camera movement or movement within the frame—the exception being the opening camera movement and the pedestrians behind the title. At the same time, Bass juxtaposes images and text metaphorically. Thus, the title sequence's second multiple exposure of building facades resembles an expressionist set from *The Cabinet of Dr. Caligari* (1919), indicating that the narrative has an uncertain grasp on reality. The image of the building facade behind Carroll Baker's credit is divided along the vertical axis, half in light and half in darkness, followed by the camera's plunge to the street, prefiguring her own somewhat schizophrenic emotional state and subsequent fall after the rape and kidnapping (she is held in a basement apartment). The credit for Ralph Meeker, who plays an anonymous loner, is accompanied by a visually chaotic and truncated image of pedestrians' legs and feet. Finally, the centered and stable image of the sun as a phenomenon of nature in the man-made chaos of the city reflects the film's central narrative conceit: that humanity and human goodness can survive, even in the most horrific circumstances, allowing love to shine, like the lights of Broadway.

City Lights

The city at night has fascinated filmmakers since at least the 1920s. Avant-garde films, whether Walter Ruttmann's *Berlin Sinfonie einer Grossstadt*

(1927), Pierre Chenal's *Paris Cinéma* (1928), Alain Tanner and Claude Goretta's *Nice Time* (1957), or William Klein's *Broadway by Light* (1958), discovered the intense visual possibilities of electric city lights, making them a theme for modernist explorations of urban space. Bass carried on that tradition in his live-action images of the city in the titles for *Something Wild* and *Casino*, turning the latter into a visual symphony of Las Vegas glitz. But he also created a visual shorthand for graphically signifying city lights, as embodied in theater marquees. The marquee signifies an urban environment—specifically, New York City and Broadway—with all the implications of being an entertainment capital, but it is also generalized enough in design to function on Main Street in small-town America. In the Bass universe, marquee lights signify the hopes and dreams of the common person, as in *The Sale of Manhattan*, where the Jewish peddler dreams of Broadway, or in the musings of a product in Bass's two-minute infomercial for Olin Mathieson, *The History of a Package* (1960), which take form as the "Great White Way" in dot-matrix lights. The lights in Bass's graphic versions are abstract, logocentric, and indexical, utilizing dot-matrix patterns to depict the mass of lightbulbs on a movie marquee or a news ticker. An early trade ad for *A Star Is Born* (1954) features the film's title created with dots, as if blazing in Broadway lights, on a black background, with Judy Garland below.[63] The same year, Bass designed an album cover for Elmer Bernstein's *Blues & Brass* that used colored circles on a black background to imagine a highly abstracted image of city lights and traffic. Virtually the same design concept, execution, and even color scheme were recycled in a 1959 brochure for Lightolier, a company specializing in decorative lighting.[64] A monochromatic moving-image version of abstracted headlights in traffic, the slightly soft-focus circles appearing in various shades of gray—Bass called them "circles of diffusion"—was also utilized for Bass's opening and closing titles for *Patterns of Life* (1957). This science program, produced at the University of Southern California and broadcast on an educational TV channel in Los Angeles, opened and closed with a jazz score by Elmer Bernstein.[65] Bass also reused the out-of-focus headlights in the opening title images for an Olin Mathieson–sponsored television series called *Small World* (1959). But Bass perfected his methodology with the introduction to the TV series *Playhouse 90*, which begins with the identical image of abstracted car headlights and then transitions to a graphic design consisting of a dot-matrix pattern.

Produced for CBS television, *Playhouse 90* (1956–1960) was not the first omnibus-type TV program, but it was one of the most famous. It lasted for 133 episodes over four seasons after premiering on 4 October 1956 with a Rod Serling–scripted drama. The show featured first-rate talent behind the camera, such as John Frankenheimer, Sidney Lumet, Franklin Schaffner, Fred Coe, Arthur Penn, Frank D. Gilroy, Horton Foote, Abby Mann, and Paul Monash, as well as in front of it, including Mickey Rooney, Jack Palance, Charles Laughton, Polly Bergen, Teresa Wright, and June Lockhart. Each show had its own producer, cast, crew, and story. *Playhouse 90* started out as a live show with a live opening title sequence: the orthicon cameras focused on large white Moravian stars that turned around their own axes, then cut to the TV stars in the upcoming episode as they stood looking at the camera from between paper stars hanging from visible strings. The end credits were then keyed in over a static image of the same group of Moravian stars. That was not a Bass design. The program eventually transitioned to videotape production, although some shows were actually filmed, but the opening stayed pretty much the same throughout its four seasons.[66] Even reruns of the show, hosted by Richard Boone, do not include the Bass-designed opener. So it is unclear for what iteration of *Playhouse 90* Bass created the titles found in the Bass Collection. It is possible that the twenty-five-second Bass title was used merely as a teaser or promo for the show.

The title begins with extremely out-of-focus lights that form perfect circles. Traffic noise cues the viewer to the fact that these are automobile headlights moving through urban traffic. The circles form patterns in various shades of gray, depending on the brightness of the lights, but moving either horizontally or vertically. The dots of light start to form patterns in straight lines, indicating that Bass has subtly switched to graphically generated white circles, as the word "PLAYHOUSE" is written with dots. With the appearance of the title, introductory music commences—a bouncy, going-to-the-theater melody. "PLAYHOUSE" fades out, while larger white circles re-form to create "90" in the center of the frame. "PLAYHOUSE" and "90" then blink alternately onscreen as if they were Broadway lights.

Here, Bass brings together two kinds of urban light. The title opens with nighttime automobile traffic, streetlights, and traffic noises, suggesting that people are on the move, entering the city or leaving it. These patterns of circular light are then mixed with graphic circles that are a visual trope for Broadway marquee lights, indicating that a theatrical experience awaits the viewers of *Playhouse 90*. The flashing two-part title also mimics an electronic marquee. According to a document in the Bass Papers, "The general intent is to create an active, night-life, atmosphere reminiscent of the visual stimuli associated with theatre-going."[67] Its simplicity of design is its greatest strength; it is both highly abstract and concrete—hallmarks of the Bass brand.

In fact, Bass had been playing with the idea of depicting an urban landscape through a dot-matrix screen since his work on *Edge of the City*, although only in his preferred version of the titles, not in the actual release prints. There, Bass uses what can only be characterized as white and gray computer punch holes overlaid onscreen to abstractly depict the urban landscape traversed by film's hero in the live-action images. Likewise, Bass's posters for the same film feature the computer punch cards; however, Bass does not yet cover the entire screen with a dot matrix to produce typography. The dot-matrix pattern communicates modernity, whether through its association with computers or the news ticker. Creating a graphic for typography and images based solely on a dot matrix would come with Bass's next television project after *Playhouse 90*.

In the spring of 1961 the Westinghouse Corporation premiered a ninety-minute videotaped, late-night talk show, *PM East/PM West*, which was cohosted by Mike Wallace and Joyce Davidson in New York (*PM East*) and Terrence O'Flaherty in San Francisco (*PM West*). The show premiered on 12 June 1961 on the Group W Network and was then syndicated to other television stations in Chicago, Washington, D.C., New York, and Los Angeles. It lasted only one season (until 22 June 1962) and failed, in part, because audiences were expecting Wallace, who was famous for attacking and bloodying interviewees on his previous ABC talk show, *The Mike Wallace Interview* (1957–1959), to do the same on this show. However, *PM East/PM West* focused on show-business personalities who had to be cajoled to appear on the program, so Wallace remained as gentle as a lamb, causing audiences to abandon the show in droves.[68] Bass may have been contracted to do the titles through Westinghouse, which had already used him for an advertising campaign.[69]

The titles for *PM East/PM West* survive in various forms and differ slightly, since the show ran on both the East and West Coasts. Bass uses a dot-matrix pattern to signify the Broadway news ticker format. Rectangular white forms on a black background are ordered in straight rows from the top of the screen to the bottom. A description in the Bass Papers, probably written after the fact but approved by Bass, has the title image beginning with Bass's proverbial sunset: "We open on a setting sun slowly sinking into the horizon. As it begins to disappear, the night lights of the city begin to wink on . . . building into the skyline configuration of New York . . . the skyline goes higher and higher, until the light pattern covers the screen . . . then breaks down to form 'PM East,' which blinks on and off . . . as we fade into the beginning of the show."[70] Before the sun has completely set, individual lights flash on and off and then form a suspension bridge as the suns sets beneath it. Next, the lights slowly form a slightly abstract image of the New York skyline; the outline of the buildings grows larger as the lights continue to flash, and the shapes of the buildings expand upward until the screen is completely filled with white lights. Lights are then slowly extinguished from the edge of the frame toward the center, until the image morphs into very large block letters, "PM," that cover the top two-thirds of the screen; "EAST" and "WEST" appear in letters half the size, covering the lower third of the screen. Graphically, "EAST" and "WEST" share the same "PM," each carrying the visual weight of the other. Yet they are also apart because although they share the same format, they have different hosts, different lengths (sixty versus thirty minutes), and, of course, different time zones.

These marquee lights clearly broadcast the show's intention to entertain late-night audiences on both coasts with show-business personalities relaxing and hopefully sharing gossip with established broadcast and print journalists. A late-night show implies more "adult" content, as indicated by the setting sun. City lights here are reduced to the Times Square news ticker and the marquee lights of Broadway. But Bass is also playing with the space created through the lights, for example, when he fills the television screen with little white lights in straight rows—a self-reflexive gesture pointing to the medium itself and to the fact that light allows the artist to create pictures and make art. Ironically, prior to producing the *PM* design, Bass had created a more technically and aesthetically complex iteration of the dot-matrix marquee as a trope for the glitz of Las Vegas in *Ocean's Eleven.*

Frank Sinatra hired Saul Bass to do the titles for the *Frank Sinatra Show* (1957) and then hired him again in 1960 for *Ocean's Eleven.* By then, the film already had a long production history. As early as April 1956, Matador Productions announced that it would produce *Ocean's*

Eleven with director Gilbert L. Kay and producer Earl Colbert.[71] The project either remained dormant or could not get financing, because actors Peter Lawford and Frank Sinatra bought the rights to the screenplay in December 1957.[72] Sinatra's Dorchester Productions and Lawford's Kenlaw Productions were still planning to make the film nine months later, but production had to be postponed due to Sinatra's commitments elsewhere; meanwhile, Richard Breen was working on the script.[73] When Lewis Milestone was brought in as producer and director sometime in 1959, he discarded much of the film's plot but kept the basic premise of a group of ex-army buddies robbing five Las Vegas casinos.[74] With a distribution deal from Warner Brothers, the film was shot in Las Vegas at the Sands (partially owned by Sinatra), the Sahara, and the Riviera casinos and on the Warner lot in Burbank between January and March 1960. The exceedingly complex animation needed for the titles was done by Art Goodman, Dirk Barlow, Bill Hurtz, and Jim Hiltz. Executive producer Sinatra apparently allotted $65,000 for Bass's titles, although, according to a *Hollywood Reporter* article, titles usually cost only $2,500 to $5,000. But, as the article noted, "Frank's gasser-type titles are animated slot machines, roulette wheels and crap tables, and that's The Hard Way."[75] Since the end credits are conventional images of the Rat Pack, except for the final "The End" in white dot matrix, it is possible that the money ran out. Again, the cost of Bass's titles had become an issue in the press.

Ocean's Eleven premiered on 3 August 1960 in Las Vegas, but when the film opened in New York and Los Angeles a week later, it received mixed to poor reviews. *Variety* was charitable, as usual, pointing out that although the film had major weaknesses, including a doubtful premise, a contrived script, uncertain direction, and a group of actors essentially playing themselves, it would be a moneymaker. Bass got another rave review: "Main titles by Saul Bass are as clever as anything that follows."[76] In fact, *Ocean's Eleven* became the highest-grossing film of Frank Sinatra's career, taking in more than $5.5 million and reaching eighth place for the year.

The title sequence begins with an abstract white dot matrix—basically, a horizontal pattern that keeps changing shape on the Cinemascope screen until it becomes a large "1" just to the left of the vertical axis. The "1" slowly disappears and is replaced by a gray-green "2" slightly to the right of the vertical axis, then by a brighter blue "3" on the extreme right side of the screen, while "FRANK SINATRA" appears in white capitals on the horizontal axis and butted up against the "3." The titles then continue the count, up to "11," in pink, orange, and yellow, while the names of the other stars (Dean Martin, Sammy Davis Jr., Peter Lawford, Angie Dickinson, and Richard Conte) are displayed in white on the horizontal axis, ending with the film's title. Nelson Riddle's orchestral score brilliantly identifies the names in lights with leitmotifs.[77] Bass next creates an orange and pink rectangular frame with multiple lines, placing the costarring credits in white dot matrix in the center, followed by a sideways blue and pink "8" with more actors' credits in white in both holes of the number. An elaborate movie marquee design by Art Goodman, which Bass reused in black and white for *The Sale of Manhattan*, accompanies the centered credits for Red Skelton and George Raft. A zigzag arrow that moves across the full length of the wide screen in green and blue allows Bass to place the screenplay and story credits in the black spaces in between, before the arrow disappears. The following frame creates a pattern of vertical lines, columns, and circles that frames two face cards—the queen of diamonds and king of hearts—while the technical credits appear in white dot matrix over the design. Next, the design slowly disappears and is replaced by a dot-matrix design of a slot machine; the four windows, containing a lemon, a bell, cherries, and an orange, are now solid images on a white background. Bass lets the slot machine rip, and the images move rapidly on their vertical wheel, coming to a stop on two cherries and the image of a man and a woman kissing (the two right windows), before a black window shade is pulled down over the third window and white technical credits are seen. The slots then spin into action again, as three blue martini glasses come up and a gray-green balloon appears in the fourth window; the balloon rises out of frame, and a drunk holding the string appears, followed by black credits on a white field. Again the slots rotate, coming to a stop on four white bells in a blue square with black technical credits below them; the fourth window states, "titles designed by SAUL BASS." The dot matrix then forms a highly stylized American eagle, while the musical credits appear in three sets of circles within the design. Finally, two solid white dice bounce onto a white dot-matrix table and are removed by a solid croupier's stick. Then another set of dice lands with Lewis Milestone's credit handwritten and printed inside the white field. The film dissolves to a live-action shot as the dice are removed again with the croupier's stick.

By the late 1950s, Las Vegas had become a gamblers' paradise in the eyes of most Americans. It was also a town dominated by the organized crime syndicates that had built the first great postwar casinos after Nevada legalized gambling in the 1930s. Bass plays with many Las Vegas signifiers here, beginning with the count-up of Arabic numbers, which points to the many casino marquees along the Vegas Strip and provides a convenient way to list all the above-the-title stars. Like the subsequent rectangular frames and curly eights, the pastel colors of the constantly moving and changing dot-matrix patterns refer to Las Vegas's particular kind of gaudy ambience, reinforced by a musical theme that mimics the flashing "lights." In keeping with Las Vegas's emerging reputation as an entertainment city, the end credits have the principals walk past a marquee on which their names appear—a self-reflexive advertising moment for sure. Of course, the playing cards and slot machine represent the very essence of Las Vegas gambling and casino culture, but interestingly, the playing-card title reprises a similarly designed composition in *Around the World in 80 Days*. The slot machine design, in contrast, allows Bass to insert a few visual jokes, one being the dropping of the window shade before a couple engages in sexual activity, an idea he had played with in *The Moon Is Blue* and *Love in the Afternoon* and may have been inspired by a Paul Rand advertisement. The drunk who floats up with a balloon in one hand and a bottle in the other is wearing a nineteenth-century black stovepipe hat, again referencing *Around the World in 80 Days*. The white bells on a blue background that pop up on the slot machine are almost identical to the Bell Telephone logo Bass sold to AT&T as a brand-new design eight years later.[78] The abstracted blue American eagle references the fact that all the thieves had been members of the same army unit in World War II. And finally, the roll of the dice, which comes up first as seven and then as Milestone's credit, may be Bass's signature joke on the director, visualizing the fact that every film production is a crapshoot. Like the subsequent film narrative, the opening titles for *Ocean's Eleven* are jokey, fun, and not very deep. The animation required to create the titles, however, was technically complex and labor intensive, given that each change in the dot matrix necessitated a new cell. The solid images of the playing cards, slot machines, and dice make the gambling motif more concrete and legible, since casinos at the time were all about gambling, drinking, and sex (all three activities referenced in the titles), unlike today, when they also advertise family tourism.

Casino (1995) was the fifth collaboration between Martin Scorsese and Elaine and Saul Bass since Scorsese first rediscovered Saul in 1989, when he saw the titles for *War of the Roses*.[79] One of Scorsese's favorite films is *Ocean's Eleven*, so the Basses were a natural fit for the director's film about Las Vegas and the Mafia's dominance of the great casinos. Completed in the last year of Saul's life, the titles for *Casino* reveal the extent to which he was deferring to Elaine in determining the design elements. Thus, although the typography and its placement within the screen frame still conform to the Bass style, the preponderance of diagonals and the abandonment of geometric design principles are likely attributable to Elaine. Elaine Bass's abstract symphony of Las Vegas light is an ecstatic burst of abstract color. According to Saul, "We attempted to create a metaphor for the Las Vegas of betrayal, twisted morality, greed, hubris, and in the end, self-destruction. The descent into Dante's Inferno."[80] Some of the city lights footage for *Casino* had in fact been shot thirty years earlier for the *Something Wild* title sequence.[81]

Apparently, the Basses were shown the first, last, and middle reels of *Casino* before designing the title sequence.[82] Planning of the sequence was well under way in September 1994, when Bass received some stock footage of explosions. By that time, the titles' main theme had apparently been set, although earlier memos indicate that at some point, a much more expansive, touristy view of Las Vegas had been considered, including images of eagles, tarantulas, sidewinder snakes, scorpions, traffic lights (red-yellow-green), and well-known Vegas sights. A month later, Bass sent Scorsese a memo in which he literally sketched out the "scale of body to frame in 2:35," as well as noting the fact that the flying body following the car explosion would be in silhouette.[83] Postproduction work apparently occurred in June 1995, with final approval for the title cards coming in October. The total cost for the *Casino* main title sequence, credits, and end credits was $111,316.56, not including the fees for the services of Saul and Elaine Bass. In a letter to Barbara De Fina, Scorsese's producer, Bass outlined the reasons for the high cost. In particular, he maintained that a lot of experimentation was necessary to manufacture a continuous fireball out of only two seconds of explosion. Utilizing an Avid System, they created "twelve 2–3 second units which collapse into 18–20 seconds, due to overlapping dissolves, flops and different framings, etc."[84] Another problem seems to have been the scale and trajectory of the flying figure, which had to be achieved optically with the eighteen to twenty seconds of footage they had at their disposal. The conception of the sequence had apparently been worked out well before production began, since much of the discussion seems to have been about finding a proper font for the titles.

Opening simultaneously in New York and Los Angeles on 22 November 1995, *Casino* was not viewed as an unqualified success. Indeed, although many reviewers acknowledged Scorsese as America's greatest living director and noted that the film's strengths (e.g., the explosive violence, the intensity of emotion) are present in all his work, they complained that Scorsese had covered this territory before. Speaking of the actors' performances, Mick LaSalle observed in the *San Francisco Chronicle*: "De Niro and Pesci are good, but this time they know they're good, and the inspiration is gone. They have one eye on us and one affectionate eye on themselves."[85] Janet Maslin in the *New York Times* and Peter Travers in *Rolling Stone* focused more on the film's journalistic aspects, both noting that Nicholas Pileggi's book and script detail the rise and fall of Mafia influence in the Las Vegas casinos in the 1970s and early 1980s and that Scorsese was interested in depicting a historical canvas rather than individual fates. Maslin wrote: "With its rivers of cash and mountains of neon, its high rollers and lowlife hoods, 'Casino' luxuriantly explores the anatomy of America's gaudiest (and now most cinematically popular) playground."[86]

Casino's nearly three-minute title sequence begins with a black screen and white sans serif typography announcing the production company and informing viewers that it is a true story from 1983. Ace Rothstein (Robert De Niro) is then seen leaving a casino and is heard speaking offscreen: "When you love someone, you gotta trust them. There is no other way. . . . And for a while, that's the kind of love I had." He gets into his car and turns on the ignition, and the car explodes in a fireball. As the above-the-title credits for Scorsese, De Niro, and Sharon Stone fade in, Rothstein's body hurls through an inferno of flames, which dissolves to the red lights of a Las Vegas marquee; the body continues to fall as Joe Pesci's name fades in. The film's title card follows, with "*Casino*" moving diagonally up the screen while staying on a horizontal line. The remaining major actors' credits, as well as credits for the major behind-the-scenes talent, fade in and out on a changing array of abstract compositions of pure color, crafted from cutout views of the Las Vegas Strip light shows. The lights transition back to red, and the camera pans down an arched grid, as the falling body and the flames reappear for Barbara De Fina's producer's credit; the screen dissolves to pure flames for Scorsese's director credit, before the image dissolves to the interior of a casino and Ace Rothstein's narration.

Elaine and Saul's design concept consists of two elements, with the first bracketing the second: the flying body of Ace Rothstein after the explosion and the marquee lights of Las Vegas. Rothstein's body falling through an inferno of fire marks the Jewish gangster's descent into hell's flames. Wearing an intense coral-orange sports jacket, shirt, and tie with white pants and shoes, Rothstein is visually divided in the first shot—an innocent angel with one foot in hell. With the explosion, his body tumbles through the flames in a diagonal but steadily downward trajectory, finally entering the visual space of Las Vegas, which is both glitzy, thanks to the colored lights, and a marker of hell, with red arches of light. The human body falling through the flames clearly references the iconography of medieval paintings of souls being sucked into hell's fire, as in Hans Memling's triptych *The Last Judgment* (1467), the Limbourg brothers' illustration *Hell* (circa 1412), or Duc de Berry's *Book of Hours*. Finally, the diagonal movement of the body from the upper left to the lower right sets up an arc that is reversed in the following movement of the film title and the lights behind it, the casino being the mechanism for the hero's rise before his fall. The movement of the body also connects the vision of hell to another kind of hell—namely, the Las Vegas Strip. The intense reds of the Las Vegas lights as Joe Pesci's name appears onscreen identify his character as another one of the fallen, as is the character played by Sharon Stone. When the flames return near the end of the title sequence, so too does the body falling through space, although now the movement is much more vertical than diagonal, and the flames themselves are in close-up, almost identical to the flames in the last frames of the *Exodus* titles.[87] But here the flames are seemingly more abstract, similar to the white cloth in *War of the Roses*—that is, more for the sake of pure design than semantic content. Is Scorsese placing himself in the same hell as his characters?

The Christian (specifically, Catholic) interpretation of these opening images of the descent into hell is reinforced by the sound track. At the moment of the explosion, Bass cuts to the final chorale from Johann Sebastian Bach's *St. Matthew Passion* (1727), which is called *Wir setzen uns mit Tränen nieder*. Bach may have been a devout Lutheran, but the music, text, and images in the chorale speak of death and exhaustion, not the redemption that Christian theology teaches. Here, the grave, visualized through the horizontal lines of Rothstein's vehicle, morphs a moment later into the driver's funeral pyre. As in Billy Wilder's *Sunset Boulevard* (1950), the central character seemingly narrates from beyond the grave via Bach's libretto:

Wir setzen uns mit Tränen nieder und rufen dir im Grabe zu:
Ruhe sanfte, sanfte ruh! Ruht, ihr ausgesogenen Glieder!
Euer Grab und Leichenstein soll dem ängstlichen Gewissen ein
bequemes Ruhekissen und der Seelen Ruhstatt sein. Höchst
vergnügt schlummern da die Augen ein.

We sit down with you in tears, call to you in your grave:
Rest gently, gently rest! Rest you exhausted limbs
Your grave and tombstone for our fearful conscience shall be
a comfortable pillow, and the place where our souls find
rest with the greatest content, there our eyes will close in sleep.

Indeed, all the principal characters—Rothstein, his partner Nicky Santoro, and his wife Ginger—are "sinners," committing larceny, murder, and adultery, respectively. And they will all die—or at least that is the supposition after seeing Rothstein blown up. The religious music elevates the intensity of the light's color scheme, translating the images into the emotional intensity of the moment, which subsequently morphs into a secular ecstasy.

The diagonal movement of the abstract light show in the title frame, with the title typography also moving on a diagonal trajectory, is unique in the Bass canon and can probably be attributed to Elaine's influence, as can the abstract light play. The Basses present close-up compositions of marquee lights in such a way as to make their texts illegible and thereby abstract. Ironically, the film's formalist center can also be seen as a tribute to the abstract color films of Jordan Belson, the Whitney brothers, and Moholy-Nagy. The lights of this city take on an almost otherworldly quality, like a surreal dream or a Zen exercise. Thus, the red and yellow light play that accompanies James Woods's credit seemingly references computer data (long before *The Matrix*), whereas the purple and orange lights for Kevin Pollack and L. Q. Jones, respectively, duplicate the Broadway news ticker seen in so many other Bass titles; these have become pure indexical signs of urbanity, but they still adhere to a spatial geometry based on the x- and y-axes. Subsequent titles vacillate between predominantly blue light and red light—between heaven and hell. Some frames feature rainbow light, such as the Elaine and Saul Bass credit; this makes sense, given that rainbows were central to the Bass/Yager corporate logo and design. But the title then morphs again into an electronic version of Paul Klee's fields of abstract color, recalling the Bass of yore. Thelma Schoonmaker's credit is dominated by diagonal shafts of red light from the right, as if it were streaming in through the windows of a Gothic cathedral, while Pileggi's book credit, in diagonal blue light, is reminiscent of Leni Riefenstahl's monumental *Lichtsäulen* at Nuremberg, which also created cathedrals of light. Indeed, eight of the thirteen light compositions (62 percent) incorporate diagonal lines—a staggering number, given the dearth of such compositions in Bass's earlier work.

Light and color are expressions of emotion, but here, the emotions (like the light) remain on the surface. The primary colors are intense but too abstract to function as motors of empathy, just as the film's narrative seemingly lacks any inner depth. Rothstein's suits in rainbow colors are the only available insight into his character. Ironically, the overall montage of successive light compositions contrasts large areas of screen color: blue versus rainbow prisms of light; red, blue, and black diagonal stripes. The privileging of rounded edges and the repetition of line, shape, and color follow a more rhythmic logic than the strict geometric patterns prevalent in most of Bass's other work. Like *The Age of Innocence*, *Casino*'s title sequence marks the evolution of the Bass brand to one that expresses Elaine's more rounded and (dare I say) more feminine design sense.

The Sale of Manhattan

The Sale of Manhattan (1962), Saul Bass and Art Goodman's short animated film, takes us back to Bass's original style and humor, while conforming to an image of New York City that emphasizes Broadway. Stan Freberg wrote the script, and the film was produced as a segment for his ABC special, *Stan Freberg Presents the Chun King Chow Mein Hour: Salute to the Chinese New Year*, which was originally broadcast on 4 February 1962. The skit had previously appeared on a record album, *Stan Freberg Presents the United States of America: The Early Years*.[88] The five-minute animated film tells a humorous version of the sale of the island of Manhattan in 1626 to Peter Minuit, director general of the New Netherland colony, for sixty Dutch guilders, or approximately $1,000 (not the $24 of legend). However, according to a caption accompanying twenty frames reproduced in a design publication, "This film, entitled *The Sale of Manhattan*, is a musical parody on the historic transaction whereby the island of Manhattan was sold by the Red Indians to Peter Stuyvesant [*sic*], then Governor of New York, for the paltry sum of 24 dollars."[89] Although Freberg's show got mixed reviews, the animation received some favorable comments: "The program had its better moments, a Sid Caesarian operation involving old movie clichés had several good funnies, . . . and even an animated version of the sale of Manhattan Island."[90]

In the film, a typical Jewish, cigar-smoking New York talent agent negotiates the sale of Manhattan between a cigar-store Indian and a Dutch straight man. It opens with a very large Native American chief perched on a pedestal with wheels, standing next to a coonskin cap–wearing pioneer who ostensibly owns the store. They meet a Dutchman with a heavy accent who says he saw a listing in the paper for the sale of the island. The store owner offers to do all the talking for the Indian, and when the colonist asks about the price, the "agent" shuts up his client and changes into a suit and a bowler hat, now looking more like a nineteenth-century Jewish merchant. When the Dutchman sees the forest covering the island, he says $32.50 in junk jewelry is too much to pay and walks away, but the agent pulls him back and says the island may not look like much now, but someday. . . . Behind them, rectangles suddenly turn into a skyscraper skyline; then the lights of the marquees for the Roxy, Paramount, Empire, and State theaters appear. The agent trades his bowler for a top hat as a chorus line of squaws dances in the background. As the agent dances with a line of male and half-naked female dancers, the Dutchman agrees to the sale, whereupon the agent has the trees hauled away. When the Dutchman asks what's happening to the trees, he's told that he didn't pay for a furnished island. The last laugh is on him, the Indian says, because the whole island is solid concrete. All three ride a freight elevator down to below street level as Bass cuts to a furious live-action montage of New York traffic.

Utilizing the simple line drawing style that was a hallmark of Art Goodman's animation, *The Sale of Manhattan* plays with both history and the viewer's knowledge of present-day Manhattan, the humor arising over the postmodern clash of various subject positions. Knowing that they are reproducing a legend—the Ur-myth of the great city's founding—rather than a historical reality, Bass and Freberg consciously traffic in ethnic stereotypes that were common fixtures in early-twentieth-century vaudeville but probably offended many when the program aired in 1962. A case in point is the Native American, who is visualized as the cliché European Americans made of him: a giant in a loincloth whose feet are glued together to maintain the cigar-store pose. The "Red Indian" towers over both the agent and the colonist, his physical presence emphasized by his sizable naked chest—a threat on many fronts. But he is symbolically castrated, immobilized, dependent on others to push him around, which may have been a point worth making for liberal humanists like Freberg and Bass, given the abject poverty and lack of opportunity for Native Americans at the time.

The Dutch colonist looks like a historical figure, but he has the accent and personality of a "Dutch" vaudevillian comedian, who was really a cliché of the slow-witted German immigrant. The Dutchman gets to play the straight man, and it seems to be a natural fit. Small and very round, the Dutchman eats well but is frugal. However, as the narrative demonstrates, he is also susceptible to erotic visual pleasure. So he buys the island but realizes, after its defoliation, that it won't attract any colonists. He, like the cigar-store Indian, is a character in a giant vaudeville show that slips into burlesque.

The joke in the master narrative is that it is the Jewish impresario who literally directs the historical events (by dominating the deal) and the vaudevillian performance (consisting of a comedy routine, followed by a big musical number, and then more comedy). A foundational myth of the United States, involving the civilizing European and the noble savage, is played out in 1626 Manhattan, but it has a so-called alien—a Jewish immigrant and Lower East Side street peddler—transforming himself (as did Louis B. Mayer, Harry Cohen, Marcus Loew, Carl Laemmle, and others) into the quintessential Broadway agent Roxy Rothapfel, orchestrating the show. Throwing off his camouflage, the Jewish character changes into his bowler just when the Dutchman asks about sale price. But he is also the architect of New York's identity as the capital of musical theater, another cliché transposed to the 1600s and visualized by the new impresario. His next costume change to top hat and tails introduces the musical show, including a burlesque finale of close-ups of very round behinds. And indeed, the lights of Broadway and their potential for spectacle (i.e., visual pleasure) seduce the colonist into making the purchase. Eroticism, or the satisfaction of the male gaze, closes the deal. The show then closes down, leaving only a final ethnic slur. The colonist realizes that the whole island is concrete, the trees merely props that can be carted off the Broadway stage at a moment's notice. The image of concrete feeds into Middle American prejudices about the city, summed up by the wooden Indian: "Nice place to visit, but who would want to live here?" Somewhat disconcertingly, the Jewish agent, created by liberal Jews, can be understood to represent all the prejudices of WASP Americans living in the hinterlands and their belief that New York City is dominated by Jews who will sell you anything and cheat you on top of it. One wonders how much of this was a form of self-loathing, not uncommon among Jewish intellectuals, reflecting the feelings of the transplanted westerner Saul Bass.

National Bohemian Beer

Bass's visualization of urban landscapes is invariably architectural, graphic, macrocosmic, and metaphoric. Whether a bird's-eye view from above, as in *West Side Story* or *Alcoa Premiere*, or from street level, it is all about the movement of traffic, as in *Something Wild* or *Why Man Creates*, of people as mass. Nowhere do we see individualized faces in the crowd. His city lights work to abstract the urban environment even further, obliterating natural space and reducing it to the metaphor of theatrical entertainment and colored light shows. Human beings, if they are visible at all, are visualized as a mass—pedestrians crossing the street, entering and leaving office buildings, on the move. With his "Andy Parker aka Regular Joe" television commercials for National Bohemian beer, Bass places an individual identity at the center of his urban landscape for the first time, but he keeps Andy invisible. Instead, the audience sees the spaces where Andy works and plays. Bass takes the camera to actual inhabited environments, but he shows merely a microcosmic view of interiors, as contrasted to the public macrocosmic view of *West Side Story*.

Bass's first assignment for National Bohemian was redesigning the label for its twelve-ounce bottle. He also completed a series of wordless newspaper and magazine advertisements for the company that used only pictographs. Photographs of various men, both blue collar and white collar, were placed on a white background; above them are dialogue bubbles to which the subject is adding bottles of National Bohemian beer. The dialogue bubbles also appeared in ads in which pairs of men are engaged in some activity, such as bowling, and four more ads in which a heterogeneous couple is doing household chores, such as washing the dishes or painting.[91] Bass next produced a series of television commercials for National Bohemian (1957), one-minute spots called "Lights Out," "Peanut," and "Don't Touch that Dial," all of which play with the fact that National Bohemian's light beer had to be brewed in the dark.[92] A second set of National Bohemian commercials (1963–1965) was released in one- and two-minute versions and featured Andy Parker aka Regular Joe. Bass would later direct commercials for Rainier beer (1966), but the authorship of Olympia beer commercials (1970s) in the Bass Collection is in doubt.[93]

Like the Mennen Baby Magic commercials, the Andy Parker National Bohemian beer commercials are all about parts rather than wholes.[94] The one-minute spot begins with a close-up of a clock and the off-camera speaker announcing, "It's the end of a working day." Next, Bass cuts together images of hands as they shut down an office—covering a typewriter, closing a file drawer, hanging up a phone, and so forth. Andy Parker is introduced as a white-collar office worker, but we see only the back of his head, his feet as he walks out the door, and his hands as he pays for a newspaper. The camera follows him as he walks down the street past a sign announcing the sale of mechanical toy dogs, making him "wonder if Tommy would like a toy." Next we see the man's reflection in a store window as the announcer chirps, "He knows a store window was made to straighten ties." The man enters through a steel door, and the commercial dissolves to a close-up of beer being poured into a tall glass, then cuts to a silhouette of the man at the bar as the bartender puts the glass in front of him. The next shot dissolves to a close-up of the bartender's hand wiping the counter as the announcer states, "Andy Parker knows the value of a good day's work." The final shots zooms in on a bottle of National Bohemian beer as Andy walks out the door in the background and the announcer concludes, "Like you, he knows the taste of quality. Maybe like Andy Parker you'll enjoy National Bohemian beer. That taste of pleasant living at the end of the day."

The Andy Parker–Regular Joe commercial is a film of body parts that creates a narrative surrounding the tired office worker having a quick beer before facing traffic and the kids at home. In the office, Bass creates a montage of hands, feet, and torsos from the secretarial pool, their purses and high heels the markers of their gender. Andy Parker is never seen in a frontal shot; rather, the camera catches the back of his head, his hands, arms, and feet, as he strolls through the cityscape. Even the city itself is not shown in long shots with the architectural sweep of *North by Northwest*; rather, it is depicted through urban way stations—the newspaper stand, the shop window, a street vendor, the local watering hole—spots rather than vistas. Later in the bar, which is typically dark, the white-collar worker is recognizable only by his suit and tie; his face is in shadows, his body merely a shadow as he walks back out into the light to face his commute after a moment of alcoholic respite. The television viewer thus sees and experiences the city from the point of view of the commuter, the camera functioning as a surrogate for both subject and object. Here, then, Bass is attempting to negotiate viewer identification with the office worker by keeping the latter's individuality indistinct and by placing the viewer in his position.

"The taste of pleasant living" had been National Bohemian beer's advertising slogan for decades, but here, Bass modernizes the brand by jettisoning its mascot—a one-eyed cartoon figure named Natty Boh that had been designed in 1936—and by implying that the beer is perfect for the new postwar, urban, gray-flannel-suit crowd. Indeed, a two-minute version of the same commercial does nothing more than add visual details, while making it clear that Andy Parker is a stereotype, one of thousands of male commuters who leave the office after a hard day's work, making the point with an image of swishing briefcases flying past the camera. Andy Parker is an urban flaneur, taking an indirect route to his suburban commuter train, tarrying at shop windows, and relaxing with a beer. In the longer version, Bass interpolates shots of men and women exiting an elevator as the door opens, feet and legs standing at a pedestrian crosswalk waiting for the light to change, and several commuters drinking beer and eating popcorn in the bar while the announcer intones, "The companionship of others who know the taste of quality."[95] Finally, the visual contrast between the light outside and the darkness inside the bar references another set of much shorter National Bohemian beer commercials (thirty-second spots) that Bass produced.[96] These spots were based on the notion of the beer achieving greatness by being brewed in the dark but drunk in the light, with a match or candle illuminating the National Bohemian label.

The narrative structure of the Andy Parker National Bohemian beer commercials is built around a journey from the office to the local bar and then, by implication, home to the wife and kids. The subject is visualized as a series of images of body parts that act as metonymies for the whole. Bass and his client believed their audience consisted of a suburban, white-collar, mostly male workforce that was not averse to having a beer at the local bar after work. The trek through the city at rush hour is communicated through specific way stations that isolate the subject, rather than showing him in the crowd. The narrative trope of a journey must have fascinated Bass, because he used it again and again in his credit sequences, commercials, and films, often imbued with a sense of discovery. Indeed, the journey allows the traveler to see a multitude of things and environments and, ideally, to acquire knowledge in the process.

6

Journeys of Discovery

Seeing Is Knowledge

A journey takes one to new places and allows one to see new things. Travel broadens horizons, changes perspectives, forces new points of view through the unavoidable confrontation with previously unknown geographies, environments, and peoples through the simple act of perception. Seeing is therefore a form of knowledge. Travel (whether actual or virtual) and acquisition of knowledge about the world are indelibly linked. We tend to forget that before the twentieth century, individuals who were not members of the ruling class rarely traveled and had few concepts of what the world looked like beyond their own horizon. The invention of the railroad in the nineteenth century began to democratize travel and made it much faster and more convenient as well. Steamships and better road systems also did their part. Almost simultaneously, the invention of photography in the mid-nineteenth century further changed perceptions of the world. Indeed, the age of modern travel and the birth of photographic media occurred at roughly the same moment in history, and both became primary manifestations of modernity.

The late-nineteenth-century advent of cinema and the automobile also occurred simultaneously, and both inventions accelerated the collapse of space and time. The world suddenly seemed much smaller. News and images that once took months, even years, to reach the masses were now available within a matter of days. The images may have been in black and white, but they moved. The earliest cinema audiences hungered for scenes of street life in New York, Paris, Moscow, Tokyo, and Jerusalem; the sugar fields of Cuba; the rubber plantations of Malaysia; the coal mines of Birmingham; and contemporary events such as the funeral of President

McKinley, the coronation of Czar Nicholas II, and the Boxer Rebellion. All this and more were captured by the first cameramen of Auguste and Louis Lumiere, who fanned out over the globe between 1896 and 1900 to shoot exotic and everyday sights; they screened the work on location to finance the journey and then sent the material back to Paris for worldwide distribution. The cinema brought a cornucopia of new sights in rapid succession, just as the experience of the urban landscape had. The cinema was a child not only of technology but also of rapid and largely unchecked urbanization. In the great cities of New York, Paris, and London, speed manifested itself in a time lapse of perception due to the compression of space, whereby humans, architecture, and traffic created a chaos of conflicting movement. The fragmentation of seeing resulted in a changed vision that not only transformed modernist art but also influenced early cinema's depiction of those phenomena.[1] The express purpose of Albert Kahn's *Archives de la Planète* was to collect travel film and photographic documents as a form of knowledge.

Saul Bass realized very early on the potential of the journey as a narrative device for both his titles and his films. Travel invariably involves a goal, both geographic and conceptual, but more often than not, the journey itself is the goal, as if the mere accomplishment of the quest leads to the acquisition of knowledge. This is certainly true for Saul and Elaine Bass's most mature manifestation of the travel narrative in *Quest*, where the completion of the journey leads magically and inexplicably to enlightenment. However, it is also true for Bass's previous short films and his title sequences, even if, in those cases, knowledge of the world seems more a by-product of than the raison d'être for the quest. Indeed, during such journeys, knowledge is gained sequentially and serendipitously, like Walter Benjamin's urban flaneur or like Bass's boy walking along the beach.

Titles on the Move

By the 1970s, having a character on the move in the title sequence, either leaving for or arriving from somewhere else, had become cliché. Such title sequences could introduce the characters or even create identities, while keeping the plot on hold until the title sequence ended and the story proper began. In the late 1980s, when Elaine and Saul Bass first returned to creating credit sequences, they produced a number of titles that employed this strategy but were, for the most part, too nondescript to even be recognized as Bass titles. For example, the titles for *Big* (1988, Penny Marshall) feature a twelve-year-old boy walking home from school, giving few indications in terms of style and content that Saul Bass designed them. The same can be said for the Basses' titles for *Doc Hollywood* (1991, Michael Caton-Jones) and *A Bronx Tale* (1993, Robert De Niro), although in the latter, an opening montage of wise guys hanging out on street corners in the Bronx, precisely cut to the tune of Dion and the Belmonts' "I Wonder Why" (1958), bears Saul's unmistakable signature, especially in terms of its repetitive motion. It had not always been so. When Saul Bass created his first title sequences in the mid-1950s, the trope of the journey had not yet ossified into a cliché.

Ironically, Bass's title sequence for Martin Ritt's *Edge of the City* (1957), his first to use the narrative trope of the journey, also inserts his typical designs for graphic city lights over the live-action images. Bass thus doubles the view of New York City, showing the Manhattan skyline at night in the live-action journey, and using abstract white rectangles to symbolize the city between the typography. This bifurcation of the urban environment may refer to the moral choices the hero must make. Indeed, the ferryboat ride in the dark takes the central character to his future workplace, where, over the course of the narrative, he will grow in moral stature—standing "ten feet tall," in the words of one character—because he has stood up to evil while remaining true to his friend and colleague.

Edge of the City is based on a teleplay, "A Man Is Ten Feet Tall," written by Robert Alan Aurthur, directed by Robert Mulligan, and broadcast on NBC's *Philco Television Playhouse* on 2 October 1955. David Susskind, who produced the teleplay with Aurthur, took the project to Metro-Goldwyn-Mayer for a big-screen version. (He was hoping to repeat the theatrical success of *Marty*, another *Philco* show. Originally broadcast in May 1953 at the end of the program's sixth season, *Marty* became a huge box-office hit in April 1955, eventually winning an Oscar for Ernest Borgnine.) Sidney Poitier, who received his first costar billing in *Edge of the City*, was the only actor to be carried over from the television production, and his performance marked the first time an African American starred in a dramatic role on American television. Poitier was paid only $15,000, while blacklisted director Martin Ritt earned a mere $10,000. These extremely miserly salaries reflected the fact that the studio was not willing to budget more than $500,000 for the production because of its racial content. Shot on location in the Bronx and Harlem, the film ran into trouble with the Motion Picture Production Code Administration because of the possible homosexuality of the central character, Alex Nordman, played by John Cassavetes. According to internal memos, the Breen office asked that at least two scenes be changed because they communicated the hero's "almost psychopathic aversion to women."[2]

The film received rave reviews from a preview audience, and even the reviews in the mainstream New York press were very positive, complimenting the liberal-minded producers, all of whom were first-time filmmakers. Calling it a "courageous, thought-provoking and exciting film," the critic for *Variety* noted that despite the interracial relationship at the heart of the narrative, it was not a film "about the Negro problem."[3] Bosley Crowther in the *New York Times* also considered the film an earnest effort but thought the drama too often fell into the patterns of American television, while the story itself was too imitative of *On the Waterfront* (1953).[4] According to the *Village Voice*, the film had qualities reminiscent of the best Italian Neorealist films and was an important example of Hollywood's attempt to insert some social significance into its products; however, it was marred by a "happy ending" that allowed the weak hero to defeat the bully who was twice his size.[5]

The black-and-white titles for *Edge of the City* open with Alex Nordman (Cassavetes), dressed in work clothes, running toward the camera as a metal gate is being closed. Alex jumps the barrier and leaps onto the ferry, just as it is pulling away from the dock into the night. As "Metro-Goldwyn-Mayer Presents" appears in white lettering on the screen, Alex strolls out onto the deck in silhouette, lighting a cigarette against the New York skyline, followed by the film's title in Times New Roman font, with "Edge" just below the horizontal axis, "of" just above, and "the City" twelve points below the axis. The words appear individually and disappear the same way, replaced by the names of the costars, Cassavetes and Poitier, in caps well below the axis; at the same time, graphic lights are stacked vertically, forming what can be interpreted as three high-rise buildings. The supporting players' names appear in right-justified caps, screen right, as does the screenwriter credit, while the camera tracks the ferryboat passing through the night, accompanied by changing patterns of white rectangles. Having reached the shore, Alex crosses the railroad tracks and walks up a ramp as the musical and technical credits appear, including "Titles designed by Saul Bass," with more rectangles to the right of the left-justified credits. Surprisingly, for the final credits for Susskind and

Ritt, the white rectangles form horizontal lines as borders for the names as Alex walks back down the rail-yard ramp (having asked for directions, one assumes), past the camera, and toward the door of an office.

The serif typography shoots out from the screen as if typed, reinforcing the film's journalistic aspects: it tells a socially critical story, ripped from the headlines. Carrying a bag, Alex Nordman is clearly in a hurry as he barely makes it onto the departing ferry traversing the East River, as the skyline in the background indicates. The silhouetted figure might indicate that he is a person with a dark past, one who has made poor moral choices and now hopes to correct them. However, with his face in shadows, except for a brief pass by the camera at the end of the title sequence, Alex remains a solitary working-class figure, facing the lights of the city and a dark industrial landscape. The city's contours and character are unknowable in the darkness, allowing the audience to question what is to come, just as Alex may be doing in his reverie. The long tracking shot of the ferry focuses on the narrative on a journey, although the boat itself is hardly visible in the darkness; its interior lights form a horizontal pattern that is distinguishable from the lights of New York in the background only by its movement. The ferry lights are mirrored later in the white rectangles accompanying the producer credits. Clearly, the abstract graphic forms presented with the credits are the title's most interesting innovation, although they are missing from release prints in circulation.[6] Saul Bass himself had a somewhat elaborate and complicated explanation for the use of these graphic forms:

> Against the live-action background play a series of animated rectangles. At the beginning, they create a sense of "drive" (as the protagonist runs down the pathway to a ferry) by popping on and off the screen in long, horizontal patterns. Later (as the figure crosses the river on the ferry) they assume a symbolic representation of the lights of the Manhattan skyscrapers as they flicker on and off the screen. They once again resume the horizontal "drive" character (as he moves through the freight yard on the other side of the river) interspersed with random flickering "thought" patterns near his head. Finally, they lead us visually to the bright light of the hiring office door and end as our story begins.

While such an interpretation may have been clear in the designer's mind, it was probably not so apparent to contemporary audiences; they were already attempting to read the live-action images and the credits, leaving little cognitive energy to analyze the graphic permutations of the abstract forms. Only in the middle, when the background is less busy, can the rectangles be read as abstract reflections of the skyline.

The key to the graphic element may be in Bass's poster design. His posters for *Edge of the City* (the one-sheet, three-sheet, and half-sheet) all feature a pencil drawing of a man running on Bass's signature red background. The man's torso is cut off at the chest by the top of the image, while a much smaller woman is seen running behind him. Although the red background gives no sense of perspective, the size of the figures creates perspective; this is reinforced by small yellow rectangles in the background, making it appear as if they are running away from the city. The film's title below is laid out architecturally, as if it is another building, but it also balances the composition. The poster thus communicates that the story takes place at the edge of the city, which is true in the sense that it is set in the rail yards, away from the city center. Interestingly, in the three-sheet version, the male protagonist is cut off a bit lower, revealing that he is wearing a tie, which misrepresents his status as a member of the working class. The poster clearly identifies the rectangles as city lights. Therefore, the doubling of the city lights in the titles may be understood as a visualization of the contrast between the harsh reality of the city and the idealized graphic version. Likewise, there is the protagonist's moral choice between facing the reality of his situation as an army deserter and bringing his friend's killer to justice, and holding on to the illusion that he can live outside of social reality. The titles thereby reflect the deeply political choices the socially conscious filmmakers are offering their protagonist.

While the titles for *Edge of the City* visualize a journey in an urban environment, Bass's titles for William Wyler's *The Big Country* (1958) depict an endless journey through the nineteenth-century American West. The titles communicate the slowness of travel, rather than speed. Attempting to visualize the isolation of the ranching community that is the locale for the film's narrative, Bass focuses on a stagecoach, which is dwarfed by the endless landscape of the American plains. As Bass states in *Bass on Titles*: "I tried to establish the notion of an island of people in a sea of land, the vastness of which is penetrated by a stagecoach. After an endless journey it reaches this isolated people and only then does the story begin."

A year later he admitted that critics had told him the *Big Country* titles were nice but not very Bass-like.[7]

The Big Country, a big-budget western epic, was based on the novel *Ambush at Blanco Canyon* by Donald Hamilton, which had been serialized in the *Saturday Evening Post* in February 1957. It is the story of a feud between two families over water rights in the parched high plains of the American West. No fewer than five writers were credited on the movie script, although there were actually seven writers, including Leon Uris.[8] Apparently, none of them delivered a satisfactory script, forcing the team to begin production without one.[9] Bass was brought in during preproduction in April 1957, after Gregory Peck told Leon Roth of United Artists that he wanted to hire Bass: "He will design trade ads, newspaper and magazine ads, billboards, special stationery, invitations, various announcements, etc. He will undertake to find a keynote or trade-mark by which the picture can be readily identified. And, he will design the titles for the picture."[10] Shot on location at the Drais Ranch near Stockton, California, and at Red Rock Canyon, Jawbone Canyon, and the Mojave Desert, as well as at the Goldwyn studios, the film was in production from 30 July to 18 November 1957.[11] The location shooting devoured $35,000 a day, and the whole film was completed at a cost of $3.1 million, making it one of the most expensive westerns ever produced.[12] The film was formatted in the relatively new Technirama process, which, like VistaVision, utilized an eight-perforation, horizontal anamorphic image at a ratio of 2.25:1; it was then reduced to 2.35:1 on 35mm and stretched to 2.21:1 on 70mm road-show prints with a stereo track, the latter sold as Super Technirama 70.[13] Bass employed the second unit in Stockton to get the images he needed for the title sequence.[14] The film opened at the Astor in New York on 1 October 1958.

Due to its huge costs and a first-run gross of only $4 million, *The Big Country* broke even but hardly produced any income for Peck and Wyler, who were each entitled to 25 percent of the profits.[15] It did earn a Best Supporting Actor Oscar for Burl Ives and a nomination for its music, but little else. It was, however, the top box-office performer in the United Kingdom in 1959. Critic W. R. Wilkerson actually predicted that the film would lose money because its extreme length prohibited speedy audience turnover, resulting in lower ticket sales.[16] Bosley Crowther complained that this was the most bellicose and violent film about peace ever made, thereby referencing Peck's and Wyler's previous pacifist outing in *Friendly*

Persuasion (1956).[17] Another critic also cited the pacifist angle as a way of blowing up the film into a "long and ambitious western" but concluded, "for the most part the approach is pedestrian and superficial."[18] *Time* magazine, in contrast, called the film "a starkly beautiful, carefully written classic western that demands comparison to *Shane*."[19] None of the reviewers chose to comment on Bass's titles.

Saul Bass was hired to do both the titles and some of the publicity. He produced what was apparently intended to be the film's logo: a huge yellow sun, painted in the style of Van Gogh, on an orange background. The high art connection was purposeful, given that the studio was marketing the film as an arty western with major stars, not as a Saturday matinee "oater." The logo appeared on Bass's B-style one-sheet, the half-sheet, a Japanese re-release poster from 1966, the sound-track album, and the press book, while the majority of the United Artists publicity featured head and body images of the large cast of stars.[20] Like the titles, all the Bass images are composed to emphasize the vastness of the landscape in relation to the tiny stagecoach on the horizon. The large sun logo and the horizon are placed in the bottom quarter of the frame, while orange sky fills the remaining space above.

Taking advantage of the wide screen, Bass opens the titles with a racing stagecoach pulled by six horses and with two riders atop it. The image fills the length of the screen and moves left; the camera holds the composition as "UNITED ARTISTS PRESENTS" appears in white sans serif capitals, justified screen right. Credits in a slightly larger sans serif font with shadow highlights for Gregory Peck, Jean Simmons, and Carroll Baker follow on the same line, just above the horizontal axis, as does the credit for Charlton Heston, as the image cuts to a close-up of thundering horses' hooves. The shot continues for William Wyler's above-the-title credit just below the horizontal axis, then cuts to a wide-screen vista of the open landscape; the stagecoach and horses are dwarfed on a road that traverses the frame at the horizontal axis, as the film's title appears below. The stagecoach continues its journey on the road for Burl Ives's and Charles Bickford's credits, then dissolves very slowly to a high-angle close-up of the giant moving wagon wheel; the axle is at the frame's exact center, and credits for the supporting cast appear on the horizontal axis and then justified in a column at screen left. For the script and musical credits, Bass again dissolves to an extreme long shot of the stagecoach, meandering toward the camera; this dissolves again to a close-up of the horses' legs for Franz Planer's credit as cinematographer. The remaining technical credits fade in and out, while Bass utilizes long dissolves between extreme long shots and close-ups of the stagecoach. After Wyler's credit as director, the stagecoach rolls away from the camera, up the vertical axis, and toward a distant town on the horizon.

The superwide screen gave Bass a proper canvas to capture those endless golden plains in his 2:39-minute title sequence. Cinematographer Franz Planer desaturated the image further to give the landscape a dried-out look. Indeed, the subsequent narrative involves an irrational feud over water in this moisture-deprived landscape. Just as the poster is monochromatic in orange, yellow, white, and black, Bass limits his color palette in the titles to a golden yellow, the brown-black of the horses, a pale blue sky, and the white typography, again emphasizing the dryness of the landscape through a poverty of color. Meanwhile, on the sound track, Jerome Moross's score pounds out grandiose western themes to accompany the journey. Everything is done on an epic scale in Wyler's western, so Bass chooses a thick font to give the white typography weight against the mostly golden background.

The wide-screen vistas again emphasize the vastness of the landscape. The horizon moves up and down but is always above and exactly parallel to the horizontal axis, thus taking advantage of the Technirama screen. Surprisingly, Bass had this to say about wide-screen cinematography: "The wide screen works extremely well with panoramic vistas such as in *The Big Country*. . . . On the whole it works against our interests except for horizontal figures and that provides us with certain advantages."[21] The last image shows the stagecoach driving up the vertical axis of the frame, the town nestled at the top of the screen, on the horizon, creating a visual *T* that marks the journey's end point.

Bass cuts from the long shots of the stagecoach to close-ups of the horses' heads, the wheels, and the hooves, keeping these images compositionally steady (the camera tracking to keep the objects centered), yet their intense movement gives the impression of speed. Bass contrasts the slow movement of the stagecoach in the extreme long shots with the kinetic speed of the close shots, utilizing long dissolves to emphasize the contrast even further. The designer is thus playing with onscreen space through the variable movement of the stagecoach in the long and close shots, contrasting speed and stasis. Interestingly, Bass excludes images of any human beings, except for the tiny stagecoach drivers seen briefly in the first shot, thus emphasizing the isolation and emptiness of the town that is the stagecoach's destination. It is an alien environment that must be penetrated but offers little relief to the traveler. It is also possible that Bass and Wyler wanted to avoid showing any of the riders in the stagecoach to heighten the mystery of who would be making such a long and tedious journey. Only when the stagecoach stops in the town is it revealed that it is the easterner, Gregory Peck, who has come to shake things up in this intractable family feud. Having passed his first test by just getting there, he will be further tested over the course of the narrative.

If *The Big Country* is all about open spaces, then Otto Preminger's *The Cardinal* (1963) is metaphorically about closed-off spaces, about a lack of horizons and the limited choices available to a representative of the Catholic Church. Like Preminger's previous films about institutions (e.g., *Anatomy of a Murder*, *Advise and Consent*), *The Cardinal* delivers an exemplary analysis of the church by following the career of a lowly priest who is eventually elected to the College of Cardinals in Rome. Bass's credit sequence marks the priest's journey on foot through the streets of the Vatican to the meeting where he will be told of his ascension to cardinal. According to Bass, the walk gives the character the opportunity to reminisce about his past life, shown in flashback in the narrative proper, but ironically, the title sequence gives no indication what he is really thinking about.

The rights to Henry Morton Robinson's 1950 novel had been languishing at Columbia since 1955, after Louis de Rochemont's intention to turn it into a film failed.[22] Columbia dropped the project because of fierce opposition from Cardinal Spellman of New York, who was convinced the central character was modeled on him.[23] This left the field open for Preminger, who announced in August 1961, while *Advise and Consent* was still in production, that *The Cardinal* would be his next project. Beginning in the summer of 1962, he worked with Robert Dozier to produce a script from the sprawling novel, but blacklisted writer Ring Lardner Jr. and Gore Vidal both did rewrites without credit. Preminger was probably responsible for a key scene that is not in the novel; it takes place in 1938, at the time of the Anschluss in Vienna, and illustrates the Catholic Church's cowardly attitude toward the Nazis.[24] Production commenced in February 1963, with much of the film shot on location in Boston, Rome (the Vatican), and Vienna, as well as at Revue Studios in

North Hollywood, and it wrapped on 10 May 1963.[25] The Vatican liaison for the film was a young Joseph Ratzinger, who would become Pope Benedict XVI. After private screenings at the Vatican, which may have financed a portion of the film, *The Cardinal* had its world premiere in Paris in November and opened in Boston on 12 December as a benefit for Cardinal Cushing. Initially road-showed at premium prices, *The Cardinal* had box-office receipts in excess of $7 million by May 1964 and would eventually gross over $11 million.[26]

The reviews were decidedly mixed. Bosley Crowther spent more than half his review musing about the film it might have been if Preminger had focused on the old cardinal played by John Huston, concluding that the hero was totally colorless, even if the film had lots of pageantry.[27] Irene Thirer wrote in the *New York Post*: "The story of a man, rather than a priest, played with true humility by Tom Tryon, is pictorially exquisite, intelligently cast, and painstakingly, if not thrillingly directed."[28] Hollis Alpert remarked that the cardinal "seems more Protestant than Catholic. . . . They seem to have forgotten to include in him signs of genuine zeal, fervor, and a sense of mission." Ironically, in one of the few reviews that mentions the titles, Preminger gets credit for their style: "He had Saul Bass create a main title which is exclusively Preminger and it has become his trademark."[29]

As with other Preminger projects, Bass was responsible for elements of the publicity campaign and the premiere invitation, as well as the credit sequence. For the logo, Bass chose to use the title itself, with "The" casting a giant shadow behind the word "Cardinal" at the bottom of the image. Bass places this logo on his trademark red-orange background, covering the top three-fourths of the one-sheet poster; below, the word "Cardinal" in white transitions to a white field that captures the remaining credits in black typography and acts as a pedestal for the logo.[30] Inside "The," Bass creates a montage of photographic images of actor Tom Tryon and his almost love interest, played by Romy Schneider; a couple dancing the tango; and a Nazi parade. "The" has been interpreted as the giant shadow of the church and its power, but why Bass eschewed an iconographic logo in this case is unclear. One explanation may be that he wanted to avoid the use of any overtly religious symbolism that could have been identified with the Catholic Church but might have limited audience appeal. *Logos* means "word" in Greek, and it is indeed the words of the New Testament and the writings of the church fathers that are the basis of Catholicism's beliefs, rules, and regulations; therefore, using a word-based image as a logo makes some sense, given that the film is about the strictures of the Catholic Church. The images within the word, in contrast, seem to conform to Hollywood publicity maxims, since the focus on heterosexual relations (along with a little controversial political commentary) makes little sense, given the film's actual narrative. For the window insert, Bass used the logo at the bottom of the frame, keeping the article as a black shadow; he then added five photographic images in a broken window design, as he had done in the trade advertising for *Death of a Salesman*, again highlighting nonexistent heterosexual sex. However, Bass's design must have been considered successful, because it was used for all the various poster sizes as well as for trade advertisements and other collateral. Years later, Bass would reuse the idea of a logocentric design for his poster of Stanley Kubrick's *The Shining* (1980), inserting a ghostly image within another "The" that dwarfs "Shining."

Bass's titles for *The Cardinal* are among his most beautiful. The visual design adheres to a strict grid structure, in terms of both the live action and the placement of typography. Interestingly, the live-action shots are uncommonly long in the 3:10-minute sequence, averaging ten seconds, yet the graphic titles themselves conform completely to the Bass brand. To highlight the overall graphic design of the live-action shots, Bass composes his images to emphasize horizontal and vertical lines and patterns that are inherent in either the Roman pavement or his framing. The movement of the actor through these spaces is either horizontal (parallel to the lines of the titles and the composition) or vertical, but in such a way as to obliterate any sense of depth. Likewise, the titles on the horizontal axis either directly parallel the lines of the action or form crosses with the vertical lines of the composition, adding to the impression of flatness. A number of other titles are placed on monochromatic fields without strong vertical or horizontal lines. Bass plays with the flatness of the design by reducing his color palette to a virtually monochromatic brown, beige, white, and black.

The first long take, lasting twenty-one seconds, could have been shot by Preminger. As the cardinal leaves his house, the camera tracks him as he walks past and crosses the street. It is the only image in which the central character's features are visible, in which he is identifiable as an individual. In all subsequent shots, the priest is seen from behind, from the side, as a fleeting black-robed figure barely visible in an alley, as a shadow on the pavement, as an upside-down reflection in a pool of water, or in an extreme long shot as nothing but an exclamation point in a largely mono-chromatic pattern—in other words, as a stereotypical priest. Like the trav-elers in *Edge of the City* and *The Big Country*, the churchman remains a cipher. For example, the sequence's third shot, after the character is intro-duced, uses the shadows of stone columns to create black vertical and horizontal bars that form squares through which the priest passes; he is seen only walking away from the camera, seemingly moving without movement because of the use of a telephoto lens to flatten space. In another shot, Bass films Tryon in the background, tracking him with the camera as lines of vertical columns pass in the foreground, accentuating horizontal movement. Bass brilliantly exploits the wide screen by compos-ing images of stairs that cover the screen with parallel lines; at other times he shoots slightly downward, so that only the pavement and its patterns are visible. Indeed, the figure of the priest is constantly framed by vertical and horizontal patterns. Only a single short shot visualizes the priest walk-ing up stairs that are placed diagonally in the composition, indicating that he is "on the way up," but even here, he remains a shadow. Why does Bass use this level of abstraction to depict a journey to one of the Catholic Church's highest offices?

Bass's titles demonstrate that *The Cardinal* is decidedly not the biog-raphy of an individual priest rising to the top of the church hierarchy; rather, it is about the history of the Catholic Church as experienced by one of its members. Like many of Preminger's other films, *The Cardinal* focuses on the functioning of an institution, not on the individual psy-chology of its characters. Furthermore, during the course of the narrative, the cardinal is shown to be a weak character who consistently bows to the edicts of the church, even when his sister's life is at stake. In fact, his suc-cess as a churchman is based on his weakness, on his inability to break out of the rutted path the church has planned for him, even when he momen-tarily falls in love with a woman. Surprisingly, Bass's description of the title sequence gives quite a different impression: "The film opens just prior to his becoming a Cardinal, and then moves back in time to review his life. The title shows him walking through Rome . . . through the Pagan and Christian landmarks of the Eternal City . . . as he meditates on his past life."[31]

But in fact, the cardinal must conform to the patterns he traverses (on either the horizontal or the vertical axis) if he wishes to achieve his goals within the church. For this reason, the central character is depicted as wandering through a rigid maze, a cipher who is virtually invisible in the grid that represents church doctrine. (Interestingly, Bass reuses many of these images in the title sequence for his unused finale for *Phase IV* and in *Quest*, where the compositional grid also represents a new world order.) Ironically, the sequence's last split image—with the church on one side and "il Duce" graffiti on the other—may be Bass's trademark joke, this time on Preminger, whose name fades out on the image. While ostensibly signaling the film's historical time frame, it could also be a comment on Preminger's well-publicized mistreatment of Tom Tryon, who left the acting profession as a result of the experience.

Bass's titles for *A Walk on the Wild Side* (1962), directed by Edward Dmytryk and based on a 1956 novel by Nelson Algren, may be his most celebrated, receiving more press than virtually any others. Apart from their undeniable excellence, reviewers were struck by the contrast to the mediocre film that followed. Indeed, even Dmytryk acknowledged in his autobiography that Bass's titles were "a masterpiece," although he also claimed the film had been well received.[32] Since most of the film's narrative takes place in a New Orleans bordello, Bass visualizes a journey of a different sort here: a promenade by an alley cat through its turf in the urban jungle. Steven Spielberg later told Bass that he tried to re-create the title sequence with his 8mm camera and his pet dog after seeing that black cat in *A Walk on the Wild Side*.[33]

Charles K. Feldman bought the rights to the novel, looking for a vehicle to make the European actress Capucine a star.[34] He then hired several scriptwriters to turn the digressive and virtually plotless novel into a workable script and to get the controversial material past the Motion Picture Production Code Office. According to published statements by actor Laurence Harvey after the film opened, he blamed Feldman for bringing in new writers who destroyed the script by watering it down.[35] Shot on location in New Orleans, as well as at Columbia studios in the summer of 1961, the film was supposed to premiere in New Orleans, but the event was canceled when the city fathers apparently objected to the film; instead, the film opened in New York on 21 February 1962.[36]

Before shooting the title sequence, Bass first did tests in 16mm using his own cat. As he later commented: "You could talk to that cat and it would do anything on demand." However, Bass's cat died before filming actually commenced. The sequence eventually took three or four days to shoot, including faking the cat fight by having people wear gloves and hold the cats.[37] Bass was apparently not involved in any of the publicity designs, although the black cat is featured on the posters and on Elmer Bernstein's sound-track album. According to Bernstein, after meeting with the producers about the score, he had no idea what to do, but Bass's storyboards of the cat fight inspired him.[38] Bass's own statements about why he used the cat are contradictory. In one description he notes: "The film is set in New Orleans in the early Thirties. And is about the disenfranchised, tough, seamy characters of a despairing time. Symbolic of this is the cat in these titles credits."[39] Ten years later he exclaimed: "The cat was the symbol of the basic variability and changeability of the women who were the central characters. So the cat was right for the theme and mood of the film."[40]

The reviews for *Walk on the Wild Side* were mixed, due in no small part to the fact that many critics, such as Hedda Hopper and Brendan Gill, were uncomfortable with the subject of prostitution.[41] They saw the film as vulgar at best and as catering to European depravity at worst. Other reviewers noted that the film failed to hold up to the titles Bass had created.[42] There were also some genuinely positive reviews that praised both the film and Bass's titles, including Hazel Flynn: "So we have here what really amounts to an exposé comparing vice to a black panther prowling the back alleys of a city, state or nation . . . in search of the innocent to prey upon with all the cunning and voracious appetite of the wild and savage beast."[43] Finally, there was Judith Crist, the "critic most hated by Hollywood,"[44] who caustically demolished the film (but praised Bass): "The complicated plot, which aspires to being at most 'adult' and at least naughty, winds up as bathetic, foolish and dreary, a muddled mélange of vacuous characters and naïve pseudo-psychology."[45]

The titles begin with Elmer Bernstein's award-winning tune and an arresting image of stacked concrete pipes. The largest one in the center reveals a black cat as the camera zooms into the darkness of the pipe, where two cat's eyes are visible just above the film's title in white sans serif capitals on the horizontal axis. The cat's eyes stay onscreen in a slow dissolve as Bass cuts to an extreme high-angle shot of a black cat walking down the vertical axis, while the stars' names appear left-justified. Another dissolve reveals the cat strolling horizontally, its black body filling the frame, while Barbara Stanwyck's credit appears left-justified on the horizontal axis. Perfectly matching a cut on action, Bass dissolves to an even closer shot from the same angle of the cat's paws, as the supporting players are listed left-justified. Another dissolve has the cat walking straight toward the camera, which must have been placed on the pavement, as the major behind-the-scenes credits fade in and out. Bass next dissolves to a shot of the cat walking horizontally to the right, then behind a wooden fence, so that the animal is visible only in the cracks. It then moves in front of the fence, as Bass zeroes in on a close-up of the cat's head, framed by credits for the production designer and associate producer above and below. Walking behind a chain-link fence and between some pipes, the cat continues to wander as more credits appear. Finally, seeing a white cat, the black cat attacks, leading to a quick montage of a cat fight before the "hero" emerges victorious. An extreme close-up of the cat's head and eyes marks the moment, before it resumes its stroll as the credits for the producer and director appear.

Formally, the 2:48-minute sequence, consisting of thirty-eight shots, is constructed very similarly to the title sequence for *The Cardinal*, except that here the protagonist is consistently moving to the right instead of to the left. Like the later title, *Walk on the Wild Side* begins with a long twenty-one-second shot, zooming in on the "hero" rather than tracking him. All the remaining shots, however, are much shorter, as was Bass's usual style. One anomaly in the graphics is the use of a decorative feminine line design separating the principal actors' credits. The lighting in the black-and-white film is extremely high key, indicating that it is nighttime. A strong sidelight illuminating the openings of the pipes, which form stark circles, is reminiscent of the *Alcoa Premiere* sequence, which Bass was producing almost simultaneously. Utilizing invisible nighttime light sources, Bass divides his screen horizontally between the light pavement and the dark background, so that the cat's body is often invisible in the darkness, except for the eyes in frontal shots. The cat's walk was clearly shot at significantly more than twenty-four frames per second, giving its movements a languid, lazy, slow-motion feeling, especially in connection with the slow dissolves. In contrast, the cat's movement is accentuated when it walks behind a wooden or chain-link fence or behind pipes in the foreground, a device Bass also used in *The Cardinal*. Bass intercuts longer and closer shots, again to vary the perception of movement even though the action is continuous, as he did in *The Big Country*.

The cat fight consists of twenty-four separate shots in a blur of white and black fur; each shot is only a fraction of a second long, so the battle is over almost before it begins. The feline altercation is, of course, Bass's trademark surprise at the end of the title sequence. Here, it becomes all the more graphic through the contrast between the black and white cats. Given that the central conflict in the film is between a naïve country bumpkin come to the big city and a hard-boiled madam of a whorehouse, one might, as Bass did later, see the cat fight as a metaphor for the film's narrative. Bass, of course, is playing with a slang term for a house of prostitution—namely, a cathouse—and he ends the title sequence with a literal cat fight—also a slang term for an altercation between two women fighting "in a vicious, cat-like manner, esp. by scratching, pulling hair, and biting."[46] While the black cat successfully defends its turf against the intruder and continues its journey, the end of the cinematic narrative is both violent and deadly.

Interestingly, thanks to several close-ups of its face and eyes, the cat has more personality than any of the human characters in Bass's other title sequences constructed around journeys. The cat's body movements, particularly in close-ups focusing on the front paws, have a grace that not only cat lovers find appealing, especially accompanied by Elmer Bernstein's jazzy crossover hit. The first and longest image of the sequence gives a lot of face time to the cat, making it abundantly clear that this is a good-looking cat that has the right moves—a "character" the audience can identify with. Whereas the black cat is well groomed for stardom, the white cat is covered with street dirt; it is, after all, an urban alley cat. The black cat appears not only in the title sequence but also in the end credits, where it walks over an old newspaper announcing the fate of the jealous madam. Constructed of outtakes, the end sequence shows the cat walking in the opposite direction from the opening, its body filling the frame through the end credits and a final "The End." The cat's "humanity" makes the sequence work, as indicated by the critical response.

What *Walk on the Wild Side* demonstrates by its implementation of the mechanisms of identification is how little identity is given to the characters in other Bass titles. They remain shadows, figures trapped in the geometry of Bass's landscape designs. The titles contain not a single close-up—the very thing actors fight for. Is this a case in which the formal challenge—that is, to prepare for the beginning of the narrative proper without actually beginning it—forces Bass to deny any possibility of identification, thus bringing his project within the realm of avant-garde cinema? Just as his titles continue to be constructed along a grid, his characters are strictly limited to horizontal and/or vertical movements, parallel to the frame's axes. This rigid formalism functions only to call attention to the artificiality of the image itself, again countering the aesthetic thrust of Hollywood narrative cinema, which makes artifice invisible. We can therefore theorize that in Bass's titles about journeys, it is not the characters themselves or their symbolic stand-ins who acquire knowledge through travel; it is the audience. In contrast, Saul Bass's films either create characters for identification or construct subjective views for the audience that visualize the acquisition of knowledge through travel, through the quest.

From Here to There

Sponsored by United Airlines, Saul and Elaine Bass's first film together, *From Here to There* (1964), was produced for the Transportation and Travel Pavilion at the New York World's Fair and was shown at United Airlines' Jetarama Theater from 22 April 1964 through 17 October 1965.[47] Though slightly less than nine minutes long, the film had a huge impact in terms of both its reception by hundreds of thousands of viewers at the World's Fair and its awards at international festivals. Technically innovative in its use of both 35mm Academy aperture (in monochrome sepia) and 35mm Cinemascope (in color), the film is conceptually simple—an airplane journey from Los Angeles to New York, or. from here to there. Yet it is brilliantly executed, turning vision from the air into a kaleidoscope of abstract art images. Indeed, the film embodies the notion that travel broadens human perception by allowing travelers to see the United States as they have never seen it before. Bass himself described the film as follows: "The film deals, in kaleidoscopic form, with the air travel experience—the excitement, the love, the poignancy—of partings and greetings, and the unique visual experience of aerial flight."[48]

Although no documentation survives revealing how Bass won the commission to make the film, the idea to shoot straight down from the air onto the landscape probably came from his experience working on the opening of *West Side Story*. Indeed, some of the later images in *From Here to There*, such as when the plane is circling New York to land, could have been outtakes from the earlier film. *From Here to There* was independently produced by Saul Bass & Associates, directed by Saul Bass, and "conceived and designed" by Elaine and Saul Bass. Albert Nalpas edited the film with Saul, and Jeff Alexander composed the music. The aerial photography was shot by William Garnett from a Cessna aircraft; one camera was mounted to point through a side window, and another camera shot footage through a port cut in the bottom of the plane.

After the New York World's Fair closed, the film was shown at numerous festivals and was distributed through Pyramid Films, although the 16mm nontheatrical Pyramid prints did not open up to a wide-screen view, as the 35mm version did.[49] The film won the Gold Medal Award from the Art Directors Club of Los Angeles, the Golden Eagle Award from CINE (Council on International Non-Theatrical Events), and prizes from the Chicago International Film Festival, the International Film Festival of New York, the Rio de Janeiro International Film Festival, the Cracow International Festival of Short Films, and the Melbourne Film Festival.

The reviews were extremely complimentary to Saul Bass. Shortly after the fair opened, the critic for *Cue Magazine* wrote: "Evidently Mr. Bass, so well-represented at Eastman Kodak, cannot complete an assignment without artistry. The little introduction and epilogue are as humorous and poignant as the meetings and partings of all humanity."[50] The *Hollywood Reporter* positively gushed: "One thing Bass demonstrates brilliantly is that the art form serves its creator or interpreter to the degree that the artist knows his art. Bass is a master and an innovator in film because he knows film's limitations and elasticity." Meanwhile, a review in the *Los Angeles Herald Examiner* reminds us that air travel was still a rare experience for many Americans in 1964: "For more than 150 million Americans, jet travel has only been a dream. And for those who have never flown, a unique visual experience awaits them at the United Airlines exhibit at the New York World's Fair."[51]

From Here to There opens at Los Angeles International Airport as passengers arrive with their bags, wait in the terminal for their flights, and bid farewell to their friends, relatives, and lovers. Bass then cuts to a close-up of a jet engine, followed by shots of a United Airlines jet moving down the runway and taking off. Two minutes into the film, the aperture opens up to a wide-screen vista as Bass transitions to a subjective view from the plane itself. He then alternates between highly abstracted views of the American landscape taken from 35,000 feet in the air, looking straight down, and images of the same or similar scenes taken from the ground. For example, Bass cuts from an image of the meandering Mississippi River to a shot of a steam-powered riverboat, or from a composition of big trees to aerial shots of logs floating in formation downriver to a logger on the river, then back to the aerial view. Whereas the images taken from the plane steadily but slowly track right, as if traveling from west to east, the images on the ground often involve movement within the wide-screen frame. Finally, as the plane approaches the runway at Idlewild Airport, shown in a subjective view from the air, the screen narrows again to Academy aperture. People are waiting at the gate as the passengers begin to arrive, carrying the same packages and suitcases seen earlier. Next, Bass creates a montage of reunions, including a close-up of Bass himself holding a giant stuffed panda and greeting a small child who runs into his arms. Finally, the scene focuses on a little girl watching a set of small mechanical birds hopping toward the exit. "Presented by United Airlines" is written on one bird, while another features "Produced by Saul Bass & Associates" around its button eye—Bass's trademark closing joke.

Although financed by United Airlines, *From Here to There* is more of an advertisement for air travel in general than for the carrier itself. Apart from the final credit, the United Airlines name and logo are seen only in extreme long shots of planes on the tarmac. The one exception is a rectangular matte shot after the plane lands that blocks out everything except its tail (featuring the old UA logo, ten years before Bass designed a new one). And given that the film is underscored with music but contains no voice-overs or dialogue or any words at all, there are no opportunities for promotion at that level. The nontheatrical Pyramid prints even eliminated the last mechanical bird shot with the United Airlines logo, another attempt by Bass to obfuscate the film's sponsored origins. On the narrative level, the film obviously reproduces Bass's own journey from Los Angeles to New York to attend the World's Fair. Yet Bass's film is in fact structured around vision as a form of knowledge; it makes the secondary point, by means of the airport scenes at the beginning and end of the film, that air travel brings people together quickly and efficiently. For each aspect, Bass develops a different aesthetic strategy.

For the opening and closing sequences in the airports' departure and arrival lounges, Bass uses a monochromatic, sepia-toned film stock in Academy aperture because he wants to emphasize the human emotions inherent in separations from and reunifications with family and friends. As noted earlier, Bass was not a big fan of wide-screen processes; like many classical Hollywood filmmakers, he considered wide screen too big for close-up views and therefore ineffective in capturing intimate moments that foster viewer identification. Indeed, both airport sequences are perfectly matched montages of specific visual details, with Bass relying on extreme close-ups that eliminate the surrounding context. In the opening at the Los Angeles airport, Bass edits together a series of bags and suitcases, cut on movement, as the passengers carrying them are tracked by the camera. He follows that up with a montage of close-ups of passengers and those being left behind, hugging, kissing, shaking hands, waving. In between, Bass adds a visual joke: he includes a shot of a little girl releasing a helium balloon, then shows groups of people staring up at the balloon out of the frame. In the New York airport, Bass again cuts together extreme close-up shots of people looking around and awaiting the arrival of passengers. Again he uses matched cuts as people find each other and hug and kiss, including an image of Bass himself kneeling on the floor to hug an arriving child. Elaine Bass is seen in another close-up, waving to an imaginary passenger. Bass inserts another joke: a girl opens a jack-in-the-box and gets whacked by her mother. Then come the mechanical birds as a final coda for the film's only credits, which serve to remind the audience that, unlike these hopping birds, they have just experienced real flight. The use of close-ups and matched cuts that emphasize effortless and smooth transitions (figuratively and literally) succeeds in creating moments of identification and empathy in the audience, bringing back to a human scale the celestial experience of flight.

The use of two different screen formats also brings into stark relief the contrast between the abstract experience of jet airplane travel and the human outcomes of travel itself. Interestingly, Bass transitions between the two, at both the beginning and the end, by cutting together images of the plane taking off and landing. These cinematographic images were achieved with a supertelephoto 1000mm lens, allowing close-ups of the plane's wheels, engines, and wings as it took off; however, this also completely flattened space, so the jet appears to be moving without movement. Bass repeats this design element in the views from the air, where the landscapes appear to be passing very slowly beneath the plane. The widescreen color images of flight not only visualize a unique perspective but also communicate the rich variety of natural and man-made landscapes and even moments of American history. As Bass learned from his experience creating the titles for *The Big Country* and *West Side Story*, the Cinemascope screen allows the camera to capture the sheer size of the

American continent, while also replicating the experience of looking down on an abstracted landscape and wondering what is actually down there. For his bird's-eye-view images, Bass may have drawn inspiration from aerial photographs reproduced by Kepes and Moholy-Nagy in their respective books, both noting that such views from on high destroy the Renaissance perspective and a stable horizon, allowing the establishment of spatial relationships that compress space.[52] Bass's aerial views are almost completely abstract, the various topographies of the landscape morphing into visual patterns, such as the checkerboards of the grain fields in the midwestern plains or the irregular shapes, lines, dots, and spots that make up the image of the Hoover Dam. While the former recalls Paul Klee, the latter could be mistaken for an Abstract Expressionist painting.

The urban landscapes, too, are like abstract canvases. One shot features a highway cutting the screen in half at the horizontal axis while an image of the Brooklyn Bridge is superimposed, adding a strong vertical design element. In another, an image of a highway interchange looks like a giant bow, then dissolves to an abstract pattern of parked cars. These aerial views alternate with shots from the ground that make concrete what was previously abstract—for instance, the Hoover Dam image is intercut with shots of water flowing through giant turbines. Here, Bass is presenting a lecture in vision and imagination, in seeing from afar and from up close, in learning to read abstracted images and imagining what they mean. At one point, Bass even superimposes vertically and horizontally composed images of fields over what appears to be a historical image of the Cimarron land rush, a nod to the way the continent was populated. We can thus interpret the wide-screen middle section, particularly the abstracted images of topography, as an invitation to discuss the semiotics of photographic images. Just as the air traveler looks down and attempts to read the landscape to discover what is below, Bass affords the audience the opportunity to read abstracted images and decode their meaning. Cutting to images on the ground that decode the actual semantic meaning of the previously seen images reinforces the visual play between close and far; it allows viewers to "check their work," so to speak, and communicates the notion that seeing through travel is a form of knowledge. Finally, the utilization of two screen formats in one film makes the constructed nature of the cinematic experience apparent to even the most naïve viewer, foregrounding vision the way the best avant-garde films do.

The Searching Eye

While *From Here to There* was premiering at the United Airlines Pavilion at the 1964 New York World's Fair, *The Searching Eye* was opening at the Eastman Kodak Pavilion. The two films can be seen as companion pieces, and not only because of the geographic and temporal proximity of their release. Both films oscillate between Academy and wide-screen formats, as tropes of different kinds of vision, and are essentially meditations on vision and travel. Both films were financed by corporate clients, but they do not advertise specific products. Rather, they encourage the desire to engage in specific behaviors that can be facilitated by the products and services offered by the sponsoring companies. However, while *From Here to There* presents a discourse on sight in the subtext, *The Searching Eye*, as the title indicates, is *expressis verbis* about vision, employing a whole catalog of cinematic techniques to illustrate various forms of cinematic perception. Bass moves from the macrocosmic world of air travel in the former film to the microcosmic vision of a young boy walking and playing on an ocean beach. Whereas the former can create empathy only in the narrative frame, *The Searching Eye* much more overtly instrumentalizes mechanisms of identification to engage the audience, making it a hybrid that vacillates between Hollywood narrative technique and the avant-garde.

The Searching Eye was part of a massive pavilion that included an eighty-foot tower with screens projecting the world's largest color photographs, visible from anywhere on the fairgrounds. The Kodak Pavilion itself housed fifteen exhibit halls, including two theaters. According to the 1964 World's Fair website, the pavilion was conceived with three goals in mind: "to demonstrate the wealth of experience to be gained from photography, to provide scenes for on-the-spot picture-taking, and to show the influence of photography on various aspects of modern life, among them science, leisure, medicine, industry and education."[53] The film was shown every half hour to as many as 35,000 people a day in a large circular theater built into the base of the picture tower.[54] Records indicate that the Basses produced three different versions of the film. The version shown at the World's Fair utilized two 70mm projectors simultaneously.[55] The 70mm film may or may not be identical to the twenty-three-minute 35mm version. A 16mm version, cut to seventeen minutes, included a completely different narration and many alternative shots and was released by Pyramid in 1969.[56]

When ground was broken for the Kodak Pavilion in August 1962, the company was planning to make a twelve- to fourteen-minute motion picture, according to a press release, but the producers are not mentioned.[57] Saul Bass's involvement actually began much earlier: he had made a bid to design the whole pavilion, as indicated by an undated photo of a model on an index card in the Bass Papers, and he eventually sued the commission responsible for the World's Fair when he failed to win the bid.[58] Interestingly, the design submitted by Herb Rosenthal and Saul Bass could be mistaken for the ground level of the design chosen by Kodak's architects.

Elaine and Saul began work on *The Searching Eye* sometime before September 1963, having hired Walter Lane, the ten-year-old son of actor Rusty Lane, to appear in the film.[59] Bass was ideal for the job. There were more experienced filmmakers around, but Kodak wanted its World's Fair exhibit to be cutting edge. Bass gave the company street credibility because he was much more than a filmmaker; he was a designer, and he was avant-garde without being threatening. Maybe most important, Bass was not just a producer of images but also an intense consumer of them. As a graphic designer and a filmmaker, Bass virtually imbibed images. Previous references to images from Moholy-Nagy's and Kepes's books clearly indicate that everything Bass viewed was used as grist for his mill. *The Searching Eye* was Bass's first independent film—that is, one that allowed him to utilize his own growing archive of virtual and real stock shots and craft a montage of heterogeneous material. Numerous images can convey the consumer's desire for photographs, so Bass's concept of a film about vision—in other words, the conscious perception of photographic and cinematic images—perfectly matched Kodak's goals.

An undated publicity text about *The Searching Eye*, printed on Saul Bass & Associates stationery, picks up an idea that was central to 1920s German avant-garde filmmaking—namely, that the camera is an extension of human vision. Bauhaus artists and film theoreticians made it the structuring principle of the seminal *Film und Foto* exhibition that opened in Stuttgart in May 1929 and was curated by Moholy-Nagy and Hans Richter.[60] A central metaphor of that exhibit was the "camera eye" as a new form of perception attuned to the modern age. Thus, Dziga Vertov's *Man with the Movie Camera* (1929), shown at the exhibition, was a symphony of images demonstrating that the photographic camera expands the physiological and emotional parameters of human optics. Vertov had previously completed forty-five *Kino-Eye* newsreels that purported to show the real lives of workers and farmers in the new Soviet state, even as he espoused the notion in various theoretical texts that the camera eye is a more perfect form of human vision that can investigate the chaos of visual appearances. Franz Roh and German designer Jan Tschichold, who almost single-handedly invented modern-style typeface and was strongly influenced by the Bauhaus, even though he trained in Dresden, published *Foto Auge, Photo-Eye, Oeil et Photo* in 1929, which likewise uses metaphor to visually explicate the "New Vision" in photography. Very much in the spirit of these texts, Bass wrote: "Man has devised many different instruments to extend the limits of our 'highest privilege.' . . . The telescope to penetrate the infinite limits of space . . . the microscope to penetrate the finite limits of matter . . . and the camera, to record what 'the searching eye,' aided or unaided, has found. All learning, all thinking, the doing of man starts first with . . . sight!"[61]

Sight is a continuous human experience, but one that few actively and consciously pursue. Bass wanted everyone to really see the world, whether on a walk along the beach or a journey across the continent in a plane or automobile. In an interview with David Sohn, Bass made this point explicitly: "Everything in the film was approached from that point of view—to take the ordinary, unexotic expressions of these things and find a way of looking at them that would reveal the known as the unknown."[62] Just as in his title sequences, Bass wanted to point out the extraordinary in everyday objects, and here, he wanted to expand the concept to all forms of photographic vision.

The film's reception by the press was not only extremely positive but also quantitatively staggering, given that it was a short film at an event that encompassed hundreds of attractions. The *New York Times* alone mentioned *The Searching Eye* in no fewer than four articles between April and September 1964.[63] It also published a sixteen-page supplement about the Kodak Pavilion that included two pages of illustrations from the film.[64] The most positive review in the *Times* came from Jacob Deschin, published days before the fair opened: "For sheer visual excitement, boldly inventive imagination, and technical virtuosity, it has rarely been equaled. Its poetic message, the exaltation of the familiar and the commonplace, will be appreciated by audiences on all levels."[65] James Powers in the *Hollywood Reporter* also focused on Bass's self-assured manipulation of the medium: "Bass brilliantly demonstrates that the art form serves its creator or interpreter to the degree that the artist knows his art."[66] Finally, a reviewer in *Modern Photography* noted that Bass scrupulously circumvented a naïve interpretation, even though his subject is a young boy: "Bass avoids the usual cliché of a boy discovering the world. While he shows the boy looking and seeing, he also shows that there's much that the untutored eye can't see."[67] The film garnered more film festival prizes than *From Here to There. The Searching Eye* won the Lion of St. Mark at the Venice Film Festival, as well as the Golden Gondola Award from the International Committee for the Diffusion of Artistic and Literary Works by the Cinema (CIDALC). The film also captured prizes from the Chicago, San Francisco, New York, and Edinburgh Film Festivals in 1964 and received a CINE Golden Eagle Award. Eastman Kodak was extremely happy with the film's reception; it played to consistently packed houses, as indicated in a press release after the fair closed.[68]

The Searching Eye opens with the film's logo—an abstracted eye design consisting of white rectangles and a rainbow pie as a pupil—above the title.[69] The eye turns into an orange globe that grows and shrinks onscreen, then goes black. A montage of close-ups of various animal and human eyeballs follows. Only then does Bass introduce his star, an approximately ten-year-old blond boy. The boy walks through marshy fields to the beach, where he jumps into the surf. At that point, the screen expands from Academy ratio to a wide-screen format, and the camera plunges into the ocean to reveal the underwater world. The film returns to the smaller format when the boy continues to explore the beach and various rocks along the shore, then it goes wide again when he watches a flock of seagulls flying by; a sequence on animal and human flight follows. Next, the boy builds a sand castle, and the camera zooms in to reveal a microscopic shot of a grain of sand; Bass then inserts a wide-screen montage of the geologic origins of the earth. Bass reserves the Academy-sized images to depict the boy and his journey, while the wide-screen images illustrate what the boy sees—or what he doesn't see but Bass wants the audience to see. The boy continues his journey to a pier, as Bass inserts wide-screen sequences of water drops falling in extreme slow motion and flowers blooming in fast motion. Finally, the boy returns home and looks out the window, using a piece of paper to create a "telescope." Bass then cuts to wide-screen images of the sun before returning to the boy, who closes the window and ends the film. The short version eliminates several of the wide-screen explorations and ends on a completely different shot.

The most important formal feature of *The Searching Eye*, like *From*

Here to There, is the intermixing of two formats: 35mm Academy aperture and 70mm wide screen. The latter also allows for impressive split-screen images. Bass employs the 1:1.33 Academy ratio to bring the boy's quest, or just his serendipitous exploration of a seashore environment, closer to the viewer. Here, Bass chooses classical Hollywood composition and continuity editing to create a bond between the boy and the audience, most of whom remember similar moments in their own lives. He walks along the beach, he builds a sand castle, he gets his photograph taken on the pier—these are iconic "Kodak moments" in the life of almost every boy and girl in America. The adventure with the photographer gets its own tagline: "So we try to preserve the image as a tangible memory." In another endearing sequence, we see the boy imitating a seagull on the beach as he tries to sneak up on them. Visual interest in the boy is not diminished by the fact that he is extremely photogenic; in fact, a Hollywood producer was willing to offer him a long-term contract after the film opened.[70] Bass credited Elaine with getting a naturalistic performance from the boy, who was, after all, an untrained actor. Bass also used very long lenses, shooting the boy from very far away so he wouldn't be so conscious of the camera, but also optically isolating him within the frame because of the extremely short depth of field (focus).[71] The light, too, adds to the sense of nostalgia for one's own childhood, especially in the scene where the boy is shown in close-up, eating an apple, as the bright late-afternoon light puts a yellow glow on the scene. Finally, by cutting away continually to the boy looking at the camera and then at what he sees, or vice versa, Bass places the subject in the position of the onscreen boy. For example, Bass inserts an extreme close-up of a dragonfly's head as it cleans itself, then cuts away to the boy looking at it before the dragonfly flies away. However, many other sequences transition to the wide-screen view, which, through subsequent editing, clearly tells the audience that this is not necessarily what the boy sees.

Indeed, at the same time and in apparent contradistinction to Bass's aesthetic of classical Hollywood crosscutting, he employs the wide-screen sequences to communicate directly with the audience—a strategy that cannot but help make the audience conscious of the techniques employed. Indeed, the wide-screen images are visual lectures articulating the film's thesis that the camera is an important technological extension of the human eye. The fact that the screen is repeatedly opening and closing its field of vision adds a level of self-reflexivity to the film, taking it into the realm of the avant-garde. In fact, the film's opening shots can be construed as a Constructivist exercise in screen size and perception: an orange globe grows and shrinks, followed by a cut to utter blackness, demonstrating that relative size on a flat surface can be translated into the perception of distance. The optical illusion of the undulating circle on a black background creates a visual metaphor for the theoretical possibilities of screen composition, just as the subsequent blackness establishes the parameters of the format and creates a yin to the yang of actual moving images on the screen.

Bass also cuts away periodically to sets of human and animal eyes, some of them from works of art, again pointing to the act of vision and its depiction in art. In another wide-screen sequence, Bass again articulates the notion of the camera as an expansion of human vision, visually analyzing the movement of a drop of water through extreme slow motion, through stroboscopic freeze-frames of a drop's splash, through vertical split screens presenting the movement of raindrops, as the narrator intones, "We learn how to slow down truth, so we can see and understand." The freeze-frame of a drop hitting the water's surface is a staple for illustrating the expansion of the eye's physiological properties, going back as far as Hans Richter's *Film Enemies of Today—Film Friends of Tomorrow* (1929). In other words, Bass never strays far from his central topic—namely, the nature of vision, which he defines as the perception of the real world through camera-produced images.

Mediating between the two screen formats and the two points of view—the limited, first-person view of the boy and the wide-screen, omniscient point of view—is the offscreen narrator. His soothing voice both ingratiates the boy to the audience (reproducing some of his thoughts) and expertly communicates scientific facts and theses. The narrator moves effortlessly from third-person omniscient to first-person plural, the not so royal *we* inviting the audience to identify with him: "Searching always for a more perfect perception of reality, impatient with the limits of our vision, we learn how to slow down truth, so we can see and understand." Knowledge is thus communicated not through identification with the boy, as in the visual design and the Hollywood classical narrative, but through the narrator's decorporalized voice of science and reason; in other words, it is a body of knowledge from the world of adults.

Each of the wide-screen sequences maps out a different science project. The in-the-surf scene expands to wide screen when the boy jumps in

292

the water; the shots of the surf are already accentuating the wideness of the view through horizontal compositions. Plunging underwater, the camera reveals the hidden and mysterious world of sharks, sardines, and other colorful fish. The underwater view then transitions to shots of microscopic organisms floating in water. The microscopic close-ups are accompanied by the intonation: "To enlarge his vision, to reveal what he can't see with the unaided eye, so that he might know and understand." Within the diegetic frame, the "he" refers to the boy, but the images are visible only to the audience. The wide screen also allows Bass to construct multi-image panels across the screen space, going from four images of the same floating, spinning organisms to what seem to be hundreds. Having delved into the mysteries of water, the film's next wide-screen foray is into the air, as Bass demonstrates the natural flight of birds and attempts to visualize the mechanics of flight. The next wide-screen sequence takes the viewer into the earth, where images of lava flows are multiplied again in multiple split screens before Bass constructs a planetary creation myth, with stormy seas and ultimately dried-out riverbeds in a desert landscape. Bass would later remake this particular sequence for *The Solar Film*. The subsequent aerial shots of a typography designed by humans who have plowed fields, built roads, and constructed cities directly references *From Here to There* and may even include a shot from that film, given that both films were produced simultaneously. From the natural signs of the universe—water, air, and earth—Bass moves on to the growth of plant and animal life, the former visualized by fast motion: multiscreen imagery of seedlings pushing up from the soil and growing, riots of flowers blooming, strawberries and tomatoes ripening, barren trees acquiring and then shedding leaves, the lines of a cut tree revealing its age. From water, air, and earth signs to the circle of life on our planet, the audience's exploration of natural phenomena concludes almost inevitably with wide-screen images of the sun (and the fire sign), the nuclear explosions on its surface and the reddish-orange deity setting into the ocean's endless horizon. Shot on a California beach, *The Searching Eye* embraces both scientific methodology and ancient mysticism, childlike innocence and self-assured experience, a nostalgic Hollywood narrative of our collective childhood memories and a self-reflexive, avant-gardist meditation on the practical and theoretical implications of camera vision.

In particular, the sand-castle scene—where first the surf and then the boy destroy his creation—offers Bass the opportunity to visualize the boy's fantasy of medieval knights and engage the audience in an intense reverie of their own. Bass inserts a brief faux animation sequence of knights in armor fighting for the sand castle (achieved through ultraquick cuts), as the boy looks on from one of its windows. Bass would use this montage of two different levels of narrative within the same compositional frame again in *Windows* (1977), a promotional film for Warner Brothers that he recut to create the less overtly commercial *Notes on the Popular Arts*. The whole sand-castle sequence, with its wide-screen intercuts, crystallizes through image and word Bass's important statement about the connection between imagination and creativity, a topic he returns to repeatedly in film and print media. As the boy's sand castle disappears into the surf, the narrator consoles: "Man struggles to preserve his vision and his dreams." He continues: "Man recognizes the strength of reality. He accepts it and becomes a part of it." In other words, creativity is possible only through failure. It is an idea Bass develops further in *Why Man Creates*.

Ultimately, then, *The Searching Eye* offers two journeys of discovery. One is made by the boy, whose sense of playful exploration reflects the audience's own childhood experience. The other journey is made by the audience; guided by the narrator, the viewers explore the planet's natural phenomena through wide-screen and other cinematic techniques, including slow-motion, time-lapse, stroboscopic, microscopic, and telescopic photography. The film's self-reflexive discourse on vision and the mechanical tools and techniques available to the photographer and filmmaker adds a critical dimension, in keeping with the project's overall goal of creating a film appropriate for Kodak Pavilion audiences. The question, however, is why Elaine and Saul Bass chose the narrative frame of a child's walk on a California beach, given the fact that they had been working for several years on an unidentified New York film that seemingly was more in keeping with the modernism communicated by the Kodak Pavilion's architecture. The answer may be that, after two decades in California, Bass was succumbing to the nature-oriented, sun-burnt, quasi-mystical, West Coast mumbo-jumbo culture of fruits, nuts, and flakes. Certainly, *Quest* (1983), made almost two decades later, supports this explanation.

Quest

Six years after directing *Phase IV* (1974), Bass returned to fiction filmmaking (and to science fiction) for the second and last time. Working with

Elaine, Saul directed a thirty-minute film that not only utilizes the narrative structure of a journey to communicate intellectual content and experience but actually portrays a fictional journey (a quest) that can be understood as an allegory. Financed by a Japanese religious cult and therefore overtly conveying mystical forms of spiritual thought, *Quest* is based on a story by Ray Bradbury; it is about the journey of a male member of the religious community to find "the light," firmly placing the narrative in the realm of metaphor rather than realistic depiction. Indeed, the film's star is not its central character but rather its art direction, resulting in a phantasmagoric landscape utilizing miniatures, mattes, lighting, superimpositions, and other technical effects. Although the film was screened at film festivals in the United States and was eventually distributed nontheatrically by Pyramid Films, its reach was limited by its producers, except in Japan, where the film was shown eight times a day over a four-year period at the headquarters of M. Okada International Association in Atami.[72]

Herb Yager was the initial contact for the *Quest* production. While in Japan, he was invited to Atami (outside Tokyo), one of the three sites chosen by Mokichi Okada for his churches because of the "harmonious unity of natural beauty and aesthetic man-made features." The cult had built a shrine on a mountaintop, requiring pilgrims to take two incredibly long escalators to reach it. When Yager saw the amphitheater-like space, he suggested that Saul Bass could make a film to be shown to the church's congregation. Bass initially felt uncomfortable with the religious subject, but he eventually agreed with Yager that it could be a purely metaphoric vision without proselytizing for the church, just as his other sponsored films had avoided product placement.[73] Church officials may have been impressed by the 1979 special issue of the Japanese design magazine *IDEA*, which was dedicated solely to Saul Bass & Associates, and they agreed to let Bass make "a positive film, a film that doesn't view life as a prelude to disaster."[74]

The Church of World Messianity (reorganized in 1980 as the M. Okada International Association) had been founded in January 1935 by Japanese amateur philosopher Mokichi Okada (1882–1955). Okada claimed that in 1926 he had received a divine revelation from God that empowered him to channel God's healing light, called *Johrei*. Okada hoped to "develop a civilization that allows us to regain those pure and refined sensitivities that help us to live rich and fulfilling lives, rediscover the meaning of life, recognize how blissful it is to be alive, and find new ways of living based on the true meaning of humanity."[75] If the cult's name change can be seen as part of a new identity campaign, rebranding its spiritual ideology in a more secular framework, then Bass was the right man to make the film. Although the church's theological interpretation of *Johrei* and Bass's cinematic understanding of light may have been only tenuously connected, it was the promise of artistic freedom that attracted the designer: "Once agreement had been reached on the script and budget, Saul and Elaine . . . would be left entirely to themselves during the production."[76] Clearly, Bass hoped that the Japanese church fathers would function the way United, Kodak, and Kaiser had, supplying money but not insisting on advertising their religious beliefs.

In any case, Bass sent a film proposal to Okada International in late November 1980. Two weeks later, he began discussions with Ray Bradbury about writing a science fiction script for the project, apparently already aware that the Japanese were willing to fund a production budget of $1 million for the short film. In March 1981 the budget was approved at $1.1 million, with $250,000 going to Bass/Yager and $748,000 for the actual production.[77] However, Bass was worried because, "in recent years there have been a bunch of very big budget features that have established a level of expectation in the special effects area."[78] He therefore suggested that Bradbury set the story on earth rather than in outer space. Bradbury ended up adapting an old short story of his called "Frost and Fire" (first published in 1946 in *Planet Stories* under the title "The Creatures that Time Forgot"). As he had done on all his previous film projects, Bass designed extremely detailed storyboards for every shot in the film, in some cases creating multiple storyboards for longer, more complicated shots. According to Elaine Bass: "We evolved a landscape, a physical landscape of the world and the journey. We built into the landscape many of the visual ideas that had fascinated us over the years."[79] Given the need to hold costs down, the film was shot on a 50- by 150-foot rented sound stage in Hollywood, with much of the set décor and landscape provided by rear projection, superimpositions, animation, and models.[80] Costs were further curtailed by eschewing almost all synchronous sound; only the early scenes were narrated, and much of the film had no dialogue at all. The music by Berington Van Campen, with additional music from Gustav Holst's orchestral suite *The Planets* (1916), was recorded in February 1983. Despite the best intentions, the film went over budget by more than half, forcing the firm to eat the cost overruns.

The film premiered in Japan on 15 June 1983, at a festival sponsored by Okada International. Over the next four years, the film played eight times a day at the church's headquarters. Bass had to constantly make new 35mm prints because the old ones wore out. When Okada switched from carbon to zenon lamps in its projectors, changing the color balance, a whole new round of lab tests followed, and new prints had to be made because Bass was such a stickler for color.[81]

Beginning in August 1983, the film was sent to numerous film festivals and enjoyed immediate success, winning gold medals at the International Film and TV Festival of New York, the International Film Producers Festival, and the International Film Council. According to Herb Yager, film distributors were anxious to purchase the rights, but the Japanese feared political repercussions if the religious film were commercialized, leading Saul's partner to complain that they were losing income every day.[82] As a result, the film continued to play only film festivals throughout 1984, including Cannes, Bilbao, Moscow, Houston, Chicago, London, and San Antonio. When the film played at Filmex in Los Angeles, it was reviewed by *L.A. Weekly*, which noted: "The effects choreography and wide-angle composite shots are outstanding. The sequence with Holst as the boy runs to a pyramid is galvanizing."[83] Once the film was released nontheatrically through Pyramid in 1985, it received some strong support from George Lucas, who had worked with Bass in the late 1960s. Lucas wrote in Pyramid's press package: "What makes *Quest* so extraordinary is the especially inventive use of special effects. As the hero pursues his quest, we too, are taken on a journey through another world, created through original and imaginative effects, and an evocative soundtrack. *Quest* is a beautiful and thought-provoking film."[84]

Quest relates the story of a people apparently locked behind a cosmic gate; because they lack sunlight and vegetation, their life span has been reduced to eight days. According to an elder, many have tried to make the journey to open the gate, but they all died before they got there. One child is selected at birth to make the trek and is trained accordingly. On the second day, he is sent out "to dispel the darkness." Wandering through both barren natural landscapes and the architecture of long-extinct cultures, the boy/man confronts a sloth-like monster in a cave, traverses a sea of sand, plays a board game with a violent ape-man, and makes his way through a maze and a surfboard game before finally, on the seventh day, finding and opening the giant gate. He wanders out into the real world, where the normal life span is 20,000 days. The light shines on his own people behind the gate, supposedly bringing them peace, happiness, and long life.

The Basses structured the film as a journey, as a mythical quest narrative in the sense of Vladimir Propp's *Morphology of the Folktale*, whereby the hero is posed a challenge and is sent out into the world to overcome it; he is confronted with a series of trials that require him to fight, and his journey finally ends in victory.[85] In keeping with the archaic quest narrative, the doomed people in *Quest* are dressed in biblical gray robes and gowns, the men and women wearing black and gray head coverings like the ancient tribes of Israel. Unlike Bradbury's completely secular science fiction story, the Basses' film looks more like a fantasy or a sword-and-sandal epic. Indeed, the hero in the Bradbury story is a member of a marooned spaceship team that has to hide in caves because the planet's environment has been polluted by radiation; he must travel to another spaceship in less than an hour's time, and the life span of the other survivors has been reduced to eight days. Little else remains of the Bradbury story.

Thus, the first one-third of the thirty-minute film entails choosing a baby to fulfill the quest and preparing the young hero to do so. He (as well as the viewer) is told the reasons for his quest. Listening to the heart of his elder and his own heart, the baby is told: "We are locked away in a world where our lives speed through time in eight days. No time to see, to feel, to know, it's time." He is taught to fight with a spear, to strategize, to think with the help of objects that simulate games of logic; he is also given some magical totems that will help him on his journey. As in many foundational myths (including the birth of Jesus Christ), the birth is witnessed by many of the tribe's elders, the lighting on the mother's pregnant belly and then on the child visualizing a nativity scene involving a messianic figure. Even though some of the onlookers express doubt— "Is this the one?" "It's too early to tell"—the hero has the markings of the "chosen one." Later, when the question is asked again, the baby has been brought to a table that is lit like an alter from above, creating the aura of a divine light pointing the way. The infant has no name, imbuing him with the quality of an Everyman who will lead the way to the light, but also metaphorically representing any human journey to enlightenment.

On the second day of his life, the boy leaves the confines of the cave, crosses a barren landscape, and enters yet another dark cave, where he confronts and kills a giant sloth with his spear. He has passed his first test. Interestingly, the monster's screams can still be heard after the battle, and the young hero looks around, bewildered, and then screams, "No." He says no again, and the sound disappears, as if the monster were just a figment of his imagination, like the psychic id in *The Thing*. Indeed, as Paul Ricoeur notes, quest fairy tales often send the hero into some dark forest where he must face a beast: "These initial episodes do more than merely introduce the mischief that is to be suppressed; they bring the hero or heroine back into a primordial space and time that is more akin to the realm of dreams than to the sphere of action."[86] Given that the elders, including his birth mother, accompany him spiritually on the journey, whispering to him not to be afraid, the monster may be seen as a physical embodiment of the fear he must overcome if he is to be successful in his quest. Again, the lighting plays a key role, indicating that his fight against the primordial creature may be a mental one. In part because Bass had no money to construct a full-sized monster, only parts of the sloth are seen—specifically, its mouth and claws, with the former possibly being created through rear projection. The battle takes place in the darkness, shown with quick crosscutting and clever lighting of the hero, as Bass did with the cats in *Walk on the Wild Side*.

The hero must next wade through a flat sea of pure white sand, which sometimes reaches up to his neck, before he is crushed by a giant floating rock with a castle on top. Here, Bass reproduces René Magritte's 1959 painting *The Castle in the Pyrenees*, which depicts a giant, realistic-looking rock, with a castle on top, that seems suspended above (or is falling into?) the sea. This painting, which defies all logic of gravity, conforms to the surrealist tenet to make the ordinary strange, forcing the viewer to see it anew. In the case of the Magritte painting, Elaine confessed that it had long been Saul's wish to find a use for that particular image.[87] A similar image of a rock suspended in space had already been tested in Bass's original *Phase IV* finale. The suspension of gravity (in the painting) also implies the obliteration of time, but in *Quest*, the hero must race against time to avoid getting crushed by the boulder (short term) and to open the gate before he dies (long term). Furthermore, while Magritte's boulder consciously resembles an egg, which in the surrealist canon symbolizes rebirth and fertility, Bass not only throws gravity back into the mix but also turns the female egg into its opposite, a phallus that ultimately penetrates the soft sand. The fact that one of the elders, seen earlier during the boy's training, looks like Salvador Dali is another Bass joke on surrealist art.

The hero reaches the far shore's architectural structures, consisting of three monuments: a hand held up in greeting, the face of an old man, and a bird's head with a large beak. The still-descending rock touches down like a spaceship, throwing dust storms into the air and causing the giant statues to start to collapse. The bird monument is, in fact, another form of prophecy of the coming messiah, since at the film's end, we see the hero in the real world, surrounded by flocks of birds. Thus, the earthquake bringing about the destruction of the monuments is another part of the divine plan for the hero. One of the smaller falling monuments resembles the ant towers in *Phase IV*, one of several visual quotes from that film. Another recalls *The Searching Eye*: one of the huge stone eyeballs falls out and nearly kills the hero, who explores the stone cavern inside the statue's head as the other eyeball falls out behind him; the two empty eye sockets, with their view of the landscape beyond, create another visual metaphor for sight. As everything begins to crumble, the hero is suddenly surrounded by stars and is able to see the whole universe; this allows him to notice a small entrance, which he jumps into at the last moment, before being crushed by debris.[88] As the hero proceeds through a classical Greek–style temple, the moving camera work is strongly reminiscent of a similar scene in *The Cardinal*. The hero then meets his predecessor, who is preparing to die; he tells the hero to climb the pyramid visible on the horizon, rather than trying to go around it. This is a classic fairy-tale interdiction, addressed to the hero.

At the top of the pyramid, the hero, now with a beard, is tested again. He must engage in a game of electronic chess with an ape-man, where the game's cones and cubes shoot lasers to destroy their opponents.[89] For Bass, language is an essential measure of intelligence, so it is not surprising that, despite initially losing half his pieces, the hero outwits the ape, who pounds his fist on the table, causing sparks to fly, while the hero makes his escape over a magically appearing causeway. The notion of an ape-man who can only growl playing a high-tech board game is patently ridiculous in terms of a logical, realistic narrative, so again the question becomes, is the hero playing with the animalistic and brutal side of his own psyche? Next, he finds himself inside the same computer game, where he is the prey for two opposing cones. Again, he outwits the power manipulating the pieces. First, he causes one to kill off the other; then he uses the mirror given to him by the elders to deflect the laser back at the attacker, thus destroying the remaining cone. This magical totem from the elders saves the day, allowing the hero to "channel the light," as Mokichi Okada claimed to have done in 1926.

On the seventh day—another biblical reference—the hero arrives at the slit in the world and opens the gate by finding the indented palm prints that exude light. The gate, which at one point resembles a Christian cross, opens, flooding the people with light. The yellow light moves over the people below, like the sun rising on a new morning. Jesus Christ reportedly exclaimed, "I am the light of the world," so here we see Bass borrowing Christian metaphors as the hero literally brings light into the world. The final image of the hero at the crest of a hill in front of an orange-red setting sun returns the viewer to Bass's own canon of iconographic images. Okada's healing light, or *Johrei*, and Bass's more pagan mysticism may not be so far apart. As demonstrated in both *The Searching Eye* and *The Solar Film*, Bass repeatedly depicts the sun—or, rather, sunlight—as the beginning of all life on the planet. Another point of intersection between Okada's church and Bass is the concept that nothing in life is easy. Bass formulates that thesis in connection with creativity in *The Searching Eye* and, as we will see, in *Why Man Creates*.

The church interpreted *Quest*'s narrative as follows: "Confronted with a world of hardship and difficulties . . . , the film vehemently asserts that barriers during our journey are the passage ways that must be traversed and the doors that must be opened."[90] Any reading of *Quest*, then, must consider it an allegory for Mokichi Okada's teachings and therefore a theological text. Church representative Masa Miura makes this explicit: "The film can be regarded as a joint creation of Saul Bass and Mokichi Okada. . . . Above all, the journey of the boy full of ordeals can be construed as a symbolic rendering of the life of great men as Mokichi Okada." Miura goes on to state that the film will advance the causes of the M. Okada International Association, which is "now on the verge of embarking on a renewed mission on a worldwide basis."[91] Bass explicitly objected to sharing credit with Okada, but the film had not yet been shot at that point, so additional discussions about the film's ideological thrust may have occurred. Against this proselytizing impetus, the Basses later attempted to contextualize the film in more secular terms. The Pyramid study guide, for example, notes: "The boy in *Quest* as well as Luke Skywalker, James Bond, the Hulk *et al.* function in exactly the same way for contemporary society. Through their adventures they come 'to serve as powerful picture language for the communication of traditional wisdom.'"[92]

Whether the teachings of the Church of World Messianity constitute "traditional wisdom" rather than cult worship is open to debate. However, what has been neglected in the discussion up to this point is the role of the art direction in *Quest*. In fact, Saul and Elaine saw the film as an opportunity to play: "We built into the landscape many of the visual ideas that had fascinated us over the years."[93] In fact, utilizing front and rear projection, painted mattes, bipack silhouettes, miniatures, and overcranking of the camera, Bass re-creates many of the visual designs first seen in the "lost" ending to *Phase IV*. This includes a landscape of what can only be described as upside-down pyramids, an image Bass reused for the cover of a psychology textbook.[94] Other designs, such as the endless stairs or the line patterns in the sand, recall both *Phase IV* and *The Cardinal*. The point is that each and every composition is consciously arty, just as the references to surrealist art denote that the environments depicted are landscapes of the mind. In the same vein, the consistent use of three-dimensional geometric shapes, whether squares, cones, or pyramids, harks back to the Bauhaus elementary design course. And just as the boy plays with marble pieces that will later morph into a deadly game of survival on a vast electronic board game, he also constructs a model from steel girders that he will later have to navigate, an image recalling M. C. Escher.[95] Except for the electronic board game, no computer graphics were used, making the film's visual achievements all the more astounding.[96]

Apart from the overt art history references, how do we interpret the film's overall design? It is apparent that *Quest* is only partially a chronological journey through space in time; it is equally a journey through time in space. Interestingly, some of Bass's sketches for the journey resemble the landscapes of chronological time created for *The Solar Film* and *100 Years of the Telephone*, whereby the present is seen in the foreground and the future is on the horizon.[97] The negative evidence for such a reading lies in the fact that the spatial relations within the narrative construct make little to no sense in a realistic context. Where is the gate in relation to the cave where the people dwell? Why doesn't the mother travel halfway to the gate before her child is born? How can the light fall directly into the cave if the gate is a seven-day journey away? Looking more closely at the sets, they take the hero from primitive caves to classical Greek temples to computer landscapes, a journey ostensibly through time rather than space. This notion fits with Ricoeur's critique of Propp's morphology of thirty-one different functions of the narrative quest, noting that the chronological dimension is more or less supplanted by conceptual segmentation: "The chronological dimension was not abolished, but it was deprived of its temporal constitution as plot. The segmenting and the concatenating of functions thus paved the way for a reduction of the chronological to the logical."[98] A reading that sees the quest as a journey through time, the hero as an allegorical figure for all humanity, conforms to a theological interpretation of the text. This "story of mankind," ending in an embrace of the church's teachings, communicates the institution's belief that it embodies the highest stage of human development, allowing complete freedom and harmony with nature. The film's final images of the hero, the sun, and the birds signify a reestablishment of balance between man and nature, a concept that both the M. Okada International Association and the Basses could agree on.

Bass's narratives of the journey always imply the acquisition of knowledge and experience through the act of looking. And yet, while the actors engaged in the journey function as stand-ins for the audience, Bass often blocks that identification by privileging his overall visual design, resulting in a self-conscious audience. The actual act of seeing and of acquiring knowledge is thereby displaced onto the audience. Indeed, common to all the characters in the titles and films discussed here is their silence, their lack of verbal language to express their own thoughts and emotions. They are merely stand-ins for the audience, which the filmmaker addresses directly through words and images. For Saul Bass, language and the ability to communicate through language ultimately define civilization.

7

Civilization

Organizing Knowledge through Communication

Saul Bass's *Why Man Creates* (1968) begins with an animated scene of "prehistoric" cave dwellers attempting to kill a steer-like animal more than twice their size. After the first attempt fails, because the animal is too big and they are afraid of it, they discuss the matter and decide that one of them will act as bait while the others spear the animal from behind as it chases the lone hunter. The dead steer's image is then reproduced on the wall of a cave, like the cave paintings in Spain and France dating from the Aurignacian period onward. In this thirty-second sequence, Bass and Art Goodman visualize the beginning of civilization, defining it as the moment when a group of individuals in a community discusses and formulates a joint plan of action for the common good and then documents in art and narrative the success of that strategy, making it available to future generations. For Bass, then, art is a way for one generation to speak to the next. To use the term "prehistoric" is in fact incorrect, since that image is also the first act of historiography.

Bass's work is predicated on the supposition that civilization is based on the development and implementation of language as a mode of communication, whether spoken or pictographic, and that much of that communication is about human history. As banal as it sounds, language allows people to exchange thoughts, feelings, ideas, and emotions and to understand the point of view of their immediate neighbor. Language is about getting people together to take common action for the common good. But it is also about creating traces of our own individual existence and about writing history. Human history demonstrates our forward move-ment, and as a liberal humanist experiencing the post–World War II boom in American power, society, and economy, Bass believed that civilization had progressed over the last ten millennia and would continue to develop. It is no accident that all of Bass's narratives about the historical develop-ment of society, whether in *Why Man Creates* or *100 Years of the Telephone* or *The Solar Film*, are structured as journeys to the far horizon; they are about traveling straight ahead into the future. Despite hiccups, such as the energy crisis detailed in *The Solar Film*, Bass believed in human progress, both social and technological. Indeed, even that film argues that there are rational solutions to the energy crisis, if we can only agree to implement them. Even a mystical film like *Quest* (which takes the hero beyond the horizon) suggests that the most intractable problems can be solved if obstacles are faced one at a time and if the knowledge of a civilization is communicated to its children.

For Bass, all design is about communication, and communication is what defines civilization. Communication is seen as a creative and intel-lectual process that is dependent on finding the best possible solution to a design problem. This is accomplished by focusing attention on the audi-ence's needs and desires, as well as on the message to be communicated. The exchange of knowledge is paramount. Communication occurs when an addressee is taken from something he or she knows and understands to something he or she doesn't know. As one journalist noted early in Bass's career: "He starts with the premise that the creative act is one that brings about a new relationship between existing objects or ideas. Mr. Bass strives, in his work, to share with the consumer or viewer a creative experi-ence."[1] In visual design work, that moment is more telegraphic, even as it suggests narrative. The same can be said for some of Bass's title work, although the element of narrative moves to the fore in many other Bass titles. In his advertising, promotional, and narrative films, Bass transports knowledge through narrative, both fictional and nonfictional. Indeed, just as Bass hoped audiences would see the everyday anew through the act of consciously seeing, he hoped to rearrange and contextualize commonly known facts to create an understanding of relationships between things or to create a narrative explicating the complex social and political processes at work in society.

However, the focus for Bass is always on the microcosm, on the pro-cess and the immediate issue at hand, not necessarily on the theoretical construct. In this sense, Bass is a conceptualist, seeing each problem as a unique puzzle with its own set of practical and rational solutions, rather than a theoretician who approaches issues through an ideological construct. This, of course, is in keeping with his antitheoretical and anti-intellectual public pronouncements, although even his historical narratives, which appear to be nothing more than a collection of chronologically ordered facts, are a priori inflected with ideology. In Bass's case, that ideology can be characterized as a positivist, socially responsible, and capitalist one; it ascribes agency to individuals rather than to social forces beyond human control. Even a film like *Quest* is strangely agnostic, never visualizing or speaking the name of God. Communication and education are the linchpins of progress, so it is not surprising that many of Bass's films analyze difficult problems and find simple solutions but eschew concrete answers. For his title sequences involving historical subjects, Bass attempts to set the stage by visualizing events and objects that can contextualize the narratives that follow. In his short films, Bass tackles complex subjects and plays with direct audience address, crafting essays that pose many questions and only seldom offer concrete answers. It therefore behooves us to look at *Why Man Creates* and *Phase IV* as exceedingly complex and fragmented narratives whose modernism invites an open-ended dialogue with the audience but avoids ideological absolutes.

Cowboys and War

Saul Bass's titles for Delmar Daves's *Cowboy* (1958) set the stage for another adult western that purports to be a realistic look at the history of the American West during the great cattle drives of the 1870s. Millions of cattle were driven north from Texas to the railroad lines in Kansas for transport to Chicago for slaughter and processing. In fact, according to the *Oxford English Dictionary*, the word *cowboy* originated in this period to describe that particular occupation. Given that Hollywood had already produced oodles of westerns built around cattle drives, Howard Hawks's *Red River* (1948) being the most famous, the film's challenge was to avoid the clichés of the genre. Likewise, Bass's titles consciously attempt to undercut any heroic stylization, which the western genre was prone to, especially to satisfy the Saturday matinee market. Among 1950s westerns, *High Noon*, *Shane*, and *Johnny Guitar* led the way in this arena. Bass therefore created animated graphic titles that both play to the genre's clichés by utilizing stereotypical western music and humorously deflate the western cowboy myth by "reading" an advertisement from a Chicago newspaper, dated 25 March 1872, offering mail-order western goods so that any tenderfoot can turn himself or herself into a cowboy.

Cowboy was based on a semiautobiographical novel by Frank Harris, *My Reminiscences as a Cowboy* (1930), which tells the story of a hotel clerk who goes west to join a cattle drive from Mexico. The film's extremely long preproduction history was no doubt partly the result of Harris's meandering plot and the novel's sexually explicit content, which the Motion Picture Production Code would have found objectionable. John Huston bought the rights to the novel in the 1940s and was planning to produce the film with Sam Spiegel and Horizon Pictures, starring his father, Walter Huston, and Montgomery Clift. However, Walter died before the production team completed its other project, *The African Queen* (1951), so the property languished. In January 1953 the project was turned over to Ranald MacDougall, a writer-producer at Columbia; eighteen months later it was given to producer Jerry Wald, with Peter Viertel as scriptwriter and Spencer Tracy chosen to play the lead.[2] By July 1956, Gary Cooper and Alan Ladd were being mentioned as possible leads.[3] Eventually, the project landed with Julian Blaustein, who had previously produced *Storm Center* and *The Racers* and would hire Bass again for *The Four Horsemen of the Apocalypse*. Bass was hired to do the *Cowboy* titles, Jack Lemmon and Glenn Ford landed the leads, and Delmar Daves was chosen to direct. Given the extreme heterogeneity of the poster designs and other publicity, it is unlikely that Bass was involved in the film's marketing. The animation, however, is very much in keeping with the style of *Around the World in 80 Days*, so one can assume that some of the same individuals worked on *Cowboy* as well. The script was completed by Dalton Trumbo, who received no credit as a result of being blacklisted; Edmund H. North fronted for him.[4] Daves, who also directed the classic western *3:10 to Yuma* with Glenn Ford, later claimed that *Cowboy* was his favorite western because of its realism.[5] The film premiered on 7 January 1958 in Oklahoma City and then opened in New York on 19 February 1958.

Cowboy received mostly tepid reviews. For all the talk about the film being a realistic look at the hard lives of cowboys on the cattle trail, the actors looked too well-fed, and the color film was too pretty. Whereas James Powers was generally positive about Delmar Daves's indifferent direction, Bosley Crowther went for the jugular, noting that the film was a "routine herd-trailing saddle saga" that made Jack Lemmon look like a fugitive from the "Hasty Pudding Club."[6] The British *Monthly Film Bulletin* took a more balanced view: "to the familiar, romantic elements of the great cattle trek, the film brings something almost iconoclastic: the group of men on the trail are shown to be a raw and lawless lot . . . the film fails in its last third, and gives way to stock revisions of character to ensure a happy ending."[7] Indeed, reviewers generally agreed that Lemmon was miscast in the role of the tenderfoot who becomes a hardened trail hand.[8]

Bass's titles open completely abstractly, similar to his opening for *The Seven Year Itch*. Here, a series of six blue and olive-green bars of slightly different widths fills the frame horizontally; they are overlaid with a variety of black embroidery stitch patterns before "Columbia Pictures presents" appears above the horizontal axis. The six bars morph into three thicker bars in three different shades of blue, and the title appears in wide, white, serif type at frame left, encased in a rectangle composed of a black double-stitch pattern. As the title fades out, the spatial geometry of the color fields changes to two horizontal rectangles and a vertical one (right frame), the stitch pattern now resembling an old-style picture frame around the credits for Glenn Ford and Jack Lemmon, along with an oval frame around "starring." Additional lead actors' credits appear in frames as the background is divided into five rectangles in various blue hues. The color field then dissolves to a reproduction of the *Chronicle*, a Chicago newspaper on a yellow-brown field to simulate old paper, while the remaining acting credits appear center-justified in white capitals on three lines below the horizontal axis. As the white credits fade out, the camera zooms in on a close-up of an advertisement for a western saddle; Edmund North's credit is listed above and the credit for the serialized novel is listed below in the same-style serif typography. The camera then pans right to an advertisement for men's hats, while the musical credits are overlaid in white sans serif capitals. All but one of the hats fades out, and the cowboy wearing that hat fades in while the monochromatic color turns to a wine red; a white lasso flies horizontally over the screen, dragging a black cowboy boot back into view as the cinematography credits appear in white. The boot in the same position becomes part of a newspaper advertisement for boots with white spurs and then dissolves to a blue field; the spurs morph into stars, and secondary technical credits appear frame left and left-justified, then frame right and right-justified (including Bass's title credit). The brief 1:28-minute sequence ends, after an interlude with various cattle brands filling the screen, when Blaustein's and Daves's respective credits appear in white in front of a newspaper illustration of a Jersey cow on a red field.

The titles for *Cowboy* function on two graphic levels: the color field and the textual design with the mock newspaper are at the center, while the narrative details float freely between design elements. Throughout the credits, Bass references various everyday objects and aspects of the cattle drive, characterizing this stereotypical nineteenth-century genre piece as just another day's labor for ordinary working men. The opening color scheme, with its preponderance of blues and grays, references the Civil War and possibly the colors of men's clothing, while the horizontal embroidery stitch patterns can be read as a synecdoche for the blue jeans worn by the cowboys. The constellation of old-time rectangular and oval picture frames around the names of the major actors playing these long-dead cowboys is a device Bass uses again in both *That's Entertainment II* and *A River Runs through It*. Here (as there), the design communicates both a sense of nostalgia and a sense of home and family, something most cowboys didn't have. The theme of cowboy fashion is continued in the following newspaper section, which not only reveals the film's historical time frame but also catalogs other accessories, including saddles, hats, and boots. The specific order of the objects in the titles chronicles the transformation of an eastern city slicker into a cowboy—the early hats are mostly for city dwellers, until a cowboy appears wearing a cowboy hat. The narrative continues in the following titles as the color field transitions to Bass's trademark red, placing visual emphasis on the action that follows: a lasso in an unseen hand ropes a boot, and its spurs dissolve into an image of open skies on the cattle drive. Finally, Bass incorporates his trademark joke by first visualizing a cow separated into its various cuts of meat for Blaustein's credit, maybe indicating that, as producer and holder of the purse strings, he is a manager of parts rather than the whole. Daves's directorial credit is accompanied by the whole living cow before it is led off to slaughter.

Thus, Bass's graphic, animated titles communicate historical knowledge through a number of different visual tropes and typographic devices. Bass's method is to take one detail and carry it into the next frame: a cowboy hat is suddenly worn by a cowboy, one boot dissolves into an advertisement for many boots, the spurs become stars in the sky over an open range. The effect is to create smooth transitions that encourage a narrative reading. The UPA-style animation, which matches flat color fields with very simple animated objects, is perfectly suited to Bass's purpose, which is to keep the focus on the credits while inviting the audience to combine the narrative details communicated in the titles and construct the beginnings of a western narrative. At the same time, the visual focus on details—that is, the objects of everyday life—communicates Bass's understanding that these are the historical artifacts that survive—old picture frames, clothing, newspapers—allowing us to extrapolate images and knowledge of the past from these historical documents.

In light of what film curator Stephen Harvey called "a bad idea that became deadlier at every step," it is probably better that Bass's montage sequences for *The Four Horsemen of the Apocalypse* (1962) were eventually jettisoned in favor of much shorter, less obtrusive, and less violent montages.[9] Yet Bass's original montages are interesting in two ways: as an attempt to integrate graphic design elements and live-action newsreel images in a montage sequence, and as templates for his subsequent prologue for *The Victors*. In fact, that prologue reutilizes virtually the same edit as one of the *Four Horsemen* montages (along with some additional shots), attempting to communicate both historical and ideological knowledge about World War II. Here again, we see Bass's willingness to take ideas he pitched unsuccessfully to one client and sell them to another.

While producing a remake of its biggest hit from the silent period, *Ben Hur* (1959), someone in the front office at Metro-Goldwyn-Mayer came up with the idea to remake *The Four Horsemen of the Apocalypse* (1921), which had been Rudolph Valentino's break-out film for Metro Pictures. It is the story of a young Argentine playboy in Paris who learns the meaning of sacrifice and responsibility in the trenches of World War I. The original film's success depended almost wholly on the smoldering star's rendition of the tango, which set off a dance craze in the United States. In July 1958 Julian Blaustein was brought in to produce the remake, and Vincente Minnelli was set to direct.[10] Scriptwriter Robert Ardrey threw out 90 percent of the original Vicente Blasco Ibáñez novel, turning it into the story of a playboy in Nazi-occupied France who must choose between collaboration and resistance. Unfortunately, studio bosses Sol Siegel and Joseph Vogel decided to cast forty-two-year-old Glenn

Ford in the lead, who was too old and certainly lacked the androgynous sexual fire of Valentino; Ingrid Thulin, the Swedish star of Ingmar Bergman films, was equally miscast as the romantic heroine. Minnelli and Blaustein fought when the budget ballooned from $4.75 million to $7.5 million owing to the director's overshooting on location in Paris. In August 1960 Bass was hired "to prepare a montage of posters, newsreels, press cuttings and photographs from war-time records that will be inserted as the story unfolds, giving historical backgrounds to the narrative's events."[11] Five months after production began in Paris in October 1960, the film wrapped in Culver City at the Hal Roach Studios in March 1961.[12] The film flopped miserably, losing close to $6 million.

It is likely that Bass spent several months in 1961 producing four war montages, as well as designing some trade advertisements.[13] These montages—"Sports Palace," "Warsaw," "Rotterdam," and "La Martinique"—were supposed to be interspersed throughout the narrative of *The Four Horsemen of the Apocalypse*. According to Mike Lonzo, Bass's assistant, they later served as the basis of the titles for *The Victors*.[14] Jean Douchet's contemporary description claims that the montages were not completely eliminated but only drastically shortened, so that their character as historical evidence was mitigated: "The scenes from newsreels (Nazi meetings, aerial squadrons, bombardments, etc.) are shattered, anamorphosed, vividly colored—in short dismembered like cubist Picassos. Visible reality is willfully denied."[15]

In the first three montages, each running about 1:20 minutes, Bass experiments with juxtaposing graphic texts or symbols with historical newsreel footage in order to make an ideological point about the nature of World War II. The "Sports Palace" sequence refers to Adolf Hitler's famous *"Deutschland ist nun erwacht"* (Germany has awakened) speech, given at the Berliner Sportpalast on 8 April 1933. The newsreel footage, however, comes almost exclusively from Leni Riefenstahl's *Triumph of the Will*, which postdates the sports palace event by more than a year.[16] In the sequence, Bass moves from close shots of recognizable individuals in the crowd to arms raised in the Nazi salute to groups of Nazi supporters and finally to an amorphous mass. That mass is next seen in long shots of crowds that have been geometrically ordered as phalanxes, ending with the infamous image of Hitler and his lieutenants marching down a human corridor created by tens of thousands of followers at the Nuremberg Party rally in 1935. Bass intercuts these images with graphics of Nazi swastikas, in ascending order from three to six to twelve to forty-eight swastikas on the screen; then he transitions to swastikas forming larger swastikas to swastikas in rows, as if on parade. Interestingly, neither the propaganda minister nor any of the Nazi Party leaders are integrated into the montage (Hitler is heard on the sound track), nor are their supporters visualized as an amorphous mass oppressed by the Nazi leadership, as in many documentaries. Instead, through the progressive montage from individuals to masses to militarily ordered masses, Bass emphatically declares that the German people, made up of individual citizens, enthusiastically support the Nazi regime and are willing to subjugate themselves to the will of the Nazi leaders. The swastika graphics, then, become a symbol of that thesis, as swastikas multiply and Bass lines them up in marching formations, symbolically visualizing the ever-increasing number of Germans subsumed under the Nazi banner.

The next two montages, encapsulating the Nazi blitzkrieg in Poland in September 1939 and Holland in June 1940, are similarly constructed of alternating images and graphics. Both focus on the bombing of cities and the mass killing of innocent civilians by the German Luftwaffe, rather than on military actions between opposing armies. The "Warsaw" montage opens with photographs of Hitler in various poses as he gives one of his war-mongering speeches, the camera moving ever closer to his face until only his gaping mouth fills the screen (a shot similar to the crying baby in the Mennen Baby Magic commercial, and presaging the final shot of the *Seconds* title sequence). Bass then cuts from the screaming voice of Hitler to an explosion, followed by numerous other explosions. Bass inserts a shot of a woman running down the street and falling, as buildings collapse in rapid succession. (The shots of collapsing buildings were culled from the MGM feature film *San Francisco* [1936], about the famous 1906 earthquake. By freezing the image, one can see that the people in the shot are wearing clothing from the pre–World War I era.)[17] Bass then interlaces various French and other foreign newspaper headlines announcing the bombing of Warsaw, but in negative, so that the headline is white on a black background. He completes the sequence with images of corpses intercut with explosions and the sound of warplanes on their bombing runs.

The planes are only heard in the "Warsaw" montage, whereas the "Rotterdam" montage begins with shots of bombers and Stukas in formation in the skies, culminating in a striking image of a Stuka diving vertically through the frame, superimposed on a close-up of a woman's anguished face looking up to the sky. As another explosion is heard, Bass cuts to a montage of graphics, "HOLLAND BOMBED—HOLLAND'S NEUTRALITY VIOLATED," in white sans serif capitals on a black background. Intercutting more images of explosions, buildings burning uncontrollably, and victims (including children) running, Bass then superimposes an image of a dead woman's face on a shot of Hitler dancing a jig, which grows larger as he dances. The jig was re-created with a step printer from a few frames of Hitler in Paris after the French surrender, since the original shots were apparently too decomposed.[18]

Both blitzkrieg sequences argue that the German war machine is driven by invisible forces (no pilots are shown); the bombing wreaks havoc and destruction on civilians with no regard for human decency. Images of piles of corpses, as well as close-ups of outstretched, bloody hands, are particularly brutal, encapsulating the anguish of the civilian population. Images of Hitler bracket the two montages, symbolically indicating that he not only ordered the attacks but also rejoiced in the destruction his Luftwaffe inflicted. Taken together, then, the three montages establish that the Nazis enjoyed popular support and that the German people, along with their leaders, were responsible for starting the most brutal war ever fought against civilian populations up to that time.

The final montage, "La Martinique," begins with a shot of Glenn Ford entering a party filled with French women and Nazi officers. Ford works his way through the crowd as the revelers drink champagne and kiss. Bass cuts to a close-up of a bald man laughing, then to an extreme close-up of his gaping mouth, before inserting a newsreel image of a machine gun muzzle rapidly firing and the German soldier operating the gun. After cutting back to the open mouth drinking a glass of champagne, Bass inserts a shot of a tank's treads rolling over a dirt road, followed by more explosions and images of tanks. Bass then returns to Ford's character in the crowd. The juxtaposition between the Nazi bacchanalia in a Parisian villa and the images of war further reinforces the brutality and the insensitivity of the Germans, who wage war against France and then celebrate late into the night. Unlike the other montages, which probably would have been stand-alone sequences inserted into the fictional narrative, the final montage is integrated into the film's narrative. The inclusion of this montage on the surviving reel clearly establishes that all four montages were created for *The Four Horsemen of the Apocalypse*.

Saul Bass's two-minute prologue for *The Victors* is a much more sophisticated reediting of material from the *Four Horsemen* montages, as well as additional material.[19] Unlike the war montages, which juxtapose the mass destruction of the Nazi blitzkrieg and civilian casualties, the prologue of *The Victors* telegraphs in visual shorthand that the rise of Nazism and World War II can be attributed to missed opportunities at the end of World War I. The prologue transitions directly to the two-minute title sequence, which employs newsreel footage of Allied soldiers marching down the Champs-Elysées on parade after the liberation of Paris, as well as other victory parades. This creates a bracket for the narrative that follows, which concerns the actions of American troops from the Battle of Britain in 1942 to the occupation of Berlin in the spring of 1946.

Carl Foreman had been a hugely successful Hollywood scriptwriter before being blacklisted in 1951, during the second wave of hearings by the House Un-American Activities Committee. Like Ring Lardner Jr., Cy Endfield, Joseph Losey, and others, Foreman moved to the United Kingdom, where he cowrote the Oscar-winning script for *The Bridge on the River Kwai* (1956) with fellow blacklistee Michael Wilson, although neither received screen credit or an Oscar. In 1960 he signed a deal with Highroad Productions and Columbia to write and direct six pictures.[20] *The Guns of Navarone* (1961), for which Foreman was both producer and scriptwriter, was nominated for a Best Picture Oscar; like his other films, this was a British production. Bass and Foreman knew each other well; they had both worked for Stanley Kramer on such films as *Champion* (1949), *The Men* (1950), and *Cyrano de Bergerac* (1950). In 1957 Foreman bought the rights to Alexander Baron's *The Human Kind* (1953), a volume of short stories about ordinary British soldiers during the war. In adapting the work, Foreman changed the soldiers to Americans. Preproduction began in 1960, while he was still completing *Guns of Navarone*. The film was shot in England, Sweden, France, and Italy between April 1962 and February 1963; it had an international cast, while Foreman functioned as producer, director, and writer. The three-hour film premiered in London in November 1963 and opened in New York a month later on 19 December.

Unfortunately, *The Victors* did not do well at the box office, coming on the heels of the hugely successful World War II epic *The Longest Day* (1962). Indeed, *The Victors* can be considered a film noir version of *The Longest Day*, focusing less on heroic battles against fascism—no actual combat footage is seen, other than in Bass's prologue—than on the loss of American fighting men due to the scandalous conditions behind the lines. Foreman links the individual episodes that take the American troops from London to Italy, Paris, Belgium, and Berlin through newsreel montages that present the course of the war at home and on the front from an official Allied perspective. In contrast is the unofficial narrative of what goes on behind the lines, where we see racist white American soldiers killing their African American comrades, boys attempting to sell themselves to the soldiers, and scores of women of every nationality offering sex for food or money. The film ends with a Russian soldier and an American soldier in occupied Berlin killing each other in a knife fight because neither can understand what the other is saying. Given its dark vision of the "good war," most American critics panned the film, including Bosley Crowther in the *New York Times* and Arthur Knight in the *Saturday Review.*[21] Many of the reviewers commented on the insertion of newsreels into the film, especially the inclusion of a segment with Bess Truman trying unsuccessfully to break a bottle of champagne during the christening of a troop ship.[22] Bass was apparently not responsible for these interludes, but he received praise for his prologue and titles from at least one British reviewer, who wrote: "Saul Bass's job is considerably larger than usual. He has to cover the major military and political events in Europe from about 1914 to 1963, convey the brutality and uselessness of war and do it within a short prologue to the Foreman film. He succeeds."[23]

Bass opens his prologue with a fake newsreel; it is actually a fictional sequence from *All Quiet on the Western Front* (1930). The camera moves laterally along a World War I trench as machine guns (ostensibly behind the camera) slaughter the soldiers attacking the trench. The camera movement is so fast that the shot seems continuous, but it is in fact made of up numerous jump cuts of material that has been optically repeated and speeded up. Meanwhile, Bass keeps the eye centered on the never-ending stream of bodies being mowed down. The camera movement ends with a stark photograph of a pair of disembodied hands gripping barbed wire, all that remains of a soldier. This image is held onscreen for a full four seconds, allowing the eye and mind to rest briefly before cutting to cheering crowds as an insert of a newspaper headline announces, "GERMANY SURRENDERS." Small American flags identify the nationality of the next crowd, with confetti parades and cheering dominating the sound track. This is followed by newspaper photographs of Lloyd George,

Woodrow Wilson, and Georges Clemenceau, then more crowds intercut with newspaper photographs of their disembodied hands signing the Versailles Treaty. The camera zooms in on the final photo as the cheering gives way to Hitler's famous "Germany has awakened" speech, although the subsequent images of Hitler are from another event. In fact, Bass cuts together thirty separate photographs (or freeze-frames) of Hitler in less than ten seconds. The camera zooms in until the last five images reveal a giant mouth, moving but out of sync with the words screamed on the sound track. The Hitler segment is identical to the segment in the *Four Horsemen* war montages, and like the latter, the first minute of the prologue ends with explosions. The second minute begins with shots of fighter and bomber squadrons in the air, engines screeching, then cuts to the vertical dive-bomb of a Stuka. This dissolves to a multiple exposure of a woman looking up at the sky in anguish—these twelve seconds taken from the "Rotterdam" montage. The following montage of people fleeing, explosions, and buildings falling down reworks the *Four Horsemen* montages, adding flash-frames of disembodied and partially mangled hands reaching up or out and a shorter edit of Hitler dancing a jig over the image of a dead woman's face. After several more explosions, the screen dissolves to black and the film's first title.

The film's title is captured in white sans serif typography on a black background. All the remaining titles also appear in white, but the background consists of army newsreel footage of various Allied armies marching in parades, all in the same direction and seemingly at the same speed. Only the uniforms change from British to American to Australian to French to Russian, while the credits fade in and out and a military march blares on the sound track. The title sequence lasts less than two minutes, so the whole opening clocks in at four minutes of screen time. The original prologue was apparently much longer, but Bass was forced to cut it.[24] Bass's original storyboards for *The Victors* reveal that the designer was still experimenting with typographical elements moving around the screen, integrated into the newsreel footage, and sometimes even on top of it, as in the "Rotterdam" title over a sky full of planes or the disembodied hands raised in the air behind "ARMISTICE." However, his storyboards jettison the rather one-dimensional use of newspaper mock-ups in favor of pure typography laid out graphically rather than in real space.[25]

The official description of the prologue in the Bass Papers reads as follows: "The prologue outlines in documentary form the historical background to this war: the destruction during World War I, the Versailles Peace, the rise of Hitler, his attack on Europe, and the battle of Britain . . . where the story begins."[26] Although this description is technically correct, it hardly describes what is actually seen. First, it should be noted that 60 percent of the prologue involves images of war, as Bass juxtaposes the senseless slaughter of men in combat during World War I with the targeted killing of civilians in World War II. The ominous drum heard at the beginning of the epilogue sounds like it is playing a funeral march for victims in both wars. Whereas the machine-gun sequence from World War I begins without warning, just as that war had no rational cause, World War II is ascribed directly to Adolf Hitler. Hitler seemingly proclaims war, a bomb explosion actually emanating from his facial orifice. Bass ends the prologue with the haunting image of a corpse superimposed over a process shot of Hitler dancing a jig. The optically printed Stuka attack that initiates the World War II sequence resembles a ballet of death, with its repetition of overlapping action shots. Here, Bass takes a page from Sergei Eisenstein's playbook: in *October*, the opening of a drawbridge illustrates the theoretical point that such a montage extends cinematic time for dramatic emphasis. The next image, a dive-bombing Stuka superimposed on an old woman looking up, perfectly encapsulates the prologue's ideological point: that Hitler has ordered his war machine to target civilians. The remaining war sequence is an expressionist montage of war victims running for cover—including the de rigueur woman with a baby (again recalling Eisenstein, but this time, *Potemkin*)—bombs exploding, and buildings collapsing, all signifying the chaos of war. Bass also intercuts flash-frame images of disembodied hands reaching in from various sides of the film frame, yet another expressionistic, *pars pro toto* device to signify pain, suffering, and death without actually showing the last. Unlike the war montages from *Four Horsemen*, no actual corpses are seen, except for the final close-up of the woman in whose image Hitler dances a jig before more explosions introduce the titles. For those in the know, Hitler danced that jig on 22 June 1940 as the French army surrendered outside the General Foch railway car in the forest of Compiègne, the same place where the armistice ending World War I had been signed. Thus, the prologue actually ends historically with the fall of France. Strikingly, the prologue contains no images of actual soldiers, Nazi or otherwise, only the unrelenting attack of seemingly unmanned warplanes. Ultimately, Bass's images of war are drained of all but the most elementary of historical markers, gliding into the stereotypical. Bass's editing, resulting in an average of one image per second, creates a kinetic movement that appeals directly to the audience's emotions through the dichotomy of aggressor and victim.

Bass's images of peace are of a different sort. He intercuts cheering crowds the moment peace is declared, as well as throughout the "Versailles" sequence introducing the national leaders. The masses are clearly identified by nationality, so peace is depicted as an international project. The peace demonstrations disappear on both the sound track and the screen when Hitler's voice is heard, indicating that popular support does not extend to the German dictator. Even though the signatories of the Versailles Treaty are identified, their disembodied hands as they sign it remain anonymous, curiously draining their actions of agency. This impression is strengthened by the fact that Hitler's voice overwhelms the silent hands. Hitler, in contrast, is invested with an incredible amount of vitality and force, thanks to the animation of his hands and mouth; like the German words he is screaming, his actions are unintelligible but threatening nevertheless. The image of the gaping and agitated mouth is a horror vision, and as noted earlier, Bass will use it again in *Seconds* and *Phase IV*. In the latter, the round entrance to the ant colony perfectly matches these previous images, but in *The Victors*, the orifice signifies the mouth of a cannon firing its deadly load.

If Bass's editing of the prologue communicates the chaos, death, and destruction of war through compositional juxtapositions of movement, action, and form, then his title sequence communicates peace as nothing more than preparation for another war. Whereas the prologue is all jump cuts, the title sequence employs the principles of continuity editing to create a seamless parade of soldiers from all the nations participating in the Allied victory. All the men, regardless of their uniform, appear happy, while their regulation marching and Bass's cutting on form create a sense of unity. The parade is transparently a montage of many different parades of armed soldiers, each marching separately in his own physical space, as indicated by the environments visible at the fringes of the film frame. The irony lies in the martial spirit of the marching band heard on the sound track, supporting the elegant, formal design of military bodies in motion crashing against the actual reality of the war, which did not end but rather morphed into the Cold War. Whether Bass constructs one victory parade or many new parades for the Cold War era, he anticipates the film's final ironic scene in which former allies kill each other simply because they can't communicate.

The prologue and title sequence thus perfectly complement each other. Bass uses the formal tools of film montage to communicate complex historical processes in a minimum amount of time. As a matter of course, historical processes are merely telegraphed through stereotypical signification, yet their aesthetic force more than compensates. Ideologically, the Bass sequence makes a strongly pacifist argument by demonstrating the horrors of war on the one hand and the support for peace on the other. At the same time, the opening montage articulates a "great man" theory of history—that is, national leaders define the course of events. Meanwhile, the political and social forces that brought Hitler to power are invisible, unless one considers the jump cut from Versailles to Hitler to be a definitive statement that his rise was the direct result of the harsh peace negotiated there. Of special interest is the fact that the peace is communicated through newspaper headlines, yet the newspaper as a mode of communication disappears in the war segments; even the typographic communications suggested in the storyboards are gone.

Bass's titles for *Cowboy* and his various war montages for *The Four Horsemen of the Apocalypse* and *The Victors* attempt to communicate complex historical processes through the visual shorthand of film montage, whereby highly iconographic images from history are juxtaposed in a semantic chain. With his short films, Bass would go even further in developing his editing skills to communicate complex information about the world.

Apples and Oranges

Completed in 1962 as a promotion for the Columbia Broadcasting Network (CBS), *Apples and Oranges* is a thirteen-minute live-action and animated work that extols for advertisers the virtues of the relatively new medium of television.[27] It compares television's reach to the numbers achieved by supposedly less efficient traditional print media such as magazines. Based on a scientific marketing study commissioned by CBS and executed by Audits and Survey Company and Eugene Gilbert & Company over a two-year period in 1960–1961, *Apples and Oranges* clearly demonstrates television's superiority.[28] The study was the brainchild of Jay Eliasberg, director of CBS-TV's Research Department, and it was obviously conceived to increase CBS's advertising revenue.[29] Bass was hired to make the short through the intervention of Louis Dorfsman, creative director of CBS-TV and a longtime friend. The goal was to transform the forty-five-page market analysis into an "easily digestible film form for advertising executives."[30] Bass probably designed the cover and promotional material for the study as well, since the cover image depicting half an apple and half an orange held together with a measuring tape is pure Bass.[31] According to one industry trade periodical, Bass designed the film, but it was produced and directed by Dorfsman and George Bristol, head of advertising and sales promotion.[32] As Bass noted in an article on the film: "We had to make a story of research. This meant that we had to first understand the message ourselves. Then we used our creativity as a vehicle for delivering it clearly and concisely."[33] Part of the problem was that many advertising executives did not accept the premise that print and TV advertising were comparable. They believed the two media were like apples and oranges—hence the title. Beginning in February 1963, the film was screened for advertising agency executives in New York and ten other major cities.

Apples and Oranges begins by making the point that measuring the actual numbers of households or individuals reached by television and by print media is not a valid comparison. In fact, Bass stacks the deck from the beginning. In discussing magazines, Bass uses moving typography that has been split on its own horizontal axis (in the style of *Psycho*), remaining largely illegible; then he cuts to invisible hands flipping through magazines and a montage of printing presses. The sequence ends with a large pair of scissors cutting a string that holds a bundle of magazines together (reverberations of *The Shrike*), punctuating the fact that television is now competing with magazines for advertising dollars. Television, viewers are told, has penetrated 50 million homes, with potential consumers paying much more attention to television than to newspapers or magazines; these statements are accompanied by an exciting montage of television content. Placing film images in a television vignette, Bass seamlessly intercuts shots of Judy Garland, Danny Kaye, Red Buttons, Lucille Ball, Jackie Gleason, Jack Benny, and Ed Sullivan; news images of Nikita Khrushchev, Fidel Castro, and Jackie Kennedy; and scenes of sporting events, all of which make a much more immediate impression. The introduction concludes that even though television reaches millions of households each evening, "these were audiences you could barely compare, like apples and oranges."

SAUL BASS

After filling the screen with numbers, a device Bass would use again in *Why Man Creates* and *The Solar Film*, the piece transitions to an animated sequence of apples and oranges being sliced in front of the numbers. Meanwhile, the audience is told that a new CBS study of audiences "moves beyond this stalemate to focus on the total advertising effect of each medium." Indeed, the film proclaims that rather than studying the medium itself, this analysis focuses on the effect achieved by each advertisement, regardless of medium. In other words, *Apples and Oranges* employs the tools and language of empirical communications research, as it developed in the post–World War II United States. To make the study look even more scientific, Bass invokes a mathematical formula: size of audience (x) times response per unit of audience (y) equals total advertising effect (E), or (x)(y) = E. In this equation, variables can change, but the effect remains the same. Bass visualizes this equation with extremely simple graphics, placing white heads with smiley faces in cubes on vertical and horizontal axes, with either a rectangular television screen or turning pages in each square.

According to *Apples and Oranges*, the CBS study identified four ways in which people respond to advertisements: awareness of the product, belief in the product, evaluation of the product, and desire to buy the product. In the study, CBS marketing researchers sought to measure the effect of thirteen different products advertised in various print media and on eighteen different television shows on all three networks. To measure actual changes in attitudes, carefully selected interviewers questioned more than 6,000 interviewees nationwide, including wives, husbands, and parents, to establish a baseline before exposure to advertising media; the participants were then reinterviewed after exposure. Bass visualizes the CBS interviewers as silhouetted figures with hats who bear a strong resemblance to the gangster icons Bass created for advertisements for KLH Research and Development Corporation (1957) and *Some Like It Hot* (1959).[34] However, the silhouetted design likely also reminded viewers of the newly popular "Spy vs. Spy" cartoon characters created by Antonio Prohías for *Mad Magazine*. The spy connection was not unintentional, as Bass noted: "Research of this type is really a socially approved kind of spying."[35] Interviewees were questioned immediately after exposure to advertisements in magazines and five minutes after television viewing. The total audience response was then divided by the number of advertising dollars spent. After crunching the numbers, indicated onscreen by moving computer punch holes, television turned out to be 25 percent more effective than magazines in increasing product awareness, 42 percent more effective in creating belief in a product, and 100 percent more effective in product evaluation and encouraging a desire to buy. While the actual study named the advertised products under scrutiny (e.g., Bayer aspirin, Dial soap, Ford Falcon, Kellogg's corn flakes), the film lists no brand names, the goal being to speak to all advertisers.

Clearly, the actual study and the filmic presentation by CBS were addressed to companies that might be potential advertisers. For Bass, this short film was his first attempt at an essay film, a form he would perfect with *Why Man Creates*. The essay film implements heterogeneous media and varied cinematic forms and styles to communicate complex systems of knowledge. Mixing various media or juxtaposing graphics, photography, painting, and typography was an important aesthetic strategy at the Bauhaus and one that Bass would repeatedly use. In *Apples and Oranges*, Bass utilizes moving and layered typography to suggest the visual confusion of print media, just as he uses live-action documentary images to suggest the real-world immediacy of television and animated graphs and symbols to visualize outcomes. Basic shapes such as squares, diamonds, circles, crosses, arrows, and asterisks signify different responses to different media, while pictographs such as sliced apples and oranges in a slot machine image (like the one Bass used for *Ocean's Eleven*) signify that vendors are gambling with their advertising dollars if they don't analyze scientific data on the effectiveness of their work. Human heads that look more like white spoons represent interviewees, with television interviewees slightly rounder than their news-reading counterparts; abstract images of flipping pages and a round-edged TV screen further specify readers and viewers, respectively. Indeed, the spoon heads made an appearance as actual spoons with faces in Bass's advertisement for Manufacturers National Bank a year earlier.[36] The hat- and coat-wearing "spies" represent the legions of interviewers, identified in some shots by CBS's eye logo under a hat. An outstretched and disembodied hand also comes into play, pointing to data, as do Bass's trademark computer punch holes, signifying the crunching of data.[37] At another point, Bass employs the graphic map from *Four Just Men*, consisting of lines and house symbols, to visualize the distribution of households interviewed. Finally, as in the case of the trade ads for *Some Like It Hot*, Bass injects many humorous moments, such as when a very tall interviewer opens his coat to reveal that he is sitting on the shoulders of a colleague.[38] Later, Bass animates scores of interviewers tiptoeing across the screen in straight rows, going in opposite directions. Other visually inventive and humorous tricks include combining slices of apples and oranges into one fruit or coloring an interviewee in various rainbow colors to indicate willingness and desire to buy a product.

Apples and Oranges thus utilizes heterogeneous cinematic devices, including animation, live-action documentary images, moving typography, graphs, and even clearly defined segments, to visualize and communicate complex intellectual concepts emerging from an empirical study. It is the form Bass would come to prefer for his own independent films, always mixed with an ample amount of humor.

100 Years of the Telephone

In celebration of the centenary of Alexander Graham Bell's invention of the telephone—or, more accurately, the founding of the Bell Telephone Company in 1877—the company commissioned Bass to make a short film to demonstrate the telephone's place in the history of the United States. Bass was a natural for the project, given that he had coordinated Bell's corporate identity makeover in 1969. According to dates on various treatments for the project, Bass was first approached sometime before November 1975. The first treatment indicates that Bass initially proposed a much longer live-action film called *The One Hundred Year Old Man*. That film would have started with a live-action interview with a 100-year-old man who had won an essay contest in 1889 at age of thirteen, a plot structure similar to that of the popular Arthur Penn film *Little Big Man* (1970). The script then proposed presenting a series of flashbacks of his memories, including attending the St. Louis World's Fair (1904), participating in the Lafayette Escadrille during World War I (1917), and serving as an air-raid warden in World War II (1940). Another of the eight different draft scripts and treatments in the Bass Papers developed live-action historical vignettes around various telephone models: the Butterstamp wall telephone (1878), a Blake desk set (1880), a magnet wall set (1907), a pedestal desk set (1910), a desk set with combined receiver (1930), a 500-type color desk set (1954), a princess phone (1959), Touch-Tone (1968), and so forth.[39] Although no correspondence with the sponsor survives, one can assume that such a live-action film would have cost much more than Bell was willing to spend. A production schedule reveals that a preproduction story meeting was to be held on 10 December 1975, where it was agreed that final delivery of a two-inch high-band videotape would take place sometime in March 1976.[40] It is unknown whether that schedule was maintained, but the Bass office sent the completed three-minute animated film to the Journées Internationals du Cinema d'Animation–Festival d'Annecy in June 1977 and to the Melbourne International Film Festival in August 1978. The film's production date is 1977, so one can assume that production continued well into 1976.[41]

The style of *100 Years of the Telephone* is similar to the animation Bass and Art Goodman would design two years later for the historical time line in *The Solar Film*. The structure, however, is identical, with the camera (image) moving from the foreground to the horizon (background) through time, just as the upward camera movement in *Why Man Creates* signifies the passage of time by creating a temporal chronology from the floors of a building. Likewise, the Bass-Goodman animated sequences have similar lengths of three minutes (*Telephone* and *Solar*) and four minutes (*Why Man Creates*). In *100 Years of the Telephone*, the actual years are carved in huge stone edifices, marking the passage of time, while historical scenes are embedded in the rock or take place at the foot of the stone cliff. Thus, the film fades in on Alexander Graham Bell with an "entrepreneur" who wants him to give up on his invention and invest in an industry with a future—namely, high-button shoes—as a huge granite 1876 looms in the background. Next, a covered wagon with a Bell Telephone logo on it rides up to the stone edifice, and a cable is pulled from the back to hook up to the number. For 1879, Thomas Edison, holding a lightbulb, obsesses about being a failure until he plugs it into the wall, after which he screams, "I'm a success." The opening of the Brooklyn Bridge literally connects 1883 and 1884, while 1888 sees the inauguration of the Statue of Liberty with fireworks; everything is washed away by the Johnstown flood in 1889, and Teddy Roosevelt's Rough Riders make an appearance in 1898. In 1905 Albert Einstein calls his mother to tell her he has invented the theory of relativity, while in 1909 Admiral Robert Peary and Roald Amundsen argue about whether they are to meet at the North Pole or the South Pole.[42] Other historical markers include Woodrow Wilson's Fourteen Points (1919), the Scopes monkey trial (1925), the introduction of talking pictures (1929), a GI in a telephone booth (1943), the moon landing (1969), the American bicentennial (1976), and finally a new Bell Telephone truck hooking up a giant Touch-Tone phone in front of the 1977 edifice, completing a full 100 years.

Like the Einstein and Wilson panels, many of the events depict individuals talking on the telephone with their mothers or spouses, giving Bass the opportunity to inject healthy portions of humor into the proceedings. For example, when Einstein says, "I have just discovered the theory that could change the entire conception of the universe," his mother says, "That's all right, son, so long as you keep in touch with your mother." An astronaut's mother tells him much the same thing when he calls from the moon. This stereotype of the overbearing mother is a universal one, but it also had a specifically Jewish connection for Bass and Goodman. In other humorous episodes, a reporter calls his editor during the Scopes trial and says: "No, get this, chief, in the famous evolution trial John Scopes today made his boldest statement ever!" "Well, I'll be a monkey's uncle." "Yeah! That's just what he said!" Other jokes are more visual, such as when the 1929 edifice cracks and crumbles to the ground, symbolizing the stock market crash. Another visual joke involves a GI telephoning home during World War II (1943): as he stands in the phone booth, a large poster behind him warns, "The Enemy Is Listening," and features Hitler's oversized ear. For the bicentennial year 1976, the edifice is draped in American flag patterns, while a rally and celebrations take place at its base. The telephone is invariably placed in the center of well-known historical events that have affected the course of the nation. The events chosen range from those instigated by "great men" and those social events affecting large parts of the population, such as the migration to California during the Great Depression and the migration to suburbia (and the advent of drive-in theaters) during the 1950s. Although the chronology theorizes that the telephone was central to American history, the construction is artificial, since virtually none of the events depicted depended on the telephone per se. Indeed, the film merely demonstrates that the telephone could have been instrumental in communicating these events to the rest of the world. The chronological movement of history is thus connected to communication in general and to the telephone in particular, implying that civilization's body of knowledge is itself a function of communication.

Why Man Creates

Saul Bass deservedly won an Academy Award for his short film *Why Man Creates* (1968), which is undoubtedly his greatest achievement as a filmmaker.[43] Creating a free-form essay that directly addresses audiences, Bass utilizes an extremely heterogeneous set of formal elements to probe and question the nature of creativity, without providing any definitive answers; instead, he develops an open-ended structure that engages the audience. Eschewing an actual head title, Bass writes the subtitle in pencil on a piece of paper in the first image: "A series of explorations, episodes & comments on the nature of creativity," immediately indicating that his personal and subjective essay film will be both nonlinear in its narrative and experimental in its form. As one critic noted: "Bass relished in the open-ended and fragmentary nature of his subject matter, taking every opportunity to explore and play with ideas, while avoiding the need for a unifying or stridently singular metaphorical thread throughout."[44] The irony and the beauty of *Why Man Creates* are that its open-endedness is as much a product of Bass's aesthetic concept as it is the outcome of the preview process by corporate executives and others consultants, who in their sheer numbers formed a significant audience.[45]

Bass started thinking seriously about creativity in the mid-1950s, especially after the Russians sent *Sputnik* into orbit and Americans began to worry about the nation's education and science gap. Bass participated in various conference programs; in 1958 he attended the New York Art Directors Club Visual Communications Conference on Creativity, and in 1959 he spoke at a Westinghouse-sponsored conference on creativity at Stanford University.[46] In "A Definition of Creativity," Bass theorized tongue-in-cheek to his old Jewish *mamele* that creativity is getting someone else to do your work for you, to execute your ideas. More seriously, he wrote in the same piece: "If we understand the act to be an insight that establishes a new relation between existing concepts or objects, each creative act is a nonconforming act."[47] Indeed, this vacillation between off-the-cuff, even flippant humor and the seriousness of his purpose also characterizes *Why Man Creates*. Bass apparently believed that humor was a necessary part of the learning process if boredom leading to noncommunication was to be avoided. As Bass noted in an interview: "If you laugh with an idea you are opening yourself to it."[48] But Bass also considered nonconformity to be essential for creativity. In an article published in the British *Journal of the Royal Society for the Encouragement of Arts*, the designer wrote: "The creative personality is essentially non-conforming. If we understand the creative act to be an insight that establishes a new relation between existent concepts or objects, then we must accept the fact that to one degree or another, each creative act is a non-conforming act. The creative personality sees something that is not seen by others, and this insight may or may not be in conformity with the general view on the matter."[49]

Originally the brainchild of Robert Sandberg, Kaiser Aluminum and Chemical Company's vice president of public relations and advertising, and inspired by several issues of Kaiser's company magazine,[50] the film was apparently in preproduction by September 1966. According to Bass: "This was intended to be essentially a recruiting film. It was aimed at scientists and engineers in the East—Silicon Valley didn't exist in those days. Kaiser's theory was if they could show how aluminum was being used creatively and how Kaiser was a hell of a great place to be, then that would be exciting for a creative engineer or scientist."[51] It is interesting to speculate whether Sandberg went to Bass because of his track record with rival ALCOA. In any case, Bass wrote to William Riley of Young & Rubicam to get advice on the proposed "Kaiser film." Among other issues, Bass worried that creativity was too broad a topic: "This general area of ideas is so vast that there is a great danger that the film may degenerate into a marvelous but incohesive [*sic*] stew of goodies."[52] What becomes clear from the surviving production files is that this film, presumably like Bass's other sponsored films, was influenced by the sponsors and other opinion leaders Bass trusted. Though not exactly produced by committee, *Why Man Creates* went through a lengthy and intense preview and revision process that rivaled anything the major motion picture studios had done in the classical era.

Bass started by making undated and seemingly random notes to himself about the film. Some of these bear quoting because they give insight into the designer's creative process. On one page Bass writes: "Creativity not a joy, not rational—messy—not like picking a diamond, more like sitting in a room full of junk." The junk Bass refers to is the infinite variety in the world and the depth of our historically accumulated knowledge and art, which feeds into the present. This may have been the germ of the idea for a section called "The Edifice." Some of his notes morph into images that Bass will utilize in "The Edifice," such as "Beethoven's chord, 3rd symphony," or a drawing of two telegraph operators sending messages to each other from adjacent tables. On another page, Bass scribbled an idea that would become his "Judgment" sequence:

Indian arrows/grand central
Cowboy shootout/Wilshire shoppers demonstrate "cause and effect
    relationship" (Ideas of yesterday have they an effect today?)

Civilization

On another page he put down two ideas that would evolve into the "Parable" and "Judgment" sequences: "Ball rolling . . . Argument between two points of view (society vs. individual)." On yet another piece of paper: "Not a story as such but a series of episodes which the viewer relates to each in his own way and it will be different for some from others. Thus, you will become part of the film and complete the process."[53] Here, Bass is consciously designing a film that maximizes audience subjectivity—a much more radical notion of creativity than that envisioned by the Kaiser executives, who may have tended toward a Tolstoyan view of art, or something akin to art for Everyman. Thus, even before a script was completed, Bass was already focusing on a more open-ended structure that would not predigest content for the viewer but present ideas for each viewer to process individually, effectively constructing his or her own film.

On 19 December 1966 Kaiser Aluminum and Chemical Company and Saul Bass signed a design and film production agreement that obligated Kaiser to finance a film on creativity.[54] By February 1967, a first script had been completed and sent to Kaiser for comment, consisting of the following parts: "The Stimulus. The Process. The Judgment. The Problem. The Beginning. The Mark."[55] Production must have started almost immediately, because the first edit of the film was finished by November.[56] Since the original storyboards presented to Kaiser survive on twenty-nine eight- by ten-inch photographic contact sheets, we have a good idea of Bass's initial proposal. Utilizing actors who did not appear in the final film, and structured around a countdown, the story opens with a go-go dancer and then intercuts various modes of communication—typewriters, telephones, switchboard panels, and computers—before transitioning to a jumping-jacks sequence in traffic. A body builder training at Muscle Beach is followed by a series of images of industrial pipes. The remaining images follow the outline below, reflecting the November 1967 edit. Some key images from the original concept have already been removed (as indicated by the gaps in the numbers), including a sequence of a child growing up juxtaposed with shots of a Jewish ghetto child (who doesn't grow up); a man shooting an arrow into the heavens, followed by a rocket penetrating space; a very short animated sequence with an ant and a tree; and some modern art reproductions.[57]

1. Main title 33.5 sec
2. Head Openings 1 min 35 sec

4. All together 50 sec
5. Gastro-Intestinal 51.5 sec
7. Eggs Cracking 18.5 secs
8. Number Dialogue 33.5 secs
10. Anatomy lecture 25 secs
12. Human Forms Nature 26 secs
13. Process (includes creators) 5 min 6.5 secs
14. Seeds 46.5 secs
15. Judgment 2 min 43 secs
16. Parable 2 min 41 secs
17. Digression 20 secs
18. Edifice 3 min 50 secs
19. Problem 4 min 21 secs
20. Mark 4 min 11.5 secs
21. The End 48 secs[58]

The film was shot on 16mm color reversal film, which Bass hoped to blow up to 35mm for theatrical distribution, thus qualifying the film for the Oscars.[59] According to once source, the production budget was approximately $200,000; however, Kaiser's total outlay, including the cost of prints and promotion, eventually exceeded $400,000, of which Kaiser needed to recoup $298,988.36.[60]

Once the first edit was completed, the film began an intensive period of previews. First, it was shown to numerous executives from Kaiser and Young & Rubicam at the latter's headquarters on 21 February 1968. After the screening, Bass removed the original head title, which consisted of white sans serif typography on a black background: "Documents under the general heading . . . why . . . man . . . creates." He also removed the typographic digits for the chapter headings, which left the audience at sea as to what was coming next but also objectified the segmentation.[61] It was Bass's friend Lou Dorfsman who suggested eliminating the countdown at the end of the film and "telling it straight" in the titles. Both he and Don Fabun from Kaiser also complained about the excessive length of the "Parable" and "Judgment" chapters. Others commented that the footsteps in the sand at the end of the film were depressing and anticlimactic.[62] In fact, Bass's intention had been to engage the viewer as a potential artist-creator (supporting a Tolstoyan Everyman point of view) with a final direct invitation inserted after the footsteps in the sand. In the final script, a Teletype machine spews out the following message: "VISION NEEDED . . . CREATIVE IMPULSE UNIVERSAL . . . CULTIVATED WITH CURIOSITY . . . FREEDOM INTENSITY . . . WONDERFUL THINGS CAN HAPPEN . . . STARTING WITH YOU . . . REGARDS." Following the Teletype, Bass inserted images of fingers on piano keys, a brush on a canvas, and a beaker with a flame that grows until it fills screen (shades of *Exodus*). However, executives found this ending confusing, and they were unsure of Bass's purpose. And indeed, although the three images signify three areas of human creativity, and the growing flame visualizes the increasing passion for creativity, there are too many final messages here. Thus, it is possible that the previewed film ended with only the footsteps in the sand.

Kaiser was apparently uneasy about the innovative ellipses, seeming non sequiturs, and staccato montage cutting, and it needed authoritative reassurance about the film's corporate value.[63] It is not known whether there was any critique of the human forms sequence, which featured female art nudes, but that part was also omitted in the final cut. Finally, a corporate statement of purpose by Kaiser prefacing the film was eliminated in favor of a program guide, at the suggestion of executives from Lamb Kelley and Young & Rubicam.[64] As a result, Kaiser published a fancy, full-color twelve-page brochure that included reproductions of approximately fifty frames from the film and a note by Kaiser's president, T. J. Ready Jr., to clarify the company's position.[65] Subsequently, Bass made further cuts, including the gastrointestinal sequence, made up of shots of industrial pipes in a factory while a speaker discusses food; changed the ending, adding handwritten title cards; and, possibly most important, moved "The Edifice" sequence to the front of the film.

By the spring of 1968, Kaiser had distributed the film through Modern Talking Pictures to hundreds of schools, churches, and civic groups, always carefully documenting audience numbers and comments. While some negative comments remained, the film's reception was now largely positive. By the summer, the film was also being reviewed in mainstream newspapers. In August 1968 *Why Man Creates* had its Los Angeles theatrical premiere at the Laemmle Los Feliz, sharing the bill with Jacques Demy's *Les Demoiselles de Rochefort*; however, it was advertised as *Thoughts on Creativity*.[66] The film played for two weeks, possibly to qualify for the Academy Awards, but further theatrical screenings never materialized.[67] Probably thanks to Lou Dorfsman, "The Edifice" was shown on nationwide television during the 24 September premiere of CBS's *60 Minutes.*[68]

Once *Why Man Creates* won an Academy Award, it really took off. Indeed, as reviews began to appear in various magazines devoted to education, it became clear that teachers were embracing the film. It also helped that the Educational Film Library Association gave *Why Man Creates* an award as best commercial public relations film.[69] One reviewer wrote: "I think that this little film does pretty well what it sets out to do— suggest that we relax, let our imaginations have free rein once in a while, and, stop looking at the world one way."[70] In *Art Education Magazine*, another reviewer wrote: "One cannot help but feel strains of Moliere's satire, of Shakespeare's humanism, of surrealist incongruity, and of the playful but profound paintings of Paul Klee."[71] However, it was a series of articles by David A. Sohn (at least one of which was republished in Pyramid's catalog) that really helped the film reach its audience of educators.[72] As noted on one website, the film was screened in elementary and high schools throughout the 1970s: "Many adults who were schoolchildren during this time have extremely fond memories of Bass' film."[73]

The film's huge success led to more tensions with Kaiser. The company had been distributing the film more or less for free, and Bass thought his design firm should be participating in profits beyond a net 25 percent.[74] In the summer of 1969 Pyramid was given a nonexclusive contract to distribute the film to the nontheatrical market.[75] Unlike in the theatrical market, where earnings start high and taper off as the film runs its course, earnings in the nontheatrical market tend to increase over time, as more and more schools and colleges purchase or rent the film for classroom use. Indeed, according to the *Hollywood Reporter*, the film had grossed more than $1.3 million through rentals and the sale of about 4,000 copies by late 1977.[76] For Bass & Associates, this meant that it initially received checks from Pyramid totaling about $15,000 a year (in 1971); by 1975, fourth-quarter earnings alone reached $8,444, and in 1976 it earned $35,991.53 over the course of the year.[77] One can assume that earnings continued at this level at least until the 1980s, when video began to affect the market, although even then, video sales were probably brisk in the nontheatrical market as schools and universities made the switch from 16mm film to VHS. Even today, the film remains hugely popular: *Why Man Creates* has been watched on YouTube more than 166,000 times.

Surprisingly, the title *Why Man Creates* never appears in the film. Bass considered it too pretentious and favored the more modest title *Notes on Creativity.*[78] Bass offered the sponsor no fewer than thirty-eight different titles, but Kaiser insisted on *Why Man Creates.* Unable to convince company executives to change their minds, Bass omitted the title altogether, adding only a generic "Kaiser Aluminum and Chemical Company presents" head title before beginning in medias res.[79] In a 1988 seminar for AT&T executives, Bass minced few words: "It was a title I really felt uncomfortable with at the time. . . . And almost 20 years later, still do. It makes a promise that just can't be kept. . . . And that title served the film—and Kaiser—badly."[80] In Bass's opinion, the worst thing about the title is that it implies there is an answer to the question, whereas Bass's whole aesthetic strategy and philosophy are that there are no monocausal answers, no theoretical precepts. He thought film titles were already too semantically constricting. As Academy archivist Sean Savage has remarked, Bass had a real problem with film titles: some had two titles, like *Windows/Notes on the Popular Arts,* while others had none at all on the physical print. Bass preferred titles with the word "Notes" in them, communicating something unfinished and open-ended; he didn't want any title to carry the semantic or aesthetic weight of defining his film. He envisioned the film experience as a journey of discovery for the audience, and he used humor and cinematic form to engage them in a discussion on the nature of creativity, where there are no final answers, just as there are no titles.

Bass in fact implements a similar strategy in *Notes on the Popular Arts* (his own version of *Windows*), after removing the corporate good news to stock traders of the Warner Brothers–Kinney conglomerate.[81] In that film, Bass utilizes a typewriter (with a close-up on disembodied hands) to type out the film's title in caps. He also uses notes, each of which is subsequently crossed out with typed double x's: "When we consider the popular arts today. . . ." Crossed out. "As Emerson wisely said. . . ." Crossed out. "Popular arts. . . ." Crossed out. The head title's notes thus succumb to silence, leaving the film with a title but no beginning, other than a transition to the first episode. Here again, we see Bass's aversion to theory, manifested in his inability (comically feigned) to make definitive or generalizing statements about his topic, the so-called popular arts. Unwilling to define what his overall conception might be, he allows the audience to enter into the discussion without any preconceptions, allows each viewer to create his or her own film from the images and sounds he has created. *Why Man Creates* demonstrates the same resistance to articulating ideas in words but is infinitely more successful, as it is not forced to find humorous commonalities among all its corporate sponsor's products.

From the very first image of *Why Man Creates*, Bass communicates that his essay film is personal, the musings of the artist. We see Bass's disembodied hand in extreme close-up (actually, only the fingers) writing with a pencil on a sheet of white paper: "A series of explorations, episodes & comments on creativity."[82] As Bass's colleague Al Kallis noted, staring at a blank sheet of paper is always the moment of truth for a designer, who must create something out of nothing and come up with an idea that will spark communication between the designer and the audience. That image visualizes the hand of the artist, which must execute and form visual ideas coming from the brain, from the mind's eye. Bass returns to the writing hand throughout the film, marking the various chapters of his work and presenting the end credits. Here, then, we return to a quintessential Bauhaus image—that of the hand in action, the hand at work creating art. This is evident in Jan Tschichold's Bauhaus-influenced photomontage on the cover of *Foto-Auge*, juxtaposing the artist's head (in particular his eye), the hand holding a compass for drawing, and graph paper.[83] One can also read the use of pencil and paper here as purposefully low tech, indicating that anyone can create; they are also the first tools of a designer. Finally, the writing hand is the visual equivalent of a direct address to the audience. Indeed, *Why Man Creates* eschews the "voice of God" narration of many other documentary films of the period, which presuppose a passive audience; instead, Bass attempts to engage viewers in an active process of questioning and exploration. Significantly, *Why Man Creates* never directly answers the central question of its title, freeing each audience member to take away his or her own thoughts after seeing the film.

The film is broken down into seven sections, or chapters: (1) The Edifice, (2) Fooling Around: Some Ideas Start that Way, (3) The Process, (4) The Judgment, (5) A Parable, (6) A Digression, and (7) The Search: Work in Progress on New Ideas. The first and last sequences are the longest, at five and seven minutes, respectively; the others run about four minutes, except for "The Judgment" (three minutes) and "A Digression" (thirty seconds). "The Edifice" and "A Digression" feature animation by Art Goodman and Pantomime, while "A Parable" employs stop-motion animation. The other sequences are constructed as live-action montages with nonsynchronized and synchronized sound. As in so many Bauhaus-influenced design solutions, whether for a single page or a syntagmatic ordering of film images, Bass's film fragments perception through its conglomeration of diverse media. The heterogeneity of its aesthetic media, as well as its nonlinear narrative, forces the viewer not only to continually rethink what is being said but also to adjust to how it is being said, promoting an active reading. Each chapter is self-contained, yet it also relates to those before and after it.

"The Edifice" presents a history of the world through the filter of its greatest creators and thinkers. This is imagined as a house in which succeeding generations add floors, as the camera slowly tracks up through the building (and through the ages). At the beginning of this chapter, I mentioned the cave paintings that make up the ground floor of the edifice. Bass then chronicles humanity's subsequent technical and intellectual achievements in a humorous fashion: One man invents a lever to lift weights; another invents the wheel. Further up, masses of slaves move giant stones for the Egyptian pyramids, while someone on the next floor calls out "bronze" and "iron," referring to those respective ages. Next, Euclid is mentioned by name, while the Greek philosophers are identified by the questions they asked: "Who shall rule the state?" (Plato). But Bass is not so naïve as to think that history is only an upward movement characterized by unadulterated progress. There are always hiccups. For example, when a toga-wearing figure responds to Plato's question by saying, "All the people," he is promptly impaled on a sword by a colleague. The fall of Rome is visualized by a temple that cracks and then falls (an idea Bass used in *Spartacus* and would use again in *100 Years of the Telephone*). When the Dark Ages arrive, Bass tints the image blue and has yellow light emanating from Gothic archways, where we see and hear Gregorian monks chanting:

What is the shape of the Earth?
Flat.
What happens when you get to the edge?
You fall off.
Does the Earth move?
Ne-ev-ev-er.

With the arrival of Copernicus and Galileo (identified by their statements), the darkness disappears, allowing Michelangelo to paint the ceiling and

Leonardo da Vinci to paint the floor; the latter is identified by the *Mona Lisa*, which he hangs on the wall.

The chronology is not always accurate. For instance, in the film, the invention of the lightbulb (1879) precedes Darwin (1859), and Freud on the couch (1899) precedes Alfred Nobel's invention of dynamite (1863). Rather than strictly chronologically, Bass groups events by the nature of the endeavor: Darwin and Freud, Beethoven and Tchaikovsky, Nobel and Pasteur, Washington, Lincoln, Marx, Wilson, Roosevelt, and so forth. Bass's typical humor infuses each level of the edifice. For example, a black spot bounces through the floor chanting, "I'm a bug, I'm a germ"; then, when it sees Louis Pasteur, the spot changes its tune, "I'm not a bug, I'm not a germ." The closer to the modern era Bass gets, the more negative the images become. Indeed, the edifice ends as a dystopia: after the Wright brothers' biplane lands on top of the building, Bass creates a junkyard pile of airplanes, automobiles, and television sets, ending the sequence with a cloud of smoke and an atom symbol hovering over the mountain of metal as a voice coughs and screams, "Help." In other words, Bass is saying that throughout the history of the world, humanity's creativity has undoubtedly led to progress, as well as to the invention of many things that are now destroying the planet. This slightly dystopian version of human history certainly runs counter to the sponsor's feel-good intentions, but it is couched in humor to soften the blow. It is indeed a moment of real Jewish self-deprecating humor—always seeing *shvartz* in the good—that came naturally to Bass and Goodman but not to the WASP suits at Kaiser.

Chapter 2, "Fooling Around," presents a series of non sequiturs connected by swish pans: disembodied hands opening a chicken egg and finding crude oil or a butterfly, an analysis of a bald pedestrian's cranium visually divided into USDA prime meat cuts, a female and male exchanging the many numbers we must remember in our daily lives (which appear on the screen until it is completely blackened by numbers), pedestrians doing jumping jacks on signal at a city crosswalk, a party and its guests. The humor in this chapter takes its cue from Dadaism, privileging nonsense and intuition; its images tend toward the absurd, the incongruent, and the playful. Interestingly, the last section, where the heads of three party guests are opened like jars, originally came at the beginning: the go-go dancer gets two scoops of ice cream and milk, a somewhat misogynistic visual joke, just for fun; the bearded hippie is revealed to be a mama's boy (another Jewish joke); and the straitlaced, middle-class matron is just an empty-headed drunk. It is the Dadaist incongruence of the images that engages the audience, especially children, to think about creativity. As the chapter ends, the narrator asks, where do ideas come from? The answer: "From looking at one thing and seeing another, fooling around, playing with possibilities." Bass then cuts to a series of multiple exposures: a girl jumping rope over an extreme low-angle shot of pedestrians or a bird's-eye view of New York and the surf flooding a beach. The heterogeneity of the photomontages defies easy categorization; they constitute "fooling around," just as much of the previous film did. And that leads to something worth saving and expanding; "that is where the game stops and the real work begins." Bass thus theorizes that all creation is based on experimenting, on trying various tactics, on exploring parameters to find the middle, on juxtaposing total opposites, whether in ideas or in media. All this can be fun, but ultimately, it must end in the hard work necessary to truly engage in the material.

"The Process" presents a young man attempting to create something out of oversized building blocks, but he fails, and the structure (which seemingly defies gravity) collapses. Bass then intercuts on the sound track an original interview with Thomas Edison, talking about failing repeatedly before he succeeded, while photographic portraits of Edison at various ages flash onscreen. The young man tries again, but again his structure collapses, and Ernest Hemingway appears in portraits and talks about "fighting like hell" when he tries to write. While the on-camera talent inadvertently punches his hand through a building block, Bass cuts to portraits of Albert Einstein, who notes that a solution cannot be achieved by brute force, but with patience, it might eventually present itself. Suddenly the young man has an epiphany: he attaches body parts (hands, arms, legs) from a clothing store mannequin to his building blocks to create a moving sculpture. The artist's shrill wife then enters the scene to comment that his creation needs American flags, Bass again injecting humor into these mostly serious proceedings. Bass implies, through this little bit of theater, that the creative process involves continual experimentation and hard work, yet the final outcome may be dependent on serendipity, chance, luck. The intercutting of Edison, Hemingway, and Einstein undergirds the notion that hard work is an essential element of the creative process.[84]

In "The Judgment," Bass takes aim at society's critics, whom he sees as more or less useless in "contributing to the creative process." He accomplishes this by editing together almost exclusively negative comments made by ordinary people looking at an invisible work of art. Indeed, the first words heard are, "What a piece of garbage that is!" In fact, Bass is restaging well-known television footage of Chicagoans being interviewed after the unveiling of a Picasso sculpture in front of the Richard Daley Civic Center on 15 August 1967. At the time, the publicly financed sculpture in downtown Chicago caused a huge controversy.[85] In the film, one gentleman says the artwork represents the decline of the West, obviously referring to Oswald Spengler, and the crowd turns into an ugly mob, apparently ready to lynch the artist; one person actually says, "Let's hang 'em." Bass cuts to the young man from the previous chapter, now dressed as a cowboy, who takes aim at the audience and shoots, "killing" two on-the-street critics. In turn, he is shot with words of damnation, momentarily reviving when an offscreen housewife notes that she likes the piece. Bass's closing joke, though, is that she likes the artwork because the material used is worth "at least $100." Here, Bass is not only poking fun at the uselessness of critics (perhaps including his own critics in the Kaiser executive suites); he is also warning the artist that listening to the mob is dangerous. More important, as Bass repeatedly stated in interviews, creativity is an act of nonconformity, of moving beyond conventional wisdom. Society is often an impediment to change and to creativity (a thought taken up again in "A Digression").

"A Parable" illustrates the notion of nonconformity by following the "career" of a Ping Pong ball that is rejected in the production line when it bounces too high in a test. It bounces out into the world—Bass apparently voiced the ball's bounce, "POING"—eventually ending up in a large field where other rejects have gathered. But instead of sitting around and giving in to its fate, it bounces higher and higher until it disappears. Bass then ends with a somewhat bombastic, tongue-in-cheek roll title in dead silence:

There are some who say he's coming back and we have only to wait. . . .

There are some who say he burst up there because ball was not meant to fly. . . .

And there are some who maintain he landed safely in a place where balls bounce high.

The roll title and the silence—fixtures in the science fiction and adventure genres—imbue the sequence with an epic, even mythological, quality, thereby humorously spoofing film genres while visualizing the life and times of a Ping Pong ball that may have become the messiah.

Surprisingly, Bass spends a significant amount of screen time on the factory production process, cutting together shots of moving balls and machines on an assembly line, an homage to Walter Ruttmann's montages in *Berlin, Symphony of a City*, but also emphasizing standardization. Here, Bass is once again stressing by example the necessary element of nonconformity and the need for artists to take risks, regardless of social concerns. The parable of Ping is the story of an artist or an explorer who dares to enter unchartered waters and becomes the stuff of legend.

The relationship between society and the individual artist is also the subject of the next chapter, "A Digression." In this thirty-second animated sequence, two snails meet. One asks, "Have you ever thought that radical ideas threaten institutions, then become institutions and in turn reject radical ideas which threaten institutions?" When the second snail responds in the negative, the first one says, "Gee, for a moment there I thought I had something." In fact, this notion of the cyclical nature of radical ideas is a truism for art and politics. What is radical and new in one generation may become conservative or reactionary in the next. As the literary and social critic Irving Howe, a contemporary of Bass, wrote: "In the war between modernist culture and bourgeois society . . . the middle class has discovered that the fiercest attacks upon its values can be transposed into pleasing entertainments, and the avant-garde writer or artist must confront the one challenge for which he has not been prepared: the challenge of success. Contemporary society is endlessly assimilative, even if it tames and vulgarizes what it has learned, sometimes foolishly to praise."[86] By the late 1960s, Bass could say much the same about his own work in film titles. That which had appeared revolutionary and new in the mid-1950s had become acceptable industry practice.

The final chapter, "The Search," is not only the longest but also the most complicated and heterogeneous. In fact, it consisted of two distinct chapters in earlier edits. First, Bass interviews scientists working on long-term projects; then he creates a montage of art that mirrors the intellectual history of "The Edifice." As the chapter begins, an offscreen speaker is interviewing a cancer specialist, who explains what he is doing and concludes that in five years he will know more. Some of the footage seems to be taken from Bass's IBM cancer research spot. The offscreen speaker notes that Dr. Dulbecco has been working on cancer research for twenty years.[87] And this is the point of all the subsequent interviews with scientists: they are working on long-term problems, and there is no instant gratification—just decades of hard work. One scientist admits he has reached a dead end after seven years of research and is at a loss what to do next. Bass films the scientist packing up his briefcase and turning off the hall lights, plunging the screen into darkness. Again, Bass is emphasizing that some problems are difficult, and finding solutions may take decades or longer. Having once again fallen into a depressing (albeit realistic) state of mind, as he had at the end of "The Edifice," Bass tries to invoke some positive energy by asking, "Why does man create?"

Bass then cuts to a yellow sun slowly rising on an orange horizon, as a stick figure that could be a Giacometti sculpture fades in. This image inaugurates the chapter's final section: a montage of the history of art. The image itself (which is also used for the poster) is hauntingly beautiful, mixing nature with modernist art in a way that emphasizes the mystical aspects of creation rather than modernism's clear-eyed rationalism or the nonsense of Dada. It is an image that only the mature Bass could have created, remaining true to the modernist notions of Moholy-Nagy and Kepes in terms of its design elements, but now melded through an image of the sun to a more nature-oriented aesthetic, bound up with his California home.

Bass structures this journey through art with a series of statements by the narrator, which are then illustrated with paintings or cutouts of paintings. As the narrator intones, "Men have struggled against time, against decay," Bass interweaves multiple-exposure images of ancient art (with a Picasso thrown in), depicting the gods (in man's image) with lightning, water, fire, and earth. He is thus interpreting the will to create art as a struggle against the natural environment. This is a riff on a similar creation sequence in *The Searching Eye*, but now centered on humanity's rather than nature's creation. Bass then implies that man's technological advancement defies nature, even while providing benefits to humanity. This point is emphasized as Bass fades to black on a spaceship, then cuts to his signature image of birds flying away from the sun at center screen—the designer's personal trope for human freedom. Next, Bass cuts together ancient and modern paintings of men and women rather than gods, including a Peter Paul Rubens (*Dance of Italian Villagers*, 1636), a Pieter Brueghel

(*Wheat Harvest*, 1565), and a Pablo Picasso (*Maternity*, 1905), all of which focus on human secular subjects. Curiously, Bass's cropping of well-known paintings indicates that he is not necessarily interested in maintaining the integrity of the art, as an art historian would be; rather, he treats the visual material as a designer who is willing to use any visual resource. Indeed, the cropping is severe enough to dehistoricize the paintings, lifting their subjects into the timeless realm of myth. Oddly, Michelangelo's finger of God from the Sistine Chapel is seen behind a cross matte, a Christian interpretation of the theology behind the image. This seems out of character for Bass, who seldom (if ever) employed religious symbolism in his work and whose public Jewishness remained secular. One wonders whether the cross was simply a nod to all the medieval and Renaissance art inspired and financed by the Catholic Church, or perhaps to the conservative WASPs at Kaiser. When Bass cuts to signatures of Rembrandt, Picasso, Mark Twain, and others, they become metonymies for the great art, literature, and music created by these individuals.

Interestingly, Bass's next montage is of street graffiti, some of which was shot for *West Side Story*, as the sound track notes, "Some have spoken inarticulately." Bass ends the sequence with two words painted on a brick wall, "I am," indicating that even graffiti is a legitimate form of human communication and a means of self-expression, no matter how raw. By extension, Bass exclaims that art can be created by anyone, regardless of their training, education, or status.[88] In his final image, Bass slowly zooms out from the head of a male statue, then dissolves to a shot of a boy on the beach chasing seagulls, taken from *The Searching Eye*.

Bass thus ends the film not only with an image of freedom but also with the profound statement that to create is to communicate, and to communicate is the essence of humanness. Human beings, unlike any other creatures on earth, have the ability to speak articulately and to assert their individuality through language. And there is no better medium for asserting one's uniqueness than art. But Bass also understands that creating anything new is a complicated process involving imagination, thinking outside the box, and continual experimentation, as well as hard work and the ability to block out the noise of the mob. In one image, missing from the final cut, a number of visitors look at a piece of modern art in a museum, with one man in a suit standing on his head to view the painting. It is a joke on modern, nonrepresentational art but also a theoretical statement about the fact that art, once it is created, belongs to the audience, which may choose to read the work in any number of ways. In *Why Man Creates* Saul Bass is both funny and deadly serious, because his subject calls for it. Creating something original demands a playful attitude, on the one hand, and lots of serious hard work, on the other. Not without reason, he cut at least three important sequences from the film into his 1969 AT&T identity campaign film, which was intended to sell the new company design and colors to middle managers; these scenes called attention to themselves and intellectually engaged the audience, which was necessary to get a buy-in from AT&T's staff.[89]

Through his collage technique, Bass communicates theses and seemingly random thoughts, often articulating them nonverbally through the juxtaposition of images, whether of his own creation or borrowed from the great masters. The collage technique also allows an open-ended structure, giving audience members great freedom to create their own film from Bass's shards, elevating communication from a sender-receiver situation to a reciprocal, two-way dialogue. In doing so, Bass acknowledges that we are all products of what has come before, but we also have the freedom to be ourselves and do nothing more than chase birds on the beach. In *Phase IV*, Bass's only feature film, the designer further explores the social aspects of human communication. That film focuses not on individual identity formation but on social microcosms, concluding that the survival of the planet may be in jeopardy if humans don't relinquish their self-centered individual desires.

Phase IV

Ironically, Saul Bass's poster for *Why Man Creates* can be read as a science fiction image, the spindly Giacometti figure in the foreground matching some popular images of aliens—human-like without being human—indistinct in the glare of the rising yellow sun. Bass's only full-length feature film would in fact be a science fiction film about ants taking over the world. Made in the wake of *The Hellstrom Chronicle* (1971), *Night of the Lepus* (1972), *Invasion of the Bee Girls* (1973), and other films about nature gone wild, *Phase IV* was marketed in much the same way: as a horror film. More appropriately, given its lack of any sustained action sequences and its high-art design, it should have been categorized with Stanley Kubrick's *2001: A Space Odyssey* (1968), a film it resembles in more ways than one, or with George Lucas's *THX 1138*

(1971) or *Fantastic Planet* (1973) or Nicholas Roeg's *The Man Who Fell to Earth* (1976). As a result of Paramount's mishandling of the film, *Phase IV* was a failure at the box office, although eventually, it almost broke even.[90] Today, the film is considered a typical *film maudit*, or "cursed film"—one that was unjustly ignored or undervalued at the time of its release but has now been rehabilitated. And while the designer's uncertainty in directing actors and sustaining dialogue is apparent, the film's graphically stunning images and open-ended narrative more than compensate the audience. *Phase IV*'s overall design therefore deserves a reevaluation, especially in light of the recently rediscovered original ending, which Paramount had rejected in favor of a shorter but no less ambiguous finale.

The idea for *Phase IV* was apparently hatched over cocktails in 1971. Peter Bart, then vice president in charge of production at Paramount, was having dinner with producer Paul Radin. When Bart asked Radin what was cooking, the latter responded off the top of his head, even though nothing was actually in the works: an ant story. Paramount green-lit the idea almost immediately. Radin called Bass, who happened to have a friend who worked with ants, and he liked the idea.[91] In September 1971 a press release went out announcing the film with Bass as director and Mayo Simon as scriptwriter. Bass's fee for directing was $30,000; however, all but $5,000 would be withheld until the film was completed on budget.[92] This may have been a precaution because Bass had never directed a feature film, although he had put his name in the hamper for *A Man Called Horse* (1970), and Ingo Preminger had suggested him at Fox for *M*A*S*H* (1970).[93] By June 1972, the script was apparently finished, and preproduction was proceeding, with shooting scheduled to take place in California and the Arizona desert.[94] However, within weeks, the *Hollywood Reporter* announced that the film would be produced in London, with location shooting in Kenya, possibly because Radin's production company for his TV series *Born Free* was located there.[95] Bass storyboarded and numbered virtually every shot in the film, even going so far as to block out the actors' movements within the shot.[96] Production began on 30 October 1972 at London's Pinewood Studios, with an approved budget of $1 million; it continued through February 1973, and postproduction dragged on in London until November 1973.[97] The film was given a PG rating by the MPAA, after a hearing in January 1974 reversed the original R rating.[98]

Paramount apparently couldn't decide what to do with the film. As early as September 1973, while the film was still in postproduction, Bass and Radin were sounding the alarm bell, complaining about Paramount's lack of communication and foot-dragging in terms of devising a release campaign, despite "the tremendous enthusiasm on the part of Paramount's executives and staff towards the picture."[99] For nine months the film sat on the shelf as Bass pleaded with Robert Evans and Frank Yablans to release it, but Paramount was skittish because previews had garnered mixed results.[100] For example, a New York City preview in August 1974 netted the following comments: "Poor. Walk-out. General appreciation of Saul Bass' artistry, but no involvement with plot or theme of film. Most women do not like the film, in contrast to men who liked and approved of it."[101] Meanwhile, Bass and Paramount were reediting the film. Bass complained that Paramount's publicity was selling *Phase IV* as a straight horror film, attracting audiences that would be disappointed with a film that did not really belong in that genre. Ultimately, Paramount had so little confidence in the film that it opened in Los Angeles without any press screening or fanfare on the bottom of a double bill.[102]

Ironically, the film poster was not designed by Bass, and it was certainly not modern. It features an old-style, realistic hand in close-up with ants climbing out of a hole in the palm.[103] At a London preview attended by friends of Bass, several audience members wondered whether the film was European in origin, and Bass certainly believed the film would have had a better chance if it had been sold that way.[104] It is unclear whether the film at that point included Bass's original ending, which, like Kubrick's *2001*, consisted of a montage of the future of the planet under the guidance of a new ant-directed intelligence. By the time of the film's American release, the ending had been drastically cut to just a few short shots.[105]

As noted earlier, the reviews for Saul Bass's first feature film were decidedly mixed. On the positive side, the exhibitors' trade journal *Box Office* predicted substantial earnings for the film, concluding: "So amazing are the images on the screen and the picture's total effect that one is shocked afterward to realize how few special effects there are."[106] In fact, numerous reviewers commented on the startling ant footage and the beauty of Bass's compositions, but they also complained that the film's narrative was unrealistic if not silly.[107] Jay Cocks at *Time* magazine also praised the film: "*Phase IV* is good, eerie entertainment, with interludes of such haunted visual intensity that it becomes, at its best, a nightmare incarnate. It can also be quite wobbly, with ripely absurd dialogue."[108] Bass's handling of the actors and the dialogue were seen by many critics as fatal weaknesses, leading *Variety* to call the film mediocre horror and to go for the designer's jugular: "On the basis of the evidence here, he is not going to be as trail-blazing as a director."[109] However, Kevin Thomas in the *Los Angeles Times* lambasted Paramount for its mishandling of the film, which he declared to be visually stunning: "All this is made gaspingly credible under Bass' inspired direction, abetted by K. Middleham's remarkable photography. . . . Never do Bass and his gifted associates ever go for cheap horror effects . . . it emerges as a stunningly effective warning than man must learn to live in harmony with nature—if it's not already too late."[110]

Likewise, a number of English critics realized that the film was more akin to art than horror. As Nigel Andrews wrote in London's *Financial Times*: "But Bass' film is something else altogether: a surreal poem in which the landscapes seem to have sprung from a Dali painting—hard shapes and contours drooping in the yellow desert heat—and in which the visual effects . . . represent cinematic sleight-of-hand of the first order."[111] In the almost forty years since the film's original release, and especially since its appearance on DVD, such critical points of view have prevailed, and the film is now considered a cult classic.[112] As one critic noted in 2010: "*Phase IV* is much more than the sum of its parts and worthy of (re)visiting now that it has found second life on DVD."[113]

Phase IV's plot is deceptively simple: Cosmic phenomena cause a change in the behavior of ants in the Arizona desert. Making a giant evolutionary leap, the ants begin to communicate and behave tactically, taking over whole communities and killing all human and animal life in their path. Biologist Ernest Hubbs (Nigel Davenport) and mathematician and game theorist James Lesko (Michael Murphy) are sent to the desert to study the ants and take appropriate measures to end the threat. There, they set up a hermetically sealed laboratory. When they are attacked by the ants, they spray a yellow poison that inadvertently kills a farm family attempting to flee to the lab. However, a young girl, Kendra (Lynne Frederick), survives, and the scientists take her in. The ants then miraculously develop into a new species that is impervious to the poison. Hubbs becomes increasingly irrational after being bitten by an ant; he refuses to retreat and is killed by the insects. Lesko, meanwhile, has learned to communicate with the ants via electric radio signals and is eventually accepted by them, as is Kendra. The couple is designated to be the progenitors of a new human-ant hybrid that will take over the planet.

Phase IV conforms to Hollywood's generic expectations, insofar as its plot centers on a beleaguered group of white men surrounded by "aliens"— whether Indians, as in westerns like *The Indian Fighter* (1956); creatures from outer space, as in science fiction films like *Aliens* (1986); or hostile gang members, as in crime dramas like *Fort Apache, the Bronx* (1981). And although classic sci-fi film fans and critics tend to favor realistic narratives, the charm of many such films is in their art direction, cinematography, special effects, and visual design. It is no accident that some of the most interesting science fiction films have been directed by art directors such as William Cameron Menzies (*Things to Come*, 1936) and Nathan Juran (*The Preying Mantis*, 1957), animators such as George Pal (*War of the Worlds*, 1953), special-effects wizards such as Ray Harryhausen (*First Men on the Moon*, 1964) and Douglass Trumbull (*Silent Running*, 1971), or cinematographers such as Rudolph Maté (*When Worlds Collide*, 1951). These artists, who were schooled visually and understood how to compose an image, often gravitated to science fiction because it offers possibilities to create alternative worlds rather than dress up the contemporary landscape. Bass, in this regard, seemed like a natural choice for the film, even though he felt challenged by the visual design problems posed by a science fiction film.[114] And visual acuity is indeed a requirement for the genre, according to Vivian Sobchack: "The major visual impulse of all SF films is to pictorialize the unfamiliar, the non-existent, the strange and the totally alien—and to do so with a verisimilitude which is, at times, documentary in flavor and style."[115] A preferred landscape for science fiction, then, is the desert, because its barren harshness emphasizes man's vulnerability and exposure, in contrast to the aliens that inhabit it.[116]

The film is narrated by Lesko (the preview version had no narration, but audiences were apparently confused). He first describes the changes in the ants' behavior as Bass cuts from images of the universe to individual ants running through tunnels and then gathering in larger groups. At this point, the music gives way to the deafening sound of the ants' high-pitched squeal. As the ant footage continues, we hear warnings of a biological imbalance, because traditionally antagonistic ant species are now working together to eliminate all their predators. It is seven minutes into the film before any human life is shown, consisting of a vehicle being driven through a depopulated landscape. Thus, from the very beginning,

Bass is juxtaposing the natural world of ants with their extraordinary power to communicate. For Bass, communication is the first sign of intelligence, separating human from animal (suggested by the opening animation of *Why Man Creates*). As subjective ant shots indicate, Bass assigns these creatures the ability to see and gain knowledge before acting, just as he did with human subjects in *The Searching Eye* and *From Here to There*. At one point, after the ants have short-circuited the scientists' air conditioner, Lesko asks, "How do they know?" The viewer already knows that the ants can see. As the narrative continues, Lesko begins to send radio signals of a square, arguing that geometry is a universal language of intelligent beings. As Bass notes, the ants communicate through structures—that is, architecture becomes a language.[117] Unlike in other horror films, where the threat from aliens is violently mindless, *Phase IV*'s ants are rational.

Utilizing high-key lighting to backlight the colorfully translucent ant bodies, Ken Middleham's microscopic photography is fascinating and beautiful. The play of light on the ants' bodies provides a veritable light show—extreme colors from red to blue to green, huge eyes reflecting blue light, the camera zooming in until the eye is an intricate mass of light blue dots in three dimensions. Here, Bass and Middleman are carrying on a long tradition of nature films that were championed by the avant-garde because they aestheticized nature, such as the films of Jan Mol and Jean Painlevé in the 1920s. The seemingly vast networks of tunnels are used not only for transportation but also as communications highways. The insects' actions are strangely affecting, such as the sequence in which a whole string of ants sacrifice themselves to carry a ball of poison to the queen, who consumes the yellow chemical to immunize her offspring. In another scene, accompanied by funeral music, the ants line up corpses of their fallen comrades.

In many ways, the ants seem more sympathetic than the humans, who are depicted as weak, insensitive, and duplicitous. Hubbs shows virtually no emotion when he realizes that they have killed the farm family, and he hinders rescue efforts for selfish motives. In fact, Lesko and Hubbs represent the two poles of scientific discourse: while Lesko hopes to understand the ants and thus work in harmony with nature, Hubbs is only interested in trying to overpower and control nature. Clearly, from Bass's mid-1970s ecological perspective (further developed in *The Solar Film*) the former strategy is preferable. An early draft of the film's conclusion included the title "Man at One with Nature (Paradise Regained)," which was supposed to follow a highly metaphoric sequence in which Kendra gives birth to a sun, after she and Lesko have made love in an ant tunnel.[118] Bass's use of visual metaphors of nature finds its correlative in the way he measures time: not in hours but in sunrises and sunsets, in moonrises and moonsets. The orbs of the sun and the moon are a recurring visual leitmotif, mirrored graphically in the entrance to the ant queendom and its tunnels, the laboratory, the holes in the hands of the human victims, the eyes of the ants, and the circle of light out of which Kendra rises as if from the dead, a symbol of life.

Phase IV is indeed a feast for the eyes. The film constantly surprises the viewer with striking images of the brightly colored phantasmagoria of Middleham's ant colony, as well as images of the desert. In an opening shot, Bass utilizes an extremely long lens, held for more than a minute, to present an image of the yellow desert heat and haze that resembles nothing if not an Abstract Expressionist painting. Fast-motion images of the desert landscape follow, its ever-changing light from rising suns and full moons reflecting a constantly shifting field of visual details. Finally, there are images that simply arrest the mind: the slow zoom on a blue star cluster; the fast-motion wilting of a blue cactus flower; the blue-tinted oscilloscope image of ant sounds (Lissajous spirals from *Vertigo*); the black ant obelisks against a blue sky,[119] their heads tilting up toward the heavens like some kind of primitive gods; the blue honeycomb of the ant queen's eye; the poisoned yellow desert landscape;[120] the shattering of glass beakers and obelisks in slow motion; the stop-motion decomposition of a desert mouse on a television screen; the multiple exposures of Lesko's final trek to the ant queen; the step-and-repeat opticals of humans mating. These images offer a veritable catalog of experimental film techniques. Many of Bass's images, such as the abandoned desert towns with street grids for developments that were never constructed or the poisoned yellow landscape, can be read as contemporary news images of ecological disasters. And, given Bass's interest in ecological issues, such references are probably intentional.

Nevertheless, there is an interesting paradox in the film's overall view. The unseen human institutions of power are shown to be shortsighted and unable to comprehend the seriousness of the problem. Hubbs, a representative of the scientific establishment supported by the institutions of power, is self-serving and is willing to risk lives to achieve his own ends. In other words, it is dangerous to rely solely on these larger social structures. But therein lies the paradox, because the film's nonconformist and antiauthoritarian messages are relativized by what follows. Both Kendra and Lesko "sacrifice" themselves for the common good, which is precisely why the ants allow them to survive. They are thus seen as pure of heart. Bass may be implying that our own society is too invested in individual bourgeois privileges and that de-emphasizing individuality for the sake of species survival would lead to better communication and a more smoothly functioning society. In an interview while the film was still in production, Bass stated: "When we started the script we agreed that ants were more adaptable than man, they had more discipline and social will. All they really lacked was individual will and technology. So we gave them those two things. And Jesus! What we wound up with was a question of who has domination over the planet!"[121]

At the end of the release version of *Phase IV*, the chosen couple submits to the will of the new ant intelligence, which is nothing if not authoritarian. One can imagine that science fiction audiences in 1974 would have found it hard to swallow that the humans essentially lose out to the monsters. Forty years later, such a downbeat ending is much more acceptable. Louis Dorfsman sent Bass a razor-sharp ideological analysis of the film: "Actually the message as I chose to interpret it is that a disciplined, structured society will eventually beat the shit out of our so-called free society. No?"[122] Before deciding whether this is the case, it might be productive to analyze Bass's original six-minute conclusion to the film, which survives in verbal descriptions, storyboards, and actual footage. The release ending is identical to the first twenty-one shots of the original ending, but the final shot of Kendra and Lesko standing and waiting for instructions is shot 96 in Bass's original cut. What comes in between is a much more dire visualization of humanity's fate under the ant dictatorship, even as the montage of images remains mysterious, bringing the film back to its original antiauthoritarian and nonconformist impulses.

Some have compared Saul Bass's original ending to Stanley Kubrick's finale for *2001: A Space Odyssey*.[123] But Bass is putting on much more than a light show for hippies tripping on acid. In ninety-eight shots over 5:50 minutes, Bass creates a vision of humanity reduced to specimens in a giant breeding farm controlled by ants. Initially, Bass accomplishes this by cutting together twelve images of Kendra and Lesko walking and running through huge, open architectural spaces that have the feel of de Chirico paintings but the look of Oscar Niemeyer's reinforced-concrete Brasilia: large, modernist hexagonal structures with flat plazas as roofs; square, layered buildings with endless ramps. As in the ants' message to the scientists, the ants here use architecture, structure, and form as language. The landscape turns sinister when it is revealed that some buildings are divided into open cells that contain humans, with the ants watching over them. Bass's camera zooms in on the cells from above, so that the buildings resemble boxes with square compartments to hold buttons or butterfly specimens. Another shot reveals endless rows of open windows with human silhouettes in them. Bass seems to be implying that modernist architecture has a dehumanizing aspect, because the dimensions of space dwarf humans and make the environment inhospitable. In a number of images, Lesko and Kendra are seen as tiny specks fleeing but never getting anywhere.

In another series of fifteen flash cuts, Bass edits together close-ups of individual humans with "QUAD 37/47741" and other numbers tattooed on them, indicating locations. One shot of Bass himself in rubber and metal sunglasses directly quotes Chris Marker's totalitarian scientists in *La Jetée* (1962). Human beings in this brave new world are visualized as laboratory specimens subject to numerous experiments: fingers boring a hole in a man's forehead, fingertips on fire, and so on. Finally, Bass metaphorically visualizes the human mating process by opening with a composite image, half of Kendra's face and half of Lesko's face, followed by multiple exposures of a nude Kendra giving birth to a circular symbol of life. Then he cuts to naked bodies in the surf; tadpoles swimming in blue water, symbolizing sperm; and a blue rose opening in stop motion, symbolizing female genitalia. Next, Bass cuts in a multiple exposure of a man diving and an eagle flying. (This image from *The Searching Eye* is reutilized in *Quest*, where it symbolizes freedom. But here it has ominous undercurrents of danger, as it does in *Cape Fear*.) The futility of flight is ultimately revealed when Bass concludes the sequence with the couple standing and holding hands while the ants watch over them, the same image of submission that concludes the release ending. Thus, Bass creates a dystopian view of the future, envisioning a society in which individual desire is subsumed by the interests of the social organism as a whole, here represented by the ants. In an interesting paradox, the ants communicate through form and structure, just as Bass does in his designs in general and in the original ending of the film in particular. Accompanied only by music, the original ending of *Phase IV* thus conveys its knowledge purely visually, allowing each viewer to interpret the quick flow of images individually.

After the original ending was reconstituted, Bass, with the benefit of hindsight, admitted that he understood why it had been shortened. He acknowledged that it was too long and too abstract, and no one would have understood what it all meant.[124] Indeed, Bass himself was never able to explain what it signified. As in the case of *Phase IV*'s original ending, much of Bass's film work was driven by graphic design, by formal considerations, rather than by the semantics of editing. In the aftermath of *Phase IV* and the many changes he was forced to make, Bass gave up on producing Hollywood feature films. He thought it was just too difficult to work with unions and producers. He told a British journalist that directing a feature film is "like attaching a pencil to the scoop of a bulldozer and then trying to draw a sensitive portrait with it. You're in the driver's seat, but the controls are imprecise. You've got a million people on the set, alarms are going off and the till is jangling. It's a matter of survival to complete it."[125]

Now, more than forty years after its initial release, Saul Bass's *Phase IV* is considered a much more interesting film than many critics at the time realized. Within the context of the science fiction genre, Bass not only warns against our continued destruction of the planet and our disharmony with nature but also theorizes that the essence of humanity is the ability to communicate intelligently—a skill that must be utilized much more often for the common social good. Finally, in using a whole catalog of innovative cinematic devices, Bass has crafted a film that aspires to high art rather than satisfying the lowly standards of genre, thus elevating the medium, as he had done for titles and commercials and in his short films.

When contemplating Saul Bass's fifty-eight-year design career, it becomes apparent what an extraordinary achievement it was. Of all the modernist graphic designers in post–World War II America, Bass was the only one to negotiate two more or less separate careers: his corporate design business, and his involvement in all that was cinema, whether trade advertisements, posters, titles, commercials, or films. No other nationally known graphic designer straddled the two industries: Ray and Charles Eames stuck to avant-garde films, and Paul Rand and Erik Nitsche were part-timers when it came to Hollywood poster designs. For Bass, the corporate side of his business was often used to finance the cinema side, especially toward the end of his career, when his film projects lost money due to undercapitalization. Cinema and filmmaking were, by all accounts, Bass's passion. Indeed, Bass perfectly embodies the kind of work described so eloquently by David James in *The Most Typical Avant-Garde*, documenting careers that crossed the borders between Hollywood and the avant-garde.[126] Whereas artists such as Oscar Fischinger, Pat O'Neill, and Morgan Fischer worked in the industry to finance their art, Bass consistently undermined Hollywood's standard operating procedures by insisting on high-art standards for his designs. In the former cases, Hollywood indirectly subsidized avant-garde art film production, but in the latter, avant-garde technique and aesthetics were integrated into Hollywood's commercial work flow. Bass didn't always get his way, as demonstrated by his catalog of rejects and the existence of his own gallery versions of previously published work, but he got his way more often than anyone else did. A brand was born.

Saul Bass was the right person at the right time, and he knew how to seize the opportunity presented to him by American cultural history. Essentially an autodidact, Bass used willpower, determination, and his vociferous reading of design texts and images (in particular, the design books by Laszlo Moholy-Nagy and Gyorgy Kepes) to climb out of his ethnic (Jewish) and professional (cut and paste) ghetto and enter the rapidly professionalizing field of graphic design, previously the exclusive domain of white, Anglo-Saxon Protestants. Growing up poor in the Bronx, with only limited educational opportunities beyond high school, Bass endured a ten-year apprenticeship in East Coast sweatshops before heading west for Hollywood, where he would reach the top of his profession and achieve international fame and recognition. Bass's trajectory resembled that of the Hollywood moguls, who founded an industry and rose to the top of the social hierarchy.

The world was changing in the aftermath of World War II. Thanks to the influx of mostly European, modernist, Jewish refugee artists and designers both before and after the war, the level of sophistication of American design was forever altered for the better. Suddenly, modernist design was being supported by major capitalist institutions, in no small part due to the influence of Bauhaus émigrés who elevated design to the level of art but also insisted on practical solutions that would be good business. The Bauhaus aesthetic of clean and simple lines, circles, and squares was easily adapted to the needs of American corporate advertising, projecting an image of capitalism that was modern and forward thinking. This created new opportunities for an ambitious young designer, and Bass struck out on his own, moving to California when it was essentially virgin territory for modernist graphic designers. Bass carved out a lifelong career by draping himself in that European modernist mantle, but with a romantic American touch, and then selling that aesthetic to the Hollywood entertainment industry as a form of moral uplift. Bass was able to accomplish this feat because he started at the bottom in the film industry and had a deep understanding of its psychology.

Another historical transition working in Bass's favor was the slow but continual breakdown of the classical Hollywood studio system, whereby all aspects of production, distribution, and exhibition were controlled by a vertically and horizontally organized corporation. With the outlawing of block booking, young, independent producer-directors sought product differentiation in the newly competitive film market by raising their non-generic aesthetic standards. With his own newly acquired high-art credentials as a modernist graphic designer documented in feature stories in European design magazines, Bass appealed to this new generation of independent producers and directors. Despite the intransience of the film industry power structures, Bass managed to create a unique and historically significant body of work across multiple media. That work was of its time yet also outside of it, made for commercial imperatives but imbued with the integrity of the artist. Despite the Taylorized production system, which often discouraged aesthetic ambitions or artistic signatures, Bass's film work is instantly recognizable and capable of inducing intense visual pleasure. Using avant-garde techniques, Bass integrated popular and high art, elevating the former through the latter. With rare exceptions, Bass worked only on projects that were true to his liberal American politics and social ideology. No designer did that longer or more effectively than Saul Bass. That is his legacy.

The key to Bass's success is that he developed an instantly recognizable brand, one that created specific expectations in his clients but still managed to give them something unique. It was a lesson he learned from his Hollywood apprenticeship: audiences want the same thing over and over again, yet somehow different and surprising. Bass's brand relied on Bauhaus principles, which the designer had internalized to such a degree that they became like intuition: relying on a modernist grid, composing images from simple geometric shapes, devising logo-like icons for product identity, and developing his montage skills. These formal devices allowed Bass to communicate efficiently, while still giving audiences the freedom to read images subjectively. Over time, Bass began to integrate images of nature and the natural environment into his modernist designs, moving beyond the cold rationalism of European modernist design to a more romantically inflected aesthetic featuring sunsets and rainbows. A question for future research may be to what extent other modernist American designers translated modernism into a specifically American form. In any case, Bass's best graphic designs for cinema directly reference modernist art: his posters for *Man with the Gold Arm, Bonjour Tristesse, Saint Joan,* and *Anatomy of a Murder.* His films and titles, in contrast, utilize avant-garde compositions and cinematic techniques, as well as montage, to construct open-ended narratives that privilege audience subjectivity. In his best cinematic work, *Why Man Creates,* Bass constructs a free-form essay film that depends on conscious audience participation to convey its multidimensional levels of meaning, making it truly a work of the modernist avant-garde. As a result, Bass's work remains as fresh today as when it first emerged from his studio.

Saul Bass embraced the Bauhaus aesthetic and ethic, focusing his most serious attention on the layout and composition of the image, yet also considering graphic design, typography, animation, stop motion, split screen, and all the other camera and laboratory technologies that call attention to the painterly construction of the frame. The two-dimensional frame became the canvas on which Bass telegraphed key words and images that communicated as efficiently as today's search engines. Many of his logos and images have entered into our collective cultural memory, whether *Vertigo*'s Lissajous spiral form, the "corpse" from *Anatomy of a Murder,* or the disembodied arms from *Exodus* and *Spartacus.* Young designers continually employ the "Bass look" to differentiate their work stylistically. References to specific Bass images also abound; for example, a 2014 commercial for Nikon cameras shows a young boy building a New York skyline from wooden building blocks, the image of the finished sculpture with the creator in the background replicating Bass's opening credits for *Alcoa Premiere* or, more specifically, a still of Bass and his set published in Bass and Kirkham's coffee-table book.

According to Lev Manovich, digital cinema has been transformed from a nineteenth-century pre-cinema art of hand-painted images to a twentieth-century realist art of indexical images to a twenty-first-century art of computer animation.[127] Thus, it becomes evident that understanding graphic art and painting is essential for both producing and reading images in the digital world. Maybe this is the ultimate key to Saul Bass's success and the element that made (and makes) him modern: in constructing a brand that embraced animation, moving graphics, legible typography, the geometric construction of screen space, and montages of moving images that could have been stills, and by employing almost exclusively formal elements in a two-dimensional frame, Bass's visual design anticipated our modern digital world. Ours is a world of split frames, moving graphics, and computer-generated animation; a world of iconic rather than indexical signs, of images cut at machine-gun speed; a world of instant product identification and of logos worth dying for. The clean modernist graphics, the open color fields, the interpolation of words and images that we associate with Saul Bass and, by extension, with the post–World War II era of *Madmen* are suddenly in style because they are appropriate to the digital environment and because they teach today's designers of films, television shows, and computer games how to communicate with the audience. Finally, Bass's best work challenges today's designers to create free spaces for audiences where they can not only consume images but also participate in the construction of their meaning. In this sense, Bass's legacy couldn't have been greater.

Acknowledgments

This specific project began in the early 1990s when my colleague, poster dealer Bob DePietro, first made me aware of Saul Bass's magnificent film posters. He sold me an *Advise and Consent* poster, which led to the purchase of *Bonjour Tristesse* and *Saint Joan* posters. My wife and I gave *Saint Joan* to my mother-in-law, Janet Schirn, a well-known interior designer, who had it hanging in her foyer for many years. However, my interest in Gestalt theory began two decades earlier, when I was a graduate teaching assistant for Donis A. Dondis in her Introduction to Communications course at Boston University. Today, scholars consider Dondis's *A Primacy for Visual Literacy* (1973), which was our class text, the most important interpretation of Gestalt art theory after Rudolf Arnheim and Gyorgy Kepes. In 1979 I co-curated a reconstruction of the 1929 German exhibition "Film und Foto," originally organized by Hans Richter and Laszlo Moholy-Nagy and heavily influenced by Gestalt theory, so I was already attuned to Bass's work when I discovered his posters a decade later. In June 1996 I participated as a film programmer at the Aspen International Design Conference, which held a memorial tribute to Bass that year. Six years later, while I was curator at the Hollywood Entertainment Museum, I organized a Saul Bass poster and lobby card exhibition, "Saul Bass: Designer." It ran from 20 February to 13 April 2003 and concluded with an evening reception for many of Bass's former students and coworkers. At the time I was already planning to write a book about Bass, but then a new job as director of the UCLA Film and Television Archive kept me busy elsewhere. However, after being named an Academy Scholar by the Academy of Motion Picture Arts and Sciences in 2006, I knew I had to get to work.

First and foremost, then, I would like to thank the Academy of Motion Picture Arts and Sciences, which allowed me to conduct the research for this project. Thanks in particular to Shawn Guthrie and the members of the Academy Scholars committee. The Margaret Herrick Library and the Academy Film Archive now house the collections from

Bass's estate, and the staffs of those two institutions could not have been more helpful over the years. I thank them all for their kindness and good-will. In particular, at the Herrick, I would like to thank Barbara Hall (now director of the Warner Brothers Archives), Jenny Romero, Faye Thompson, Brad Roberts, Jeanie Braun, Kristine Kreuger, Janet Lorenz, Elizabeth Eiben, and all the wonderful people at the special collections desk: Andrea Battiste, Marisa Duron, Michael Hartig, Mona Huntzing, Charlie Qualls, Jonathan Wahl, Kevin Wilkerson, and Galen Wilkes. At the Academy Film Archive, I would like to thank May Haduong, Cassie Blake, Mike Pogorselski, and Sean Savage. May Haduong was more than generous with her time during the research phase of this project. Sean Savage, the resident archivist responsible for processing the Saul Bass Collection, was invaluable not only in finding materials but also in serving as a discussion partner, and his ideas directly impacted this book.

Next, I would like to thank the friends and colleagues of Saul Bass who spent time discussing his life's work with me: Herb Yager, Al and Trudi Kallis, Arnold and Isolde Schwartzman, James Hollander, Mike Lonzo, Paula Goodman, Jeff Goodman, Jack Garfein, and Owen Edwards. Mr. Kallis and Mr. Hollander, in particular, provided key images that helped me formulate my overall narrative. I also had fruitful personal and e-mail conversations with Bob DePietro, Foster Hirsch, Henning Engelke, Justus Nieland, Neil Jaworski, Louise Sandhaus, and Melissa Dollman.

I would like to thank my staff at the UCLA Film and Television Archive, all of whom were supportive, but some of whom went beyond the call of duty to track down films, images, and rights holders, especially Todd Wiener, Joe Hunsberger, Nina Rao, Megan Doherty, Jeff Bickel, Randy Yantek, and Mark Quigley. Former staff member Dino Everett, now director of the Hugh Hefner Film Archive at the University of Southern California, provided some important shows from that collection. The staff at the UCLA Library Special Collections and interlibrary loan desk were invaluable in tracking down sources and in making the Stanley Kramer Papers available, especially Peggy Alexander, Amy S. Wong, Cesar Reyes, Sandra Farfan-Garcia, and Cindy Hollmichel. At the American Film Institute, I would like to thank librarian Robert Vaughn for making a crucial Saul Bass Oral History available to me. Research queries to the University of Illinois' Aspen International Design Conference Archive were professionally handled by Gretchen Neidhardt, while Naomi Lederer at Colorado State Library and Carol Ellis of the University of South Alabama Archives responded promptly to queries. Much of the preliminary research was conducted with the help of my graduate assistant at UCLA, Alexandra Schroeder, and my summer intern Adam Burnstine spent hours combing through the *Hollywood Reporter.*

At the University Press of Kentucky I would like to thank my editor, Anne Dean Dotson, and her assistant, Bailey E. Johnson, as well as copyeditor Linda Lotz. For permissions, I would like to thank Paul Ginsburg and Roni Lubliner at NBC-Universal; Andrea Kalas and Larry McCallister at Paramount Pictures; Grover Crisp and Margarita Diaz at Sony Pictures; Julia Heath at Warner Brothers; Megan Bradford at Metro-Goldwyn-Mayer; Andrea Fischer from the Artists Rights Society (ARS), New York; and Juliet Kepes Stone, Ty Mattson, and Heidi Frautschi at the Paul Klee Zentrum, Zurich.

Finally, I'd like to thank my wife, Martha (Mindy) F. Schirn, and my daughter, Gianna Mei Li Horak, for their unwavering support while I spent hour upon hour at my computer and, of necessity, neglected their needs. Their indulgence is greatly appreciated.

Filmography

The Dark Mirror (1947, Robert Siodmak)	Trade advertisements
The Snake Pit (1947, Anatole Litvak)	Trade advertisements
Temptation (1947, Irving Pichel)	Trade advertisements
Champion (1949, Mark Robson)	Trade advertisements
Home of the Brave (1949, Mark Robson)	Trade advertisements
Without Honor (1949, Irving Pichel)	Trade advertisements
The Admiral Was a Lady (1950, Albert S. Roegell)	Trade advertisements
All About Eve (1950, Joseph Mankiewicz)	Trade advertisements
Cyrano de Bergerac (1950, Michael Gordon)	Trade advertisements
The Men (1950, Fred Zinnemann)	Trade advertisements
No Way Out (1950, Joseph Mankiewicz)	Trade advertisements
The Sound of Fury (1950, Cy Endfield)	Trade advertisements
Death of a Salesman (1951, László Benedek)	Trade advertisements
Decision before Dawn (1951, Anatole Litvak)	Trade advertisements
Hard, Fast, and Beautiful (1951, Ida Lupino)	Trade advertisements
M (1951, Joseph Losey)	Trade advertisements
The Scarf (1951, E. A. Dupont)	Trade advertisements
Androcles and the Lion (1952, Chester Erskine)	Trade advertisements
The Big Sky (1952, Howard Hawks)	Trade advertisements
Clash by Night (1952, Fritz Lang)	Trade advertisements
The Four Poster (1952, Irving Reis)	Trade advertisements
The Happy Time (1952, Richard Fleischer)	Trade advertisements
High Noon (1952, Fred Zinnemann)	Trade advertisements
The Lusty Men (1952, Nicholas Ray)	Trade advertisements
Member of the Wedding (1952, Fred Zinnemann)	Trade advertisements
My Six Convicts (1952, Hugo Fregonese)	Trade advertisements
The Sniper (1952, Edward Dmytryk)	Trade advertisements
The Moon Is Blue (1953, Otto Preminger)	Trade advertisements
Return to Paradise (1953, Mark Robson)	Trade advertisements
Carmen Jones (1954, Otto Preminger)	Poster, publicity, titles

Magnificent Obsession (1954, Douglas Sirk)	Trade advertisements
Riot in Cell Block 11 (1954, Don Siegel)	Trade advertisements
A Star Is Born (1954, George Cukor)	Trade advertisements
Vera Cruz (1954, Robert Aldrich)	Trade advertisements
The Big Knife (1955, Robert Aldrich)	Titles
The Desperate Hours (1955, William Wyler)	Trade advertisements
Kiss Me Deadly (1955, Robert Aldrich)	Trade advertisements
The Man with the Golden Arm (1955, Otto Preminger)	Poster, publicity, titles
Mister Roberts (1955, John Ford, Mervyn LeRoy)	Trade advertisements
My Sister Eileen (1955, Richard Quine)	Trade advertisements
Night of the Hunter (1955, Charles Laughton)	Trade advertisements
Not as a Stranger (1955, Stanley Kramer)	Trade advertisements
Pearl of the South Pacific (1955, Allan Dwan)	Trade advertisements
The Racers (1955, Henry Hathaway)	Trade advertisements, titles
The Rose Tattoo (1955, Daniel Mann)	Trade advertisements
The Seven Year Itch (1955, Billy Wilder)	Titles
The Shrike (1955, José Ferrer)	Trade advertisements, titles
Speedway (1955, TV)	Television commercials, advertising
Trial (1955, Mark Robson)	Trade advertisements
The Virgin Queen (1955, Henry Koster)	Trade advertisements
Around the World in 80 Days (1956, Michael Anderson)	Titles
Attack! (1956, Robert Aldrich)	Trade advertisements, titles
The Conqueror (1956, Dick Powell)	Trade advertisements
Giant (1956, George Stevens)	Trade advertisements
Johnny Concho (1956, Don McGuire)	Titles
On the Threshold of Space (1956, Robert D. Webb)	Trade advertisements
Playhouse 90 (1956, TV)	Bumpers
Somebody up There Likes Me (1956, Robert Wise)	Trade advertisements

Storm Center (1956, Daniel Taradash)	Trade advertisements, letterhead, promotional material, titles
Sun Detergents (1956, TV)	Television commercial
This Week (1956, TV)	Titles
Trapeze (1956, Carol Reed)	Titles
Blitz beer (1957, TV)	Television commercials
Edge of the City (1957, Martin Ritt)	Poster, trade advertising, promotional material, titles
Frank Sinatra Show (1957, TV)	Bumpers, titles
Love in the Afternoon (1957, Billy Wilder)	Poster, trade advertisements
National Bohemian beer (1957, TV)	Advertising, television commercials
Patterns of Life (1957, TV)	Titles
The Pride and the Passion (1957, Stanley Kramer)	Trailer, promotional material, premiere invitation, titles
Saint Joan (1957, Otto Preminger)	Poster, trade advertisements, promotional material, television spot, titles
The Young Stranger (1957, John Frankenheimer)	Promotional material, titles
The Big Country (1958, William Wyler)	Poster, titles
Bonjour Tristesse (1958, Otto Preminger)	Poster, letterhead, promotional material, titles
Cowboy (1958, Delmar Daves)	Titles
The Defiant Ones (1958, Stanley Kramer)	Trade advertisements
The Naked Eye (1958, Louis Clyde Stouman)	Poster, trade advertisements
2nd San Francisco International Film Festival (1958)	Poster
Vertigo (1958, Alfred Hitchcock)	Poster, advertising, titles

Anatomy of a Murder (1959, Otto Preminger)	Poster, advertising, letterhead, promotional material, television spot
Porgy and Bess (1959, Otto Preminger)	Titles (unfinished)
Faces and Fortunes (1959, Morton Goldsholl and Millie Goldsholl)	Assistant director
Four Just Men (1959, TV)	Titles
North by Northwest (1959, Alfred Hitchcock)	Titles
Olin Mathieson Small World (1959, TV)	Titles
San Francisco International Film Festival (1959)	Poster
White King (1959, TV)	Television commercial
Exodus (1960, Otto Preminger)	Poster, trade advertising, letterhead, titles
The Facts of Life (1960, Melvin Frank)	Titles
History of Packaging (1960, TV)	Television commercial
Magnificent Seven (1960, John Sturges)	Trade advertisements
Ocean's Eleven (1960, Lewis Milestone)	Titles
Psycho (1960, Alfred Hitchcock)	Pictorial consultant, titles
Rainier beer (1960, TV)	Television commercials
San Francisco International Film Festival (1960)	Poster
Some Like It Hot (1960, Billy Wilder)	Trade advertisements
Spartacus (1960, Stanley Kubrick)	Design consultant, titles
The Sundowners (1960, Fred Zinnemann)	Trade advertisements
Alcoa Premiere (1961, TV)	Titles
5th San Francisco International Film Festival (1961)	Poster
Judgment at Nuremberg (1961, Stanley Kramer)	Poster, letterhead
One, Two, Three (1961, Billy Wilder)	Poster, trade advertisements
PM East/PM West (1961–1962, TV)	Bumpers, titles
Something Wild (1961, Jack Garfein)	Titles
West Side Story (1961, Robert Wise)	Poster, prologue, visual consultant, titles

Advise and Consent (1962, Otto Preminger)	Poster, promotional material, trade advertisements, titles
Band-Aid (1962, TV)	Television commercial
Apples and Oranges (1962, Lou Dorfman and George Bristol)	Visual design
The Best of Bolshoi (1962, TV)	Animated preludes
Birdman of Alcatraz (1962, John Frankenheimer)	Window cards
The Four Horsemen of the Apocalypse (1962, Vincente Minnelli)	Montage sequences, trade advertisements
History of Invention (1962, IBM)	Television commercial
Icarus Montgolfier Wright (1962, Osmond Evans)	Titles
Men against Cancer (1962, IBM)	Television commercial
Mennen Baby Bath (1962, TV)	Television commercial
Mennen Baby Magic (1962, TV)	Television commercial
Orientation IBM (1962, IBM)	Television commercial
The Sale of Manhattan (1962, TV)	Animated sequence
Walk on the Wild Side (1962, Edward Dmytryk)	Titles
Andy Williams Show (1963, TV)	Titles
The Cardinal (1963, Otto Preminger)	Posters, promotional material, titles
It's a Mad, Mad, Mad, Mad World (1963, Stanley Kramer)	Poster, promotional material, titles
National Bohemian beer, Andy Parker— Regular Guy (1963–1965, TV)	Television commercials
Nine Hours to Rama (1963, Mark Robson)	Letterhead, trade advertising, titles
Seven Days in May (1963, John Frankenheimer)	Titles (uncredited)
7th San Francisco International Film Festival (1963)	Poster
The Victors (1963, Carl Foreman)	Prologue, titles
8th San Francisco International Film Festival (1964)	Poster
From Here to There (1964, Saul Bass)	Producer, director
Hallmark Hall of Fame (1964, TV)	Titles

Filmography

Profiles in Courage (1964, TV)	Titles
The Searching Eye (1964, Saul Bass)	Producer, director
2nd New York Film Festival (1964)	Poster
Bunny Lake Is Missing (1965, Otto Preminger)	Poster, promotional material, trade advertisements, titles
In Harm's Way (1965, Otto Preminger)	Poster, promotional material, advertising, titles
Grand Prix (1966, John Frankenheimer)	Montage sequences, titles
Not with My Wife, You Don't (1966, Norman Panama)	Visual consultant, titles
Seconds (1966, John Frankenheimer)	Poster, promotional material, titles
Hurry Sundown (1967, Otto Preminger)	Sound-track album cover
The Two of Us (1967, Claude Berri)	Poster, promotional material, book cover
Bridgestone tires (1968, TV)	Television commercial
Fireman's Ball (1968, Milos Forman)	Poster, promotional material
The Fixer (1968, John Frankenheimer)	Poster, promotional material
RCA "The Kid" (1968, TV)	Television commercial
Very Happy Alexander (1968, Yves Robert)	Poster, promotional material
Why Man Creates (1968, Saul Bass)	Producer, director
Mattel Baby Tenderlove (1969, TV)	Television commercial
Tell Me That You Love Me, Junie Moon (1970, Otto Preminger)	Poster
Such Good Friends (1971, Otto Preminger)	Poster, promotional material
10th Chicago International Film Festival (1973)	Poster
11th Chicago International Film Festival (1974)	Poster
The Party (1974, Bob Adler)	Producer
Phase IV (1974, Saul Bass)	Director

Filmography

The Taking of Pelham 1 2 3 (1974, Joseph Sargent)	Titles
Dixie Cups (1975, TV)	Television commercials
Rayovac batteries (1975, TV)	Television commercial
Rosebud (1975, Otto Preminger)	Poster, promotional material
NBC: The First 50 Years (1976, TV)	Opening sequence
That's Entertainment II (1976, Gene Kelly)	Titles
Bass on Titles (1977, Saul Bass)	Poster, director
Brothers (1977, Arthur Baron)	Poster, promotional material
Girl Scout cookies (1977, TV)	Television commercial
Looking for Mr. Goodbar (1977, Richard Brooks)	Titles (unused)
100 Years of the Telephone (1977, Saul Bass)	Producer, director
Windows aka *Notes on the Popular Arts* (1977, Saul Bass)	Poster, producer, director
Apocalypse Now (1979, Francis Ford Coppola)	Photographer
The Double McGuffin (1979, Joe Camp)	Poster
The Human Factor (1979, Otto Preminger)	Poster, promotional material
Security Pacific Bank (1979, TV)	Television commercial
The Shining (1980, Stanley Kubrick)	Poster, promotional material
The Solar Film (1980, Saul Bass)	Poster, producer, director
Filmex '81 (1981)	Poster
Quest (1983, Saul Bass)	Poster, producer, director
20th Chicago Film Festival (1984)	Poster
Filmex Los Angeles (1985)	Poster
Broadcast News (1987, James L. Brooks)	Titles
Big (1988, Penny Marshall)	Titles
Talk Radio (1988, Oliver Stone)	Poster
Tonkô/The Silk Road (1988, Jun'ya Satô)	Poster, titles
National Film Registry, Library of Congress (1989)	Animated logo

Return from the River Kwai (1989, Andrew V. McLagen)	Poster
6th Israel Film Festival in the USA (1989)	Poster
The War of the Roses (1989, Danny DeVito)	Titles
Goodfellas (1990, Martin Scorsese)	Titles
Matushita (1990, TV)	Television commercial
Cape Fear (1991, Martin Scorsese)	Titles
Doc Hollywood (1991, Michael Caton-Jones)	Titles
Preminger: Anatomy of a Filmmaker (1991, Valerie A. Robins)	Titles
63rd Academy Awards (1991)	Poster
Israel Film Festival (1992)	Poster
Motion Picture Centennial (1992)	Poster
Mr. Saturday Night (1992, Billy Crystal)	Titles
The Age of Innocence (1993, Martin Scorsese)	Titles
A Bronx Tale (1993, Robert De Niro)	Titles
Schindler's List (1993, Steven Spielberg)	Poster, advertising
65th Academy Awards (1993)	Poster
Cancion de Cuna (1994, José Luis Garci)	Poster
66th Academy Awards (1994)	Poster
30th Chicago Film Festival (1994)	Poster
Under Suspicion (1994, Simon Moore)	Titles
Beyond the Clouds (1995, Michelangelo Antonioni)	Titles (unrealized)
Casino (1995, Martin Scorsese)	Titles
Higher Learning (1995, John Singleton)	Titles
A Personal Journey with Martin Scorsese through American Movies (1995, Martin Scorsese)	Titles
67th Academy Awards (1995)	Poster
68th Academy Awards (1996)	Poster
Psycho (1998, Gus Van Sant)	Titles (based on Bass)

Notes

Abbreviations

AMPAS   Academy of Motion Picture Arts and Sciences
CSULB   California State University at Long Beach
MPAA   Motion Picture Association of America

Introduction: *Qui êtes-vous*, Saul Bass?

1. Saul Bass Academy Award Acceptance, 16mm black-and-white clip, Saul Bass Collection, Academy Film Archive, AMPAS.

2. Interview with James Hollander, 31 October 2012, Burbank, CA.

3. In 1989 Bass actually designed the moving image logo for the National Film Registry.

4. AT&T seminar manuscript, 1988, Saul Bass Papers, Margaret Herrick Library, AMPAS.

5. Hollander interview, 2012.

6. Interview with Arnold Schwartzman, 20 February 2013, Los Angeles. Schwartzman went on to direct the Academy Award–winning documentary *Genocide* (1982). See Arnold Schwartzman, *A Persistence of Vision: Arnold Schwartzman Profiles of His Work in Graphic Design and Film* (Mulgrave, Australia: Images Publishing, 2005).

7. "A Discussion with Producer Cara McKenney, and Creative Directors Steve Fuller and Mark Gardner," in *The Art of the Title*, 19 September 2011, http://www.artofthetitle.com/title/mad-men/. See also a review of *Mad Men* that calls the Bass-inspired title sequence one of the best ever: http://www.ellistabletalk.com/2013/01/02/the-way-we-were-matthew-weiners-mad-men/.

8. David Geffner, "First Things First," *Filmmaker Magazine* 6, no. 1 (Fall 1997), http://www.filmmakermagazine.com/issues/fall1997/firstthingsfirst.php.

9. See "Dexter Intro by Ty Mattson," YouTube, https://www.youtube.com/watch?v=n9adZ0HRu04.

10. David Peters, "Every Frame Counts," *Eye Magazine* 66 (Winter 2007), http://www.eyemagazine.com/feature/article/every-frame-counts.

11. Geffner, "First Things First."

12. Jeffrey Wells, "Saul Bass in 'Devil' Poster," *Hollywood Elsewhere*, http://www.hollywood-elsewhere.com/2007/09/saul_bass_in_de.php.

13. *An Interview with Saul Bass—Outstanding 20th Century Designer Series,*

directed by David Cronister, 3 May 1979, DVD 7932-2-1, Saul Bass Collection, Academy Film Archive, AMPAS.

14. Saul Bass, "A Definition of Creativity," *Design: The Magazine of Creative Art* 60 (March–April 1959): 144. See also Saul Bass, "Creativity in Visual Communication," in *Creativity: An Examination of the Creative Process,* ed. Paul Smith (New York: Hastings House, 1959), 122–23, in which the anecdote is repeated word for word.

15. Lorraine Wild, "That Was Then, and This Is Now: But What Is Next?" *Émigré* 39 (1996), http://www.emigre.com/Editorial.php?sect=1&id=18. See also Lorraine Wild, "Europeans in America," in *Graphic Design in America: A Visual Language History,* ed. Mildred Friedman et al. (New York: Harry Abrams, 1989), 152–69.

16. David Badder, Bob Baker, and Markku Salmi, "Saul Bass," *Film Dope* 3 (August 1973): 6.

17. Owen Edwards, "Saul Bass" (unpublished manuscript, ca. 1992), 55, box 21A, file 10, "Biography," Saul Bass Papers, Margaret Herrick Library, AMPAS. Bass redlined the quote, possibly indicating that it revealed too much.

18. Ibid., 56.

19. Schwartzman interview, 2013.

20. Interview with Mike Lonzo, 19 September 2012, Hollywood.

21. Schwartzman interview, 2013.

22. Bass, "Creativity in Visual Communication," 127.

23. I'm grateful to Richard Walter, my colleague at the UCLA School of Theatre, Film, and Television, for this anecdote.

24. Mamoru Shimokochi, "Art Goodman. A Tribute," *Graphic Design USA* 5 (May 2009): 82. Goodman was born on 18 May 1925 and died on 2 October 2008 in Los Angeles.

25. Ibid. When Goodman retired in 1993, Bass apparently refused to make an announcement or throw him a retirement party. Bass didn't want anyone to know that Goodman was gone. The mythology that Bass did everything had to be maintained.

26. Lou Dorfsman, interview with Andreas Timmer, 6 November 1997, quoted in Andreas A. Timmer, "Making the Ordinary Extraordinary: The Film-Related Work of Saul Bass" (PhD diss., Columbia University, 1999), 31.

27. Interview with Herb Yager, 27 February 2013, Ojai, CA.

28. Ibid.

29. Interview with Jeff Okun, 23 March 2012, Hollywood.

30. Jennifer Bass and Pat Kirkham, *Saul Bass: A Life in Film and Design* (London: Laurence King Publishing, 2011), 23.

31. Ibid.

32. In both films, Elaine received credit for conception and design, but Saul took sole credit for direction. In the case of *Notes on the Popular Arts* (1977), Elaine Bass received credit as coproducer.

33. Jack Solomon Agency, "Elaine Bass. Biography," n.d., *Solar Film* file, press materials, Saul Bass Papers, Margaret Herrick Library, AMPAS.

34. *American Film Institute Seminar with Saul Bass, 16 May 1979* (Beverly Hills, CA: Center for Advanced Film Studies, 1979). This forty-page, single-spaced document is available only at the American Film Institute's Louis B. Mayer Library.

35. Telephone interview with Owen Edwards, 18 January 2013.

36. "Saul Bass [Interview]," *Designer Magazine*, May 1980, 10.

37. Joe Morgenstern, "Saul Bass" (unpublished manuscript, 1994), 33, box 21A, file 2, "Biography—Manuscript," Saul Bass Collection, Margaret Herrick Library, AMPAS.

38. Lonzo interview, 2012.

39. See Wild, "Europeans in America," 159.

40. Saul Bass, "Cover," *Arts & Architecture* 65, no. 11 (November 1948): 2.

41. Saul Bass, "Film Advertising. Filmwerbung. La publicité pour le film," *Graphis* 9, no. 48 (1953): 276–89.

42. See Herb Yager, "Saul Bass," *Graphis* 33, no. 193 (1977–1978): 392; Henry Wolf, "Saul Bass," *Graphis* 41, no. 235 (January–February 1985): 28. For a history of *Graphis*, see its website: http://www.graphis.com/history/.

43. Catherine Sullivan, "The Work of Saul Bass," *American Artist* 18, no. 8 (October 1954): 31.

44. "The West Coast: A Designer's View," *Industrial Design* 4, no. 10 (October 1957): 74.

45. Bass and Kirkham, *Saul Bass*, 10–11.

46. "Bass Badly Hurt on Way to Awards," *Variety*, 21 February 1949, 3.

47. See AIGA Medal, http://www.aiga.org/medalist-saulbass/.

48. Reyner Banham, ed., *The Aspen Papers: Twenty Years of Design Theory from the International Design Conference in Aspen* (New York: Praeger Publishers, 1974), 5.

49. See "IDCA Bare Bones Filmmaking," VHS tape, 13077-1, Saul Bass Collection, Academy Film Archive, AMPAS.

50. That year I hosted a German avant-garde film series at the conference and was able to attend the event honoring Bass.

51. Fred Hift, "And that Cramps Film Ads—Bass," *Variety*, 20 November 1957, 7.

52. This is based on an informal and wholly unscientific study in which illustrations of Bass's work from all known publications were tabulated.

53. Given the rise in Hitchcock's critical reputation in the last thirty years, those figures would probably look different today.

54. *American Film Institute Seminar*, 1–2.

55. Letter from Saul Bass to Margaret Kaplan, Harry Abrams & Co., 8 May 1980, box 21A, file 7, "Biography Correspondence," Saul Bass Collection, Margaret Herrick Library, AMPAS.

56. Yager interview, 2013.

57. Founded in 1978, *American Photographer* ceased publication in 1989, so the book series Documents of American Design probably started immediately afterward. The only book published was *Alexey Brodovitch/Andy Gruenberg* (New York: H. N. Abrams, 1989). Edwards telephone interview, 2013.

58. Yager interview, 2013. According to Yager, Edwards was on Bass's payroll.

59. Edwards, "Saul Bass."

60. Although Morgenstern's unpublished manuscript at AMPAS is dated 18 October 1994, this was apparently the second draft. There is another undated draft that, based on correspondence, was delivered in April 1994.

61. Letter from Don Congdon to Saul Bass, 13 October 1994; letter from Gillian Casey Sowell (Simon and Schuster) to Don Congdon, 29 November 1994, box 21A, file 7, "Biography Correspondence," Saul Bass Collection, Margaret Herrick Library, AMPAS.

62. Memo from "Wendy" to Saul Bass and Herb Yager, 15 April 1994, ibid.

63. Letter from Herb Yager to Joe Morgenstern, 22 July 1994, ibid.

64. Timmer, "Making the Ordinary Extraordinary," 227.

65. Noell Wolfram Evans, "Saul Bass: A Film Title Pioneer," *Digital Media F/X*, http://www.digitalmediafx.com/Features/saulbass.html.

66. Emily King, "Taking Credit: Film Title Sequences, 1955–1965" (master's thesis, Royal College of Art, 1994), http://www.typotheque.com/articles/taking_credit_film_title_sequences_1955–1965_9_conclusion.

67. See, for example, Mary Beth Haralovich, "Motion Picture Advertising: Industrial and Social Forces and Effects, 1930–1948" (PhD diss., University of Wisconsin–Madison, 1984), and Mark Thomas McGee, *Beyond Ballyhoo: Motion Picture Promotion and Gimmicks* (Jefferson, NC: McFarland, 1989).

68. Emily King, *A Century of Movie Posters, from Silent to Art House* (London: Mitchell and Beasily, 2003).

69. Ross Melnick, *American Showman: Samuel "Roxy" Rothafel and the Birth of the Entertainment Industry, 1908–1935* (New York: Columbia University Press, 2012).

70. François Truffaut, *Hitchcock* (New York: Simon and Schuster, 1967), 207–8.

71. Philip Oakes, "Coming On: Bass Note," *London Sunday Times,* 9 December 1973, 36.

72. *American Film Institute Seminar,* 40.

73. Stephen Rebello, *Alfred Hitchcock and the Making of* Psycho (New York: Dembner Books, 1990), 112.

74. See, for example, Philip J. Skerry, *The Shower Scene in Hitchcock's* Psycho: *Creating Cinematic Suspense and Terror* (Lewiston, NY: Edwin Mellon Press, 2005).

75. Stephen Rebello, *"Psycho," Cinefantastique* 16, no. 4/5 (October 1986): 48–77; Rebello, *Hitchcock and the Making of* Psycho.

76. See *Hitchcock* (2012), directed by Sacha Gervasi, script by John J. McLaughlin, starring Anthony Hopkins and Helen Mirren. Wallace Langham is credited with playing the role of Saul Bass in the film, but he only lurks in the background; if he had a speaking line, I missed it.

77. Pat Kirkham, "Reassessing the Saul Bass and Alfred Hitchcock Collaboration," *West 86th Street* 18, no. 1 (Spring 2011), http://www.west86th.bgc.bard.edu/articles/kirkham-bass-hitchcock.html.

78. Raymond Durgnat, *A Long Hard Look at 'Psycho'* (London: BFI Publishing, 2002). See also excerpts at http://sensesofcinema.com/2002/20/durgnat_psycho/.

79. Mary Glucksman: "Saul Bass: Due Credit," *Screen International,* 13 May 1994, 28.

80. David James, *The Most Typical Avant-Garde: History and Geography of Minor Cinemas in Los Angeles* (Berkeley: University of California Press, 2005), 14–15.

81. Miriam Bratu Hansen, "The Mass Production of the Senses: Classical Cinema as Vernacular Modernism," *Modernism/Modernity* 6, no. 2 (1999): 59–77.

82. According to Andrew Tracy, the essay film has only recently been identified and named by film scholars. Apart from the films of the filmmakers mentioned in the text, Tracy lists Vigo's *À propos de Nice* (1930), Ivens's *Rain* (1929), Buñuel's *Las hurdes* (1933), Resnais's *Night and Fog* (1955), Rouch and Morin's *Chronicle of a Summer* (1961), Akerman's *Je, Tu, Il, Elle* (1974), Welles's *F for Fake* (1973), Straub and Huillet's *Trop tôt, trop tard* (1982), Getino and Solanas's *The Hour of the Furnaces* (1968), Portabella's *Informe general . . .* (1976), and Andersen's *Los Angeles Plays Itself* (2003). Andrew Tracy, "The Essay Film," http://www.bfi.org.uk/news-opinion/sight-sound-magazine/features/deep-focus/essay-film.

83. Quoted in ibid.

84. See Lev Manovich, *The Language of New Media* (Cambridge, MA: MIT Press, 2002), 250, http://www.manovich.net/LNM/Manovich.pdf.

85. Interview with Jeff Okun, 6 June 2011, Studio City, CA.

86. See *6 Chapters in Design: Saul Bass, Ivan Chermayeff, Milton Glaser, Paul Rand, Ikko Tanaka, Henryk Tomaszewski* (San Francisco: Chronicle Books, 1997).

1. Designer and Filmmaker

1. See *An Interview with Saul Bass—20th Century Designer Series*, directed by David Cronister, 3 May 1979, DVD PF4720, 7932-2-1, Saul Bass Collection, Academy Film Archive, AMPAS.

2. Ibid.

3. "The World Masters 1: Saul Bass," *IDEA* 38, no. 219 (March 1990): 20.

4. Douglas Bell, "An Oral History with Saul Bass," 20, 39 (Oral History Project, 1996), Margaret Herrick Library, AMPAS.

5. Peter Bogdanovich, *John Ford* (Berkeley: University of California Press, 1978).

6. *Interview with Saul Bass*, 1979, written, directed, and produced by Prof. Archie Boston Jr., CSULB, Saul Bass Collection, Academy Film Archive, AMPAS.

7. Interview with Albert and Trude Kallis, 26 July 2012, Beverly Hills, CA.

8. Lewis Blackwell, "Bass Instinct," *Creative Review* 15 (1 May 1995): 48.

9. *Interview with Saul Bass*, 1986, written, directed, and produced by Prof. Archie Boston Jr., CSULB, Videotape PF4719, 20459-3, Saul Bass Collection, Academy Film Archive, AMPAS.

10. Interview with Arnold Schwartzman, 21 February 2013, Los Angeles. See also Philip Thompson and Peter Davenport, eds., *Dictionary of Visual Language* (London: Bergstom and Boyle Books, 1980), 23, which juxtaposes Rand's 1946 advertisement for Orbach's with Bass's *Love in the Afternoon* (1956) poster, both of which utilize text on a shade that has been pulled down.

11. The best source for biographical information is Pat Kirkham's authorized essay in Bass and Kirkham, *Saul Bass*, 3–25.

12. "Saul Bass & Associates," special issue of *IDEA* (1979): 128. See also Sally

Anderson-Bruce, *Childhood Fantasies: Champion Kromekote 2000* (Stamford, CT: Champion International Corporation, 1991), in which Bass poses as an archaeologist.

13. Founded in 1875, the Art Students League boasts a stellar list of former students and instructors. The former category includes Winslow Homer, Norman Rockwell, Jackson Pollock, Alexander Calder, Helen Frankenthaler, Roy Lichtenstein, Georgia O'Keefe, Man Ray, Ben Shahn, Red Grooms, Frank Stella, and many others.

14. Morgenstern, "Saul Bass," 6.

15. See Bell, "Oral History with Saul Bass," 8–9.

16. Bass and Kirkham, *Saul Bass*, 8.

17. Lee Kerry, "The Man with the Golden Mind," *Adweek*, 14 September 1987.

18. A *Film Daily* story notes: "Representing the Guild in the demonstration, given before a large crowd in the street outside, were Ben (RKO) Rogers, Bob (Warner) Fels, and Saul (Warner) Bass." See Phil M. Daly, "Along the Rialto," *Film Daily* 82, no. 116 (June 1942): 4.

19. See Gyorgy Kepes, *The Language of Vision* (Chicago: Paul Theobald, 1944).

20. Catherine Sullivan, "The Work of Saul Bass," *American Artist* 18, no. 8 (October 1954): 31.

21. See Laszlo Moholy-Nagy, *The New Vision: From Material to Architecture* (New York: Brewer, Warren and Putnam, 1930).

22. Bell, "Oral History with Saul Bass," 10.

23. Quoted in Edwards, "Saul Bass," 14. Both Edwards and Morgenstern repeat the same anecdote. See also *An Interview with Saul Bass—20th Century Designer Series*.

24. Quoted in Gerard van der Leun, "That Old Bass Magic," *United Mainliner* 25, no. 3 (March 1981): 63.

25. Buchanan & Company advertisement in *Variety*, 13 May 1947, 10. See also "3½ Million Bally Coin Back of IP Pix," *Film Daily*, 22 July 1946, 12, which announced International Pictures' publicity budget for the coming season, with Bass and Rudin participating in the campaigns.

26. Meredith Keeve, "Saul Bass," *Zoom* 34 (February 1988): 63.

27. "Bass Badly Hurt on Way to Awards," *Variety*, 21 February 1949, 3.

28. Edwards, "Saul Bass."

29. "Bass Breezes Back," *Daily Variety*, 12 July 1950, 9.

30. "'Group Think' Killing Selling Slants?" *Variety*, 11 February 1959, 3.

31. See reproductions for *Death of a Salesman*, *Decision before Dawn*, and *The Sniper* in Saul Bass's first documented, published essay: Saul Bass, "Film Advertising; Filmwerbung, La publicité por le film," *Graphis* 9, no. 48 (1953): 279. See also the premiere invitation to *Death of a Salesman*, 20 December 1951, Warner Beverly Hills Theatre, box 336, Scrapbook, Collection 161, Stanley Kramer Papers, UCLA Special Collections.

32. See reproductions of trade ads in Bass and Kirkham, *Saul Bass*, 16–19.

33. "Chatter," *Variety*, 27 August 1951, 6.

34. See Ken Coupland, "Saul Bass: The Name behind the Titles," *Graphis* 54, no. 316 (July–August 1998): 102; Mary Glucksman, "Saul Bass: Due Credit," *Screen International*, 13 May 1994, 27.

35. Kallis interview, 2012.

36. Bass and Kirkham, *Saul Bass*, 21n83.

37. See "The West Coast: A Designer's View," *Industrial Design* 4, no. 10 (October 1957): 74; Sullivan, "Work of Saul Bass," 67.

38. Interview with Mike Lonzo, 20 September 2012, Hollywood, CA.

39. Interview with James Hollander, 31 October 2012, Burbank, CA.

40. Both Edwards and Morgenstern name Elaine as the first employee Bass hired. According to Edwards, Bass met Elaine, who was a design student, at the 1957 Aspen Conference and hired her there. He claims Bass's marriage to Ruth was already shaky because she didn't appreciate or understand Saul's work. See Morgenstern, "Saul Bass," 32; Edwards, "Saul Bass," 50.

41. Bass and Kirkham, *Saul Bass*, 24.

42. Yager, for his part, maintained that Marsh knew nothing about marketing. When Yager came on board in 1974, Marsh insisted on reading and correcting every letter Yager wrote. When Yager resisted, Marsh complained to Bass, but Marsh soon realized that Bass had given Yager authority over all financial matters, so he left the firm voluntarily. Interview with Herb Yager, 27 February 2013, Ojai, CA.

43. Sullivan, "Work of Saul Bass," 28.

44. See reproductions in ibid., 29–31; Ludwig Ebenhöh, "Saul Bass, USA," *Gebrauchsgraphik* 27, no. 11 (November 1956): 12–21; Georgine Oeri, "Saul Bass," *Graphis* 11, no. 59 (1955): 258–65.

45. Quoted in R. Roger Remington and Barbara Hodik, *Nine Pioneers in American Graphic Design* (Cambridge, MA: MIT Press, 1989), 4.

46. See van der Leun, "That Old Bass Magic," 64.

47. For example, according to a Bass account executive, they were billing Rockwell International $75,000 to $90,000 a month, for a total of almost $2 million, in 1968. See LogoDesignLove, "The Cost of a Bass Logo," http://www.logodesignlove.com/saul-bass-logo-cost.

48. Adam Duncan Harris, "Extra Credits: The History and Collection of Pacific Title and Art Studio" (PhD diss., University of Minnesota, 2000), 222.

49. Ebenhöh, "Saul Bass, USA," 12.

50. Press book for *Carmen Jones* (20th Century–Fox, 1954), 4, microfilm, Margaret Herrick Library, AMPAS.

51. Joanne Stang, "Movie (Title) Mogul," *New York Times*, 1 December 1957, D1.

52. Quoted in Pamela Haskin, "Saul, Can You Make Me a Title?" *Film Quarterly* 50, no. 1 (Fall 1996): 11.

53. Ibid., 12.

54. Truffaut, *Hitchcock*, 207–9.

55. "Saul Bass: Portfolio of a Versatile Designer's Work," *Print* 15, no. 3 (May–June 1961): 35–46.

56. "West Coast: A Designer's View," 74.

57. See Ebenhöh, "Saul Bass, USA," 20: "Saul Bass who works as a designer in Hollywood is a typical representative of even that American style." See also Sullivan, "Work of Saul Bass," 28.

58. Richard Caplan, "Designs by Saul Bass," *Industrial Design* 5, no. 10 (October 1958): 88.

59. "Andy Parker aka Regular Joe," National Bohemian beer commercial, 1 minute, 217268-1, Saul Bass Collection, Academy Film Archive, AMPAS.

60. See *Business Screen Magazine* 24, no. 4 (1963): 381.

61. See "*Apples and Oranges*—Food for Thought. How CBS Sells a Concept," *Telefilm* 8, no. 5 (May 1963): 30–31, 38.

62. According to Klynn's obituary, "Herbert Klynn, former UPA President and longtime president of Format Productions collaborated with Ted Geisel (Dr. Seuss), Saul Bass, and Ray Bradbury" on the film, but Bass may have done only the titles at the end of the film. See "Herbert Klynn Obituary," *Variety*, 8 February 1999, 91.

63. See Mina Hamilton, "N.Y. World's Fair Film Preview," *Industrial Design* 11 (April 1964): 35–36, 40–43; Mina Hamilton, "Films at the Fair II: A Comparative Review," *Industrial Design* 12 (May 1964): 40–41.

64. Bass also traveled to the Philippines in 1974 to photograph the Major Kurtz headquarters set, where the film's climax occurs. Approximately 178 35mm slides of the shoot survive. See "*Apocalypse Now*—On Set Photography," Saul Bass Papers, Margaret Herrick Library, AMPAS.

65. James Powers, "Saul Bass Plans Short Feature on Social Changes," *Hollywood Reporter* 217, no. 7 (19 July 1971): 2.

66. "Cable Column: An Interview with Saul Bass," *Z Magazine* 2, no. 3 (August–September 1975): 21.

67. "Saul Bass Busy Writing, Directing Theatrical Project," *Hollywood Reporter* 253, no. 7 (September 1978): 8.

68. See Telex from Yamaguchi to Saul Bass, 1 July 1983, *Quest* Data Service File, Saul Bass Collection, Academy Film Archive, AMPAS.

69. "Saul Bass & Associates Changes Its Moniker," *Daily Variety*, 13 October 1978, 6; "Saul Bass & Associates," special issue of *IDEA* (1979): 132.

70. Steven Heller, "Why Design Declined at CBS: A Conversation with Lou Dorfsman," *Print* 44, no. 6 (November–December 1990): 100. Although Dorfsman doesn't specify dates, one negotiation apparently took place in 1973, after Dorfsman's mentor at CBS, Frank Stanton, retired.

71. Bass also did the initial title designs for Steven Soderbergh's *Sex, Lies, and Videotape* (1989), but his concept of having a woman wrapped in videotape or showing videotape from a VHS cassette unspooling to form the image of a woman was not pursued by Soderbergh or Harvey Weinstein, the film's producer. See box 111A, file 9, "*Sex, Lies, and Videotape*—titles," Saul Bass Papers, Margaret Herrick Library, AMPAS.

72. Yager interview, 2013.

73. See the English translation of the original German at http://bauhaus-online .de/en/atlas/das-bauhaus/idee/manifest.

74. Lorraine Wild, "Europeans in America," in *Graphic Design in America: A Visual Language History*, ed. Mildred Friedman et al. (New York: Harry Abrams, 1989), 168.

75. Lazlo Moholy-Nagy, *Vision in Motion* (New York: Paul Theobald, 1965).

76. See Jan-Christopher Horak, "The Films of Moholy-Nagy," *Afterimage* 13, no. 1/2 (Summer 1985), reprinted in Jan-Christopher Horak, *Making Images Move: Photographers and Avant-Garde Cinema* (Washington, DC: Smithsonian Press, 1997).

77. "Brooklyn Drafts New Art Policy," *New York Times*, 10 May 1942.

78. Lorraine Wild, "Modern American Graphics II: The Birth of a Profession," *Industrial Design*, July–August 1983, 56.

79. Sullivan, "Work of Saul Bass," 31.

80. Moholy-Nagy, *New Vision* (1930), 14, 60.

81. Timmer, "Making the Ordinary Extraordinary," 13–14.

82. *Interview with Saul Bass* (CSULB, 1986). See also Moholy-Nagy, *New Vision* (1930), 58.

83. Moholy-Nagy, *New Vision* (1930), 30, 35.

84. Ibid., 32.

85. Kepes, *Language of Vision*, 13.

86. Gyorgy Kepes, "Education of the Eye," *More Business* 3, no. 11 (November 1938), quoted in Hans M. Wingler, *The Bauhaus: Weimar, Dessau, Berlin, Chicago* (Cambridge, MA: MIT Press, 1969), 197.

87. Bell, "Oral History with Saul Bass," 5.

88. Ibid., 10.

89. Kepes, *Language of Vision*, 221.

90. Ibid., 17–27.

91. Ibid., 44–51.

92. Ibid., 59.

93. Ibid., 20; *Daily Variety*, 1 November 1950, 16.

94. Bell, "Oral History with Saul Bass," 28.

95. Kepes, *Language of Vision*, 67.

96. Ibid., 98.

97. Ibid., 130.

98. Ibid., 200.

99. Ibid., 207.

100. Ibid.

101. Ibid., 92, 220; Bass and Kirkham, *Saul Bass*, 161.

102. See a reproduction of the advertisement in Dick Hess and Marion Muller, *Dorfsman & CBS* (New York: American Showcase, 1987), 68.

103. See Kepes, *Language of Vision*, 87, 183. See also Bass and Kirkham, *Saul Bass*, 19, 33.

104. Kallis interview, 2012.

105. Janet Staiger, "Announcing Wares, Winning Patrons, Voicing Ideals: Thinking about the History and Theory of Film Advertising," *Cinema Journal* 29, no. 3 (Spring 1990): 8.

106. See a selection of silent and early sound movie ads in Russell C. Sweeney, *Coming Next Week: A Pictorial History of Film Advertising* (New York: Castle Books, 1973).

107. Emil T. Noah Jr., *Movie Gallery: A Pictorial History of Motion Picture Advertisements* (Fort Lauderdale, FL: Noah Communications, 1980), 11.

108. See a reproduction of the ad in Joe Morella, Edward Z. Epstein, and Eleonor Clark, *Those Great Movie Ads* (New Rochelle, NY: Arlington House, 1972), 294.

109. Ibid., 81.

110. Sullivan, "Work of Saul Bass," 28.

111. Advertisement for *Hard, Fast, and Beautiful* in *Daily Variety*, 6 September 1951, 6.

112. Reproduced in Ebenhöh, "Saul Bass, USA," 18.

113. "Fatalistic Fugue: *Bonjour Tristesse*," *Newsweek*, 20 January 1958, 89–90, quoted in Lowell E. Redelings, "The Hollywood Scene," *Hollywood Citizen News*, 22 January 1958, 7–8.

114. *Interview with Saul Bass* (CSULB, 1986).

115. James Woudhuysen, "Bass Profundo," *Design Week*, 22 September 1989, 17.

116. Bass and Kirkham, *Saul Bass*, 43.

117. See "Rainbow Bass—alphabet," box 37A, file 9, Saul Bass Papers, Margaret Herrick Library, AMPAS. A letter dated 5 May 1983 from Art Goodman (box 37A, file 38, "Art Goodman," ibid.) indicates the typography was submitted for an award but didn't win.

118. Fred Hift, "And that Cramps Film Ads—Bass," *Variety*, 20 November 1957, 7.

119. Bass and Kirkham, *Saul Bass*, 42, 214–15.

120. Interview with Jeff Okun, 23 March 2012, Hollywood, CA.

121. Rudolf Arnheim, *Art and Visual Perception: A Psychology of the Creative Eye* (Berkeley: University of California Press, 1967), 167.

2. Film Titles: Theory and Practice

1. Bass was probably involved in the credits for *The Taking of Pelham 1-2-3* (1974) but did not receive credit, and he certainly contributed to the credits for *The Human Factor* (1979), which uses elements from Bass's poster for the film.

2. See Army Archerd, "Just for Variety," *Daily Variety*, 15 February 1966, 2; "Ray, Wilson to Film 'The Alien' for Col.," *Daily Variety*, 12 June 1967, 1.

3. Interview with Jeff Okun, 6 June 2011, Studio City, CA.

4. Interview with Mike Lonzo, 20 September 2012, Hollywood, CA.

5. Interview with Saul Bass, KTTY Channel 11 Los Angeles, 27 November 1977, Saul Bass Collection, Academy Film Archive, AMPAS.

6. Saloment Cort, "'The Compleat Filmmaker'—From Title to Features," *American Cinematographer* 58, no. 3 (March 1977): 289.

7. *American Film Institute Seminar*, 3.

8. For example, see Hazel Flynn, "*Something Wild* Is Strange Enigma," *Los Angeles Citizen News*, 18 May 1962, clipping files, Margaret Herrick Library, AMPAS.

Flynn wrote: "The main titles are by Saul Bass and they are the most original item about the whole production."

9. Mike Fessier Jr., "Lay 'Em in the Aisles with a Title," *Daily Variety*, 27 October 1964, 39. Bass continued to design posters and other graphic materials for Wilder.

10. "Movies: Man with a Golden Arm," *Time*, 16 March 1962, 46.

11. Ken Coupland, "Saul Bass: The Name behind the Titles," *Graphis* 54, no. 316 (July–August 1998): 104.

12. Michaela Williams, "Satire of a World Premiere," *Chicago*, 13 November 1965, *The Searching Eye* reviews, box 10A, file 44, Saul Bass Papers, Margaret Herrick Library, AMPAS.

13. "Do Film Critics Extol 'Bass Credits' to Slur (by Contrast) the Director?" *Variety*, 17 June 1964, 5.

14. Arnold Schwartzman, "Saul Bass: Anatomy of a Mentor," *Baseline International Typographics Journal* 22 (1996): 21.

15. As *Time* magazine noted as early as 1962: "At 41 Bass is easily the highest priced man in his field." "Movies: Man with a Golden Arm," 46.

16. The Margaret Herrick Library's Bass Collection contains budgets only from films made in the 1980s and later.

17. Letter from Saul Bass to Tom Andre (Anthony-Worldwide production manager), 11 June 1957, Gregory Peck Papers, Margaret Herrick Library Special Collections, AMPAS.

18. Lowell A. Bodger, "A Modern Approach to Film Titling," *American Cinematographer* 40, no. 8 (August 1960): 477.

19. See, for example, memo from Al Tamarin to Myer P. Beck, "Advertising and Publicity Budget," 10 December 1956, box 14, Stanley Kramer Papers, UCLA Library Special Collections.

20. Rebello, *Hitchcock and the Making of* Psycho, 100.

21. Henry Wolf cited a figure of $50,000 for *Spartacus*. See Henry Wolf, "Saul Bass: Some Short Takes on a Long Friendship" (unpublished manuscript on Henry Wolf stationery), box 39A, file 41, "Henry Wolf," Saul Bass Papers, Margaret Herrick Library, AMPAS. See also Bodger, "Modern Approach to Film Titling," 477; Fessier, "Lay 'Em in the Aisles," 39; A. D. Murphy, "Only a Pittance for Pix Titling," *Daily Variety*, 31 October 1967, 46.

22. "Pix Owe Much to Credits. Opening Runoff Now Getting Lotsa Flair, Flash, Mood-Setting Motifs," *Variety*, 11 September 1957, 7, 19.

23. Fred Foster, "New Look in Film Titles," *American Cinematographer* 43, no. 6 (June 1962): 357, quoted in Jason Gendler, "Saul Bass and Title Design: Intention and Reception, and Production Integration" (paper presented at Society of Cinema and Media Studies Conference, Los Angeles, March 2010).

24. Vincent Canby, "Panic: An Industry Staple," *Variety*, 21 September 1960, 4.

25. Pauline Kael, "Fantasies of the Art House Audience," *Sight & Sound* 31, no. 1 (Winter 1961–1962): 8.

26. Joseph Mathewson, "Titles Are Better than Ever," *New York Times*, 16 July 1967.

27. Coupland, "Saul Bass: Man behind the Titles," 104.

28. See Jean Firstenberg, "From the Director's Chair: Credit Where Credit Is Due," *American Film* 9, no. 6 (April 1984): 80.

29. Cort, "'The Compleat Filmmaker,'" 291.

30. *That's Entertainment II* file, box 13A, file 30, Saul Bass Papers, Margaret Herrick Library, AMPAS.

31. *Interview with Saul Bass* (CSULB, 1986).

32. Mary Glucksman, "Saul Bass: Due Credit," *Screen International*, 13 May 1994, 28.

33. Cort, "'The Compleat Filmmaker,'" 290.

34. "Saul Bass [Interview]," *Designer Magazine*, May 1980, 24.

35. Jack Haley's *That's Entertainment!* (1974) used no fewer than eleven different narrators, including Astaire, Kelly, Bing Crosby, Frank Sinatra, and Elizabeth Taylor.

36. This whole sequence was originally planned to come at the end of the titles, after the head title. See *That's Entertainment II* file, box 13A, file 29, Saul Bass Papers, Margaret Herrick Library, AMPAS.

37. The Bass estate possesses a complete set of storyboards for *A River Runs through It*, which envisioned a montage of images and crosscutting between shots of the river, a desk with family photographs, and various homemade flies on the desktop. Much of this was reworked in the early titles before the sequence transitions to historical photographs of the town. See *A River Runs through It* file, box 26, folder 498, Saul Bass Papers, Margaret Herrick Library, AMPAS. The long tracking shots along a nineteenth-century desk holding books, portraits, and artificial flies survive as 35mm rushes in the Saul Bass Collection, Academy Film Archive, AMPAS.

38. Laszlo Moholy-Nagy, *The New Vision* (Mineola, NY: Dover Publications, 2005), 46.

39. For an early example of this style of head title, see *Her Man* (1930), cited in Deborah Allison, "Beyond Saul Bass: A Century of American Film Title Sequences," *Film International*, 30 January 2011, http://filmint.nu/?p=202.

40. Originally, Donald O'Connor's name was supposed to appear on the gong. See *That's Entertainment II* file.

41. See George Stanitzek, "Vorspann (Titles/Credits, Générique)," in *Das Buch zum Vorspann*, ed. Alexander Böhnke, Rembrent Hüser, and Georg Stanitzek (Berlin: Vorwerk, 2006), 14. For the English translation, see George Stanitzek, "Reading the Title Sequence (Vorspann, Générique)," *Cinema Journal* 48, no. 4 (Summer 2009): 44–58.

42. Charles Michener with Martin Kasindorf, "Old Movies Come Alive," *Newsweek*, 31 May 1976, 48.

43. Gordon Cow, *Films and Filming*, August 1976, 39. See also Stephan Farber, *New West*, 24 May 1976, 97; Penelope Gilliat, *New Yorker*, 24 May 1976, 134; Vincent Canby, *New York Times*, 17 May 1976, 40; Hollis Alpert, *Saturday Review*, 29 May 1976, 46.

44. Quoted in Pamela Haskin, "Saul, Can You Make Me a Title?" *Film Quarterly* 50, no. 1 (Fall 1996).

45. Merle Armitage, "Movie Titles," *Print* 5, no. 2 (1947): 44.

46. Joanne Stang, "Movie (Title) Mogul," *New York Times*, 1 December 1957, D1.

47. Fessier, "Lay 'Em in the Aisles," 39.

48. "Saul Bass," short segment, American Movie Classics Channel, 1994.

49. David Bordwell, Janet Staiger, and Kristin Thompson, *The Classical Hollywood Cinema: Film Style & Mode of Production to 1960* (New York: Columbia University Press, 1985), 25.

50. Bodger, "Modern Approach to Film Titling," 476.

51. See "Pix Owe Much to Credits," 7; Fred Hift, "And that Cramps Film Ads— Bass," *Variety*, 20 November 1957, 7, 24.

52. Quoted in Jaan Uhelszki, "Film: The Art of Motion Graphics in Film," *Soma* 18, no. 7 (September 2004): 86.

53. Grant Tume, "Design for Living," *Detour Magazine*, March 1996, 32.

54. André Gardies, "Am Anfang war der Vorspann," in Böhnke et al., *Das Buch zum Vorspann*, 21.

55. The Chop Suey Alphabet font was designed by Ross F. George in 1935. See Harris, "Extra Credits," 134.

56. Thierry Kuntzel, "Die Filmarbeit, 2," *Montage/AV* 8, no. 1 (1999): 25–84.

57. Bordwell, Staiger, and Thompson, *Classical Hollywood Cinema*, 25.

58. Tom Conley, *Film Hieroglyphs: Ruptures in Classical Cinema* (Minneapolis: University of Minnesota Press, 1991), ix.

59. Gardies, "Am Anfang war der Vorspann," 27.

60. Conley, *Film Hieroglyphs*, ix.

61. See "The True Story behind MGM's Main Title Design," http://www.mgm-movie-titles-and-credits.com/main-title-design.html.

62. See Deborah Allison, "Promises in the Dark: Opening Title Sequences in American Feature Films of the Sound Period" (PhD diss., University of East Anglia, 2002); Harris, "Extra Credits"; and Gemma Solana and Antonio Boneu, *Uncredited: Graphic Design & Opening Titles in Movies* (Amsterdam: BIS Publishers, 2007).

63. Pat Kirkham, "Reassessing the Saul Bass and Alfred Hitchcock Collaboration," *West 86th* 18, no. 1 (Spring 2011), http://www.west86th.bgc.bard.edu/articles/kirkham-bass-hitchcock.html.

64. Peter Hall, "Opening Ceremonies: Typography and the Movies, 1955–1969," in *Architecture and Film*, ed. Mark Lamster (New York: Princeton Architectural Press, 2000), 129.

65. Coupland, "Saul Bass: Man behind the Titles," 103.

66. Solana and Boneu, *Uncredited*, 13.

67. Allison, "Beyond Saul Bass."

68. Peter Decherney even argues that duping was part of the early industry's business model. See Peter Decherney, *Hollywood's Copyright Wars: From Edison to the Internet* (New York: Columbia University Press, 2012).

69. Julia May, "The Art of Film Title Design throughout Cinema History," *Smashing Magazine*, 4 October 2010, http://www.smashingmagazine.com/2010/10/04/the-art-of-the-film-title-throughout-cinema-history/. See also Yael Braha and Bill

Byrne, *Creative Motion Graphic Titling for Film, Video, & the Web* (London: Focal Press, 2011), 47.

70. Bordwell, Staiger, and Thompson, *Classical Hollywood Cinema*, 26.

71. Adam Duncan Harris, "Das goldene Zeitalter de Filvorspanns: Die Geschichte der Pacific Title and Art Studios," in Böhnke et al., *Das Buch zum Vorspann*, 123. See also Harris, "Extra Credits."

72. Allison, "Beyond Saul Bass."

73. See http://www.shillpages.com/movies/index2.shtml.

74. Armitage, "Movie Titles," 43.

75. Allison, "Beyond Saul Bass."

76. Deborah Allison, "Innovative Vorspanne und Reflexivität im klassischen Holllywoodkino," in Böhnke et al., *Das Buch zum Vorspann*, 94–101.

77. Everett Aison, "The Current Scene: Film Titles," *Print* 19, no. 4 (July–August 1965): 29.

78. Ibid.

79. Saul Bass, "Film Titles—A New Field for the Graphic Designer," *Graphis* 16, no. 89 (May–June 1960): 209.

80. Harris, "Das goldene Zeitalter de Filvorspanns," 126.

81. Braha and Byrne, *Creative Motion Graphic Titling*, 48.

82. Angela Aleiss, "The Names behind the Titles," *Variety*, 8 December 1997, 86.

83. Ibid., 56.

84. David Geffner, "First Things First," *Filmmaker Magazine* 6, no. 1 (Fall 1997), http://www.filmmakermagazine.com/issues/fall1997/firstthingsfirst.php.

85. Ellen Lupton and J. Abbott Miller, *Designs Writing Research: Writing on Graphic Design* (New York: Princeton Architectural Press, 1996), 5.

86. *Interview with Saul Bass* (CSULB, 1986).

87. Paul Rand, *Design Form and Chaos* (New Haven, CT: Yale University Press, 1993), 3.

88. Peter Bil'ak, "In Search of a Comprehensive Type Design Theory," *Typotheque* .com,http://wwtypotheque.com/articles/in_search_of_a_comprehensive_type_design_theory.

89. Lupton and Miller, *Designs Writing Research*, 62.

90. Robert Bringhurst, *The Elements of Typographic Style*, 3rd ed. (Vancouver: Hartley and Marks, 2005), 19.

91. Ibid., 20–24.

92. Jim Supanick, "Saul Bass: To Hit the Ground Running . . . ," *Film Comment* 33, no. 2 (March–April 1997): 73.

93. Memo from Morrie Marsh to Saul Bass, 9 March 1973, "Bass on Titles" box, Saul Bass Papers, Margaret Herrick Library, AMPAS. See also Title Reel memo, 3 October 1968, ibid.

94. Memo from Saul Bass to Morrie Marsh, Re: Dave Adams distributed Title Reel, 6 January 1972, "Bass on Titles" box, Saul Bass Papers, Margaret Herrick Library, AMPAS.See also memo, Pyramid Films, 10 May 1977.

95. Okun interview, 2011.

96. "Gleanings from a Gondola," *Variety*, 8 September 1982, 7.

97. Review of *Bass on Titles*, *EFLA* (1978): 10, 109.

98. Kimberly Elam, *Expressive Typography: The Word as Image* (New York: Van Nostrand Reinhold, 1990), 1.

99. John R. Biggs, *Basic Typography* (London: Faber and Faber, 1968), 15.

100. Elam, *Expressive Typography*, 32.

101. Ibid., 31.

102. Biggs, *Basic Typography*, 40.

103. Dawn Ades, "Function and Abstraction in Poster Design," in *The 20th Century Poster: Design of the Avant-Garde* (New York: Abbeville Press, 1984), 61.

104. Martin Solomon, *The Art of Typography: An Introduction to typo.icon.ography* (New York: Watson-Guptill, 1986), 148.

105. I'm referring not to typographic color here, which indicates the intensity of the type as set en masse, but to its conventional usage. Michael Beaumont, *Type: Design, Color, Character & Use* (Cincinnati, OH: Northern Lights Books, 1987), 78.

106. Alan Casty, *The Dramatic Art of the Film* (New York: Harper and Row, 1971), 57. See also James Monaco, *How to Read a Film: The Art, Technology, Language, History and Theory of Film and Media* (New York: Oxford University Press, 1977), 86.

107. Kepes, *Language of Vision*, 54, critiqued the golden mean because he saw it as an absolute value that was supposedly based on nature; this hindered the free expression of dynamic rhythm on the page—a rhythm based on sensory relationships rather than mathematics. Bass also had little use for the golden mean. See Bell, "Oral History with Saul Bass," 38.

108. Philip B. Meggs, *A History of Graphic Design* (New York: Van Nostrand Reinhold, 1983), 379.

109. Bringhurst, *Elements of Typographic Style*, 23.

110. Meggs, *History of Graphic Design*, 380.

111. Solomon, *Art of Typography*, 15, 42.

112. Rebello, *Hitchcock and the Making of* Psycho, 57, 100–101. Bass asked for and got three 16mm prints of the *Psycho* titles for his personal archive. This must have become standard practice for Bass & Associates, because the estate collection includes 16mm titles for most of Bass's films.

113. Bass and Kirkham, *Saul Bass*, 404n87.

114. *Psycho* file, box 6A, file 33, Saul Bass Papers, Margaret Herrick Library, AMPAS. Bass's published description of the titles is slightly shorter.

115. Raymond Durgnat, *A Long Hard Look at "Psycho"* (London: BFI Publishing, 2002), 20.

116. James Counts, "Just the Beginning: The Art of Film Titles," http://www.twenty4.co.uk/03-articles/ArtofFilmTitles/main.htm (no longer available). I'm grateful to Melissa Dollman, who pointed me to this source in her unpublished paper "Moving Words" (UCLA, 2005).

117. Hitchcock had previously used an image of venetian blinds being raised and lowered behind the credits for *Rear Window* (1953), which also addresses the issue of voyeurism.

118. *Higher Learning* file, box 4A, file 2, Saul Bass Papers, Margaret Herrick Library, AMPAS. The file also includes a diagonal grid drawn in pencil on cardboard.

119. Ibid., box 3A, files 39, 40, 41. The production had a budget of $40,000, but it actually cost only $25,357. The design firm received $30,000, payable in installments at contract signing, approval of final design, and completion.

120. Ibid.

121. Ibid.

122. Bass and Kirkham, *Saul Bass*, vi.

123. Martin Scorsese, "Saul Bass 1920–1996: A Celebration of an Extraordinary Life" (unpublished manuscript, 1996), quoted in Kirkham, "Reassessing the Saul Bass and Alfred Hitchcock Collaboration."

124. Coupland, "Saul Bass: Man behind the Titles," 105.

125. Martin Scorsese, interview by the British Film Institute, 11 February 1993, VHS tape, Saul Bass Collection, Academy Film Archive, AMPAS.

126. Timmer, "Making the Ordinary Extraordinary," 121.

127. *Goodfellas* file, box 3A, file 37, Saul Bass Papers, Margaret Herrick Library, AMPAS.

128. Ben Brantley noted in his film review: "From its opening credits, which whizz off the screen like souped-up getaway cars, Martin Scorsese's *Goodfellas* stays in breathlessly high gear." *Elle*, November 1990, clipping in *Goodfellas* production file, Margaret Herrick Library, AMPAS.

129. Josh Wolski, "*Goodfellas*, Not Coming to a Theater Near You," 8 August 2005, http://notcoming.com/saulbass/caps_goodfellas.php.

130. Bass and Kirkham, *Saul Bass*, 271.

131. Ibid.

132. Bass described his titles for *Saint Joan* as follows: "The title opens with bell symbols, in the form of bell clappers, swinging back and forth across the screen. They swing and advance towards the viewer and fade as they enlarge to screen-filling size. In the interim, new clappers emerge from the background and swing across the screen. They too advance and grow in size. This process is repeated throughout the title as the credits appear and disappear. However, the general effect is one of the screen filling more and more with the ethereal, swinging bell symbols, until finally a few white clappers are introduced, one of which advances and dominates the entire screen. At the apex of this clapper's forward movement the symbol for the film (a figure holding a broken sword) materializes within it, followed by the final credit." "*Saint Joan* titles description," box 10A, file 25, Saul Bass Papers, Margaret Herrick Library, AMPAS.

133. Tom Eckersley, *Poster Design* (London: Studio Publications, 1954), 35.

134. Joanne Stang, "Movie (Title) Mogul," *New York Times*, 1 December 1957, 86.

135. "Behind the Title," *Newsweek*, 20 January 1958, 89–90, box 1A, file 46, Saul Bass Papers, Margaret Herrick Library, AMPAS.

136. Gene Moskowitz, "*Bonjour Tristesse*," *Variety*, 15 January 1958, 6.

137. "Titles Description," box 2A, file 48, Saul Bass Papers, Margaret Herrick Library, AMPAS, first published in Bass, "Film Titles," 209.

138. Josh Wolski, "*Bonjour Tristesse*, Not Coming to a Theater Near You," 8 August 2005, http://notcoming.com/saulbass/caps_bonjourtristesse.php.

139. Memo from Myer P. Beck to Stanley Kramer, 18 December 1956, box 14, Publicity folder, Stanley Kramer Papers, Collection 161, UCLA Library Special Collections.

140. Memo from Al Tamarin to Myer P. Beck, "Advertising and Publicity Budget," 10 December 1956, box 14, Stanley Kramer Papers, UCLA Library Special Collections.

141. *The Pride and the Passion*, box 6A, file 27, Saul Bass Papers, Margaret Herrick Library, AMPAS.

142. See Mark Vallen, *Art for a Change* blog, http://art-for-a-change.com/blog/2010/06/goya-los-caprichos-in-los-angeles.html.

143. See *The Pride and the Passion* production file at the Margaret Herrick Library, AMPAS, reproduced in part in Bass and Kirkham, *Saul Bass*, 170.

144. Bass and Kirkham, *Saul Bass*, 163, 191.

145. See the original trailer at http://www.tcm.com/mediaroom/video/196871/Pride-and-The-Passion-The-Original-Trailer.html. Fredenthal's sketches were also published in *Life* magazine and the exhibitors' manual, and they were available for purchase through the National Screen Service. Fredenthal (1914–1958) was a well-known American watercolorist and illustrator (e.g., he illustrated the novel *Tobacco Road*). The trailer cost $7,500, according to the publicity budget for the film. See memo from Al Tamarin to David V. Picker, "Overall Campaign," 8 February 1957, box 14, "The Pride and the Passion" production files, Stanley Kramer Papers, UCLA Library Special Collections.

146. Bass and Kirkham, *Saul Bass*, 397n10.

147. Bass, "Film Titles," 209. The article reproduced thirty-six color frames from the film.

148. "Behind the Title," *Newsweek*, 20 January 1958, 90.

149. Art Cohn, *Michael Todd's* Around the World in 80 Days *Almanac* (New York: Random House, 1956), 11–16.

150. Strictly speaking, the *Oxford English Dictionary* traces the etymology of *cameo*'s meaning as "a bit part in a film" to a 1950 novel by Edmund Crispin. Todd was apparently the first to use the term to denote major stars in walk-on parts, although this has yet to be accepted by the *OED*.

151. See Morgenstern, "Saul Bass," 44.

152. "Bass Obtains Release from '80' Ad Chore," *Daily Variety*, 19 July 1956, 2.

153. Richard Warren Lewis, "Box Office Bait by Bass: A Designer Masters the Fine Art of Hooking an Audience," *Show Business Illustrated*, 23 January 1962, 50.

154. Jack Harrison, "*Around the World in 80 Days*," *Hollywood Reporter*, 18 October 1956, 3. See also Fred Hift, "*Around the World in 80 Days*," *Variety*, 24 October 1956, 6; Sherwin Kane, *Motion Picture Daily*, 18 October 1956, 6.

155. D. R., "*Around the World in Eighty Days*," *Monthly Film Bulletin* 24 (1957): 94.

156. Hollis Alpert, "What Goes on Here," *Woman's Day*, March 1961.

157. See, for example, http://filmfanatic.org/reviews/?p=15567; http://www.afilmcanon.com/journal/2009/6/20/anderson-around-the-world-in-eighty-days-1956.html.

158. "Suit Charges Todd 'Pirated' Epilog for '80,'" *Daily Variety*, 28 December 1956, 2.

159. "Saul Bass Answers 'Plagiarism' Charge with Suit for 600G," *Daily Variety*, 18 January 1957, 2.

160. "250G '80 Days' Suit over Epilog Settled," *Daily Variety*, 8 July 1958, 3.

161. Noell Wolfram Evans, "Saul Bass: A Film Title Pioneer," http://www.digitalmediafx.com/Features/saulbass.html.

162. Reprinted in Georgine Oeri, "Saul Bass," *Graphis* 11, no. 59 (1955): 260.

163. Gerard Blanchard, "Saul Bass: Génériques et Languages," *Communications et Languages* 40 (1978): 78, 80.

164. A document in the production file, "Credit Provisions," contains five pages of notes on specifications for text size and billing for the actors' credits. See Gunther Schiff to Stanley Kramer, 21 January 1963, box 62, "It's a Mad, Mad, Mad, Mad World," Stanley Kramer Papers, UCLA Library Special Collections.

165. *It's a Mad, Mad, Mad, Mad World* reviews file, Saul Bass Papers, Margaret Herrick Library, AMPAS.

166. Bass and Kirkham, *Saul Bass*, 41–42.

167. See http://en.wikipedia.org/wiki/It%27s_a_Mad,_Mad,_Mad,_Mad_World.

168. The high costs of making three-camera, wide-screen films led the Cinerama company to stop production of its original system after the release of *How the West Was Won* (1962). Cinerama continued the brand with Ultra Panavision 70, which used anamorphic lenses to project onto the curved screen. *It's a Mad, Mad, Mad, Mad World* was the first single-camera Cinerama film. See http://www.widescreenmuseum.com/widescreen/wingup2.htm.

169. Bob Allen, "Designing and Producing the Credit Titles for 'It's a Mad, Mad, Mad, Mad World,'" *American Cinematographer* 44, no. 12 (December 1963): 706–7. The same color scheme as a monochromatic background strongly suggests that Bass created the last twenty seconds of the *It's a Mad, Mad, Mad, Mad World* trailer, where the title appears word by word as the title song is heard. See http://www.youtube.com/watch?v=Sla845GW9YM.

170. It is also odd that Stanley Kramer, who worked with Bass on numerous projects over a fifteen-year period, never mentions the designer in his autobiography. See Stanley Kramer with Thomas M. Coffey, *A Mad, Mad, Mad, Mad World: A Life in Hollywood* (New York: Harcourt, Brace, 1997). Bass is also missing from Donald Spoto, *Stanley Kramer: A Life* (New York: Putnam, 1978).

171. Philip K. Scheuer, "'It's a Mad World Challenge to Sanity," *Los Angeles Times*, 5 November 1963, pt. 4, 11.

172. Tube, "*It's a Mad, Mad, Mad, Mad World*," *Daily Variety*, 5 November 1963, 5.

173. Gene Arngel, "Mad Money Millions for Kramer and UA," *Film Daily*, 5 August 1965, 1, 5. See also memo from Leon Goldberg to Arthur Krim, 11 May

1966, Re: Stanley Kramer Pictures, box 127, folder "Sale Correspondence MW," Collection 161, Stanley Kramer Papers, UCLA Library Special Collections.

174. Allen, "Designing and Producing the Credit Titles," 707. Normally, theatrical curtains rose in four or five seconds.

3. Creating a Mood: *Pars pro toto*

1. Morella, Epstein, and Clark, *Those Great Movie Ads*, 44.

2. Harris, "Extra Credits," 227.

3. Fred Hift, "And that Cramps Film Ads—Bass," *Variety*, 20 November 1957, 24.

4. *AT&T Corporate Program* (1969), 16mm film, Saul Bass Collection, Academy Film Archive, AMPAS. *A New Look for the Bell System* is the Academy's title for the film.

5. Morella, Epstein, and Clark, *Those Great Movie Ads*, 44.

6. Foster Hirsch, *Otto Preminger: The Man Who Would Be King* (New York: Alfred A. Knopf, 2007), 195–96.

7. Otto Preminger, *An Autobiography* (New York: Doubleday, 1977), 109. See also Hirsch, *Otto Preminger*, 196. There is some controversy about whether Preminger is remembering the story correctly. Bass denied working on *The Moon Is Blue*. See Bell, "Oral History with Saul Bass," 67. Andreas A. Timmer quotes Bass's assistant, Brad Roberts, who said Bass designed the birds for the VHS release of the film in 1980. See Timmer, "Making the Ordinary Extraordinary," 134n4.

8. "Chatter," *Variety*, 9 December 1955, 11.

9. "Chatter," *Variety*, 13 December 1955, 9.

10. See *Bass on Titles*. See also Hirsch, *Otto Preminger*, 244. Bass and Kirkham, *Saul Bass*, 398, includes a photo of the Fox Wilshire marquee in Los Angeles, showing only the symbol for *Exodus*.

11. See Saul Bass interview, *Man with the Golden Arm*, typed transcript, box 4A, file 21, Saul Bass Papers, Margaret Herrick Library, AMPAS; Hirsch, *Otto Preminger*, 242.

12. See Robert M. Wendlinger, "Strong 'Arm' Methods: Roger Lewis of UA Discussed Unusual Ad Campaign for 'Golden Arm,'" *Hollywood Reporter*, 1955, in box 4A, file 21, Saul Bass Papers, Margaret Herrick Library, AMPAS; "Saul Bass," short segment, American Movie Classics Channel, 1994.

13. "*The Man with the Golden Arm*," *Hollywood Reporter*, 27 December 1955, 5–11.

14. Robert J. Landry, "Anatomy of a Campaign," *Variety*, 10 June 1959, 7.

15. See the trailer at http://www.youtube.com/watch?v=YljTxWFTtCk.

16. Art Goodman drew the *Advise and Consent* poster, but it was Bass's idea. Bass said the film would blow the lid off Washington, leading Goodman to suggest opening up the dome of the Capitol. Interview with Mike Lonzo, 20 September 2012.

17. Bass and Kirkham, *Saul Bass*, 149.

18. Bell, "Oral History with Saul Bass," 44.

19. King, "Taking Credit," http://www.typotheque.com/articles/taking_credit_

film_title_sequences_1955–1965_6_musical_statues_spartacus_1960. See Bass and Kirkham, *Saul Bass*, 192.

20. Hift, "And that Cramps Film Ads—Bass," 24.

21. Ibid.

22. Morella, Epstein, and Clark, *Those Great Movie Ads*, 109.

23. "Bureau of Missing Business," *Variety*, 20 August 1958, 12.

24. Ervine Metzl, *The Poster: Its History and Its Art* (New York: Watson-Guptill, 1963), 18.

25. John Barnicoat, *Posters: A Concise History* (London: Thames and Hudson, 1985), 7.

26. Maurice Rickards, *The Rise and Fall of the Poster* (New York: McGraw-Hill, 1971), 20.

27. Epes Winthrop Sargent, "Ten Years of Film Advertising," *Moving Picture World* 31, no. 10 (10 March 1917): 1489.

28. Steve Schapiro and David Chierichetti, *The Movie Poster Book* (New York: E. P. Dutton, 1979), 9.

29. Universal Film Manufacturing Company advertisement in *Moving Picture World* 19, no. 8 (21 February 1914): 909.

30. Sargent, "Ten Years of Film Advertising," 1489.

31. See Epes Winthrop Sargent, "Advertising for Exhibitors," *Moving Picture World* 11, no. 10 (9 March 1912): 860; "The Question of Posters," *Moving Picture World* 12, no. 3 (20 April 1912): 205; Abraham Nelson, "Posters Cause Comment," *Moving Picture World* 25, no. 5 (31 July 1915): 856.

32. J. B. Clymer, "Posters, Pertinent and Impertinent," *Moving Picture World* 14, no. 8 (23 November 1912): 778; W. Stephen Bush, "New Lights on Posters," *Moving Picture World* 28, no. 5 (29 April 1916): 777.

33. "New 'Pearl White' Poster," *Moving Picture World* 14, no. 12 (12 December 1912): 1179.

34. "Paramount's Convertibles," *Moving Picture World* 36, no. 9 (1 June 1918): 1282.

35. "History of the Movies and the Movie Poster," http://www.fffmovieposters.com/movieposterhistory.php.

36. Schapiro and Chierichetti, *Movie Poster Book*, 14. See also Gregory J. Edwards, *The International Film Poster* (Salem, NH: Salem House, 1985), 68–69; Edwin Poole and Susan Poole, *Learn about Movie Posters* (Chattanooga, TN: iGuide Media, 2002), 310–14.

37. Eugene A. Hosanksy, "The Current Scene: Film Posters," *Print* 19, no. 4 (July–August 1965): 22.

38. Bruce Hershenson, "A History of Movie Posters," http://www.reelclassics.com/Articles/General/posters-article.htm.

39. Stephen Rebello and Richard Allen, *Reel Art: Great Posters from the Golden Age of the Silver Screen* (New York: Abbeville Press, 1988), 118.

40. "*Carmen Jones* Art," in *34th Annual of Advertising and Editorial Art and Design* (New York: Longmans, Green in association with Art Directors Club of New

York, 1955), n.p. [303]. See also Judith Salavetz, Spencer Drate, and Sam Sarowitz, eds., *Art of the Modern Movie Poster: International Postwar Style and Design* (San Francisco: Chronicle Books, 2008), 440, which names *Carmen Jones* as Bass's first poster design. Kallis and Bass won an Art Directors Club Award for a Quanta Airlines advertisement in 1956. See *35th Annual of Advertising and Editorial Art and Design* (New York: Longmans, Green, 1956), n.p. [no. 60].

41. Edwards, *International Film Poster*, 73.

42. Hosanksy, "Current Scene," 20.

43. Toot Buj, "Buy American," *Film Comment* 44, no. 3 (May–June 2008): 20. Williams argues the same point in reference to Bass's title designs. See David E. Williams, "Initial Images," *American Cinematographer* 79, no. 5 (May 1998): 92.

44. Salavetz, Drate, and Sarowitz, *Art of the Modern Movie Poster*, 440.

45. The poster design of silhouettes was also used for other materials, including the premiere invitation and billboards. What convinced me that Bass must have designed the poster is the fact that a whole campaign was organized around the image; in addition, the design for United Artists' press releases includes a square image of a map of Nuremberg (red and black) split into fifteen fragments, a design feature seen in many Bass designs, including the end titles for *The Big Knife* and *Four Just Men*. See *Judgment at Nuremberg* press releases, box 38, folder "Publicity Jan," Collection 161, Stanley Kramer Papers, UCLA Special Collections.

46. It has been argued that Bass did not design the poster for *West Side Story*. See Bass and Kirkham, *Saul Bass*, 107.

47. Some Bass one-sheet posters now sell for more than $1,000: a very good quality *Vertigo* poster was sold at auction in 2011 for more than $4,900, *The Man with the Golden Arm* sold for $1,500 in April 2012, and *Anatomy of a Murder* went for $2,400 in 2010. See the auction history site at eMovieposter.com, http://www.emovieposter.com/agallery/search/film%253A%2520VERTIGO%2520%28%2758%29/archive.html.

48. Quoted in Hosansky, "Current Scene," 20.

49. Armin Hofmann, "Thoughts on the Poster," in *The 20th Century Poster: Design of the Avant-Garde*, ed. Dawn Ades (New York: Abbeville Press, 1984), 91.

50. The artist for *The Big Country* was Morton Dimondstein. See AIGA Archives, http://designarchives.aiga.org/#/entries/Saul%20Bass/_/detail/relevance/asc/34/7/16212/big-country/1.

51. Quoted in Selden Rodman, *Conversations with Artists* (New York: Devin-Adair, 1957); later published in "Notes from a Conversation with Selden Rodman, 1956," in *Writings on Art: Mark Rothko*, ed. Miguel López-Remiro (New Haven, CT: Yale University Press, 2006).

52. See Lynn Spigel, *TV by Design: Modern Art and the Rise of Network Television* (Chicago: University of Chicago Press, 2008), 52.

53. "The West Coast: A Designer's View," *Industrial Design* 4, no. 10 (October 1957): 129.

54. Phyllis Tanner and Maury Nemoy are credited as artists on the poster. See

AIGA Archive, http://designarchives.aiga.org/#/entries/Saul%20Bass/_/detail/relevance/asc/50/7/17655/the-man-with-the-golden-arm/1.

55. See *37th Annual of Advertising and Editorial Art and Design* (New York: Longmans, Green, 1958), n.p. [nos. 64, 65], which lists Saul Bass and Henry Markowitz as the artists. The same source credits Goodman and Bass for the *Love in the Afternoon* poster.

56. Bass and Kirkham, *Saul Bass*, 128; http://www.moviepostershop.com/bonjour-tristesse-movie-poster-1958. The actual one-sheet poster in the author's possession confirms that the reproduction in Bass and Kirkham is accurate.

57. The last 40 seconds of the 1:36-minute trailer features the face in blue and pink, as the credits silently pop in and out; it ends with the message: "Next Attraction in This Theater" in the Bass type for *Tristesse*. Previously, the trailer showed several scenes without comment. https://www.youtube.com/watch?v=Z-RCRulvXgQ .

58. As Martin Scorsese notes in reference to *Bonjour Tristesse*'s logo: "This suggests Modigliani and Matisse but also recalls haute couture and the sophisticated advertising design of the time." Martin Scorsese, "Anatomy of a Synthesist," *New York Times Magazine*, 29 December 1996, 44.

59. "*Porgy and Bess*, Unused Production Elements," 16mm, color reversal, 4:45 minutes, 16778-2-1, Saul Bass Collection, Academy Film Archive, AMPAS.

60. Bass and Kirkham, *Saul Bass*, 165.

61. See Stanley Wolpert, *Nine Hours to Rama* (New York: Random House Books, 1962).

62. Steven Heller, "The Man with the Big Book Look," *Print* 56, no. 2 (March–April 2002): 48.

63. *Hollywood Reporter*, 16 January 1962, 3. See also Bass and Kirkham, *Saul Bass*, 398.

64. Bass and Kirkham, *Saul Bass*, 148.

65. Stanley Wolpert, *Nine Hours to Rama* (New York: Bantam Books, 1963).

66. Metzl, *The Poster*, 170. Metzl's prejudice against credits, expressed at least twice in the text, is a bit odd, given his invocation that posters be both advertising and art.

67. Purchased from the Bass estate by Jim Northover, the posters for *Grand Prix*, *Exodus*, and *The Fixer* were among those exhibited. See http://www.oipolloi.com/bass-notes-the-film-posters-of-saul-bass.

68. "Preminger Picture Nearly Flawless," *Hollywood Reporter*, 14 December 1955, 3. See also "*Man with the Golden Arm*," *Motion Picture Herald*, 17 December 1955, 706.

69. Quoted in Leo Goldsmith, "*The Man with the Golden Arm*, Not Coming to a Theatre Near You," 2005, http://www.notcoming.com/saulbass/caps_manwgoldenarm.php.

70. Harris, "Extra Credits," 228.

71. Wendlinger, "Strong 'Arm' Methods."

72. "*Man with the Golden Arm*," box 4A, file 27, Saul Bass Papers, Margaret Herrick Library, AMPAS.

73. For example, five MPAA companies abstained from voting on the film. See W. R. Wilkerson, "Trade Views," *Hollywood Reporter*, 9 December 1955, 1. Meanwhile, a second scene of Sinatra preparing heroin with a spoon and matches was cut to appease with New York State censor. See "Preminger Voluntarily Cuts Scene from 'Arm,'" *Variety*, 14 December 1955, 37. See also "L.A. Radio Stations Refuse to Air Spot Plugs for 'Man with Golden Arm,'" *Daily Variety*, 19 December 1955, 9. Finally, the Legion of Decency gave the film a B rating. See "Legion 'B'-Rates Preminger Pic, Denied Seal," *Variety*, 28 December 1955, 13.

74. "*The Man with the Golden Arm*," typed manuscript, n.d., box 4A, file 19, Saul Bass Papers, Margaret Herrick Library, AMPAS.

75. Jack Moffitt, review of *Man with the Golden Arm*, *Hollywood Reporter*, 14 December 1955, 3. Gene Moskowitz wrote: "Novel titles have been produced by Saul Bass." See his film review in *Variety*, 14 December 1955, 6.

76. Jan-Christopher Horak, *Lovers of Cinema: The First American Film Avant-Garde* (Madison: University of Wisconsin Press, 1995), 35–36.

77. Bass and Kirkham, *Saul Bass*, 66.

78. Ibid., 55.

79. Hirsch, *Otto Preminger*, 219.

80. "Pickford to Star in *The Library*," *Variety*, 21 November 1951. See also "Mary Pickford Hops out of Stan Kramer's 'Fire' Because It Isn't Tinted," *Variety*, 19 September 1952, 1; *Hollywood Reporter*, 25 September 1952, 1.

81. See "Polishing Library," *Daily Variety*, 1 June 1955, 8; "Upcoming Pic, 'The Library' to Sneer at Book-Burners' Fear of Ideas," *Variety*, 6 July 1955, 1.

82. "Legion of Decency 'Separately' Classifies Col's STORM CENTER," *Daily Variety*, 10 July 1956, 1.

83. "Inside Stuff—Pictures," *Variety*, 8 July 1959, 17.

84. Hirsch, *Otto Preminger*, 284–85. Uris's novel remained on best-seller lists for eighty weeks and sold 400,000 hardback and 3 million paperback copies.

85. There is some controversy about whether Otto Preminger or Kirk Douglas broke the blacklist. Preminger first announced publicly in January 1960 that Trumbo would receive credit for *Exodus*. Trumbo had earlier written the script for *Spartacus*, under a pseudonym, but Douglas did not make a similar announcement until September 1960. Nevertheless, it was Douglas who received an award from the Writers Guild for breaking the blacklist. See Hirsch, *Otto Preminger*, 327–28. Ceplair confirms that Douglas overstated his case. See Larry Ceplair, "Kirk Douglas, *Spartacus*, and the Blacklist," *Cineaste* 37, no. 1 (Winter 2012): 11.

86. See "Add Preminger Pros & Cons," *Variety*, 3 February 1960, 24; advertisement in *Hollywood Reporter*, 29 March 1960, 29, reprinted in Bass and Kirkham, *Saul Bass*, 139.

87. See "*Exodus* Production Elements Unused Title Sequence," 16mm, black and white, 5812-2-1, Saul Bass Collection, Academy Film Archive, AMPAS. Images of the surf would reappear in Preminger's *In Harm's Way*.

88. See Doug Bennett, "Military Stencil Typeface History," http://www.imagemaking.us/2011/10/military-stencil-typeface-history-by.html.

89. The trailer also ends with yellow flames engulfing the screen after the *Exodus* logo appears in white and the title in pink on a blue background, reprising an earlier title shot at the beginning of the trailer. See http://www.youtube.com/watch?v=gmcjfCQMKfA.

90. "Man with Gold Arm (Navy Rank), Plus Guts' Cue to Prem's World Sell," *Variety*, 31 March 1965, 13.

91. *In Harm's Way*, "Script Covers," box 4A, file 9, Saul Bass Papers, Margaret Herrick Library, AMPAS.

92. *In Harm's Way*, "Titles Description," box 4A, file 12, Saul Bass Papers, Margaret Herrick Library, AMPAS.

93. All quotes in this paragraph are from review sheet, "*Cape Fear* Storyboards for Promotion," box 2A, file 8, Saul Bass Collection, Margaret Herrick Library, AMPAS.

94. Thomas Krag and Tim Volsted, eds., *Title Sequence Seminar: Saul and Elaine Bass, 25 April 1995* (Copenhagen: National Film School of Denmark, 1995), 46.

95. The logo was used in the poster and on all advertising. Bass also designed an elaborate press book for the campaign, which was made to look like a congressional attaché case. The press book was included in my 2002 exhibition "Saul Bass—Designer" at the Hollywood Entertainment Museum.

96. U.S. House of Representatives, *Our Flag* (Washington, DC: Government Printing Office, 1989), http://www.usflag.org/colors.html.

97. See "Robson Adds '9 Hours' to His 20th Slate," *Daily Variety*, 3 October 1961, 1; *Hollywood Reporter*, 16 January 1962, 13.

98. James Powers, "*Nine Hours to Rama*," *Hollywood Reporter*, 18 February 1963, 3; Harrison Carroll, "*Nine Hours to Rama* Powerful," *Los Angeles Herald Examiner*, 9 May 1963; Philip K. Scheuer, "Gandhi Story Makes Powerful Screen Epic," *Los Angeles Times Calendar*, 3 March 1963, 3; Tube, "*Nine Hours to Rama*," *Variety*, 20 February 1963, 6; Raymond Levy, "*Nine Hours to Rama*," *Motion Picture Herald*, 6 March 1963, 762.

99. John Coleman, "Bass Relief," *New Statesman*, 1 March 1963.

100. Interview with Jeff Okun, 6 June 2011, Studio City, CA. The biggest challenge was finding a bulk fabric that looked like a handkerchief.

101. Stuart Klawans, "Film," *Nation*, 1 January 1990.

102. Jason Woloski, "Not Coming to a Theatre Near You," http://www.notcoming.com/saulbass/caps_warroses.php.

103. Quoted in John Naughton, "Credit Where Credit's Due . . . ," *Empire* 57 (March 1994): 54.

104. Quoted in Krag and Volsted, *Title Sequence Seminar*, 47.

105. "Shirley Thomas from Hollywood," radio broadcast, 23 October 1955, 5:30 p.m., KFI-NBC, transcript in *The Big Knife*, "Publicity File," box 1A, file 43, Saul Bass Papers, Margaret Herrick Library, AMPAS.

106. Jean-Pierre Piton, *Robert Aldrich* (Paris: Edilig, 1985), 41.

107. Bass and Kirkham, *Saul Bass*, 35.

108. Allan Sekula, "The Body and the Archive," in *The Contest of Meaning: Critical Histories of Photography*, ed. Richard Bolton (Cambridge, MA: MIT Press, 1992), 343.

109. The play opened on 15 January 1952 and closed on 1 May 1952, after 161 performances. Universal supposedly paid six figures for the film rights. See *Hollywood Reporter*, 23 February 1954, *The Shrike* production file, Margaret Herrick Library, AMPAS.

110. According to an unsubstantiated note on the Internet Movie Database (IMDb), Bonner literally died onstage in July 1955, playing the same role at the Carthay Circle Theatre in Los Angeles, less than ten days after the film opened.

111. *The Shrike* (1955) publicity brochure, production files, Margaret Herrick Library, AMPAS.

112. Blogger "The Siren" argues that misogyny is at the very core of the film, despite June Allyson's strong performance. See http://selfstyledsiren.blogspot.com /2012/01/shrike-1955.html.

113. A. H. Weiler, "*The Shrike* (1955) Tamed 'Shrike'; Film Wife Less Deadly than One in Play," *New York Times*, 8 July 1955, http://movies.nytimes.com/movie/rev iew?res=9D00E0DD103AE53BBC4053DFB166838E649EDE.

114. Murray Schumach, *The Face on the Cutting Room Floor: The Story of Movie and Television Censorship* (New York: William Morrow, 1964).

115. David Badder, Bob Baker, and Markku Salmi, "Saul Bass," *Film Dope* 3 (August 1973): 2.

116. The next Bass title on the list of the 250 greatest films of all time is *Goodfellas*, at 171. See http://explore.bfi.org.uk/sightandsoundpolls/2012/critics/.

117. See Timmer, "Making the Ordinary Extraordinary," 131n62. Timmer quotes a letter from Bass to Herb Coleman, dated 26 February 1959, describing Whitney's work as well as the color timing of the sequence.

118. Tom Sito, *Moving Innovations: A History of Computer Animation* (Cambridge, MA: MIT Press, 2013), 26–28.

119. According to Emily King, *Vertigo* and *Psycho* were made with the help of Harold Adler, who worked at National Screen Service (where *The Seven Year Itch* was also produced). Adler comments on the precision of Bass's storyboards but notes that Bass needed help translating them to film, which may or may not have been true. See King, "TakingCredit," http://www.typothequecomarticlestaking_credit_film_ title_sequences_1955–1965_5_spiralling_aspirations_vertigo_1958.

120. Quoted in Pat Kirkham, "The Jeweller's Eye," *Sight & Sound* 7, no. 4 (April 1997): 18.

121. Donald Spoto, *The Art of Alfred Hitchcock: Fifty Years of His Motion Pictures* (Garden City, NY: Dolphin Books, 1976), 299–300.

122. See Moholy-Nagy, *New Vision* (2005), 175.

123. *Vertigo*, "Title Description," box 13A, file 39, Saul Bass Papers, Margaret Herrick Library, AMPAS. Strangely, Bass insists that the opening shots of the title sequence were in black and white before being tinted red. The original trailer for *Vertigo* also employed the Lissajous light form, which appears immediately after a close-up of a dictionary definition of *vertigo* (almost matching Bass's definition here), followed by the film's title shot. See the *Vertigo* trailer at https://www.youtube.com/ watch?v=Z5jvQwwHQNY.

124. Robin Wood, *Hitchcock's Films* (New York: Paperback Library, 1970), 78.

125. Franz Roh and Jan Tschichold, *Foto-Auge, Photo-Eye, Oeil et Photo* (Stuttgart: Akademischer Verlag GmbH., 1929).

126. Although John and Penelope Motimer received screen credit, the original novel by Miriam Modell was adapted by Walter Newman, Charles Beaumont, Ira Levin, Dalton Trumbo, and Arthur Kopit. See Hirsch, *Otto Preminger*, 400–401.

127. See "*Bunny Lake Is Missing*," *Daily Variety*, 9 April 1965, 5. The ad reproduced the poster with a note to the left in Bass's own hand: "Starts shooting in London today."

128. See "*Bunny Lake Is Missing*," *Box Office*, 18 October 1965; Robe, "*Bunny Lake Is Missing*," *Daily Variety*, 5 October 1965, 3, 10. The latter writes: "The simple but effective titles by Saul Bass, will, as usual, carry over into the film's entire advertising and promotion campaign."

129. *Bunny Lake Is Missing* title description file, Saul Bass Papers, Margaret Herrick Library, AMPAS.

130. In *Spartacus*, the palm rather than the back of the hand is visible, but otherwise, the image is identical.

131. Bass and Kirkham, *Saul Bass*, 54.

132. Andrew Sarris, *The American Cinema: Directors and Directions 1929–1968* (New York: E. P. Dutton, 1968), 106. See also Andrew Sarris, *Confessions of a Cultist: On the Cinema, 1955/1969* (London: Simon and Schuster, 1971), 212–14.

133. Frankenheimer abandoned scriptwriter Lewis John Carlino's happy ending, which united the subject with his original family, and instead made him a victim of the malevolent corporation he had hired. See Stephen Bowie, "John Frankenheimer," http://www.sensesofcinema.com/2006/great-directors/frankenheimer/. See also Peter Wilshire, "A Key Unturned: *Seconds*," http://archive.sensesofcinema.com/contents/01/18/seconds.html.

134. *Seconds*, "Storyboards," box 11A, file 4, Saul Bass Papers, Margaret Herrick Library, AMPAS.

135. Okun interview, 2011.

136. Lonzo interview, 2012.

137. All the footage was apparently shot first with a normal lens, then projected onto a distorted mirror surface and rephotographed while moving the mirror to create further distortions.

4. Modernism's Multiplicity of Views

1. Philip B. Meggs, "Saul Bass on Corporate Identity," in *Design Culture: An Anthology of Writing from the AIGA Journal of Graphic Design*, ed. Steven Heller and Marie Finamore (New York: Allworth Press, 1997), 72.

2. Sergei Eisenstein, "A Dialectical Approach to Film Form," in *Film Form: Essays in Film Theory* (New York: Harvest Books, 1949), 54.

3. Bell, "Oral History with Saul Bass," 12. See also Mary Glucksman, "Saul Bass: Due Credit," *Screen International*, 13 May 1994, 27.

4. Reproduced in Ludwig Ebenhöh, "Saul Bass, USA," *Gebrauchsgraphik* 27, no. 11 (November 1956): 18.

5. It is possible that Bass met Nalpas while working on *The Seven Year Itch* at National Screen Service. Interview with Mike Lonzo, 20 September 2012.

6. "Saul Bass [Interview]," *Designer Magazine*, May 1980, 10.

7. *American Film Institute Seminar*, 24.

8. Lars-Olaf Beier and Walter Midding, *Vorspann: Zum Werk von Saul Bass* (Hamburg: North German Television [NDR], 1991), VHS tape, 28308-1, Saul Bass Collection, Academy Film Archive, AMPAS.

9. Moholy-Nagy, *Vision in Motion*, 44.

10. Amos Gitai, *Carmel* (Tel Aviv: Munio Gitai Weintraub Architecture Museum, 2012), 40, 42.

11. *Looking for Mr. Goodbar*, "Title Art," Richard Brooks Papers, Margaret Herrick Library, AMPAS.

12. Beth Laski, "Art Rings 'Clockers' Alarm: Ads Redone after Gripes from Preminger Films," *Daily Variety*, 24 September 1995, 1, 17.

13. E-mail from Sean Savage, Academy Film Archive, to the author, 21 September 2012. A 16mm negative of the sequence, completed up to the cinematographer's credit, survives in the Saul Bass Papers. Rebello quotes an unnamed Bass employee as the source for the existence of these *Anatomy* credits but notes: "Bass contends the story is untrue, and that the only similarity between the sequences was the use of 'bars' as a graphic motif." See Stephen Rebello, "*Psycho*," *Cinefantastique* 16, no. 4/5 (October 1986): 74.

14. See http://www.emovieposter.com/agallery/archiveitem/10998570.html. The French poster doesn't include the corpse, which is visible at the bottom of the frame of the American half-sheet.

15. *Anatomy of a Murder*, "Record of Work Done" file, Saul Bass Papers, Margaret Herrick Library, AMPAS.

16. Ibid.

17. Timmer, "Making the Ordinary Extraordinary," 75.

18. See the original trailer for *Anatomy of a Murder* at http://www.youtube.com/watch?v=54muV-xIhIU.

19. Winfried Günther, "A Shot Conveys an Outlook," in *Stanley Kubrick* (Frankfurt: Deutsches Filmmuseum, 2004), 57.

20. See "Kubrick 'Spartacus' Director; Mann Out," *Daily Variety*, 16 February 1959, 1, 4. The battle scenes were apparently shot in both the San Fernando Valley and Spain. I have found no sources that actually list Bass as having directed the battle scenes, although he may have been present at the California shoot. Reproductions of the *Spartacus* storyboards indicate that Bass also designed a gladiator sequence and the gladiator cages. See *Spartacus*—sequence storyboard illustrations by Saul Bass, box 13A, file 21, Saul Bass Papers, Margaret Herrick Library, AMPAS.

21. Martin M. Winkler, Spartacus: *Film and History* (London: Wiley-Blackwell, 2007), 4.

22. B. D., "*Spartacus*," *Monthly Film Bulletin* 28, no. 324 (January 1961): 6. See

also Bosley Crowther, "*Spartacus*," *New York Times*, 7 October 1960, 28. For a positive review, see Brendan Gill, "Love and Slavery," *New Yorker*, 15 October 1960, 133.

23. Bass was hired to do the battle scenes, which were originally supposed to be merely hinted at: "I was working on the battle, because at first, it wasn't going to be a big epic picture, just reasonable . . . 2 or 3 million dollars. So they thought it would be very interesting to do a symbolic battle, and they thought symbolic battle . . . that's Saul Bass, so they called me in and I was working on a symbolic battle. Then things started getting a little out of hand, budget rising—it was now about 4 or 5 million—so they said, let's have a little more . . . let's do an *impressionistic* battle. So I redid the whole thing. Well, they were enlarging the picture, putting more and more things in, and finally they said—Well gee, we can't go down the line and then have somebody look through the window and say 'That's a helluva battle going on down there' . . . what we need is an all out battle. So by this time I was the battle expert, and that's how I wound up doing what for me is this most unlikely thing." Quoted in King, "Taking Credit," http://www.typotheque.com/articles/taking_credit_film_title_sequences_1955–1965_6_musical_statues_spartacus_1960, and in Bass and Kirkham, *Saul Bass*, 197.

24. Bass and Kirkham, *Saul Bass*, 193–94.

25. King, "Taking Credit," http://www.typothequecomarticles/taking_credit_film_title_sequences_1955–1965_6_musical_statues_spartacus_1960.

26. "Injury Jinx Plagues Film," *Los Angeles Examiner*, 6 July 1960, *Facts of Life* production file, Margaret Herrick Library, AMPAS.

27. See Tube, "*The Facts of Life*," *Daily Variety*, 14 November 1960, 3; "*The Facts of Life*," *Limelight*, 17 November 1960, production file, Margaret Herrick Library, AMPAS.

28. "Sexy Eyes over Hope's Shoulder," *Life*, 17 March 1961, 109.

29. Based on their style, Art Goodman was probably responsible for executing the *Facts of Life* titles, as he was for the *Advise and Consent* poster.

30. The Saul Bass Papers include production elements of the following commercials: Speedway 79 (1955), Sun detergent (1956), National Bohemian beer (1957), Olin Mathieson (1960), Band-Aid (1962), Mennen baby products (1962), Rainier beer (1968), Mattel Toys (1969), Bridgestone tires (1968), Chevrolet OK cars (1971), RCA (1968), Michigan Bell (1972), Olympia beer (1975), Dixie Cups (1975), Rayovac batteries (1975), Girl Scout cookies (1977), Matushista (1978), Security Pacific Bank (1979), Millar Gooseberries (n.d.), and Hallmark cards (n.d.). Bass may have produced more commercials, but these are the only ones that survive.

31. Bass and Kirkham, *Saul Bass*, 96.

32. See *Business Screen Magazine* 24, no. 4 (1963): 381.

33. The Mennen Baby Magic commercial is on YouTube: http://www.youtube.com/watch?v=20zxateRV44&feature=fvwrel.

34. See this Mennen Genteel Baby Bath soap commercial on YouTube: http://www.youtube.com/watch?v=_T-C6bMp1Vw.

35. Bass's Mennen Genteel Baby Bath soap commercial survives in the Saul Bass Collection, 22403-1, Academy Film Archive, AMPAS.

36. The Bass Collection has sixty- and thirty-second commercials for Mattel's Toy and Hobby Book, Peanuts wind-up toys, and Toot Sweet, all from the same period, but they may have been used only for reference.

37. RCA "The Kid" commercial, 16mm color, 1 minute, 84138-1, Saul Bass Collection, Academy Film Archive, AMPAS.

38. It has been argued that this commercial was not produced by Bass, but there is no documentary evidence either way. Given that it was found in the Bass Collection, I believe there is enough formal evidence to claim that it was produced by Bass. See e-mail from Jennifer Bass to the author, 6 April 2013.

39. Kepes reproduces Marcel Duchamp's *Nude Descending the Stairs* (1912), Herbert Matter's advertisement for the Container Corporation of America, and Harold E. Edgerton's photograph "Golfer" (n.d.). See Kepes, *Language of Vision*, 180–82.

40. Most of the posters and advertisements for the film have a decidedly un-Bass-like look to them, but Bass's record of work for the film indicates that he designed at least one trade advertisement. See *Attack!* "Record of Work," box 1A, file 26, Saul Bass Papers, Margaret Herrick Library, AMPAS.

41. David Badder, Bob Baker, and Markku Salmi, "Saul Bass," *Film Dope* 3 (August 1973): 1.

42. Edwin T. Arnold and Eugene L. Miller, *The Films and Career of Robert Aldrich* (Nashville: University of Tennessee Press, 1986), 69.

43. Super Panavision 70mm was in fact almost identical to Todd-AO. *West Side Story* was also produced in Super Panavision 70. See http://www.widescreenmuseum.com/widescreen/wingsp1.htm.

44. "Saul Bass Gets Tricky," *Hollywood Reporter*, 20 October 1966, 13.

45. "Bass Doing Effects," *Hollywood Reporter*, 29 June 1966, 9. See also "Dialogue on Film: John Frankenheimer," *American Film* 14, no. 5 (March 1989): 24. Bass stated that Albert Nalpas edited the sequences with him. See *American Film Institute Seminar*, 8.

46. "Cinerama Makes Deal with Frankenheimer/Lewis," *Hollywood Reporter*, 30 November 1964, 1, 4; "'Grand Prix' 1st Film Securing Cinerama Mantling sans Release," *Daily Variety*, 30 November 1964, 1; "MGM to Finance Release Cinerama Prod'n, 'Grand Prix,'" *Daily Variety*, 10 September 1965, 1.

47. "Casting 'Prix' on MGM Lot; Pic Rolls May 22," *Daily Variety*, 15 February 1966, 20.

48. *Grand Prix*, box 3A, file 33, Saul Bass Papers, Margaret Herrick Library, AMPAS.

49. "*Grand Prix*," *Film Daily*, 5 August 1966. In addition, a new 70mm, high-speed color film processor was used at MGM labs for release prints. See "MGM Using New 'Prix' Processor," *Daily Variety*, 1 December 1966, 3.

50. "*Grand Prix* Gross Tops Mil in Cinerama Dome Run," *Daily Variety*, 23 October 1967, 3; "Cinerama to Earn More than $5 Million," *Hollywood Reporter*, 21 April 1967, 1, 3.

51. "Ways of Winning," *New Yorker*, 31 December 1966, 60; Pry, "*Grand Prix*," *Daily Variety*, 22 December 1966, 3, 15.

52. Pauline Kael, "A Sense of Disproportion," *New Republic*, 14 January 1967, 41–42.

53. Bosley Crowther, "Screen: Flag Is Down at Warner for 'Grand Prix,'" *New York Times*, 22 December 1966, http://movies.nytimes.com/movie/review?res=9F07E7D8123CE43BBC4A51DFB467838D679EDE.

54. Stephen Bowie writes on the Senses of Cinema website: "The indifference of the all-not-quite-star-cast toward the material is matched by Frankenheimer's indifference toward them, as if the director didn't want the Ferraris upstaged by any showy acting. See http://www.sensesofcinema.com/2006/great-directors/frankenheimer/.

55. According to some sources, it was apparently Elaine Bass's idea to have the screen go silent.

56. See Hal Hinson, "*Mr. Saturday Night*," *Washington Post*, 25 September 1992, http://www.washingtonpost.com/wp-srv/style/longterm/movies/videos/mrsaturdaynightrhinson_a0a79f.htm; Peter Travers, "*Mr. Saturday Night*," *Rolling Stone*, http://www.rollingstone.com/movies/reviews-mr-saturday-night-20010227.

57. Jeffrey Wells, "Another Battle between Artistic Truth and Mass Appeal: And the Loser Is . . . ," *Los Angeles Times Calendar*, 18 October 1992, *Mr. Saturday Night* production files, Margaret Herrick Library, AMPAS.

58. Marilyn Moss, "*Mr. Saturday Night*," *Box Office*, December 1992, R-87, *Mr. Saturday Night* production files, Margaret Herrick Library, AMPAS.

59. Julie Salamon, "*Mr. Saturday Night*," *Wall Street Journal*, 24 September 1992. See also Todd McCarthy, "*Mr. Saturday Night*," *Daily Variety*, 14 September 1992, 3, 12, who writes: "The title sequence by Saul and Elaine Bass hilariously sends up the preparation of Jewish food faves." Janet Maslin characterized the title sequence as "vivid," "complete with cabbage stuffing." See Janet Maslin, "Billy Crystal, in Directorial Debut, Stars as Obnoxious Stand up Comic," *New York Times*, 23 September 1992, http://movies.nytimes.com/movie/review?res=9B06E3D6123AF930A1575AC0A964958260.

60. Michael Sragow, "Shtick Shifts," *New Yorker*, 5 October 1992, 162–64.

61. The hands reportedly belonged to Elaine Bass, who had a huge hand in creating the title sequence (no pun intended).

62. The Basses were apparently not happy with Billy Crystal's abrasive commentary. They subsequently created the sequence as a stand-alone film without narration and with different music. Their version, dated 1993–1994, remains in the Bass Collection, Academy Film Archive, AMPAS. See e-mail from Sean Savage to the author, 15 March 2013.

63. V. I. Pudovkin, *Film Technique and Film Acting* (New York: Grove Press, 1970), 97.

64. The whole film takes place on one empty set with the actors mingling as the camera roams between them, intercut with photos and other visual material to illustrate points the speakers are making. Bob Aller, who worked as a production assistant on *Bass on Titles*, directed. It is also possible that Gene McGarr directed at least some of the film, as he was the announced director in *Variety*. "Gene McGarr will direct a Westinghouse promo film for Saul Bass & Ass., marking the first time in the 20 year

history of Bass' company that someone other than Bass will direct one of its films." Both the announced writer and cameraman were credited in the film. See "Pix, People, Pickups," *Daily Variety*, 3 May 1976, 3.

65. Interview with Herb Yager, 27 February 2013, Ojai, CA. The first physical indication of Bass's involvement is a telephone memo from a secretary to Bass dated 3 January 1978, in which Michael Britton (Wildwood Productions) confirms an honorarium of $10,000 for Bass and $15,000 for a writer on project. The first letter of agreement is dated 25 January 1978. See also letter from Michael Britton to Herb Yager, 1 March 1978, re "Alternative Energy Source Film," *Solar Film*, "Film Agreements," box 12A, file 87, Saul Bass Papers, Margaret Herrick Library, AMPAS; "Saul Bass Busy Writing, Directing Theatrical Project," *Hollywood Reporter*, 7 September 1978, 8.

66. Allan Richards, "Lola Redford and Ilene Goldman: Consumer Action Now," *Mother Earth News*, July–August 1972, http://www.motherearthnews.com/nature-community/interview-redford-goldman/zmaz72jaztak.aspx.

67. *Solar Film* script dated 22 November 1976: "Caging the Sun." The final approved script is called "Solar Energy" and is dated 1 May 1979, box 12A, file 53, Saul Bass Papers, Margaret Herrick Library, AMPAS.

68. The budget was allocated as follows: live-action sequences, $82,549; animation, $114,300; postproduction, $120,850. See letter from Rafael de la Sierra (Warner Communications) to Michael Britton (Wildwood Productions), 10 April 1979, "Film Agreements," box 12A, file 87, Saul Bass Papers, Margaret Herrick Library, AMPAS.

69. Clarke Taylor, "Redford's *Solar Film* Screens," *Los Angeles Times*, 6 March 1980, production file, Margaret Herrick Library, AMPAS.

70. See *Solar Film*, "Log Book Dailies, Shot Charts," box 12A, file 105, Saul Bass Papers, Margaret Herrick Library, AMPAS.

71. Nancy Collins, "Redford Shines at Premiere of His 'Solar Film,'" *Los Angeles Herald Examiner*, 18 March 1980, A10.

72. Lee Grant, "Robert Redford Finds a Place in the Sun," *Los Angeles Times*, 29 March 1980, 8.

73. Among its film festival awards were the Golden Cine Eagle Award; Gold Medal, Chicago Film Festival; Golden Mercury, Venice Film Festival; Bronze Medal, Huesca Short Film Fest (Spain); Golden Cindy IFPA (Information Producers of America); Bronze Medal, Columbus Film Fest; Diploma Ekofilm International Fest (Czechoslovakia); and Diploma Aspen International Film Fest.

74. Lee Grant, "Robert Redford Finds a Place in the Sun," *Los Angeles Times*, 29 March 1980, 8.

75. Charles Champlin, "*Solar Film* Having an Extended Run," *Los Angeles Times*, 9 May 1980, production file, Margaret Herrick Library, AMPAS.

76. Dale Pollack, "Live Action Shorts up for Award," *Los Angeles Times*, 29 March 1980, sec. 2, 9.

77. Stanley Mason, "Saul and Elaine Bass: A New Film on Solar Energy," *Graphis* 37, no. 232 (September–October 1981): 156–59.

78. Robert Redford noted in a letter to Saul Bass dated 25 November 1980: "The issue of theatrical distribution is much more complex. I agree with you that there is more to be done here and that our original expectations were never really met." Box 12A, file 95, Saul Bass Papers, Margaret Herrick Library, AMPAS.

79. See letter from Lyn Adams (Pyramid Films) to Saul Bass, 5 November 1980, *Solar Film*, "Pyramid," box 13A, file 8, Saul Bass Papers, Margaret Herrick Library, AMPAS.

80. Letter from Sheldon Renan (Pyramid) to Saul Bass, 20 March 1980, box 13A, file 8, Saul Bass Papers, Margaret Herrick Library, AMPAS. Pyramid offered 22.5 percent on the gross dollar for normal print sales and rentals, 50 percent of the net on sublicensing, and $5,000 against royalties, payable no later than eighteen months after the nontheatrical release. However, Warner's legal department blocked the deal for months, even though Pyramid was already promoting the film.

81. Letter from Michael Britton (Wildwood) to Lyn Adams (Pyramid), 8 June 1981, *Solar Film*, "Pyramid," box 13A, file 8, Saul Bass Papers, Margaret Herrick Library, AMPAS.

82. *The Solar Film*, press release, Wildwood Enterprises, production files, Margaret Herrick Library, AMPAS.

83. Interestingly, as Sean Savage from the Academy Film Archive has confirmed, all 16mm prints still bore the original title, although the credits were changed to add Elaine Bass's directorial credit. See e-mail from Sean Savage to the author, 15 March 2013. In a letter from Saul Bass to Michael Britton, 14 August 1980, he acknowledged Elaine's contribution to the film: "The fact is, as you know, that the film is overwhelmingly a product of my work and Elaine's work." In fact, Bass credited Elaine in a way he never did for other designers working in his office, even when they took the lead on projects. See "Correspondence with Various Subcontractors," box 14A, file 95, Saul Bass Papers, Margaret Herrick Library, AMPAS.

84. Interview with Jeff Okun, 23 March 2012, Hollywood, CA.

85. Earlier outlines and treatments of the film apparently included at least one more animated section—a dialogue about solar energy, similar to the "A Digression" dialogue between snails in *Why Man Creates*. Another outline included at least three animated sections. *Solar Film*, "Press Materials," box 13A, file 6, Saul Bass Papers, Margaret Herrick Library, AMPAS.

86. The "Big Trouble" animation sequence originally included the following before getting to the discovery of coal as an energy source: cottage industries, water power, population explosion, inventions, steam, and wood. See letter from Saul Bass to Stan Hart, 11 September 1978, and script attachment, box 12A, file 24, Saul Bass Papers, Margaret Herrick Library, AMPAS.

87. The actual roll text in the print does not end with a question mark.

88. Krag and Volsted, *Title Sequence Seminar*, 67.

5. The Urban Landscape

1. Quoted in Marjorie Perloff, "The Avant-Garde Phase of American Modernism," in *Cambridge Companion to American Modernism*, ed. Walter B. Kalaidjian (Cambridge: Cambridge University Press, 2005), 195.

2. See Jan-Christopher Horak, "Paul Strand and Charles Sheeler's *Manhatta*," in Horak, *Lovers of Cinema*, 267.

3. Sergei Eisenstein, *The Film Sense* (London: Faber and Faber, 1948), 83, quoted in Scott McQuire, "Immaterial Architectures: Urban Space and Electric Light," *Space and Culture* 8 (2005): 126.

4. Kepes, *Language of Vision*, 154. Opposite this discussion, Kepes reproduces a Bernice Abbott photograph, "Night View" (1932), taken from a high angle looking down on nighttime New York.

5. Interview with James Hollander, 31 October 2012, Burbank, CA.

6. Sullivan, "Work of Saul Bass," 67.

7. Bass and Kirkham, *Saul Bass*, 3.

8. See Mike Connolly, "Rambling Reporter," *Hollywood Reporter*, 16 December 1952, 2. See also the production history of the film in the *American Film Institute Catalog of Motion Pictures*, http://www.afi.com/members/catalog/DetailView .aspx?s=&Movie=51652.

9. See "Feldman Pays 225G for '7 Year Itch,'" *Hollywood Reporter*, 20 February 1953, 1; *Los Angeles Daily News* clipping, 8 March 1953, and unidentified clipping, 12 May 1954, *Seven Year Itch* production files, microfilm, Margaret Herrick Library, AMPAS.

10. "Main Titles by NSS!" *Variety*, 10 August 1955, 17.

11. According to George Axelrod, who was interviewed for the DVD edition of the film, he and Wilder fought huge battles with Joseph Breen's MPPC Office and were forced to eliminate or rewrite numerous lines of dialogue.

12. Land, "*The Seven Year Itch*," *Daily Variety*, 8 June 1955, 6.

13. Jack Moffitt, "*The Seven Year Itch*," *Hollywood Reporter*, 3 June 1955, 3; the *Showman's* and *Motion Picture Daily* reviews are quoted in "Main Titles by NSS!"

14. Quoted in Lowell E. Redelings, "Men behind the Scenes," *Los Angeles Citizen News*, 24 October 1955, box 23A, file 8, "Clippings," Saul Bass Papers, Margaret Herrick Library, AMPAS.

15. In *Billy Wilder's Filme* (Berlin: Verlag Volker Spiess, 1980), 389, Neil Sinyard and Adrian Turner argue that the opening and closing of boxes refer to the game of confusion in Feydeau's farces.

16. Susan Reed and Doris Bacon, "Director Billy Wilder Puts His Legendary $22 Million-or-So Art Collection on the Auction Block," *People*, 13 November 1989, http://www.people.com/people/archive/article/0,,20115935,00.html.

17. See "*Four Just Men*," Dinosaur TV website, http://www.78rpm.co.uk/tv4 .htm.

18. Titles for *Four Just Men*, 16mm print, 11693-1, Saul Bass Collection, Academy Film Archive, AMPAS.

19. Bass and Kirkham, *Saul Bass*, 44.

20. Apparently, Bass produced a title sequence for *The Young Stranger* that consisted solely of graphics; it is in the Saul Bass Collection, 57998-1, Academy Film Archive, AMPAS. Like the published version, Bass's original begins with the camera zooming in and around a close-up pencil drawing of a young man's face; then it con-

tinues panning to a close-up of the eye before cutting to a second pencil-drawn image of a young man walking away, his back to the observer, while the camera zooms in on the back of his head for Frankenheimer's directorial credit. The final version dissolves to a young male student walking on campus, immediately after the costarring credits. It is highly likely that Bass removed his name from the final credits—which are included in the original version—due to these changes. Was Frankenheimer unable to pay for all the designs, or did he think they were too weird, leading him to abbreviate the graphic portion? Although the Bass Papers include photos of the graphic designs, no correspondence survives to clear up this issue. See "The Young Stranger," box 14A, file 40–41, Saul Bass Papers, Margaret Herrick Library, AMPAS.

21. See Leonard J. Leff, "Hitchcock at Metro," *Western Humanities Review* 37, no. 2 (Summer 1983): 97.

22. In Bass and Kirkham, *Saul Bass*, 182, this image is still overlaid with a grid, but it isn't in the film.

23. The elevator metaphor is evoked by Bass himself in his official description of the sequence; see *North by Northwest*, "Title Description," box 4A, file 35, Saul Bass Papers, Margaret Herrick Library, AMPAS. Beth Gilligan's description of the sequence doesn't mention the element of the counterweight; see *North by Northwest*, 2005, http://www.notcoming.com/saulbass/caps_nxnw.php.

24. Spoto, *Art of Alfred Hitchcock*, 353.

25. "Violent green" is Bass's adjective in the official description of the titles, box 4A, file 35, Saul Bass Papers, Margaret Herrick Library, AMPAS.

26. Hitchcock is seen most famously as an annoyed reader on the London subway in *Blackmail* (1929), in Victoria Station in *The Lady Vanishes* (1938), on a train in *Shadow of a Doubt* (1943), leaving a train with a cello case in *The Paradine Case* (1947), boarding a train with a bass in *Strangers on a Train* (1951), and sitting on a bus in *To Catch a Thief* (1955).

27. Art, "*Alcoa Premiere*," *Variety*, 18 October 1961, 35, reprinted in *Variety Television Reviews 1923–1988* (New York: Garland Publishing, 1989).

28. See http://www.imdb.com/title/tt0054513/plotsummary; Tim Brooks and Earle Marsh, eds., *The Complete Directory to Prime Time Network and Cable Shows: 1946–Present* (New York: Ballantine Books, 1999), 7, 24.

29. See Connie Bruck, *When Hollywood Had a King* (New York: Random House, 2003), 162, 186; Dennis McDougal, *The Last Mogul: Lew Wasserman, MCA, and the Hidden History of Hollywood* (New York: Crown Publishers, 1998), 189–91, 193.

30. See *Al-Zalean*, March–June 1963 and September–October 1964; e-mail from Carol Ellis, director, University of South Alabama Archives, 6 May 2011.

31. See Bass and Kirkham, *Saul Bass*, 294. The brochure's cover features a highly abstract, modernist design of green, blue, and purple bars, similar to the design concept for Frank Sinatra's album *Tone Poems of Color* (1956) and Bass's *Psycho* titles.

32. Alcoa advertisement, *Wall Street Journal*, 21 February 1963, 12.

33. See "Alcoa Changes Its Trademark," *Industrial Marketing* 38 (February 1963): 120; "Alcoa's Public Relations Department Played Key Role in Introducing New Logo," *PR News*, 23 December 1963, reprinted in David P. Bianco, ed., *PR*

News Casebook: 1,000 Public Relations Case Studies (Detroit: Gale Research, 1993), 1574.

34. Bass and Kirkham, *Saul Bass*, 296.

35. See "Alcoa New Mark TV Commercial," 15014-1, 16159-1, Saul Bass Collection, Academy Film Archive, AMPAS.

36. "In London," *Daily Variety*, 24 August 1965, 4.

37. Reprinted in Bass and Kirkham, *Saul Bass*, 295.

38. The *Hollywood Reporter* notes that the main titles would be completed the week of 26 June. See "'West Side' Windup," *Hollywood Reporter*, 27 June 1961, 10.

39. Bass recalled that the opening for *West Side Story* was "a take-off on the earlier title design for *North by Northwest*." See Morgenstern, "Saul Bass," 42.

40. In an extra on the 2003 DVD release, Robbins states that he had been trying to produce a modern version of Shakespeare's play since the 1940s. However, since Robbins had no film directing experience, he was relegated to codirector status. See also Lars-Olav Beier, *Der unbestechliche Blick. Robert Wise und Seine Filme* (Berlin: Bertz Verlag, 1996), 87.

41. "*West Side Story*," *Filmfacts*, 3 November 1961, 245–48. See also *Daily Variety*, 7 December 1960. Robbins completed the prologue and the musical numbers "America," "Cool," and "I Feel Pretty." See Beier, *Robert Wise und Seine Filme*, 88.

42. Arthur Knight, "Romeo Revisited: *West Side Story*," *Saturday Review*, 14 October 1961, 40.

43. See James Powers, "*West Side Story* Hailed as B.O. Smash, Great Film Work," *Hollywood Reporter*, 6 October 1961, 3; Whit, "*West Side Story*," *Variety*, 27 September 1961, 6.

44. Todd McCarthy, "Jets Have Their Way Onscreen," *Daily Variety*, 5 June 2009, 8. See also James D. Ivers, "*West Side Story*," *Motion Picture Herald*, 4 October 1961; Frank Leyendecker, "*West Side Story*," *Box Office*, 4 October 1961, all in production files, Margaret Herrick Library, AMPAS.

45. It has been suggested that the dancing figures, visible in the production's letterhead, were altered by the studio to be more figurative. See Bass and Kirkham, *Saul Bass*, 199.

46. See the auction history and images for *West Side Story* at http://www.emovieposter.com/agallery/film_title/WEST%2520SIDE%2520STORY%2520%28%2761%29/archive.html.

47. Bass and Kirkham, *Saul Bass*, 200–201. Ascertaining credit here is as complicated as the sequences Bass designed for *Psycho* and *Spartacus*.

48. See the anecdote in T. J. Edwards, "*West Side Story*, 1961 Road Show Feature," Cinema Sightlines website, http://cinemasightlines.com/roadshow_westsidestory.php.

49. Marino Amoruso and John Gallagher, "Robert Wise: Part One 'The RKO Years,'" *Grand Illusions* (Winter 1977), quoted in Frank Thompson, *Robert Wise: A Bio-Bibliography* (Westport, CT: Greenwood Press, 1995), 82.

50. David Badder, Bob Baker, and Markku Salmi, "Saul Bass," *Film Dope* 3 (August 1973): 4.

51. See the sequence on YouTube: http://www.youtube.com/watch?v=A7tL7-gXjPk. I'm grateful to Arnold Schwartzman for alerting me to this film.

52. Although there is no documentation, the trailer's construction indicates that Bass may have been involved. See *West Side Story* trailer, http://www.youtube.com/watch?v=5G31aw3R0x4.

53. Eugene Archer, "Capturing Something Wild for the Camera," *New York Times*, 8 July 1960, production files, Margaret Herrick Library, AMPAS.

54. See *Hollywood Reporter*, 3 June 1961.

55. Interview with Jack Garfein, 19 September 2010, Los Angeles.

56. Albert Johnson, "Jack Garfein: An Interview," *Film Quarterly* 17, no. 1 (Autumn 1963): 36.

57. "*Something Wild*," *New Yorker*, 30 December 1961, 45.

58. "Films of the Quarter," *Film Quarterly* 15, no. 3 (Spring 1962): 71.

59. See, for example, J. Hobermann's 2006 review in the *Village Voice*, http://www.villagevoice.com/2006–12–19/film/method-to-her-madness/.

60. Hazel Flynn, "*Something Wild* Is Strange Enigma," *Los Angeles Citizen News*, 18 May 1962, production files, Margaret Herrick Library, AMPAS.

61. Johnson, "Jack Garfein," 36.

62. Flavia Wharton, "*Something Wild*," *Films in Review*, February 1962, 110.

63. *A Star Is Born* (1954), trade advertisement, reproduction in the possession of Al Kallis.

64. Bass and Kirkham, *Saul Bass*, 52, 396.

65. Thanks to Dino Everett, director of the Hugh Hefner Film Archive at the University of Southern California, who graciously gave me access to the show.

66. See *Playhouse 90: Journey to the Day*, broadcast 22 April 1960, tape available at Archive Research and Study Center, UCLA Film and Television Archive.

67. See *Playhouse 90* opening description, box 16A, file 28, Saul Bass Papers, Margaret Herrick Library, AMPAS.

68. Hal Erickson, *Syndicated Television: The First Forty Years, 1947–1987* (Jefferson, NC: McFarland, 1989), 168–69.

69. See the Westinghouse magazine advertisement in Bass and Kirkham, *Saul Bass*, 49.

70. "*PM East* [TV] Opening Description," box 16A, file 29, Saul Bass Papers, Margaret Herrick Library, AMPAS.

71. Tube, "*Ocean's Eleven*," *Variety*, 10 August 1960, 6.

72. For a detailed history of the film's production, as reflected in the press, see *The American Film Institute Catalog of Motion Pictures Produced in the United States*, vol. 6, *Feature Films, 1961–1970* (Berkeley: University of California Press, 1971).

73. See "Lawford to Vegas," *Daily Variety*, 31 October 1958, 5; "*Ocean's* Start Date," *Daily Variety*, 25 November 1958, 18; "Bill of the Year ('60): Frankie, Dino & Sammy," *Weekly Variety*, 4 November 1959, 1, 58.

74. See *Los Angeles Examiner*, 7 August 1960, 9, 12.

75. Unidentified *Hollywood Reporter* clipping, "*Ocean's Eleven*, Clippings," box 4A, file 77, Saul Bass Papers, Margaret Herrick Library, AMPAS.

76. Tube, "*Ocean's Eleven*," *Variety*, 10 August 1960, 6.

77. Blog post by Mark Webster, *Ocean's Eleven*, 23 April 2009, http://motiondesign.wordpress.com/.

78. According to James Hollander, the Bass office created hundreds of drawings to visualize the creative process of designing a new corporate logo for executives at AT&T. Interview with James Hollander, 31 October 2012, Burbank, CA.

79. Martin Scorsese, interview by the British Film Institute, 11 February 1993, VHS tape, 15163-1-1, Saul Bass Collection, Academy Film Archive, AMPAS.

80. Quoted in Pat Kirkham, "Bright Lights, Big City," *Sight & Sound* 6 (January 1996): 12–13.

81. E-mail from Sean Savage to the author, 15 March 2013.

82. Beier and Midding, *Vorspann: Zum Werk von Saul Bass*.

83. Letter from Douglas Owens (Universal Pictures) to Saul Bass, 21 September 1994; letter from SEB to Martin Scorsese, 26 October 1994 (includes Bass's actual sketch below the designers' signatures), "Letterhead," box 2A, file 2, Saul Bass Papers, Margaret Herrick Library, AMPAS.

84. Letter from Elaine and Saul Bass to Barbara De Fina, 19 June 1995, sent via fax, "Casino Costs," box 2A, file 18, Saul Bass Papers, Margaret Herrick Library, AMPAS.

85. Mick LaSalle, "Scorsese's 'Casino' Comes up Broke/Stone's the Only Ace in a Bad Hand," *San Francisco Chronicle*, 22 November 1995, http://www.sfgate.com/movies/article/Scorsese-s-Casino-Comes-Up-Broke-Stone-s-the-3018766.php.

86. Janet Maslin, "A Money-Mad Mirage from Scorsese," *New York Times*, 22 November 1995, 9; Peter Travers, "*Casino*," *Rolling Stone*, 22 November 1995, http://www.rollingstone.com/movies/reviews/casino-19951122. Travers wrote: "With *Casino*, based on material from Nicholas Pileggi's nonfiction book (names have been changed and events altered for the film), Scorsese tries to weave visual poetry out of warped ambitions."

87. In the correspondence for *Casino*, the Basses specifically request to see the footage of the *Exodus* flames, which may or may not have been recycled here.

88. The Capitol Records album (SM-1573) was released in 1961. See http://www.discogs.com/Stan-Freberg-Presents-The-United-States-Of-America-Vol-1-The-Early-Years/master/281065. The show's bumper was also produced by Bass and included the same extreme low-angle shot of pedestrians found in *Something Wild*.

89. Walter Herdeg, ed., *Film and TV Graphics: An International Survey of Film and Television Graphics* (Zurich: Graphis Press, 1967), 79.

90. Tube, "Stan Freberg Presents Chinese New Year's Eve," *Daily Variety*, 6 February 1962, 16.

91. "National Bohemian Beer—Record of Work Done," box 62A, file 20, Saul Bass Papers, Margaret Herrick Library, AMPAS.

92. "Lights Out," "Peanut," and "Don't Touch that Dial," 16mm, 21768-1, Saul Bass Collection, Academy Film Archive, AMPAS.

93. There were numerous commercials for Rainier beer, including "Awakening" (twenty seconds), "Storm and Clearing" (thirty seconds), and "Aerial" (one minute), dated 28 December 1966. See "Rainier Brewing Company Storyboard Descriptions," box 64A, file 29, Saul Bass Papers, Margaret Herrick Library, and the 16mm color prints, 17608-1, Saul Bass Collection, Academy Film Archive, AMPAS. These are the least Bass-like of any of his work, so he may have been only minimally involved in their production.

94. "Andy Parker aka Regular Joe," National Bohemian beer, 16mm, 21768-1, Saul Bass Collection, Academy Film Archive, AMPAS.

95. Ibid., 78788-1.

96. See "Burnt Match," "Peanut," and "Lights Out," National Bohemian beer, 16mm, 21874-1, Saul Bass Collection, Academy Film Archive, AMPAS.

6. Journeys of Discovery: Seeing Is Knowledge

1. The literature on this phenomenon is voluminous. See Tom Gunning, "An Unseen Energy Swallows Space: The Space in Early Film and Its Relation to American Avant-Garde Film," in *Film before Griffith*, ed. John L. Fell (Berkeley: University of California Press, 1983), 355–66.

2. Letter from Geoffrey Shurlock (MPAA/PCA) to David Susskind, 16 March 1956, Production Code Administration files, Margaret Herrick Library, AMPAS.

3. "*Edge of the City*," *Daily Variety*, 26 December 1956, 3.

4. Bosley Crowther, "*Edge of the City*," *New York Times*, 30 January 1957, http://movies.nytimes.com/movie/review?res=9D04E6DF143EE23BBC4850DFB766838C649EDE.

5. Edwin Fancher, "Movies: *Edge of the City*," *Village Voice*, 3 April 1957, http://news.google.com/newspapers?id=Pd4QAAAAIBAJ&sjid=EIwDAAAAIBAJ&pg=6609,4662036&dq=movies&hl=en.

6. The DVD version of *Edge of the City*, distributed by Warner Brothers Home Video, is missing the rectangular light patterns.

7. *American Film Institute Seminar*, 14.

8. "Uris Scripts Wyler Film," *Hollywood Reporter*, 9 May 1957, 2.

9. Jan Herman, *A Talent for Trouble: William Wyler* (New York: G. P. Putnam's Sons, 1995), 382.

10. Letter from Gregory Peck to Leon Roth, 11 April 1957, Gregory Peck Papers, Margaret Herrick Library Special Collections, AMPAS, quoted in Jason Gendler, "Saul Bass and Title Design: Intention and Reception, and Production Integration" (paper presented at Society of Cinema and Media Studies Conference, Los Angeles, March 2010).

11. *The Big Country* press book, production files, Margaret Herrick Library, AMPAS.

12. Axel Madsen, *William Wyler* (New York: Thomas Y. Crowell, 1973), 333.

13. For technical details about Technirama, see http://www.widescreenmuseum.com/widescreen/techniramaspecs.htm.

14. Saul Bass, "Thoughts on Film," in *Communication: The Art of Understand-*

ing and Being Understood, ed. Robert O. Bach (New York: Hastings House, 1963), 23.

15. Herman, *Talent for Trouble*, 392. See also Michael Freedland, *Gregory Peck* (New York: William Morrow, 1980), 151.

16. W. R. Wilkerson, "Trade Views," *Hollywood Reporter*, 25 August 1958, 2.

17. Bosley Crowther, "War and Peace on Range in 'Big Country'; Gregory Peck Stars in Wyler's Western; Action-Packed Film Scores Violence," *New York Times*, 2 October 1958, 44.

18. P. J. D., "*The Big Country*," *Monthly Film Bulletin*, 12 November 1958, 14.

19. "*The Big Country*," *Time*, 8 September 1958, 96, quoted in Madsen, *William Wyler*, 333.

20. The *Big Country* poster reproduced in Bass and Kirkham, *Saul Bass*, 174, is not one of the release posters; it is Bass's own preferred silk-screen design.

21. "Graphics—Mr. Saul Bass," in *International Television Design Conference* (London: BBC Television Centre, 1962), 8.

22. Chris Fujiwara, *The World and Its Double: The Life and Work of Otto Preminger* (New York: Faber and Faber, 2008), 299.

23. "Report Cardinal Spellman Frowns on 'Cardinal' Film as Invasion of Privacy," *Daily Variety*, 10 August 1955, 2.

24. Hirsch, *Otto Preminger*, 370.

25. "Two Soviet Directors Arrive to Observe Preminger Megging 'The Cardinal' Here," *Daily Variety*, 6 May 1963, 1.

26. "Cardinal Rentals Pass $7 Million Mark," *Hollywood Reporter*, 22 May 1964, 1.

27. Bosley Crowther, "Episodes of a Man of the Cloth: 'The Cardinal' Opens at the DeMille," *New York Times*, 13 December 1963.

28. Irene Thirer, "*The Cardinal*," *New York Post*, 13 December 1963, quoted in Hirsch, *Otto Preminger*, 385.

29. Hollis Alpert, "A Cardinal's Chronicle," *Saturday Review*, 7 December 1963, 32. See also Hazel Flynn, "Otto Preminger Oozes Optimism," *Los Angeles Citizen News*, 8 December 1963, box 2A, file 11, "Clippings," Saul Bass Papers, Margaret Herrick Library, AMPAS.

30. In the strangest placement of a Bass design in any trailer, the logo and poster are shown twice, but only briefly in the background as set decoration. Was this done to avoid the payment of further royalties? See *The Cardinal* trailer, which is a mini "making of" movie, at http://www.youtube.com/watch?v=mdH2ivqB1Uc.

31. See *The Cardinal*, "Titles Description," box 2A, file 15, Saul Bass Papers, Margaret Herrick Library, AMPAS.

32. Edward Dmytryk, *It's a Hell of a Life but Not a Bad Living* (New York: New York Times Books, 1978), 247.

33. Michael Bierut, "Catching the Big One," *ID: The International Design Magazine* 42, no. 1 (January–February 1995): 48.

34. "Feldman Packaging 'Wild Side' for UA; Capucine to Star," *Daily Variety*, 24 January 1961, 1.

35. "Actor Harvey No Fan of Feldman," *Variety*, 9 May 1962, 5.

36. "Feldman Cancels Wild New Orleans; Complains of City Fathers' Hostility," *Daily Variety*, 20 February 1962, 1.

37. Nic Francis, "Bass PHASE IV," *Screen 'n' Heard*, March 1973, 10.

38. Interview with Arnold Schwartzman, 20 February 2013, Los Angeles.

39. *Walk on the Wild Side*, "Titles Description," box 13A, file 49, Saul Bass Papers, Margaret Herrick Library, AMPAS.

40. Quoted in Francis, "Bass PHASE IV," 10.

41. See Hedda Hopper, "Old World Charm Seen as Decadence," *Los Angeles Times*, 15 February 1962, pt. IV, 20; Brendan Gill, "*Walk on the Wild Side*," *New Yorker*, 24 February 1962, 111.

42. See Philip K. Scheurer, "*Walk on the Wild Side* Tame?" *Los Angeles Times*, 8 March 1962; "*Walk on the Wild Side*," *Show Business Illustrated*, April 1962.

43. Hazel Flynn, "'Wild Side' Film Suspense Shocker," *Los Angeles Citizen News*, 8 March 1962. See also James D. Ivers, "*A Walk on the Wild Side*," *Motion Picture Herald*, 7 February 1962; Lawrence H. Lipskin, "*A Walk on the Wild Side* Strong*," *Hollywood Reporter*, 29 January 1962, 3.

44. Dennis McLellan, "Judith Crist Dies at 90; Film Critic 'Most Hated by Hollywood,'" *Los Angeles Times*, 8 August 2012.

45. Judith Crist, "This Week's Movies," *TV Guide*, n.d., clipping in "*Walk on the Wild Side*," box 13A, file 44, Saul Bass Papers, Margaret Herrick Library, AMPAS.

46. See the entry in *Oxford English Dictionary*, http://www.oed.com/view/Entry/266205#eid43330280.

47. A photo of the theater and a brief description of the film are available on the 1964 World's Fair website, http://www.worldsfairphotos.com/nywf64transportation-travel.htm.

48. *From Here to There*, "Awards," box 3A, file 24, Saul Bass Papers, Margaret Herrick Library, AMPAS.

49. See the Pyramid Films catalog description. The 16mm film rented for $15 and could be purchased outright for $130.

50. "*From Here to There*," *Cue Magazine*, 11 July 1964.

51. Undated review from *Hollywood Reporter*, *From Here to There*, "Clippings," box 3A, file 25, Saul Bass Papers, Margaret Herrick Library, AMPAS; "Turn Your Dream to Reality," *Los Angeles Herald Examiner*, 12 July 1964. See also "New York Fair," *Time*, 3 July 1964.

52. See Moholy-Nagy, *New Vision* (2005), 38, 183, 202; Kepes, *Language of Vision*, 74.

53. See http://www.worldsfairphotos.com/nywf64/kodak.htm.

54. "Saul Bass' 'Searching 1-Eye' Spotlights Eastman Kodak's Tiptop Exhibit," *Variety*, 29 April 1964, 178. A second industrial film, produced in-house by Kodak, was shown in a smaller theater in the pavilion, also on the half hour.

55. Myron A. Matzkin, "Movie Maker," *Modern Photography*, July 1964, 111.

56. Sean Savage notes in a 15 March 2013 e-mail: "The film was projected first as a 35/70 interlocked projection onto a single screen. The imagery is checker-boarded

between the two strands of film, one falling away to make room for the other. And as for versions, I'm pretty convinced a shorter dual-system edit replaced the first version during its run in the Kodak Pavilion. There was a third, possibly unfinished single-strand 35mm version, and the 16mm Pyramid version had a completely new narration."

57. See Kodak publicity brochure, *Groundbreaking at the New York World's Fair, 1964–65* (New York: New York World's Fair Corporation, 1962), 6, http://www .worldsfairphotos.com/nywf64/booklets/kodak-groundbreaking-8-21-62.pdf.

58. The index card states: "Photo, pavilion proposal." See "Eastman Kodak Co.—Record of Work Done," box 50A, file 21, Saul Bass Papers, Margaret Herrick Library, AMAPS. See also Bass and Kirkham, *Saul Bass*, 92–93; *Saul Bass & Associates v. United States*, no. 373-68, U.S. Court of Claims, July 19, 1974, http://www.leagle.com/decision/19741891505F2d1386_11626.xml/SAUL%20BASS%20&%20ASSOCIATES%20v.%20UNITED%20STATES.

59. "Saul Bass Producing Eastman Kodak Short," *Hollywood Reporter*, 19 September 1963, 8; "Moppet Lane 'Eye-d,'" *Daily Variety*, 1 October 1963, 3.

60. See Ute Eskildsen and Jan-Christopher Horak, eds., *Film und Foto der zwanziger Jahre* (Stuttgart: Verlag Gerd Hatje, 1979); Jan-Christopher Horak, "Film and Foto: Towards a Language of Silent Film," *Afterimage* 7, no. 5 (December 1979).

61. *The Searching Eye*, "Misc. 1970," box 10A, file 38, Saul Bass Papers, Margaret Herrick Library, AMPAS.

62. Quoted in David A. Sohn, "The 'Eyes' Have It," in Pyramid Films, *The Searching Eye* brochure, reprinted in *Media & Methods*, September 1970.

63. See Jacob Deschin, "Novel Pavilion Has Various Program of Shorts and Picture Services," *New York Times*, 19 April 1964; Bosley Crowther, "The Screen: Creative and Exhilarating," *New York Times*, 23 April 1964, 1, 12; Bosley Crowther, "Advance in Art of Cinema Seen in Film at World's Fair," *New York Times*, 10 May 1964; Bosley Crowther, "Once More to the Fair," *New York Times*, 5 September 1964.

64. "Come to the Fair. Meet Me at the Kodak Picture Tower," *New York Times*, 26 April 1964, sec. 11.

65. Deschin, "Novel Pavilion"; *The Searching Eye*, "Clippings," box 10A, file 36, Saul Bass Papers, Margaret Herrick Library, AMPAS.

66. James Powers, "H'wood Mastery Marks World's Fair Films," *Hollywood Reporter*, 29 May 1964 , 3.

67. Matzkin, "Movie Maker," 111. See also Ralph Miller, "Kodak Opens Fair Exhibit with Bass' 'The Searching Eye,'" *New York World-Telegram and Sun*, 16 April 1964, 44; "World's Fair 'Sells' Photography," *Photo Weekly*, 27 April 1964; Judith Crist, "Guilded Tokens and New Techniques," *New York Herald Tribune*, 31 May 1964, 21; "Lens Lines," *Camera* 35 (June–July 1964); Irving Desfor (Associated Press), "Imaginative Movies Fascinate Fairgoers," *Pomona Progress Bulletin*, 21 June 1964.

68. "Kodak Pavilion a World's Fair Success," Kodak press release, 15 October 1965, http://www.nywf64.com/easkod10.shtml.

69. The logo later appeared on Kodak's mid-1960s 16mm Pageant projectors. See http://cdn.krrb.com/post_images/photos/000/104/824/P1120391_large .jpg?1362076100.

70. See "Sol Lesser Signs Sandy Lane," *Box Office*, 3 August 1964, production files, Margaret Herrick Library, AMPAS.

71. See Sohn, "The 'Eyes' Have It."

72. According to an article published in September 1986, the film was "not yet in theatrical release." See "The Making of *Quest*," *Step-by-Step Graphics* 2, no. 5 (September–October 1986): 36.

73. Interview with Herb Yager, 27 February 2013, Ojai, CA.

74. See "Saul Bass & Associates," special issue, *IDEA* (1979). See also the statement by Saul and Elaine Bass in Marsha Jeffer and Pauline G. Weber, *Study Guide to* Quest (Santa Monica, CA: Pyramid Films, 1985), 3.

75. Quoted on the M. Okada International Association website, http://www .moainternational.or.jp/en/intro/intr01.html.

76. Bass and Kirkham, *Saul Bass*, 253.

77. "Production Budgets QUEST, Dated March 1981," box 9A, file 4, Saul Bass Papers, Margaret Herrick Library, AMPAS.

78. Letter from Saul Bass to Ray Bradbury, 8 December 1980. Per a signed letter of agreement dated 24 December 1980, Bradbury was paid $22,500 for the first and final shooting scripts. See "Ray Bradbury," box 7A, file 33, Saul Bass Papers, Margaret Herrick Library, AMPAS.

79. Quoted in Jeffer and Weber, *Study Guide to* Quest, 3.

80. In a letter to Takahiro Yamaguchi dated 24 July 1981, Saul Bass reported on his preproduction work to church officials, noting that "adhering to our budget creates still more work—that is finding unique ways to achieve very costly effects at a price we can afford, without a loss of quality." See "Overseas Data Service," box 8, file 27, Saul Bass Papers, Margaret Herrick Library, AMPAS.

81. Interview with Jeff Okun, 23 March 2012, Hollywood, CA.

82. Telex from Herb Yager to Takahiro Yamaguchi, 7 November 1983, "*Quest* Film Festivals," box 8A, file 6, Saul Bass Papers, Margaret Herrick Library, AMPAS.

83. See "*Quest* Film Festivals," box 8A, file 6, Saul Bass Papers, Margaret Herrick Library, AMPAS.

84. The Pyramid print of *Quest* is available on YouTube in its entirety: http:// www.youtube.com/watch?v=Zcb-M5a4Uy8&feature=related.

85. Vladimir Propp, *Morphology of the Folktale* (Austin: University of Texas Press, 1968).

86. Paul Ricoeur, "Narrative Time," *Critical Inquiry* 7, no. 1 (Autumn 1980): 184.

87. Jeffer and Weber, *Study Guide to* Quest, 3.

88. The falling rocks were slowed down by overcranking to as much as sixty-four frames per second. See "The Making of *Quest*," 46.

89. Bass inserted a similar game between a baboon and a child in shot 87 of the deleted original ending for *Phase IV*. I'm grateful to Sean Savage for pointing this out to me. E-mail from Sean Savage to the author, 15 March 2013.

90. Memo from Masa Miura to Dick Huppertz, 25 November 1981, "Overseas Data Service," box 8A, file 27, Saul Bass Papers, Margaret Herrick Library, AMPAS.

91. Ibid.

92. Jeffer and Weber, *Study Guide to* Quest, 4.

93. Ibid.

94. Carole Wade and Carol Tarvris, *Psychology*, 3rd ed. (New York: HarperCollins, 1993). The cover is reproduced in Bass and Kirkham, *Saul Bass*, 377.

95. Carole Cox, "Electric Media: New Short Films for the Humanities," *English Journal* 74, no. 7 (November 1985): 96.

96. See "The Making of *Quest*," 40.

97. See the landscape drawing in ibid., 38.

98. Ricoeur, "Narrative Time," 184.

7. Civilization: Organizing Knowledge through Communication

1. "Print Personality: Saul Bass," *Print* 11, no. 6 (May–June 1958): 18.

2. See "Col Acquires 'Cowboy' from Horizon Pictures," *Daily Variety*, 15 January 1953, 6; Mike Connolly, "Rambling Reporter," *Hollywood Reporter*, 21 June 1954, 2.

3. See *Los Angeles Times*, July 1956, quoted in the American Film Institute catalog, http://www.afi.com/members/catalog/DetailView.aspx?s=&Movie=52509.

4. Dalton Trumbo's writing credit was reinstated by the Writers Guild in 2000. See *Hollywood Reporter*, 4 August 2000.

5. Jean-Louis Rieupeyrout, "Au pays du Western," *Cinéma 61*, quoted in Will Wehlig, ed., *Delmar Daves* (Oberhausen: Verlag Karl Maria Laufen, 1972), 101–2.

6. James Powers, "Cowboy," *Variety*, 12 February 1958, 6; Bosley Crowther, "Cowboy," *New York Times*, 20 February 1958. See also "Thank You Note to Critics," *Daily Variety*, 13 March 1958, 7–11.

7. Derek Prouse, "Cowboy," *Monthly Film Bulletin* 25, no. 290 (1958): 31.

8. See *Newsweek*, 17 February 1958, 106; *Time*, 17 February 1958, 64; *New Yorker*, 1 March 1958, 107; *Saturday Review*, 1 March 1958, 26.

9. Stephen Harvey, *Directed by Vincente Minnelli* (New York: Museum of Modern Art/Harper and Row, 1989), 263.

10. "'4 Horsemen' Reins Handed Blaustein," *Daily Variety*, 11 July 1958, 1.

11. Thomas Quinn Curtiss, "Four Horsemen to Ride Again," *New York Herald Tribune Paris*, 17 August 1960, *Four Horsemen of the Apocalypse*, production files, Margaret Herrick Library, AMPAS.

12. Harvey, *Directed by Minnelli*, 264.

13. See *Four Horsemen of the Apocalypse* trade advertisement in *Daily Variety*, 13 September 1961, 29. It uses the torn-paper design Bass would later use for *Bunny Lake Is Missing*.

14. The montages survive in the Saul Bass Papers; see *The Four Horsemen of the Apocalypse*, "Production Elements, Unused War Montages." It has been argued that Elaine and Saul spent months looking for World War II footage for *The Victors*, yet Mike Lonzo, who worked on the *Victors*, has no memory of Elaine being around. In

fact, Elaine Bass may have been misremembering which film she worked on, having pulled the material for *Four Horsemen* instead. See Bass and Kirkham, *Saul Bass*, 210; interview with Mike Lonzo, 19 September 2012; Mike Lonzo posting, 4 September 2007, http://www.filmscoremonthly.com/board/posts.cfm?threadID=44652& forumID&.

15. Jean Douchet, "The Red and the Green: *The Four Horsemen of the Apocalypse*," in *Vincente Minnelli*, ed. Joe McElhaney (Detroit: Wayne State University Press, 2009), 42.

16. Existing footage from the actual speech shows a crowd made up exclusively of uniformed Nazi storm troopers, while Hitler himself is seen only in long shot, neither of which suited Bass's purposes. See the newsreel excerpt at http://www.youtube.com/watch?v=JI9fpBiRCMw.

17. See Bass and Kirkham, *Saul Bass*, 210. The authors confirm that images from *San Francisco* were used, but again, they suggest that the images were intended for *The Victors* prologue, for which they were also used.

18. Ibid.

19. In the mid-1960s Bass was seemingly becoming a montage specialist, much as Slavko Vorkapich had been in classical Hollywood. For example, it was announced that he would do an opening prologue for George Roy Hill's *Hawaii* (1966) and the titles and special effects for Blake Edwards's *The Party* (1968). See Army Archerd, "Just for Variety," *Daily Variety*, 15 February 1966, 2; "Ray, Wilson to Film 'The Alien' for Col," *Daily Variety*, 12 June 1967, 1.

20. "Carl Foreman Turns to Directing," *Daily Variety*, 7 December 1960, 1, 4.

21. Bosley Crowther, "*The Victors*," *New York Times*, 20 December 1963; Arthur Knight, "*The Victors*," *Saturday Review*, 14 December 1963, 24.

22. See Harrison Carroll, "*Victors* Grim Film," *Los Angeles Herald Examiner*, 23 December 1963, B-4; Richard Gertner, "*The Victors*," *Motion Picture Herald*, 27 November 1963; PGB, "*The Victors*," *Films & Filming*, January 1964.

23. J. S., "*The Victors* Prologue by Saul Bass," *Cinema*, February–March 1964.

24. According to Mike Lonzo: "I recall that we worked, off-and-on, nearly six months on this prologue. As it exists now in the film, it is only about half its original work print length. It was a very detailed visual essay on WWI, the aftermath, the rise of the political postwar developments in Germany, the rise of Hitler, and the beginning of WWII—all of which led into the Main Title, and then, in effect, was the historical setup for the film." Lonzo posting, 2007.

25. The storyboards for *The Victors* are reproduced in Bass and Kirkham, *Saul Bass*, 212–13.

26. "*The Victors*—Title Description," box 13A, file 42, Saul Bass Papers, Margaret Herrick Library, AMPAS.

27. Unfortunately, the prints available in the Saul Bass Collection, Academy Film Archive, AMPAS, are completely red, so it is impossible to tell what parts of the film were in black and white and what parts were in color.

28. "How to Compare Apples and Oranges," *Broadcasting Magazine*, 28 January 1963, 30.

29. Arthur Perles, "TV Sales-Muscle Kayos Mags," *Radio Television Daily*, 28 January 1963, 1, 3.

30. "*Apples and Oranges*—Food for Thought. How CBS Sells a Concept," *Telefilm* 8, no. 5 (May 1963): 30.

31. See the cover image in Dick Hess and Marion Muller, *Dorfsman & CBS* (New York: American Showcase, 1987), 138. See also *Radio Television Daily*, 13 February 1963, 6–7. For a similar design concept, see General Control Company advertisement (1956) in Bass and Kirkham, *Saul Bass*, 51.

32. Perles, "TV Sales-Muscle Kayos Mags," 3. The shooting was handled by Format Films, according to this source. See also "How to Compare Apples and Oranges," 34.

33. "How to Compare Apples and Oranges," 31.

34. Bass and Kirkham, *Saul Bass*, 77, 156–57.

35. "*Apples and Oranges*—Food for Thought," 31.

36. Bass and Kirkham, *Saul Bass*, 47.

37. The computer punch-hole design would appear as early as 1957 in Bass's posters and titles for *Edge of the City* and in a report for the California Test Bureau (1957). However, the design is most obvious in two infomercials made for IBM in 1962, "The History of Invention" and "Cancer Research." See Bass and Kirkham, *Saul Bass*, 80, 97.

38. Bass had used a coat-wearing figure exposing himself for an advertisement for KLH Research and Development in 1957. See Bass and Kirkham, *Saul Bass*, 77.

39. "AT&T, One Hundred Years of the Telephone," box 44A, files 10, 15, 19, Saul Bass Papers, Margaret Herrick Library, AMPAS.

40. "Pantomime Pictures Inc. Tentative Production Schedule *100 Years of the Telephone*," box 44A , file 18, Saul Bass Papers, Margaret Herrick Library, AMPAS.

41. "100 Years Film Festivals," box 44A, file 42, Saul Bass Papers, Margaret Herrick Library, AMPAS; Bass and Kirkham, *Saul Bass*, 102, 408. These sources give two different dates: 1976 and 1977.

42. In fact, Peary claimed that he reached the North Pole in 1909, but Amundsen did not reach the South Pole until 1911.

43. The Academy Film Archive has now fully restored the film, as previous prints were badly faded. The unrestored version is still being distributed by Pyramid Films and can be seen at https://www.youtube.com/watch?v=euh0kEU20V4.

44. Jason Woloski, "*Why Man Creates*," http://notcoming.com/reviews/whymancreates/.

45. The same year Bass produced *Why Man Creates*, IBM financed its own film about creativity and human endeavor, *Transformations*. Produced and directed by Ralph Sargent, later the owner of Film Technology Inc., the seventeen-minute film was recently screened at "The Real Indies: A Closer Look at Orphan Films" at the Academy Film Archive.

46. "Print Personality: Saul Bass," *Print* 11, no. 6 (May–June 1958): 17. See also "Pros & Cons on TV Conformity," *Variety*, 30 September 1959, 31.

47. Saul Bass, "A Definition of Creativity," *Design: The Magazine of Creative Art* 60 (March–April 1959): 144.

48. Quoted in Bass and Kirkham, *Saul Bass*, 382.

49. Saul Bass, "Thoughts on Design. An Oration," *Journal of the Royal Society for the Encouragement of Arts* 113, no. 5112 (November 1965): 992.

50. Shirley Smith, "PR Films Coming or Going?" *Business Screen* 31, no. 5 (May 1970): 34.

51. Morgenstern, "Saul Bass," 65. Morgenstern is apparently paraphrasing an unidentified manuscript in the Bass Papers, thought to be a seminar for AT&T marketing executives in 1988. Thanks to Sean Savage for making this document available to me.

52. Letter from Saul Bass to William Riley (Young & Rubicam), 30 September 1966, "*Why Man Creates* Y + R Previews #21," box 15A, file 5, Saul Bass Papers, Margaret Herrick Library, AMPAS.

53. See "*Why Man Creates* Script #1," box 14A, file 30, Saul Bass Papers, Margaret Herrick Library, AMPAS. The file contains more than thirty unnumbered and mostly undated sheets of paper with handwritten notes. One, on Saul Bass & Associates letterhead and dated 2 October 1967, contains more than thirty suggested titles for the film, including *Why Man Creates*.

54. See letter from Robert A. Sandberg (Kaiser) to SB, 10 December 1970 (which mentions the original contract agreement date), "*Why Man Creates* Legal," box 14A, file 53, Saul Bass Papers, Margaret Herrick Library, AMPAS.

55. Memo from Don Fabun (*Kaiser Aluminum News*) to SB, 13 February 1967, "*Why Man Creates* Script #1," box 14A, file 30, Saul Bass Papers, Margaret Herrick Library, AMPAS.

56. Although Erik Daarstad is credited as cinematographer, some slates on outtakes indicate that Laszlo Kovacs also shot footage for Bass. See e-mail from Sean Savage to the author, 15 March 2013.

57. "*Why Man Creates*—Storyboards, Presented to Kaiser," box 14A, file 50, Saul Bass Papers, Margaret Herrick Library, AMPAS.

58. This outline is dated 20 November 1967. See "*Why Man Creates* Early Notes," box 14A, file 32, Saul Bass Papers, Margaret Herrick Library, AMPAS. The final script by Mayo Simon and Saul Bass is dated February 1968 and corresponds to this version, but according to Bass's handwritten note on the script from 14 July 1975, "Final changes after film shoot may never have been incorporated in an actual updated script version." See "*Why Man Creates* Final Script," box 14A, file 37, Saul Bass Papers, Margaret Herrick Library, AMPAS.

59. Interview with James Hollander, 31 October 2012, Burbank, CA.

60. "Kaiser Film Wins Plaudits (and $s)," *California Business*, n.d. [March 1969?], "*Why Man Creates* Press Clippings," box 14A, file 44, Saul Bass Papers, Margaret Herrick Library, AMPAS.

61. *Why Man Creates*, alternative version, 16mm color reversal positive, 82654-1-1, Saul Bass Collection, Academy Film Archive, AMPAS.

62. See "*Why Man Creates* Y + R Previews #21," box 15A, file 5, Saul Bass Papers, Margaret Herrick Library, AMPAS.

63. Morgenstern, "Saul Bass," 66.

64. Memo from Hugh Morris to Robert Sandberg, 26 February 1968, "*Why Man Creates* Y + R Previews #21," box 15A, file 5, Saul Bass Papers, Margaret Herrick Library, AMPAS.

65. See *Why Man Creates* brochure, "*Why Man Creates* Programs," box 14A, file 59, Saul Bass Papers, Margaret Herrick Library, AMPAS.

66. See press release, Laemmle Theatre, 23 August 1968. See also Richard Whitehall, "The Film Scene," *Open City*, 6–12 September 1968, "*Why Man Creates* Reviews," box 14A, file 44, Saul Bass Papers, Margaret Herrick Library, AMPAS.

67. See Joe Broady, "Sugar Coated Blurb Pix Big Biz," *Daily Variety*, 28 October 1969, 150.

68. The edifice sequence was subsequently broadcast on 8 July 1970 on the *Smothers' Brothers Summer Show*. See "Television Review," *Daily Variety*, 9 July 1970, 7; "*Smothers Brothers Summer Show*," *Women's Wear Daily*, 10 July 1970, clipping, "*Why Man Creates* Reviews," box 15A, file 1, Saul Bass Papers, Margaret Herrick Library, AMPAS.

69. See *Business Screen* 30, no. 7 (July 1969): 500. "Kaiser Film Wins Plaudits (and $s)" notes that, after the film's Oscar win, Modern Talking Pictures produced 500 new prints.

70. Yaffa Draznin and Hugh Marsh, "Movie Provokes Opposing Views," *Los Angeles Technograph* 10, no. 4 (March–April 1969): 5.

71. [Beverly Jeanne Davis], Review of *Why Man Creates*, *Art Education Magazine*, October 1969, 49.

72. See David A. Sohn, "See How They Run," *Film News* 26, no. 5 (October 1969): 20–21; David A. Sohn, "The Eye of the Observer: Films to Make You See," *Science Activities*, January 1970, 10–12.

73. Jason Woloski, "*Why Man Creates*," http://www.notcoming.com/reviews/whymancreates/.

74. See letter from Robert A. Sandberg to SB, 10 December 1970; memo from Morrie Marsh to SB, 15 December 1970, "*Why Man Creates* Legal," box 14A, file 53, Saul Bass Papers, Margaret Herrick Library, AMPAS. Marsh writes that Kaiser's public relations firm would have distributed the film for free forever, regardless of the $225,000 it invested.

75. The Pyramid agreement was signed on 1 July 1969. See letter from Sandberg to SB, 8 November 1971, "*Why Man Creates* Legal," box 14A, file 53, Saul Bass Papers, Margaret Herrick Library, AMPAS.

76. "Bass Moneymaker," *Hollywood Reporter*, 21 November 1977, 11.

77. See letter from Ainsworth (Pyramid) to Morrie Marsh, 11 May 1972, "*Why Man Creates* Legal," box 14A, file 53, Saul Bass Papers, Margaret Herrick Library, AMPAS. The letter included a royalty check for $37,296.65, which amounted to 25 percent of Pyramid's income ($149,186) for the period 1969–1971. See also Ainsworth (Pyramid) to Morrie Marsh, 14 February 1973, "*Why Man Creates* Rentals," box 15A, file 2, Saul Bass Papers, Margaret Herrick Library, AMPAS. This letter included a check for $9,850.43 for the fourth quarter of 1972. Later earning statements indicated the following: $8,4440.93 for fourth-quarter 1975; $10,118.41 for

first-quarter 1976; $10,456.75 for second-quarter 1976; $8,426.60 for third-quarter 1976; $9,399.90 for fourth-quarter 1976; and $6,989.77 for first-quarter 1977.

78. See Morgenstern, "Saul Bass," 64; AT&T seminar manuscript, 1988, Saul Bass Papers, Margaret Herrick Library, AMPAS.

79. The note with the typed titles is dated October 1967 and is on Saul Bass & Associates letterhead. See "*Why Man Creates* Script #1," box 14A, file 30, Saul Bass Papers, Margaret Herrick Library, AMPAS.

80. AT&T seminar manuscript, 1988, Saul Bass Papers, Margaret Herrick Library, AMPAS.

81. Saul Bass had designed the corporate logo for Warner Brothers, which Herb Yager characterized as DOA because it put the *W* in a television frame, just as the company was transitioning to a transmedia conglomerate and changing its name from National Kinney Corporation to Warner Communications. Yager thought Bass just wasn't paying attention when he designed the logo. Nevertheless, Bass apparently went to the head of National Kinney Corporation and suggested a film that would demonstrate to Wall Street that the diverse entertainment businesses now at the company's center all fit together. Interview with Herb Yager, 27 February 2013, Ojai, CA.

82. Significantly, Bass used the same introduction for *Notes on the Popular Arts*, but with disembodied hands typing on a typewriter. This less personal approach was more in keeping with that film's commercial goals.

83. Roh and Tschichold, *Foto-Auge, Photo-Eye, Oeil et Photo*, cover.

84. The first edit, shown in February 1968, also included Frank Lloyd Wright in the mix. Sean Savage informs me that there are also outtakes of old-time portraits of "Saul as Old Creator," indicating that Bass considered placing himself in the pantheon. E-mail from Sean Savage to the author, 15 March 2013.

85. This is confirmed by a photocopy of an article about the Chicago Picasso controversy in the Bass Papers. See D. J. R. Bruckner, "Chicago Unveils, Hails Its Puzzling, 50 Ft. Picasso," *New York Times*, n.d., "*Why Man Creates* Script #1," box 14A, file 30, Saul Bass Papers, Margaret Herrick Library, AMPAS.

86. Irving Howe, *Literary Modernism* (Greenwich, CT: Fawcett Publishers, 1967), 24.

87. Dr. Dulbecco would eventually win a Nobel Prize for his work in medicine in 1975. See http://articles.latimes.com/2012/feb/21/local/la-me-renato-dulbecco-20120221.

88. This final sequence is named "The Mark" in previous iterations of the script and cutting continuity, and it refers to humanity's take on nature.

89. The three sequences are the jumping-jacks scene in traffic, the social worker scene with a cascade of numbers, and the brain surgery scene. Later in the AT&T film he uses a short version of the Hitler montage from *The Victors*. See AT&T Corporate Program (1969), 16mm print, 1499-1, Saul Bass Collection, Academy Film Archive, AMPAS. The Academy calls the film *A New Look for the Bell System*; there is no title on the original film.

90. According to Paramount distribution reports from 1985, the film's overall shortfall was $372,622, after subtracting income from expenses. However, there was apparently a lot of "creative accounting" on Paramount's side, since it sold the film to

television in November 1975 for $1.1 million, when the balance was $1.6 million in the red; a month later, the balance remained at $1.6 million. See Paramount Financial Reports #1 (2 December 1974), #5 (20 December 1975), #20 (31 August 1985), "*Phase IV* Distribution Reports," box 5A, file 28, Saul Bass Papers, Margaret Herrick Library, AMPAS.

91. Nic Francis, "Bass PHASE IV," *Screen 'n' Heard*, March 1973, 11.

92. See "Phase II for Par," *Variety*, 22 September 1971, 2; "Saul Bass Will Direct 'Phase II' for Paramount," *Hollywood Reporter*, 22 September 1971, 1. Simon received $10,000 for his script, but he complained in a letter to the editor of the *Los Angeles Times* that his role had been ignored in an article on the making of the film. See letter to the editor, *Los Angeles Times*, 17 March 1973, clipping in *Phase IV* production files, Margaret Herrick Library, AMPAS. See also letter from Ben Margolis to Morrie Marsh, 30 November 1972, and letter from Eric Weissmann (Law Offices of Kaplan, Livingston, Godwin, Berkwitz & Stein) to Eugene Frank (Paramount), 28 June 1972, "*Phase IV* Legal," box 6A, file 2, Saul Bass Papers, Margaret Herrick Library, AMPAS.

93. Hollander interview, 2012. See also Bell, "Oral History with Saul Bass."

94. A. H. Weiler, "Bass's Bugs," *New York Times*, 30 June 1972. The final shooting script, dated 3 September 1972, consisted of 106 pages of dialogue and 544 shots. See "*Phase IV* Script," box 5A, file 21, Saul Bass Papers, Margaret Herrick Library, AMPAS.

95. "*Phase IV* Will Roll in London for Par," *Hollywood Reporter*, 19 July 1972, 4.

96. See "*Phase IV* Storyboards," box 6A, file 22, Saul Bass Papers, Margaret Herrick Library, AMPAS; interviews with Jeff Okun, 6 June 2011, Studio City, CA, and 23 March 2012, Hollywood, CA.

97. See "Film Prod. Pulse," *Variety*, 15 November 1972, 34. This chronology is based on an article stating that Bass left London in late November 1973, after thirteen months behind the camera and in the editing room. See Philip Oakes, "Coming On: Bass Note," *Sunday Times*, 9 December 1973, 36.

98. MPAA news release, 22 January 1974, *Phase IV* production files, Margaret Herrick Library, AMPAS.

99. Letter from Saul Bass and Paul Radin to Charles Glenn, VP Advertising Publicity & Promotion, 20 September 1973, "*Phase IV* Publicity," box 6A, file 14, Saul Bass Papers, Margaret Herrick Library, AMPAS.

100. Three months after completing the film, Bass wrote: "All goes well on PHASE IV and distribution plans are proceeding apace—having been held up by the problems created at Technicolor by your state of crisis. . . . Our economy is fairly rocky—and this makes for cautious attitudes in business circles, having its inevitable effect on all of us." Letter from Saul Bass to Arnold Schwartzman, 21 February 1974. On 18 April Bass wrote to Radin: "Still don't have a release date." Then again on 7 June: "The picture's in Yablans' hands. Evans considers it his (Yablans') baby now. I am awaiting word as to his intentions about the release date and a release plan." On 1 October Radin wrote to Bass: "If the picture hasn't in fact opened anywhere, do you think they will ever release it? I cannot believe it is that bad." Finally, in a letter to Radin on 28 October,

Bass confessed: "*Phase IV* opened in forty theatres in New York (and is apparently not doing too well). I have not talked to Paramount; I have given up on that completely." All the letters are in "*Phase IV* Correspondence," box 5A, file 27, Saul Bass Papers, Margaret Herrick Library, AMPAS.

101. New York City preview, 12 August 1974, "*Phase IV* Previews," box 6A, file 1, Saul Bass Papers, Margaret Herrick Library, AMPAS.

102. Kevin Thomas, "*Phase IV*," *Los Angeles Times*, 13 June 1975, pt. IV, 15.

103. See letter from Saul Bass to Paul Radin, 1 September 1974; Bass's aide-mémoire about a meeting with Yablans and Glenn, attached to Telefax from Saul Bass to Frank Yablans, 10 October 1974; letter from SB to Barry Day, McCann-Erickson Advertising Ltd., London, 11 November 1974, all in "*Phase IV* Correspondence," box 5A, file 27, Saul Bass Papers, Margaret Herrick Library, AMPAS. As Bass noted in the letter to Day regarding the film's publicity: "I am pleased you liked it and can only hasten to assure you that I had nothing to do with the posters or the ad campaign generally (although there were a lot of battles between Paramount New York and me)."

104. Bass's friends wrote: "Some people at the theatre stopped Leon to ask him if you were an Englishman because the picture had a foreign feeling!" Letter from Julia and Leon Winston to Saul Bass, 27 January 1974: "*Phase IV* Correspondence," box 5A, file 27, Saul Bass Papers, Margaret Herrick Library, AMPAS.

105. For many years, the ending montage sequence was believed to have never been made, but it turned up in the Bass Collection at the Academy Film Archive. According to Jeff Okun, the sequence is not the original; rather, Okun re-created it in 16mm in the late 1970s. However, Sean Savage, the Academy's Bass archivist, questions the veracity of Okun's statement, given that Paramount's separation masters of *Phase IV* have the montage intact. See Bass and Kirkham, *Saul Bass*, 257; Okun interview, 2012; e-mail from Sean Savage to the author, 15 March 2013.

106. "*Phase IV*," *Box Office*, 16 September 1974.

107. See "*Phase IV*," *Motion Picture Production Digest*, 18 September 1974; "*Phase IV*," *Audience* 75 (September 1974): 15; John Dorr, "*Phase IV*," *Hollywood Reporter*, 2 October 1974, 8; William Wolf, "*Phase IV*," *Cue*, 28 October–3 November 1974; "*Phase IV*," *Seventeen* 33, no. 11 (November 1974); "*Phase IV*," *Playboy* 21, no. 12 (December 1974); J. R., "*Phase IV*," *Oui* 4, no. 1 (January 1975).

108. Jay Cocks, "*Phase IV*," *Time*, 14 October 1974, 10–11.

109. Har., "*Phase IV*," *Variety*, 9 October 1974, 18. See also Frank Rich, "*Phase IV*," *New York Times*, 4 October 1974; Robert C. Cumbow, "*Phase IV*," *Movietone News* 37 (November 1974): 31–32.

110. Thomas, "*Phase IV*," 15.

111. Nigel Andrews, "Ant Action," *Financial Times*, 18 October 1974. See also Jonathan Rosenbaum, "*Phase IV*," *Monthly Film Bulletin* 41, no. 489 (October 1974): 228.

112. A sign of the film's growing critical status is its inclusion in a new film series at the Los Angeles County Museum of Art, "Beyond the Infinite: Science Fiction after Kubrick." See https://www.lacma.org/series/beyond-infinite-science-fiction-after-kubrick.

113. Graham J. Murphy, "*Phase IV*," *Science Fiction Film and Television* 3, no. 2 (Autumn 2010). See also Thomas Scalzo, "*Phase IV*," *Not Coming to a Theatre Near You*, http://notcoming.com/reviews/phase4/; "*Phase IV*—A Film by Saul Bass," *The Hauntological Society*, http://thehauntologicalsociety.blogspot.com/search? updated-min=2011-01-01T00:00:00Z&updated-max=2012-01-01T00:00:00Z&max-results=50. Numerous other reviews of the film on DVD can be found on the Internet Movie Database, http://www.imdb.com/title/tt0070531/externalreviews.

114. In retrospect, Bass commented on his experience with *Phase IV*: "I think *Phase IV* was an interesting but not entirely successful film. Still as a life experience, it was absolutely extraordinary. On the one hand full of anxiety, frustration and even despair. On the other hand, exhilarating and energizing. Talk about life on the edge! Even when it drives you nuts, you are stimulated and engaged. Until then all my work had been relatively short forms: titles, sequences, short films. Long forms are another kind of creative experience. They represent a different sort of creative problem, qualitatively as well as quantitatively. Especially when you have never done it before." Krag and Volsted, *Title Sequence Seminar*, 20–21.

115. Vivian Sobchack, *Screening Space: The American Science Fiction Film* (New York: Ungar Publishing, 1987), 88.

116. Ibid., 112.

117. Beier and Midding, *Vorspann: Zum Werk von Saul Bass*.

118. See "*Phase IV* drawings," box 5A, file 29, Saul Bass Papers, Margaret Herrick Library, AMPAS. According to Sean Savage (personal communication, 25 January 2013), the role of Kendra was reduced because Lynne Frederick's performance was stilted and because Paramount executives were worried there might be some inappropriate sexual chemistry between the underage Frederick and Murphy.

119. This shot, particularly its soundscape of an abstract buzzing noise, immediately recalls the alien slabs at the beginning of *2001*.

120. Bass described the toxic yellow desert as a "strangely threatening, but strangely beautiful landscape." See *American Film Institute Seminar*, 32.

121. Quoted in Philip Oakes, "Coming On: Bass Note," *Sunday Times*, 9 December 1973, 36.

122. Memo from Louis Dorfsman (CBS Broadcast Group) to Saul Bass, 10 December 1974, "*Phase IV* Correspondence," box 5A, file 27, Saul Bass Papers, Margaret Herrick Library, AMPAS.

123. See John Brosnan, *Future Tense: The Cinema of Science Fiction* (New York: St. Martin's Press, 1978), 228. Brosnan argues that *Phase IV* tries too hard to emulate *2001*, but he only had access to the abbreviated ending, "with the two humans being transformed, either by the ants or by the intelligence guiding them, into a new form of life."

124. Bass apparently lost the original ending, and Jeff Okun claims he re-created it for demonstration purposes. Okun interview, 2012. However, Sean Savage from the Academy Film Archive found the original ending at Paramount and has begun showing the film with that ending.

125. Bart Mills, "The Anty Hero," *Arts Guardian* (London), 10 February 1973, 10. Thanks to Sean Savage for pointing out this quote.

126. David James, *The Most Typical Avant-Garde: History and Geography of Minor Cinemas in Los Angeles* (Berkeley: University of California Press, 2005).

127. See Manovich, *Language of New Media*, 250, http://www.manovich.net/LNM/Manovich.pdf.

Selected Bibliography

About or by Saul Bass

Adair, Gilbert. "Let the Good Titles Roll." *Sunday Times*, 14 April 1996.

Aison, Everett. "The Current Scene: Film Titles." *Print* 19, no. 4 (July–August 1965): 26–30.

———. "Saul Bass: The Designer as Filmmaker." *Print* 23, no. 1 (January–February 1969): 90–94, 129–30, 133.

"Alcoa's Public Relations Department Played Key Role in Introducing New Logo." *PR News*, 23 December 1963. Reprinted in David P. Bianco, ed., *PR News Casebook: 1,000 Public Relations Case Studies* (Detroit: Gale Research, 1993).

Allen, Bob. "Designing and Producing the Credit Titles for *It's a Mad, Mad, Mad, Mad World*." *American Cinematographer* 44, no. 12 (December 1963): 706–7, 728–30.

Alpert, Hollis. "What Goes on Here." *Woman's Day*, March 1961.

American Film Institute Seminar with Saul Bass, 16 May 1979. Beverly Hills, CA: Center for Advanced Film Studies, 1979. Available only at American Film Institute.

Anderson-Bruce, Sally. *Childhood Fantasies: Champion Kromekote 2000*. Stamford, CT: Champion International Corporation, 1991.

Anon. *28th Annual of Advertising and Editorial Art and Design*. New York: Longmans, Green, 1949.

———. *29th Annual of Advertising and Editorial Art and Design*. New York: Longmans, Green, 1950.

———. *30th Annual of Advertising and Editorial Art and Design*. New York: Longmans, Green, 1951.

———. *32nd Annual of Advertising and Editorial Art and Design*. New York: Longmans, Green, 1953.

———. *33rd Annual of Advertising and Editorial Art and Design*. New York: Longmans, Green. 1954.

———. *34th Annual of Advertising and Editorial Art and Design*. New York: Longmans, Green, 1955.

———. *35th Annual of Advertising and Editorial Art and Design*. New York: Longmans, Green, 1956.

———. *37th Annual of Advertising and Editorial Art and Design*. New York: Longmans, Green, 1958.

———. *38th Annual of Advertising and Editorial Art and Design*. New York: Longmans, Green, 1959.

———. *40th Annual of Advertising and Editorial Art and Design*. New York: Longmans, Green, 1961.

———. *41st Annual of Advertising and Editorial Art and Design*. New York: Longmans, Green, 1962.

———. *61st Annual of Advertising and Editorial Art and Design*. New York: Longmans, Green, 1982.

———. *65th Annual of Advertising and Editorial Art and Design*. New York: Longmans, Green, 1986.

———. *67th Annual of Advertising and Editorial Art and Design*. New York: Longmans, Green, 1988.

"*Apples and Oranges*—Food for Thought. How CBS Sells a Concept." *Telefilm* 8, no. 5 (May 1963): 30–31, 38.

Assayas, Oliver. "Hommage à Saul Bass." *Cahiers du Cinema* 426, (1981): x.

Auiler, Dan. Vertigo: *The Making of a Hitchcock Classic*. New York: St. Martin's Press, 1998.

Avrich, Barry. "A Friendship by Design: Remembering Saul Bass." In *Classic Film Festival, Hollywood 2012*. TCM Festival Program, 66–71.

Badder, David, Bob Baker, and Markku Salmi. "Saul Bass." *Film Dope* 3 (August 1973): 1–6, 10.

Bandon, Alexandra, and Abbott Combes. "A Question for: Saul Bass." *New York Times Magazine*, 10 March 1996, 21–25.

Bass, Jennifer, and Pat Kirkham. *Saul Bass: A Life in Film and Design*. London: Laurence King Publishing, 2011.

Bass, Saul. "Cover." *Arts & Architecture* 65, no. 11 (November 1948): 2.

———. "Creativity in Visual Communication." In *Creativity: An Examination of the Creative Process*, ed. Paul Smith, 121–30. New York: Hastings House, 1959.

———. "A Definition of Creativity." *Design: The Magazine of Creative Art* 60 (March–April 1959): 144–45, 170.

———. "Edge of the City—Color Poster." In Charles Rosner, "AIG, 3rd Exhibition." *Graphis* 13, no. 71 (July 1957): 312.

———. "Film Advertising. Filmwerbung. La publicité pour le film." *Graphis* 9, no. 48 (1953): 276–89.

———. "Film Titles—A New Field for the Graphic Designer." *Graphis* 16, no. 89 (May–June 1960): 208–15.

———. Foreword to *The Album Cover Art of Sound Tracks*, ed. Frank Jastfelder and Stefan Kassel, 5–7. New York: Little, Brown, 1997.

———. "How I Got the Idea." In *A Smile in the Mind: Witty Thinking in Graphic Design*, ed. Beryl McAlhone and David Stuart, 170–71. London: Phaidon Press, 1996.

———. "The Making of *Quest*." *Step-by-Step Graphics* 2, no. 5 (September–October 1986): 36–47.

———. "Movement, Film, Communication." In *Vision + Value*. Vol. 6, *Sign, Image and Symbol*, ed. Gyorgy Kepes, 200–201. New York: George Braziller, 1966.

———. "Poster—Music Center Unified Fund." In Kit Hinrichs, "AIGA: California Graphic Design." *Graphis* 39, no. 224 (March–April 1983): 40.

————. "Some Thoughts on Motion Picture Film." In *Design Forecast 2*, ed. Laurence S. Sewell, 20–26. Pittsburgh, PA: Aluminum Company of America, 1960.

————. "Thoughts on Design: An Oration." *Journal of the Royal Society for the Encouragement of Arts* 113, no. 5112 (November 1965): 991–94.

————. "Thoughts on Film." In *Communication: The Art of Understanding and Being Understood*, ed. Robert O. Bach, 23–32. New York: Hastings House, 1963.

"Bass Instinct." *Creative Review* 15, no. 5 (1 May 1995): 47–49.

"Bass Notes." *Creative Review* 16 (3 June 1996): 11.

Beegan, Gery. "Directed by Saul Bass." *Dot, Dot, Dot* 11 (September 2005): 18–22.

"Behind the Title." *Newsweek*, 20 January 1958, 90.

Beier, Lars-Olav, and Gerhard Midding. *Teamwork in der Traumfabrk. Werkstattgespräche*. Berlin: Henschel Verlag, 1995.

Beier, Lars-Olaf, and Walter Midding. *Vorspann: Zum Werk von Saul Bass*. Hamburg: North German Television (NDR), 1991. VHS tape, 28308-1, Academy Film Archive, Academy of Motion Picture Arts and Sciences.

Bell, Douglas. "Oral History with Saul Bass." Unpublished manuscript, 1996. Saul Bass Collection, Margaret Herrick Library, Academy of Motion Picture Arts and Sciences.

Beneson, Laurie Halpern. "The New Look in Film Titles: Edgy Type That's on the Move." *New York Times*, 24 March 1996, 22.

Berthomé, Jean-Pierre. "Les inconnus du générique." *Cinéma* 70, no. 142 (January 1970): 32–42.

————. "Saul Bass et Alfred Hitchcock: Trios mariages et un enterrement." *1895*, no. 57 (April 2009).

"Better than the Film." *Creative Review* 29 (4 August 2009): 28.

Bierut, Michael. "Catching the Big One." *ID: The International Design Magazine* 42, no. 1 (January–February 1995): 48.

Billanti, Dean. "The Names behind the Titles: Saul Bass." *Film Comment* 18, no. 3 (May–June 1982): 61–71.

Blackwell, Lewis. "Bass Instinct." *Creative Review* (Marketing Week) 15 (May 1995): 48–49.

Blanchard, Gerard. "La lettre et la cinématographe." *Revue du Cinema* 312 (December 1976): 96–102.

————. "Saul Bass: Génériques et Languages." *Communications et Languages* 40 (1978): 76–96.

Bodger, Lowell A. "A Modern Approach to Film Titling." *American Cinematographer* 40, no. 8 (August 1960): 476–78.

Brown, David R. "Saul Bass." AIG, 1982. http://www.aiga.org/content.cfm?contentalias+saulbass.

Buj, Otto. "Buy American." *Film Comment* 44, no. 3 (May–June 2008): 20.

"Cable Column: An Interview with Saul Bass." *Z Magazine* 2, no. 3 (August–September 1975): 21.

Caplan, Richard. "Designs by Saul Bass." *Industrial Design* 5, no. 10 (October 1958): 88–93.

Cavestany, Juan. "Saul Bass. El hombre de los créditos." *El Pais Semanal*, 11 August 1996, 10–11.

Champlin, Charles. "Sunny Side of Saul's Film Job." *Los Angeles Times*, 14 March 1966.

Cherchi Usai, Paolo. "Il migliore e Saul Bass con 'Vertigo.'" *Segnocinema: Rivista Cinematografica Bimestrale* 14 (September 1984): 11.

Cohn, Art, ed. *Michael Todd's* Around the World in 80 Days. New York: Random House, 1956.

Coleman, John. "Bass Relief." *New Statesman*, 1 March 1963.

Collins, Keith. "Pic Graphics Pioneer Saul Bass Dies." *Daily Variety*, 26 April 1996, 5, 47.

———. "Saul Bass Obit." *Variety*, 29 April 1996, 128.

Connah, Roger. "Graphics: Mood or Mode; Saul Bass, Arthur Guiness, Günter Grass." *Form Function Finland* 2 (April 1993): 8–18.

Cooper, V. "Observations from the Outback." *Boulder County Business Report* 7, no. 7 (July 1988): 2.

Cornand, André. "Le Festival d'Annecy et les Recontres internationales du cinema." *Image et Son* 313 (January 1977).

Cort, Saloment. "'The Compleat Filmmaker'—From Title to Features." *American Cinematogapher* 58, no. 3 (March 1977): 288–91, 315, 325–27.

Coupland, Ken. "Saul Bass: The Man behind the Titles." *Graphis* 54, no. 316 (July–August 1998): 102–5.

Cox, Carole. "Electric Media: New Short Films for the Humanities." *English Journal* 74, no. 7 (November 1985): 96.

Coyne, Richard S. "Saul Bass & Associates." *CA Magazine: The Journal of Communication Arts* 10, no. 4 (August–September 1968): 14–31.

———. "Saul Bass Interview." *Communication Arts*, 1968/1971. www.commarts.com/creative/bass/index.html.

Cumbow, Robert C. "*Phase IV.*" *Movietone News* 37 (November 1974): 31–32.

Davis, Beverly Jeanne. "*Why Man Creates.*" *Art Education Magazine*, October 1969, 49.

De Benedetto, David. "Moving Texts: The Film Titles of Saul Bass." http://www.reddye.com/writing_saulbass.html.

Dillon, David. "Notes on Creativity, the Visual Arts, and Some Educational Implications." *Language Arts*, November–December 1981.

"Do Film Critics Extol 'Bass Credits' to Slur (by Contrast) the Director?" *Variety*, 17 June 1964, 5.

Dorfsman, Louis. "Saul Bass, a Combination of Intellect and Emotion." In *The Master Series: Saul Bass, 11 March–5 April 1996*, 6. New York: Visual Arts Museum at the School of Visual Arts, 1996.

Draznin, Yaffa, and Hugh Marsh. "Movie Provokes Opposing Views." *Los Angeles Technograph* 10, no. 4 (March–April 1969): 4–5.

Dunn, Linwood. "Effects and Titles for 'West Side Story.'" *American Cinematographer* 42, no. 12 (December 1961): 736–38, 757.

Durgnat, Raymond. *A Long Hard Look at "Psycho."* London: BFI Publishing, 2002.

Ebenhöh, Ludwig. "Saul Bass, USA." *Gebrauchsgraphik* 27, no. 11 (November 1956): 12–21.

Edgar, Ray R. "Micro Film." *World Art* 18 (1998): 24–29, 84.

Evans, Noell Wolfram. "Saul Bass: A Film Title Pioneer." http://www.digitalmediafx.com/Features/saulbass.html.

Everschor, Franz. "Ich strebe nach Einfachheit." *Film-dienst* 64, no. 26 (December 2011).

"Experimental Letterheads by Saul Bass: A Portfolio of Eight Exciting New Designs." *Print* 16, no. 5 (September–October 1962): 30–32.

"Fatalistic Fugue: *Bonjour Tristesse.*" *Newsweek*, 20 January 1958, 89–90.

Favermann, Mark. "Two Twentieth-Century Icons." *Art New England* 18 (April–May 1997): 15.

Fessier, Mike, Jr. "Lay 'Em in the Aisles with a Title." *Daily Variety*, 27 October 1964, 39, 118.

"First for Saul Bass: Illustrations from Henri's Walk to Paris." *Print* 16, no. 5 (September–October 1962): 55.

Firstenberg, Jean. "Credit Where Credit Is Due." *American Film* 9, no. 6 (April 1984): 80.

Fischer, Dennis. "Saul Bass." In *Science Fiction Film Directors 1895–1998*, 92–94. Jefferson, NC: McFarland, 2000.

Foster, Fred. "New Look in Film Titles." *American Cinematographer* 43, no. 6 (June 1962): 357–73.

"Four Advertisements." *Graphis* 13 (July 1957): 312–45.

Frischauer, Willi. *Behind the Scenes of Otto Preminger.* London: Michael Joseph, 1973.

Frolick, Stuart. "Saul Bass—Nothing Less than a Legend." *Graphis* 47, no. 276 (November–December 1991): 94–105.

"*From Here to There.*" *Industrial Design Magazine*, April 1964, 40–43.

Fujiwara, Chris. *The World and Its Double: The Life and Work of Otto Preminger.* New York: Faber and Faber, 2008.

Fullmer, Berne. "The Logo and the Trademark in the World of Merchandising." *Image* 3, no. 4 (August 1968): 4–5, 13.

Gendler, Jason. "Saul Bass and Title Design: Intention and Reception, and Production Integration." Paper presented at Society of Cinema and Media Studies Conference, Los Angeles, March 2010.

Gerle, Jörg. "Intermediale Lektionen." *Film-dienst* 63, no. 15 (July 2010).

Gett, Trevor. "Saul Bass HonRDI." *RSA Journal* 144, no. 5470 (June 1996): 10.

Gid, Raymond. "Saul Bass: New Film Titlings and Promotional Films." *Graphis* 19, no. 106 (1963): 150–59.

Giles, Dennis. "Saul Bass." *Film Reader* 1 (1975): 76–77.

"Giving Credit Where Credit Is Due. Mr. Bass Is an Artist with Titles." *National Observer*, 16 August 1965, 18.

Glover, Kara. "Saul Bass Is a Designing Man." *Los Angeles Business Journal* 12, no. 36 (3–9 September 1990): 20–21.

Glucksman, Mary. "Due Credit: Saul Bass." *Screen International*, 13 May 1994, 27–28.

"Graphics—Mr. Saul Bass." In *International Television Design Conference*, 8–9. London: BBC Television Centre, 1962.

Hackworth, Nick. "Brutally Seductive Simplicity." *Evening Standard*, 19 July 2004.

Hales, Linda. "Creation Myths." *Architect* 96, no. 14 (December 2007): 81.

Hall, Peter. "Memorable Bass Lines." *Design Week* 11, no. 21 (1996): 13.

Hamilton, Mina. "Films at the Fair II: A Comparative Review." *Industrial Design* 12 (May 1964): 32–41.

———. "N.Y. World's Fair Film Preview." *Industrial Design* 11 (April 1964): 36–43.

Harbord, Jane. "Bass Takes the Credit—But Not for *Psycho*." *Broadcast*, 18 April 1986, 17.

Harper, Laurel. "The Man with the Golden Designs." *How: The Bottomline Design Magazine* 11, no. 3 (May–June 1996): 90–95.

Harris, Adam Duncan. "Extra Credits: The History and Collection of Pacific Title and Art Studio." PhD diss., University of Minnesota, 2000.

———. "Revolution in Context: The Golden Arm of Saul Bass [abstract]." *Michigan Academician* 29, no. 3 (1997): 277.

Harwood, J. "*Phase IV*." *Variety*, 9 October 1974, 18.

Haskin, Pamela. "Saul, Can You Make Me a Title? Interview with Saul Bass." *Film Quarterly* 50, no. 1 (Fall 1996): 10–17.

Heathcote, Edwin. "Poster Boy for American Film." *Financial Times*, 16 July 2004.

Heesch, Klaus. "Film Titles and Credits Shouldn't Be an Afterthought." *Juice Box* 1, no. 2 (May 2007). http://klausheesch.com/stuff/uploads/general/JuiceBox_v01n002.pdf.

Heller, Steven. "Saul Bass." In *Graphic Design in America: A Visual Language History*, ed. Mildred Friedman et al., 18–19. New York: Harry Abrams, 1989.

———. "Saul Bass 1920–1996." *Print* 50, no. 4 (July–August 1996): 110.

Herdeg, Walter, ed. *Film and TV Graphics: An International Survey of Film and Television Graphics.* Zurich: Graphis Press, 1967.

Hift, Fred. "And that Cramps Film Ads—Bass." *Variety*, 20 November 1957, 7, 24.

Hinchcliff, Rob. "Saul Bass." *Grafik* 119 (2004): 60–63.

Hirsch, Foster. *Otto Preminger: The Man Who Would Be King.* New York: Alfred A. Knopf, 2007.

Hogenkamp, Maaike. "*The Man with the Golden Arm*." *Skrien* 165 (April–May 1989): 46–47, 68.

Hollinger, Hy. "Man with the Golden Graphic: Saul Bass Dies." *Hollywood Reporter*, 26 April 1996, 12, 77.

Hosanksy, Eugene A. "The Current Scene: Film Posters." *Print* 19, no. 4 (July–August 1965): 20–25.

"How to Keep a Creative Man Creative." *Printer's Ink*, 11 April 1958, 51–52.

Hundley, Jessica. "A Sharp Eye for Design." *Los Angeles Times*, 20 February 2003.

Hüser, Rembert. "(Hand)writing Film History: Saul Bass Draws Martin Scorsese in a Title Sequence and Writes His Name Underneath." In *Sign Here! Handwriting in the Age of New Media*, ed. Sonja Neef, José van Dijck, and Eric Ketelaar, 164–79. Amsterdam: Amsterdam University Press, 2006.

"In Memoriam: Saul Bass." *Graphis* 53, no. 307 (1997): 107.

Jackson, Frank. "*Phase IV:* . . . Individualists Are Likely to Find a Disturbing Dream." *Cinefantastique* 3 (1974): 31.

Jeffer, Marsha, and Pauline G. Weber. *Study Guide to* Quest. Santa Monica, CA: Pyramid Films, 1983.

Jenkins, Bruce. "Making the Scene: West Coast Modernism and the Movies." In *Birth of the Cool: California Art, Design, and Culture at Midcentury*, ed. Elizabeth Armstrong. New York: Orange County Museum of Art/Prestel, 2007.

Johns, Ian. "The Man Who Made It Big in Pictures." *Times of London*, 1 July 2004, 4.

Kamekura, Yusaku. "Recent Works of Saul Bass, 1961–1963." *Graphic Design* 13 (October 1963): 27–40.

———. "Saul Bass Passed Away." *IDEA* 44, no. 258 (1996): 106–9.

Kane, Bruce, and Joel Reisner. "A Conversation with Saul Bass." *Cinema* 4, no. 3 (Fall 1968): 30–35.

Karamath, Joe. "Overtures and Psychotic Symphonies." *Eye Magazine* 39 (Spring 2001). http://www.eyemagazine.com/feature/article/overtures-and-psychotic-symphonies.

Kaye, Joyce Rutter. "Saul Bass' Moving Icons." *U&lc* 23, no. 3 (Winter 1996): 22–23.

Keeve, Meredith. "Saul Bass." *Zoom* 34 (February 1988): 62–65.

Kelly, Frank. "You've Seen His Work around Town, But Do You Know Who Saul Bass Is?" *Washington Post*, 23 February 1986, G2.

Kerry, Lee. "The Man with the Golden Mind." *Adweek*, 4 September 1987.

King, Emily. "Taking Credit: Film Title Sequences, 1955–1965." Master's thesis, Royal College of Art, 1994. http://www.typotheque.com/articles/taking_credit_film_title_sequences_1955-1965.

King, Susan. "Hollywood's Man behind the Title." *Los Angeles Times*, 28 January 2002.

Kingsley, Canham. "*Phase IV.*" *Federation of Film Titles* 2 (October 1974): 18.

Kirby, Tim. "How Saul Bass Makes His Mark." *Campaign*, 9 May 1986.

Kirkham, Pat. "Billy Wilder and Saul Bass in Conversation." *Sight & Sound* 5 (June 1995): 18–21.

———. "Bright Lights, Big City." *Sight & Sound* 6 (January 1996): 12–13.

———. "The Jeweller's Eye." *Sight & Sound* 7, no. 4 (April 1997): 14–19.

———. "Looking for the Simple Idea—Interview with Saul and Elaine Bass." *Sight & Sound* 4, no. 2 (February 1994): 16–17, 20.

———. "The Man with the Golden Pencil." *Blueprint* 129 (June 1996): 16.

———. "The Personal, the Professional, and the Partner(ship)." In *Feminist Cultural Theory*, ed. Beverly Skeggs, 207–26. Manchester, UK: Manchester University Press, 1995.

———. "Reassessing the Saul Bass and Alfred Hitchcock Collaboration." *West 86th*

Street 18, no. 1 (Spring 2011). http://www.west86th.bgc.bard.edu/articles/kirkham-bass-hitchcock.html.

———. "Saul Bass, a Life in Design and Film: Elaine Bass, a Collaboration in Film and Life." In *The Banham Lectures: Essays on Designing the Future*, ed. Jeremy Aynsley and Harriet Atkinson, 143–55. London: Berg, 2009.

Klein, Lenore. *Henri's Walk to Paris.* New York: W. R. Scott, 1962. Reprint, New York: Rizzoli, 2012.

Klein, Nancy Hopkins. "Saul Bass: On the Real Priorities." *Design Firm Management* 41 (1994): 1–6.

Koenig, Rhoda. "All Credit to the Master." *Independent*, 15 July 2004.

Kothenschulte, Daniel. "Overtüren des Kinos. Sau Bass—Meister des Vorspanns." *Film-dienst* 47, no. 1 (January 1994): 8–11.

Krag, Thomas, and Tim Volsted, eds. *Title Sequence Seminar: Saul and Elaine Bass, 25 April 1995.* Copenhagen: National Film School of Denmark, 1995.

Lally, Kevin. "Arresting Images." *Film Journal* 99, no. 3 (March 1996): 22–23.

Lapinsky, Stan, et al. "Saul Bass." *Skrien* 210 (October–November 1996): 38–47.

Latorre, José Maria. "Saul Bass: Diseñador." *Dirigido por . . .* 399 (April 2010).

Lentz, Harris, III. "Saul Bass Obituary." *Classic Images* 252 (June 1996): 56–59.

Lewin, Richard. "Saul Bass in Memoriam." *Graphis* 53, no. 307 (January–February 1997): 105.

Lewis, Richard Warren. "Box Office Bait by Bass: A Designer Masters the Fine Art of Hooking an Audience." *Show Business Illustrated*, 23 January 1962, 48–51.

Liberti, Fabrizio. "L'uomo che uccise il popcorn time." *Cineforum* 37, no. 5 (June 1997): 10–11.

Mack, Elin. "Saul Food." *Visuelt* (Norway), 2004, 12–15.

"Le magician des génériques." *Télérama*, 12 January 1982.

Mallerman, Tony. "Saul Bass, You Said It!" *Television Mail*, 10 October 1969, 14–15.

"*Man with the Golden Arm* Has a Top Credit Rating." *Australian*, 28 August 1976, 3.

Mason, Stanley. "Saul and Elaine Bass: A New Film on Solar Energy." *Graphis* 37, no. 232 (September–October 1981): 156–59.

Matzkin, Myron A. "Movie Maker." *Modern Photography*, July 1964, 111.

McAsh, Iain F. "Saul Bass: One Black Rose over a Crimson Flame." *Films Illustrated* 2, no. 21 (March 1973): 22–23.

McDowell, David. "*Phase IV.*" *Photon* 26 (1975): 11–12.

McVicker, George. "The Long Arm of a Dream." *Artists Guild of Chicago*, 7 February 1963, 5–6.

Meggs, Philip B. "Saul Bass on Corporate Identity." In *Design Culture: An Anthology of Writing from the AIGA Journal of Graphic Design*, ed. Steven Heller and Marie Finamore, 71–77. New York: Allworth Press, 1997.

Miller, K. "Saul Bass." *Times Literary Supplement*, 13 August 2004.

Miller, Robert. "Designer's Talent Transcends Any Job Category." *Dallas Morning News*, 7 February 1986, 3D.

Mills, Bart. "Ants Take over the World in PHASE IV, a First Feature for Director Saul Bass." *Los Angeles Times*, 18 February 1973, 22.

———. "The Anty Hero." *Arts Guardian* (London), 10 February 1973, 10.

Mogg, Ken. "Deaths of Saul Bass and William K. Everson." *MacGuffin* 19 (May 1996).

Mörchen, Roland. "Saul Bass." *Film-dienst* 52, no. 19 (September 1999).

Morgenstern, Joe. *Saul Bass: A Life in Film and Design*. Unpublished, Los Angeles, 1997.

"Movies: Man with a Golden Arm." *Time*, 16 March 1962, 46.

Murat, Pierre, and Bernard Genin. "Saul Bass. Le bon genie des génériques." *Banc-Titre* 40 (April 1984): 7–11.

Murphy, Graham J. "*Phase IV*." *Science Fiction Film and Television* 3, no. 2 (Autumn 2010).

Murphy, Paul. "Credit Rating." *Design Week* 11, no. 13 (28 March 1996): 18–20.

Naughton, John. "Credit Where Credit's Due. . . ." *Empire* 57 (March 1994): 54–55.

Nicolin, Paola. "Un anno con la XIV—creare nel Grande Numero: Saul Bass." *Abitare* 461 (2006): 1–100.

Niece, Robert C. *Art: An Approach*. Dubuque, IA: William C. Brown, 1963.

Nourmand, Tony. "Films in a Frame. The Multitalented Saul Bass Could Capture a Movie in a Single Image." *Patek Phillippe* 9 (Spring–Summer 2001): 73.

———. "Reel Art." *Art Review* 48 (March 1996): 50–51.

Oakes, Philip. "Bass Note." *Sunday Times*, 9 December 1993, 36.

Oeri, Georgine. "Saul Bass." *Graphis* 11, no. 59 (1955): 258–65.

Oliver, Myrna. "Saul Bass: Innovative Film Title Designer." *Los Angeles Times*, 27 April 1996.

Omasta, Michael. "Saul Bass." *EPD Film* 13 (June 1996): 17.

Penny, Mark. "*Phase IV*: Saul Bass' Directorial Debut." *Offscreen* 12, no. 5 (May 2008).

"*Phase IV*." *Independent Film Journal* 74 (18 September 1974): 8.

"Pioneers: Saul Bass." *Communication Arts* 41, no. 287 (March–April 1999): 164–65, 242.

Pipes, Alan. *Production for Graphic Designers*. 5th ed. Upper Saddle River, NJ: Prentice Hall, 2009.

Piton, Jean-Pierre. "Lexique des réalisaurs de films fantastiques américaines—Saul Bass." *Revue du Cinéma* 360 (April 1981): 121–26.

Pollack, Ben. "Credit Where Credit Is Due—To Titlemakers." *Los Angeles Times*, 28 August 1966.

Ponant, Pierre. "Saul Bass: Un graphiste générique particulier." *Beaux Arts* 244 (2004): 36.

Porter, Bob. "Bass Keeps One Foot in Business World, Other in Films." *Dallas Times Herald*, 16 February 1986, 6C.

Powers, James. "Saul Bass Plans Short Feature on Social Changes." *Hollywood Reporter*, 19 July 1971.

"Prem Helps Bass Make Title Grade in Public Retro." *Variety* 6, no. 3 (1981): 6.

Preminger, Otto. *Preminger: An Autobiography*. New York: Doubleday, 1977.

"Print Personality: Saul Bass." *Print* 11, no. 6 (May–June 1958): 17–38.

Prolsdorfer, R., and S. Brock. "*Quest.*" *Sightlines* 18, no. 3 (Spring 1985).

Pryor, Thomas M. "Hollywood Dossier." *New York Times,* 23 January 1955, X5.

"Public Sees Creative People as Responsible for Environmental, Social Effects, Warns Saul Bass." *Graphics: USA,* September 1970, 1, 21.

Purtell, Tim. "Credits Where Credit Is Due." *Entertainment Weekly,* 1 December 1995, 43.

"Q&A with Saul Bass." *Marquee* 1, no. 1 (Spring 1990).

"A Question for Saul Bass." *New York Times Magazine,* 10 March 1996.

Racine, Robert W. "Short Films: *Why Man Creates.*" *Mass Media Ministries* 7, no. 7 (10 August 1970): 1–2, 8.

Rebello, Stephen. *Alfred Hitchcock and the Making of* Psycho. New York: Dembner Books, 1990.

———. "*Psycho.*" *Cinefantastique* 16, no. 4/5 (October 1986): 48–77.

Redelings, Lowell E. "Men behind the Scenes." *Los Angeles Citizen News,* 24 October 1955.

Relph-Knight, Linda. "The Momentary Magic of Saul Bass's Film Titles." *Design Week* 19, no. 30 (22 July 2004): 4.

"RIT's Annual William A. Reedy Memorial Lecture: Saul Bass on Purpose." *Rochester Institute of Technology News & Events* 11, no. 19 (10 May 1979): 4–5.

Robbins, Valerie. *Preminger—Anatomy of a Filmmaker.* New York: Otto Preminger Films, 1991.

Rockman, Arnold. "It's All a Matter of Credit." *Toronto Daily Star,* 30 June 1962.

Rodman, Howard. "Coastlines: The Name behind the Title." *Village Voice,* 12 July 1988, 57–58.

Romney, Jonathan. "'Let It Roll! He Wrecked 'Popcorn Time' and Turned the Humble Credit Sequence into a Film-goer's Fetish: All Hail Saul Bass, the Matisse of the Movies. . . .'" *Independent,* 18 July 2004. http://enjoyment.independent.co.uk/low_res/story.jsp?story=542645&5dir=21.

Rosenbaum, Jonathan. "*Phase IV.*" *Monthly Film Bulletin* 41 (October 1974): 228.

Ross, Chuck. "Saul Bass Returns in Big Way." *San Francisco Chronicle,* 18 June 1988, C3–5.

Rossner, Ed. "Saul Bass." *Cinema Papers* 11 (January 1977): 238–39.

Rutledge, James. "Time to Give Credit to a True Master." *Daily Telegraph,* 17 July 2004.

Ryan, Tom. *Otto Preminger Films Exodus: A Report.* New York: Random House, 1960.

Saada, Nicholas. "Saul Bass, l'art de l'ouverture. L'homme qui promettait des rêves." *Cahiers du Cinéma* 504 (July–August 1996): 34–39.

Salavetz, Judith, Spencer Drate, and Sam Sarowitz, eds. *Art of the Modern Movie Poster: International Postwar Style and Design.* San Francisco: Chronicle Books, 2008.

"Saul Bass." *Communication Arts* 11, no. 4 (August–September 1969): 16–19.

"Saul Bass." *Communication Arts* 32, no. 2 (March–April 1990): 5–6.

"Saul Bass." *Design Journal* (Korea) 8 (1988): 36–37.

Selected Bibliography

"Saul Bass." *Graphis* 46, no. 46 (May–June 1990): 9–10.

"Saul Bass." *IDEA* 18, no. 100 (May 1970): 76–77.

"Saul Bass." *IDEA* 41, no. 240 (September 1993): 130–31.

Saul Bass. Tokyo: Ginza Graphic Gallery, 1993.

"Saul Bass [Interview]." *Designer Magazine*, May 1980, 10, 24.

"Saul Bass: Animation in Design." *Vital—The International Animation Festival*, 13 June 1998, 1.

"Saul Bass: Inventor of Graphic Film Titling." *The Pad. Art Directors Club of Phoenix Newsletter*, May 1966, 2–8.

"Saul Bass: Portfolio of a Versatile Designer's Work." *Print* 15 (May–June 1961): 35–46.

"Saul Bass & Associates." Special issue, *IDEA* (1979).

"Saul Bass Dies at 75; Invented Movie Title Genre." *Graphic Design: USA* 32, no. 6 (June 1996): 20.

"Saul Bass en el cine." *Creatividad* 25 (May–June 1977): 18.

"Saul Bass Interview." *Popular Photography* 55, no. 7 (July 1964): 108.

"Saul Bass 1920–1996." *AIGA Journal of Graphic Design* 14, no. 2 (1996): 54.

"Saul Bass on Corporate Identity." *Step-by-Step Graphics* 2, no. 5 (September–October 1986): 44–45.

Saul Bass Portfolio. Cohoes, NY: Mohawk Graphics Collection, 1985.

"Saul Bass' 'Searching 1-Eye' Spotlights Eastman Kodak's Tiptop Exhibit." *Variety*, 29 April 1964, 178.

Scheuer, Philip K. "Titles Need Not Be Bore. Curse Removed from Screen Credits by Designer Bass." *Los Angeles Times*, March 6, 1958, 11.

Schwartzman, Arnold. "A Moving Experience: The Art of Motion Picture Title." In *Graphic Design since 1950*, ed. Ben Bos and Elly Bos, 661–67. London: Thames and Hudson, 2007.

———. "Passings." *International Documentary* 15, no. 4 (June 1996): 22–23.

———. "Saul Bass: Anatomy of a Mentor." *Baseline International Typographics Journal* 22 (1996): 17–24.

Scorsese, Martin. "Anatomy of a Synthesist." *New York Times Magazine*, 29 December 1996, 44–45.

——— "Film by Elaine and Saul Bass." *IDEA* 41, no. 241 (November 1993). 66–71.

———. "Giving Credit to Saul Bass." *IDEA* 43, no. 5 (September–October 1996): 28.

———. "Martin Scorsese on the Talent of Saul Bass." *Telegraph*, 30 October 2011. http://www.telegraph.co.uk/culture/art/art-features/8855960/Martin-Scorsese-on-the-talent-of-Saul-Bass.html.

———. "Saul Bass: L'homme qui promettait des rêves." *Cahiers du Cinema* 504 (July–August 1996): 40–41.

———. "Saul Bass as a Designer of Films." In *The Master Series: Saul Bass, 11 March–5 April 1996*, 4. New York: Visual Arts Museum at the School of Visual Arts, 1996.

———. "Saul Bass 1920–1996: A Celebration of an Extraordinary Life." Unpublished manuscript, May 1996.

———. "Saul Bass's Cinematic Art: Director Martin Scorsese Remembers the Designer's One-of-a-Kind Movie Posters." *Architectural Digest* 67, no. 3 (March 2010): 44–48.

———. "When the Lights Go Down. Saul Bass Turned Opening Titles into an Exquisite Art." *Guardian*, 9 July 2004.

"The Searching Eye." *CA Magazine: The Journal of Communication Arts*, 1964.

Shay, Don. "The Microcosmic World of Ken Middleham." *Cinefex* 3 (December 1980): 58–71.

Silver, Alain Joel. "Robert Aldrich: A Critical Study." Master's thesis, UCLA, 1973.

Silver, Alain, and James Ursini. *Whatever Happened to Robert Aldrich? His Life and Films*. New York: Limelight, 1995.

6 Chapters in Design: Saul Bass, Ivan Chermayeff, Milton Glaser, Paul Rand, Ikko Tanaka, Henryk Tomaszewski. San Francisco: Chronicle Books, 1997.

Skerry, Philip J. *The Shower Scene in Hitchcock's* Psycho: *Creating Cinematic Suspense and Terror*. Lewiston, NY: Edwin Mellon Press, 2005.

Sohn, David A. "The Eye of the Observer: Films to Make You See." *Science Activities*, January 1970, 10–12.

———. "See How They Run." *Film News* 26, no. 5 (October 1969): 20–21.

Solana, Gemma, and Antonio Boneu. *Uncredited: Graphic Design & Opening Titles in Movies*. Amsterdam: BIS Publishers, 2007.

Sommese, Lanny. "Saul Bass." *Novum Gebrauchsgraphik* 59, no. 6 (June 1988): 4–11, 59.

Spoto, Donald. *The Art of Alfred Hitchcock: Fifty Years of His Motion Pictures*. Garden City, NY: Dolphin Books, 1976.

Stang, Joanne. "Movie (Title) Mogul." *New York Times*, 1 December 1957, 86.

Steen, Tom. "Checklist 60—Saul Bass." *Monthly Film Bulletin* 35, no. 415 (August 1968): 128.

———. "Saul Bass Title Designer." *Skoop* 5, no. 4 (March 1968): 37–48.

Stein, Irwin. *Saint Joan*. Text by Marjorie Mattern. New York: Feature Books, 1957.

Stevenson, Jay. "Saul Bass Obituary." *Cinefantastique* 28, no. 1 (1996): 6.

Stremfel, Michael. "Veteran Logo Artist Sketches for 'Expo.'" *Los Angeles Business Journal*, 21 August 1989, 12.

Sullivan, Catherine. "The Work of Saul Bass." *American Artist* 18, no. 8 (October 1954): 28–31, 67–68.

Supanick, Jim. "Saul Bass: . . . To Hit the Ground Running." *Film Comment* 33, no. 2 (March–April 1997): 72–77, 93.

Swire, Sidney. "Creative Process Is Key to Designer/Director Saul Bass." *Larchmont Chronicle* 32, no. 3 (March 1994): 12.

"Take Two. A Man of Many Titles." *NEO: Innovation and Discovery* 4 (Fall 1995): 7–12.

"A Talk with Saul Bass." *Graphics Today* 2, no. 2 (March–April 1977): 30–36.

Terek, Tomislav. "Saul Bass: The Man behind the Titles." *Filmwaves* 8 (Summer 1999). http://www.filmwaves.co.uk/Filmwaves_files/01_14/8sbass.htm.

Thomas, Robert McG., Jr. "Saul Bass, 75, Designer, Dies; Made Art out of Movie Titles." *New York Times*, 27 April 1996, 30.

Thomson, David. "The Man with the Golden Pen." *Independent on Sunday*, 21 June 1998, 19–20.

Thomson, David, and Ian Christie. *Scorsese on Scorsese*. London: Faber, 1996.

Timmer, Andreas A. "Making the Ordinary Extraordinary: The Film-Related Work of Saul Bass." PhD diss., Columbia University, 1999.

"Top Drawer. A 'First' for Saul Bass." *Print* 16, no. 6 (November 1962): 55.

Tume, Grant. "Design for Living." *Detour Magazine*, March 1996, 32.

Tylski, Alexandre. "Saul Bass: Les films d'un grand cinéaste." *Positif* 601 (March 2011): 63–67.

Uffelen, René van. "Saul Bass 1921–1996." *Skrien* 209 (August–September 1996): 78.

Uhelszki, Jaan. "Film: The Art of Motion Graphics in Film." *Soma* 18, no. 7 (September 2004): 39, 86.

Vallee, Julien. "My Design Classic: Saul Bass—'Anatomy of a Murder.'" *Computer Arts* 199 (2012).

van der Leun, Gerard. "That Old Bass Magic." *United Mainliner* 25, no. 3 (March 1981): 61–64.

Via, Baldo. "Saul Bass: All'inizio era il titolo." *CineCritica* 4, no. 13/14 (1999): 60–62.

Viviani, Christian. "*Quest*." *Positif* 281–82 (July–August 1984): 98.

Waugh, John C. "The Art of Film Credits." *Christian Science Monitor*, 18 July 1961.

Weiler, A[be]. H. "*Phase IV*." *New York Times*, 21 October 1974, 48.

Weinstock, Neal. "A Graphic Worth a Thousand Words." *Millimeter* 12, no. 6 (June 1984): 80–82.

"The West Coast: A Designer's View." *Industrial Design* 4, no. 10 (October 1957): 44–76, 128–29.

Whitehall, Richard. "The Film Scene." *Open City* 68 (6–12 September 1968).

Whitman, M. "*Phase IV*." *Films Illustrated* 4 (November 1974): 84.

"*Why Man Creates* by Saul Bass." *Art Education* 22, no. 7 (October 1969): 49.

Williams, David E. "Initial Images." *American Cinematographer* 79, no. 5 (May 1998): 92–98.

Wilson, William. "Saul Bass . . . Virtuoso of Useful Art." *Los Angeles Times Calendar*, 29 December 1968, 8

Wolf, Henry. "Saul Bass." *Creation* 18 (1993): 34–57.

———. "Saul Bass." *Graphis* 41, no. 235 (January–February 1985): 28–35.

"The World Masters 1: Saul Bass." *IDEA* 38, no. 219 (March 1990): 20–28.

Woudhuysen, James. "Bass Profundo." *Design Week* 4, no. 38 (22 September 1989): 16–17.

Yager, Herb. "Saul Bass." *Graphis* 33, no. 193 (1977–1978): 392–407.

Yager, Herb, and Saul Bass. "Questions, Answers, Evasions." In "Saul Bass & Associates," special issue, *IDEA* (1979): 128–29.

Zeitlin, David. "Seen Any Good Titles Lately?" *Life*, 7 February 1964, 99–101.

About Movie Publicity

Ades, Dawn. *The 20th Century Poster: Design of the Avant-Garde*. New York: Abbeville Press, 1984.

Barnicoat, John. *Posters: A Concise History*. London: Thames and Hudson, 1985.

Les Belles affiches du cinema. Paris: Atlas, 1986.

Bresler, Jerry, et al. "The Journal Looks at Motion Picture Advertising." *Journal of the Screen Producers Guild*, June 1961, 3–31.

Byrne, Bridget. "The Art of Film." *Box Office* 134 (July 1998): 26.

Ciment, G. "A Critical Bibliography of Movie Posters." *Positif* 311 (January 1987): 57–60.

Del Costello, Mark. "Big Boom in Movie Posters." *American Film* 4 (July–August 1979): 20–24.

Doff, John. "Making Film Ads." *Films and Filming* 1, no. 5 (February 1955): 10.

Eckersley, Tom. *Poster Design*. London: Studio Publications, 1954.

Edwards, Dianna. *Picture Show: Classic Movie Posters from the TCM Archives*. San Francisco: Chronicle Books, 2003.

Edwards, Gregory J. *The International Film Poster*. Salem, NH: Salem House, 1985.

Everett, Diana Difranco. *Movie Posters: 75 Years of Academy Award Winners*. Atglen, PA: Schiffer, 2002.

Fischer-Nosbisch, Fritz. "Film Poster Today." *Camera* 45, no. 5 (May 1966): 40–47.

Frank, S. "Hollywood's Ballyhoo Boys." *Saturday Evening Post*, 11 December 1948, 34–35.

Fuller, Kathryn H. *At the Picture Show: Small Town Movie Audiences and the Creation of Movie Fan Culture*. Washington, DC: Smithsonian Press, 1996.

Games, Abram. "The Poster in Modern Advertising." *Royal Society of Arts Journal* 110, no. 5069 (April 1962): 323.

Golding, David. "Keep the Drums Rolling." *Journal of the Screen Producers Guild*, November 1956, 10.

Goodman, Mort. "Ad Agencies Dust off Old Show Biz Tricks, Reap a Rich Harvest." *Daily Variety*, 25 October 1966, 232.

Gordon, Jay E. "There's Really No Business Like Show Business." *Quarterly of Film, Radio and Television* 6, no. 2 (Winter 1951): 173–85.

Haralovich, Mary Beth. "Film Advertising, the Film Industry, and the Pin-up: The Industry's Accommodations to Social Forces in the 1940's." *Current Research in Film* 1 (1985): 127–64.

———. "Motion Picture Advertising: Industrial and Social Forces and Effects, 1930–1948." PhD diss., University of Wisconsin–Madison, 1984.

Hershenson, Bruce. "A History of Movie Posters." 1998. http://www.reelclassics .com/Articles/General/posters-article.htm.

"History of the Movies and the Movie Poster." http://www.fffmovieposters.com/ movieposterhistory.php.

"Hollywood's Clamour Boys." *American Mercury* 54 (January 1942): 85–92.

Holston, K. Review of *A Century of Movie Posters, from Silent to Art House. Library Journal* 129, no. 2 (February 2004): 88.

Johnson, Keith F. "Cinema Advertising." *Journal of Advertising* 10, no. 4 (Winter 1981): 11–19.

King, Emily. *A Century of Movie Posters, from Silent to Art House.* London: Mitchell and Beasily, 2003.

Kobal, John. *50 Years of Movie Posters.* London: Hamlyn, 1973.

———. *Foyer Pleasure: The Golden Age of Cinema Lobby Cards.* New York: Delilah Communications, 1983.

Koszarski, Richard. *History of American Cinema 3. An Evening's Entertainment: The Age of the Silent Feature Picture, 1915–1928.* New York: Scribner's Sons, 1990.

Lederer, Richard. "I Don't Know Anything about Advertising, But. . . ." *Journal of the Screen Producers Guild*, September 1969, 25–27.

Lockwood, C. "Movie Memorabilia—Old Movie Posters." *Connoisseur* 208, no. 836 (1981): 114–17.

Luk, Tiiu. *Movie Marketing: Opening the Picture and Giving It Legs.* Beverly Hills, CA: Silman-James Press, 1997.

"Macy's vs. Movies." *Time*, 18 January 1932, 22.

Madalena, Batiste. *Movie Posters: The Paintings of Batiste Madalena.* New York: Abrams, 1985.

Maynell, Francis. "This Publicity Business." *Sight & Sound* 5, no. 19 (Autumn 1936): 6–68.

McGee, Mark Thomas. *Beyond Ballyhoo: Motion Picture Promotion and Gimmicks.* Jefferson, NC: McFarland, 1989.

Metzl, Ervine. *The Poster: Its History and Its Art.* New York: Watson-Guptill, 1963.

Montini, F. "Posters and Movie Publicity." *Cineforum* 22, no. 1–2 (1982): 35–38.

Morella, Joe, Edward Z. Epstein, and Eleonor Clark. *Those Great Movie Ads.* New Rochelle, NY: Arlington House, 1972.

"Movie Promises and Performance." *Christian Century* 48 (25 February 1931): 360.

"Movie Promotion Up." *Business Week*, 8 June 1940, 47.

Muller, Eddie. *The Art of Noir: The Posters and Graphics from the Classic Era of Film Noir.* New York: Overlook Press, 2002.

Noah, Emil T., Jr. *Movie Gallery: A Pictorial History of Motion Picture Advertisements.* Fort Lauderdale, FL: Noah Communications, 1980.

Nourmand, Tony, and Graham Marsh. *Film Posters of the 50s: The Essential Movies of the Decade.* New York: Overlook Press, 2001.

———. *Film Posters of the 60s: The Essential Movies of the Decade.* Cologne: Evergreen/Taschen, 2005.

Novin, Guity. "A History of American Movie Posters." In *A History of Graphic Design.* http://guity-novin.blogspot.com/2011/09/chapter-46-history-of-american-movie.html.

Poole, Edwin, and Susan Poole. *Collecting Movie Posters: An Illustrated Reference Guide.* Jefferson, NC: McFarland, 1997.

———. *Learn about Movie Posters.* Chattanooga, TN: iGuide Media, 2002.

Rebello, Stephen. "National Screen Service." *Cinefantastique* 18, no. 2/3 (1988): 76.

————. "Selling Nightmares: Movie Poster Artists of the Fifties." *Cinefantastique* 18, no. 2/3 (1988): 40–75.

Rebello, Stephen, and Richard Allen. *Reel Art: Great Posters from the Golden Age of the Silver Screen*. New York: Abbeville Press, 1988.

Resnick, Ira M. *Starstruck: Vintage Movie Posters from Classic Hollywood*. New York: Abbeville Press, 2010.

Rickards, Maurice. *The Rise and Fall of the Poster*. New York: McGraw-Hill, 1971.

Rotzoll, Kim B. "The Captive Audience: The Troubled Odyssey of Cinema Advertising." In *Current Research in Film: Audiences, Economics, and Law*, 72–87. Norwood, NJ: Ablex, 1987.

Sarowitz, Sam. *Translating Hollywood: The World of Movie Posters*. New York: Mark Batty Publisher, 2007.

Schapiro, Steve, and David Chierichetti. *The Movie Poster Book*. New York: E. P. Dutton, 1979.

Scott, Kathryn Leigh. *Lobby Cards: The Classic Films*. Los Angeles: Pomegranate Press, 1987.

Selling Dreams: British and American Film Posters 1890–1976. Cardiff: Welsh Arts Council, 1977.

Slide, Anthony. *Now Playing: Hand-Painted Poster Art from the 1910s through the 1950s*. Santa Monica, CA: Angel City Press, 2007.

Snedaker, Kit. "The Image-Dealers." *Los Angeles Herald-Examiner California Living*, 29 August 1971, 18–24.

Staiger, Janet. "Announcing Wares, Winning Patrons, Voicing Ideals: Thinking about the History and Theory of Film Advertising." *Cinema Journal* 29, no. 3 (Spring 1990): 3–31.

Sweeney, Russell C. *Coming Next Week: A Pictorial History of Film Advertising*. New York: Castle Books, 1973.

Timmers, Margaret, et al., eds. *The Power of the Poster*. London: V&A Publications, 1998.

Vance, Malcolm. *The Movie Ad Book*. Minneapolis, MN: Control Data Publishing, 1981.

Webb, M. "Art—Vintage Movie Posters." *Architectural Digest* 54, no. 1 (April 1994): 256–65.

Weill, Alain. *The Poster*. New York: G. K. Hall, 1985.

Williams, John Elliot. "They Stopped at Nothing." *Hollywood Quarterly* 1, no. 3 (April 1946): 270–78.

Willis, F. H. "Hans Hillmann's Film Posters." *Graphis* 15 (July 1959): 344–49.

Wyatt, Justin. *High Concept: Movies and Marketing in Hollywood*. Austin: University of Texas Press, 1994.

Zreik, Serge. *Souvenirs d'Hollywood: Affiches du cinéma américain, 1925–1950*. Paris: Editions Alternatives, 1986.

About Credit Sequences

Abrams, Janet. "Beginnings, Endings, and the Stuff in Between." *Sight & Sound* 4 (December 1994): 22–25.

Aison, Everett. "The Current Scene: Film Titles." *Print* 19 (July–August 1965): 2.

Aleiss, Angela. "The Names behind the Titles." *Variety,* 8 December 1997, 86.

Allison, Deborah. "Beyond Saul Bass: A Century of American Film Title Sequences." *Film International,* 30 January 2011. http:///filmint.nu/?p=202.

———. "Catch Me If You Can, Auto Focus, Far from Heaven and the Art of Retro Title Sequences." *Senses of Cinema* 26 (2003). http://www.sensesofcinema .com/2003/26/retro_titles/.

———. "Novelty Title Sequences and Self-Reflexivity in Classical Hollywood Cinema." *Screening the Past* 20 (2006). http://www.latrobe.edu.au/screeningthe past/20/ novelty-title-sequences.htmlBottomofForm.

Armitage, Merle. "Movie Titles." *Print* 5, no. 2 (1947): 38–44.

Billson, Anne. "Credits Where Credits Are Due." *Independent* (London), 2 June 1988, 23.

Blanchard, Gérard. "Le scriptovisuell ou Cinémato-Graphe." In *L'Espace et la lettre: Écitures, typographies,* 393–438. Paris: Union générale editions, 1977.

Böhnke, Alexander. "Handarbeit, Figuren der Schrift in SE7EN." *Montage/AV* 12, no. 2 (2003): 9–18.

———. "Der Vorspann." In *Gesichter des Films,* ed. Johanna Barck and Petra Löffler. Bielefeld: Transkript Verlag, 2005.

Böhnke, Alexander, Rembrent Hüser, and Georg Stanitzek, eds. *Das Buch zum Vorspann* [The Title Is the Shot]. Berlin: Vorwerk, 2006.

Boin, David J. "The History and Art of Motion Picture Title Production." Unpublished manuscript, 1963. Margaret Herrick Library, Academy of Motion Picture Arts and Sciences.

Bordwell, David, Janet Staiger, and Kristin Thompson. *The Classical Hollywood Cinema: Film Style & Mode of Production to 1960.* New York: Columbia University Press, 1985.

Bowser, Eileen. *Transformations in Cinema: 1907–1915.* Berkeley: University of California Press, 1994.

Boxer, Sarah. "Making a Fuss over Opening Credits." *New York Times,* 22 April 2000, A15, 17.

Calhoun, John Leroy. "Where Credit Is Due: The Heads and Tails of Title Design." *Theatre Crafts* 21, no. 7 (August September 1987): 79–82.

Charney, Leopold Joseph. *Just Beginnings: Film Studies, Close Analysis and the Viewer's Experience.* Ann Arbor, MI: UMI, 1993.

Conley, Tom. *Film Hieroglyphs: Ruptures in Classical Cinema.* Minneapolis: University of Minnesota Press, 1991.

Croal, N'Gai. "Where Credits Are Due." *Newsweek,* 10 November 1997, 92.

D'Angelo, Aldo. "La grafica e cinema nella television." *Bianco e nero* 29, no. 9–10 (September–October 1968).

de Mourgues, Nicole. *Le générique de film.* Paris: Méridiens Klincksieck, 1994.

Dorfsman, Louis. "Film Titles and Captions." In *Film and TV Graphics 2: An International Survey of the Art of Film Animation,* ed. Walter Herdig, 172–95. Zurich: Graphis Press, 1976.

Emerson, John, and Anita Loos. "Title Technique." *Motion Picture Magazine* 21, no. 6 (July 1921): 30, 82, 86.

Gardies, André. "Au commencement était le générique." In *Le conteur de l'ombre. Essais sur la narration filmique*, ed. André Gardies, 12–23. Lyon: Aléas, 1999.

Geffner, David. "First Things First." *Filmmaker Magazine* 6, no. 1 (Fall 1997). http://www.filmmakermagazine.com/issues/fa111997/firstthingsfirst.php.

Geibel, Victoria. "Images in Motion." *Design Quarterly* 144 (1989): 1–30.

Goss, Tom. "On Air, on Screen, Type over Time." *Print* 40 (November 1986): 72–78.

Halas, John. "Graphics in Motion." *Novum Gebrauchsgrafik* 9 (September 1982): 14–19.

Halas, John, and Roger Manvell. *Design in Motion.* New York: Hastings House, 1962.

Harris, Adam Duncan. "Das goldene Zeitalter de Filvorspanns: Die Geschichte der Pacific Title and Art Studios." In *Das Buch zum Vorspann*, ed. Alexander Böhnke, Rembrent Hüser, and Georg Stanitzek, 123–36. Berlin: Vorwerk, 2006.

Harvey, Francis. "Type and the TV Screen." *Print* 8 (1954): 91–116.

Heller, Steven. "Quick Cuts, Coarse Letters, Multiple Screens (Mr. Roughcut)." *Eye Magazine* 32 (Summer 1999). http://www.typotheque.com/articles/quick_cuts_coarse_letters_multiple_screens.

———. "Reel Classics." *ID: The International Design Magazine* 46 (March–April 1999): 64–69.

Henning, Michael. "Der Vorspann im Film." Unpublished Diplomarbeit, FB Design, Universität Köln, 1997.

Herdeg, Walter, ed. *Film and TV Graphics II: An International Survey of the Art of Film Animation.* Zurich: Graphis Press, 1976.

Inceer, Melis. "An Analysis of the Opening Credit Sequence in Film." Senior thesis, University of Pennsylvania, May 2007. http://repository.upenn.edu/cgi/viewcontent.cgi?article=1080&context=curej.

Johnson, Grady. "Credits Ledger: Film Title-Making Is Inventive Business." *New York Times*, 16 October 1955, X6.

Kaufmann, Debra. "The Name behind the Titles: At 75, Pacific Title & Art Studio." *Hollywood Reporter*, 23 March 1994, 3, 10.

King, Emily. "Taking Credit: Film Title Sequences, 1955–1965." Master's thesis, Royal College of Art, 1994. http://www.typotheque.com/articles/taking_credit_film_title_sequences_1955–1965.

Kirkham, Pat. "Dots and Sickles: Maurice Binder's Bond Titles." *Sight & Sound* 5 (December 1995): 10–13.

Kramer, Stanley, with Thomas H. Coffey. *A Mad, Mad, Mad, Mad World: A Life in Hollywood.* New York: Harcourt, Brace, 1997.

Kreck, Joachim. *Spielfilm-Titel. Eine Dokumentation der XIV Westdeutschen Kurzfilmtage Oberhausen.* Oberhausen: Westdeutsche Kurzfimtage, 1968.

Kuntzel, Thiery. "The Film Work." *Enclictic* 2 (Spring 1978): 39–61.

———. "The Film Work 2." *Camera Obscura* 5 (1980): 6–68. In German: "Die Filmarbeit, 2." *Montage/AV* 8, no. 1 (1999): 25–84.

Levy, Raymond. "The Art of Film Titles." *Motion Picture Herald*, 4 March 1964, 16.

Limcaco, Jad. "100 Years of Movie Title Designs." http://designinformer
.smashingmagazine.com/2010/02/03/100-years-movie-title-stills/.

Mathewson, Joseph. "Titles Are Better than Ever." *New York Times*, 16 July 1967, J1.

May, Judith. "The Art of Title Design throughout Cinema History." *Smashing Magazine*, 4 October 2010. http://www.smashingmagazine.com/2010/10/04/
the-art-of-the-film-title-throughout-cinema-history/.

McCort, Kristinha. "Titles throughout Time: The Evolution of Film Title Design."
Millimeter 30, no. 77 (July 2002): 25–26, 28.

Milne, Peter. "The Development of the Sub-title." *Photoplay* 28, no. 5 (October
1925): 132.

Murphy, A. D. "Only a Pittance for Pix Titling." *Daily Variety*, 31 October 1967, 46, 179.

Pearlman, Chee. "Roll Call." *ID: The International Design Magazine* 37, no. 2
(March–April 1990): 38–45.

Peters, David. "Every Frame Counts." *Eye Magazine* 66 (Winter 2007). http://www
.eyemagazine.com/feature/article/every-frame-counts.

"Pix Owe Much to Credits. Opening Runoff Now Getting Lotsa Flair, Flash, Mood-
Setting Motifs." *Variety*, 11 September 1957, 7, 19.

Pollack, Ben. "Credit Where Credit Is Due—To Titlemakers." *Los Angeles Times*, 8
August 1966, 10, 41.

Re, Valentina. *Al Margini del Film: Incipit e titoli di testa*. Pasian di Prato: Campa-
notto Editore, 2006.

Rosentswieg, Gerry. "Please Read the Titles to Yourself." *Show: The Magazine of Films
and the Arts* 1, no. 2 (February 1970): 55–62.

Ross, Chuck. "Saul Bass Returns in 'Big' Way." *San Francisco Chronicle*, 18 June
1988, C3, C5.

Saignes, Michel. "Pour un cinema graphique." *Banc-Titre* 1–2 (April 1978): 4–5.

Scheuer, Philip K. "Title Art Occupies World of Its Own." *Los Angeles Times*, 29
August 1961, 7.

Spinrad, Leonard. "Titles: There's More to Them than Meets the Eye and Ear." *Films
in Review* 6, no. 4 (April 1955): 168–70.

Stanitzek, George. "Reading the Title Sequence (Vorspann, Générique)." *Cinema
Journal* 48, no. 4 (Summer 2009): 44–50.

"The Story behind Screen Titles." *Production Design: The Magazine of the Society of
Motion Picture Art Directors* 3, no. 1 (1953): 28–36.

Straw, Will. "Letters of Introduction: Film Credits and Cityscapes." http://
strawresearch.mcgill.ca/LettersofIntroduction.pdf.

Tarleau, Ellen D. "The Illustrated Title." *Motion Picture Magazine*, March 1920, 38,
94, 96.

"Titles: Coming on Strong." *Newsweek*, 8 July 1968, 64–65.

Tylski, Alexandre. *Le générique de cinéma: Histoire et fonctions d'un fragment hybride*.
Toulouse: Presses universitaires du Mirail, 2008.

Vernet, Marc. "The Filmic Transaction: On the Openings of Film Noirs." *Velvet Light
Trap* 20 (Summer 1983): 2–9.

Weed, Peter. "What's in a Title?" *Movie Maker* 14, no. 70 (Summer 2007): 30–32.

Wright, Benjamin. "Death of the Title Sequence." In *Aspect Ratio.* 2008. http://aspectratio.wordpress.com/2008/03/19/death-of-the-title-sequence/.

Yu, Li. "Typography in Film Title Sequence Design." Paper 11366, University of Iowa, 2008. http://lib.dr.iastate.edu/etd/11366.

Zagala, Anna. "The Edges of Film." *Senses of Cinema,* 21 May 2002. http://sensesofcinema.com/2002/feature-articles/titles/.

Zeitlin, David. "Seen Any Good Titles Lately?" *Life,* 7 February 1964, 99–101.

General

Aynsley, Jeremy. *Pioneers of Modern Graphic Design.* London: Michael Beazley, 2005.

Hayles, N. Katherine. "Virtual Bodies and Flickering Signifiers." *October* 66 (1993): 69–91.

James, David. *The Most Typical Avant-Garde: History and Geography of Minor Cinemas in Los Angeles.* Berkeley: University of California Press, 2005.

Poulin, Richard. *The Language of Graphic Design.* Beverly, MA: Rockport Publishers, 2012.

Remington, Roger. *Nine Pioneers in American Graphic Design.* New York: W. W. Norton, 1989.

Index

Abbott, Bernice, 227, 401n4

ABC (American Broadcasting Corporation), 42, 235, 249, 258

Abstract Expressionism, 24, 30, 142, 143, 167

Academy Awards (Oscars), 1, 2, 3, 5, 9, 43, 45, 120, 140, 197, 201, 212, 215, 219–20, 230, 239, 267, 271, 315, 326, 330–32, 368, 369n6

Adler, Harold, 38, 102, 192, 393n119

advertising, trade, 35, 36–37, 56–65, 70, 104, 116, 126, 130–31, 139–40, 144, 160–61, 179, 185, 191–95, 205, 276, 312, 351, 361–65

Advise and Consent (1962), 16, 41, 84, 96, 99, 132, 140, 149, 168–69, 197, 201, 274, 365, 387n16

Age of Innocence, The (1993), 11, 45, 95, 100, 168–69, 174, 176–77, 258, 368

Albers, Annie, 26, 47, 49

Albers, Josef, 47, 49, 143; *Homage to a Square* (1950), 143

ALCOA (Aluminum Company of America), 39, 45, 143, 174, 235–38, 243, 328, 402n33

Alcoa Premiere (TV series), 217, 229, 235–38, 261, 280, 354, 364

Aldrich, Robert, 42, 61, 64, 178, 179, 208–10, 362; *Vera Cruz* (1954), 64,178, 208, 362

Algren, Nelson, 152, 278

All About Eve (1950), 37, 56, 361

American Cinematographer (magazine), 73, 74, 79

American Film Institute (AFI), 12, 17, 22, 72, 192, 358

Anatomy of a Murder (1959), 6, 16, 30, 41, 58, 97, 104, 131–32, 141–42, 144, 163, 194–96, 202, 229, 233, 274, 354, 364

Anderson, Howard, 89, 187

Anderson, Michael, 124, 362

animation, 2, 5, 20, 27, 30, 78, 82, 87, 92, 110, 114, 119, 121–23, 145, 152, 184, 196, 218, 220, 222, 251, 253, 259, 294, 296, 308, 311, 319, 324–25, 334, 347, 354–55; computer, 20, 182, 355; stop-motion, 207, 334

Apocalypse Now (1979), 43, 367

Apples and Oranges (1962), 31, 43, 126, 320–24, 365

Arakaki, George, 39

Argo (2012), 6

Arnheim, Rudolf, 47, 67, 91

Around the World in 80 Days (1956), 27, 73, 95–97, 119, 120, 125, 149, 210, 253, 308, 362

Art Directors Club of Los Angeles, 14–15, 37, 42, 283

Art Directors Club of New York, 13–15, 42, 50, 138, 327

Art Nouveau, 95, 135

Arts & Architecture (magazine), 14

Art Students League, 35, 374n13

Astaire, Fred, 76, 235–36, 380n35
AT&T (American Telephone and
    Telegraph), 2, 13, 39, 43, 45,
    129–30, 253, 333, 342
Attack! (1956), 57, 73, 97, 104,
    117, 193, 202, 208, 362

Bacon, Paul, 147
Bad Education (2004), 6
Baker, Carroll, 244–46, 272
Balsmeyer, Randy, 90
Band-Aid commercial (1962), 205,
    207–8, 365
Bass, Andrea, 35
Bass (Makatura), Elaine, 1, 11–12,
    17–19, 26–28, 38–39, 44–45,
    97, 105–6, 166, 173–75, 199,
    203–4, 215–17, 220–21, 254,
    256–58, 266, 282, 285, 288,
    291, 294–96, 299, 302, 370n32,
    375n40, 398n61, 400n83,
    411n14
Bass, Jeffrey, 39, 206
Bass, Jennifer, 39
Bass, Robert, 35
Bass (Cooper), Ruth, 35, 38–39,
    375n40
Bass, Saul: biography, 34–46, 227;
    brand of 4–5, 7–8, 11, 13–21,
    25–29, 34, 36, 56, 58, 61,
    63–67, 94, 106, 124, 154, 177,
    182, 195, 240, 249, 258, 276,
    353, 355 ; corporate design work
    by, 9–10, 12–13, 17–18, 28, 30,
    39, 42–45, 63–65, 71, 129, 236,
    324, 351; design theory, anti, 34,
    51–52, 91–92, 334
Bass on Titles (1978), 12, 17, 43,
    72, 92–94, 168, 170, 218, 241,
    270, 367, 398n64
Bass/Yager & Associates, 7, 11, 63,
    65, 220, 258, 296. *See also* Saul
    Bass & Associates
Bauhaus, 8, 13, 15, 24–27, 29, 36,

46–51, 53–56, 60–61, 63–65,
    68, 95–96, 98, 101, 129, 138,
    163, 191, 193–94, 225, 231,
    238, 288–89, 302, 323, 334–35,
    352–54; philosophy of, 50–53,
    54–58, 95, 163
Bayer, Herbert, 15, 47, 58, 96
Bazin, André, 27, 218
Beall, Lester, 57
Beese, Lotte, 26
Bell, Douglas, 33–34, 56
Bell Telephone campaign film
    (1969), 43, 129, 194–95,
    416n89
Belson, Jordan, 184, 257
Benny, Jack, 77, 321
Bernstein, Elmer, 131, 143,
    150–51, 165–66, 196, 243, 247,
    279, 281; *Blues & Brass* (1954),
    247
Bernstein, Leonard, 239–40
Big (1988), 108, 267, 367
Big Country, The (1958), 68, 73,
    93, 99, 140, 202, 270–74, 277,
    280, 285, 363; poster, 132, 138,
    140
Big Knife, The (1955), 97–98,
    177–79, 192, 208, 362
billboards, 7, 87, 125, 131, 136,
    142, 194, 233, 271, 389n45
Binder, Joseph, 57
Binder, Maurice, 20, 83, 89
Blaustein, Julian, 61, 151, 158, 308,
    310
Blodgett, Thurston, 3
Bogeaus, Benedict, 62, 192
Bonjour Tristesse (1958), 16, 41, 64,
    110–14, 132, 134, 363; poster,
    141, 144–45, 149, 354
Bordwell, David, 79, 86
Bradbury, Ray, 43, 44, 295–96,
    298, 376n62, 410n78
Brakhage, Stan, 24
Brandt, Marianne, 47

Braque, Georges, 58
Bredendieck, Hin, 49
Breuer, Marcel, 47, 49
British Film Institute (BFI), 148, 181–82
Broadcast News (1987), 71, 367
Broadway, 62, 87, 120, 126, 131, 145, 178, 189, 208, 228, 230, 239, 246–47, 248–50, 257–58, 260–61
Brodovitch, Alexey, 15
Brooklyn College, 15, 35, 49
Brooks, James L., 45, 367
Brooks, Richard, 71, 194, 367
Brothers (1977), 133, 141, 194, 367
Brownjohn, Robert, 89
Bruhwiler, Paul, 3
Buchanan & Company, 36–37
Bunny Lake Is Missing (1965), 16, 41, 95–97, 108, 132, 177, 185–86, 194, 366
Burn after Reading (2008), 6
Burrows, Hal, 84, 136
Burtin, Will, 10, 15, 50, 57

Cannes Advertising Film Festival, 43, 203
Cape Fear (1991), 11, 45, 99, 163, 165–68, 183, 350, 368
capitalism, 46, 57, 308, 352–53
capital letters, 89, 96–97, 103, 106, 108–11, 113, 124, 126, 147, 151, 157, 159, 161 62, 164, 166, 169, 173, 185–86, 188, 196, 198, 210, 212, 216, 233–34, 236–37, 241, 252, 268, 272, 279, 309, 314, 333
Cardinal, The (1963), 16, 99, 108, 132, 147–48, 240, 274–80, 280, 300, 302, 365
Carmen (Bizet), 118
Carmen Jones (1954), 16, 38–41, 61, 73, 97–98, 100, 130, 132, 138–40, 153–57, 160, 179, 361

Carra, Vincent, 3
Casados, John, 3
Casino (1995), 5, 26, 45, 97, 154, 162, 229, 247, 254–58, 368
CBS (Columbia Broadcasting System), 43, 45, 58, 217, 248, 320–23, 332
Champion, The (1949), 33–34, 37, 61, 63, 315, 361
Chermayeff, Ivan, 29
Chermayeff, Serge, 49
Chicago Film Festival, 72, 149, 367–68
Cinemascope, 73, 98, 111, 116, 230, 251, 282, 285
Cinerama, 97, 125–26, 210–12, 386n168
circles, 26, 50, 55, 58, 67–68, 111–13, 116, 122, 155, 187, 210, 224, 232–33, 237, 247–48, 252, 280, 292–93, 323, 348, 352
Clarke, Stanley, 107
color, use of, 26, 36, 53–55, 61, 63–68, 74, 82, 89, 97, 111–12, 122, 130, 140, 144, 155–57, 162, 171, 175, 217, 231, 242–43, 254, 258, 273, 276, 297, 310, 347, 355; and typography, 85, 96, 104, 114
Container Corporation of America, 15, 47, 58
Continental Airlines, 13
Cooper, Kyle, 6, 90, 107–8; *Se7en* (1995), 6
Cowboy (1958), 95, 97, 307–10, 320, 363
Cox, Jeremy, 90
Crosby, Bing, 77, 380n35
Crystal, Billy, 215–16, 368
Cukor, George, 85, 362
Culhane, Shamus, 119
Curtis, Tony, 1, 198

Dandridge, Dorothy, 61, 138, 156
Darwin, Charles, 222, 336
Daves, Delmar, 307–8, 310, 363
Davis, Bette, 146, 158, 160
Death of a Salesman (1951), 37, 179, 199, 276, 361
Decision before Dawn (1951), 37, 58, 60, 194–95, 361
De Fina, Barbara, 108, 254, 256
Deren, Maya, 25, 154
DeVito, Danny, 173–74, 368
Dietz, Howard, 84, 88,
Dimondstein, Morton, 3
Director's Guild of America (DGA), 116, 148
Dmytryk, Edward, 37, 72, 278, 361, 365
Dondis, Donis A., 357
Dorfsman, Louis, 10, 39, 45, 321, 330–31, 349, 376n70
dot-matrix pattern, 247, 249, 250, 251–53
Double McGuffin, The (1979), 133, 141, 367
Drewes, Werner, 49
Duchamp, Marcel, 207, 227, 397n39
Dunn, Linwood G., 86
Durgnat, Raymond, 22, 102

Eames, Charles and Ray, 11, 212, 351
Eastman Kodak Company, 10, 43, 218, 283, 287–91, 294, 296
Edge of the City (1957), 98, 140, 193, 249, 267–70, 277, 363, 413n37; poster, 149, 270
Edwards, Owen, 12, 17–18
Ed Wood (1994), 6
Ehrman, Marli,
Eisenstein, Sergei, 22, 24, 30, 62, 191, 197, 203, 205, 227, 318; *October* (1927), 197, 318; *Potemkin* (1925), 191, 318

Eittel, Clifford, 57
Ellington, Duke, 142, 196
Elliot, Melissa, 90
Engel, Jules, 39, 42
Everett, Mimi, 90
Exodus (1960), 16, 41, 96–97, 132–33, 148–49, 154–55, 160–62, 194–96, 200, 210, 256, 331, 354, 364, 391n85, 392n89

Facts of Life, The (1960), 6, 194, 200–202, 364
Feher, Joseph, 57
Feininger, Lux, 47, 50
Feininger, Lyonel, 46, 47, 50
Feldman, Charles K., 229–30, 278
Ferrer, José, 180, 362
Ferro, Pablo, 89, 211
film titles, 4–6, 11, 16–17, 27–28, 40, 45, 71–75, 78–80, 97–101, 111, 119, 145, 157, 170, 197, 208, 229, 243, 252, 266, 281, 306, 351, 361–68, 382n132; history, 84–90; theory, 21–22, 80–84, 90–92
Fischinger, Oskar, 145, 207, 352
Fitzgerald, Wayne, 76, 89–90
Fixer, The (1968), 146, 366
Fong, Karin, 90
Foote, Cone & Belding, 37, 38
Foote, Emerson, 37
Foote, Horton, 248
Foreman, Carl, 23, 315–16, 365
Four Horseman of the Apocalypse, The (1962), 43, 308, 311–15, 317–18, 320, 365, 411n14
Four Just Men (1959), 229, 232, 323, 364
Frank, Melvin, 200, 364
Frankenheimer, John, 6, 23, 42, 187–88, 210–14, 233, 248, 363, 365–66, 394n133, 401n20
Frank Sinatra Show, The (1957), 42, 252, 363

Freberg, Stan, 43, 127, 258–60
Fredenthal, David, 115, 118, 385n145
Freeman, Bob, 90
Freud, Sigmund, 81, 158, 177, 180–81, 185, 336
Friedman, Hal, 9
From Here to There (1964), 11, 27, 43, 53, 203, 218, 282–86, 287, 290, 293, 347, 365
Fruchtman, Jerry, 39

Gabo, Naum, 49
Gandhi, Mahatma, 147, 170–71
Ganis, Sid, 41
Garfein, Jack, 243–46, 364
Garland, Judy, 62, 77, 247, 321
Garza, Augustine, 3
Gavin, John, 104, 198
General Film Company, 135
Gestalt theory, 53–55, 67, 91, 129, 133, 154, 357
Giacometti, Alberto, 69, 141, 145, 232, 340, 342
Glaser, Milton, 29, 137
Godard, Jean-Luc, 24–25, 208
Goldsholl, Morton, 57, 364
Goodfellas (1990), 45, 97, 99, 101, 107–8, 168, 185, 368
Goodman, Art, 5, 8–10, 12, 18, 27, 39, 50, 119, 133, 140–41, 148–49, 163, 187–88, 194, 221, 223, 251–52, 258 59, 305, 325–26, 334, 336
Gorin, Jean-Pierre, 25
Goya, Francisco, 114–18
Grand Prix (1966), 19, 43, 93–94, 146, 187, 210–14, 366
Graphis (magazine), 13–14, 17, 88, 220
Green, Pamela B., 6, 90; *The Kingdom* (2007), 90
Greenberg, Richard, 90
Greenberg, Robert, 90

grids (design), 30, 65, 95, 98, 101, 103–7, 110, 114, 124, 159, 162, 164, 199, 202, 210, 227–28, 231, 233–35, 255, 276, 278, 282, 353
Griffith, D. W., 86; *The Birth of a Nation* (1915), 59
Gropius, Walter, 24, 46–47, 49

Halprin, Lawrence, 49
Hanna-Barbera, 66
Hansen, Miriam, 24–25
Hard, Fast, and Beautiful (1951), 60, 65, 361
Hellstrom Chronicle, The (1971), 44, 342
Herrmann, Bernard, 103, 165, 234
Higher Learning (1990), 97, 101, 105–7, 233, 368
Hirschfeld, Al, 136
History of a Package, The (1960), 247
Hitchcock, Alfred, 16–17, 19, 21–22, 38, 41, 45, 101–2, 104–5, 140, 181–84, 191, 193, 195, 200, 233–36, 243, 363–64, 374n53, 383n117
Hitler, Adolf, 312–14, 317–20, 326, 412n16
Hollywood Reporter, 120, 131, 153, 166, 171, 230, 251, 283, 289, 332, 343
Holocaust (Shoah), 55, 150, 155, 159–60, 162
Hope, Bob, 182, 200
House Un–American Activities Committee (HUAC), 158, 315
Hughes, Howard, 37–38, 60
Human Factor, The (1979), 133, 141, 233, 367
Hurry Sundown (1967), 69, 194, 366

IBM, 39, 43, 203, 212, 340, 365
Icarus Mongolfier Wright (1962), 43, 365

IDEA (magazine), 13, 17, 66, 295
In Harm's Way (1965), 93–94, 96–97, 132, 137, 140, 148, 163–65, 194–95, 366
Institute of Design (Illinois Institute of Technology), 49
International Design Conference, Aspen (IDCA), 15
It's a Mad, Mad, Mad, Mad World (1963), 67, 93, 119, 125–27, 132, 141, 168, 194–95, 201, 210, 365, 386n169

Jarmuth, Jack, 86; *The Jazz Singer* (1927), 86
jazz music, 107, 142–43, 150–51, 196, 247, 281
Jews and Judaism, 7–9, 29, 31, 34, 39, 43, 54, 140, 154, 155, 160, 162, 215–16, 247, 256, 259–61, 326–27, 329, 336, 341, 352
Johnson, Albert, 244
Johnson, Philip, 49
Judgment at Nuremberg (1961), 139, 364, 389n45

Kael, Pauline, 74, 212
Kaiser Aluminum and Chemical Corporation, 2, 43, 296, 328–33, 336, 338, 341
Kallis, Al, 34, 38, 58, 60–61, 138–39, 156, 192, 202, 334, 388n40
Kallis, Maurice, 137–38
Kandinsky, Wassily, 47, 50, 53
Katz, Joel, 3
Kelly, Gene, 75–76, 367, 380n35
Kepes, Gyorgy, 15, 19, 24, 29, 33–36, 46, 50–55, 59–60, 63, 91, 154, 228, 231, 286, 288, 340, 352; biography, 48–49; *The Language of Vision*, 46, 56–58, 91, 207, 383n107, 397n39
King, Emily, 20, 393n119

Kirkham, Pat, 19, 22, 25, 35, 60, 84, 107, 202, 239, 354
Klee, Paul, 26, 47, 50, 96, 145, 231, 258, 286, 332; *Farbtafel* (1930), 231; *Flora in the Sand* (1927), 26, 231
Klynn, Herbert, 39, 43, 221, 376n62
Kodak. *See* Eastman Kodak Company
Kramer, Stanley, 23, 37, 42, 61, 73, 114–18, 124–27, 139, 158, 179, 315, 358, 362–65, 386n170
Kubrick, Stanley, 23, 42, 148, 197–200, 276, 349, 364, 367; *2001: A Space Odyssey* (1968), 15, 342, 344, 349
Kuntzel & Deygas, 6

Las Vegas, 26, 163, 229, 247, 249–51, 253–56
Lee, Karen, 3
Lee, Spike, 6, 195; *Clockers* (1995), 6, 195
Legion of Decency (Catholic), 159, 230, 391n73
Leone, Sergio, 83
Lewis, Edward, 198, 211
lines, in design, 26, 50, 55, 68, 100, 102–4, 108, 112, 142, 144, 149–51, 155, 173, 178–79, 232–33, 241, 248, 252, 258, 276, 302, 352
Litvak, Anatole, 37, 60, 361
lobby cards, 41, 84, 89, 135, 240
logos, 62–63, 65, 129–34, 140–42, 149, 161, 168, 354–55; corporate, 3, 13, 17, 28, 39, 45, 65, 67, 85–86, 129
Lonzo, Mike, 8, 71, 312, 411n14, 412n24
Looking for Mr. Goodbar (1977), 71, 194, 202, 367
Los Angeles, 1, 4–5, 6, 9, 14–15,

40, 42, 45, 125, 131, 148, 161, 228, 247, 249, 251, 255, 282, 284, 297, 331, 344

Love in the Afternoon (1957), 130, 194–95, 253, 363

Lucas, George, 1, 297, 342; *THX 1138* (1971), 342

Lumet, Sidney, 6, 248; *Before the Devil Knows You're Dead* (2007), 6

Lupino, Ida, 61, 180, 361

Lynes, Russell, 15

Magnificent Obsession (1954), 62, 192, 362

Magnificent Seven, The (1960), 117, 146, 364

Magritte, René, 299

Manhatta (1921), 227

Manovich, Lev, 27, 354

Man with the Golden Arm, The (1955), 16–17, 20, 38, 41, 65, 73, 80, 93, 100, 118, 130–32, 134, 148–53, 194, 196, 362; poster, 138, 141, 143

Marker, Chris, 25, 350; *La Jetée* (1962), 350

Markowitz, Henry, 3, 390n55

Marsh, Morrie, 39, 71, 92, 375n42, 415n74

Marx, Karl, 158, 200, 336

Matisse, Henri, 141, 145, 390n58; *Blue Nude II* (1952), 141

Mattel Baby Tenderlove commercial (1969), 205–6, 366

Mattel Toy Company, 42, 205, 396n30, 397n36

Matter, Herbert, 15, 397n39

Mattson, Ty, 6; *Dexter* (TV series), 6

McFetridge, Geoff, 79

McLaren, Norman, 207

Melendez, Bill, 39, 125–26

Melnick, Ross, 21

Men, The (1950), 37, 315, 361

Mennen Baby Magic commercial (1962), 43, 76, 188, 193–94, 203–6, 262, 313, 365, 396n34

Mercer, Johnny, 202

Mercer, Ray, 89

Metro-Goldwyn-Mayer (MGM), 75–76, 84, 87–89, 136, 160–61, 171, 211–13, 229, 233–34, 267–68, 311

Meyer, Hannes, 47, 193

Mies van der Rohe, Ludwig, 47, 49

Minnelli, Vincente, 23, 311–12, 365

Mister Roberts (1955), 62, 362

MOA International Corporation (Church of World Messianity, M. Okada International Association), 44, 295–97, 301–3

modernism, 24–25, 30, 40, 42, 87, 96, 144, 154, 191, 294, 307, 340, 354

Moholy, Lucia, 47–48, 194

Moholy-Nagy, Laszlo, 15, 24, 26, 29, 36, 50–52, 54, 59, 63, 68, 154, 176, 194, 238, 257, 286, 288, 340, 352; biography, 47–49; *Leda* (1926), 121; *A Lightplay: Black, White, Grey* (1930), 172; *The New Vision*, 35, 46, 52–53, 76, 183, 193; *Vision in Motion* (1947), 48; *Yellow Circle* (1921), 68

Mondrian, Piet, 36, 50, 143, 150, 181

montage, 22–23, 25, 27, 30–31, 43, 62, 76, 86, 99, 159, 164, 168, 187–88, 191–93, 199, 203, 205, 208–12, 214, 217–18, 224, 259, 262, 284, 290, 311–20, 331, 339, 349, 354–55, 365–66, 412n19

Moon Is Blue, The (1953), 130, 253, 361, 387n7

Morgan Litho Company, 136
Morgenstern, Joe, 18, 35, 372n60
Motion Picture Production Code,
    130, 152, 230, 268, 278, 308
Mr. Saturday Night (1992), 11, 27,
    97, 194, 215–17, 368
Mucha, Alphonse, 135
My Six Convicts (1952), 124, 361

Nagata, Dave, 3, 171
Nalpas, Albert, 192, 282, 395n5,
    397n45
National Bohemian Beer
    commercial (1957), 31, 42, 193,
    202, 261–64, 365
National Film Registry, 2, 66, 367
National Screen Service (NSS), 72,
    89, 101, 137, 192, 229,
    385n145
Nazis (German National Socialist
    Party), 36, 47, 49, 274, 314–15
NBC (National Broadcasting
    Corporation), 69, 267
NBC: The First 50 Years (1976), 53,
    69, 367
Nemoy, Maury, 38
Neutra, Richard, 15
New Bauhaus, Chicago, 15, 49
New York City, 24–25, 34–36, 72,
    84, 109, 135, 161, 174, 191,
    225, 227–28, 231–35, 238–41,
    243–44, 247–51, 255, 257–61,
    265–69, 271, 278, 282, 284–85,
    297, 308, 315, 321, 337, 344,
    354
New York Times, 40, 75, 79, 111,
    180, 212, 244, 255, 268, 289,
    316
New York World's Fair (1964), 10,
    43, 210, 212, 282–84, 287–88
Nine Hours to Rama (1963),
    93–94, 97, 132, 141, 146–47,
    168, 170–73, 365
Niven, David, 111, 112, 122, 123

North by Northwest (1959), 5, 16,
    41, 93, 98, 101, 181, 202, 229,
    233–36, 238, 241, 243, 263,
    364
"Notes on Change" (ca. 1965), 44
Notes on the Popular Arts/Windows
    (1977), 19, 43, 70, 128, 219,
    294, 333, 367, 370n32,
    416n82
Not with My Wife, You Don't
    (1966), 96–97, 128, 366
No Way Out (1950), 37, 62, 137,
    361

Ocean's Eleven (1960), 87, 130,
    229, 250–54, 323, 364
Ogilvy Public Relations, 10
Okada, Mokichi, 295, 301
Okun, Jeff, 67, 71, 93, 221, 358,
    418n105, 419n124
Olin Mathieson Company, 42, 247,
    364, 396n30; *Small World*
    (1959), 247, 364
Once upon a Time in the West
    (1968), 83
One, Two, Three (1961), 132, 141,
    194, 364
100 Years of the Telephone (1977),
    31, 96, 302, 306, 324–26, 335,
    367
O'Neill, Pat, 25, 39, 352
On the Threshold of Space (1957),
    62, 362

P+A/Mojo, 6
Pabco paint, 39, 65, 194
Pacific Title and Art Studio, 86,
    89–90, 99
Paepcke, Walter, 15, 49, 58
Palance, Jack, 68, 178–79, 209, 248
Panama, Norman, 200, 366
Pantomime Pictures, Inc., 334
Paramount Consent Decree (1948),
    4, 40

Paramount Pictures Corporation,
36, 40–41, 44, 134, 136–37,
259, 343–45, 416n90, 419n118

Pars pro toto, 129, 147, 149, 168,
177, 189, 191, 217, 224, 318

Party, The (1968), 71, 218, 366

Patterns of Life (1957), 247, 363

Pearl of the South Pacific (1953), 62,
192, 362

Peck, Gregory, 73, 271–72, 274

Perri, Dan, 90

Phase IV (1974), 16, 19, 21, 23, 28,
31, 36, 41, 44–45, 70, 155, 166,
177, 184, 194, 205, 217, 278,
294, 299–300, 302, 307, 319,
342–51, 366, 419n114

photography, 26, 47–48, 92, 171,
179, 265, 283, 287, 323, 345,
347

photomontage, 57–58, 60, 148,
191, 194, 227, 334, 337

Picasso, Pablo, 58, 113, 142,
144–45, 232, 312, 338, 340–41;
Maternity (1905), 341; *Le Visage
de la Paix* (1950), 144

Piegdon, Ted, 3

Playhouse 90 (TV series), 236,
247–49, 362

Playhouse Pictures, 125

PM West/East (1961), 249–50, 364

Porgy and Bess (1959), 41, 145,
182, 364

posters, film, 6, 28, 11, 15, 55, 59,
129, 131, 134–38, 138–45,
146–49, 157, 168, 198, 229,
240, 270, 342, 354, 357,
361–68

pre-Columbian art, 9, 38, 141

Preminger, Ingo, 183, 381

Preminger, Otto, 16–17, 19, 23,
30, 40–42, 45, 57, 71–73, 87,
89, 110–15, 118, 130–31,
133, 140–46, 149, 150–55,
160–65, 168–70, 182,

185–86, 195–96, 200, 208,
233, 274–78, 343, 361–68,
387n7, 391n85

press books, 40, 84, 126, 272,
393n95

Pride and the Passion, The (1957),
65, 73, 95, 97, 110, 114–19,
363, 385n135

Psycho (1960), 16, 19, 21, 41, 43,
73, 99, 101–6, 166, 181, 193,
195, 198, 200, 203, 233, 321,
364, 368, 383n114

Pyramid Films, 12, 92, 220–21,
283–84, 287, 295, 297, 301,
332, 400n80, 415n77

Quest (1983), 27–28, 44, 69–70,
155, 217, 266, 278, 294–303,
306–7, 350, 367

Racers, The (1956), 62, 97, 179,
192, 208, 308, 362

Radin, Paul, 36, 343–44, 417n100

Rand, Paul, 15, 29, 37, 49, 52, 58,
91, 137, 253, 351

Randolph, Paul, 49

Rank, J. Arthur, 77

RCA "The Kid" commercial
(1968), 194, 206, 366, 397n37

Rebello, Stephen, 22, 73, 395n13

Redford, Robert, 43, 76, 219–20,
400n78

Reinecke, Gay, 3

Reinhardt, Ad, 142–43

Rembrandt, 145, 341

Return to Paradise (1953), 56, 138,
361

Richter, Hans, 48, 176, 288, 292

Riley, Michael, 90

Ritt, Martin, 267, 363

River Runs Through It, A (1992),
76, 310, 380n37

RKO Radio Pictures Corporation,
37–38, 60–61, 137, 180

Robson, Mark, 37, 170–71, 361–62, 365
Rockwell, Norman, 137, 374n13
Roper, Burns W., 15
Rosebud (1975), 132, 194, 367
Rothko, Mark, 142
Ruttmann, Walter, 22, 102, 145, 246, 339; *Berlin—Die Sinfonie einer Großstadt* (1927), 246, 339

Sagan, Françoise, 111
Saint Joan (1957), 16, 41, 73, 96–97, 110, 114, 132, 134, 141–42, 144–45, 149, 354, 363, 384n132
Sale of Manhattan, The (1962), 43, 127, 247, 252, 258–59, 365
sans serif typefaces, 52, 56, 95–96, 98, 103, 106, 108, 111, 126, 146–47, 159, 161, 164, 166, 169, 172–73, 187, 201, 212, 231, 233–34, 240, 245, 272, 279, 309, 314, 317, 330
Sarofsky, Erin, 90
Sato, Gary, 3
Saul Bass & Associates, 5, 8–9, 28–29, 63, 282, 284, 288, 295. *See also* Bass/Yager & Associates
Scandal Sheet (1952), 88
Schindler's List (1993), 146, 368
Schlemmer, Oskar, 47
Schwartzman, Arnold, 3, 8–9, 369n6
Scorsese, Martin, 19, 45, 72, 96, 107–10, 162, 166, 168, 174–76, 254–56, 368, 390n58
Screen Publicists Guild, 35
Searching Eye, The (1964), 11, 17, 25, 28, 31, 43, 53, 69, 72, 154, 176, 218, 222, 287–94, 300–301, 340–41, 347, 350, 366
Seconds (1966), 71, 93, 95, 146, 166, 177, 187–89, 204, 313, 319, 366

self-reflexivity in film, 25, 87, 186, 214, 250, 253, 291, 293–94
serif typefaces, 95–96, 116, 118, 124, 157, 175, 210, 216, 230–31, 269, 309
Seven Year Itch, The (1955), 25–26, 38, 72–73, 84, 93, 96, 100, 149, 179, 229–32, 309, 363
Shimokochi, Mamoru, 3, 9
Shining, The (1980), 141, 148, 276, 376
Shrike, The (1955), 139, 177, 179–81, 208, 321, 362
Silk Stockings (1957), 89–90
Simon, Mayo, 44, 343, 414n58
Simon, Norton, 199, 219–20
Simon and Schuster, 18
Sims, Art, 6, 195
Sinatra, Frank, 42, 114, 116, 131, 152, 250–52, 380n35; *The Poems of Color* (1956), 402n31
Singleton, John, 105–7, 368
Skelton, Red, 58, 252
Smith, G. Dean, 3
Sniper, The (1952), 37, 361
Solar Film, The (1980), 12, 27, 31, 43, 69, 154, 217–25, 293, 301–2, 306, 322, 325, 347, 367, 400n85
Something Wild (1961), 69, 97, 229, 237, 243–47, 254, 261, 363
Sony Pictures Corporation, 259
Spartacus (1960), 16, 19–20, 43, 74, 93, 95, 132–34, 149, 161, 179, 194, 197–200, 335, 354, 364, 379n21, 395n20, 396n23
Spielberg, Steven, 6, 45, 133, 278, 368; *Catch Me If You Can* (2002), 6
split screen, 124, 188, 211–14, 291–93, 254
squares, design, 26, 55–56, 68,

142–43, 150, 155, 231, 237, 242, 277, 302, 323, 353

Star Is Born, A (1954), 62, 247, 362

Steiner, Ralph, 164–65, 167, 172, 192; *H₂O* (1928), 164–65, 167, 192; *Mechanical Principles* (1930), 172

Storm Center (1956), 16, 73, 97–98, 146, 148, 154–55, 157–60, 162, 193, 308, 363

Such Good Friends (1971), 132, 141, 366

Sundowners, The (1960), 74, 364

Sutnar, Ladislav, 57

Swanson, Carla, 90

Tanaka, Ikko, 29

Tanner, Phyllis, 38, 389n54

Taradash, Daniel, 61, 155, 158, 363

Technicolor, 62, 114, 117, 417n100

Tell Me That You Love Me, Junie Moon (1970), 185, 366

That's Entertainment II (1976), 69–71, 75–80, 84, 310, 367, 380n36

Times New Roman (typeface), 105, 116, 181, 268

Timmer, Andreas A., 19

Todd, Michael, 119–22, 124, 385n150; Todd AO, 122, 210, 397n43

Toffoli, Jay, 3

Tomaszewski, Henryk, 27

Tonkô/The Silk Road (1988), 141, 146, 194, 367

Toulouse-Lautrec, Henri de, 135

Tracy, Spencer, 77, 125–26, 308

Trafton, Howard, 33, 35

Truffaut, François, 21, 208

Tschichold, Jan, 96, 99, 183, 289, 334

20th Century–Fox Film Corporation, 35, 41, 88, 136, 156, 229

typography, 7, 19, 30, 38, 46, 59–60, 62–63, 66, 76–78, 82, 85, 87, 90–92, 97–100, 108–13, 118, 122–24, 132–33, 138–41, 147–48, 151, 155, 157–58, 162–63, 164, 166, 169, 173, 182–83, 186, 196, 198–201, 210, 231, 234, 237, 240, 247, 249, 254–57, 267, 269, 273, 275–76, 293, 309, 317, 321, 323–24, 330, 354–55

United Airlines, 18, 43, 45, 65, 218, 282–84, 287

United Artists Film Company (UA), 35, 37, 115, 126, 130–31, 161, 208, 240, 244, 271, 272, 389n45

United Nations Building, 241, 243, 245

United Productions of America (UPA), 121, 311, 376n62

United Way, 45, 66

Universal Pictures Film Company, aka NBC-Universal, 74, 86, 89, 134, 135, 137, 180, 195, 197, 393n109

Uris, Leon, 160–61, 271, 391n84

Vargas, Alberto, 137

Variety, Daily, Weekly, 15, 36, 73–75, 111, 126, 131, 153, 163, 171, 230, 235, 239, 251, 268, 345

Venice Film Festival, 93, 290, 399n73

Vertigo (1958), 16, 20, 41, 53, 101, 132, 134, 140, 160, 167, 177, 181–85, 348, 354, 363, 393n123

Vertov, Dziga, 25, 197, 288

Victors, The (1963), 76, 93, 194–95, 311–12, 315, 320, 365, 411n14, 412n24

Viola, Steve, 90

Virgin Queen, The (1954), 62, 363

VistaVision, 114, 271

von Lauderbach, Nancy, 39

Vorkapich, Slavko, 4, 43, 76, 164, 412n19

Wagenfeld, Wilhelm, 47

Walker, Todd, 3

Walk on the Wild Side, A (1962), 11, 16, 72, 93, 95, 97, 150, 240, 278–82, 299, 365

Warner Brothers (Warner Communications), 35, 43, 45, 49, 59–60, 88–89, 108, 133, 137, 219–20, 251, 294, 333, 416n81

War of the Roses (1989), 27, 97, 108, 169, 173–74, 217, 254, 256, 368

WASPs (White, Anglo–Saxon Protestants), 36, 261, 336, 341

Weiner, Matthew, 5; *Mad Men* (TV series), 5

Weller, Don, 3, 7

Wellman, William, 59

Westinghouse, 13, 218, 249, 327, 398n64

West Side Story (1961), 11, 6, 43, 93–94, 96, 132, 140, 143, 217, 229, 331, 237–43, 261, 282, 285, 341, 364, 389n46, 403n39

Whitney, James and John, 25, 39, 145, 161, 182, 184, 257; *Variations on a Circle* (1942), 145

Why Man Creates (1968), 1–2, 5,

16, 19, 25, 27–28, 31, 43–44, 50, 69–70, 88, 96, 105, 128, 141, 145, 154, 166, 177, 194, 261, 294, 301, 305–7, 322–23, 325–34, 342, 347, 354, 366, 400n85, 414n58; poster, 342

wide-screen formats, 90, 94, 97–98, 111–12, 121, 125, 157, 210, 210, 214, 273, 282–83, 286–87, 290–94, 386n168

Wild, Lorraine, 8

Wilder, Billy, 23, 25, 42, 72, 87, 101, 131, 140–41, 149, 229–32, 257, 362–64, 379n9, 401n11; *Sunset Boulevard* (1950), 87, 257

Williams, Richard, 20

Willoughby, Bob, 39

Winkler, Irwin, 108

Wise, Robert, 239–42, 362, 364

Wolf, Henry, 14

Wolpert, Stanley, 147, 171

Women, The (1939), 85

World War II, 8–9, 14, 24, 28, 46, 50, 60, 82, 95, 98, 165, 208, 232, 253, 306, 311–12, 315, 318, 322, 326, 351–52, 355

Wyler, William, 68, 99, 270–74, 362–63; *Ben Hur* (1959), 311

Yager, Herb, 10–12, 14, 17–18, 39, 41, 44–45, 71–72, 93–94, 295, 297, 375n42, 416n81

York, Howard, 3

Young Stranger, The (1957), 187, 200, 233, 363, 401n20

Yu, Garson, 90

Zanuck, Darryl F., 88

Zinnemann, Fred, 37, 361, 364; *High Noon* (1952), 37, 307, 361

SCREEN CLASSICS

Screen Classics is a series of critical biographies, film histories, and analytical studies focusing on neglected filmmakers and important screen artists and subjects, from the era of silent cinema to the golden age of Hollywood to the international generation of today. Books in the Screen Classics series are intended for scholars and general readers alike. The contributing authors are established figures in their respective fields. This series also serves the purpose of advancing scholarship on film personalities and themes with ties to Kentucky.

SERIES EDITOR
Patrick McGilligan

BOOKS IN THE SERIES
Mae Murray: The Girl with the Bee-Stung Lips
Michael G. Ankerich

Hedy Lamarr: The Most Beautiful Woman in Film
Ruth Barton

Rex Ingram: Visionary Director of the Silent Screen
Ruth Barton

Von Sternberg
John Baxter

Hitchcock's Partner in Suspense: The Life of Screenwriter Charles Bennett
Charles Bennett, edited by John Charles Bennett

Dalton Trumbo: Blacklisted Hollywood Radical
Larry Ceplair and Christopher Trumbo

The Marxist and the Movies: A Biography of Paul Jarrico
Larry Ceplair

Warren Oates: A Wild Life
Susan Compo

Jack Nicholson: The Early Years
Robert Crane and Christopher Fryer

Being Hal Ashby: Life of a Hollywood Rebel
Nick Dawson

Bruce Dern: A Memoir
Bruce Dern with Robert Crane and Christopher Fryer

Intrepid Laughter: Preston Sturges and the Movies
Andrew Dickos

John Gilbert: The Last of the Silent Film Stars
Eve Golden

Saul Bass: Anatomy of Film Design
Jan-Christopher Horak

Pola Negri: Hollywood's First Femme Fatale
Mariusz Kotowski

Mamoulian: Life on Stage and Screen
David Luhrssen

Maureen O'Hara: The Biography
Aubrey Malone

My Life as a Mankiewicz: An Insider's Journey through Hollywood
Tom Mankiewicz and Robert Crane

Hawks on Hawks
Joseph McBride

William Wyler: The Life and Films of Hollywood's Most Celebrated Director
Gabriel Miller

Raoul Walsh: The True Adventures of Hollywood's Legendary Director
Marilyn Ann Moss

Charles Walters: The Director Who Made Hollywood Dance
Brent Phillips

Some Like It Wilder: The Life and Controversial Films of Billy Wilder
Gene D. Phillips

Ann Dvorak: Hollywood's Forgotten Rebel
Christina Rice

Arthur Penn: American Director
Nat Segaloff

Claude Rains: An Actor's Voice
David J. Skal with Jessica Rains

Buzz: The Life and Art of Busby Berkeley
Jeffrey Spivak

Victor Fleming: An American Movie Master
Michael Sragow

Thomas Ince: Hollywood's Independent Pioneer
Brian Taves

Carl Theodor Dreyer and Ordet: *My Summer with the Danish Filmmaker*
Jan Wahl

CPSIA information can be obtained
at www.ICGtesting.com
Printed in the USA
BVHW042330201122
652047BV00011B/188/J